M000100885

Catastrophe and Contention in Rural China

This book documents how China's rural people remember the great famine of Maoist rule, which proved to be the worst famine in modern world history. Ralph A. Thaxton, Jr., sheds new light on how China's socialist rulers drove rural dwellers to hunger and starvation, on how powerless villagers formed resistance to the corruption and coercion of collectivization, and on how their hidden and contentious acts – both individual and concerted – allowed them to survive and escape the predatory grip of leaders and networks in the thrall of Mao's authoritarian plan for a full-throttle realization of communism – a plan that engendered an unprecedented disaster for rural families. Based on his study of a rural village's memories of the famine, Thaxton argues that these memories persisted long after the events of the famine and shaped rural resistance to the socialist state, both before and during the post-Mao era of reform.

Ralph A. Thaxton, Jr., is a Professor of Politics and the Chairman of the East Asian Studies Program at Brandeis University. He is the author of *Salt of the Earth: The Political Origins of Peasant Protest in China* (1997) and *China Turned Rightside Up: Revolutionary Legitimacy in the Peasant World* (1983). He was named a Post-Doctoral Fellow at the University of California (Berkeley) Center for Chinese Studies (1974–75) and a Fellow at the Institute for Advanced Study (2002) and has won numerous prizes and fellowships, including a National Endowment for the Humanities University Teachers' Fellowship, a Harry Frank Guggenheim Fellowship, a Chiang Ching-kuo Foundation International Fellowship, and the United States Institute of Peace Fellowship.

Cambridge Studies in Contentious Politics

Editors

Jack A. Goldstone *George Mason University*
Doug McAdam *Stanford University and Center for Advanced Study in the Behavioral Sciences*
Sidney Tarrow *Cornell University*
Charles Tilly *Columbia University*
Elisabeth J. Wood *Yale University*

Ronald Aminzade et al., *Silence and Voice in the Study of Contentious Politics*
Javier Auyero, *Routine Politics and Violence in Argentina: The Gray Zone of State Power*
Clifford Bob, *The Marketing of Rebellion: Insurgents, Media, and International Activism*
Charles Brockett, *Political Movements and Violence in Central America*
Gerald F. Davis, Doug McAdam, W. Richard Scott, and Mayer N. Zald, *Social Movements and Organization Theory*
Jack A. Goldstone, editor, *States, Parties, and Social Movements*
Doug McAdam, Sidney Tarrow, and Charles Tilly, *Dynamics of Contention*
Sharon Nepstad, *War Resistance and the Plowshares Movements*
Kevin J. O'Brien and Lianjiang Li, *Rightful Resistance in Rural China*
Silvia Pedraza, *Political Disaffection in Cuba's Revolution and Exodus*
Sidney Tarrow, *The New Transnational Activism*
Charles Tilly, *The Politics of Collective Violence*
Charles Tilly, *Contention and Democracy in Europe, 1650–2000*
Stuart A. Wright, *Patriots, Politics, and the Oklahoma City Bombing*
Deborah Yashar, *Contesting Citizenship in Latin America: The Rise of Indigenous Movements and the Postliberal Challenge*

Catastrophe and Contention
in Rural China

MAO'S GREAT LEAP FORWARD
FAMINE AND THE ORIGINS
OF RIGHTEOUS RESISTANCE
IN DA FO VILLAGE

RALPH A. THAXTON, JR.

Brandeis University

CAMBRIDGE
UNIVERSITY PRESS

CAMBRIDGE UNIVERSITY PRESS
Cambridge, New York, Melbourne, Madrid, Cape Town, Singapore, São Paulo, Delhi

Cambridge University Press
32 Avenue of the Americas, New York, NY 10013–2473, USA

www.cambridge.org
Information on this title: www.cambridge.org/9780521722308

First published 2008

Printed in the United States of America

A catalog record for this publication is available from the British Library.

Library of Congress Cataloging in Publication Data

Thaxton, Ralph, 1944–
Catastrophe and contention in rural China : Mao's Great Leap forward famine and the origins of
righteous resistance in Da Fo Village / Ralph A. Thaxton, Jr.
    p. cm.
Includes bibliographical references and index.
ISBN 978-0-521-89749-5 (hardback) – ISBN 978-0-521-72230-8 (pbk.)
1. Famines – China – Da Fo Cun (Henan Sheng) – History – 20th century.   2. Government,
Resistance to – China – Da Fo Cun (Henan Sheng) – History – 20th century.   3. Peasant uprisings –
China – Da Fo Cun (Henan Sheng) – History – 20th century.   4. Communism – China – Da Fo
Cun (Henan Sheng) – History – 20th century.   5. Da Fo Cun (Henan Sheng, China) – Economic
conditions.   I. Title.
HC428.D34T43   2008
330.951′18–dc22   2007043011

ISBN 978-0-521-89749-5 hardback
ISBN 978-0-521-72230-8 paperback

To my mentors – Edward Friedman, Maurice Meisner, and James C. Scott –
in partial return for all they have taught me about China
and the agrarian world

Contents

Contents

Photos follow Chapter 7.

Acknowledgments

This work owes too many debts to too many gracious colleagues to cover here. For now, I wish to thank my great mentors, Edward Friedman, Maurice Meisner, and James C. Scott, who educated me at the University of Wisconsin, later befriended me, and also supported me in too many ways to mention across the years. I only hope that this work begins to live up to their impossibly high standards of scholarship. In particular, I was most fortunate to be able to study with Edward Friedman and James C. Scott, both of whom have established themselves as intellectual giants among Western and world scholars who deal with popular resistance in agrarian Asia. By standing on their shoulders and taking inspiration from each of them, I was able to penetrate the social and political world of Chinese villagers even more than I myself originally had imagined. *Catastrophe and Contention in Rural China* unashamedly draws from and builds on their wisdom. Hopefully, it adds to the knowledge they and their counterparts in agrarian studies have established.

While at Wisconsin, I was especially privileged to have studied with Edward Friedman, who has supported my scholarly endeavors come rain or shine, and who, in the case of this book, has provided scholarly materials and offered priceless advice on key issues in rural Chinese politics. Looking back, I also was most fortunate to have studied with Professors Donald McCrone, Charles Cnudde, Richard M. Merelman, and the late Murray Edelman, all of whom taught political psychology and political behavior. I could not have achieved the depth of this scholarly probe without remembering their teaching and that of my mentors. I am especially grateful to professors Friedman, Scott, and Merelman for helping me grasp the limits of top-down political science approaches to political change and social protest.

Cai Jiming, Chen Yixin, Han Dongping, Li Huaiyin, Liu Jundai, Lu Huilin, Wang Shuobai, Wu Chongqing, Yu Honglian, and Zhao Shukai have been wonderful colleagues, and each has contributed greatly to my knowledge of rural China. Lu Huilin, whom I befriended at Harvard University in the late stages of research for this book, helped me better understand some aspects of the practice of public criticism in the Mao era, and I am grateful for his input.

Eleven good colleagues read and offered insightful criticisms on an early, tortuously longer, unpolished version of *Catastrophe and Contention in Rural China* – or on parts of it – and so I especially want to thank Thomas P. Bernstein, Lucien Bianco, Alfred L. Chan, Bruce Gilley, Benedict J. Tria Kerkvliet, Steven I. Levine, Julia Strauss, Patricia (Tia) Thornton, Jonathan Unger, Susanne Weigelin-Schwiedrzik, and Felix Wemheuer for their intellectual generosity and guidance, all of which I took advantage of in revising and reducing the original manuscript. Alfred L. Chan, Steven I. Levine, and Susanne Weigelin-Schwiedrzik went beyond the call of duty in offering constructive advice on the original work, and so they deserve a special note of my gratitude. Additionally, I am indebted to Gail Hershatter, William A. Joseph, Benedict J. Tria Kerkvliet, and Arthur Kleinman for commenting on one of the last revised versions of this work; I especially want to thank Gail Hershatter for her insightful critique and helpful advice.

Thomas P. Bernstein and Charles Tilly, the two "anonymous readers" for Cambridge University Press, provided critical analyses of the manuscript and thereby prodded me to struggle with both the small and big issues they raised. Their questions and insights also helped me place some of the key chapters in comparative perspective and, in the end, to hone the historical narrative and the underlying theoretical framework. I am most grateful for their insights, and I hope that my response to their wisdom does not disappoint either of them.

Ao Qun, Gregor Benton, Thomas P. Bernstein, Lucien Bianco, Marc Blecher, Alfred L. Chan, Sherman Cochran, Jerome A. Cohen, Myron Cohen, Roger Des Forges, Neil J. Diamant, Bruce J. Dickson, Lowell Dittmer, Michael Dutton, Stephan Feuchtwang, Joseph Fewsmith, Karl Gerth, Bruce Gilley, Christina Gilmartin, Merle Goldman, Steven M. Goldstein, Linda Grove, Han Dongping, Han Xiaorong, Harry Harding, Kathleen Hartford, Ronald J. Herring, Gail Hershatter, Hui-Tam Ho tai, Andre Janku, Gary Jefferson, Kay Ann Johnson, William A. Joseph, Benedict J. Tria Kerkvliet, William Kirby, Edward Kissi, Pierre-François Landry, Steven I. Levine, Li Huaiyin, Li Lianjiang, Perry Link, Lu Huilin, Lu Xiaobo, Roderick MacFarquhar, Richard Madsen, Kimberley Ens Manning, Robert Marks, Barrett McCormick, Ethan Michelson, Erik Mueggler, Klaus Mühlhahn, Ramon H. Myers, Andrew J. Nathan, Kevin J. O'Brien, Suzanne P. Ogden, Jean C. Oi, Pei Minxin, Tamara Perkins, Elizabeth J. Perry, Paul G. Pickowicz, Kenneth Pomeranz, Carl Riskin, Antonius Robben, Stanley Rosen (whose good humor has helped keep me sane over the years!), Les Ross, Robert Ross, Gregory Ruf, Anthony Saich, Janet W. Salaff, Mark Selden, Peter J. Seybolt, Vivienne Shue, Helen Siu, G. William Skinner, S. A. Smith, Dorothy J. Solinger, Jonathan Spence, Julia Strauss, Lawrence Sullivan, Scot Tanner, Sidney Tarrow, Patricia (Tia) Thornton, Charles Tilly, Tu Wei-ming,

Acknowledgments

Jonathan Unger, Frederic Wakeman, Jr., Andrew Wedeman, Suzanne Weigelin-Schwiedrzik, Robert Weller, Felix Wemheuer, Lynn White III, Tyrene White, Martin King Whyte, Brantley Womack, Aida Yuen Wong, R. Bin Wong, Wu Jieh-min, Wu Kaiming, Dali Yang, and David Zweig have been wonderful colleagues. I am indebted to each one of them for our friendship as well as their admirable scholarship.

I am especially grateful to Thomas P. Bernstein for all that he has taught me and done for me since our first encounter, when I was studying Chinese and conducting dissertation research in Taiwan. Last but not least, I am deeply indebted to the late Frederic Wakeman, Jr., and to the late John King Fairbank. Each of these magnanimous individuals helped me find joy and security in studying modern China. Hopefully, this book is worthy of their indefatigable efforts to create a field of China-focused research in which a hundred flowers could bloom.

I also want to thank all of the China scholars who have struggled with and written about the Great Leap Forward. Frederick Teiwes and Warren Sun, whose pioneering work on the Great Leap disaster is well known, were kind enough to give me their take on the Anti–Five Winds Campaign in 1960, and Kimberley Ens Manning and Felix Wemheuer have given useful advice on many important aspects of the Great Leap Forward in rural China. I cannot offer enough praise for Edward Kissi, whose insightful comparative analyses of state-driven famines, and generous advice, helped me focus more sharply on the politics engendering the Great Leap disaster.

I am much indebted to the National Endowment for the Humanities, to the Harry Frank Guggenheim Foundation, and to the Chiang Ching-kuo Foundation for the fellowships and grants that facilitated this research. A fortunate turning point in my intellectual development came during my interaction with twelve other Harry Frank Guggenheim scholars in late 1990s' workshops on memory and violence, in Portugal and Manhattan. I express deep thanks to all of them, and to Karen Colvard of the Harry Frank Guggenheim Foundation and the organizers of each of the workshops, for making me think hard about state repression, trauma, and memory. I wish to thank the Institute of Sinology at the University of Heidelberg, where I spent several weeks writing and speaking on the Great Leap Forward in the summer of 2002, and the Institute for Advanced Study School of Social Science at Princeton, where I was able to make some progress in writing this book in the fall semester of 2002. I also am grateful to the Columbia University Weatherhead East Asian Institute Seminar and to the Yale University Program in Agrarian Studies Colloquium for the opportunities to present some of my early work on the Great Leap to their students and scholars in 2003 and 2004, respectively. My interactions with scholars in these forums helped me improve this book, and I especially benefited from the reflections of Myron Cohen at Columbia and Nathalie Gravel and Jonathan Spence at Yale.

Finally, I am impossibly indebted to Starry Eyes and the wonderful gang of conspirators in whom we find great happiness – Paco, Honey Rabbit, Maddy,

Kitty-Legs, Doodle, Boo, Siddy, and Willy! Willy, my yellow Labrador retriever, who also goes by the name of Mr. Mischief, did everything he could to sabotage this book, including eating a hard copy of Teiwes and Sun's *China's Road to Disaster*. Well, Will, at least you ate a good book! All of these characters were there for me in the years when this project, much like rural China under Mao, took a great leap backward.

Now that the book is finished, it is time to thank the inhabitants of Da Fo for giving us their humanity and their history, and to move on to how they see the revolutionary past and the reform present. Because this book relies on their voices to narrate their history, I have attempted to protect them from any future penalty for their collaboration by using pseudonyms for the names of the key places, people, and officials in the rural county of this study. Whereas I have used pseudonyms for some of the key actors and villages beyond the boundaries of this county, I have used the real names of the county, prefectural, provincial, and national units, actors, and events that were linked with the fate of the people of Da Fo and Dongle County.

Waltham, MA
March 1, 2008

Cast of Characters

DA FO VILLAGE (GREAT BUDDHA), 1920–1993

Communist Party Secretary Bao Zhilong and His Network of Clients

Bao Zhilong: Uneducated leader of the Communist Party–led militia in 1938 and head of the militia during and after World War II. Da Fo Communist Party secretary in the early 1950s, vice-director of Liangmen district between 1951 and 1954, and the vice-director of the Liangmen People's Commune in 1958–61. Da Fo party secretary for the post–Cultural Revolution period, into the early 1990s.

Bao Yibin: Son of Bao Yidai (popular Peasant Association leader in the 1945–47 period) and a graduate of the Public Security Bureau training academy in Dongle County. Da Fo party secretary in Da Fo during the Great Leap and its famine.

Bao Zhigen: Son of a landless manure collector and illiterate ruffian and opportunist. Client and toady of militia chief and party secretary Bao Zhilong.

Pang Lang: Corrupt Da Fo brigade accountant. Provoked the "dumpling rebellion" of early collectivization. Client of Bao Zhilong.

Pang Siyin: Member of the Bao Zhilong–led Chinese Communist Party (CCP) militia in World War II and later vice-secretary of the Da Fo CCP.

*Liang Xiaolu: Wife of Bao Zhilong. Extremely corrupt. Did not engage in manual labor in the Great Leap Forward. Leaked Bao Yibin's affair with another woman to his wife.

* Denotes female member of the cast of characters.

Other Important Characters

Bao Guangming: Alienated farmer. Opponent of Bao Zhilong in the Great Leap famine.

Bao Hongwen: Younger brother of Great Leap–era party secretary Bao Yibin. Mistreated and betrayed returned People's Liberation Army (PLA) veteran.

Bao Huayin: Returned college student and a CCP leader of the county-level anti-Japanese resistance during World War II. Rose to high-level state position in Beijing in the late 1940s. Embittered by Mao Zedong's Great Leap Forward.

Bao Rulong: Son of Da Fo party boss Bao Zhilong. Studied martial arts in Luoyang in order to defend his father against angry villagers in the reform era.

Bao Tiancai: Graduate of Daming Seventh Normal College, returned student and founder of the Da Fo Communist Party branch in 1938.

Bao Yizhao: Da Fo party leader who rose to a prominent position in the Anyang prefecture government after the Civil War. Led an investigation into the causes of the Great Leap famine in Xinyang prefecture. Accused of being a rightist by Wu Zhipu.

Bao Yuhua: Benevolent landholder in the Bao lineage and leader of the educated and enlightened elite of Da Fo village in the pre-1949 period.

*Du Rutai: Lost her one-year-old son to measles because party leaders insisted that she continuously work in the collective fields during the Great Leap.

Guo Weili: Arch Maoist, outsider, and Cultural Revolution terrorist.

*Huang Fengyan: Female participant in Bao Zhigen's First Harvest Company in the Great Leap. Denied sick leave and embittered by inhumane treatment.

*Ji Danying: Victim of the practice of Communist Party–connected leaders sleeping with the wives of farmers chained to collective fields during the Great Leap Forward.

*Liu Jing: Spouse of imprisoned Bao Sunyuan, former Kuomintang party secretary of Dongle County. Target of Guo Weili and the Red Artists. Murdered in the Cultural Revolution.

Pang Chengling: *Baozi* seller and defiant participant in state-forbidden marketing during the Cultural Revolution.

Pang Zhonghua: PLA officer and Korean War veteran. Returned to Da Fo in the Cultural Revolution from working in a top-secret nuclear weapons research site.

*Ruan Yulan: Conscripted production team leader in the Great Leap. Criticized by party leaders for allowing her exhausted female team members to catch up on sleep in the sweet potato fields.

Tang Guoyi: Farmer and composer of the doggerel ridiculing the watered-down soup of the public dining hall.

Tang Weilan: Farmer. Beaten mercilessly by Communist Party leaders at the Tong Tin River Dig labor camp in the Great Leap. Worked with work team to struggle against Bao Zhilong and party leaders in the aftermath of the Great Leap famine, both in the *fan wufeng* campaign and the Four Cleanups.

Zhao Jinjiang: Smallholder. Staunch defender of the independence of family-based farming and opponent of the land-pooling associations.

Zheng Daqing: Co-leader of prewar protest movement and member of the Eighth Route Army and PLA.

Zheng Tianbao: Son of Zheng Daqing. Worked for the Eighth Route Army during World War II and served in the Liangmen People's Commune Cultural Education Department during the Great Leap.

Zheng Yunxiang: Member of the Da Fo brigade militia in the late 1950s. Leader of an armed raid on the collective fields of another brigade during the Great Leap.

Chronology of Important Events

1911	Qing dynasty falls; Republican period begins
1920–21	North China Famine
1928, Nov.	Nationalist government established
1931–35	Dongle County protest movement against salt police
1937, Dec.	Japanese invasion reaches Dongle County
1938, Mar.	Da Fo branch of CCP founded
1938, Apr.	Da Fo militia organized
1938, Fall	CCP tax reform; Japanese Army first appears in Da Fo
1939, Dec.	Puppet Army occupies Da Fo
1942	Henan Famine
1945, Apr.	Japanese forces defeated and driven out of Dongle County
1945, Aug.	Japanese surrender
1946, May	CCP land reform begins in Da Fo
1946–47	Civil War begins
1949–50	Communist victory in the Civil War; People's Republic of China created
1950	Korean War begins
1951, late summer	Mutual aid agriculture groups begin in Da Fo
1952, late year	Land-pooling associations begin in Da Fo
1953	Unified purchase and sale begins in Da Fo
1955	Agricultural production cooperatives (APC) formed in Da Fo; later that year, five-village APC established
1956	Wei River flood; APC disbanded
1958	Liangmen People's Commune established; public dining halls created in August; Mao's rectification movement reaches the countryside in December 1957–January 1958

1958–61	Great Leap Forward
1959, late	Grain ration reduced to 0.5 *jin* per day; high tide of Mao's anti-rightist campaign
1960, spring	Great Leap famine at full force
1960, late	*Fan wufeng* campaign
1962	Mao forced to give up chairmanship of CCP to Liu Shaoqi
1964	Socialist Education Movement
1964–65	Four Cleanups campaign
1966–73	Cultural Revolution in Da Fo
1966	Deng Xiaoping removed from power
1968–69	Liu Shaoqi expelled from Communist Party; dies in captivity
1973	Bao Zhilong returned to position of party secretary for Da Fo
1976	Mao Zedong dies
1978	Deng Xiaoping returns to power; Reform era begins with Deng's introduction of reforms at the Third Plenum of the 11th Party Congress
1982–85	Liangmen People's Commune disbanded
1982	Land division in Da Fo returns the village to individual household farming

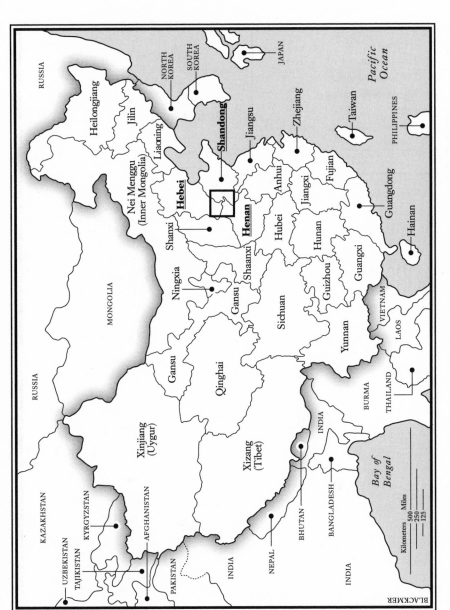

Map 1. Provinces of China, neighboring countries, and area of study. Map by Kate Blackmer.

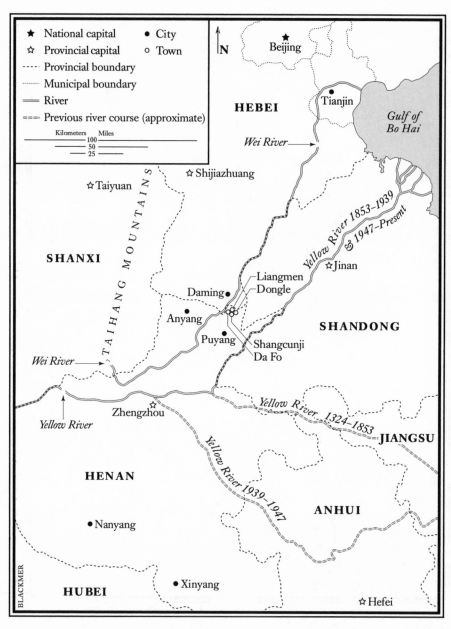

Map 2. Hebei-Shandong-Henan border area, showing location of Da Fo village. Map by Kate Blackmer.

Introduction

The Great Leap Forward Famine and Chairman Mao's Catastrophe

Denied entry into the U.S.-dominated global economy, in the middle of 1958, less than one decade after seizing national state power through a rural-based insurgency, Mao Zedong and the Chinese Communist Party (CCP) initiated a political campaign known as the Great Leap Forward. Aimed at promoting self-reliant economic growth and building a modern competitive state through rapid industrial development and the collectivization of agriculture, this campaign also was driven by Mao's desire to pilot a great leap from socialism to communism, an ideological goal that had implications for policy implementation and ultimately stoked fanaticism at all levels of governance. In the end, the Great Leap fell short of its economic and political goals and spawned a disaster in the Chinese countryside.

Mao Zedong and other key members of the Central Party Committee were forewarned of the disaster. Between mid-August and late October 1958, they received written petitions from rural farmers in Henan province. The petitions, some of which were penned by members of the Communist Youth League, pleaded with central party politicians to correct problems created by cadres in charge of the Great Leap locally. An August 11 petition addressed to Tan Zhenlin, who had fought under Mao's command in Hunan during the late 1920s and on whom Mao relied to push his rural policies in the Great Leap, complained that party cadres were falsely overreporting the harvest output so they could justify appropriating more of the food crop for the party-state and thereby achieve greater glory in the eyes of their superiors.[1] A second anonymous

---

[1] On Mao's connection to Tan Zhenlin, see MacFarquhar, *Origins of the Cultural Revolution*, 2:60–61, 82–84. On the first petition, see Yu Xiguang, *Dayuejin Kurizi Shangshuji*, 41–43, 61–64.

petition, sent to Mao on October 20, 1958, documented another problem: cadres were consistently breaking the law by severely beating farmers who did not obey their orders, targeting especially those who accurately reported the harvest output.[2]

For the first time, this second petition revealed to Mao Zedong the severity of some of the social problems engendered by the Great Leap Forward. In responding to it on November 29, 1958, however, Mao did not look for the causes of cadre behavior in government institutions or in his own national policies, but rather fell back on his premise that such events had occurred in no more than 10 percent of China's villages and were the result of local power falling into the hands of "a few counterrevolutionaries." Ignoring the petitioner's request for an independent, centrally directed investigation, he directed his followers in the Henan Provincial Communist Party Committee to look into the problem.[3]

The matter did not end there: between October 1958 and March 1959, Mao received internal reports of food shortages from junior party officials in Henan, Shandong, Anhui, Hunan, Jiangsu, and Hebei, and in late April 1959 shocked Politburo leaders informed Mao that a great famine had spread to fifteen of China's provinces and that 25 million rural people were facing starvation.[4] Mao did not mobilize state resources to manage this emergency. Instead, he compounded it. On the one hand, while on provincial inspection tours, Mao usually asked the first provincial level Communist Party secretaries about local grain production – not about local grain supply. On the other hand, Mao relied on these same party secretaries, all of whom were under pressure to produce a big surge in agricultural production, to provide information about potentially serious problems in communal food supply, and they invariably evaded specific revelations of the extent of the grain shortage crisis in the countryside.[5] Thus, while acknowledging that overzealous local party leaders had surrendered rural farm people to hunger, Mao declined invitations to visit besieged villages in remote interior provinces in the months following the late April 1959 famine alert. At the July 1959 Lushan Conference, in which defense minister Peng Dehuai warned Mao of the serious social and political consequences of the famine, the leader of the Communist Party refused to acknowledge he was making a great mistake and insisted on unconditional obedience to his Great Leap policy.[6] Shortly thereafter, Mao accelerated the Great Leap campaign by initiating an anti-rightist movement aimed at silencing party and nonparty opponents of the rapid transition to large-scale collective agriculture and the commune takeover of private farm household assets.[7]

[2] Yu Xiguang, *Dayuejin Kurizi Shangshuji*, 64–65.
[3] Ibid.
[4] Ling Zhijun, *Lishi bu Zai Paihuai*, 79–80.
[5] Huang Jun, "1960–61 Mao Zedong dui Lianghuang Wenti de Renzhi Jiqi Zhengce Diaozheng."
[6] Becker, *Hungry Ghosts*, 87–88; Teiwes and Sun, *China's Road to Disaster*, 202–05.
[7] Bernstein, "Mao Zedong and the Famine," 421, 423–24, 429–37, esp. 433–34.

Introduction

Whether Mao single-mindedly pursued his Great Leap agenda without regard to its cost to rural dwellers and, unlike Stalin, attempted to draw tillers to his vision without inflicting massive human suffering is a much debated issue. Initially, Mao proclaimed that his Great Leap was aimed at rescuing the rural poor from a marginal existence,[8] and it seems that the Maoist system of procurement was designed to mitigate the social cost of squeezing primitive capital from the farm population.[9] Yet this system, which in theory was aimed at returning food back to the villages by reselling a part of the state-appropriated harvest at a "reasonable price," had a deleterious impact on per capita consumption in rural China.[10] Whereas the miscarriage of this system has been attributed to misinformation based on seriously flawed communication between central government leaders and rural cadres, Mao Zedong himself was substantially responsible for the misinformation crisis of the Great Leap. According to local knowledge, in the first decade of the People's Republic of China (PRC), Mao and his local party base systematically dealt with voiced popular complaints over grain extraction by instituting public criticism of county- and village-level dissenters – a process that devastated the ageless practice of addressing the misrule of high and mighty officials through deferential petitions. As this study indicates, the suppression of such complaints correlated strongly with Maoist government attempts to gain control over the grain harvest.[11]

To be sure, Mao Zedong argued for an agricultural collectivization that would restore prosperity to rural people and make them equal with urban workers and urban cadres. However, Mao's industrial policy not only maintained the unequal economic disparities between rural and urban China, it also reinforced social and political discrimination against country people.[12] Throughout most of the collective era, and especially during the Great Leap Forward, Chinese farm households were trapped in an apartheid system. This system, which was called the people's communes, was aimed at maximizing production for provisioning the cities and constructing offices, factories, schools, and social insurance systems for urban-dwelling workers, cadres, and officials. Rural people who criticized it were labeled dangerous. Those who attempted to escape it were denied exit by party-orchestrated public struggle, which, in the end, further jeopardized survival.

Although leading scholars have shown that Mao did act to curb some excesses of the Great Leap from time to time, it is important to place the Great Leap and the horror it produced in the villages of China in the context of the Mao-led

---

[8] For this view, see Meisner, *Mao's China*, 191, 196, 207–08.
[9] See Bernstein, "Stalinism, Famine, and Chinese Peasants"; Ash, "Squeezing the Peasants"; and Bernstein, "Mao Zedong and the Famine," 427. According to Bernstein, Mao told cadres attending a Zhengzhou conference that peasant livelihood was important and farmers would need to conceal a portion of their harvest if they were to survive.
[10] Ash, "Squeezing the Peasants," 960–61, 971–72, 975.
[11] Zhou Weihai, interview, August 29, 1993.
[12] Wemheuer, "Grain Problem," 13–18.

revolutionary takeover of state power beginning in 1945. From the perspective of this historical process, it seems that Mao was consistently pushing for radical transformation on all fronts, and that any retreats to moderate policy on Mao's part were the product of his penchant for quick change and imperious trickery: he gave in momentarily to ultimately get his way, and his retreats were ebbs within a systematic pattern of resolute advance.[13] When, for example, Mao launched the 1946–47 land reform, he had to pull back because he could not afford to alienate conservative smallholders while the Civil War raged. When Mao attempted to nationalize the grain market through unified purchase and sale in 1953, he was forced to retreat by reports of rural cadre skepticism and popular discontent over this veiled form of procurement. In mid-1955, when Mao launched the agricultural production cooperatives, he again was compelled to retreat from this move against the proprietary rights of tillers, in part because the smallholding "middle peasants," whom Mao labeled "malcontents," refused to sell their surpluses to the state and wanted to back out of the big production cooperatives to farm their own land.[14] Then, in 1957–58, after starting the anti-rightist movement in the countryside and then pushing ahead with the Great Leap Forward in poor interior provinces, Mao himself acknowledged that his own aspirations and the zealous acts of his cadre base had combined to produce chaos and food supply problems.[15] Yet when implored to pull back by Marshal Peng Dehuai, Mao Zedong reacted by crushing Peng and reinventing the repressive anti-rightist policies of the past. As Thomas P. Bernstein has shown, this development created a political climate that allowed the Great Leap to quickly generate a disaster in much of the countryside.[16] Seen in this context, the calamity of the Great Leap seems to resonate with Mao's long-standing belief in the necessity of the radical transformation of rural society.[17] Thus, even though Mao expressed compassion for rural people, he had been hardened by Kuomintang state violence, and he had come to understand both pre- and post-1949 China as a huge country with pockets

---

[13] I am much indebted to Edward Friedman for helping me grasp this point and the political history that demonstrates it. Personal correspondence, May 1, 2007. Also, on Mao's incessant push of his own transcript, which began even prior to unified purchase and sale, see Strauss, "Morality, Coercion and State Building," 893–912, esp. 912.

[14] On this point, also see Mao, *Jianguo Yilai Mao Zedong Wengao*, 5:208–11, where Mao admits to seeing multi-province reports on the detainment of "middle peasants" who complained about collectivization. The smallholders refused to sell grain surpluses to the state and wanted to leave the cooperatives to farm on their own land. Though many of them voiced fears of food shortages, Mao accepted official reports that these "middle peasants" were "malcontents" who actually were not suffering. Three of these cases were from Henan villages, and Mao referred each case to "Comrade Wu Zhipu" for review.

[15] Teiwes and Sun, *China's Road to Disaster*, 162–63, 164–67.

[16] Bernstein, "Mao Zedong and the Famine," 421–23, 431–32, 445.

[17] Here I have benefited from correspondence with Edward Friedman (May 1, 2007) and Alfred L. Chan (May 20, 2007). Still, the basic starting points for this interpretation are in the works of Tsou, "Revolution, Reintegration, and Crisis," 307; MacFarquhar, *Origins of the Cultural Revolution*, 2:333, 3:275–83; and Chan, *Mao's Crusade*, 15.

of famine and flood disaster, so he was accustomed to massive human suffering. After seizing national power, Mao convinced himself that he could extract huge amounts of grain from rural China, and, after all was said and done, Mao allowed his cadre base to compel farm households to endure a life of semi-starvation so that he could promote internal economic colonization and enable China to catch up with the global powers quickly.[18]

Championed by Mao himself, the supreme leader of the newly established PRC, and impressed on the countryside by means of Mao's autocratic style of policy making and his revival of wartime structures and strategies to force the advancement of collective agriculture, the Great Leap Forward engendered the worst famine in modern world history.[19] This famine took the lives of 40 to 55 million rural people;[20] at least 32.6 million people died as a result of food deprivation alone.[21]

The History of a Single Rural Village

As Gregory Ruf observes, the trauma of the Great Leap Forward "had a profound influence on the shaping of popular consciousness," particularly on how China's village people viewed – and still view – the Communist Party.[22] Yet official party historiography in the PRC has presented the catastrophe of the Great Leap Forward with little reference to the trauma it inflicted on individuals, families, and communities or to the damage it did to the Communist Party's legitimacy in the countryside.[23] This book takes us inside the disaster of the Great Leap Forward through examination of a single rural village in which Maoists achieved supremacy. It is the first of two linked volumes about how China's rural people

---

[18] See Mao, *Jianguo Yilai Mao Zedong Wengao*, 5:190–210, 8:336–38. In a July 5, 1959, essay, Mao urged rural people to eat less and said they should be prepared to suffer one, two, even three more years. Clearly, he was looking to solve the problem of grain production through their suffering. To be fair, Mao also said private vegetable plots should be restored. However, because this *Wengao* information was to be disseminated only among cadres, ordinary villagers were not likely to catch wind of it, and, in any event, the drift of Mao's thinking most likely reinforced an official culture in which the welfare of the state superseded that of rural people. Compare with Chang and Halliday, *Mao*, 392, 426–27.

[19] MacFarquhar, *Origins of the Cultural Revolution*, vol. 2; Friedman, Pickowicz, and Selden, *Chinese Village*; Teiwes and Sun, *China's Road to Disaster*; Smil, "China's Great Famine," 1619–21; Yang, *Calamity and Reform in China*, vii; Chan, *Mao's Crusade*, 28–30, 40–42, 48–49. On Mao's policy of war communism as the originator of the famine, see Friedman, Pickowicz, and Selden, *Chinese Village*, 219–35, and Spence, *Mao Zedong*, 133–45. For a brilliant analysis of the Great Leap as a Maoist military campaign, see Wemheuer, personal correspondence, 2003, 1–2.

[20] The early conservative estimate was 30 million. See Bannister, "Analysis of Recent Data" and *China's Changing Population*. For an estimate of 40 million, see Jin Hui, CASS, 193; also Jian, Shen, and Jiu, *Lao Xinwen*, 1. For the estimate of 45 million, see Teiwes and Sun, *China's Road to Disaster*, 5, and for the outer limit estimate of 55 million, see Yu Xiguang, *Dayuejin Kurizi Shangshuji*, 8.

[21] Cao Shuji, "1959–1961 Nian Zhongguo de Renkou."

[22] Ruf, *Cadres and Kin*, 161.

[23] Weigelin-Schwiedrzik, "Taking the Heat Out."

remember the politics that imposed the famine of Mao's Great Leap Forward, about how some resisted and eventually escaped its grip, and about how their memory of this traumatic injustice has shaped the politics of everyday resistance ever since. Relying substantially on oral political history, it provides the first in-depth history of how one village's people experienced the ultimate catastrophe of Maoist rule. I have drawn on individual memories of encounters with the ground-level agents of Mao's Great Leap Forward to show how rural people attempted to survive and resist this formative episode of socialist state building and then, in its aftermath, strove to recover the liberties, entitlements, and enterprises they lost to its brutality.

The fundamental premise of this study is that during the Great Leap Forward Famine, the Chinese Communist Party lost its mandate to rule in the same interior rural places where it had earlier based its insurgency against Chiang Kai-shek's Nationalist government. My central hypothesis is that the individual and collective recollections of the style of Communist rule that crystallized in this formative phase of state making – autocratic, brutal, corrupt, and distrustful – when combined with the plunder, forced labor, and starvation of the famine itself, turned Chinese villagers against the Communist Party, in which they had earlier placed their trust, and motivated them to seek basic social rights and local self-governance through protracted resistance to Communist rule. The persistence of this resistance and the memories of state-delivered pain that made it necessary have complicated the efforts of post-Mao reformers to regain political legitimacy with village dwellers in the agricultural interior. As I will explore in the second volume of this study, the memory of loss and suffering in the Great Leap famine has conditioned Chinese villagers to think about their relationship with the Communist Party in ways that do not bode well for the continuity of socialist rule, though the degree to which popular memories of the famine have been attenuated, or transformed, over time for post–Great Leap generations remains an open question.

Trained in agrarian studies and Chinese politics, I had long aspired to under-take a research project on how Chinese villagers experienced the waves of state intrusion of the twentieth century. When I first began my field work in rural China in the 1980s, my interest was in how Mao and the Communist Party won control over the Chinese mainland from the Kuomintang (Chinese National-ist Party) following World War II and how village people saw Kuomintang state interventions in their lives. Two experiences shifted my focus and led to my inter-est in the Great Leap campaign as a famine-inducing state failure. First, while interviewing in remote villages during the late 1980s, I found that villagers would respond to questions about the 1942 Henan Famine with stories of their personal suffering in the radical scarcity of 1958–61. I began to understand that they had been impoverished by two different famines, the first during the era of Nation-alist governance and the latter after the Communist party-state had supposedly resolved the food insecurity of the past. Later, as I interacted with scholars who were studying the impact of war, famine, and repression on popular memory in other societies, I began to realize that I was positioned to play a role in uncovering the story of how Chinese villagers experienced the greatest trauma of Maoist politics: the Great Leap and its famine. This led to my interest in presenting an oral history of how the people of one village remember their experiences with socialist rule under Mao.

This volume is based on interactive interviews and intimate discussions with both ordinary villagers who suffered from the Great Leap famine and village-level Communist Party leaders who participated in and sometimes imposed the politics engendering the famine. Between 1989 and 2007, I conducted and/or supervised approximately four hundred in-depth interviews with villagers aged twenty-one to eighty-five in Da Fo, or "Great Buddha," village, a rural market village situated on the North China Plain in Dongle County, Henan province. I chose to conduct research on the long-term history of this village on the advice of farmers in another village in Dongle County where I was interviewing during the late 1980s. They told me that if I wanted to discover how the Communist Party succeeded in the Anti-Japanese War of Resistance of 1937–45 and to learn more about the fate of the party in the post-1949 period, then I should go to Da Fo. When my official Dongle County hosts learned of the farmers' suggestion, they turned pale and protested that *they* could find a more appropriate village for me to study. I soon learned that Da Fo was nicknamed "the old headache" by both Kuomintang and Communist Party cadres. On sensing the official reluctance to allow me to go to Da Fo, I played a hunch and dug in my heels. Fortunately, the local Dongle County historian whom I had befriended and worked with in studying the rise of the Communist Party in the pre-1949 countryside supported my choice.

Da Fo's location in the interior of Henan province, where present-day rural village living standards are on par with those in rural Albania and the Philippines,[24] offered distinct advantages for my research. First, the province had been assailed by radical Maoist initiatives during the Great Leap Forward, as Wu Zhipu, the first party secretary of Henan, sought to please Mao by imposing the Chairman's Great Leap transcript on the countryside to the extent that the famine's death rate soared. In addition, through my previous research in this remote area of rural Henan province, I had won the trust of many rural people in the region. I could talk with them frankly, and I had learned the agrarian history of the triprovincial North China border area where they and their ancestors lived.[25]

Although it would be difficult to establish the "representativeness" of Da Fo for all of China – and although it is clear that "the old headache" and the rest of Henan were subject to comparatively radical repression due to Wu Zhipu's

[24] Heilig, "Poverty Alleviation in China."
[25] For my previous study of this border area, see Thaxton, *Salt of the Earth*.

enthusiasm for implementing Mao's Great Leap Forward – the village certainly shared a number of features with thousands of other twentieth-century villages in the larger area where it is located: Its soil grew acutely saline over the course of the twentieth century, causing grain crop yields to decline. In consequence, villagers became increasingly reliant on off-farm market income for subsistence and developed well-honed family strategies for surviving famine. The village suffered violence serially at the hands of bandits, warlords, Kuomintang agents, Japanese occupiers, and Communist Party cadres. It produced its fair share of locally raised party leaders who under normal circumstances should have been more benevolent toward villagers than imported cadres. Its inhabitants suffered a great disappointment with Maoist-style politics, and, since the founding of the PRC, they have resorted to ageless modalities of resistance to misrule and deprivation.[26]

Da Fo was attractive for another reason: Unlike Wugong village, a model socialist village studied by Edward Friedman, Paul G. Pickowicz, and Mark Selden for their seminal work *Chinese Village, Socialist State*, Da Fo village never became a model socialist pacesetter, nor did it become the headquarters of the people's commune to which its people were forced to belong. Choosing it for study thus gave me a unique opportunity to clarify the unofficial relationship of one rural community to the people's commune, the lower tip of the party-state. By choosing Da Fo, I could begin to penetrate the inner layer of what James C. Scott has called "everyday resistance" to the death grip of the Great Leap in one village, a task that eluded Friedman and his associates because, as they point out, Wugong village benefited from its position in the communal state hierarchy, and hence Mao's Great Leap did not force its residents into the forms of desperate resistance taken up in villages in which the famine was far worse.[27] In recording this inner history, I revisit Dali Yang's pathbreaking work, *Calamity and Reform in China*, and I show how the resistance unfolded on the ground, why it became entwined with contention, and how it provided a way out of the Maoist disaster. Following in Yang's footsteps, *Catastrophe and Contention in Rural China* better positions us to explicate the relationship between popular resistance to socialist dictatorship in the Great Leap era and the coming of reform in the short- and long-term aftermath of this calamity.[28]

---

[26] I am indebted to Julia Strauss (October 14, 2003) and Steven I. Levine (February 11, 2006) for helping me struggle with this section.

[27] Although Friedman, Pickowicz, and Selden spin a rich, eye-opening narrative of the resistance of rural people, their most telling examples of resistance to the Great Leap famine are derived not from Wugong village itself but from different villages under the domination of Wugong commune party leaders and from villages across Raoyang County. A great strength of their work is that it shows there was resistance in many villages, both within the commune and across the county, and that in Wugong and Raoyang discontent with Maoist collectivization persisted and fueled resistance well after the famine officially ended. See *Chinese Village*, 224–25, 230–31; see also Friedman, Pickowicz, and Selden, *Revolution, Resistance, and Reform*, 7, 10, 12, 214–16.

[28] Yang, *Calamity and Reform in China*, 1–67.

Introduction

The two linked volumes that are the result of my long-term study of Da Fo together form a political history of one rural community's evolving relationship with pre-Maoist, Maoist, and post-Maoist rulers. I have explored this relationship through interdisciplinary research occurring at the intersection of political sociology, cultural anthropology, and political psychology. Hence, this first volume focuses substantially on how villagers remember their encounters with Communist Party agents of the Maoist state during the Great Leap episode, but in order to do so its narrative necessarily reaches back to the periods of Nationalist rule, Japanese occupation, and civil war, during which the local Communist leadership style took shape, and forward to the 1980s and 1990s, when hidden resentments against Da Fo's Great Leap–era Communist Party leaders finally began to be more openly expressed. The story thus sheds new light on the nature of the legitimacy crises that developed under three different regimes – those of the Kuomintang, the Japanese (administered through their Puppet Army), and the Communists. During the Japanese occupation of the Second World War and in the subsequent years of civil war, Da Fo village became a bastion of Communist Party power. By studying it, I began to grasp how and why the party was able to sink deep roots in one rural community. I then looked at how Mao's grand design affected those roots in the decades following the Communist victory of October 1, 1949.

Although the documented memories of the Great Leap survivors expose the politics of Maoist delusion and deception, this book does not present an open-and-shut case against the unprecedented violence of socialist rule. Though some of its voices support such an interpretation, others, particularly those of village power wielders, do not. In the final analysis, this book shows that village history both before and after 1949 has been enveloped in violence and that, tragically, the acknowledged horrors experienced by rural villagers in the pre-1949 era in some ways prepared the ground for the unbelievable horrors of the Maoist disaster.

Even if my findings on Da Fo are correct, a single case study cannot prove a thesis. Da Fo might be an exception to the general pattern of why and how rural contention has developed in China. The value of any case study is that it can help us generate new theories, disprove overly deterministic ones, and shed light on previously unknown causal processes. *Catastrophe and Contention in Rural China* does not seek to disprove any deterministic theory of rural contention. Instead, it develops a new approach – an approach that is grounded in historical memory – that might be used and refined by others to understand why contemporary rural China is such an incendiary place. It also shows in depth the relationship between memory, resistance, and protest during and long after an episode of massive state cruelty, thereby inviting further reflection on how important memory is to contention and where memory works specifically to inform the discursive framework through which rural dwellers press rulers to repair the past by righting wrongs and admitting their imperfections. In this respect, this book is also about the learning process that can open up a public conversation over inherited state violence, which Roger I. Simon reminds us is essential to the successful invention of elementary forms of democratic life.[29]

Although this book is focused largely on one village, I value comparison. Thus, I have drawn on data from several villages and counties in the Hebei-Shandong-Henan border area in which Da Fo is located and from several other Chinese provinces in order to make a few comparisons that highlight both the typical and the atypical features of Da Fo's experience with socialist rule. There are more than a million villages in rural China. Surely not all of them were affected by the Great Leap Forward Famine in the same way, and popular responses to the famine as well as memories of the famine and its damage most likely vary from place to place. Surely too, however, the narrative of this one village's political history, woven together largely from individual memories of the most traumatic episode of the Mao era, contains threads of a historical relationship with agents of the Maoist party-state that were shared with scores of other rural villages. I hope that this work will challenge future scholars to further explore the distinctions and similarities between the political experiences of rural communities more or less transformed by the Great Leap and its famine.

Memory, Politics, and Oral History Methodology

Despite the fact that Da Fo village was savaged by three different regimes and experienced three different famines – the North China Famine of 1920–21, the Henan Famine of 1942, and the Great Leap famine of 1958–61 – it had an unusually high number of survivors who were in the fifty-five to eighty-five age group at the time of my study. Most of them had clear and keen memories of the past, and they gave me reliable oral testimony that reflected the changing history of the village over most of the span of the twentieth century. Following Paul Thompson, I especially needed these aged "voices of the past" to get beyond "haphazard reminiscence" and construct a coherent historical narrative of village life before Mao's Great Leap.[30]

I treat these individual trauma survivors as members of complex family and community relationships, probing several dimensions of popular memory. My research seeks to extend the work of many Western scholars of contemporary rural China who have relied on personal histories to understand villagers as individuals.[31] The Maoists attempted to suppress and erase popular memory of the famine, but, as Daniel L. Schacter has pointed out, memories of war, famine, repression, and other traumas often persist in popular consciousness long after the actual traumatic event itself. "The intrusive memories that result from such

[29] Simon, *Touch of the Past*, 6–7.
[30] Thompson, *Voice of the Past*, 23, 182.
[31] Chan, Madsen, and Unger, *Chen Village*; Huang, *Spiral Road*; Friedman, Pickowicz, and Selden, *Chinese Village*; Ruf, *Cadres and Kin*; Mueggler, *Age of Wild Ghosts*.

experiences," Schacter informs us, "usually take the form of vivid perceptual images, sometimes preserving in minute detail the very features of a trauma which survivors would most like to forget."[32] The interviews I conducted for this book confirm that many villagers still live with the traumatic Maoist past.

In working with the narrative memories of villagers I encountered, I drew from Paul Connerton's wisdom and considered how the Maoist famine was experienced individually and collectively by villagers according to three categories of perception: the semantic memory acquired through assimilation of moral teachings about proper conduct; the memory formed by bodily presence, appearances, and movement, resulting in embodied memory; and the habitual memory that is formed from quotidian life-serving performances.[33] The oral testimonies in this study help us understand how day-to-day experiences with the political agents of the Great Leap campaign affected these various forms of memory and how each form of memory shapes the social and political activities of villagers today. Though I do not explicitly discuss particular categories of memory in the chapters that follow, I have drawn on them in developing my analysis.

I also have explored the political worldviews of villagers through the concept of differentiated memory, seeking to find out why people who survived the same political event hold different memories of it. For instance, I have asked why and how local Communist Party leaders were able to gain followers in the years before the Great Leap by manufacturing a generalized official memory of Maoist sacrifice for a new socialist polity aimed at serving the rural poor but were subsequently unable to use official memory to structure how all villagers saw the socialist polity after the famine (though they were able to influence the memories of some villagers). The radical practices of the Communist Party enforcers of Maoist rule in the Great Leap Forward altered the ways in which villagers remembered, and hence perceived, the party-state.

I take seriously Eric Selbin's observation that "there is a societal memory which is up for grabs, a battlefield where various groups struggle to protect and extend their interpretations of society's past."[34] *Catastrophe and Contention in Rural China* shows that rural China's survivors of the Great Leap Forward Famine hold obstinate memories of pain and loss inflicted on them by agents of the Communist Party and that they use these memories to question the legitimacy of the post-Mao political order. As I will explore in a subsequent volume, some of the disputes over the tax burden, family planning, and entitlement to education in the post-1978 reform era occur in the context of constantly remembered past injustices, and the preserved memory of the worst episode of socialist-inflicted pain and

---

[32] Schacter, *Seven Sins of Memory*, 174.
[33] On semantic memory, see Madsen, *Morality and Power*, and Schwarcz, *Bridge Across Broken Time*. On embodied memory, see Stoller, "Embodying Colonial Memories," and Feldman, "Punition, Retaliation." On habitual memory, see Connerton, *How Societies Remember*, esp. 34–35, and Thaxton, *Salt of the Earth*.
[34] Selbin, "Agency and Culture," 82.

loss is drawn upon to direct protest and contention in the present.[35] The present volume reminds us that the memories of injustice and loss in the Great Leap episode contain, as Jun Jing has argued, "some highly explosive energies."[36] We cannot fully grasp the evolution of contentious struggle in the Chinese countryside without reference to the catalytic power of the memory-driven emotions of the trauma survivors we meet in this book.

For the most part, Western scholarship on the origins of protest under reform in rural China relies upon printed sources, but politics in rural Chinese villages is still by and large a verbal, orally documented phenomenon. It cannot be fully understood by relying mainly on inscription, in part because much of what is voiced in interaction between the sub-county agents of China's contemporary Leninist political order and village dwellers is not recorded. Oral history is, in the words of Paul Thompson, "the *first* kind of history," and it offers a way of narrating the past through interaction with country people whose knowledge of facts and patterns is based on memory.[37] *Catastrophe and Contention in Rural China* is in part an attempt to rescue this older mode of oral history from its long-standing subordination to documentation through inscription. To be sure, I have attempted to supplement and corroborate the interview data with printed Chinese sources, including articles on provincial- and county-level history, local history materials and local county gazetteers, secret inner party documents and inner party reference materials, a few personal memoirs, a village party branch report, and the Great Leap Famine Archive on the Internet.[38] Nonetheless, attempting to write this village history made the need for a return to oral history quite obvious: the evidence from official documents, particularly in post-1949 China, often seemed inadequate or politically slanted. It seems that the socialist state collected information on the Great Leap's crash mainly from the county level and that the details of the famine and popular resistance to it in rural villages usually did not find their way into official documents. Communist Party censors continue to screen and suppress much of what makes its way into print, and this, too, limits the availability of primary source materials about the Great Leap famine. Through oral history, however, Chinese villagers speak to us from minds stockpiled with memories of their actions, thoughts, and feelings, most of which were previously voiced, if at all, within the framework of local oral tradition.

The bias against relying on rural dwellers to help us create historical representations of state and revolution in twentieth-century China is strong among Chinese intellectuals, many of whom disdain popular memory and seldom question whether the official Communist Party–crafted history of revolution and reform is in accordance with the habitual memory of rural people. My research

[35] Ibid., 82–83. On this approach, also see Kleinman, "How Bodies Remember," 703–23.
[36] Jing, *Temple of Memories*, 167.
[37] Thompson, *Voice of the Past*, 25, 26–37.
[38] Da Jihuang Dang An (The Great Leap Famine Archive), Xin Guancha, (New Observations), 2000, http://www.xgc2000.com, hereafter referred to as GLFA.

demonstrates, however, that China's rural people have placed their memories of political history in significantly different frameworks than those offered by scholars whose focus is on national historical moments and campaigns, globally driven political events, or reform-era protest issues and events. In particular, in popular memories, the state intrusion of the Great Leap was interpreted at the village level as a greater *systemic* challenge to the permanency of peasant livelihood and culture than any other twentieth-century political intrusion in China. Bruce Gilley cautions that these memories constitute a volcano of pent-up grievances, and, if China's Leninist dictatorship falls, they will leap to the front to provide a graphic picture of how China's "little people" suffered under socialist rule.[39] *Catastrophe and Contention in Rural China* reveals that this process is already underway in one part of the remote countryside. It provides us with a ground-level view of how popular memory has directed the efforts of villagers to settle scores with the perpetrators of the Great Leap's harm, and it makes us aware that memory of past injustice has shaped subsequent attitudes toward the party-state.

Because I am aware that oral testimony is subjective and subject to influence and manipulation, I used several methodological procedures to depoliticize and maximize the reliability of the interviews. In order to avoid ending up with a biased sample of pre-selected respondents chosen by the Da Fo Communist Party secretary and his close network of cadres and clients, I insisted on and won the freedom to choose my interviewees from any household. I was able to conduct more than 90 percent of the interviews without supervision or monitoring by any PRC authorities (university hosts, foreign affairs bureau officials, or provincial- and county-level historians). My Chinese research assistant, who was trained in Western social science research techniques of in-depth interviewing and who grew up in a rural Chinese village, assisted in most of the interviews. Together or separately, we made approximately twenty-two trips to Da Fo village between 1989 and 2007. On only two occasions did a local historian or a local foreign affairs official accompany us to the village. Part of the reason I gained such accessibility was the trust we had won from interviewing people in scores of villages within this northern Chinese border area during the 1980s.

Of course, as all China scholars who attempt to do field work in the PRC know, it is difficult to conduct research in a village completely free of state controls.[40] Rural China is not rural Mexico. One can not just walk into a village and start interviewing villagers without going through certain political networks and protocols, and power holders often attempt to monitor and inhibit research. Fortunately, before I took up this study of Da Fo, I had had more than a few encounters with monitors and inhibitors, so I was prepared to deal with some – though certainly not all – of these problems. When I interviewed in Cheng Guan village, Puyang County, between 1985 and 1987, for example, I was placed under

[39] Gilley, *China's Democratic Future*, 221.
[40] See Friedman, "Learning About a Chinese Village," 2.

the supervision of a county-level party historian who insisted on sitting in on some of my interviews. His purpose was to ensure that I interviewed local village people who remembered pre-1949 history in line with the Communist Party's interpretation of a small, early 1930s peasant rebellion that was officially led by the party. On one occasion, when I ventured away from the usual interview site and located a fragile, aged ex-beggar who had played a role in leading this rebellion against the Kuomintang police state, the county party historian seemed to panic. When I insisted on interviewing such nonparty old-timers, he frowned and sulked for days on end. He was alarmed and upset by my incursion into "incorrect history."

Nor did my kind provincial-level hosts, both of whom were party historians and hence connected with the ruling party-state, facilitate all of my research, some of which, ironically, they only imagined I intended. When I interviewed in Qi Ji village, in Hua County, in 1987, they were horrified that I had found out that this village existed. The village's Catholic farmers had mounted fierce resistance to the Kuomintang police state in the early 1930s, and it was they who had taken the lead in what supposedly was a Communist Party–led rebellion. My hosts did not want to go with me to this wretchedly poor, remote place, which we had to find by soliciting verbal directions from farmers in different villages. At this point, I was only interested in studying how the Communist Party had brought rural people under its banners in the pre-1949 period, and I had made this clear to my hosts. Out of fear that I would stumble onto prohibited information, however, they overreacted. In attempting to inhibit me from getting at such information, they actually drew me to it. One insufferably hot June afternoon, I decided to break away from household interviews earlier than usual and go check in with the village chief – someone I liked immensely. As I approached the outer wall of the village chief's home courtyard, I overheard the voice of one of the party historians. Unaware of my presence, he was admonishing the village chief: "You can tell him anything you like about what happened here before 1949, but do not dare tell him one damn thing about what happened here after 1949!" Several years later, on one of my return visits, the village chief and several of Qi Ji's farmers told me that two hundred people – at least one-ninth of the village's inhabitants – had died in the Great Leap famine. This episode stimulated my interest in what happened in rural China after 1949.

The problem of party monitoring and blocking is an intractable one for Western scholars of China, but, in studying Da Fo village, I got lucky, and I was quick to seize on this luck and turn it to my advantage. I started my research in Da Fo and in Dongle County four years after I had done extensive oral history interviewing in many other villages and several other counties. Toward the end of this interview work, I befriended a competent and knowledgeable local county historian whose chance for a full life had been ruined by the Cultural Revolution. We instantly hit it off. I listened to him. I realized he had vast and deep knowledge of local history. I came to respect him. In private, he told me that he agreed with my approach – that is, he felt that I was right to rely on rural people and their memories and not the printed materials of the Communist Party. I learned that he had to be careful about what he could help me to learn and see, but in working with him I found a way to get beyond monitoring. This sympathetic county historian "supervised" several interviews without unduly restricting our freedom to question villagers, and, in due time, my Chinese research assistant and I were allowed to interview villagers with or without the county historian present. Once I established mutual trust with this county historian, official blockage also was less and less an issue. For one thing, my provincial-level hosts, the party historians, gladly stayed in the rapidly modernizing Puyang City to engage in rest and recreation rather than accompany me to hot, dirty Da Fo, with its drab food and dirt toilets. These city-based party historians had no desire to return to the grimy and impoverished world of village China, a world they associated with Mao-era deprivation.

Eventually, I learned to work within and outside of the local party-state. By the early 1990s, I was interviewing villagers without being chaperoned by provincial or county-level actors. But what surprises me, in retrospect, is how little village party leaders, including the Da Fo party secretary, did to inhibit my interviewing. Perhaps this had something to do with the fact that I genuinely showed interest in their personal lives and that I listened to their perspectives on their triumphs and disappointments, all of which were influenced by war, famine, and Mao's state. As *Catastrophe and Contention in Rural China* makes clear, their memories of the Great Leap's human cost often were conditioned by their ties to the party-state, but their collaboration helped me better grasp both the official and unofficial roots of China's current crisis.

To be sure, China is a country in which a dominant single-party state has attempted to maintain controls on memory in order to prevent the emergence of political opposition from below.[41] Knowing the allegiances of different groups, particularly among villagers, is of great importance in grasping the politics driving the Maoist leap into the famine, and knowing the extent to which different villagers actually shared Mao's enthusiasm for revolutionary socialism is also important, for this has influenced how various groups of villagers remember the direction of the Great Leap – to some, it was progress, but to others, it was an incapacitating setback. This point cannot be overemphasized, because, in the early 1950s and the years building to the Great Leap Forward, the Communist Party introduced a new political language portraying and praising China as a revolutionary nation and a society utterly and totally committed to "class struggle," the targets of which became those who reacted negatively to the ways in which Mao's designs affected their lives. According to Zhang Letian, this revolutionary

---

[41] Beja, "Forbidden Memory, Unwritten History," 1.

language colored everyday discourse at the village level, and it apparently was used incessantly by village-level party activists in charge of the Maoist campaigns against "rightists" and "class enemies"; this same language was used to legitimate the creation of the people's communes at the outset of the Great Leap Forward.[42] Whether it significantly influenced popular consciousness – particularly how nonparty ordinary villagers received and responded to the Great Leap and its institutions – remains to be discovered. I suspect that by asking questions with words drawn from the official revolutionary language of the Maoist era, one can easily understate resistance to Mao's utopian experiment, though by not using the words of the dominant party-state, one has to be careful not to overestimate the extent to which the weak and the powerless could resist. By and large, I have relied on the latter strategy of getting at popular memory. While keeping in mind that the language of Maoist ideology mattered, I wanted to encourage those I interviewed to tell me how they conducted their lives in ways that were not framed and directed by the state-organized expressions and events so impressively covered in conventional approaches to China under socialist rule, and I also sought to encourage them to voice how they saw and remembered their everyday attempts to survive a long period of political extremity.[43]

In order to achieve this goal, I first chose interview subjects by the technique of "snowball sampling" outlined by Earl R. Babbie.[44] Each individual informant helped me build up a network of native villagers who had participated in, witnessed, and somehow survived the Great Leap Forward and its famine. Many of them also had memories of the decades of history before and after this calamity. This technique helped me to draw in villagers from all walks of life and from different lineages, villagers who had spent their entire lives in Da Fo and those who had left it for both short and long periods, and villagers who had a range of knowledge about resistance to state injustice at the village, township, and county levels from 1920 to 2007. It also allowed me to build up a database that avoided the pitfalls of Communist Party–controlled sampling. During multiple trips to this village, my research assistant and I were able to engage in extensive conversations with individuals and conduct many small group discussions. Approximately 25 percent of the people we interviewed were either members of the Communist Party or of party-state networks, and many of them were implicated in the politics that imposed this disaster. The other 75 percent had no history of direct party involvement, though some people in this nonparty sample were connected to party members by virtue of marriage and kinship ties.

[42] Zhang Letian, "Guojia Huayu de Jieshou Yu Xiaojie," 1–2. On this point, see also Kimberley Ens Manning's important essay, "Marxist Maternalism," 349–50, 357–59, 364–66, 371. On the importance of formal language as an instrument of state power, see Schoenhals, *Doing Things with Words*, 1–29.
[43] Here I build on Kerkvliet's insightful approach, though he is not dealing with the exceptional or with extremity. *Everyday Politics in the Philippines*, 9–11.
[44] Babbie, *Practice of Social Research*, 214–15.

Introduction

In the course of studying villagers' memories, my research assistant and I paid attention to the organizing principles they used in relating their stories.[45] This was a challenging task, but one that was eased by understanding who the respondents were. In struggling with this issue, we came to see that different groups often organized their stories around different principles. The structural narratives of many key village Communist Party leaders seem to have been influenced by a dual identity. This identity was tied up with wartime sacrifice, an experience that apparently increased their involvement with networks of armed Communist power seekers while decreasing their relations with village-based kin, and, furthermore, increased their mobility. As young, poor, semi-rooted people on the move, they had frequent encounters with local and regional Communist Party opponents of intrusive predatory armies – an experience that prepared them to associate war and revolution with Communist order. In contrast, many of Da Fo's ordinary, nonparty farmers were less inclined to organize their personal narratives by the principles of this local party network. They focused more on day-to-day and year-to-year efforts to preserve the entitlements of their households, and when they spoke of a collapsed past, they sometimes implicated the local party leaders, as well as the train of other violent intruders, in this collapse. For many party leaders, post-1949 Chinese history held the promise of a new beginning, and they perceived the difficult times of the Mao years as correctable and behind them. But ordinary farmers tended to relate their stories of the past in terms of a series of disruptions that continued after the Communist revolutionary victory. They not only spoke of how family life had been turned upside down in the Mao years but also voiced fears that the bad road of the past might leap ahead of them, once again leaving them to face new party-orchestrated disaster.

We interviewed village women as well as men. The great majority of some fifty female interviewees (approximately one-eighth of the interview sample) were not connected to the dominant Communist Party families in the village. I found that interviews with female villagers yielded a deeper layer of unofficial popular memory of the Great Leap as an episode of terror and hunger. Rural men, especially the male village party leaders who had learned to present the past in speech bounded by politically correct terminology, often tend to organize their memories around Communist Party–influenced narratives of grand national events, such as the Anti-Japanese War of Resistance, the Cultural Revolution, or the Deng Xiaoping–led reform. In contrast, the markers around which village women organize their memories of the past are more those of unofficial everyday domestic life experiences – when a child was born or died, for example. Thus, in comparison to village men, Da Fo's women were, for the most part, more inclined to express their individual and family past in language that was more immune to party-state efforts to promote forgetting and misremembering. They

---

[45] In constructing this section, I have benefited from personal correspondence with Charles Tilly, March 5, 2007, and from Bearman and Stovel, "Becoming a Nazi," esp. 69, 75, 85–89.

were also more inclined to give vivid, precise, and accurate testimony about how they survived the Maoist famine and endured in its aftermath.[46] In *Catastrophe and Contention in Rural China*, rural women give us portraits of how they suffered from the Great Leap campaign of the predominantly male-directed local Maoist party-state, whose leaders imposed the famine and its hidden politics of sexual predation, and of how they survived and even resisted it.

Rural people are inclined to remember their individual histories as part of a pattern of interaction with family.[47] Following this wisdom, my Chinese research assistant and I interviewed the majority of respondents in their homes, either alone or with a few family members present, placing them within the framework of family memory.[48] This permitted me to grasp the extent to which individual encounters with the agents of the socialist state were entwined with the struggles of small kin groups sharing terrain and habits threatened by state aggrandizement. As scholars of agrarian studies constantly remind us, in the most fundamental sense, peasant politics is about the attempts of rural farm households to avoid appropriation of resources by outside power holders.[49] It is not surprising that people in Da Fo hold keen memories of their own avoidance of the party-state's incursions into family and village life. *Catastrophe and Contention in Rural China* seeks to help us grasp how the Maoists attempted but failed to put an end to this avoidance in the Great Leap Forward, and it prepares us to more fully appreciate the deeper origins of the crisis of state legitimacy in the contemporary post-Mao countryside.

In my research, I have acknowledged the potential unreliability and variability of memory itself. I used three methods to address this problem. First, my research assistant and I usually did not ask specific questions about the Great Leap Forward or the famine – we rarely used these terms in our interviews. Rather, we allowed the life narratives of those we interviewed to guide our conversations, and the villagers' memories about the Great Leap era and the famine emerged within the context of these narratives. Second, rather than ask villagers "why" they and others behaved in a certain manner, we simply invited them to remember their lived everyday experience in refined detail. As Wendy Hollway and Tony Jefferson have pointed out, asking people to explain "why" they acted in a certain way tends to invite justifications rooted in defensive anxieties about the past, and thus to

[46] I have borrowed from, and learned from, the interview methods of Hui-Tam Ho Tai. Personal correspondence, February 25, 2003. For a different approach to gendered memory, see Gail Hershatter's wonderful essay on the difficulties of understanding and interpreting female memories of the 1950s. "Gender of Memory," 2002, esp. 64–68.

[47] Halbwachs, *On Collective Memory*, 52–59, 65–71, 82–83.

[48] Here I built on methods pioneered in a previous work. See Thaxton, *Salt of the Earth*, xvii.

[49] See Hanks, *Rice and Man*; Scott, *Moral Economy of the Peasant, Domination and the Arts of Resistance*, and *Seeing Like a State*; Adas, "From Avoidance to Confrontation"; Friedman, Pickowicz, and Selden, *Chinese Village*; Zhou, *How the Farmers Changed China*; Thaxton, *Salt of the Earth*; White, "Domination, Resistance and Accommodation"; and Thornton, "Comrades and Collectives."

sometimes produce highly selective and self-serving constructions of historical agency.[50] Our strategy was to invite villagers, with and without ties to state power, to freely talk about how they received and responded to state-introduced changes that spanned many decades and different regimes, and our questions did not pre-judge these regimes or their local agents. Third, we interviewed about one in every five individuals repeatedly (two, three, and more times), sometimes asking the same questions in different ways on returning to the village so that I could check the early recall of the respondent against his or her later voiced memories. And, finally, I used a small group interview technique, interviewing villagers and village party leaders I had previously interviewed individually in a group context with two to six fellow villagers. In this way, I could focus on the political life history of only one person among those present while integrating him or her into a wider group discourse on the past. I enlisted the others to nudge the targeted respondent to think harder about the past, to attempt to clarify hazy memories, and to debate whether and how some experience or incident actually happened, thereby jogging and corroborating individual memory through a freewheeling group discussion and exchange. I used this technique in the household courtyards of both powerful and powerless villagers, always paying attention to the fact that people were inclined to speak more freely when in the trusted spaces of their families and friends.

This small group interview method, while designed to check and corroborate individual memory, also gave me access to group memory and helped me grasp how individual memories differed from community memory and how the former sometimes resonated with images, feelings, and insights of the collective memory of villagers. The oral history evidence makes it clear that many individual farmers shared community remembrances that were at odds with many – but certainly not all – of the Great Leap recollections of dominant local Communist Party leaders. It also helps us grasp the process by which village party leaders attempted to take over and dominate discourse in the course of the Great Leap Forward and to insinuate a fabricated memory of the disaster that followed Mao's folly.

Book Overview

The chapters that follow are divided into roughly three parts. The opening three chapters document the formation of the Chinese Communist Party in Da Fo village during the pre-1949 period, showing how party recruitment and armed struggle created two different "poles" of party leadership and how the processes of war and revolution left village leadership in the hands of the least educated and most violent party leaders on the eve of the Communist revolutionary victory, a

---

[50] Here I have benefited from Tilly, personal correspondence, March 7, 2007, and from Holloway and Jefferson, "Biography, Anxiety, and the Experience of Locality," 169–71.

result that power holders did not intend. These are the individuals who in fact led Mao's Great Leap inside the village and helped make Mao's rushed strategy of development so lethal. Chapter 3, which follows the processes through which collective farming was introduced in Da Fo village, focuses on the political factors that turned the Great Leap into a campaign of state-induced food deprivation. It shows how popular everyday resistance to the Maoist creation of big collective units for agricultural production and state appropriation formed individually and collectively within and beyond Da Fo village in the years building up to the Maoist push for the people's communes in 1958 – the year in which the Great Leap began.

The three chapters at the heart of the book document Da Fo villagers' experiences with state-induced deprivation during the Great Leap Forward, their resistance to it, and their ultimate escape from it. Chapter 4 sheds light on how the Great Leap was experienced in Da Fo, describing the introduction of collective farming and public dining halls, analyzing the causes of the famine in Da Fo, and investigating how public criticism was used to keep villagers from retaliating. In Chapter 5, I explore how Da Fo's farmers initially attempted to survive the deprivation of the Great Leap, paying special attention to the efforts of farm households to activate ageless, family-centered strategies of acquiring food security in the face of the revved-up Maoist pressure for greater appropriation, and I also show how the party-state systematically interfered with villagers' rights to pursue these strategies, particularly the right to secure the package of food nutrients required for survival. This chapter illustrates how Da Fo's Communist Party rulers clamped down on the efforts of villagers to stave off starvation through begging, crop theft, migration, and a host of other desperate survival activities. I argue that party-state repression was a critical factor and induced what Amartya Sen would call the "entitlement failure" of the Great Leap famine.[51] This famine was not just the product of the lack of food pure and simple but rather was intimately connected with a wave of Maoist-commissioned repression that deprived villagers of their family-centered means of food entitlement. Aimed at taking away all means of private household food production, this Maoist repression induced the social catastrophe of the Great Leap.[52] This chapter sheds light on such repression in Xinyang, where Maoism became synonymous with unbelievable savagery, and on the link between this savagery and the fate of Da Fo in the crisis months of the Great Leap Forward.

In 2000, Li Ruojian published a breakthrough article on social turmoil and social control during the Great Leap, in which he documented the rise of violent resistance to the official agents of Mao's ruinous communal experiment.[53]

---

[51] Sen, *Poverty and Famines*, 51.
[52] Just as V. Smil's important essay argues. Smil, "China's Great Famine," 1619–21.
[53] Li Ruojian, "Dayuejin Yu Kunnan Shiqi de Shehui Dongdang Yu Kongzhi," 1–4.

Chapter 6 reveals how the majority of Da Fo's villagers escaped the famine of Maoist rule quite differently, through a cautious form of silent contention from below. The focus here is on how villagers employed everyday resistance to effectively resist the claims of local party leaders and how, in the final analysis, they saved themselves from starvation without the help of Liu Shaoqi and the enlightened inner-party opponents of Mao, who introduced reforms in 1961. This chapter also sheds light on the consequences of this escape from the famine for resistance, legitimacy, and reform in the immediate and long-term aftermath of Mao's Great Leap.

The final three chapters of the book examine what we might think of as the immediate legacy of the Great Leap Forward Famine in Da Fo. Chapters 7 and 8 both cover the period between the end of the Great Leap in 1961 and well into the reform era that began following Mao's death in 1976. The first focuses on politics, the second on economics. The nature and cost of the Cultural Revolution – and particularly its strong links to the Great Leap Forward – are taken up in the seventh chapter. This chapter gives special attention to how the famine survivors seized on this and earlier Maoist-inspired political movements to voice grievances against the local Maoist party leaders who perpetrated the Great Leap famine. In Da Fo, as in other rural areas, the Cultural Revolution – a rerun of the war communism that produced the Great Leap – inspired another outbreak of "vigilante socialism" by militia forces, so in the end it was left to the People's Liberation Army (PLA) to attempt to restore political order.[54] But the PLA intervention in Da Fo, though it put an end to chaos in the short term, also brought the same hated leaders of the Great Leap era back to power, ironically compromising the party's chances of regaining legitimacy through reform.

Chapter 8 explores the nature of the economic recovery and rehabilitation engineered by ordinary villagers in the decades spanning the end of the Great Leap and the fading of the Cultural Revolution. After the Great Leap failed, they resorted to their own market-focused strategies of survival and rejected active engagement with the party, which sought to rebuild trust with farmers and reintegrate village production with state revenue goals. As consumers, poor farm people turned to petty trade as their first path to survival long before Deng Xiaoping and post-Mao reformers advocated market-focused entrepreneurship, leaving Mao's successors to try to catch up with and take credit for popular market initiatives originally undertaken to escape the protracted deprivation of socialist famine.

The final chapter reveals how Da Fo villagers, having largely rejected the Communist Party's attempts to shape their memories of the Great Leap Forward, eventually acted on their latent desires to get even with local party leaders who

---

[54] Friedman, Pickowicz, and Selden, *Revolution, Resistance, and Reform*, 132–33, 136–45, 150.

perpetrated the savagery and starvation of the Great Leap.[55] The people of Da Fo inform us that this struggle to settle old unforgotten grievances irrupted again in the reform era, after Mao was gone, and that this unauthorized struggle, rather than the reform policy per se, exposed the old-guard Maoists to the villagers' hidden desire to avenge the Great Leap past.

[55] The insightful scholarship of Xin Liu, who doubts that a "hidden transcript" can be found in Chinese villages, has inspired this chapter, and I am indebted to his challenge to find it. Liu, *In One's Own Shadow*, 22.

1

The Republican Era and the Emergence of Communist Leadership during the Anti-Japanese War of Resistance

Located in rural Dongle County in the northern tip of Henan province on the lower North China Plain, Da Fo village was settled by migrants from Shanxi's Hongdong County in the first century of Ming rule. A day's journey from Beijing, six hundred miles to the northeast, Da Fo is far from the center of national power. After a seven-hour train ride from Beijing to the Anyang station in Henan province, the contemporary traveler continues eastbound by automobile into rural Anyang County. Once past the drab market stalls of Chu Wang town, in Neihuang County, the color of the earth begins to fade from light brown to pale yellow, showing traces of the acute salinization that ruined the fertile croplands of villages positioned along the old course of the Yellow River in the early twentieth century, when its tributaries flooded frequently.

Here the civilization of urban China rapidly gives way to the eternal rhythms of rural life. Within less than an hour the traveler is moving along a broken tarred road where red and yellow oxen compete with young Chinese driving jeeps and trucks. Across the Dongle County line, the fields display the products of dry zone agriculture. This agricultural zone is distinguished by its wheat, corn, and millet production; little rice is grown in this area of the North China Plain. Three hours out of Anyang, shortly after entering Liangmen (Two Gates) township, a one-*li* (0.5-kilometer) bumpy dirt trail designed by donkey carts and horse-drawn wagons passes by young people peddling live bronze, black, and gold chickens in impromptu trailside markets. Then, only a few minutes from the turbulent Wei River, Da Fo village comes into view. Lined by blue China asters, its entry road leads to red brick houses that have replaced the thatched and mud-brick huts of the past.

Da Fo derives its name from a huge Buddhist pantheon on which scores of deities were etched.[1] The story of this Buddhist temple and its multiple statues has been handed down to the villagers by their ancestors. When the village was initially settled, in the Ming period, a priest in charge of the temple seized a local girl, confined her to the temple complex, and presented her as a saint, conning villagers into giving up material possessions to receive her blessing. In time, the girl fled, declared she had been abducted, and exposed the charlatan. Angered by this discovery, villagers appealed to local officials and to the emperor to allow them to destroy the temple and drive out the priest. When the emperor hesitated, a rumor that he owed the priest for having saved his life swirled, and villagers thereupon persuaded local officials to grant the appeal. Though they destroyed the temple, they continued to refer to its grounds as the spot where the great pantheon of Buddhist gods had been. Consequently this place became known as Da Fo: the village of the Great Buddha.

In 2001, four decades after the Great Leap Forward, Da Fo village had approximately 2,800 inhabitants, twice the population of the late Republican period. A poor rural interior village with little industry, most of its families still depend on tilling the land for a living, though they also obtain income from market-focused petty trade and, increasingly, from urban-based construction work – we will encounter them as migrant workers in the next volume. As in imperial and Republican times, this remote place is barely on the political map of central government officials, if at all. Nonetheless, Da Fo played a role in the rise of the Chinese Communist Party in the pre-1949 period, just as it played a part in Mao's attempt to design a national socialist polity. To understand this role, we must first understand the aspects of Da Fo's history, economy, and ecosystem that affect villagers' expectations of their political leaders. The slighting of local political history in the Republican era – the period from the termination of the Qing dynasty in 1911 to the victory of the Communist Party over Chiang Kaishek's Nationalist government in 1949 – has limited outsiders' efforts to fully comprehend the central and enduring paradox of politics in rural China under Communist Party rule: The pre-1949 Maoist insurgency attracted rural people from all walks of life, promising them freedom from agricultural scarcity, corrupt and violent dictatorship, and pillage, rape, and murder by invading armies of various stripes. Yet the impact of state violence, famine, and war led to the rise of native local Communist leaders who practiced violent politics in their home communities and formed expectations of entitlement that proved incompatible with the promises of a Communist government that claimed to be committed to guaranteeing livelihood, building democracy, and nurturing a confident nationalism.

---

[1] As mentioned in the introduction, I have used pseudonyms for the name of the village and its denizens. In crafting this one small part of the narrative, I have altered the name of the temple. "Da Fo," or "Great Buddha," is therefore a pseudonym. Aside from this improvisation, virtually every detail of the village's history is accurate.

Though it was Mao himself who most significantly betrayed the promise of modern China's revolution, we cannot explain the speed or scope of the unbelievable savagery unleashed in rural communities during the Great Leap period without reference to Mao's willing accomplices in the countryside. In Da Fo, these accomplices first came to the fore as village leaders during the early years of the Anti-Japanese War of Resistance, when Kuomintang power had collapsed on the North China Plain and villagers looked to local men to protect their livelihoods and offer them a new vision of just governance.

Saline Earth and Earth Salt

By the time the Qing dynasty was upended in 1911, the people of Da Fo village could no longer rely solely on agriculture to guarantee the basic requirements of subsistence. Positioned on the southern end of the Zhang River in Hebei province and on the northern flank of the Wei River in Henan, Da Fo was increasingly affected by saline flood waters in the early Republican era. When it rained hard, the floods on the Xiao River went directly into the upper reaches of the Wei River, depositing tons of salt and alkaline into the soils of Da Fo. By 1925, about 70 percent of Da Fo's salt-impregnated land was layered twenty feet deep with these deposits.[2] This *jiandi*, or alkaline land, inhibited the flow of nitrogen to grain crops, so wheat, the major cereal crop of the Hebei-Shandong-Henan border area in which Da Fo is located, had an average yield of only sixty to seventy-five *jin* per *mu* in the Republican period, as compared to an average yield of six hundred to eight hundred *jin* per *mu* in the 1990s. (One *jin*, or sixteen *liang*, is equivalent to 1.3 pounds. One *mu* is equal to 0.165 acres.) Cereal yields fell as salinization intensified in the early Republican period, when government upkeep of the canal system historically designed to carry salt deposits from interior farmlands to rivers linked to the sea was totally neglected.[3]

By the time Chiang Kai-shek established the Nationalist government in Nanjing, Jiangsu province, on November 4, 1928, and then extended the reach of the Kuomintang to Dongle County in the early 1930s, only a few of Da Fo's farm households could still rely solely on grain crops grown on their small parcels for survival. Villagers indicate that during the Republican period four big landowning households owned 1,800 *mu* of the 4,000 *mu* of cropland in Da Fo. Making up less than 1 percent of the village households, these big landowners held nearly 50 percent of the land – the most fertile land in the village. About five additional wealthy farming households owned another fifty to seventy *mu* of land each, and thirty more households held approximately twenty *mu* of land, with a few holding up to thirty *mu*. This left nearly two hundred households to compete for approximately 1,500 *mu* of poor saline land. The average holding of these land-hungry

---

[2] Thaxton, *Salt of the Earth*, chs. 1–2; Seybolt, *Throwing the Emperor*, 67, 12; Seybolt, "War Within a War," 205.
[3] See Pomeranz, *Making of a Hinterland*; Thaxton, *Salt of the Earth*.

households was seven *mu*, but some owned as many as fifteen, whereas others owned only one to five *mu*. These two hundred farm households, composing nearly three-quarters of Da Fo's marginalized families, farmed small plots of the most acutely salinized and sandy land in the village. Even a fairly good harvest yield from summer wheat and autumn corn and millet was not enough to see a family of five through the year.

To offset diminishing grain yields in normal times and keep from succumbing to hunger when calamity struck, Da Fo's marginalized tillers engaged in three different types of activities to make ends meet. Most of them farmed tiny, scattered strips of land planted with winter wheat harvested in mid-June, spring corn that brought returns in August, and *gaoliang*, or sorghum, which was rotated with millet and was ripe for the taking by October.

They supplemented crop production with off-farm market earnings, producing earth salt (*xiaoyan*) by mixing the saline dirt with water and placing the muddy brew in cauldrons over fires or in family-run, solar-heated salt ponds. This primitive salt was then sold at local, periodically convened village markets, including one in Da Fo itself. The salt trade became vital to family survival, as income from it was used to purchase up to 50 percent of household food supply (and as much as 90 percent in families with only one to seven *mu* of poor saline land). Dependency on making earth salt for a living colored much of village life. Virtually every Da Fo household had a red cart to collect soil to make salt, and every household possessed one or two cauldrons for making salt.

To supplement crop production and profits from salt peddled in local markets, finally, a minority of villagers also engaged in side-occupations involving highly specialized skills. They became carpenters, stonecutters, tailors, small traders, porters, purchase agents, and animal hide dealers. Income derived from these activities, some of which required sojourning in Dongle and surrounding counties, was used to purchase as much as 10 percent of household food supply in ordinary years, enabling the poorly endowed inhabitants of Da Fo to survive the first three serious crises of the Republican era.

The Crises of the Republican Period

In the spring of 1920, a severe drought gripped the lower part of the North China Plain, settling over northern Henan, western Shandong, and southern Hebei provinces. This long drought extended into the spring of 1921. As a result, several million farmers perished in what came to be called the North China Famine of 1921. Dongle County was affected, as was Da Fo. Farmers remember that its fields were parched, and grain crop yields fell to twenty and thirty *jin* per *mu*. But the old-timers also remember that no one in Da Fo died in this famine. Born in 1905, Bao Xinyuan, a native of Da Fo, was sixteen when the famine gripped the western part of Dongle County. He recalls how people in Da Fo got through this time of extreme hunger by migrating and trading in earth salt:

I remember the famine of the ninth year of the Republic. In that year, some Bao lineage members had to migrate to Shanxi. Bao Zheng, Bao Suwang, Pang Zhanlin, Pang Huixin, and Pang Haiyin all had to go there. They went to Yueyang County to open up wasteland, and they survived by tilling crops on this reclaimed land for a year or so. Then they returned here, bringing their newborn children back with them. Actually, few people in Da Fo had to migrate, and few died, because most of us were able to rely on the money from salt trade to purchase grain to sell in other places. Buying and selling this grain helped us survive the famine.[4]

Still, at the height of the famine nearly 30 percent of Da Fo's households found themselves in dire straits, for the Dongle County government had no relief grain to distribute to villagers. Most of the grain taken via taxation from villagers had been given up to the warlord-directed central government that ruled Henan province in the 1920s, and little of it had been returned to county officials for relief purposes.[5] The Dongle County magistrate therefore agreed to cooperate with an international famine relief agency to enable the county's most desperate villagers to survive the famine. In 1921, when Da Fo's wheat harvest wilted, an American Protestant missionary from this famine relief organization accompanied several Dongle County officials to investigate which of Da Fo's households were without grain. These charitable outsiders issued relief grain tickets to nearly fifty households, whose heads turned in the tickets for millet in Handan, over the border in Hebei province.[6]

The image of China as a "land of famine" in which village dwellers invariably succumbed to starvation every time there was serious harvest failure[7] not only underestimates the resiliency of the market-focused agrarian economy in which Da Fo's smallholders operated, it also ignores the extent to which they were able to activate a host of customary family strategies of food acquisition when famine loomed.[8] Villagers recall a range of self-help strategies to cope with grain scarcity, including reliance on tuber crops such as sweet potatoes, wild vegetables, and the tender white blossoms of Da Fo's Chinese scholar trees (*huaishu*) and its willow trees (*liushu*). Begging was yet another strategy, usually undertaken during the spring hunger and sometimes extended over longer periods in settings beyond Da Fo.[9] As we have seen, migration to other less affected rural communities in Dongle County itself and in the wider triprovincial border area was also an option. Villagers speak of going to places where they had kinship connections to help them survive for a few months or longer. Before people migrated out of Da Fo on a more permanent basis, they would sell off property, including used clothes, and

[4] Bao Xinyuan, interview, August 18, 1989.
[5] Pang Xiannai, interview, August 18, 1989.
[6] Bao Xinyuan, interview, August 18, 1989; Pang Xiannai, interview, August 18, 1989.
[7] For such a representation, see Becker, *Hungry Ghosts*, 10–22.
[8] As Amartya Sen's work, *Poverty and Famines*, might predict, this system of subsistence-level entitlement was based on the ability of families to obtain food supplies by freely engaging in such strategies. *Poverty and Famines*, 45–59.
[9] Bao Zhishan, interview, August 19, 1989.

27

they also pawned land. During the period of the famine, Da Fo villagers solicited low-interest grain loans from several big landholders, including Bao Yuhua and Bao Sunyuan, although this strategy proved less efficacious when the drought proportionately reduced crop production in the fields of the wealthy landholders.

Between 1925 and 1937, a wave of banditry rocked the Wei River area, presenting Da Fo with another crisis. Several bandit armies operated in the triprovincial North China border area. The most notorious were a thousand-man force led by Yang Faxian out of Dongle, a thousand-man unit out of Neihuang under Guo Qing,[10] a two-thousand-man force under Chen Daobing and Chen Xinmeng from Hui County, and a two-thousand-man bandit network led by Zhang Jintang in Daming. Specializing in raiding village croplands and kidnapping for ransom, these bandits targeted better-off market villages.[11] In mid-1927, a forty-man contingent of Zhang Jintang's bandit army struck Da Fo, whose inhabitants had relied on the salt trade to engineer an impressive economic recovery from the 1921 famine, making the village a prized object of predatory banditry. The bandit force kidnapped the brother of Pang Xianzhi, whose family quickly sold half of its 120 *mu* of farmland in order to get the six hundred silver dollars needed to ransom him.[12]

Shortly after the Nationalist government established its presence in Dongle County in the early 1930s, the bandit Zhang Jintang was captured and put to death by the Dongle County police under the direction of the Kuomintang. Kidnapping subsided for a short period, but the Dongle County Kuomintang was unable to completely eradicate banditry in the Wei River area, and the bandit armies of Yang Faxian, Chen Daobing, and Guo Qing continued to raid relatively affluent villages and prized market towns. Robbery and kidnapping persisted around Da Fo in Dongle County and Tuxingcun village in adjacent Wei County. During this period, Yang Faxian plundered Chu Wang town in Neihuang[13] and then set his sights on Dongle's villages. Yin Fengxiu, a native of Da Niu village, since married into Da Fo, is still haunted by the memory of this banditry:

I have encountered so much hardship in my lifetime – Yang Faxian's bandit army, the Nationalist soldiers, the Japanese devils invading us. My family was robbed twice by Yang Faxian's armed men. The first time they took packages of our clothes. The second time they took the family ox. My grandfather followed them all the way to Chu Wang town, begging them to show mercy. In the end, they allowed him to take back his ox, but they also beat him with their weapons.[14]

Constantly fearful of being overrun by bandits, Da Fo's wealthier households pooled resources to build high walls around the village in the mid-1930s so that

[10] Seybolt, "War Within a War," 212.
[11] Pang Xiannai, interview, August 18, 1989; Bao Gui, interview, August 20, 1989.
[12] Pang Xiannai, interview, August 18, 1989.
[13] Seybolt, "War Within a War," 212.
[14] Yin Fengxiu, interview, July 10–11, 2002.

villagers did not need to flee every raid. In these years, Da Fo became a sanctuary for the victims of bandit assaults on surrounding villages. One hundred of these desperate outsiders declared themselves to be monks and began living in Da Fo's temples, including the Nainai temple, the Ghost temple, and the *Guandi* (war god) temple in the eastern quadrant of the village. In the late 1950s, when villagers were mobilized by the Maoists to participate in a deep-plowing campaign to improve crop yields, the ghosts of this disordered bandit past turned up. Pang Guihua recalls the discovery: "During the Great Leap Forward," says Pang, "we were digging the field deep in the east corner of the village. We dug up twenty-three human skulls there. We believed that these were the skulls of the people who had fled the bandits and become monks in our temples."[15]

In the memory of villagers, however, the greatest threat to peace and sustenance prior to World War II was neither famine nor banditry, but rather the national-level Kuomintang tax state. From the moment the Nationalist government established its presence in Dongle County in 1930, there were squabbles over the land tax, which was collected by county officials. Da Fo's residents were required to pay one silver dollar for every eight *mu* of land, a regressive tax that favored those with more land and fertile fields. The tax was due twice annually, once for summer wheat and again for the autumn harvest. Piled on top of this land tax was a host of surtaxes, including the infamous *gongzhai*, or bond tax, which the Kuomintang required all villagers with fifty *mu* of land to pay.[16]

But the land tax and the bond tax were only minor annoyances compared to the salt tax. After seizing control of the state in 1928, Chiang Kai-shek's Nationalist government attempted to create a powerful, unified, fiscally sound national political order. High Kuomintang officials looked to the Ministry of Finance to carry out revenue policies aimed at producing new state wealth. Operating from Nanjing, the Nationalist government's fiscal leaders projected their fiscal claims into distant rural counties, towns, and villages by capturing intermediate-level regional institutions like the Changlu (North China) Salt Company, a merchant-run salt firm that historically had been the indirect state instrument for collecting the salt tax in North China. In effect, the Kuomintang national leadership attempted to transform China's salt tax administration into an expanded profit-gathering enterprise at the expense of rural dwellers.

Two facets of this process had grave political implications for the people who produced and marketed earth salt in Da Fo. Their earth salt undersold the "official" salt from which Nationalist government leaders wanted to bolster revenue flow. To force rural consumers to purchase official salt, which came from the government-held oceanic salt pans along China's more industrialized east coast, Chiang Kai-shek's officials declared the production and sale of earth salt – which had been permitted and only loosely supervised in the last decade of the Qing

---

[15] Pang Guihua, interview, July 11, 2002.
[16] Pang Xiannai, interview, August 18, 1989.

dynasty and the first years of the Republic – to be illegal. Their efforts to enforce this monopoly invariably undermined the sale of cheaper earth salt in the markets of Dongle, Daming, Weixian, and other counties of the deep interior. Ministry of Finance officials labeled the sale of earth salt "smuggling" and then proceeded to justify the crackdown on this petty trade as a campaign against black market activity harmful to state revenue growth. Ultimately, the attempt by the Nationalist government to increase the volume of maritime salt sent into this remote border area and to raise the price of salt distributed through government-operated shops backfired. Local people from all walks of life began to rely even more on cheaper earth salt markets, which mushroomed throughout the early 1930s. Their lack of compliance gave the Nanjing-based Ministry of Finance a pretext to rely on greater force to enforce its salt monopoly campaign.

Beginning in 1930, Kuomintang finance minister T. V. Song transformed a "salt investigation force" conceived by warlord Yuan Shikai in 1915 into a full-fledged national tax police force, the Shuijingtuan. First established in the Shanghai area, this centrist police force extended the reach of the central government–controlled North China Salt Tax Bureau from Tianjin deep into the remote counties along the old course of the Yellow River – a place where poor farmers, village teachers, minor gentry figures, and even local government personnel had a stake in the lower-priced earth salt. The Shuijingtuan was an independent 45,000-man police instrument of the Kuomintang fiscal center. Armed with handguns, modern rifles, and a machine gun, and riding horses or bicycles, each of its forty-five-man police units was responsible only to the Kuomintang Ministry of Finance and had no obligations to people in the salt land villages. On June 15, 1932, the Ministry of Finance ordered every county magistrate in Hebei, Shandong, and Henan to cooperate with its salt tax force to remove the "illegal salt makers" from their lands and to arrest those who resisted. Two years later, the Kuomintang Department of Civil Affairs, bowing to pressure from the Ministry of Finance, exempted the salt tax police from responsibility for injuring or killing people who dared to organize collective resistance to government efforts to ban the production and sale of earth salt.[17]

In the spring of 1930, a unit of the salt tax force established its presence in Dongle County town and then set out to repress salt making in the villages of western Dongle. Da Fo and Shangcunji, where Da Fo's salt makers frequently traded, became targets of the salt tax police. The police first invaded Da Fo on bicycle, just after they had initiated an attack on people trading earth salt in Shangcun market. Armed with rifles and bayonets, they broke the salt makers' cauldrons, dumped confiscated earth salt in village streets, and levied fines on households engaged in production of the contraband.[18] The villagers were

[17] Thaxton, *Salt of the Earth*, 67–68, 76–77; "Lai Han Zhao Deng" (Letter to the Publisher), *Da Gong Bao*, April 17, 1935.

[18] Ruan Yin, interview, August 18, 1989; Bao Lijun, interview, August 23, 1989; Bao Zhimin, interview, August 24, 1989; Zheng Tianbao, interview, August 24, 1989.

frightened and angry. So were Da Fo's big landholders, who also profited from marketing earth salt produced by the tenants of their poorest lands. Bao Jinsong, the village chief in 1930, warned the head of the salt tax police in Dongle town that the salt makers in Da Fo might kill the police if there were further incursions, and he teamed up with Zheng Daqing and Bao Zhilong to organize a crowd of angry salt makers to greet the police with jeers and threats of bloodshed when they came to Da Fo. The police took notice and retreated to Dongle town, but they soon resumed their violent incursions.

In the following year, Da Fo's salt makers played hide-and-seek with the police, fleeing every time the police approached and returning to the village to salvage their red carts and salt-making tools after nightfall, when the police had retired to their base in Shangcun market town.[19] In time, they also shifted their salt trade to unpatrolled market sites, which meant they gave up on trading in Shangcunji. Pang Xiannai explains: "After the police attack, we increasingly sold our salt in Huicun, Shuidi, Shitai, and Xiaolu. We no longer went to Shangcun market because the salt police were concentrated there. We had sold there often before the police came, but afterward we avoided them by going to sell in these other villages."[20] Those villagers who tried to trade their salt surreptitiously in Shangcunji were discovered, beaten, and punished. In July 1931 Bao Zheng was arrested by the salt police, along with seven other people. He managed to escape and return to Da Fo.[21]

Several months later, in autumn of 1931, thirty of Da Fo's salt makers joined with more than one hundred of their counterparts in the first transvillage collective action against the Kuomintang salt revenue police in Dongle County. Bao Zhilong, only thirteen years old at the time, joined with Zheng Daqing to coordinate a protest march from Da Fo to Shangcunji, where villagers confronted the police. Bao Zhilong explains,

I fought the salt police in 1931, and so did Zheng Daqing, a salt maker and a purchase agent. Zheng Daqing was the leader of this struggle, as he was very good at producing earth salt and nitrate. Indeed, a lot of villagers had learned how to produce earth salt and nitrate from him, and they followed him in this struggle – Pang Faliang, Bao Wusheng, Bao Peifu, and others were among his followers. Most of these people were among the better-off villagers who had improved their households by earth salt trade, which enabled them to earn money to purchase land.[22]

Da Fo's contingent of salt makers joined with counterparts from other rural places in hurling bricks at the heads of the police and seizing their bicycles, temporarily driving them from Shangcunji back to Dongle County town.[23]

---

[19] Ruan Yin, interview, August 18, 1989.
[20] Pang Xiannai, interview, August 18, 1989.
[21] Bao Zheng, interview, August 22, 1989.
[22] Bao Zhilong, interview, August 17, 1989.
[23] Ibid.

Despite the aggressive reaction of villagers, the salt tax police were relentless. In late 1934 they killed twenty salt makers near the Dongle-Daming County line and wounded many others in clashes to the north of Da Fo, Shangcunji, and Dongle County town. The violent police campaign to suppress the salt market galvanized Da Fo's poorly endowed smallholders, drawing them to popular anti-police collective actions in the countryside and then in Dongle County town, where in the spring of 1935 they joined with their counterparts from scores of other border area counties to confront the vanguard of the Shuijingtuan. In the violent clash that followed, two members of the salt tax police were killed. Three salt makers lost their lives, and scores were injured in scuffles with the police.

The next year's protest movement in Dongle alerted the Nationalist government to the persistent strength of its political rivals in this section of the North China Plain. Da Fo's salt makers were first joined by several thousand protesters from the rural salt land villages surrounding Dongle town, including Nan Fengzhuang, Qin Ling Dian, and Pingyuanzhuang to the south. They were buoyed by the arrival in early April 1935 of another three thousand members of the Transcounty Salt Makers' Association, whose leadership surrounded the county seat and who engaged in multiple acts of resistance, including a massive sit-in and a battle to keep the police from destroying salt-making ponds.[24]

The balance of power shifted to the protesters when key members of the Dongle County elite placed themselves on the side of the salt makers. Dongle was a gentry stronghold, and prominent minor gentry figures – many of whom themselves had an economic interest in the earth salt trade – feared the police attacks would force many of the poorest inhabitants of the salt land villages to turn to desperate acts of crop theft and banditry.[25] Moreover, some of the agents of the Dongle County Public Security Bureau had blood ties to the poor salt producers in Shangcunji and Da Fo. They knew the movements of the police, and they helped to prepare the salt producers in advance of police raids, reducing the raids' effectiveness.[26] The Kuomintang-appointed county magistrate, Wei Congqing, could not count on these people as reliable allies in a showdown with the salt tax police. Checkmated by this united front of local people, the magistrate called on the local gentry on April 12, 1935, and asked them to mediate the conflict between the villagers and the police. He accompanied them to a number of salt land villages, where peace talks were held, and pleaded with them to help persuade the salt makers to refrain from attacking the police. Wei promised the salt makers he would honor their major demands: the police would leave Dongle County; local people would be allowed to market earth salt; and the families of those who had been killed during the police confrontations would be compensated.[27]

[24] Thaxton, *Salt of the Earth*, 182–83.
[25] Ibid., 189.
[26] Ibid., 184.
[27] Ibid., 183; "Dongle Canan Shanhou," *Da Gong Bao*, April 17, 1935.

With news of this victory in hand, Da Fo's salt makers went back to their red pushcart operations and pondered the advantages of further collective action. Zheng Daqing and Bao Zhilong, the leaders of Da Fo's anti-police rebels, were hailed as community leaders who had fought for the basic subsistence rights of the rural poor, opposed state greed, and championed local justice. This struggle against the Nationalist government's attempts to deprive Da Fo village of one of its most important subsistence entitlements would prove important in later years.

Large Landholders in the Republican Period

The participation of Da Fo's large landholders in the actions against the salt tax police made sense in terms of the social relationships between village smallholders and large landholders during the Republican period. In the aftermath of the Communist Revolution, Mao Zedong and the Marxist theoreticians in the Communist Party wrongly ascribed the mobilization of impoverished peasants into the revolutionary movement to their having been exploited by cruel landlords. This paradigm of horizontal class-based conflict does not accurately capture popular memory of the relationship of Da Fo's big landowners to the marginalized salt land smallholders during the Republican period, which served to sustain the village as a viable economic and social unit.

The Bao lineage, whose members originally settled the village, was the largest of seven descent kin groups in Da Fo, comprising 65 percent of the village households. The descendents of the Pangs, Zhengs, and Ruans made up another substantial cluster of "patrilineal kin" groups, after which there were three or four other small descent groups.[28] At the time of the transition from dynastic to Republican rule, four Bao households owned nearly half the land in the village. Big landholder Bao Yuhua was one of them. It was said that Bao Yuhua's grandfather had possessed several thousand *mu* and that a decline in his household fortunes started when Bao Yuhua's father sold off land under the pressure of agricultural degradation and government tax claims, leaving his family with only four hundred *mu* by the early 1920s.

A notable person in Da Fo and in Dongle County, Bao Yuhua not only managed the economy of his own household but also presided over a host of rituals, community services, and work relationships with other Bao kin group members, including many of the poor tillers of the salt lands. He was the most influential figure in the dominant Bao kin group and a pivotal player in village politics. When a Bao lineage member died, for example, Bao Yuhua often was consulted about funeral rites. He sometimes helped the family of the deceased to plan the funeral ceremonies and prepare a proper burial, acquire a coffin, hire musicians, and arrange for the pallbearers.[29] Each year on Hanshi, the spring day when villagers

---

[28] On the importance of such groups, see Ruf, *Cadres and Kin*, 11.

[29] On the importance of this process in solidifying the unity of the descent group, see Watson and Rawski, *Death Ritual*, and Ruf, *Cadres and Kin*, 17.

visited their ancestors' tombs, the Bao lineage sponsored a banquet for its members that offered each person two *jin* of steamed bread and several bowls full of pork. The Bao lineage had fifty *mu* of temple land, and Bao Yuhua, along with other Bao lineage heads, made sure that the harvest from this land was used to underwrite the Hanshi banquet.[30] Along with the other big Da Fo landowners, Bao Yuhua also paid his share of the costs of sponsoring the traditional Land and Water Festivals, which drew people from far and wide to trade, play, and surrender themselves to the protective spell of Guangong, the war god whom many villagers revered.[31]

As the owner of four hundred *mu* of Da Fo's most fertile land, of a village winery, and of scores of rental properties in the vicinity of Shangcun market, Bao Yuhua was positioned to provide a number of benefits and services to villagers, many of whom were farmers in his lineage.[32] They responded by giving support, loyalty, and services to Bao Yuhua, whom they referred to as their *en ren*, or benefactor, the Chinese term for a good, trustworthy patron. (The word "*dizhu*," or "landlord," did not even exist in the vocabulary of the villagers at this time.) By accounts an ally of poor and rich alike, Bao enjoyed a good reputation among most of them because "he was sympathetic to poor folks."[33] During the 1920s and 1930s, Bao Yuhua provided villagers within his network with goods and services deemed essential to their survival, and stories of his good will still circulate. He was known for treating his three permanent hired hands and his dozen or so temporary workers with fairness. He frequently allowed people in Da Fo to share his farm tools, seeds, surplus crops, and his unstored harvest. Bao Zhendao, who was eighty-four years old in the summer of 2002, recalls the patronage of Da Fo's "good landlord," a term that poor villagers used to describe former benefactors after the Communist Party introduced the term "landlord" into popular vocabulary:

Bao Yuhua, one of the village landlords, was different from the other three. He was more sympathetic to the poor people. He allowed the poor villagers to glean in his fields. . . . He had a big pile of wheat straw on his threshing grounds, and he always placed a pitchfork beside the pile so people could get the straw. Usually, by the end of autumn, his big wheat straw pile was completely taken away by the poor villagers. Bao Yuhua never did anything to stop this. Because of his benevolence, everybody in Da Fo thought Bao Yuhua was a good person.[34]

This was an understatement. Bao Yuhua also was well known for issuing small, interest-free grain loans to poor tillers when their saline lands were afflicted by drought and pestilence, allowing them to pay him back when their budgets

[30] Bao Zhendao, interview, July 6, 2002.
[31] Pang Siyin, interview, August 21, 1989.
[32] Bao Peizhi, interview, June 15, 2006.
[33] Bao Zhendao, interview, July 5, 2002.
[34] Ibid.

permitted. Indeed, Bao Yuhua's interest-free hunger loans helped many Da Fo families survive the Henan Famine of 1942.[35] Villagers recall that if a few poor people pilfered a little of the crop from the edge of Bao Yuhua's grain fields, Bao never made a fuss about it, and he let people from Da Fo and Shuidi glean his wheat fields after the harvest.

Bao Yuhua was instrumental in keeping rival Bao landlords from mistreating villagers, and he also provided protection from external predatory forces. Bao was active in organizing people to defend Da Fo from roving bandit groups in the Dongle–Wei County–Daming area in the early 1930s, and he helped them resist the predatory designs of Yang Faxian's bandit army on the eve of the Japanese invasion. Bao further enhanced his reputation by paying for the school tuition of various members of the Bao lineage, thereby helping his own sublineage add status to its material wealth and improving the standing of the village in the eyes of Dongle County leaders. In the 1930s, Da Fo's students registered impressive scores in the competitive exams for Dongle County high school and regional college slots. During these years of Kuomintang ascendance, several outstanding Da Fo graduates of the Dongle County high school and the Daming Seventh Normal College (a key regional college) were among the esteemed returned student-clients of Bao Yuhua, enhancing his reputation as they graduated into leadership roles in the schools of surrounding villages and towns.

In the same period in which Bao Yuhua established himself as a benefactor of the poor, a countertrend developed among Da Fo's other three "landlords," Bao Zhihai, Bao Wenhao, and Bao Sunyuan, each of whom possessed more than four hundred *mu* of land. Bao Zhihai was the worst of the three. According to Bao Zhendao, "Bao Zhihai did not enjoy a good reputation in the village because he did not show any sympathy for poor folk." Bao Zhihai held the lowest rank of scholar (*xuicai*) in the Qing system, but after the dynasty was overthrown this title was no longer recognized, and Bao lost his stipend from the Dongle County government. Although Bao Zhihai did not hold an official post in Da Fo in the 1920s, he nonetheless is remembered as putting on haughty airs, taking advantage of many villagers, and performing few acts of philanthropy.[36]

The misdeeds of Bao Zhihai (and to a lesser extent of his son Bao Yinyuan) multiplied in the years of Kuomintang rule. Whereas many were in fact minor, they nonetheless undermined his authority and left a record of animosity. In the past, Bao Zhihai, like other big landholders, had more or less respected the basic social rights of villagers. For example, he had provided long-term employment for hired field hands. By the late 1920s, however, he began to enlist field hands on a short-term basis, to cut back on the meals once provided to them, and to pay them only after the harvest was completed and deposited on his threshing

[35] Bao Zhimin, interview, August 24, 1989.
[36] Bao Zhendao, interview, July 5, 2002.

ground, discontinuing the customary practice of advanced payment or payment in stages.[37] In the early 1930s, Bao Zhihai began charging exorbitant interest rates on loans made to villagers in the time of spring hunger. If a poor household borrowed one *dou* (thirty *jin*) in the two months before the June wheat harvest, then its members had to return two *dou*. If the debt was not settled by the end of the harvest, then the family had to pay back four *dou*. These terms represented an increase of more than two hundred percent compared with the rate on this kind of loan in the early Republican years. Loans to Bao Zhihai were to be paid back by working for him or signing over land used as collateral for the loan.[38] Bao also charged a village family an extra fee for storing the loaned grain in his bin, a cost he had covered in the past.

To be sure, Bao Zhihai still occasionally joined with other landlords in sponsoring protection for Da Fo from regional bandits and extra-village thieves and kidnappers. Yet he was more inclined to defend only the interests of his own household. He seldom assisted ordinary villagers in countering the sporadic invasions of local petty militarists. Furthermore, if someone from the village took a few crops from Bao Zhihai's fields, he would instruct his crop watchers to catch them and then afterwards fine them or beat them. For instance, Bao took away Zheng Zhun's donkey as a fine for Zheng's gathering straw and grass from his wheat fields. Similarly, on discovering that Pang Qingxian had taken just one stalk of sorghum from his fields, Bao made the old man pay him back with a rifle that was of incomparable value.[39]

Between 1928 and 1938, Bao Zhihai frequently used his connections to the Kuomintang courts to flaunt the law. His son Bao Yinyuan had bribed his way into a judgeship, and the elder Bao took advantage of this connection. Many villagers hold resentful memories of two incidents in the early phase of Kuomintang ascendance. In 1934, fancying himself as someone who should be praised for his good deeds, Bao Zhihai demanded that villagers honor him by donating money to a *bian* – a wooden board on which couplets were carved in commemoration of his benevolence to the poor. When poor farmers failed to contribute to the *bian*, Bao Zhihai fined them and destroyed their sorghum crops.[40] Understandably, the *bian* infuriated those who fell victim to Bao's system of blackmail. In 1935, Bao Bingqing, a Da Fo native, opened a small restaurant in Shangcunji. Bao Zhihai's son Bao Yinyuan frequented this establishment, often running up a liquor tab, which prompted the owner to request that the younger Bao pay the tab in cash rather than credit. Bao Yinyuan refused to pay and fought with Bao Bingqing, breaking furniture and wine carafes in the restaurant. Consequently, Bao Bingqing sued Bao Zhihai in the Dongle County court. Although the suit was

---

[37] Ibid.
[38] Pang Mingzhai, interviews, August 20, 24, 1989; Bao Gui, interview, August 20, 1989.
[39] Ruan Jinhan, interview, May 13, 1990.
[40] Bao Zhilong, interview, May 7, 1990; Pang Dongchen, interview, May 7, 1990.

dismissed, Bao Zhihai would not let the matter rest. He pressed Bao Bingqing to give him an apology banquet in Shangcunji. During the banquet, the elder Bao humiliated Bao Bingqing by making him walk outside and kneel down before a huge crowd of people at the market crossroads, an act that stirred anger and resentment among Da Fo's small traders who observed the abuse.[41]

Bao Zhihai's reputation was totally ruined during the 1942 Henan Famine (discussed in Chapter 2), when he began acquiring the lands of desperate farmers on the cheap and refused to loan grain to the poorest farm households. He went further and seized the land and homes of several families who could not repay hunger loans on time. In one instance, Bao sent his men to tear down the house of Pang Mingzhai's family and then pressed Pang to sell his eldest sister to compensate him for the loan. Eventually, Bao Zhihai would issue loans only at exorbitant rates that he calculated could not be paid back. From this point on, many villagers perceived Bao Zhihai as lacking in morality.[42] One particular episode of his "immoral landlordism" has survived in their memories. Bao Jingan recounts:

During the big famine of 1942 my brother, Bao Peishou, was assaulted by Bao Zhihai when he tried to get some leaves from Bao's willow tree to eat. While my brother was climbing the tree and picking the leaves, Bao Zhihai arrived and began waving a wooden manure pole, threatening to beat him. My brother was too frightened to come down, so I went to plead with Bao Zhihai. I managed to walk Bao away from the tree while he was cursing my brother. This willow tree was on Bao Zhihai's threshing ground, but in Da Fo it was the custom to pick leaves from any of the trees in a time of hunger. In the past, villagers had used the willow tree leaves in a recipe for famine relief soup. Bao Zhihai was the only Da Fo landlord who opposed this custom and tried to stop it during the famine of 1942.[43]

Nonetheless, the fragments of surviving oral history suggest that Bao Zhihai was still in a minority of one at the time. Most of the huge landowners among the Bao households were still held in esteem by Da Fo's farmers in the early 1930s, and most were connected with the Kuomintang. In these years, Da Fo's affluent landholding denizens actively endorsed Kuomintang founder Sun Yat-sen's Three Principles (nationalism, democracy, and livelihood), which were the basis of Kuomintang ideology, and they sent their own sons and the sons of their fellow lineage members to schools organized by the Nationalist government. Bao Yuhua, Bao Sunyuan, and even Bao Zhihai sent their offspring to private study in Da Fo's primary school, to Shangcun high school, and to Kuomintang-managed post-secondary institutions. By 1935, Da Fo village had become well known among people who treasured educational achievement in the Hebei-Shandong-Henan border area. Bao Wenping, the brother of big landholder Bao Sunyuan,

---

[41] Bao Zhilong, interview, May 11, 1990.
[42] Bao Zhendao, interview, July 5, 2002; Pang Mingzhai, interview, August 24, 1989; Pang Siyin, interview, August 21, 1989.
[43] Bao Jingan, interview, May 15, 1990.

had graduated from high school and college, had done a study abroad tour in Japan, and then returned to assume the deanship of the Seventh Normal College in Daming County, Hebei province. He was a rising star in the educational hierarchy of the Nationalist government.[44]

The jewel in the crown of the Kuomintang's higher education movement in the Hebei-Shandong-Henan border area, the Daming Seventh Normal College was the college of choice for youthful aspirants to teaching careers and public service positions in the Nationalist government in the 1930s, and Bao Wenping's leadership role at the college gave Da Fo students a leg up in the competition to gain admission. Between 1931 and 1935 the college attracted the most determined and diligent of Da Fo's students, the most accomplished of whom was Bao Tiancai, the son of a farm household blessed with fifty *mu* of land and profits from earth salt production. Not all of Da Fo's college-bound students were from affluent households. Those who were financially handicapped received small monthly tuition loans from Dean Bao, their patron during that period. Bao Huayin, for example, was the son of a landless farmer, but with Dean Bao's help he was able to graduate from the college along with his better-off peers.[45]

In the early 1930s, Bao Tiancai returned to Da Fo to teach in its primary school and practice medicine. He was followed by several good friends, including Bao Huayin, Bao Weishen, and Pang Yunding. Nearly every one of these graduates joined Da Fo's big landholders in promoting Sun Yat-sen's Three Principles, and most of them followed Bao Wenping's example by joining the Kuomintang, anticipating that they would rise up through the modernizing educational system of the Republic of China. By 1935, big landholder Bao Sunyuan had become the secretary of the Kuomintang Dongle County Committee. Bao Yinyuan, the first son of landlord Bao Zhihai, had become the secretary of the seventh branch of the Dongle County Kuomintang. Both men worked hard to recruit people from surrounding villages to the Kuomintang cause, and they were joined by Bao Tiancai, Bao Huayin, and other rural schoolteachers.[46]

Despite popular hatred for the Nationalist government's salt tax police, Da Fo's well-endowed and well-educated Kuomintang elite enjoyed a fairly good political reputation among ordinary villagers. In this still-understudied formative phase of prewar Kuomintang rural governance, the Kuomintang Army came to Da Fo only once, staying for a mere two days, during which their presence was peaceful and non-threatening. The Kuomintang-appointed Dongle County magistrate and his men had an equally good reputation, for they had worked with the Ding Shuben Twenty-Ninth Kuomintang Army to apprehend and kill the bandit Zhang Jintang.[47] Apart from the Kuomintang attack on the war god temple complex

[44] Bao Huayin, interview, August 25, 1989.
[45] Ibid., August 18, 1989.
[46] Pang Haijin, interview, August 23, 1989; Bao Weishen, interview, August 25, 1989; Bao Huayin, interview, August 25, 1989.
[47] Pang Xiannai, interview, August 18, 1989.

after the salt makers' victory, the Nationalist party was moderately successful in promoting its own version of unity and peaceful order during the years before the Japanese invasion. Elderly villagers remember that its agents did not kill anyone, not even the returning students who had embraced the Communist Party as well as Sun Yat-sen's party while in the Daming Seventh Normal College. This sense of relative political peace was not to last.

The Japanese Invasion and the Two Poles of the Resistance

In December of 1937, the Japanese Imperial Army, having conquered and occupied Shanghai, Nanjing, and Beijing, moved into the North China Plain. Invading Dongle County from their headquarters in Daming, Hebei province, the Japanese first occupied Dongle County town and then dispersed their troops west to occupy Shangcun market area, where they began a fort-building program on the banks of the Wei River sixteen *li* east of Da Fo. With no more than three hundred of their own well-trained combat troops, the Japanese could not directly hold all of the points of military and commercial importance in rural Dongle, so for the first two years of what the Chinese call the Anti-Japanese War of Resistance, Da Fo and scores of other rural Dongle villages remained unoccupied. The Japanese invasion destabilized the Kuomintang polity and fostered disorder. The main units of Ding Shuben's Twenty-Ninth Kuomintang Army put up a brief fight and then fled south along the Beijing-Hankow Railway, and Kuomintang businesspeople and officials, including the Dongle County magistrate, fled on the roads, only to be bombed by Japanese airpower.[48] With the collapse of Kuomintang power and a spate of Kuomintang Army defections in the last half of 1937 and the first half of 1938, Kuomintang warlords, regional bandits, the old landholding elite, and young pro–Sun Yat-sen party students with connections to the Communist Party began to promote their own political agendas within the villages.

In this early phase of the war, Da Fo was classified as what the Japanese termed an "unpacified zone." Situated a half day's ride by jeep from the major Japanese garrison in Anyang town on the Beijing-Hankow rail line and a three-hour march from Japanese-held Shangcunji, Da Fo became a contested village and a place where the Communist Party found support for its national resistance struggle against the Japanese. Though Chiang Kai-shek's Nationalist government had been working to suppress the Communists up until shortly before the Japanese invasion, by this time the CCP had united with the Nationalist government to fight against Japan, while retaining its separate political identity. In Da Fo, a Communist Party branch was established under the leadership of Bao Tiancai, the leader of the returned college graduates, and Bao Zhilong, one of the co-leaders of the prewar salt makers' protest and a young member of the preexisting village militia. Local political power started to shift away from the big Bao landholders,

---

[48] Bao Huayin, "Huiyi Dongle Xian Kangri Zhanzheng."

preparing the way for Da Fo to enter the Anti-Japanese War in alliance with the national resistance army of Mao Zedong, Zhu De, and their generals.

During this early chaotic phase of the Japanese invasion, the CCP-organized resistance in Da Fo was composed of a coalition of village schoolteachers and their landholding patron allies, semi-peasant salt makers, and purchase agents. Most of these players belonged to the dominant Bao lineage. They were divided into two distinct poles. Though the two poles had collaborated against the Kuomintang salt police and the bandits of the border area prior to the Japanese invasion, these two political forces were by and large independent of one another and, as the term "poles" suggests, about as different as they could have been. Significantly, only one of the two would politically survive the savagery of the Anti-Japanese War of Resistance.

The key leader of the first group was Bao Tiancai, one of the returned college graduates whose schools were closed due to the emergency caused by the Japanese invasion. A student of medicine, Bao Tiancai spent his time after he returned home to Da Fo ministering to surrounding villages as a country doctor, all the while propagating Sun Yat-sen's Three Principles and persuading villagers to follow the Communist Party in resisting Japanese aggression. He was joined by Bao Huayin, who, on returning to the village, began organizing patriotic schoolteachers in the vicinity of Da Fo, Shangcunji, and Jingdegu to forge plans for resisting the Japanese invasion. These two educated youths were supported by Bao Yuhua, the big landholding patron of Da Fo, who applauded their efforts to organize anti-Japanese resistance in western Dongle County, a process facilitated by the widespread presence of firearms in the Henan countryside.

Just after the first Japanese incursions into Da Fo, Bao Tiancai, Ruan Zhongqi, and Bao Huayin began contacting village schoolteachers, landlords, well-to-do farmers, and some of the semi-peasant salt traders to establish an Anti-Japanese National Salvation Association in the vicinity of Da Fo. The Da Fo branch of the Chinese Communist Party, founded in March of 1938, several months after the Japanese occupation of Shangcunji, grew out of this initiative. With Bao Tiancai as the party secretary, Bao Yuhua as the vice-secretary, and Ruan Zhongqi as another key party member, they secretly recruited several of the land-poor semi-peasant salt makers into the party. One of them was Bao Zhilong, the young co-leader of the prewar salt makers' resistance against the Kuomintang salt revenue police.

Bao Zhilong was a quick-tempered youth from a marginalized smallholding family that commanded little respect from Bao Yuhua and the esteemed patriarchs of the Bao lineage. The son of a poor farmer with only eight *mu* of poor saline land, Bao peddled green beans, pumpkins, and earth salt with his father to supplement the family's skimpy grain harvests. When the Wei River flooded their farmlands in the autumn of 1927, they were forced to sell four *mu* and to accentuate earth salt production for survival, sometimes earning a few silver dollars by selling homemade nitrate to firecracker makers and gunpowder producers in Zhanbeitun in Wei County. Bao Zhilong had no schooling. He was completely illiterate, and though he later held many important posts in the Communist Party, he was unable to decipher any of the party's written rules and regulations.[49] As a member of the sublineage of mean-spirited Bao Zhihai, Bao Zhilong's household was not favored by the Bao lineage elite.

Bao Zhilong's group included other salt land producers such as Bao Gui, Bao Lijun, and Pang Siyin. The members of Bao Zhilong's group relied heavily on the salt market for survival, whereas the party leaders in the more elite first pole frequently belonged to families with substantial landholdings. Being uneducated, Bao Zhilong and his illiterate counterparts depended solely on the cultural memory of the community for information and identity. The more educated and worldly-wise CCP leaders in Da Fo who looked to book learning and the law for guidance perceived Bao Zhilong's group to be uncultured. Whereas the second pole leaders had established themselves as the violent defenders of the village against the salt tax police in the previous Kuomintang regime, the leaders of the first pole, while in sympathy with the salt makers, often had protested against the Kuomintang salt tax force through reason and non-violent politics, including deferential pleas and written petitions to the Kuomintang magistrate. Thus, well before the Japanese invasion, and long before Mao's Great Leap Forward, Bao Zhilong's pole of the resistance equated militancy and collectivity with personal empowerment and political efficacy.

Admittedly, these two poles were somewhat interdependent and were part of the same Communist Party structure in the late 1930s. Bao Tiancai shared a fragment of identity with the people in the second group. Although in possession of ample fertile farm fields, his father, Bao Yiming, had profited from salt production and had supported the poor salt land producers against the salt tax police in the early 1930s. The younger Bao had thus experienced the threat posed to popular economy by Chiang Kai-shek's administrative despotism, and he wavered between his identity as a member of Da Fo's local community and his place in the Kuomintang state educational hierarchy. This tension, along with Chiang Kai-shek's appeasement of the Japanese aggressive takeover of Northeast China on September 18, 1931, was what had moved Bao Tiancai to conclude that Mao's Communist Party might better realize Sun Yat-sen's Three Principles than Chiang Kai-shek's Kuomintang.

The Da Fo Militia and the Second Pole

The Republican period saw three stages of militia development in Da Fo, the first two of them prior to the Japanese invasion. Each stage drew the poor fringe elements of the second pole into village political life. In the 1916–28 period,

---

[49] Bao Zhigen, interviews, August 14–16, 1989.

landholders Bao Yuhua, Bao Zhihai, and Bao Wenhao established a village defense corps to watch crops, prevent banditry, and defend against the tax claims of warlord intruders. Members of this village defense unit carried red-tasseled spears and were loosely affiliated with the countywide Red Spear Association. Partly underwritten by affluent business and landowning households, this rudimentary militia was manned by poor smallholders who feared crop thieves, small-time bandits, and tax-seeking militarists in the region.[50]

The second stage of militia development started around 1920 due to an internal feud between Bao Zhihai and Bao Gan, the Da Fo village chief at the time. After accumulating a small fortune in the coal transport business, Bao Zhihai set his eyes on becoming village chief. Thus, he reported Bao Gan's secretive and illegal transcounty opium dealings to the Daming prefectural government. This resulted in a prison sentence for Bao Gan. One of Bao Gan's sons volunteered to serve the prison term for his father, however, and Bao Gan was able to hit back at Bao Zhihai. He persuaded his nephew, Bao Zhitan, to organize a parallel village militia to fight Bao Zhihai and his village defense forces. A poor and landless person who lived in the Bao lineage temple, this Bao Zhitan was a village bully. Virtually everyone in Da Fo was afraid of him, and so were most of the people in the eighteen villages of Liangmen district. Bao Zhitan and one of Bao Gan's sons used the new militia to compel Bao Zhihai to donate money to purchase its weapons and then began to raid the granaries of relatively affluent households in other villages, dividing the loot among their militia buddies. By the late 1920s, this predatory militia force had five hundred members, and it was a thorn in the side of the Dongle County government.[51] Its reach extended all the way down

[50] If the Red Spears were organized by gentry figures, landholders, and small merchants, they were also mass organizations with the capacity to wage war. Reportedly, the Red Spears in northern Henan wiped out a warlord army in the Northern Expedition. This drew the attention of Communist Party leaders, who planned to mobilize this secret society and connect it with their anti-Japanese mission. Communist interest in the Red Spears stemmed from the fact that whereas some of the Red Spear militias were organized by gentry, and even bandits, still others were organized by smallholders and sometimes evolved armed self-defense arrangements independent of local power. In any case, the challenge of winning their militias over to Communist purposes was daunting. For one thing, virtually all of the Red Spear Associations were organized to oppose warlord taxation, and this took precedence over struggles with landlords. For another, many of the Red Spear associations were penetrated by the Japanese, and they were honeycombed with traitors. See Peng Zhen, "Lun Ji-Lu-Yu Hongqianghui Gongzuo," and "Chuan Guo Nongmin Yundong," 39–42. On the fate of the Red Spears in Dongle prior to the Japanese invasion, see Wang Shanzheng, "Dongle Hongqianghui de Xingqi yu Xiaowang," 55–57.

[51] Kuhn has shown that traditional state militia formation was tied up with the "militarization of village manpower" and that militia conscription was a constant front-burner issue for the magistrate. Interestingly, Kuhn's analysis, while convincingly showing the dynasty aimed to regulate militia formation, also suggests that politics and culture made for the possibility of local people forming self-defense forces that did not directly answer to the local government. He writes, tellingly, that "local militia institutions lay in the shadowy territory where state power interacted with local society and where ambiguous meaning had an indispensable role to play." *Rebellion and Its Enemies*, 24–28, 31–34, esp. 31. For a brilliant account of breakaway militias, see Wakeman, *Strangers at*

to the Shuanjing area in Puyang, where it occasionally clashed with the defense forces of rich and powerful landholders and drew the attention of Ding Shuben, the Kuomintang commander charged with pacifying banditry and secret society growth in Puyang after 1928.[52]

Stage three commenced with the Japanese invasion of Dongle County in December 1937. Shortly after the Japanese took over the Shangcun market area, the original Da Fo village defense corps collapsed, and some of the new militia fighters fled.[53] In the wake of the invasion, banditry proliferated, and political chaos produced unlikely partners. Bandits, such as the two-thousand-strong force from Hui County, robbed people in Dongle markets and villages and kidnapped rich farmers as well as landlords for ransom, while some local militia leaders secretly delivered their villages into bandit hands for a price. In Da Fo, Bao Zhitan seized on the chaos and panic stimulated by the Japanese invasion and began collecting weapons from big landholders and assimilating poor and hungry young people into his militia unit. But Bao's blind ambition eventually brought about his downfall. On linking up with a bigger, stronger armed militia in Anyang, Bao Zhitan began to betray the villages that he had pledged to defend, selling "invitations" to plunder them to bandits like Chen Ximing. When these bandits were invited to raid Da Fo, Bao Zhitan blamed their acts on the ill-prepared village militia and outrageously proposed that the Da Fo militia merge with the bandit forces. The ensuing conflicts and changing loyalties produced half a year of utter chaos and confusion, during which many desperate young people left Da Fo to join bandit units and then returned to join Bao Zhitan's new militia to survive the wave of plunder.

Most significantly, several of the younger part-time salt producers who later joined Da Fo's Communist Party and helped form its wartime militia came from households whose survival had become entwined with this transformed, predatory new militia under Bao Zhitan. Bao Zhilong's father, Bao Jilu, had joined Bao Zhitan's new militia during the first months of the Japanese invasion, and Bao Zhilong himself followed his father into the force.[54] In the following year, Bao Zhitan was seized and murdered by rival militia forces, and his deputy chief, Bao Jingang, was killed by bandits in adjacent Wei County. This rapid turn of

---

the Gate, 67–69, 79. For an insightful conceptualization of state loss of control over militias and the formation of predatory militias, as well as the complex, fuzzy relationship between militias and banditry, see Perry, *Challenging the Mandate*, 32–33. Perry suggests that the militia served as a rural power broker and that it was capable of directing social protest against the state (34). Her powerful conceptualization helps us understand how the Bao Zhilong–led militia could acquire power in the pre-1949 period and become so powerful in the 1950s, and a lot of Da Fo's political story resonates with her conceptualization. Also, on the importance of the militia in post-1949 revolutionary mobilization and state building, see Perry, *Patrolling the Revolution*.

[52] Bao Peisun, interview, July 21, 2005. Bao Peisun's great-grandfather teamed up with Bao Geng's fifth uncle to organize this militia. On Ding Shuben, see Thaxton, *Salt of the Earth*, 119–20.

[53] Bao Gui, interview, August 20, 1989.

[54] Ibid.

events occurred right before the Communist resistance army began to organize village militias in the vicinity of Da Fo village.

Knowing how Bao Zhitan had acquired his weapons and understanding which villagers were skilled in martial arts and militia maneuvers, young Bao Zhilong stepped into the power vacuum created by the Japanese invasion and Bao Zhitan's death to orchestrate the violent creation of an impromptu Communist Party–led militia of ten men in early 1938. Its members shared several characteristics: they were from smallholder households whose poor salt lands did not yield enough food for survival; they had little, if any, education; they were young – usually fifteen to twenty years old; they were bachelors; and they endorsed Bao Tiancai's plan to protect the village from violent foreigners. Whereas Bao Zhilong and his militia recruits joined with Bao Tiancai and Bao Huayin in organizing a defense of their home territory, they did not join the extra-village anti-Japanese guerrilla army units in which Bao Tiancai and other first-pole activists participated – units like the Wei River Brigade and the Fourth Detachment, which later became integrated with the 129th Division of the regular Communist resistance army.[55]

The important point here is that the core militant village-level leadership group of the wartime CCP militia had a direct lineage to the second pole, whose members hailed from a semi-*lumpen* militia and roving bandit networks filled with fierce local bullies and armed hustlers. In the militia transformations of the 1930s, these underemployed and often desperate young men found that violence was a means of empowerment and advancement as well as survival. There is little doubt that Mao Zedong, Deng Xiaoping, and Liu Shaoqi grasped the political significance of this phenomenon in the poor agricultural villages of the North China interior and established the *village-level armed mass base* of the Communist Party along the northern Henan–southern Hebei border where Da Fo is located by incorporating these bandit and militia actors into the party's emergent anti-Japanese self-defense forces and militias in the early phase of the Japanese invasion.[56] Whether the rise of the Bao Zhilong–led militia in Da Fo was part of a pattern limited to this border area remains to be seen. The absorption of marginalized and hardened youth into the party militias also occurred in Wugong village, Raoyang County, and central Hebei, and, as was the case in Da Fo, during and after the war some of these vigilante figures rose through the militia to become village party secretaries.[57] The oral history evidence from Da Fo shows that these men were only loosely connected to the anti-Japanese organizations of the more educated first-pole party leaders and that the Mao-led CCP would fall back on these fearless and forceful local party activists to compel conservative

[55] Bao Huayin, interview, July 15, 1985; Peng Yumei, interview, August 1985.
[56] Chen Lian, ed., *Kangri Genjudi Fajian Shilue*, 253–56.
[57] Focusing on the character of Zhang Duan, Friedman, Pickowicz, and Selden provide a short and somewhat disjointed but nonetheless clear picture of this historical process in *Chinese Village*, linking it to the role of "patriotic toughs" in pushing Mao's fundamentalist agenda in the aftermath of the revolutionary victory. See 37, 95, 102, 111, 182, 194–95, 231, 235–36, 256–57, and 286–87.

smallholders to join in mass political campaigns that were designed to advance the revolutionary agenda – especially the campaign of the Great Leap Forward. For the most part, official CCP history does not mention this connection between the rise of violence-prone, CCP-led wartime militia forces and the party-structured brute force that drove such campaigns, and this is precisely why we need to reconstruct the specific events of the pre-1949 era of war, famine, and revolution at the village level directly from the memories of village people, not just from party-issued history materials.

Early Communist Party Governance and Protection in Da Fo

The founding of the Da Fo Communist Party, including the militia, was intimately connected with two issues that the Kuomintang had failed to address: local corruption and unfair taxation. To ensure that Da Fo would be defended against bandits and the Japanese Army, CCP activists Bao Tiancai and Ruan Zhongqi proposed a sale of fifty *mu* of village temple land for the purpose of purchasing arms for the militia. In the past, this fifty *mu* had been rented out to marginal villagers, and the rental income had been used to support the Bao lineage festivals and the Da Fo primary school. This temple land had been ensnared in corruption for much of the Kuomintang decade. "The villagers agreed to sell the temple land," recalls Bao Zhilong,

because the income from this public temple land was mostly spent by the rich people who were in charge of public affairs. Before the war, the income from this land was to be used to run our school, but the money was less and less used to run the school. Rather, it was spent by the old village chief, Bao Weihe, for his own purpose. This Bao Weihe was corrupt.[58]

In order for the Communist defenders of the village to sell the temple land, they first had to remove the village chief from power.

Since the early 1930s, the Dongle County magistrate had enlisted village elites to promote democratic elections, so that strictly speaking the Da Fo village chief could not be dislodged without popular approval. Just how "democratic" such elections actually were is questionable: because the Communist Party had been driven underground by the Kuomintang in this border region since 1932, it could not openly run candidates for the post of village chief. The flight of Kuomintang officials in late 1937 seems to have been a key turning point in enabling Da Fo's CCP-affiliated college graduates to surface in the spring of 1938, when they openly proposed a special election for village chief. They put up Ruan Zhongqi as a candidate for village chief and Bao Tiancai as a candidate for assistant village chief. The election was conducted by written secret ballot – if people could not write in the candidate of their choice, they could ask others to do it for them. Eight hundred villagers turned out to vote for Ruan Zhongqi to replace Bao

Weihe as village chief. This post, as well as that of militia chief, was now in the hands of a Communist Party member. These members were all followers of party secretary Bao Tiancai, who had been elected assistant village chief.[59]

Several days after the election, the sale of the temple land was approved by a huge assembly of villagers. Bao Tiancai sold the land through a purchase agent to ten individual farmers in nearby Tuxingcun village, and the transaction was recorded in the land registry. Shortly thereafter, CCP militia head Bao Zhilong purchased the guns of some of the deserting Kuomintang soldiers in Dongle and armed the Da Fo militia activists, who henceforth presented themselves as the village crop watch team. In fact, their purpose was to defend the Communist Party branch and the political reforms won through collective mobilization in this fast-paced spring quarter of 1938.

Though the CCP won legitimacy in Da Fo initially through a democratic electoral struggle against corruption, its tax policy was equally important in establishing a bond of political trust with villagers, both big landholders and smallholders. In the fall of 1938, Bao Tiancai and his CCP cohorts carried out a tax reform movement known as *heli fudan*, "the reasonable and fair tax burden system." The new Communist Party tax policy allowed for each person to possess one *mu* of tax-free land, so that if a family of five owned six *mu* of land, they would pay taxes on only one *mu* of this land. With this change, the blatantly unfair tax system of the Kuomintang was overthrown. The poor smallholders owning one to seven *mu* of salt land were for the most part exempted. They included approximately 30 percent of households, or roughly the same poorest one-third of the village that had barely survived the North China Famine of 1921. Those owning up to fifteen *mu* of land received substantial relief under the new Communist Party tax policy. Significantly, under *heli fudan*, the tax was collected according to the harvest, so that if the harvest was poor, the tax was reduced. Those who faced harvest failures could ask to cancel their tax payment altogether. Farmers also had the option of paying the tax in grain, whereas Kuomintang officials had insisted it be paid in silver, thus encouraging the trade of grain for volatile currency.[60]

Affluent farmers holding twenty to fifty *mu* and Da Fo's four big landholders now had to shoulder far more of the tax burden than before. While shifting the burden of taxation to wealthy households with more than fifty *mu* of land, however, the *heli fudan* system did not seriously jeopardize the tax position of Da Fo's big landowners and richer farmers, although the great bulk of grain taxes was paid by twenty-four upscale households (including the four big landholders and fifteen affluent farmers who held fewer than fifty *mu*). The tax on 400 *mu* of land for a ten-person landlord household under the Kuomintang had been 12,000 *jin* of grain (based on one silver dollar per *mu*, which could purchase thirty *jin* of

---

[59] Pang Siyin, interview, August 21, 1989.
[60] Pang Siyin and Bao Zhendao, interviews, August 23, 1989; Bao Jingan, interview, May 15, 1990.

46

grain in the market). The tax on this same land under the CCP's *heli fudan* policy was as follows: If the landowner had more than three *mu* per capita, then he paid 30 *jin* per *mu*; if he had more than five *mu* per capita, he paid 37.5 *jin* per *mu* over and above the five *mu* per capita. The same ten-person landlord household with 400 *mu*, therefore, would have received an exemption on 50 *mu* and paid a total of 13,125 *jin* on the remaining 350 *mu*, which was an increase of 1,125 *jin* over taxes paid under the Kuomintang – less than a 10 percent tax increase. Moreover, these better-off big households also were entitled to a tax reduction if the harvest proved disappointing. And they, like the land-poor villagers, were no longer burdened by the sporadic warlord levies and the land surtaxes of the Kuomintang, so the reasonable burden system promised more predictability and security than the predatory tax regime of the past.[61]

The reasonable burden system was announced by Bao Tiancai and Ruan Zhongqi in a meeting of five hundred villagers at Da Fo's Tang Dynasty Temple and was attended by Tang Renyi, the secretary of the Dongle County CCP committee. Following this meeting, Bao Tiancai and the Da Fo party leaders gathered one hundred villagers to parade throughout the village, broadcasting the word of the benefits of the reasonable burden system. Da Fo became the only village in Dongle to effectively implement this tax policy. The reasonable burden tax system lasted until late 1939, providing Da Fo's farmers with a tax holiday that lasted over a year. "In this period," recalls Bao Zhilong, "we lived a good life."[62]

This good life was in no small way also dependent on the CCP abolishment of taxes on non-farm income, so villagers could make and market earth salt without any state claim on their profits. The Da Fo party activists, with Bao Tiancai leading the way, restored the recently threatened prerogative of market participation and bolstered the resistance army's commitment to protecting livelihood-enhancing market exchanges. In Da Fo, as in many other Dongle villages during this interlude, popular trade in salt-based products picked up and was even promoted by the resistance army, whose soldiers paid fair market prices for earth salt – a political change that endeared the army to many salt-making villagers who remembered the deadly force that the Nationalist government had used against them.

In the early phase of the Japanese occupation of Shangcunji, Da Fo's militia answered the call of the Mao-led resistance army to thwart the extension of Japanese power into the countryside. Two of the Da Fo militia's actions stand out. In mid-1938 it aligned with the militias of four other villages in west Dongle. The members of this *lianfang*, or united local defense squad, carried guns when they went to guard and work the fields, and they helped villagers to prevent Japanese plunder. The Japanese Army had built a small fort at Tuxingcun village, and

---

[61] Thaxton, *Salt of the Earth*, 257.
[62] Bao Zhilong, interview, August 17, 2002.

from this fort its patrols would seize the oxen of farmers working the croplands of these five villages and then slaughter them for meat. In response, the militia galvanized villagers to dig a six-foot-deep ditch connecting the fields with the villages. When the Japanese approached the fields, the militia spotters rushed to prod the oxen into this subway ditch system, through which the animals returned swiftly to the villages; meanwhile, militia snipers fired to distract the Japanese patrols from seizing the animals.[63] Militia leader Bao Zhilong, who was skilled in handling farm animals, helped orchestrate this resistance.

Bao Zhilong and several members of his militia also began acquiring guns to give to the Eighth Route Army of the Communist resistance during this period. They sold as much earth salt and as many farm animals as possible to acquire weapons for the resistance troops. Bao Zhilong recalls that they purchased the guns from the deserting Kuomintang Army soldiers of Ding Shuben's Twenty-Ninth Kuomintang Army right after the Japanese invaded and that he secretly purchased gunpowder for the Eighth Route Army units in Zhanbeitun, in Hebei province. Bao Zhilong also admits: "We got some guns from landlords. If the landlords refused, we beat them. In 1938 Bao Yishan and I led people to kill a landlord in another village to get his guns, and we gave the guns to the Eighth Route Army."[64] By early 1939 the Communist-led war of resistance against the Japanese invaders had drawn militia leader Bao into the politics of killing for national salvation.

Within the social structure of Da Fo, the Japanese invasion weakened the authority and influence of many of the big landholders in the Bao lineage and, to a lesser extent, of the returned college-educated Bao leaders. At the outset of the invasion, the Bao landlords entered into a tacit anti-Japanese alliance with underground leaders of the Communist Party. However, over the course of the war many of them oscillated, sometimes making damaging political mistakes. Big landholder Bao Zhihai and his son were particularly hurt by such mistakes. Immediately after the first Japanese Army appearance in Da Fo in the fall of 1938, which lasted seven days, Communist Party leaders Bao Tiancai and Ruan Zhongqi called on villagers to build a series of trenches across Da Fo's fields to facilitate Eighth Route Army troop movements to the front line and to speed up militia defensive maneuvers in case of future Japanese incursions. Approximately one hundred villagers volunteered to dig the trenches under the supervision of the militia. However, Bao Yinyuan, the son of Bao Zhihai, objected. Bao Yinyuan had already voiced reservations about the reasonable tax burden system, and now he tried to stop the trench-digging project. In response, Bao Tiancai, Bao Zhilong, and the militia leaders called a meeting of the heads of all 250 households in Da Fo, and these people took up the question of how to deal

---

[63] Bao Jingan, interview, May 15, 1990.
[64] Bao Zhilong, interviews, August 14, 17, 1989.

with Bao Yinyuan's opposition. He was denounced in a village mass assembly, and he was then "invited" to provide an apology dinner for the hundred people who had labored to dig the trench line. The apology dinner signaled Bao Yinyuan's loss of authority over village affairs. Shortly after this symbolic defeat, both Bao Zhihai and Bao Yinyuan were abducted by the resistance: Bao Zhilong and the militia had reported both men to the 386th Brigade of General Liu Bocheng's 129th Division. Such a fate was not unforeseeable: prior to their disappearance, the grapevine had been humming with a rumor that several big landholders in nearby Shangdizhuang had been abducted and killed by poor villagers in league with the resistance army when they had obstructed the armed struggle against the Japanese Army. Da Fo was now involved in that struggle.[65]

After an investigation, the Eighth Route Army released Bao Zhihai, but his son was judged a traitor to the resistance and put to death.[66] Not only had Bao Yinyuan opposed the trench-digging scheme, he had connected with forces loyal to Yang Faxian in the Liangmen area and had attempted to thwart the recruitment of people in Da Fo into the CCP-led Anti-Japanese National Salvation Association, thereby violating the terms of the united front.[67] Thus Bao Zhilong and the other pro-CCP militia fighters had cause to report Bao to the resistance army, and that is what they had done. The resistance army liaison to Da Fo said that the son went to the Yenan liberated area to study. In reality, Bao Yinyuan had been buried alive.[68] Among the four big landholders, only Bao Yuhua, who still enjoyed a strong reciprocal relationship with Bao Tiancai and the educated patriotic CCP leaders in his lineage, managed to survive the savagery of the war with his authority and esteem intact.

Investigation of the history of Da Fo village in the Republican period reveals the crucial role of the market, and particularly the petty trade in earth salt, in supplementing villagers' small agricultural yields and guaranteeing their subsistence. Chiang Kai-shek's Nationalist government largely lost the respect of Da Fo's salt makers by attacking this traditional prerogative. It was in the battle to retain the right to produce salt that new leaders emerged in Da Fo, Bao Zhilong among them. When the Japanese occupied the North China Plain and Kuomintang authority collapsed in the region in 1937, these leaders, who associated with the Communist Party, won legitimacy by granting villagers unrestricted access to the salt market, protecting them from Japanese invaders and bandits, and creating a fairer tax system. Far from a monolithic group, the Communists who ran the village in the late 1930s and early 1940s were divided into two poles,

---

[65] Pang Siyin, interview, August 21, 1989.
[66] Bao Zhendao, interview, July 24, 2005.
[67] Ibid., August 23, 1989.
[68] Ibid., July 5, 2002; Zheng Tianbao and Bao Yibin, interview, July 6, 2002.

one made up of educated elites associated with the most respected of the village's large landholders and the other associated with the illiterate, fringe elements of the village and with participation in the village militia. As early as 1939, as the power of Da Fo's traditional large landholders began to wane, the second pole of the village's Communist Party leadership had already begun using excessive force to meet its goals.

2

The Ascent of the Vigilante Militia

THE VIOLENT ANTECEDENTS
OF MAO'S WAR COMMUNISM

The Great Leap Forward was the product of a uniquely Maoist declaration of "war communism," but the disaster it spawned in some rural Chinese villages had roots in a less visible episode of warfare.[1] In the memory of Da Fo's inhabitants, the antecedents of Mao's war communism lay in the ascent of the Communist Party militia leaders during the years of anti-Japanese resistance and, after the Japanese were expelled in 1945, in the civil war between Nationalists and Communists that followed. The inhabitants of Da Fo experienced protracted violence at the hands of authoritarian leaders during this period, in which the village was first occupied by Yang Faxian's Puppet Army and later subject to waves of repression by the battling Nationalist and Communist forces. These conflicts dissipated the influence of Da Fo's educated, elite Communist leaders of the first pole at the same time that they brought the second pole to the fore and gave many of Da Fo's farmers a number of reasons to put their faith in the party-state established in 1949. Unfortunately, the same men who brought tax relief and land redistribution to Da Fo also developed, over more than a decade of fighting and political instability, a violent and authoritarian style of work and leadership that would ultimately prove harmful to villagers.

Occupation by Yang Faxian's Puppet Regime

The winter of 1939 witnessed a sudden reversal of the Communist Party's political fortunes in Dongle County and Da Fo village. By this time, the Japanese had recruited Yang Faxian, a one-time bandit, the ex-boss of a teahouse in Shangcunji, and a former commander in the Kuomintang Twenty-Ninth Army under Song

---

[1] Friedman, Pickowicz, and Selden, *Chinese Village*; Felix Wemheuer, personal correspondence, 2004. The work of McAdam, Tarrow, and Tilly anticipates my own here. See *Dynamics of Contention*, 7.

Zheyuan and Ding Shuben, to organize and run their Puppet Army (*weijun*) of Chinese collaborators in the border area. Composed of violent roving *lumpen* elements, including former bandits, drug addicts, habitual criminals, deserting Kuomintang soldiers, and the desperate teenage orphans of Japanese atrocities,[2] the Japanese Puppet Army was ridden with factional rivalries, and Yang Faxian had to deal with the problem of opportunism in this *lumpen* force, a phenomenon that the Communist-led resistance eventually would exploit. The Puppet Army grew to a thousand men by late 1939 and mushroomed to three thousand in the year to follow. During late 1939 and early 1940, this army began to conduct maneuvers with the Japanese Army against partisan guerrilla fighters in league with the Communist Eighth Route Army.

The Japanese Puppet Army was an ultrarepressive force, the key to instituting Japan's version of political order in the lower part of the North China Plain. By the time the Japanese attacked Pearl Harbor, there were 39,200 Puppet Army troops under indirect Japanese Army command in the Hebei-Shandong-Henan border area, and by late 1942 this army stood at 80,000; Yang Faxian's puppet force was loosely integrated with a massive collaborationist army that outnumbered the Communist-led resistance army by ten to one.[3]

Most treatments of the Communist Party's efforts to build up partisan resistance in the countryside during World War II fail to distinguish between the quite separate experiences of the Anti-Japanese War of Resistance as a war fought against the Japanese Imperial Army and as a war fought against Han Chinese collaborators in puppet forces. The CCP's war with the Japanese Puppet Army, however, was by far the most extreme political conflict taking place in the Hebei-Shandong-Henan border region between 1940 and 1945.[4] Peter J. Seybolt has demonstrated as much statistically, and he points out that by 1943 the party-directed partisan forces had killed, wounded, or captured at least eight times more Chinese than Japanese.[5] This lesser-known "second war" crisscrossed the Communist Party's war with the Japanese Army from the inception of hostilities.

A 1942 report by the Hebei-Shandong-Henan Regional Communist Party Committee left no doubt that the vagrants, bandits, and ex-soldiers filling the Japanese Puppet Army posed a grave threat to the CCP's border region government and that breaking up the alliance between this force and the Japanese Army was the greatest challenge of guerrilla warfare. Alarmingly, these puppet forces not only threatened the base area towns and villages where the Communist-led resistance army had gained the upper hand, they even dared to launch nibbling attacks on CCP-held places unsupported by the Japanese troops – acts that indicated that their hostile relationship with the resistance was not totally dependent

[2] Bao Weishen, interview, August 4, 1990; Ruan Yin, interview, August 18, 1989.
[3] "Ji-Lu-Yu Bianqu Gongzuode," 453; Zhonggong Henan Shengwei Dangshi Ziliao Zhengji Bianzuan Weiyuanhui Bian, "Ji-Lu-Yu Bianqu Kangri Genjudi Henan Bufen Gaishu," 13.
[4] Thaxton, *Salt of the Earth*, 211.
[5] Seybolt, "War Within a War," 221.

on Japanese tutoring.[6] The urgent goal of the resistance, therefore, was to turn these pro-Japanese forces into double-dealers and to win them over to the anti-Japanese cause.

But there was a problem. The local villagers did not always agree on how the resistance should resolve the problem of the *weijun* occupation. In the places where the resistance enjoyed superior strength and the puppet forces had done serious harm, villagers often asked the resistance army to fight the puppet forces head-on and remove their strongholds. In places where the Communist Party had not achieved superiority and where the Japanese Puppet Army separated the party leaders from the masses by carrot-and-stick policies, however, villagers were more inclined to implore the guerrilla army to *not* fight battles openly against the *weijun* forces, because these forces wantonly retaliated by burning homes and killing people.[7] In such cases, the CCP had little choice but to operate undercover and carefully seek protection from village people. Da Fo village was such a place.

In the early phase of the war, 1938–39, Yang Faxian's puppet force was based in Shangcunji, in western Dongle County. But in late 1939, Yang Faxian moved the entire one-thousand-man vanguard of this army sixteen *li* west of Shangcunji to fortify the Japanese hold on the strategically important Wei River. The village in which the Puppet Army entrenched itself for the next five years was Da Fo. Ostensibly, Da Fo was selected for its proximity to the Wei River, but the Japanese also sent Yang Faxian to this village because they were alarmed by reports of its support for partisan resistance. In December 1939 Yang Faxian encamped his puppet force on the outskirts of Da Fo and then began taking over the territory of the village. Yang himself established his headquarters and his residence in Da Fo. His commanders and cavalry troops moved into the houses, courtyards, and storerooms of big landholders Bao Yuhua and Bao Zhihai,[8] and his foot soldiers stayed in the homes of ordinary villagers for two- and three-year stints.

By 1941, Yang Faxian's puppet regime had begun to dismantle the reformist experiment that had drawn Da Fo to support the resistance and also had begun to restructure the village economy to serve the schemes of the Japanese and, more importantly, the puppet regime itself. The democratic system of election by ballot that put Communist Party leaders in power in 1938 was overthrown, and first-pole party leaders Bao Tiancai and Ruan Zhongqi fled the village. Yang's tax collectors quickly dismantled the *heli fudan* tax reforms instituted by the CCP, doubling the tax demand on villagers, and the party-guided process of reducing the exorbitant rates of interest and rent also was terminated. The production of off-farm income, both from earth salt and nitrate sales, was redirected to serve the Japanese Puppet Army mission of establishing a village arsenal. Most importantly, between late 1939 and late 1944, Yang Faxian ordered his soldiers to find and

---

[6] "Ji-Lu-Yu Bianqu Gongzuode," 395–400.
[7] Ibid., 423–28.
[8] Bao Zhendao, interview, July 5, 2002.

kill anyone who had joined the Da Fo branch of the Communist Party, so from the outset the Puppet Army unleashed a reign of terror and murder against the villagers who had participated in or cooperated with the CCP-led resistance.

During this period of occupation by the Japanese Puppet Army, the new educated and enlightened leadership pole of the Da Fo Communist Party branch was driven to death or driven out, and the village was thrown into a state of emergency that destroyed any definition of normalcy. Four instances of Puppet Army terror stand out in popular memory. Apparently, each compounded the trauma of the previous one.

The first involved the killing of teacher Bao Tiancai. Though Bao Tiancai had fled the village in the spring of 1940, he was soon apprehended by Yang Faxian. High on a Japanese "most wanted" list, Bao Tiancai was sent to Japanese headquarters in Daming, where he was interrogated and invited to work for Yang's army in its fight against the resistance army. Bao Tiancai agreed. But he ran away during a military engagement with the Eighth Route Army, eventually finding his way back to Da Fo to again take up the cause of the resistance. Subsequently, while directing the Communist Party's recruitment of people in Dongle's Minglizhuang, Shangdizhuang, and Liangmenpo villages[9] and in several villages in Wei County and Puyang County, Bao Tiancai incurred the ire of a pro–Yang Faxian landlord militia force in Puyang. In the autumn of 1940, a leader of this militia force lured Bao into a trap with the gift of a beautiful woman for Bao's pleasure. Bao was captured and subjected to torture. After blinding him with a sharp, metal-tipped stick, the pro–Yang Faxian militia buried Bao Tiancai alive in the south field of Wailu village in Puyang. Da Fo Communist Party members were stunned by this murder.

In the last three months of 1941, Yang Faxian's soldiers managed to seize seven new party recruits and bury them alive in a field west of Da Fo. Pang Qingtian, an early Da Fo party member, recalls this incident:

I joined the Communist Party with ten other people in 1940. Of these ten people, seven were buried alive by Yang Faxian in the autumn of 1941. Thereafter, we went underground, and we were afraid to organize resistance openly. As a result, I fled Da Fo and went to Puyang, returning here on only a few occasions between 1941 and 1944, when we were conducting guerrilla warfare to capture Dongle and Qingfeng County towns.[10]

For most of the resistance fighters, Da Fo was too dangerous to visit until early 1945, when the tides of war shifted decisively against the Japanese and their puppet forces.

Indeed, Yang Faxian extended his murderous rampage into the 1941–42 period, when his puppet troops answered the Japanese command to seize and kill Eighth Route Army fighters who attempted to return to their home villages.

---

[9] Bao Zhilong, interview, August 21, 1989.
[10] Pang Qingtian, interview, August 18, 1989.

In late 1941, for example, when Eighth Route Army soldier Pang Yunding came back to Da Fo on leave, someone reported his presence to Yang Faxian, whose soldiers caught Pang and buried him alive near Japanese headquarters in Shangcunji.[11] A good friend and colleague of Bao Tiancai, Pang Yunding had been an esteemed member of Da Fo's new wartime first-pole party leadership group, as he had graduated from the village primary school, Shangcun high school, and then the Dongle Teachers' Training School, after which he had helped Bao Tiancai set up the party branch in Da Fo – and now he too was dead.

A similar fate awaited Bao Zhenfa, a soldier in the resistance army. Bao was apprehended in early 1942 at Wanxiuzhuang while visiting his relatives and then buried alive outside of Yang Faxian's headquarters in Da Fo. His Communist Party comrades, along with other villagers, looked on in silent horror and did not plead for him, for "pleading for somebody who was an Eighth Route Army soldier," says Bao Zhendao, "was too risky."[12] Many of the members of the resistance army who returned to Da Fo either to check on the well-being of their families or to find out what Yang Faxian's troops were doing barely managed to escape the Puppet Army, and these brushes with death still were at the forefront of their memories when I interviewed them a half century after war's end.

The social costs of the Japanese Puppet Army occupation were undeniably severe. The war duties imposed on Da Fo after 1940 undercut the ability of village people to make earth salt products for their own benefit. In 1941 a team of Anyang-based master gunsmiths and munitions experts arrived in Da Fo to start up several Puppet Army arsenals. Yang Faxian's men forced adult males to work in these armaments factories without pay, a demand that often interfered with farm work and salt production. Forced marches to build Japanese blockhouses in Shangcunji took a toll, leaving these petty traders with less time to engage the market.

By 1942–43 war-enveloped semi-colonial villages like Da Fo were providing the great majority of the rank-and-file recruits for China's struggle for independence from Japanese rule. In 1938–39 some twenty villagers joined the resistance army, and still another eighty joined in 1943. By war's end at least one hundred of Da Fo's inhabitants had found a home in the national resistance army of Mao Zedong and Zhu De, whose North China Plain headquarters was in nearby Puyang County. Eighty percent of these men were from families whose tiny strips of saline land did not yield enough grain for payment of Puppet Army taxes or enough food for sustenance in the 1942 famine. These soldiers were young and often separated from their fathers; they had been mistreated and further marginalized by the Japanese Puppet Army; they had a history of begging, scavenging, and roving in and out of any local army that would provision and protect them; and they by and large were bachelors. The Japanese invasion, the puppet

[11] Bao Zhendao, interview, July 5, 2002; Pang Haijin, interview, August 23, 1989.
[12] Bao Zhendao, interview, July 5, 2002.

regime occupation, and the attendant food crisis of 1942 made these uprooted rural people receptive to the national salvation messages of Da Fo's more educated Communist Party members, who often provided them with introductions to the resistance army.[13]

If the search for security drove these young, rootless people into the resistance, the oral history evidence sheds light on precisely what insecurity they fled. Many of the resistance army fighters were fed up with the physical abuse they suffered from the Puppet Army's officers. Bao Qixin reflects that one reason he joined up was "because the Eighth Route Army officers did not beat their soldiers, whereas the *weijun* officers did beat their soldiers."[14] Still, the key factor motivating the rootless poor to join Mao's resistance army was food security and relief from the Henan Famine of 1942, which took the lives of at least 1.5 million people and prompted more than 3 million to flee Henan in search of food security in other parts of China.[15] In the fall of 1941 Da Fo lost most of its sorghum crop to drought. That same autumn, villagers were unable to plant the 1942 wheat crop for the spring to follow, which opened the door to famine.[16] Worse yet, locusts poured out of a coal-black sky to devour most of the sorghum and millet crops, and in Da Fo the locusts actually began to attack humans, eating their clothing. So prevalent were the locusts, and so hungry were villagers, that some people reportedly ate the locusts in the fields. Surreal comedy infused the famine and gave villagers another choice – Pang Yanyin started to make and peddle "locust bread," and villagers instantly nicknamed him "the Locust Pizza Man," a title some found humorous.[17]

The spring of 1942 saw the drought worsen. By June it was apparent there would be virtually no wheat harvest. Because the locusts had depleted the fall sorghum and millet crops, few villagers had any grain to carry them beyond early winter. In the six months ahead, roughly from the spring hunger to the fall harvest of 1942, villagers were reduced to wretchedness. Early in 1942, people got by on wild vegetables, bark, and tree leaves, and by intermittent begging, but, as the drought expanded in scope, the fallback vegetation was shriveled, and it became more difficult to beg locally.

The occupation made it more difficult for villagers to acquire grain when there was severe dearth, and this became all too apparent during the famine.

---

[13] On the importance of this *lumpen* connection to Mao's revolution, see Friedman, "Mao Zedong, Backwardness," 9–12.

[14] Bao Qixin, interview, August 19, 1989.

[15] For these figures, see Zhonggong Henan Shengwei Dangshi Yanjiushi, *Henan Kangzhan Jianshi*. Estimates of the Henan Famine's death rate must be taken with a grain of salt. Compare Song Zhixin, who gives a figure of 3 to 5 million in *1942 Henan Dajihuang*, 2. I am indebted to Felix Wemheuer for helping me obtain this data on the famine. The estimate of 5 million was originally given by White and Jacoby, *Thunder Out of China*.

[16] Pang Siyin, interview, August 22, 1989.

[17] Pang Yilu, interview, July 14, 2000; Ruan Yinchang, interview, July 15, 2000.

In Dongle County, 17,000 people, or 9 percent of the population, starved to death.[18] The puppet regime held grain taxes constant in this period of failed harvests, stabilizing its revenue at the expense of the farmers. At the same time, Yang's puppet soldiers issued residence cards to curtail movement in and out of the village, all part of an effort to carry out checks on the whereabouts of suspected partisan sympathizers. The gates of Da Fo were guarded constantly and locked each day from late afternoon until early morning to prevent liaisons between villagers and the guerrilla army. These restrictions on the freedom to leave the village to acquire food from relatives took their toll on the poorest households, whose members had no choice but to flee and risk persecution once the food crisis intensified in the fall quarter of 1942. Many adult males hit the migration trails to find work in the factories of Da Tong in Shanxi and the coal mines of Tang Shan, in Hebei province.

When the June wheat harvest failed, many of Da Fo's poorest families were at their wits' end. A few sold their female children in an effort to survive. Bao Zhidan, whose sister was married off in exchange for food, remembers, "We did not say we sold them, but it was more or less like that. This helped our family pass over the difficult year."[19] For the poorest young males, whose fathers had followed the migration trails or succumbed to emaciation and edema in Da Fo, fate was even more cruel. Many of the older villagers hold memories of dead bodies on the streets leading out of Da Fo in the famine of 1942.[20] They particularly recall that a disproportionate number of eleven- and twelve-year-old males were among the thin corpses littering the roads – some had been their village playmates.

Small wonder that so many young people, most of them eleven to eighteen, chased the Eighth Route Army units of Mao Zedong and Zhu De in the Dongle-Puyang area, pleading for a chance to find food and surrogate family during this year of war, terror, and famine. Ruan Yin was one of the desperate young village males who found his way into the resistance army during this crisis. His story reminds us that food security, not simply nationalist sentiment, was a major factor in the making of Communist Party legitimacy and power:

I joined the Eighth Route Army in 1943, right at the end of the 1942 famine. Before that . . . I served in the Puppet Army. I joined the Puppet Army only to get food to eat. In the year I joined the Puppet Army, my father was captured by the Japanese and taken to many different places, and I was left alone, so I had no way of surviving. I spent most of my time in Da Fo, and occasionally went out to carry messages to other villages. In return, the Puppet Army guaranteed my food.

---

[18] Jia Zongyi, "Dui Dongle Xian Diwei Gongzuode Huiyi," 166; "Ji-Lu-Yu Bianqu Dangshi Dashiji," 174; Peng Youqiang, *Dongle Xianzhi*, 39.

[19] Bao Zhidan, interview, June 26, 2001.

[20] Bao Yuming, interview, June 21, 2001; Zheng Jintian, interview, June 22, 2001; Bao Dongzhi, interview, June 24, 2001.

However, by the winter of 1943 my Puppet Army commander had been killed by the CCP-led resistance, and I did not have enough food to eat at home in Da Fo. So I left his army to join the Eighth Route Army. Ruan Zhongqi, my cousin, was in the Eighth Route Army. At that time, I went to work for him.[21]

Many of the recruits joined as "people on the move," that is, as uprooted villagers whose desperate pursuit of survival landed them in the resistance army. On several occasions, Pang Yilu's two elder brothers, for example, had traveled south of the Yellow River to beg during the 1942 Henan Famine, and during one of these trips they seized the opportunity to join the Eighth Route Army in the Puyang area.[22]

To be sure, there was another factor attracting these uprooted sons of China's salt lands into the resistance army: hatred of the invaders. Chalmers A. Johnson has argued that the Japanese invasion and its attendant brutality stirred the hatred that gave the Chinese Communists their chance to recruit China's rural people through the rallying cry of national salvation.[23] Some of the poor, young, *lumpen* elements from Da Fo say they listened carefully to Bao Tiancai, Bao Huayin, Bao Weishen, and the other patriotic students who preached national salvation propaganda. No doubt they were influenced by the anti-Japanese message of these educated and patriotic Communist Party firebrands. Nonetheless, their commitment to the Communist resistance army was stoked by hatred of a far more fearsome enemy: the collaborationist Chinese of the Puppet Army. Bao Gui, who joined the resistance army in wartime, explains: "I joined the Eighth Route Army in part because the Japanese had invaded our locality and the Puppet Army had helped the Japanese oppress us. I hated the Japanese, but I hated the puppet soldiers who served them even more because they were Chinese who helped the Japanese kill us Chinese."[24]

Once the balance of power shifted from the Japanese puppet forces to the Eighth Route Army, villagers were even more eager to join the armed resistance. In Dongle County this shift occurred between late 1943 and early 1945, and it was assisted by the Da Fo militia, whose members had largely remained in the village during the occupation and formed an underground home guard to resist the Japanese Puppet Army regime.

The Second Pole in Occupied Da Fo

In writing about warlordism in pre–World War II Republican China, Diana Lary and Edward McCord have noted that the brutal mistreatment of soldiers by their commanders predisposed many of them to take out their frustrations and fears on

---

[21] Ruan Yin, interview, August 18, 1989.
[22] Pang Yilu, interview, July 14, 2000.
[23] Johnson, *Peasant Nationalism*, chs. 1–2.
[24] Bao Gui, interview, August 20, 1989.

the civilian population, subjecting rural dwellers to a train of abuse and cruelty.[25] A similar pattern of violence against civilians by Puppet Army soldiers took hold in the occupied counties and villages during the Second World War. Well before Da Fo's Communist Party leaders became the targets of this violence, villagers heard stories of the ruthless modality of Yang Faxian's regime. Incidents of violence against civilians struck terror into the hearts of villagers, alerting them to the fact that Yang's men ultimately had no loyalty to anyone other than their own violent network.

One such incident occurred right after Yang Faxian's force was retrofitted to Japanese rule. After taking over Shangcunji, the Japanese began a search for young educated villagers to go to Japan to immerse themselves in Japanese language study, with an eye toward returning them to rural China to deepen the hold of Japan's occupation. The Japanese talent scouts chose Bao Shiyan, a Da Fo student. When the young Bao declared he did not want to go, Yang Faxian personally intervened and promised him a safe study abroad experience. After two years of study in Japan, Bao Shiyan returned to Shangcunji. However, Bao made a mistake. He seldom visited Da Fo, and when he did visit the village, he did not pay homage to his patron Yang Faxian. According to Bao Zhendao, "Yang Faxian felt that Bao Shiyan ignored him and was ungrateful, so one night when Bao Shiyan returned to the village, Yang sent his men to arrest Bao, after which they buried him alive near the village."[26] No one was allowed to watch, but everyone knew about this killing. Henceforth, villagers spoke about Yang Faxian's regime in the language of fear.

Some of the primary recipients of the Puppet Army's violent abuse were the future postwar leaders of the Da Fo Communist Party who wished to prevent such an outcome – mainly Bao Zhilong and the other local militia leaders in the second pole of the Da Fo party branch. For them, the savagery of the war represented an acute escalation of the level of "normal" violence that had permeated Da Fo since the 1920s. Their memories of this savagery and of how they habitually coped with it by means of painful and yet addictive counter-violence have eluded scholars of wartime China. This is unfortunate, because in villages like Da Fo the violent habits ensuring wartime survival influenced the ways in which local party leaders would relate to villagers in both the Civil War to come and the post-1949 phase of Maoist state building.

Consider the wartime experiences of militia leader Bao Zhilong and a few of his comrades. Bao Zhilong was repeatedly brutalized and traumatized by the *weijun* throughout the war. In 1941, for instance, people in Da Fo were ordered by Yang Faxian to dig ditches and repair roads to facilitate Japanese troop activities in the vicinity of Shangcunji. Bao Zhilong and other villagers objected, in part because this assignment required the removal of ancestral tombs. Yang's puppet soldiers

[25] Lary, *Chinese Common Soldiers*, 72, 87–89, 104–06; McCord, "Burn, Kill, Rape and Rob," 25.
[26] Bao Zhendao, interview, July 5, 2002.

thereupon beat Bao for orchestrating work slowdowns on this project. Following this, the *weijun* soldiers also beat Bao Zhilong thirty times with a wooden board when he arrived late for work on a Japanese fort-building project along the Wei River.[27] A year later, when Bao Zhilong failed to perform war service duties for the Puppet Army quickly, Yang's men threw Bao under a sharp-bladed hay-cutter, threatening to run it over him if he did not comply. Such brutality was commonplace.

Throughout most of the occupation period, roughly late 1939 until late 1944, open and organized resistance to this Japanese Puppet Army repression was too risky. To a significant extent, the Da Fo Communist Party branch was able to minimize the impact of the Japanese military occupation because its leaders established liaisons with the Puppet Army and carried on various forms of resistance under the cover of collaboration. Between 1940 and 1945 Bao Zhilong and the Communist Party leaders in Da Fo officially assisted Yang Faxian's army, pledging their allegiance to the flag of the rising sun. From 1940 on, however, they swore a secret oath of loyalty to the CCP and its resistance army, and they pledged to kill anyone who betrayed the unity of the party. Thus Da Fo's Communist Party cadres constructed a veritable Trojan horse within the Puppet Army occupation, discreetly forming little groups to defend the lifelines of the local economy against the puppet soldiers and to assist the guerrilla army in its anti-Japanese activities.

To survive within the war-imposed state of emergency, the party leaders had to quickly learn the arts of deception and defiance, and it seems that militia chief Bao Zhilong rose to meet this challenge when it came to helping villagers secure their basic means of livelihood, offering them crisis relief, protection, and security, and forming liaisons with the outside world. Bao Yuhua, Bao Zhilong, and other party survivors persuaded their comrades to take up a collection to pay Bao Xuqing to act as the head of the Da Fo Peace Preservation Committee, giving the Da Fo resistance its own liaison to the Japanese Army in Shangcunji. Through Bao Xuqing, the Da Fo party leaders could pursue a strategy of feigned cooperation with Yang Faxian's emergent order, embracing its presence to serve the interest of villagers and fecklessly responding to demands for corvée labor, building materials, and grain and poultry so as to minimize trouble.

By 1940, Bao Xuqing was serving on a committee established by Yang Faxian called the Forty-Seven Village Working Pacification Committee. Yang's puppet regime was heavily dependent on this committee for its procurement claims. The Communist Party leaders were able to take advantage of this dependence, using their economic leverage to secure their basic means of existence within the framework of wartime coexistence. Da Fo's old-timers recall that the war delivered two new sets of customers – those in flight from Japanese-occupied Shangcunji and the soldiers of the puppet regime – to whom they sold earth salt, pork balls, sweet melons, and cigarettes in Da Fo's enlarged market. That Da Fo's poor farmers

---

[27] Bao Zhilong, interview, August 23, 1989.

were able to recapture their salt market niche in this period had political ramifications, for the fact that they were not reduced to the point of sharp, nasty intravillage competition over food resources meant that the party leaders could promote anti-Japanese solidarity among households that were neither mired in poverty nor shredded by Japanese power. Da Fo's Communist Party leaders were able to forge forms of resistance based on a history of social trust and joint self-help among households of the larger, dominant lineage groups. To be sure, the crisis engendered by the 1942 famine made this more difficult. But even in the desperate months of 1942 fewer than 20 of Da Fo's 270 households pilfered crops from fellow villagers, and most of this pilfering, it turns out, was largely confined to the fields of the big landholders. The family-initiated crop watch teams that sprung up within this period quickly evolved into a villagewide crop watch team made up of members of the Bao Zhilong–led militia, sustained in part by their own salt-based income and in part from a small payment from the puppet village chief.[28]

Still, when famine intensified in 1942 many of the poorest villagers grew desperate, and Da Fo's underground resistance was seriously challenged. At this point, big landowner Bao Yuhua, now secretly the village Communist Party vice-secretary and publicly the chief of the district-level Japanese puppet government, was in daily contact with Yang Faxian, whom he made his blood brother. This liaison, which Bao made without renouncing his party membership, opened the door to grain supply in Da Fo during the worst moments of the 1942 Henan Famine, for it permitted Bao to assist the village party branch and the militia to ferry in small relief grain supplies through secret ties with the resistance army in Yunyan village over the Wei County line.[29] Bao Yuhua issued interest-free hunger loans to approximately 10 percent of the starving households in the spring of 1942, and in the famine that followed he issued grain to the families of the salt land tillers whose sons joined the resistance army.[30] Bao Zhigen recalls that his family received five hundred *jin* of grain from Bao Yuhua because they had a son in the Eighth Route Army.[31] Virtually everyone in Da Fo village knew that the CCP had come to power as the agent of forces mobilizing to relieve the suffering induced by the Henan Famine of 1942 and that in this unified effort Bao Yuhua had proven that he was a benefactor of the poor.[32]

It is not easy to judge how effective such Janus-faced resistance was. When it came to protecting villagers from the plunder of puppet regime taxation, however, the Da Fo party leaders certainly enjoyed a measure of success. Working through

---

[28] Pang Siyin, interviews, August 21, 22, 1989.

[29] Pang Mingzhai, interview, August 16, 1989.

[30] Bao Zhimin, interview, August 24, 1989; Bao Zhigen, interview, August 24, 1989.

[31] Bao Zhigen, interview, August 24, 1989.

[32] Crook and Crook also show that CCP-sponsored famine relief efforts helped legitimate the party in the eyes of village people in the pre-1949 period. See *Revolution in a Chinese Village*, 57–59. I am indebted to Edward Friedman (personal correspondence, October 10, 2005) and to Lillian Li (*Fighting Famine*, 353) for helping me grasp this point.

puppet village chief Bao Xuqing, they were able to alleviate some of the pressure for grain taxes. In the early phase of the war, Bao apparently managed to convince the Yang Faxian Working Committee that Da Fo deserved a tax reduction when the harvest was poor, and on several occasions he was able to protect those who temporarily fled when taxes proved unbearable. That the puppet regime needed the village for its headquarters and for building up its arsenal most likely allowed Da Fo's party leaders to keep taxes halfway tolerable when the harvest was good. As Ruan Zhaoyin put it, "Since Yang Faxian wanted to stay in the village, he did not want to turn people against him." Yang Faxian even ordered his soldiers to "be nice to people"; consequently, the soldiers occasionally stole oxen from other villages and delivered them to some of Da Fo's farmers. Thus, there was a carrot as well as a stick in the politics of the Puppet Army occupation.[33]

Nonetheless, by mid-1941 the puppet regime was demanding way too much in taxes – approximately half of the average output of 240 *jin* per *mu* over a two-crop season. This tax claim was more onerous than the previous Kuomintang tax claim, and it seemed glaringly unjust when compared to the recent CCP system of simple and fair taxation. In the end, even the big landowners in the Bao lineage opposed this claim, allowing the Communist Party to establish a united front of rich and poor along the axis of shared anger over Japanese Puppet Army tax plunder. This anger surfaced in collective action at the height of the big famine in late 1942, when Yang's puppet regime insisted that villagers meet its rigid tax claims, and the puppet soldiers came to each household to force hungry villagers to pay.[34] At this point, the Da Fo party branch, meeting in the house of Bao Yuhua and acting in coordination with the militia, provided its own version of tax relief. Bao Zhilong tells us that he led a "little war of resistance" against grain taxes. Bao initially fought with puppet soldiers over taxes, and then joined Bao Ke, the brother of CCP first-pole notable Bao Huayin, to secretly lead several villagers to steal back millet given over to the puppet granary. Increasingly, this kind of resistance flourished under the umbrella of Bao Zhilong's militia, and Bao continued to press Yang's Puppet Army commanders to reduce taxes again in 1943, when the harvest improved and the salt trade picked up.[35]

During the occupation, Bao Zhilong's militia also came to the aid of villagers who engaged in feuds with the puppet soldiers. The story of Bao Jingan, the head of Da Fo public security in the post-1949 era, illustrates this phenomenon and underscores the complex nature of wartime resistance. After the fall harvest of 1943 Bao Jingan was beaten by one of Yang Faxian's subcommanders. At the time, it was a customary practice that anyone could use the village stone roller, which belonged to Bao Yuhua, as long as it was not already in use. However, when Bao Jingan was using the roller to process his millet, one of Yang's soldiers

[33] Ruan Zhaoyin, interview, June 17, 2006.
[34] Pang Siyin, interview, August 21, 1989.
[35] Bao Zhilong, interviews, August 16, 20, 1989; Bao Huayin, interview, August 16, 1993.

interrupted his work and insisted on using it. The two got into an argument, and a fight broke out, during which Bao hit the soldier in the eye. The soldier ran back to his barracks and got another five soldiers to help him search for Bao, who had fled. Several days later, when Bao Jingan returned to Da Fo, the soldiers demanded that Bao come to their headquarters to make an apology, and Bao agreed. When he arrived, Bao was beaten by one of Yang's officers. During the beating, Bao Yilin, a member of the militia, walked by the headquarters and entered the room in which the thrashing was taking place to ask why Bao Jingan was being beaten. Grasping Bao Jingan's dilemma, Bao Yilin managed to rescue Bao Jingan by slapping him twice in front of the soldiers, as if they were in the right, and then dragging Bao outside. This small, clever act saved Bao Jingan's life.

The affair was not without political consequence. According to Bao Jingan, "This incident made me hate Yang Faxian. He beat and killed villagers, and he buried some Communist Party members alive. . . . This is why I joined the Communist militia in the battles against Yang Faxian and the Chiang Kai-shek Kuomintang Army in the spring of 1947. I wanted to get even for these beatings."[36] Clearly, the wartime protection afforded farmers who entered into feuds with the puppet soldiers was an investment in the political future of Mao's insurgency, for it brought new recruits to the militia and the PLA in the crisis moments of the Civil War.

To be sure, this protection was provided by a few bold and courageous members of the resistance. Bao Zhilong, who, despite his role as militia head, was still an unesteemed member of the Bao lineage descent group and little-known member of the Communist Party, was one of them. The spontaneous, high risk, and self-driven resistance of Bao Zhilong helped to distinguish the underground Da Fo branch of the Communist Party as an organization that could assuage the uncertainty associated with the violent presence of the Japanese Puppet Army and help villagers collectively defend their homes and families from predatory force. The small and dangerously impetuous acts of Bao and his militia followers began to position Bao for an important leadership role in postwar village politics. At times Bao's actions were motivated by self-interest and tied up with the interest of his Bao sublineage, and they apparently escalated as the hold of the Japanese Puppet Army occupation weakened in the last years of the war.

The first act occurred in late 1943, when Bao Zhilong beat the Da Fo Puppet Army village chief. During the autumn, Bao had agreed to carry a woman and her child from the Wei River area to Da Fo in a wheelbarrow. Her family paid Bao ten *yuan* in currency issued by the Nationalist government of Chiang Kai-shek. When Bao tried to change the currency with the puppet village chief, however, the chief would not recognize it, claiming it was inflated and that he was authorized to deal only in the currency of Yang's Puppet Army – paper money imprinted with black flowers and a horse-drawn plow. "Since the village head refused to

---

[36] Bao Jingan, interview, May 15, 1990.

change it," recalls Bao Zhilong, "I kicked him and beat him. I was very strong, and though the village chief might have beaten others, in fact he did not dare to beat me or report me. If he reported me to Yang Faxian, he knew I would find him and beat him again."[37] This small incident underscored the impotence of the puppet village chief and the rising importance of Bao Zhilong's emergent parallel system of underground resistance.

The second fight, which many villagers took notice of, also occurred in late 1943. One afternoon a battalion leader in the Puppet Army was beating up on one of Bao Zhilong's neighbors. Bao rushed into the fray and asked the soldier why he was beating his neighbor, whereupon the soldier told Bao it was none of his business. Taken aback, Bao Zhilong retorted, "I will show you it is my business!" Recalling this incident, Bao says,

I then threw the battalion leader to the ground, and I beat him badly. Many other villagers came to watch this fight, and about sixty of them backed me up by shouting supportive words, so that the battalion leader dared not fight back. Instead, he ran away to enlist the support of his superior officer. But I ran ahead of him and reported his mistreatment of my neighbor to the head of Yang Faxian's Puppet Army.... He dismissed the matter and instructed the battalion leader not to make trouble for me and the common people in Da Fo.[38]

Acts like this empowered villagers, who learned that Bao Zhilong and his militia counterparts could be counted on to manipulate Yang Faxian's need for stability in his village headquarters in exchange for affording protection and security to ordinary folk.

The War of Resistance also drew Bao Zhilong and the Da Fo peasant salt makers into a web of secret relations with the resistance army, a web that extended well beyond the village. Compelled to collaborate with Yang Faxian's munitions experts to produce gunpowder, hand grenades, bombs, handguns, and machine guns, Da Fo's chemical workers often smuggled these weapons out of the arsenals, selling them to resistance army liaisons inside and outside of the village.[39] By the end of 1941, the Da Fo party branch had become a veritable counterintelligence agency for the partisan resistance. Zheng Daqing, the purchase agent who had led the prewar salt maker struggle with Bao Zhilong, joined the resistance army in 1941 and thereafter served as chef, purchase agent, and intelligence correspondent. Posing as a peddler, Zheng passed by Japanese forts in Dongle, Neihuang, and Qingfeng, reporting enemy troop strength back to Eighth Route Army intelligence in Dongle so that the army could launch nighttime strikes on Japanese outposts and go into hiding after sunrise.[40] Similarly, Ruan Yin, who

[37] Bao Zhilong, interview, August 19, 1989.
[38] Ibid.
[39] Bao Zhilong, interview, August 24, 1989; Bao Zhigen, interview, August 24, 1989; Pang Qingtian, interview, August 18, 1989.
[40] Zheng Tianbao, interview, August 24, 1989.

served in the Puppet Army around 1941, joined the CCP the same year and the resistance army shortly thereafter. A member of an anonymous Communist "secret service" within the Puppet Army, Ruan was able to use his connections to the Puppet Army's commanders and prisons in order to secretly liberate high-ranking CCP superiors who had been captured by *weijun* forces and escort them to safety before they could be turned over to the Japanese.[41]

The wartime outreach of Da Fo's underground resistance also included working to acquire weapons for the Eighth Route Army, a path Bao Zhilong and other militia members had earlier trod in buying Kuomintang weapons to arm the militia. Drawing on a wealth of black market experiences generated from trading salt in the shadows of state power, after 1941 Bao Zhilong repeatedly left the village while the war was raging and risked his life to purchase weapons for the resistance army. Bao sold horses in enemy territory, used the proceeds to purchase guns and bullets from individual puppet soldiers, and then smuggled this lethal cargo to the resistance army. The head of a confraternity of these weapons traders, Bao routinely visited Tuxingcun in the war years because, he recalls, this was a place where many weapons had been left behind by Kuomintang troops fleeing south after the Japanese invaded, and Chen Daobing, a Kuomintang solider – turned – Yang Faxian puppet commander, was secretly trafficking in these leftover arms.[42]

The underground resistance activities of Da Fo's party leaders helped the Eighth Route Army weather the setbacks of war. Only a few months after the CCP had established the Hebei-Shandong-Henan anti-Japanese base area government, the Japanese Puppet Army launched a drive to crush the resistance army and capture the party's village strongholds. The drive targeted Dongle, Neihuang, and Puyang counties. On June 10, 1940, the Japanese sent thirty thousand puppet troops and 170 armored troop carriers from Zhengzhou, Anyang, and Handan against the CCP rural base area, deploying thousands of soldiers in key market towns, including nearby Liangmen. The resistance was caught in a crisis. There were soaring defections from the CCP, desertions of guerrilla fighters, and slow responses from the resistance army. A year later, on April 12, 1941, the Japanese launched another offensive against the triprovincial base area, wiping out battalion units of the Eighth Route Army's fourth regiment in Neihuang and then destroying the field hospitals, clothing factories, and arsenals of the base area government. Shortly thereafter, Yang's Puppet Army joined in the Japanese-orchestrated "Three All Campaign" (burn all, loot all, kill all) against the suspected CCP village strongholds, severely damaging the agricultural economy on which the resistance was partially based.

The rural villages in which the resistance army drew popular support to counter this Japanese Puppet Army savagery were those in which the salt market economy of the poor smallholders was still intact, in which there was a history

---

[41] Ruan Yin, interview, August 18, 1989.
[42] Bao Zhilong, interviews, August 14, 17, 1989.

of collective resistance to the predatory intrusions of the Kuomintang salt police and the bandits, and in which the Japanese did not subject the population to the unbridled ferocity of the Three All Campaign. Da Fo was such a place. Here the militia was able to provide several forms of assistance to the besieged units of the 129th Division of the Mao-Zhu regular army. In this period, roughly mid-1941 to mid-1943, Bao Zhilong and Pang Siyin, both members of the militia, secretly arranged for one or two people to help with planting the fields and gathering the harvests of those who left Da Fo to join the Eighth Route Army.[43] At the same time, Bao Zhilong repeatedly departed the village in secrecy to collect firewood and purchase grain for the resistance army, and Bao also became the leader of a stretcher-bearer squad, carrying the wounded soldiers to field hospitals far removed from the frontline fighting.

The Da Fo militia also helped to safeguard the dependents of the resistance fighters from death threats. In mid-1941, for example, Zheng Tianbao, the eleven-year-old son of Zheng Daqing, was seized by Yang Faxian's soldiers after they conducted a house-to-house search for outsiders. His father had become an intelligence agent of the Dongle County anti-Japanese resistance government, and his brother had joined the Eighth Route Army. Consequently, Zheng Tianbao had been moving in and out of a string of party-controlled safe houses in different villages to avoid the Japanese search for Communists. Unfortunately, Zheng had been returned to Da Fo on short notice, and, on discovering that he did not have a residence permit, Yang Faxian's soldiers dragged him to their headquarters. While Zheng was waiting to be interrogated, Ruan Zhichang entered the headquarters, asked Zheng to assist him in carrying water to a meeting of Yang Faxian's officers, and escorted him outside. "Then," recalls Zheng Tianbao, "as soon as we exited Da Fo, we began to run." The two managed to escape to safety. From this point on, the young Zheng took up a job as a mail carrier, delivering messages to CCP-led resistance operatives in the surrounding villages, thereby helping the resistance fighters obtain the information they needed to hide during the day and strike the Japanese Puppet Army at night. The information provided by this intimate underground internet helped the resistance hold in Dongle County.[44]

A major goal of the anti-Japanese base area government was to break up the alliance between the Japanese and their collaborationist forces so that the Eighth Route Army and its guerrilla detachments could focus on fighting the Japanese Army. This struggle unfolded in Da Fo and Dongle between 1941 and 1945. By late 1942 villagers often awoke to discover posters on Da Fo's trees and walls documenting the progress of the resistance army in thwarting Japanese aggression, thus weakening the morale of puppet soldiers and prompting villagers to consider the consequences of serving a regime that might lose the war. Above all else, this

[43] Zheng Dianchun, interview, August 23, 1989; Bao Lieri, interview, August 23, 1989.
[44] Zheng Tianbao, interviews, August 24, 1989, July 15, 2005.

struggle focused on recruiting both *weijun* soldiers and officers into the resistance army – turning them into double dealers and patriotic secret agents within the Japanese occupation regime – and Da Fo's party leaders were actively involved in this mission. As we have seen, Ruan Yin was among these double dealers, specializing in extricating members of the resistance from puppet regime prisoner-of-war camps. On two separate occasions, Ruan Yin was involved in saving the life of Li Huaming, who later rose to become a member of the CCP Central Committee in Tianjin. In the second instance, Li Huaming was seized by the Japanese Puppet Army at Xin Ba market village, in Wei County, and taken to a Japanese prison in Linzhuang. On learning of this capture through his Puppet Army connections, Ruan Yin went to the Puppet Army prison headquarters and secured his release.[45]

By the autumn of 1944, the resistance had integrated thousands of puppet forces and was growing in strength and prestige. A key turning point in this second war came in late 1943, when first-pole Communist Party leaders from Da Fo, now playing important roles in the CCP Dongle County committee and countywide National Salvation Association, recruited a bevy of puppet force subofficers who were unhappy with their pro-Japanese superiors. Zhao Dengjie, the head of the Puppet Army cavalry, and Yun Weifeng, police chief of Yueguang town, entered into concord with the Communist-led force and then helped units of the Eighth Route Army mount a counteroffensive against the Japanese and their diehard puppet allies, defeating the latter's effort to plunder grain in pro-CCP villages.[46] Collaborating with underground CCP militias in semi-occupied villages like Da Fo, the partisan resistance and its puppet force allies were able to not only foil the designs of Japanese commands but also capture more than seventy minor Japanese officers and liberate a number of border area towns from Japanese Puppet Army rule in late 1944 and early 1945.

By this point, members of the Da Fo militia were openly engaging in small non-violent acts of resistance to awaken villagers to the disintegration of *weijun* power and the ascent of the Eighth Route Army over the weakened Japanese forces. These ran the gamut from putting on anti-Japanese plays and operas, to boycotting puppet troop demands for corvée labor, to informing party operatives of puppet regime attempts to poison the water supply of partisan forces, to taunting Chinese puppet soldiers about their hopeless future.[47]

The last months of World War II brought two earthshaking changes to rural Dongle County. One was violent, the other non-violent. Each one further legitimated the Da Fo Communist Party and emboldened the young vigilantes in the militia. In March 1945 Da Fo's underground Communist Party members emerged to team up with the 129th Division of the Eighth Route Army under General Liu Bocheng, striking the weakened Japanese Army in Dongle County.

---

[45] Ruan Yin, interview, August 18, 1989.
[46] Zhang Huaiwen, "Ji-Lu-Yu Kangri Genjudi Gonggu Yu Fazhande Yuanyin Chutan," 103.
[47] Bao Yilin, interview, May 13, 1990; Bao Weishen, interview, August 4, 1990.

Bao Zhilong and the ten-man militia unit dug up the arms they had buried when the Puppet Army had taken over the village more than five years before, took over the Puppet Army's arsenal, and recruited twenty new members. On April 20 this thirty-man militia force joined with other village militias to drive sixty Japanese soldiers from their fort at Shangcun market town on the Wei River and then marched fifteen kilometers east to support General Liu's soldiers in an assault on several hundred Japanese troops and their puppet forces inside of Dongle County town. On April 24 this main force launched a second attack on Dongle town and on Long Wang temple in Daming, killing thirty-seven Japanese soldiers and capturing several thousand members of Yang Faxian's puppet army. The militia unit assisting in this battle was led by Bao Zhilong and the salt makers who had followed Bao in kicking the police out of Dongle County a decade past and who, subsequently, had joined with Bao in creating the CCP militia in 1938, underscoring the connection between the early anti-state protest and anti-Japanese resistance.[48]

Following this victory, several hundred people from Da Fo went to Dongle County town, where they participated in the election of a new magistrate, Tan Fengge, a leader of the local CCP underground. Several weeks after the election, the Dongle County Communist Party government cancelled the wartime *heli fudan* tax system and declared a three-year tax holiday. In Da Fo, everyone, including the land-poor salt producers who had suffered the tax injustice of the Puppet Army, was exempted from taxes. The village was plastered with slogans proclaiming tax exemptions for June wheat and declaring an end to all surtaxes. To be sure, there was a public grain tax, which amounted to eight *jin* per *mu* on the fall millet crop only. However, if the autumn millet crop failed, then people were automatically exempted; they could even receive some relief grain from the revolutionary government.[49] In this moment, the Communist-led victory promised a world without the tax state.

In taking over the celebration of this victory Bao Zhilong and the Da Fo militia leaders emerged to identify themselves as the militant fist of the oppressed and positioned themselves to spearhead the coming insurgency against Chiang Kai-shek's Kuomintang. After liberating Dongle County, the CCP sponsored a series of celebrations. In Da Fo, militia leaders Bao Zhilong and Pang Siyin recruited the Yu Zhu Opera Troupe from Puyang and then organized three operas a day for five days in a row. "This was in late June 1945, shortly after the wheat harvest," recalls Pang Siyin. "At that time, we held a Victory over Japan Opera, and all of the people from Da Fo attended. They were joined by ten thousand people from surrounding villages."[50] The operas, which depicted Guangong, or the war god – a

---

[48] Thaxton, *Salt of the Earth*, 268, and see *Jiefang Ribao*, May 5, 1945.
[49] Bao Lieri, interview, May 12, 1990; Bao Zhimin, interview, May 12, 1990; Bao Jingan, interview, May 15, 1999; Bao Lijun, interview, May 12, 1996.
[50] Pang Siyin, interview, August 22, 1998.

hero of the oppressed – were infused with political witticism stressing the good deeds of the resistance army.

In the course of waging resistance to the Japanese Puppet Army occupation, Bao Zhilong and his companions in the militia learned two important political lessons. The first pertained to armed struggle. "We learned through waging guerrilla war against the Japanese puppet forces," recalls Bao Zhilong, "that armed struggle was more effective than peaceful means in getting what we wanted. During the Anti-Japanese War we learned how to fight guerrilla warfare through military instructions sent by the Communist Party. We fought only when we were certain of victory. Otherwise, we would try to avoid the enemy. We also learned how to consolidate and develop our forces."[51] The other lesson was to make war without mercy: the enemy was to be annihilated, for the politics of war was a matter of life and death pure and simple, and hence politics justified killing. By the end of the war with Japan, the Communist Party had convinced its village followers that Chiang Kai-shek's army, which in this North China Plain area was rapidly assimilating the ultrarepressive armed bands of collaborators that had served the Yang Faxian Puppet Army, was committed to wiping them out, which meant that, in Bao Zhilong's words, "We had no way out but to fight to the death." Bao explained:

The Communist Party told us that if we killed one enemy, we already had paid for our life if we died; if we killed two, then when we died we had one score up on the enemy. So my comrades and I were prepared to die for our cause, which was to liberate the country, relieve the suffering of the common people, and help everyone have a better life.[52]

Da Fo's militia fighters were told not to think of themselves. They were to think only of China's poor masses, and they were to kill even their Chinese brothers who had slaughtered fellow villagers and fellow countrymen – and that is what they did.

Yet whereas the Da Fo militia leaders learned from their cooperation with the resistance army and adapted Communist Party slogans and popular culture to celebrate the resistance army's victory, their self-imagined equivalency with the Mao-Zhu army of the country people was somewhat misleading.[53] They had a poor understanding of the specific policies and rules governing the resistance army's relationship with rural dwellers. The Da Fo militia was never exposed to the CCP system of everyday pressure, reward, and punishment that turned regular army recruits into disciplined actors who practiced restraint in the use of force among the rural-based civilian population. In comparison to the Eighth Route Army, the militia attacks on opponents were sporadic episodes of ferocity,

---

[51] Bao Zhilong, interview, May 7, 1990.
[52] Ibid.
[53] See Friedman and Selden, "War Communism," 27.

and, unlike the Eighth Route Army, the militia leaders were not looking to make allies.

Due to the war-related deaths of many of the most enlightened and educated members of the Da Fo party branch, Bao Zhilong and his comrades, who considered themselves to be the heroes of the local party branch, surfaced to play an even greater role in making claims, framing identities, and mobilizing villagers in pursuit of collective action.[54] The problem was that the lethal violence of the war years had exposed Bao Zhilong and the Da Fo militia activists to repeated acts of savagery. Their reciprocal killings of known members of the violent Yang Faxian puppet regime ultimately produced a long-term memory of the war that justified using deadly violence against anyone who challenged party-centered political community. At war's end, these young militia fighters seem to have been prepared by their wartime performance to kill all suspected *weijun* sympathizers, many of whom were poor rural people like them. And whereas wartime violence is the exception to the rule in states with institutions in place for implementing peaceful domestic policy, in China the expulsion of the Japanese was followed after a few years by a civil war between Communists and Nationalists that lasted until 1949 and, following the Communist victory, a party-state led for many years by Mao Zedong, who continued to promote his style of "war communism" into the 1960s. In Bao Zhilong's experience and the experience of his militia comrades, the violent leadership style of wartime became the norm, and because these men held the reins of power in Da Fo, their often violent mode of rule prevailed in the village.[55]

The Land Revolution of 1945–1947

Following the springtime Liberation of 1945, the Da Fo Communist Party leadership supervised a two-stage land reform process. The cumulative effect of this leveling process further strengthened support for the party among the poorest farmers. In the first phase, the Da Fo party leaders redistributed land to villagers, requiring people with more than fifty *mu* of land to put their holdings up for sale in public auction. In May 1946, Da Fo's party activists put 1,100 *mu* of land up for auction, stipulating that each household could purchase no more than three *mu* per member. Apparently, this transfer of land was achieved via the public market, not confiscation.[56] But many of Da Fo's big landholders put land up for sale either because they feared it would be confiscated or because they felt they had a considerably better chance of keeping some land if they offered to sell a substantial

---

[54] In developing this section, I have benefited greatly from McAdam, Tarrow, and Tilly, *Dynamics of Contention*, 58–60.

[55] I am indebted to Steven Levine for his help in developing this line of argument. Personal correspondence, February 11, 2006.

[56] Compare with Crook and Crook, *Revolution in a Chinese Village*, 19–20, 179, and Pepper, *Civil War in China*, 248.

part of their holdings. Some farm households also lost out in this process. Pang Xiannai, who had seventy *mu* of land at the end of the Anti-Japanese War, was thirty-six at the start of the first phase. He recalls:

We were forced to give up forty *mu* to the other villagers during the first stage of the land reform. After the sale of the forty *mu* the land just barely produced enough for my family to eat.... When I sold the forty *mu* in public I said I was willing to sell, but in fact I did not want to sell. I had no other choice because it was the policy of the Da Fo Peasant Association.[57]

In practice, land to the tiller did not mean that all tillers benefited from land reform.

The Communist Party leader in charge of the public auction of prime croplands was Bao Zhilong, and this first phase primarily benefited Bao and his second-pole militia network, because these semi-peasants were in a position to compete for the lands politically and economically. Bao himself was the first person to know which particular fields were coming up for "auction," and the salt producers had the money to purchase these lands. Thus it should not surprise us to learn that Bao Zhilong was the recipient of twenty *mu* of land in the 1947 revolution and that, recalls Bao, "eighteen *mu* was good land, and the grain I got from this land was more than enough for a living."[58] Bao Qixin, a Da Fo resident who depended on salt trade for 30 percent of his total income in 1946, bought his land from money earned in the salt market. So did Bao Zhilong and other salt makers who were committed to the CCP and entrenched in the militia-infiltrated Peasant Association.

The second phase of land reform was initiated in early January and continued into late March 1947. Bao Zhilong and the Da Fo Peasant Association leaders took the lead in redistributing the remaining land and property of Da Fo's big landholders to the poor farmers, hired hands, and tenants who had been left out in the first phase. Approximately nine hundred additional *mu* was divided along these lines, or so party leaders publicly declared. The Peasant Association drew up a list of peasant households owning less than three *mu* per capita, then offered each family enough land to make up the difference. In reality, however, "the rule of three *mu* per capita was not fixed," recalls Pang Siyin: "There were other factors to consider. A family with less than three *mu* per member might have lived quite well if the quality of land was better and if they plowed adeptly. Or, conversely, a family of five with only twelve *mu* of extremely poor cropland and poor agricultural skills was entitled to more than three *mu*."[59]

Bao Zhilong and the militia activists in the second pole, apparently having decided that they deserved to receive more land than poor farmers whose war service records were not distinguished, awarded some of the best land to themselves,

[57] Pang Xiannai, interview, May 15, 1990.
[58] Bao Zhilong, interviews, May 5, 7, 1990.
[59] Pang Siyin, interview, May 8, 1990.

their relatives, and their comrades in the party committee and the party-staffed militia, so the poorly connected poorest tillers often received some of the poorest land – or none at all. Militia activist Bao Zhendao, for example, had eleven *mu* of land before the CCP seizure of power in April 1945, but his family had twenty-four *mu* by the end of the 1947 land reform.[60] Bao Yilin, another member of the original CCP militia, came out of the 1947 land reform with thirty-eight *mu* – twenty-five more than his family had owned in the spring of 1945.[61] By way of comparison, the amount of land held by many of the other poor smallholders stayed constant, or increased by only three to six *mu* at most; they therefore found themselves in possession of roughly ten to fifteen *mu* after 1947.

Some villagers saw the CCP-controlled land redistribution as a veiled form of privilege seeking and plunder, but few complained. On the one hand, Bao Zhilong and the militia fighters carried small arms, and no one dared challenge them. On the other hand, life was getting better. There was ample rainfall in the years 1945–47, so many of the poor tillers who did receive even just a little more land reaped greater harvests, and the salt market also was back, so these same poor tillers could earn extra income in the market, all of which redounded to the people who had taken charge of protecting the economy of the village: Bao Zhilong and his militia. The redistribution of land, households, and furniture placated many of these shortchanged poor households, who were still "small winners," causing them to look favorably on the CCP. After all, neither the Kuomintang nor the Japanese Puppet Army had touched the issue of land inequality, and the CCP's solution was far better than no solution at all. As the testimony of Bao Zhendao indicates, the CCP militia leaders well understood this dynamic: "Some got more than others," says Bao, "but no one complained publicly because at least they got more land than before."[62] Nonetheless, this approach also played to the biases of Bao Zhilong and his militia allies, all of whom felt that their war-related sacrifices entitled them to first claim on the fertile croplands being distributed in the second phase.

The skewed redistribution process in Da Fo may reflect a pattern of cadres' land grabbing throughout rural China in the period prior to 1949. Poor, land-short farmers in Tian Dexing village in Anhui's Jing County, for example, recall that those who determined how village resources were distributed during land reform were "persons who joined the guerrilla forces and fought for the Communist Party in wars," and they remember that it was these party militants who got the fertile lands and the best houses, leaving them with land that was not sufficient to sustain life.[63] This pattern of war-related entitlement would structure cadre

---

[60] Bao Zhendao, interview, May 7, 1990.
[61] Bao Yilin, interviews, May 13–15, 1990.
[62] Bao Zhendao, interview, May 7, 1990.
[63] Anhui interview, 2006.

decisions about who got the best work assignments and the better food during the Great Leap Forward in Da Fo and other villages in Henan, Anhui, and Shandong.

In concert with the land reform, Communist Party members took action against Da Fo's "landlords" in ritualized public encounters. During the first phase of land reform, the Da Fo Peasant Association, working closely with the militia, called a village meeting to put landlords and their property on public display. The Da Fo party leaders entered each so-called landlord household, removed all of the furniture for distribution, and, on the basis of decisions made in a prior closed party committee meeting, distributed pieces of furniture to the poorest of poor farmers in the village. The big landholders of the Bao lineage were left only their beds to sleep on. Following this, Bao Zhilong and the Da Fo militia escorted four landlords to a meeting in the old threshing grounds of the village. One thousand villagers attended. On arrival, they discovered that the militia had built a high stage from which Bao Yidai, a key party leader of the Peasant Association, was challenging them to join him in criticizing the misbehavior of the landlords. Then, after the militia took all of the landlords to the front of the stage, Bao Yidai encouraged people to ascend the stage and tell the crowd how the landlords had wronged them. Nearly twenty villagers spoke out.

Not everyone was eager to embrace the party effort to manufacture class struggle, however. Bao Yilin, a member of the militia, had reservations about treating the heads of the big landowning households badly, for he recalled that Bao Wenhao had treated his family with fairness. According to Bao Yilin,

I felt it was unfair of me to expect the landlord to give back the land that I had given him as payment for a loan I could not pay back. I took the land back because Chairman Mao instructed us to do so. This was called 'fair' because it was a Communist Party policy. After 1945, even though the landlord willingly returned the land to us, we treated him badly. This was because the Communist Party had declared that all landlords were bad and exploited villagers. This bad treatment of the landlord included accusing him in front of his house, forcing him onto the stage in village meetings, and cursing him in public.[64]

The notion that all landlords were exploiters, pure and simple, was a political distortion, and Bao Yilin knew it. But he was a member of Da Fo's militia guard, and his conflicted feelings produced silent complicity.

A discerning memory of the political track record of Da Fo's more powerful landholders played a role in militia decisions about whether to target them. Not surprisingly, the number-one target of the militia and the Peasant Association was landlord Bao Zhihai – the one big landholder whose misdeeds best fitted the paradigm of a bad landlord and who in fact had abused villagers and relied on his Kuomintang connections to mobilize the law in support of his mean-spirited behavior. That Bao Zhihai was already dead did not prevent him from being

[64] Bao Yilin, interview, May 15, 1990.

targeted. "It is true that Bao Zhihai had died before Liberation," says militia member Zheng Shan, "but in the land revolution of 1947 we dug his body out of his tomb and burned it before the villagers." According to Zheng, this act of violence was taken in revenge for the "outlandish and arrogant" behavior of Bao Zhihai, who had strutted around the village in a blue Mandarin robe and looked down on people through his crystal glasses.[65] Perhaps feelings of social antagonism could be called up from wounded hearts in cases like this one, but such cases were rare in Da Fo. Even the enraged militia members spared Bao Yuhua, the landholding patron who had treated the poor with kindness and joined the CCP against the Japanese Puppet Army in the Anti-Japanese War of Resistance.

The land revolution did not occur in a political vacuum. The CCP and the Kuomintang renewed their old hostilities following the Japanese surrender. During a brief cease-fire between late 1945 and early 1946, both sides attempted to negotiate the creation of a coalition government, but neither was ultimately willing to give up the territory they had won during the war. In the spring of 1946, the Kuomintang broke off negotiations, and the Civil War began. Under the administrative control of the CCP, the second phase of what was called the "land-to-the-tiller movement" galvanized peasant recruits and resources for the PLA campaign against the Kuomintang Army and transformed a struggle over landownership into a political war against the Kuomintang state.[66] With their newfound gains from the second distribution, poor villagers were more inclined to support the CCP against the Kuomintang, for, after receiving their own land to farm from the CCP, they feared they would suffer material loss and political retribution if the Nationalists emerged victorious. The memory of Bao Xijian underscores this point:

I was very glad to send grain to the PLA. This was because the CCP had given me a lot of land and there was more than enough to feed my family. I was quite worried that if the Kuomintang returned to power, they would take back the land that I recently had acquired. If the Kuomintang won and returned to power, I think they would have sent us to prison or killed us and returned all the land to the landlords.[67]

Bao Xijian, who got about 70 percent of his income from crops and the remaining 30 percent from selling earth salt and nitrate, voiced yet another concern about the outcome of the Civil War: "If the Kuomintang leaders had returned to power," he said, "I do not think they would have permitted us to produce earth salt. They would have established their own salt firm again. . . . This would

---

[65] Zheng Shan, interview, May 11, 1990. One school of memory in Da Fo holds that Bao Zhihai was implicated in the murder of CCP founder Bao Tiancai and that Bao Tiancai's mother and aunt, with members of the CCP-led Women's Federation, destroyed the tomb and exposed the body of Bao Zhihai in the land revolution. Bao Peisun, interview, June 15, 2006. I have not been able to verify this point, but it does not change the fact that members of the militia were major players in this incident.

[66] Pepper, *Civil War in China*, 301, 305–07.

[67] Bao Xijian, interview, May 14, 1990.

have taken us back to the time before the Japanese occupation, when the salt police came here to destroy our salt making tools."[68] Bao, like other poor salt producers, enjoyed a higher standard of living because the second land reform had boosted his total harvest, but he still made earth salt and nitrate for sale and depended on the proceeds for basic necessities and for extra spending money, and thus he feared the Kuomintang would destroy the gains derived from market participation by sending the salt police back again.

Whereas CCP propaganda normally emphasized peasant impoverishment due to inequality of landholdings and peasant zeal for settling old scores with landlord employers, in Da Fo it also paid attention to the villagers' desire to retain their access to the salt market, as Bao Zhilong makes clear:

If Chiang Kai-shek had won, the salt police would have returned and harmed our livelihood. We would have lost the good life we had gotten. By 1945 the CCP had revoked all taxes imposed by the Kuomintang, including the salt tax. Thus we held a mass meeting in the village, and we told villagers that "When Chiang Kai-shek returns he will bring back all of the old land taxes, the miscellaneous taxes, and the salt tax, and we will not have a good life." In this mass meeting, we told them that the Kuomintang would not allow us to make earth salt.[69]

This deeply felt fear was echoed in all quarters of Da Fo. Above all, villagers remember that the CCP initially legitimated itself by defending their household economies, and that Bao Zhilong and his militia stood against Kuomintang power holders who sought to convert their local marketing community into an input for the national state. The Kuomintang drive to take back territory held by the CCP border area government was therefore seen as a dire threat to a household-initiated adaptation to the continuing poverty of agriculture – as a threat to the survival of family, kin, and market community, all of which now were under the protective umbrella of the militia and the PLA. Villagers' shared memory of intrusive state violence surely made it easier for the Communist Party to enlist them in the PLA, which stood for a political order in which they could have a good life.

The Civil War and Vigilante Violence, 1946–1949

Within half a year of the Japanese surrender in August 1945, the Civil War between the Nationalists and the Communists boiled over in the Hebei-Shandong-Henan border area. The Communist resistance army, now renamed the People's Liberation Army, scored early successes, taking scores of counties.[70] Nevertheless, in mid-1946, Chiang Kai-shek sent Zhao Dongchen to serve as chief of staff of Yang Faxian's Puppet Army, which had been driven west to Anyang

[68] Ibid.
[69] Bao Zhilong, interview, May 6, 1990.
[70] Seybolt, "War Within a War," 223.

city. This Kuomintang operative began to work with Yang to organize counter-revolutionary terror against the Communists and to assimilate Yang's puppet troops into a more powerful killing machine – the dreaded Kuomintang New Fifth Army. This army was joined by nearly twenty thousand bandits from all corners of the border area, including a three-thousand-man force under Yang Faxian.[71]

The reconstituted Kuomintang Army incorporated a detachment known as the Huangxiangtuan, or "Homecoming Regiment." Its troops gained a reputation for slaughtering anyone who opposed them in their campaign to recover territory from the Communist Party and return landlords and the Kuomintang to home ground. In December 1946, Chiang Kai-shek sent the New Fifth Army and its Homecoming Regiment to attack the Communist Hebei-Shandong-Henan border region government, seeking to destroy the institutional foundations of Maoist revolutionary power in this strategic lower part of the North China Plain.[72] This ultraviolent force struck Da Fo village on New Year's Day of 1947, interrupting the Spring Festival and panicking hundreds of residents, some of whom fled to Shangcunji. Subsequently, the New Fifth Army placed black lanterns on the doors of suspected Communist Party sympathizers and began to seize the Da Fo villagers who had stored grain in secret underground bins for the PLA.

Just as the Kuomintang took no prisoners, so the Communist-led PLA under Liu Bocheng and Yang Dezhi responded with a violent counterattack to checkmate the Kuomintang invasion. The Da Fo militia was called on to assist the PLA in defending Dongle County and driving the Kuomintang Army out of the border area. In Da Fo, Bao Zhilong led the militia to provide a host of supportive war services for the PLA in this opening phase of the Civil War. They transported grain for PLA troops to Liu An village, in Puyang County, where the Communists' insurgent army was in a firefight with the Kuomintang Army. Bao also led a ten-man stretcher bearer squad to Handan, in Hebei province, carrying soldiers wounded in the battle for Si Dazhang to distant PLA field hospitals. Following this, Bao and his militia fighters went to Neihuang County, in Henan. Here they were joined by hundreds of other militia in transporting guns and artillery to PLA battle positions and in collecting high-quality weapons, which they subsequently took to a PLA base in Yanggu County in western Shandong.[73] Knowing they would become a "problem" for high-ranking Kuomintang fiscal planners and convinced that the Kuomintang government's Ministry of Finance would use violence to stop them from producing salt for the market, Da Fo's militiamen repeatedly risked body and limb to support the PLA push against Kuomintang forces.

---

[71] Bao Zhilong and Pang Dongchen, interviews, May 7, 1990; Seybolt, "War Within a War," 208, 211–12, 223.
[72] Seybolt, "War Within a War," 223.
[73] Bao Zhilong, interviews, May 6, 7, 1990.

When the Kuomintang's New Fifth Army first entered Da Fo in early 1947, Yang Faxian's Homecoming Regiment spread slogans and posted wanted notices, threatening to kill any of the villagers who fled Dongle with the PLA, whose forces were racing to sanctuary in the western part of Shandong province. The Kuomintang Army's message seemed to be that the villagers who stayed put would be spared. It was a ruse. In nearby Da Weicun village, Bai Huqian, a squad leader under Yang Faxian, seized Shi Dehai, the Da Weicun Peasant Association head, and executed him for involvement in the CCP-led land reform. Bao Zhilong and Bao Wuzhi, both of whom were active in the Da Fo Peasant Association, had befriended Shi Dehai in countywide Peasant Association meetings during land reform, and they were angered and alarmed by news of his death. Several months later, the PLA swept back into the Anyang-Dongle-Neihuang area, teaming up with Communist Party–led militias to capture Bai Huqian in the battle for Chu Wang town. In the Civil War, the Communist Party base area government practice was that the Kuomintang officers who had murdered civilians were given back to the place where the victim had been killed. When Bai was caught, his case was decided by Da Fo's Bao Yizhao, who had risen to head the CCP Fifth District in the territory of Dongle-Wei County. Bao Yizhao ordered Bai Huqian to submit to a public mass trial and then delivered him to Dongle County town jail.[74] At the time of the trial, Bao Zhilong and twenty armed members of the Da Fo militia were dispatched to the jail to escort Bai Huqian back to Da Weicun village. They delivered him to a crowd of nearly four thousand people at Liangmenpo, near the center of Liangmen township. Bao Zhilong describes his role in the outcome:

When we first got Bai Huqian we told him that we were just taking him home. But then we took him to Liangmenpo, and we bound him to a tree.

We brought Bai Huqian to this Liangmenpo because it was a big village, and because the Eighth Route Army had held meetings there during the Anti-Japanese War. At the meeting we told the local people what this Bai Huqian had done, and then we killed him. We used knives to stab him to death.

Then we invited Shi Danjun, the father of the head of the Da Weicun Peasant Association, to avenge his son's death. This Shi Danjun took a chopper and cut Bai Huqian's head open, so that his brains spilled out.

Only the militia and the masses were at this public retaliation meeting. It was a policy of the Communist Party at the time to let the common people settle the accounts with their enemies, and we also used this kind of event as a way to mobilize the common people to defend themselves.[75]

Clearly, too, the young militia leaders who had been harassed, beaten, and tortured by Yang Faxian's soldiers during the long war with the Japanese Puppet Army used these public killing field meetings to settle scores with them. As a result the meetings were affairs of power, revenge, and blood.[76] Thus it is not

---

[74] Zheng Tianbao and Bao Yibin, interviews, July 5, 2002.
[75] Bao Zhilong, interview, May 6, 1990.
[76] Ibid.

surprising that people from key Da Fo leadership networks remember that Bao Zhilong, the head of the militia at the time, organized some other members of the militia to go to the trial, and that these "members of the militia were involved in killing Bai Huqian, whereas the ordinary villagers were not."[77]

The Da Fo militia activists also took part in the most celebrated of these killing field episodes: the trial of Ding Minjie, one of Yang Faxian's regiment commanders.[78] Ding Minjie was executed before a gathering of ten thousand people near the Wei River and Shangcunji in mid-1947 for the crime of killing his uncle, Ding Wenlan, a famous marksman from Xi Dai village and a Communist Party member. Bao Zhilong, along with several other militia leaders, witnessed the killing of Ding Minjie. Bao Zhigen remembers it well:

> They held a public meeting at Shangcun market, and this Ding Minjie was put on stage. Before they killed him they tried to break the locks on his feet for a long time. While this was going on the wife of Ding Wenlan came onto the stage and cried out to the people how this Ding Minjie had wronged her husband. She shouted profanities at the nephew for nearly three hours. She denounced him as a beast. In the end, the PLA took him to a trench near the Wei River and shot him.[79]

The militia did not do physical harm to the big Bao landholders in this stage, for in mid-1946 most of the landlords fled house arrest in Da Fo to Anyang city. The wartime retaliation against the landlords began in early 1947, right before the second phase of land reform, when the Kuomintang New Fifth Army and its Homecoming Regiment stormed back into west Dongle County, driving out the pro-Communist village militias for forty days. In the ensuing reign of terror, several of the fugitive Bao landlords returned to Da Fo, threatening to harm villagers who had aided the Communist Party and allowing some of their clients to aid the Kuomintang. When the PLA launched a counterstrike and shifted the balance of power, Bao Zhilong and the militia leaders returned to the village and immediately worked hand-in-hand with the leaders of the Peasant Association to subject anyone who was connected to a pro-Kuomintang landlord household to public accusation, criticism, and punishment. Though few Western scholars have fully grasped the politics of this link between land reform and Civil War, it is a link that is of extraordinary importance: the Kuomintang Army strike against the CCP border region government and its popular base allowed the Communist Party leaders in Da Fo to heighten the latent social tensions between poor households and rich households and to use land reform as a political instrument to teach poor villagers about social inequality and political injustice.

Thus, in mid-1947, after the New Fifth Army attacked Da Fo village from Jingdian town in Neihuang County, the spiral of militia-inflicted violence against the officers of the murderous Homecoming Regiment quickly spilled into the lives

---

[77] Zheng Tianbao (with Bao Yibin), interviews, July 5, 2002.
[78] Ibid.
[79] Bao Zhigen, interview, May 6, 1990.

of the so-called landlords who had allegedly sided with the Kuomintang, and the violence of the Civil War became inseparable from the struggle over the land. For one month, the Da Fo militia leaders put Da Fo's landlords in a makeshift prison and then joined in criticizing them in public struggle meetings. In these meetings, Da Fo's party leaders played at rage, dramatizing their own power over formerly dominant landowning households in front of ordinary villagers. Militia chief Bao Zhilong was the cadre who orchestrated this public theater.[80]

The Da Fo militia targeted mainly the accused landlords who willfully aided the Nationalist government in its attempt to reassert its fiscal interest and root out CCP activists. Among the thirty or so people with direct social connections to Da Fo's major landholding households, approximately six were put to death. It seems that the militia leaders were reacting primarily to the role assumed by landlords in the Kuomintang New Fifth Army attack on their land reform gains and market profits and only secondarily to the ways in which the landlords had subordinated them as social producers. Still, whereas the evidence of all-out complicity with the Kuomintang inquisition was clear-cut in some cases, in others it was mixed and questionable. Raw wild emotions ruled as some of the Da Fo militia leaders created their own spur-of-the-moment political justice.

Those who embraced the Homecoming Regiment were put to death by Bao Zhilong's militia. Take the case of Bao Zhouchuan, a former vagrant and beggar who had worked in a host of marginal jobs – pulling boats, working in a cotton factory, and making earth salt – before purchasing twenty *mu* of land. When the Kuomintang Army returned around the 1947 New Year and the Da Fo militia leaders fled, Bao Zhouchuan led its soldiers to uncover the secret grain storage facilities in the fields of the missing salt producers – public grain that was to be sent to provision PLA battle front troops – and he hung a black lantern on the gates of the households with relatives in the CCP and the militia, all the while menacing the wives of several militia leaders. When the Homecoming Regiment retreated under PLA pressure, Bao Zhilong and Pang Siyin led the militia to arrest Bao Zhouchuan. They tied him to a tree and sliced him to death with knives, inviting women who had been assaulted by Bao to join the killing.[81]

A few "landlords" who lost their lives were actually affluent farmers who supposedly had conspired openly with the Kuomintang counterrevolution. Bao Weili was one of them. Angered by the Communist Party's plan to seize and redistribute his land and property to poor villagers, Bao had fled the village in the early phase of the land reform, when he also was asked to give back interest to local borrowers, including his uncle. When the Kuomintang raided Da Fo in early 1947, the militia and Peasant Association leaders spread word that Bao had returned with a gun. When asked to give it up, Bao refused, after which he was accused

---

[80] On the choreographing of violence by CCP leaders in the land revolution, see Levine, *Anvil of Victory*, 212–13.

[81] Bao Zhilong and Pang Siyin, interviews, May 7, 1990.

of informing Kuomintang troops of his uncle's CCP membership. The militia, in collaboration with the Peasant Association, arrested Bao and sent him to the gallows. In allegedly helping the Kuomintang identify party leaders, Bao Weili had crossed the line, setting himself up for militia violence.[82]

Still other victims of militia violence were poor farmers. Bao Juichun, a poor tiller, was killed around the same time, merely for shouting in public, "Why is it that the Communist Party Children's Regiment [gongchandang ertong tuan] does not sing on the street anymore?" – a question that was construed as disloyal.[83]

Tragically, this orgy of violence against landlords also became a war against poor women and pitted poor militia males against poor females who had entered the world of the wealthy. While targeting Bao Ming, a big landholder who had several concubines, Bao Zhilong and the militia ran into a problem: Bao Ming had fled to territory under Kuomintang control. Frustrated, they seized Lao Yu, Bao Ming's number-one concubine. Apparently, Lao Yu had a reputation for abusing hired hands and releasing her dog against village beggars, but she was not a Kuomintang agent. Nonetheless, the militia reinvented her as a "Kuomintang counterrevolutionary" and subjected her to revolutionary justice. After constructing a tall wooden gallows, they bound her hands behind her back and hoisted her up into the sky, shouting with each jerk of the rope, "There, can you see Chiang Kai-shek, can you see him now?!" Then, after she said that she could see Chiang Kai-shek, they let go of the rope, dropping her headfirst to the ground, instantly killing her.[84] In the second land revolution, the poor killed the poor, as the young, enraged, and emboldened male leaders of the party-based militia engaged in anti-human acts to reclaim frustrated rights to manhood, fitting this wanton violence into a Communist ideology that justified violence against greedy dominant landholders – and killing the innocent poor in the process.[85] Their actions set a disturbing precedent for the future.

The Disappearance of the First Pole

Between early 1947 and mid-1950, roughly the start of the Civil War to the outbreak of the Korean War, there was a further shift of power in the village from the educated and enlightened members of the Communist Party branch to the Bao Zhilong–led militia. This power shift was not planned; rather, it was delivered by the lethal impact of war on key first-pole Da Fo party leaders and by the rise of still other such leaders up the hierarchy of the Mao-led warrior polity, whose combat-efficient insurgent army was surging ahead in its quest to destroy the Kuomintang military and seize national power.

---

[82] Pang Siyin, interview, May 7, 1990.
[83] Bao Zhendao, interview, July 5, 2002.
[84] Zheng Tianbao, interview, July 15, 2005; corroborated by Bao Peizhi, interview, July 25, 2005.
[85] Here and in the following discussion, I have benefited from Hedges, War Is a Force, 3, 84–86.

Three dimensions of this shift are preserved in the memory of villagers. The first has to do with a key Civil War–related death. In mid-1947, when the Civil War heated up, the Peasant Associations in the salt land villages of the Hebei-Shandong-Henan revolutionary base area kicked off a massive army recruitment drive, exhorting young villagers to join the PLA and convening sending-off ceremonies for thousands of volunteers.[86] Da Fo sent 120 young people into the PLA. These semi-peasant warriors from the bad earth zone of the North China Plain invigorated the process whereby the PLA jolted the Kuomintang state. But there was a huge price for Da Fo. One of the first PLA recruits to die in combat was Bao Yidai, who lost his life in South China during the Civil War. The popular leader of Da Fo's Peasant Association, Bao Yidai was one of the most respected Communist Party members in the village. In the recruitment drive of 1947, Bao Yidai had approached militia leader Bao Zhilong about the importance of one of them volunteering for PLA service. The two men agreed that they needed to join the fight against the Kuomintang on the battlefield in order to defend the revolutionary gains of land reform, and they also agreed that one of them had to join the PLA in order to encourage more young people to join the army. Bao Yidai accepted the challenge himself, partly because Bao Zhilong was the only son in his family and Bao Yidai had several brothers and partly because Bao Zhilong promised Bao Yidai that he would care for his family should the latter not return to the village.[87] When Bao Yidai died in combat, Bao Zhilong began taking up some of his duties, and he quickly became the *de facto* head of the Da Fo Peasant Association. Technically, the Da Fo Peasant Association still had control of the militia, but, from roughly mid-1947 on, the Peasant Association was being transformed into an instrument of militia power.[88]

The second phase of this power shift commenced with the PLA victories of 1948 and 1949, which resulted in the rapid formation of the new People's Republic of China and hence the sudden ascent of many of Da Fo's first-pole party activists into regional and national administrative hierarchies of the Mao-led protostate, thus transferring them out of Dongle County and preoccupying them with the tasks of socialist state formation in distant urban places. In this period, Bao Qicai, Bao Tiancai's younger brother and a graduate of the Dongle Teachers' Training School, left the PLA to serve as the bureau chief of the Irrigation Department in Anyang prefecture.[89] Shortly thereafter, Bao Zhilong became the Da Fo Communist Party secretary; he was appointed, not elected.[90] In this same period, Bao Huayin, who had joined with Bao Tiancai to establish the Da Fo National Salvation Association at the outset of the Japanese invasion, had become CCP secretary

---

[86] Thaxton, *Salt of the Earth*, 313.
[87] Bao Rulong, interview, July 6, 2002.
[88] The testimony of Bao Qingchao, the youngest son of Bao Zhilong, confirms this change. Interview, July 6, 2002.
[89] Bao Peizhi, interview, July 25, 2005.
[90] Bao Zhendao, interview, July 5, 2002.

in Dongle County during the Anti-Japanese War, and had served under Zhang Linzhi, the leader of the CCP Hebei-Shandong-Henan border region during the Civil War, was transferred to Beijing to head a National Grain Exchange Office within the PRC Ministry of Commerce. Bao Weishen, who had joined the anti-Japanese struggle after graduating from the Dongle County Teachers' Training School, went to fight with the PLA in Shandong's Heze during the Civil War and then was promoted to a position within the National Bureau of Forestry in Beijing.[91]

Taking a longer view, then, between the late 1930s and the close of the Civil War, the Chinese Communist movement in Da Fo underwent an important transformation, which can most aptly be described as a "militarization." In the late 1940s, as the CCP gained the upper hand in the Civil War, the most promising local party leaders were promoted to higher positions in the emerging party-state hierarchy. This dual process left the dregs of party leadership at the village level, so the revolution inside of Da Fo was increasingly directed by ruffians and the poor riffraff in the second-pole militia, and this meant that ordinary villagers were at the mercy of people who were schooled in the poorly controlled and chaotic violence of irregular warfare.

This trend was reinforced by the outbreak of the Korean War, which inaugurated the third and final phase of the decline of the first pole. Many of the demobilized PLA veterans were called to war service, giving Bao Zhilong the chance to consolidate his power in their absence. The veterans were a threat to Bao Zhilong because they had great prestige among villagers. They shared patriotic goals learned in the army, by and large agreed on the importance of not using coercion to effect popular compliance, and formed a cohesive political reference group within the village. The Korean War undercut their leverage. Those who served, of course, were removed from the political scene, and they did not return to Da Fo until 1953. But even those who did not want to serve in Korea needed protection from Mao's call to arms, and the local politician who could most effectively sanction whatever excuse they could come up with to avoid serving was Bao Zhilong. Even if they disagreed with Bao on key issues, therefore, they had to be careful not to offend him if they were to have a chance to dodge the Maoist state mobilization of regular PLA troops to risk death on the distant, frozen battlefields of Korea.

This third development, in combination with the death of CCP Peasant Association leader Bao Yidai and the flight of Bao Huayin and other party leaders to the upper reaches of the state, left party secretary Bao Zhilong to make political decisions without consulting party members in the first pole and gave him the chance to dominate the Da Fo party branch and expand his power beyond Da Fo, which he did by assuming a district post in 1951. Thus, when the demobilized Korean War veterans returned to the village in 1953 and 1955, they faced a party leader who could thwart any threat to his power.[92] The flight of the educated and esteemed party leaders and the resistance army veterans, many of whom were skilled in the arts of democratic discourse and united front politics, had made Bao Zhilong and the young militia-based activists the logical candidates when the new Mao-led center looked for local leaders to secure its hold on Da Fo after the October 1 Revolution. As a result, the second pole – the pole of the poor, illiterate, and war-scarred semi-peasants – took power. It was increasingly these men who received, interpreted, and implemented the policies emanating from the new central government in Beijing and its agents in Henan province. It must be emphasized that in remote villages like Da Fo a state of statelessness prevailed even on the eve of the revolutionary victory; as a result there was no revenue, no public funds, no government services, and no law and order. Bao and his militia followers filled the political void. They had little if any conception of public governance for civic ends. Their art was conquest, and the Mao-led socialist state made no effort to prepare them to operate by peaceful rules of politics.

The Work Style of War

The clearest political casualty of the war turned out to be the open democratic work style that the Chinese Communist Party tried, but ultimately failed, to promote among its cadres. The Japanese Puppet Army occupation, with its slaughterhouse rules, had driven the Da Fo party branch underground, leaving party members to operate in secrecy. After the death of Bao Tiancai in 1941, Bao Zhilong and the party-based militia activists were segregated from ordinary villagers for long stretches of time, and indeed many villagers did not know who the real party leaders were, all of which made it difficult to foster a democratic work style, including tolerance for minority opinions and open, fair discussions with nonparty kin and non-kin, rich and poor, educated and uneducated villagers on the agendas of the wartime united front. Democratic discourse by and large was subordinated to the survival of party leaders, and survival required extreme secrecy. As a result, throughout the war years, political information that leaked outside of the party was seen as dangerous to revolutionary unity, and Da Fo's underground militia activists took politics as a struggle between them and us, pure and simple.[93]

This is not to say that absent the imperative of wartime secrecy an open, democratic work style would have prevailed. Notwithstanding the rhetoric of democratic centralism and mass line politics, the core ideological values and

---

[92] Neil J. Diamant has brilliantly shown that the key Communist village leaders often perceived returning veterans as a threat to their power and privileges and as such discriminated against them and abused them. Diamant notes that in cases in which the village chief was in control of the village militia, a monopolistic work style developed, with harmful consequences for the returned veterans. Diamant, "Between Martyrdom and Mischief," 172–74.

[93] On this tendency in general, see Hedges, *War Is a Force*, 10.

operational structure of Mao's Communist Party in this period was at best minimally democratic, hierarchical, and quasi-militaristic. Thus the wartime experiences of Bao Zhilong and Da Fo's second-pole party leaders only exacerbated an inherent characteristic of the Leninist polity in which they operated, causing them to further deviate from democratic values and discourse.

The legacy of this Leninist-structured and war-habituated political behavior was damaging, for it fostered two anti-democratic tendencies among Bao Zhilong and many other members of the wartime militia. The memory of war seems to have made it difficult for them to trust that people outside their own party-based network were not looking to undermine Chairman Mao's fight for a state in which poor rural people would find a better life. Hence they were inclined to withhold information from nonparty villagers and, further, to disenfranchise villagers who did not actively endorse Mao's postwar plan for state building and economic development. Moreover, the imprint of war fostered a tendency to suspend critical thinking, to portray all sacrifice, no matter how rational or irrational, as necessary for holding together the ascendant national community being crafted by Mao.[94] Hence, in the years following the revolutionary victory, Bao Zhilong insisted on blind obedience, sometimes dismissing cadres from their posts or transferring them to other positions and places when they attempted to press for democratic exchanges about party policy.[95] This authoritarian work style would infect the leadership of the Da Fo Communist Party and accelerate the decline of discourse between party leaders and common villagers in the decade prior to the Great Leap Forward.

The work style of Bao Zhilong and the Da Fo militia fighters was also conditioned by the experience of having lived in constant mortal danger. Apparently, they coped with this threat by finding security in the brutal habits formed in the course of surviving the Japanese Puppet Army occupation and thus built up an immunity to the horrors of violence, which desensitized them to human fragility. Hence in the postwar period they often relied on what seemed to them to be harmless acts of coercion to elicit compliance from party subordinates and ordinary villagers. Bao Zhilong in particular succumbed to this arbitrary and brutal work style. As the leader of the Da Fo militia, Bao's wartime experience was savage and nightmarish. We have already seen that Bao Zhilong was captured, beaten, and tortured in the early years of the Puppet Army occupation. Furthermore, on many occasions between 1942 and 1945 Bao Zhilong nearly lost his life in assisting the CCP-led resistance army. While carrying supplies and stretchers to and from the front lines, Bao was caught in ferocious battles in which only twenty or thirty yards spelled the difference between life and death; and while scavenging the battlefields for arms and ammunition in the wake of resistance army victories, Bao had to sift his way through wounded, gory, wailing bodies of

---

[94] On both points, I am indebted to Hedges. See ibid.
[95] Pang Jiaxiu, interview, September 14, 1995.

enemy soldiers, all the while making sure they would not kill him while he was acquiring war booty for the regular troops. To these wounded, dead, and sometimes decapitated battlefield opponents were added the living yet bloodied and dismembered soldiers of the resistance army, whose bodies Bao and his militia comrades carried to Communist field hospitals in the Hebei-Shandong-Henan base area all through 1947 and 1948. These wartime experiences, especially his abuse at the hands of the Japanese Puppet Army, stayed with Bao Zhilong well into the post-1949 era. In a sense, Bao Zhilong and his militia followers took war to be politics, and this predisposed them to approach politics from a kill-or-be-killed mentality, conditioning them to deal with complex issues by using quick-handed brutality and to ignore the human costs of force.[96]

Whether Bao Zhilong and the Da Fo militia veterans suffered trauma from their wartime experience is not entirely clear. It seems, as Catherine Merridale has found for Soviet Russia after the Great Patriotic War, that the memory of brutality and killing was placed in a cultural myth of sacrifice about which all villagers were cognizant[97] – the myth of the war god Guangong and his heroism. This myth, which emphasized the ability to survive violent extremity and overcome the life-threatening challenges of war, was somehow connected to the ideas Bao and many of his militia activists held about pride and personal accomplishment. The Communist Party opera players and drama teams had disseminated this myth in the anti-Japanese base area in which Da Fo was located during the Second World War. As a result, many of Da Fo's militia fighters who rose in the ranks of the local party branch after war's end experienced themselves as super-tough, patriotic heroes. They may have been victimized by the savagery of the Japanese Puppet Army and later by the Kuomintang's Homecoming Regiment, but they did not seem to manifest psychiatric damage from the violence they inflicted on opponents – surely an important reason why they would prove oblivious to the complaints of civilian farmers who suffered the deprivations of Mao's Great Leap Forward in the decade to come. Such complaints were not in keeping with the strong-willed makeup of the party's wartime heroes; they were the product of "little people" who lacked fortitude and were not prepared to help themselves survive hardship or help the revolutionary nation advance to greatness.

The war and its attendant emergencies also fostered a political work style characterized by the urgency of command and rooted in the pressure to keep up with the urgent orders of the resistance army commanders and militia leaders responding to the rapidly shifting tides of battle.[98] During the war against the Japanese puppet troops, Bao Zhilong had learned to confront militia followers immediately, directly, and adamantly in order to elicit cooperation for survival,

---

[96] On this point, see also Lary, *Chinese Common Soldiers*, 72, 87–89, 104–06, and McCord, "Burn, Kill, Rape and Rob," 23–24.
[97] Merridale, "Collective Mind," 39–40, 43–47, 52.
[98] On this work style, see Lu, *Cadres and Corruption*, 95–96.

and during the Civil War Bao militantly opposed slack discipline, foot-dragging, and defection on the part of the ordinary villagers who were mobilized to perform war service duties. The rush of war demanded spur-of-the-moment decisions, creating habits of haste, impatience, and contempt for the slow and deliberate routines of daily farm life, and the CCP did nothing to curb these habits among the militia elements who were to enforce political order and economic development in remote villages like Da Fo after its revolutionary victory.

Finally, war fostered a monopolistic work style among key Da Fo militia activists, including militia leader Bao Zhilong. For one thing, it taught Bao and his men that politics was about taking over territory and material things – behavior that, in peacetime, Da Fo's villagers perceived as evidence of their liberation heroes' greed. Thus, on returning to Da Fo after the April 1945 victory in Dongle County town, Bao and his men began taking over village territory. Bao Zhilong himself seized the household and courtyard of big landholder Bao Yuhua, turning this space into the gathering point for important CCP meetings. This act initiated an episode of taking over the living spaces of competitive and relatively upscale Bao landholders, who more or less ceded power to the fringe elements making up the second leadership pole of Da Fo's Communist Party.[99] To be sure, this takeover of the living quarters of so-called landlord enemies occurred in accordance with the official transcript of the 1945–47 land reform, but, unofficially, land reform simply became a cover for aggrandizement by Bao Zhilong and his militia warriors – all of whom benefited from Bao's guided dispensations of dismantled landlord households in the land-to-the-tiller campaign, during which Bao himself got the big house belonging to big landholder Bao Zhihai.[100] Regardless of what he called it, Bao Zhilong's seizure of the landlord's grand house looked to villagers like a sellout of the revolution's principles motivated purely by greed, and it raised some eyebrows.

For another thing, Bao Zhilong concentrated all power in his own hands and kept a tight leash on political decision making, which he carried out in a unilateral anti-democratic manner. Responding to Mao's May–December 1946 push for a violent redistribution of rural land to the poorest village people, Bao Zhilong and the tightly knit group of young killers in the second pole of the Da Fo party branch seem to have exhibited little difficulty in replacing united front politics with a zealous search for pro-Kuomintang traitors, or in overthrowing moderate agrarian reform to attack "class" exploiters and foes – real and imagined.[101] In

---

[99] The starting points for this logic are in Harris, *Cows, Pigs, Wars and Witches*, 64–65, but my line of reasoning differs significantly from that of Harris.

[100] Bao Peizhi, interview, July 25, 2005.

[101] Compare with Friedman, Pickowicz, and Selden, *Chinese Village*, 81. Friedman and his colleagues have argued that Wugong's village activists found it difficult to grasp village-level conflicts in terms of CCP-insinuated categories of "exploiter and exploited," and some of the evidence on the land revolution in Da Fo suggests this was a problem for some of the party members here also. Nonetheless, in Da Fo, the poorly educated, war-empowered young militia leaders could

the Civil War that followed, Bao Zhilong and his militia followers abandoned the practice of competitive direct elections for village leadership positions that had prevailed in the early phase of the CCP-led Anti-Japanese War. Moreover, Bao personally took over the process of placing his militia followers in key village positions without soliciting mass opinions and suggestions. So Bao appointed the leader of the Da Fo public security apparatus, for example, without democratic consultation. By the eve of the Communist military victory over the Kuomintang, the Bao-headed militia was in a position to enforce "incontestable rule" of the second pole of the Da Fo party branch.[102]

The monopolist work style of Da Fo's second-pole leaders also manifested itself in the appearance of "patriarchal heroism," which, according to Zhang Linzhi, the paramount leader of the Hebei-Shandong-Henan CCP base area government into the Civil War, was a phenomenon that invariably arose in the aftermath of China's successful peasant wars.[103] The political culture that formed among CCP-led militia activists during the war years gave rise to cadres who proclaimed themselves heroes and who attributed *all* of the successes of the revolutionary struggle to themselves, and hence expected that their interests would take priority over those of the community. This phenomenon cropped up in Da Fo at war's end, when Bao Zhilong and his men became preoccupied with expectations of entitlement that grew out of their imagined heroism – this despite the fact that few of Da Fo's militia activists fought shoulder-to-shoulder with the PLA.[104] Perhaps the destruction of Da Fo's temples contributed to their conceit of total responsibility for the outcome of the war: by the war's end, most of the village's seventy-two temples had been destroyed, some during the New Life Movement under Chiang Kai-shek and the rest in the wake of the land revolution, when local party leaders answered the call to destroy "superstitious" religious practices, such as selling incense and burning paper gods. Although the temples were gone, villagers still retained many of their old religious values and beliefs – but it is possible that the men responsible for destroying the temples felt differently, adopting for themselves some of the prerogatives once attributed to the gods.[105] In any case, well before Mao turned to these self-proclaimed and privilege-seeking "war heroes" to push the Great Leap, Bao and many of the Da Fo militia fighters were taking credit for saving the village from Kuomintang

imagine that village and extra-village oppressors were enemies of the oppressed poor, and so here the Communist Party could more successfully insinuate the language of class exploitation and class struggle into the emotional discourse of local struggle, thereby introducing a new, simplified linguistic pretext for advancing the attack on oppressors, real and imagined, understood and misunderstood – a complex issue and process about which we need to know more.

[102] See Gilley, *Model Rebels*, 91; Hinton, *Shenfan*, xxiii.

[103] Zhang Linzhi, "Yinian Laide Dang Yu Qunzhong Gongzuo."

[104] Bao Zhendao, interview, May 7, 1990; Friedman and Selden, "War Communism," 27; on expectation of entitlement among local party leaders, also see Han, *The Unknown Cultural Revolution*, 12.

[105] Bao Zhendao, interview, June 14, 2006.

takeover and looking to cash in on their superhuman contributions to the revolutionary victory. The corruption bred by this monopolistic work style was rooted in war-derived claims of entitlement, and it virtually assured that Da Fo's party leaders would run Mao's campaign for communization in 1958 to serve their interests, often at the expense of ordinary villagers.[106]

With the promise of the postwar peace, the widely shared hope of most of China's village people, including those in Da Fo, was that the strings of the lethal past would not be plucked again. But when the Korean War gave further impetus to the Cold War and China's isolation from the global community, Mao Zedong brought this past back to life, challenging his militant followers in Da Fo and elsewhere to draw on its lessons to consolidate the power of the Communist Party and build a political economy. In Da Fo, party leader Bao Zhilong and his men embraced this challenge and led villagers into folly and famine.

---

[106] See Friedman and Selden, "War Communism," 27. See also Lu, *Cadres and Corruption*, 93, 236–46. Lu does not take up this issue in detail, but his analysis suggests that the monopolistic work style of the party had a root in war-derived claims of entitlement and is not incompatible with the thrust of my argument.

3

The Onset of Collectivization and
Popular Dissatisfaction with
Mao's "Yellow Bomb" Road

In the year following the Communist Party victory of October 1, 1949, most of Da Fo's farmers settled into small-scale, family-based tilling routines, and they began to supplement family income through increased market participation. In this so-called honeymoon period, roughly late 1950 to early 1955, free trade in periodic markets, agricultural fairs, temple festivals, and martial arts contests made a comeback, and villagers focused on finding marriage partners, reuniting separated families, making babies, and reasserting the symbolic rituals associated with patrilineal descent and extended kinship. Lunar New Year banquets and Qingming festivals, in which people swept ancestral grave sites and burned incense and paper money to honor ancestors, became the order of the day.[1] During this period, Da Fo's fiercely independent smallholders equated the success of the recent Communist-led revolution with the freedom to farm their own fields. They were well positioned to plow the profits from renewed salt production back into agriculture, and they used their market proceeds to buy farm implements, plow animals, carts, and seeds.

The plans of Mao and other national Communist Party leaders threatened this hard-won agricultural independence and market-based prosperity, however. In the view of Mao and the Central Committee he directed, the new PRC faced an agricultural dilemma that posed a difficult policy choice in the early 1950s. Despite a series of bumper harvests, China was plagued by food shortages. The country's population had increased. Though harvests had improved, rural people were celebrating by consuming more food grain. And the sale of grain in rural free markets presumably was putting the price of food beyond the reach of the

---

[1] On the social and cultural revival of the so-called honeymoon years, see Friedman, Pickowicz, and Selden, *Chinese Village*, 114–15; on the importance of these extended kinship activities, see Cohen, "Lineage Organization," 509–15.

poorest farmers. Taken together, these three problems created a situation in which food was not distributed equally to all – a situation that the party-state wished to remedy by encouraging the collectivization of agriculture and introducing a procurement policy that created a state monopoly on the purchase and sale of grain.

Da Fo, like many other Chinese villages, went through several distinct stages of agricultural reorganization in the 1950s, some of which overlapped.[2] In the first stage, which ran from 1951 to 1956, peasant families still owned their own scattered farmlands. Party leaders encouraged smallholders to form household mutual aid groups on a seasonal basis. In Da Fo, some farmers did this spontaneously, or with minimal government direction. In the second stage, which began around 1954 and lasted into 1955, Mao and the party began to push for lower-order agricultural production cooperatives, which in Da Fo apparently took the form of land-pooling associations involving about ten to thirty households. In mid-1955, Mao urged tillers to join advanced (higher-level) agricultural production cooperatives, and thus a third stage, in which the private ownership of farmland was formally abolished, commenced in 1956 and lasted into 1957 in some places. This stage was somewhat of a watershed, as it marked the transition from family-based cooperation to state-dictated collectivization, often involving as many as several hundred households working state-captured lands on an involuntary basis. Finally, in 1958, these expanded collective household arrangements were merged into the people's communes, under which the party-state took over all privately held farmland and draft animals,[3] though farmers still retained private vegetable gardens and melon patches.

The disjunction between the statist direction in which the party was headed and Da Fo's farmers' view of the party as the benefactor of individual land tillage and free markets became apparent only gradually over the course of the 1950s. As the above description suggests, rural tillers were eased toward collectivization first by being encouraged to join cooperative ventures that allowed them to benefit from the efficiencies of sharing labor without giving up title to their lands or their traditional entitlement to land- and market-based survival strategies. Unified purchase and sale, introduced in Da Fo in 1953, was not exactly welcomed by Da Fo's farmers, but because it did not at first threaten either their subsistence grain supplies or their ability to earn extra income from trade, they tolerated the policy. It was only after the village joined the Liangmen People's Commune in 1958 that the conflict between the farmers' vision of the Communist Party and the true purposes of Mao's agricultural policy became strikingly clear, and by then it was too late for them to reclaim the prerogatives that had allowed their households to prosper.

---

[2] I am indebted to Thomas P. Bernstein, Alfred L. Chan, and William L. Joseph for helping me clarify the stages of this development.
[3] See Selden, *People's Republic of China*, 398, and Unger, *Transformation of Rural China*, 8.

Cooperativization: Mutual Aid Groups and Land-Pooling Associations

In the late summer of 1951, Da Fo party secretary Bao Zhilong answered Mao Zedong's call to promote cooperative agriculture as a means of overcoming the alleged "inertia" of private, family-based farm ownership and to improve harvest yields. Now the head of the Da Fo Peasant Association and the First District, in which Da Fo was located, militia chief Bao Zhilong teamed up with Bao Dongzhi to form a ten-household mutual aid group, whose members were said to be the poorest in the villages. This group increased its agricultural yields by 10 percent over the 1951–52 period, and Bao Zhilong began encouraging all of Da Fo's farmers to form household-based joint self-help groups ranging in size from four to twelve families.

For the most part, these groups were lineage-based. Bao Zhilong utilized his party position and his kinship network to call on favored Bao lineage members to follow his example. Bao Zhongxi, whose family joined with four other households of thirteen families in his lineage, recalls that the heads of these households were all his father's cousins. Of these five households, he says, "All were very loyal to the Communist Party and were willing to do whatever the party told them to do."[4] The members of mutual aid groups tilled their fields together. Human and animal labor were counted but weighed differently. At the end of the year, group accountant Bao Peijian figured out the total work points of each household and decided how the harvest would be distributed, with some families giving up a portion of their harvest to others.

Many Da Fo farmers voluntarily formed mutual aid groups because of the promise of increased labor efficiency and better harvest timing. Whereas in the past it had taken five people to take care of five farm animals belonging to five individual households, with mutual aid it required only one person to take care of five animals, freeing up four others to pursue other agricultural tasks or side-occupations.[5] The sharing of farm animals, tools, and farm hands also permitted individual households that had in the past had trouble keeping up with planting and harvesting schedules to sow and reap more effectively in rhythm with the agricultural seasons. Moreover, though land reform and the breakup of the big holdings of the dominant Bao landowners had been popular with many of Da Fo's farmers, the subsequent land fragmentation had left many families to cultivate tiny, often scattered plots. Hence, there was considerable incentive for tillers to voluntarily and spontaneously form small mutual aid groups.[6] In joining these groups, they retained ownership of land, animals, and the labor power they contributed, and they were also able to negotiate, or even veto, the timing and terms of mutual aid to sustain their food security.

---

[4] Bao Zhongxi, interview, September 12, 1993.
[5] Zheng Tianbao, interview, September 7, 1993.
[6] Vivienne Shue makes this point in *Peasant China in Transition*, 152–54.

By the summer of 1952 mutual aid had taken hold in other lineages, with mixed results. Many of Da Fo's tillers fondly remember the early years of mutual aid, for they were able to purchase donkeys and oxen with money earned from selling salt and grain surpluses, and land taxes were minimal.[7] Some mutual aid groups saw substantial gains: Ruan Renxing's dozen-member group's yields increased by nearly 50 percent between 1952 and 1955. Mutual aid in and of itself hardly accounted for the increase in yields, however. These were years of extremely favorable weather, and Ruan Renxing, through his connections to Bao Zhilong, recruited a number of newly land-rich Bao households into his group. More importantly, Ruan and many of his group members were engaged in market trade, and they reinvested their profits in their agricultural enterprises.

For the most part, however, harvest yields were about the same as in the pre-1949 era of solitary household farming and spontaneous joint household cooperation.[8] Yields in Zheng Rugui's mutual aid group, for example, remained the same as in the 1945–51 period.[9] Not everyone was in a position to claim that "life was better" with mutual aid, and it was obvious to most of Da Fo's farmers that the Bao lineage mutual aid groups had distinctive advantages over the others. Many of the Baos, through their CCP connections, had obtained the best land in Da Fo during the land redistribution process of 1945–47, so they were planting their crops in the richest soil the village had. As primitive chemists with good connections to the government industry in Dongle, moreover, Bao Zhilong and his followers were able to produce or procure fertilizers quickly and cheaply, enhancing their economic status even more. Despite the inequality of different mutual aid groups' endowments, however, those who held less land, or infertile land, may have seen the pooling of land as a benefit, and it is possible that some of Da Fo's poorest tillers saw the CCP as offering them a new, landlord-type patronage system in which they could gain protection from any future state predation by joining the movement and working in small labor groups managed by trusted lineage leaders.[10]

In any case, few of the families who participated in mutual aid groups saw them as a first step in a state-orchestrated communization of village life. It was the Maoist state-decreed move toward land-pooling associations that began to change the way Da Fo's tillers saw cooperativization. In late 1952, a year or so after the Central Committee in Beijing issued a call for local governments to

---

[7] Bao Zhengxi, interview, September 12, 1993.
[8] Pang Yilu, interview, September 2, 1993.
[9] Zheng Tianbao, interview, September 7, 1993.
[10] For a good discussion on this latter point, see and compare with Parish, *Chinese Rural Development*, 13–15, and Nee, "Peasant Household Individualism," 181. Nee found that independent small-holding "middle peasants" were in fact "reluctant to join" the collective movement and thought they were better off when engaging in family farming. Apparently, such a dynamic was at work in Da Fo, but it did not last very long. Compare with Shue, *Peasant China in Transition*, 156–57, 172–73, 188–89, 330, 335, 341, 343–44.

galvanize rural people to set up land-pooling cooperatives,[11] Da Fo's party leaders began experimenting with this form of agricultural production. Land-pooling associations were a more advanced version of mutual aid teams that involved larger numbers of farmers. Members worked in the association's common fields, in return for which they were entitled to a portion of its annual harvest. This portion was initially determined on the basis of how much land each household had contributed to the land-pooling association, but in later years it was determined partially on a per capita basis – every household in the association was entitled to a certain amount of grain on the basis of how many mouths it had to feed – and partially on the basis of work points, which association members earned by working in the group's fields, and which varied in value depending on the quality of each individual's labor.

Bao Zhilong and Ruan Jinhan set up land-pooling associations that quickly replaced the mutual aid groups with which villagers by and large were satisfied. Bao Zhilong became famous in Dongle County, as his land-pooling association became known as the best of the lot. Bao Zhigen, a member of this association, recalls,

Many people wanted to transfer to our land-pooling association. We got a great deal of support from the upper government. The county and township government leaders constantly came to Da Fo to help us. We got to know all of the important leaders in Dongle and Liangmen. If we had any difficulties, these leaders would immediately provide the help we needed. . . . So our crops did better than others.[12]

From the outset, Bao Zhilong's land-pooling association was supported by the Da Fo district Communist Party secretary and was subsidized by government loans for the purchase of animals, fertilizer, and new farm implements.[13]

Although in principle joining an association was voluntary and people had the freedom to choose which association to join, party boss Bao Zhilong applied pressure and offered special incentives for people to join his own association. He told the parents of Bao Zhenxiu, for example, that if they would join, they would not have to surrender their farm animals and carts to the association.[14] Despite such offers, many prospective recruits opted for membership in other associations, particularly the productive and popular association headed by Bao Zhendao, which after one year became the most efficient and mutually beneficial of the land-pooling associations in Da Fo.[15] Bao Zhilong's credentials as a tiller were suspect, for nearly everyone knew that prior to the land reform initiative he had made his living largely by off-farm trade. Some villagers suspected that

---

[11] Hinton, *Shenfan*, 99–100.
[12] Bao Zhigen, interview, July 29, 2004.
[13] Ruan Jinhan, interview, September 19, 1993.
[14] Bao Zhongxi, interview, September 15, 1993.
[15] Ibid.

the use of subsidies to lure their farm animals into Bao Zhilong's land association was merely a ploy to capture their highly treasured beasts in order to raise the yields of Bao's household, which, although enriched by land redistribution, still lacked animal labor.

More than a few villagers who participated in different land-pooling associations agree that harvest yields were higher than those of the mutual aid groups, partly because of more efficient use of farm animals and partly because of access to fertilizers.[16] Still, other villagers remember differently. Bao Xuqing is one of them. "During the mutual aid group time," recalls Bao, "life was better. We produced more grain than in the individual household family system of the past. However, when we moved up to the land-pooling associations, we did not produce as much grain as we did with the mutual aid groups. The majority of people barely had enough food to eat."[17] Whether or not they were more productive, the land associations were plagued by serious problems that required their leaders to make concessions to the interests of individual peasant households.[18] This cast suspicion on the integrity of the Communist Party leaders guiding the experiment and threatened this stage of collectivization.

The most fundamental problem with the associations, from the standpoint of villagers, was that people could not freely enter and exit them. "Membership in the land-pooling association was supposed to be voluntary," recalls Pang Yilu, a member of the association set up by Bao Chunfeng and Pang Xinzhen,

But in fact, once it became a fashion, many people were simply carried into the land-pooling associations by the political tide of the time, even though they were reluctant to join. If one did not join he would be an outsider. The head of a household was under a lot of pressure from his own family to join, as it was not possible to survive outside the cooperative. The Da Fo leaders said that only the majority had freedom, and they said that the individual had to sacrifice his or her freedom for the majority.[19]

In short, the real pressure was political. Party leader Bao Zhilong and the militia activists in his network were convinced that socialism would benefit the people of the countryside. According to Bao Zhigen, "Nobody doubted that at the time."[20] Bao and the party cadres who had helped bring the Communist Party to power had become "agents of the state," to use Helen Siu's term, but they could not fully comprehend that the political institution on which they depended might dictate orders antithetical to the interest of ordinary villagers.[21] Increasingly, they

---

[16] 1993 interviews with Bao Jenming, September 11; Pang Yilu, September 12; Bao Zhongxi, September 15; Bao Jingan, September 16; and Pang Guihua, September 20.

[17] Bao Xuqing, interview, June 21, 2001.

[18] As Hinton found. *Shenfan*, 100.

[19] Pang Yilu, interview, July 14, 2000.

[20] Bao Zhigen, interview, July 29, 2004. Actually, as the work of Helen Siu and Edward Friedman and his associates would argue, there were doubters. See Siu, *Agents and Victims*; Friedman, Pickowicz, and Selden, *Chinese Village*.

[21] Siu, *Agents and Victims*, 2, 6–7, 213.

kept themselves apart from tillers who took issue with the state pressure to pursue collective agriculture.

In Da Fo, more than a few tillers still cherished the freedom to farm their own family lands. Some, like Zhao Jinjiang, held out until the last minute, and their small acts of courage in the face of party pressures to put the union of community before the freedom of families are still remembered. One story about Zhao Jinjiang's resistance to the land-pooling association is still a source of humor among Da Fo's inhabitants. "Once on a rainy day during the campaign to move into the land-pooling associations," remembers Pang Yilu,

Zhao Jinjiang was walking on the village street. A Dongle County official came to Da Fo on a bicycle. It was customary for villagers to yield to officials riding bicycles on the streets. However, Zhao Jinjiang refused to yield to the county official, and as a result the official fell off his bike and landed in the mud. The county official got up and demanded that Zhao Jinjiang tell him which land-pooling association he belonged to. Zhao replied that he belonged to Zhao Jinjiang's land association. The official then asked Zhao to give him the name of the head of this land association. Zhao said that the head was Zhao Jinjiang and that the official was speaking to him. Later, when the Dongle County official arrived at village party headquarters and inquired about Zhao Jinjiang's land-pooling association, he was told the truth: Zhao was a holdout, a staunch defender of the independence of family-based farming. For a long time after this people retold the story as if it were a joke played on the official.[22]

It was the kind of joke that kept alive people's hopes that they might elude the evolving dictatorship of the collective.

Tillers who joined the land-pooling associations often had good reasons to regret making the transition. Some of the associations did not deliver on their promises. In theory, the land association managed by Bao Zhilong, which was supposed to be the model association, was to buy all of the farm animals and farm implements of participating farm households, which were to be valued at market price. Instead of cash, however, the household members were given credit on the land association's account. Bao Jenming, remembering this scam, remarks wryly: "I do not remember how and when the owners of the animals and implements were paid back by the association."[23] As word of the false promise of compensation by cash spread, it became more difficult for association heads to mobilize new members.

Another prevalent difficulty was calculating work points. "People in the land association," recalls Bao Dongzhi, "sometimes quarreled over how many work points a person should be given a day. Sometimes we had to decide by a competition who should be paid more or who should be paid less."[24] The issue was a constant headache for the association leaders. The competitions held to settle disagreements about work points frequently interrupted the progress of

---

[22] Pang Yilu, interview, July 14, 2000.
[23] Bao Jenming, interview, September 11, 1993.
[24] Bao Dongzhi, interview, September 14, 1993.

state-planned collectivization. The form of the competition was intriguing: In Da Fo, villagers who were dissatisfied with Communist Party decisions took matters into their own hands by sanctioning the right of any land association member to have the assigned worth of a work point recalculated by challenging someone else who had received the highest worth available. For example, if a field worker was assigned eight work points for a day's worth of harvesting and one of his peers received ten work points for the same work, the former could openly challenge the latter to a harvest-reaping contest. The two would cut a row of wheat to see who could finish first and bring in the most. If the former won, then the worth of his daily work points was instantly bumped up to equal that of the latter. Da Fo became famous for its harvest-cutting and weed-pulling contests, all aimed at ensuring the worth of the labor of individual family members.

Finally, the problem of size undermined the efficiency of production. Pang Guihua explains: "I felt that the land-pooling associations were not as good as the mutual aid groups. The mutual aid groups were small. They were relatively easy to manage. But the land associations were much bigger and much harder to manage. People had to wait for one another to go to work in the fields. This was a waste of time."[25] The issue of size also brought up a political problem: the leaders of the expanding land-pooling associations were progressively removed from the interests of tillers. "As the number of people in the land association increased, it became difficult to manage," recalls Zheng Tianbao. There were reports of theft of collective property that went uninvestigated. Villagers say that the leaders had no effective controls on stealing. "As far as the farmers were concerned," continues Zheng, "the land association was not as good as the mutual aid group. To the leaders, the land-pooling association was better than the mutual aid group. Their power increased greatly."[26]

This power inflation opened the door to the embezzlement of public funds and triggered one of the first voiced protests by ordinary villagers against state-induced collectivization in Da Fo. This unrecorded protest arose within the Pang-Zheng land-pooling association, which had a membership of seventy households and two hundred persons. In 1954 Pang Haijin, the head of this land-pooling association, and Pang Lang, the association accountant, were discovered to have taken the association's money. Zheng Daqing, one of the earliest Da Fo Communist Party members and a soldier in the Eighth Route Army in Dongle during the Anti-Japanese War, led a delegation of land association members to challenge the embezzlers. On the eve of the Chinese New Year the delegation called on Pang Lang, who was home making dumplings with his family. As soon as Pang saw the delegation approach, he fled, whereupon the members entered his house and took the dumplings to divide among themselves. Following this "dumpling rebellion," the land-pooling association members convened a public meeting and

[25] Pang Guihua, interview, June 28, 2001.
[26] Zheng Tianbao, interview, September 13, 1993.

demanded that Pang Lang be dismissed as the association accountant and book-keeper. Instead of turning over the books and the money to association treasurer Zheng Tianbao, however, Pang Lang took the money to party secretary Bao Zhilong, who refused to dismiss him. The land-pooling association members suspected a payoff, but the issue was never investigated. The incident embittered the members of the association and created one of the first great rifts between two of the party's veteran anti-state fighters, Bao Zhilong and Zheng Daqing.[27] It also tarnished the credibility of CCP rule in Da Fo, which was about to be further hurt by local party agents' implementation of the state's policy of unified purchase and sale.

The Introduction and Escalation of Unified Purchase and Sale

During the period of cooperativization, the introduction of unified purchase and sale limited the independence of Da Fo's farmers and changed their relationship to the state. In 1951, Chen Yun, Bo Yibo, and other central party leaders issued a report exploring whether the state's problems with food distribution could be handled by instating a policy of unified purchase and sale (*tongguo tongxiao*), which involved the state purchasing food grain from farmers below market price and selling it back at its own stipulated price. The central party leaders decided to delay implementing any plan for the state to acquire grain on its own terms because local party leaders throughout rural China warned Beijing that farmers would not be happy with state intervention in their right to freely sell their food crops in local markets. Yet, in 1953, Mao Zedong required the central party Financial Committee to come up with a policy to address the issue of how the state could requisition more food grain. Mao wanted to acquire more grain in markets dominated by private merchants and petty traders so that the state could provision people in Bejing, Tianjin, and other big cities and also export food abroad to earn foreign exchange currency. The method that would best serve these state goals, the Central Committee decided, was unified purchase and sale.[28]

The proposed implementation of unified purchase and sale posed a risk both to farmers and to the legitimacy of the new PRC government in Da Fo and in much of village China. For one thing, requisitioning grain would hinder the productive initiatives of small farmers and damage output. When told that *tongguo tongxiao* might trigger resistance and possibly engender rebellion, however, Mao claimed that conservative tillers were blind when it came to the benefits of socialism and the national interest, and he declared that high-level comrades like Deng Zihui, head of the PRC Central Committee Rural Work Department, were wrong to argue that it was important to protect the interests of individual farm households.[29] When informed that requisitioning grain from every rural

[27] Ibid.
[28] Bo Yibo, *Ruogan Zhongda Juece*, 1991 (revised 1997), 263–71.
[29] Ibid., 272.

place without exempting the poor, infertile agricultural swatches of the interior would be impractical and unwise,[30] Mao insisted that every place should be subjected to unified purchase and sale. In a subsequent 1953 Politburo Emergency Food Conference, Chen Yun warned of a huge rebellion, possibly involving 10 percent of China's million villages, if farmers no longer controlled their harvest and lost the right to sell it at the free market price. But Mao prevailed,[31] so even villages with highly saline lands – like Da Fo – were brought under the new policy.[32]

In this emergency conference, central party leaders, operating under pressure from Mao, concluded that they had to take one of two risks. The first was that of a "black bomb": if the food market could not be controlled, private merchants and petty traders would spike the price of food and subvert the state goals of provisioning the cities and earning foreign exchange currency. The second risk was that of a "yellow bomb": if the government took the path of unified purchase and sale, the farmers might resist and rebel. Mao and his men, including Chen Yun and Deng Xiaoping, chose the "yellow bomb" road, for it seemed the best way to integrate the scattered and diversified rural farm economy into the state plan for socialist development. There was, however, a third problem: it was politically dangerous to even suggest the requisitioning of grain, because rural people in north and northeast China associated such aggrandizement with the Japanese practice of food requisitioning and rationing in Manchuria during World War II, and some of Da Fo's returned PLA veterans surely knew about this onerous practice. So Mao and the top party leaders secretly agreed to frame the process of procurement in new language: the term "*tongguo tongxiao*" was substituted for any talk of "requisitioning" or "rationing."[33]

As early as 1953, the Liangmen district CCP officials began a drive for grain procurement from the villages under their jurisdiction, one of which was Da Fo. Many villagers vividly remember both the political process that brought procurement into their lives and the ways in which they responded to it during the years ushering in the Great Leap Forward and its famine. Perhaps the state grain procurement system was intended to be the Communist Party's alternative to the harsh taxation schemes of the Kuomintang state and Japanese colonizers – to be a voluntary program serving the interest of villagers.[34] Yet the oral testimonies from Da Fo show that it was imposed in a manner that mainly served Mao's socialist transcript and that villagers who opted not to participate were at risk.

When asked to comment on their feelings about grain procurement, Da Fo villagers start with June 1953 – the beginning of the end of the so-called

[30] Ibid., 271.
[31] Ibid., 273.
[32] Personal correspondence with Li Huaiyin, July 24, 2006.
[33] Bo Yibo, *Ruogan Zhongda Juece*, 1997, 273–74.
[34] For this view, see Shue, *Peasant China in Transition*, 214–15. Summaries of Shue's thesis are in Oi, *State and Peasant*, 43, and Kelliher, *Peasant Power*, 24.

honeymoon period – when a Liangmen district Communist Party official named Lao Shou came to Da Fo to convene a mass meeting in which she announced the new state policy of unified purchase and sale. This was the start of the Maoist attempt to establish a state grain monopoly, they say, and Lao Shou justified it in speeches supportive of China's Korean War involvement, which began in October 1950. "She said that our country was fighting the most powerful imperialist country in the world, that our soldiers were dying on the Korean War front to protect our country from the invasion of foreign enemies," recalls Ruan Jiang, "and that the least we villagers could do was to sell grain to the state to support our soldiers."[35] After forty-five days of relentless public meetings, most village farmers reluctantly agreed to go along with *tonggou tongxiao*.

But there were some holdouts who criticized the logic driving the *tonggou tongxiao* policy. Bao Minfu was one of them. He quickly became the target of the same kind of Communist Party–orchestrated public debate to which Da Fo's landlords had been subjected during the Civil War phase of land reform. When Korean War propagandist Lao Shou called on villagers to donate money to the government for purchasing airplanes and artillery, Bao Minfu quipped that he had only ten cents to donate, and the government could decide whether to use it to buy an airplane or an artillery shell. Offended by this sarcastic remark, Da Fo party secretary Bao Zhilong decided to debate Bao Minfu in a public criticism session. He told Bao Minfu to stand on a table in front of a public assembly, and during the meeting he overturned the table, causing Bao Minfu to fall to the ground, after which Bao could not move for a long while. According to Bao Zhigen, who witnessed this incident, "The people who were subjected to public debate were usually the ones who attempted to ridicule the government policy of the time."[36]

But there were good reasons for villagers to object to the new policy. State regulations for the unified purchase and sale of grain required tillers across China to sell to the state all of their grain crop in excess of 360 *jin* per household member.[37] Apparently, this figure of 360 *jin* per person was used for virtually every village, regardless of the fertility of its land system. According to Bao Yibin, the Da Fo CCP vice-secretary at the start of the Great Leap, the formula of one *jin* (16.8 ounces) per person per day was handed down by the Liangmen district government at the outset of grain procurement. Da Fo party leaders promised that grain sales to the state would never plunge villagers below that minimum.[38] The 360 *jin* allotment presumed that one *jin* per day would provide adequate sustenance for a single adult person. In fact, this figure fell short of the standard of subsistence-level grain consumption for Da Fo. People in every Da Fo lineage say they needed a bare minimum of 400 *jin* per capita to survive,

[35] Ruan Jiang, interview, May 7, 1994.
[36] Bao Zhigen, interview, July 29, 2004.
[37] Friedman, Pickowicz, and Selden, *Chinese Village*, 173.
[38] Bao Yibin, interview, September 14, 1993.

and there is a villagewide consensus that for adult male household members who both worked the land and traveled market circuits the per capita yearly grain consumption had stood at 420 to 480 *jin* prior to 1951.[39] Thus, although they were willing to assist the new party-state in promoting national development, Da Fo's farmers received the state definition of food security with considerable skepticism and suspicion. But because they had taken the CCP as an ally in their long-running war of resistance to Kuomintang state taxation, and because there was little in their pattern of past interaction with the Communist Party to suggest that procurement would entail an uncompromising attack on other sources of household food supply, for the most part the pre-1958 concept of procurement did not prompt them to openly protest the announcement of this new system of extraction.

Supposedly, under the *tonggou tongxiao* system villagers from each mutual aid group would *voluntarily* sell their extra grain to the state at a price below market value. In practice, however, the Liangmen district official in charge of procurement ordered Da Fo's party leaders to instruct village residents to report how much extra grain their neighbors possessed and pressed those with alleged surpluses to sell all of their extra grain to the state. As a result, the most esteemed grain cultivators in Da Fo, along with the village's twenty grain dealers, came under great pressure to give up their grain to the state. This practice angered many villagers and spread anxiety among competent grain producers.

By autumn of 1954 the people of Da Fo had all but lost the right to sell their grain on the private market due to the local Liangmen district government enforcement of unified purchase and sale. Zheng Jintian's memory of what this practice did to his family is revealing. Prior to 1953 Zheng's father, Zheng Zhanglin, had been one of the leading grain producers in Da Fo. When first pressed to sell grain to the state under unified purchase and sale, Zheng Zhanglin was careful to collect a receipt for what he sold, which he thought would protect him from further party-state pressure. Ignoring the receipt, however, Lao Shou threatened to send Zheng to a mass confessional meeting in Beitoucun, where hundreds of farmers who refused to sell grain to the state endured party-orchestrated public criticism. To avoid this embarrassment, Zheng agreed to sell the state more grain, but on the condition that he could buy it back from the local cooperative. Like many local tillers, he thereupon discovered that those who sold to the state grain shop did not immediately receive payment, and, worse, they eventually were paid only in credit slips. The slips could not be used for purchase of grain and barely covered the cost of required membership in the Liangmen district credit association itself. By the fall of 1954 the Zheng household faced a food shortage and had no money with which to purchase grain. Zheng Zhanglin's family barely survived by selling bean curd in the vicinity of Da Fo. The party-state

---

[39] Zheng Tianbao and Zheng Xu, interviews, September 13, 1993; Ruan Baozhang, interview, September 14, 1993.

mandate to comply with unified purchase and sale had compromised his family's food security. Others were less fortunate. Zheng Xu's father died in 1957 from recurring pneumonia, which he initially contracted in the raw weather at one of the mass public criticism meetings to which he was subjected for withholding grain from the state in 1954.

As these examples suggest, even though the CCP set an annual figure of 360 *jin* of grain per capita below which the state could not compel farmers to sell any grain supplies, local party leaders did not steadfastly adhere to that figure. Following the lead of Liangmen district officials, Da Fo's Communist Party members simply relied on neighbors' estimates of how much grain was left over after the harvest. As a result, implementation of unified purchase and sale remained highly arbitrary in the five years before the formal commencement of the Great Leap. "In these years," says Zheng Xu, "the state pressure was so high that timid farmers like us were scared of the mass meetings held by the Communist Party to realize unified purchase and sale."[40] The state grain procurement system engendered a long-term decline in grain retained for family consumption, and this decline raised serious doubts about the efficacy of collective agriculture among Da Fo's farmers.

By late 1953 and early 1954, the relationship between the national state and rural farmers had grown tense. Procurement signaled a violation of what James C. Scott calls the "safety-first principle" in peasant economic behavior.[41] It posed a fundamental threat to the basic food security of tillers, and, for this reason, this early phase of Maoist state grain procurement began to alienate villagers from the new party-state. Testimonies from Da Fo's villagers leave little doubt that the acute food deprivation of the Great Leap Forward began in 1953 and 1954 in the party-state's attempt to capture grain harvests to which farm households histori-cally were entitled. The next stage of collectivization, the agricultural production cooperative, did little to allay villagers' concerns about the course Mao's party was on.

The Failure of the Agricultural Production Cooperative

In the winter of 1955, several years after the land-pooling associations were formed, Da Fo joined with four other villages – Beitoucun, Taigu, Da Wei-cun, and Xiangtianzhuang – to upgrade and merge the land-pooling associations into a higher-level agricultural production cooperative (APC), or *jiti nongzhuang*. This five-village production cooperative was called the Xianfeng Yizhuang Jiti Nongzhuang, or the Number One Vanguard Collective Farm. Its leaders, chosen by each village, ordered local people to build an eight-room building in Da Fo to house the offices of the cooperative and announced that the combined harvest

---

[40] Zheng Xu, interview, September 12, 1993.
[41] Scott, *Moral Economy of the Peasant*, 15–20.

was to be shared among the villages.[42] In Da Fo and within the five-village unit, the harvest was to be distributed 70 percent according to per capita and 30 percent according to labor input. Pang Lang, one of the first accountants of this unit, remembers that the APC attempted to utilize the combined five villages as one accounting unit, so accountants from several villages were in charge of keeping harvest production reports and developing formulae for distribution of the harvest.[43]

To mark the founding of the APC, Bao Zhilong and his party associates sponsored a big celebration in Da Fo, and the Dongle County Yuju Opera Group came to the village to stage four days of plays. The collective farm leaders lined Da Fo's streets with newly purchased, shiny modern farming implements: double plows, walking plows, mechanical water pumps, grass shredders, and a huge planter. Bao and his comrades put these implements on exhibit to demonstrate the advantages of collective agriculture. Crowds of curious, excited villagers thronged Da Fo's streets for several days.

The inauguration of the APC marked a shift from "cooperativization" to "collectivization" – a shift that required villagers to risk significantly more than the shift from mutual aid groups to land-pooling associations had. For even though they had been farming collectively for some years, Da Fo's villagers still retained title to their lands – titles secured by many of them in the 1945–47 land redistribution – until the APC was inaugurated in 1955. Giving up private ownership meant relinquishing a key source of food entitlement that they had relied upon in periods of famine: with title to their own land, they could choose to rent some of it out, borrow money against it, sell it, or dismantle and sell portions of their homes – strategies that could enable them to survive until a crisis had passed. In joining the APC, they had to relinquish this security against famine and trust the party-state to look after their interests.

In Da Fo, the APC experiment did little to reward the villagers for their trust. Many remember that the APC did not perform as well as the land-pooling associations. Some say that their household income fell substantially after they were mobilized to join the advanced cooperative[44] and that the APC movement imperiled their ability to secure their family's annual food requirement – a memory that resonates with the research of Huaiyin Li, who has correlated income decline under the advanced production cooperative with peasant anger and protest in rural Jiangsu.[45] Despite the party's promise of unified accounting and technological miracles, the APC disbanded in a little more than a year.[46]

---

[42] Bao Dongzhi, interview, September 14, 1993.
[43] Pang Lang, interview, September 15, 1993.
[44] Ruan Yuanjiang, interview, September 14, 1993.
[45] Li, "The First Encounter," 145–62; and compare with his "From Righteous to Rightful: Peasant Resistance to Agricultural Collectivization in China in the 1950s."
[46] Bao Jenming, interview, September 11, 1993.

The major reason for its failure in Da Fo, according to Zheng Tianbao, was poor leadership: "The leaders ate and drank at the expense of the public fund, and consequently they did not work in the fields."[47] As there was no way to openly voice their anger, villagers sabotaged production by idling away work time in the fields. This greatly affected output, and the subsequent low yields further affected popular morale. Many villagers still believe that the agricultural production cooperative failed not because of the idea itself but because of the inferior quality of local leadership. Indeed, untrained local party leaders were challenged by the difficulty of managing such a complex organization and handling labor contribution formulae, not to mention the task of mastering accurate and transparent methods of accounting.

An even bigger part of the leadership problem involved the work style of Da Fo party secretary Bao Zhilong, who frequently resorted to blind commandism in advancing what he imagined to be the agenda of the APC movement. Villagers remember one particular example of Bao's dictatorial style. In 1955–56, Bao took the initiative in building a couple of fish ponds for the collective. These collective ponds soon became the fishing holes for Liangmen district and Dongle County party leaders. On a day when some of these upper leaders paid an "inspection visit" to the ponds, Bao Zhilong spotted the eight-year-old son of Pang Haijin taking a few fish for his own household. Though on good terms with the Pang household for many years, Bao Zhilong lost his temper and angrily reprimanded the boy. Shouting that he was going to teach the little boy a lesson that one should never take public property home – precisely what the upper-level official visitors were about to do – Bao grabbed him by the neck, heaved him into the fish pond, and then stood by the pond's edge watching the boy's frantic effort to save himself. While Bao insisted that he would not have let the boy drown, Pang's parents did not see it that way. They were incensed by the near drowning of their son, and they brought a lawsuit against Bao in Dongle County court. The Liangmen district leaders stalled and softened the lawsuit, so that the grievance was never settled. But the memory of the incident stayed with the Pang family, whose members retrieved it during the Cultural Revolution to criticize Bao Zhilong's commandism and his rigid defense of his party's claim to the public fish pond.[48] Even before the Great Leap Forward, villagers saw that this war-derived work style was linked to, and often reinforced by, the tendency of party leaders to rely on impulse, command, and force to promote an emergent Mao paradigm of a militarized communist polity.[49]

Poor accounting was a second factor contributing to the failure. During the high tide of the Great Leap Forward, the commune became the unit of accounting

---

[47] Zheng Tianbao, interview, September 7, 1993.
[48] Ruan Jing, interview, May 7, 1994; Bao Rulong, interviews, July 5–9, 2002.
[49] On the notion of Mao looking to the model of the military to promote his "paradigm of Communist life," see Schwartz, "Modernization and the Maoist Vision," 17.

and production, and commune leaders used their power to relentlessly draw resources from the production brigades and production teams for investment in industry and for provisioning the towns and cities. In the Da Fo–Liangmen area, this practice, which created administrative confusion, inefficiency, and conflict, seems to have had its lineage in the APC movement, whereby the merging of Da Fo and four other villages into one accounting unit produced a pattern of cumbersome and conflict-ridden governance. Essentially, the five-village APC was too big to be efficiently managed. The performance of its accounting unit and its agricultural production reflected this reality. In several cases, the harvest yields of these bigger units were not as good as those of the land-pooling associations, creating squabbles among the APC leaders. The croplands of Beitoucun, which was considered the pacesetter, for instance, were choked with weeds, and its leaders failed to mobilize anyone to reap the wheat on time. The disappointing production of Beitoucun prompted Da Fo's accountants to accuse Beitoucun's leaders of "doing a lousy job," a charge that triggered a quarrel over distribution of the harvest on the whole and Beitoucun's rightful share in particular.[50]

There was a third problem. The natural agricultural endowments and the income differentials of the five different villages were so unalike that the disparities in production exacerbated age-old tensions. For example, according to the agreed-on principle of distribution, the five villages were to share the wheat and cotton harvests equally. However, Da Weicun was so poorly endowed when it came to croplands and farm equipment (the village had only one wooden cart, with wooden wheels) that its harvests were persistently far smaller than those of Da Fo and several other villages. The Communist Party leaders of Da Fo and the other villages therefore had to cope with a constant barrage of complaints that Da Weicun was taking advantage of them. Because Da Weicun was notoriously bandit-infested, and because its people stole crops from Da Fo's fields right up until the founding of the PRC, farmers in Da Fo suspected that the party-state had forged a collective arrangement that permitted a more effective form of crop theft under the guise of cooperation by Da Weicun's inhabitants. Understandably, people in Da Fo and other villages balked at this type of cooperation.

Another serious flaw in the design of the agricultural production cooperative became apparent in 1956. The APC leaders had neither a plan to provide relief nor the resources to help tillers recover from natural disasters. Understandably, this particularly galled tillers who had given up their own traditional protection against such disasters in order to join the APC. By late 1955 the inter-village disagreements over planning and organizing production had snowballed, already portending the breakup of the cooperative. The crash came right after the summer wheat harvest of 1956, when a flood on the Wei River seriously threatened west Dongle.

---

[50] Pang Guihua, interview, September 10, 1993; Pang Yilu, interview, September 11, 1993; Pang Chuanyan, interview, September 13, 1993.

The Onset of Collectivization and Popular Dissatisfaction

Da Fo was endangered, and its inhabitants scurried to keep the flood waters from engulfing the village. Tang Jinlin, the head of Liangmen district, rushed to Da Fo to join the men fighting the flood. The local district and county authorities did an outstanding job of evacuating the village. Women, children, and old people were moved by pontoon boats to high ground and relocated to different villages in Dongle, none of which had been part of the five-village cooperative. Within Da Fo, however, flood waters severely damaged approximately 95 percent of farmers' homes and ruined virtually all of the recently harvested grain crop. Because the flood also had hit much of Dongle and Wei counties, members of the cooperative were cut off from Da Fo and from one another and left to fend for themselves. Da Fo, with its ties to the new party-state and its tradition of market-focused regeneration, went its own way and was consequently better off. The Liangmen district government, working with Dongle County leaders, was able to provide substantial and immediate relief. People gratefully recall that after the flood the government brought in fish and coal, plus clothes, quilts, grain, and cash.

Recovery, however, as distinguished from relief, was powered by market entry. When villagers speak of recovery, they invariably say that people were encouraged to work and engage in small business to help themselves recover from the flood. Whereas local government assigned a few villagers to work in the grain transport sector in exchange for food and pay, the majority of Da Fo's inhabitants recovered from the flood via extra-village entrepreneurship that had a familiar ring. They went to Sijiu and Yingzhuang, east of the Wei River, to collect saline soil and make salt for the market. They also sold nitrate and fertilizer made from *lu shui* (a by-product of nitrate production used to soften the land and fertilize crops) in local markets farther north, in Hebei's Zhanbeitun. In the memory of villagers, this "self-help" policy prevailed for a year after the summer 1956 flood. People renovated their homes and moved toward full recovery with income earned from salt and nitrate trade, while the party-state suspended collective controls on the market and the work point system. Significantly, recovery cannot be equated with the government dispensation of disaster recovery loans to individual households, for those who did a better job of self-help were given less grain and less cash than those who did a poor job. The lesson of the Wei River flood was clear: Da Fo's residents had saved themselves. It was true that they had relied on the connections of their party leaders to mobilize government-based political resources, but everyone knew these leaders had succeeded in addressing the crisis mainly by allowing villagers to make the most of market-structured petty trade.[51] None of this, of course, was part of the public transcript of the Maoist agricultural production cooperative.

The popular clamor for a return to petty trade was unequivocal, and it opened a new round of discourse with the political center over state pressure on the market.

[51] 1993 interviews with Bao Jiping, September 2; Zhou Weihai, August 29; Ruan Shaobing, September 1; and Pang Lang, September 15.

After the 1956 flood the central government pushed for the resumption of collective farming in Da Fo. However, Da Fo's second production team had in the meantime initiated a noodle-making business. Team members sold the noodles in Minglizhuang markets, in Hebei province. The head of the Minglizhuang brigade confiscated the noodles, and Da Fo's sellers moved to defend their interest. With the blessing of Qiu Ruiqing, the head of the Dongle County Organization Department, Bao Peijian wrote a letter to the central government requesting that Hebei province be instructed to return the three hundred *jin* of noodles to the second production team. Although each household was peddling noodles for its own ends, Bao explained, it was not private business. The noodles were produced by team members in a self-help effort aimed at tiding over the post-flood difficulties. The letter was signed in the name of the Da Fo collective brigade. Subsequently, the central government issued a document to Hebei province to ask Minglizhuang to return the noodles, and Da Fo's petty traders rushed back to market.[52]

The anecdotal evidence of this popular preference for the market during the first great crisis of state collectivization is intriguing. By late 1956 Da Fo's traders had been issued four hundred wheelbarrows by the Dongle County government explicitly for starting up small transport businesses. By the winter of 1956 and the spring of 1957 many villagers were earning four *yuan* per day by carrying grain, coal, and other items to different places. This was a lot of money at the time: grain was only ten cents per *jin*, so in one day's work time villagers could earn forty *jin* of grain. During this period, the Dongle County government also set up a refugee hotel in Dongle town. The hotel provided free lodging and low-cost meals to refugees from the flooded areas: porridge was one cent per bowl, and a steamed bread loaf cost only eight cents. Much to the consternation of Dongle's socialist rulers, Da Fo's refugees, who by now were doing well economically due to their own entrepreneurial efforts, turned their noses up at the cheap food of the refugee hotel, preferring the more expensive dumpling dishes offered at better restaurants. Some people reported to the Dongle County government that the Da Fo refugees were misusing their money, and within days the Dongle County party committee began blasting criticisms at them over the town loudspeaker system.[53] But the farmers of Da Fo saw little reason to give up their market activities and return to the collective, which in their view had been a disastrous experiment.

The Path to the Liangmen People's Commune

Regardless of what Da Fo villagers wanted, government pressure against petty trade increased, and by the fall of 1957 Da Fo's Communist Party leaders were discouraging household grain production for the market. They pressed those

[52] Bao Jenming, interview, July 4, 1994.
[53] Bao Peisun, interview, September 1, 1995.

who wanted to continue with their small businesses to obtain official permission to do so, and they urged villagers to resume the experiment with agricultural collectivization. By the following year, Mao was promoting his plan for a Great Leap Forward, the agricultural arm of which focused on implementing the large-scale collectivization of agriculture in rural China by merging existing APCs into huge communes. Between April and August 1958, the first experimental commune – the Chayashan People's Commune – was established in Henan province, and on August 6 Mao Zedong visited, praised, and chose this commune as the model for a nation-wide commune movement.[54] By the end of the year, thousands of communes had been established throughout the countryside. In the summer of 1958, the inhabitants of Da Fo, too, were wedded to a big eleven-village cooperative in Liangmen district. This unit quickly became the embryo of the Liangmen People's Commune and was expanded to include approximately twenty villages. Before the year was over, the leaders of this unit had begun to requisition more grain than ever before. Many villagers were dissatisfied, but they did not yet move to resist this new wave of Maoist state appropriation. Instead, they waded back into it, unaware that they were headed straight into a life-imperiling undertow.

Why did this reversal back to the radicalism of a bigger unit occur, and why did it meet with popular compliance when from 1955 to 1957 villagers had clearly experienced that the cooperative was an inadequate vehicle for increasing personal income and for dealing with disaster?[55] The short answer is that the majority of Da Fo's villagers still trusted the Communist Party and its leadership. Despite the sporadic pressures to adhere to the work point system and obey the dictates of procurement, the party had not consistently or wantonly attacked the major artery of extra-village economic advancement. The under-propagandized economic principle of the Mao-led pre-1949 agrarian revolution – free trade in non-farm products – was still in place. Pang Qinli remembers the persistence of this promise, and its fulfillment locally, in the years leading up to the Great Leap Forward:

Salt making had been our village business, and most people were engaged in making it. Salt was worth ten cents a *jin* on the market. We consumed some of it ourselves, and we sold the rest on the market or in the surrounding villages. The government did not stop us from making salt. The saline earth from the fields contained salt and *lu shui*. The earth from inside the village also contained nitrate. It was worth a lot of money – between two and three *yuan* per *jin*. We could make and sell these items freely, and there was no tax imposed on this trade. Each year, before the Great Leap Forward, I could make at least two hundred *jin* of salt. I ate some and sold some. I could get at least twenty *yuan* from the salt making. Other people who were good at making salt made much more money out of this than I did.[56]

Although unhappiness over the government procurement of grain was widespread, few of these "other people" in Da Fo feared that the party-state would

---

[54] Jia Yanmin, *Dayuejin Shiqi Xiangcun Zhengzhide Dianxing*, 1–3, 134–37, and 155–77.
[55] On this subject, see Domenach, *Origins of the Great Leap*.
[56] Pang Qinli, interview, September 18, 1993.

seriously invade non-farm market income or declare such customary enterprise to be in unacceptable competition with grain production. At this point, it seems, even the Da Fo Communist Party leaders who were faithful to the emerging Maoist command economy had not entertained any such possibility. The party had flaws, to be sure, but local people assumed they could offset them by scoring gains in the marketplace. That was what the October 1 Revolution had been about, and that was what most villagers presumed the CCP would continue to stand for. Da Fo's farmers-turned–salt producers had been riding a wave of economic prosperity since the early 1930s, and they had little reason to associate large, prolonged economic setbacks – as opposed to small momentary difficulties – with the governance of the CCP. The party's support for their pre-1949 struggle to preserve the market, for land redistribution, and now for improvement of agricultural technology and infrastructure all portended a continuous ascent.

A second factor that calmed popular anxiety over leaping into an ever-larger agricultural unit was the bumper wheat harvest of June 1958, which contributed to a false sense of security in communal food delivery institutions – particularly the public dining halls, which were established in August 1958 in Da Fo. In this short takeoff period of the Liangmen People's Commune, roughly the mid-June harvest to the mid-October harvest, many people in Da Fo came to marvel at the wonder of collective food supply. There was abundance, and the chefs of the public dining hall system prepared so much food that some was actually wasted. In the first three months of the people's commune, villagers were given free meals and allowed to eat as much as they pleased. Life was a fantastic pig-out.[57] Bao Dongzhi remembers: "The public dining halls provided wheat flour bread every meal, and the cooks brought the breads, meat, eggplant, and other vegetables to the fields at meal-time." Things quickly changed for the worse. In winter, rationing began, and Bao says that "some two months after the New Year, in April, we began to feel hungry."[58] People were lining up to get a second ration of reduced bread with husks added. But the leaders of the Liangmen People's Commune reassured them that the Communist Party would not abandon progress, and they offered incentives to induce villagers to give the commune a chance. In these first months of alarming shortages, the work point system of payment was abolished. Ordinary villagers were promised monthly salaries of three *yuan*, and heads of harvest companies were offered twelve *yuan* per month to stay the course of collectivization. This incentive system, which lasted only three months, temporarily allayed popular fears that obedience to political hierarchy and the moratorium on marketing would bring hunger.

As of November 1958 there was still a widespread conviction that the Liangmen district government, which Da Fo's people had helped put in power in the pre-1949 insurgency, was committed to providing a certain minimal level of food

---

[57] Pang Siyin, interview, September 19, 1993.
[58] Bao Dongzhi, interview, September 17, 1993.

security in return for willingness to join in agricultural collectivization. Most villagers still presumed that the party-state would not let them go hungry, even if there were a serious food shortage. The Communist Party's leaders and the regional Hebei-Shandong-Henan party committee had helped villagers obtain food in the famine of 1942, and the Dongle County government had provided food relief and encouraged self-help in the market after the 1956 Wei River flood – and, besides, although the APC movement had challenged private ownership of land planted with grain, Mao's cadres still had not touched the privately owned vegetable gardens that were essential to family survival. There was no precedent for this political entity abandoning local folk in a food crisis; it had come through before, and it would come through again – or so people thought.

At the local level, moreover, many villagers still perceived Bao Zhilong and the other Da Fo party leaders not as agents of the emerging unitary state but rather as local people allied with their own forms of household and village avoidance of, or resistance to, state domination. Da Fo's Communist Party leaders had been the rebel patrons of the village people. They had gained power by defending the basic social rights and the dignity of villagers against both the Kuomintang and the Japanese Army's puppet regime. Despite small acts of corruption and small-scale skirmishes over the boundaries of private proprietary rights and public collective obligations in the mid-1950s, many villagers trusted Bao Zhilong and the other local party leaders to steer them wisely and deliver benefits to Da Fo.

What few villagers fully understood in this post-1951 "honeymoon" period was that the patron-client relationship of Da Fo's Communist Party leaders to ordinary village families was undergoing a subtle but profound transformation that acted to bind top village leaders to the new party-state, to bolster their ability to build up a selective party-based political hierarchy within the village via state-structured patronage, and to encourage them to treat many ordinary villagers as if they were merely cannon fodder for socialist construction. The career of Bao Zhilong illustrates this development. As we have seen, Bao was favored by the pro-Mao revolutionary border region government even before the Communist revolutionary victory, which proved important in the era of Communist state construction. Between 1945 and 1955, Bao Zhilong became the titular leader of Da Fo and the ardent supporter of party-guided collectivization in Liangmen district. In pushing the village to move into each successive stage of collectivization, Bao was seen as successful, though some of his successes flew in the face of the practical economic designs of individual households. As the leader of the early cooperative movement in Da Fo and one of the most successful mutual aid groups in the Wei River area, Bao gained access to a number of state resources that, he said, promised improvement in villagers' lives. He used these resources to construct a network of mainly Bao and Pang lineage clients who assisted him in consolidating his power base.[59] If many farmers less and less appreciated Bao's

---

[59] Compare with Chan, Madsen, and Unger, *Chen Village*.

role in pushing the cooperatives of the early 1950s, some also perceived him as a fellow villager who could use his political connections to provide them with benefits, protection, and a growing number of brokerage services – a rising patron.

Having taken an instrumental part in dispensing land to many villagers during the 1945–47 land reform and having helped Bao Mingxian, Bao Lijun, and others leave Da Fo to find employment in government cooperatives and district offices between 1951 and 1957, Bao Zhilong continued to deliver benefits to his home village as he ascended the party ladder. Already the vice-director of Liangmen district in 1954, Bao Zhilong was able to elicit flood relief from the district government in 1956. His role in protecting the village from outside predators further endeared him to local people. His fight against the Kuomintang salt tax police, his resistance to the Japanese Puppet Army, and his support of the PLA in its defeat of the Chiang Kai-shek Army on the battlefield in 1947 were legendary, and since 1951 Bao Zhilong had afforded Da Fo protection from petty bandits and small crop thieves who found this increasingly prosperous village inviting. Further, Bao was able to arrange brokerage services for selected villagers, including subsidy payments for farm animal purchases to households joining the mutual aid groups under his direction and chemical fertilizers for land-pooling association members whom he favored. Bao's pivotal administrative position also permitted him to occasionally mobilize resources that could benefit the whole village, such as the exhibitions of agricultural implements and machinery and the technical irrigation assistance provided during the early period of the APCs in Dongle. Notwithstanding the flaws in collectivization and popular frustration over the imposition of unified purchase and sale, Bao's patronage outreaches were still in place when the Maoist call to form people's communes reached Liangmen district in 1958. The call offered an opportunity for Bao Zhilong and the loyal Communist Party members of his entourage to promise an expansion of such patronage, as well as hint at penalties for non-compliance, in order to move villagers to voice support for the new venture.

It should surprise no one, then, to learn that the campaign to resuscitate collective farming on a grand scale was based in the Bao lineage, whose members had most benefited from Bao Zhilong's patronage, and was powered by youthful and militant Bao party zealots who had only a secondhand understanding of the nodes of pre-1949 CCP credibility and who had not been hurt by the failure of the early cooperative movement.

At the pinnacle of the Da Fo party network on the eve of the Great Leap Forward stood party boss Bao Zhilong himself. The son of an impoverished farmer with only four *mu* of poor saline land in the 1930s, Bao and his family survived by selling earth salt in regional periodic markets right up to the land revolution of 1945–47. Completely illiterate, Bao Zhilong was unable to decipher any of the written rules and regulations of the Communist Party.[60] When I first

[60] Bao Zhigen, interviews, August 14–16, 1989.

visited Da Fo in August 1989, Secretary Bao still could not read his own name. At the time, Bao asked me to show him a piece of American money. I presented a George Washington quarter. Bao had no idea who the first president of the United States was, and although he had a good understanding of Chiang Kai-shek and his politics, he had little if any knowledge of Confucius and his political wisdom.[61]

Ruling Da Fo village from his post in Liangmen district in the 1950s, boss Bao Zhilong developed a small network of political clients. He picked Bao Yibin, a nineteen-year-old graduate of Da Fo's elementary school and of a Dongle County Public Security Bureau training school, to act as the village party secretary *in situ* from 1958 to 1961 – the entire span of the Great Leap Forward. Bao Jiping, boss Bao's cousin and choice for the post of Da Fo vice–party secretary in 1958, was only twenty-two years old. An orphan, Bao Jiping had been raised by his blind brother and had never been to school; he too was illiterate. Then there was the twenty-four-year-old Pang Lang. He had failed to finish middle school, could barely handle simple math, and was utterly corrupt. Yet Pang Lang was chosen to serve as the Da Fo brigade accountant over former "good landlord" Bao Yuhua, the honest, competent, and willing candidate for the post. With this decision, boss Bao Zhilong and his network further marginalized Bao Yuhua and the remaining first-pole leaders of Da Fo's party branch.

Additionally, Bao Zhilong frequently enlisted the help of thirty-year-old Bao Zhigen, an illiterate and landless hooligan from the outer fringe of village society – Bao Zhigen's parents were habitual beggars in the pre–World War II decade.[62] Chronically unemployed, Bao Zhigen had survived as a youth by helping his father sell donkey and horse manure scooped up from Dongle County roads in the 1930s and had then served the destructive interest of the Yang Faxian Japanese Puppet Army during the war years. The ultimate opportunist, Bao Zhigen was not a Communist Party member. But he had assisted Bao Zhilong and his militia followers in the last days of the Civil War and then joined boss Bao's cooperative in the early 1950s, all the while exploiting the need of party leaders to control local turf and contain popular dissent. Fearless and street-smart, Bao Zhigen was quick to turn every party-mandated experiment with collectivization into an enterprise to benefit himself. By the eve of the Great Leap Forward, villagers referred to him as the "second-tier government."[63]

Together, these young, poorly educated, and rough-edged Communist Party leaders managed to drown out the voices of older and wiser members of the village. Individuals who cautioned prudence in collectivizing private means of household production were silenced by Bao Zhilong and his second-pole clients,

---

[61] Compare this with Seybolt's similar portrait of another village party secretary in this border region. *Throwing the Emperor from His Horse.*

[62] Ruan Zhaoyin, interview, June 17, 2006.

[63] Bao Zhigen, interview, July 29, 2004. On the importance of *liumang*, or semi-criminal fringe elements, in Chinese local politics, see Barme, *In the Red*, 62–89, esp. 66.

many of whom joined with boss Bao in relying on hustlers like Bao Zhigen to help them facilitate Mao's rush to communize agriculture.

In a sense, villagers had little choice but to obey boss Bao Zhilong and his militant clients, because at the outset of the Great Leap Forward these brigade leaders derived political support, and gained political prestige, from Mao's *san tong* policy, which required county-level government leaders to work in villages for stints of several months. This policy, which sent county-level government leaders to eat the same food, live in the same quarters, and do the same work in the fields as villagers, brought Liu Junyin, the head of the Dongle County Public Security Bureau, to Da Fo at the start of the Great Leap, and he was joined by Dai Yantang, the future Dongle County police chief, and by Yan Dong, the future police chief of Anyang County, both of whom periodically were stationed in Da Fo during the Great Leap. Whereas villagers occasionally interacted with these upper-level power holders and came to trust that they were in Da Fo to break down barriers between the state and local people, they also understood that these county-level cadres were agents of an emergent police state that, before the famine hit the police themselves, had a somewhat cozy relationship with Da Fo's party leaders. Hence, the appearances of these police figures gave villagers more reason to accept the leadership of Bao Zhilong and his militant political network.[64]

In stressing Da Fo's party leaders' practical and self-interested reasons for pushing Mao's Great Leap Forward, it is important to remember their genuine hope in the promise of Mao's initiative. After all is said and done, men like Bao Zhilong, Bao Yibin, Bao Zhigen, and their comrades in Da Fo were poor rural people whose parents and grandparents had been the victims of official neglect and the diversion of state investment away from the bad alkaline soils of their peripheral fields and farms; of state predatory tax forces; of the failures of fiscally strapped and sometimes corrupt national, regional, and local administrative elites to prevent food shortages; and of rural proletarianization, all of which combined with memories of drought, harvest failures, and a series of famines.[65] Conscious that millions of their marginalized and overtaxed counterparts had succumbed to the famines of 1920–21 and 1942, the people of this Henan village lived with the intrusive memories of these past unnerving wars over sustenance,[66] which in part reflected the cumulative social consequences of Chinese state subordination to a Darwinian system of international military power.[67]

Each of Da Fo's land-poor Communist Party leaders had a story to tell about how a family or lineage member had attempted to cope with famine – especially

---

[64] Bao Zhanglin, interview, July 6, 2006.

[65] Pomeranz, *Making of a Hinterland*; Bianco, "Peasant Movements" and "Peasant Responses"; Wong, *China Transformed*, 197, 228; Thaxton, *Salt of the Earth*; Huang, *Peasant Economy*.

[66] For the conceptual underpinnings of this argument, see Schacter, *Seven Sins of Memory*, 174–75, and Davis, *Late Victorian Holocausts*, 13.

[67] See Wong, *China Transformed*, 173–74, and Thaxton, *Salt of the Earth*.

the Henan Famine of 1942. In that year, Bao Dongzhi's younger brother, Bao Wenxue, died at age twelve from emaciation and an edema-related illness, and Bao is still haunted by memories of his playmates starving in Da Fo's back streets. Bao Zhidan's father starved to death, and his mother had to marry off both of his younger sisters in return for food to survive the crisis of 1942, during which time he joined his mother in begging for food in Da Fo's market. Zheng Ziyan's brother also died in the 1942 famine, when Zheng was eleven, and Zheng is still troubled by the memory of poor families from other villages selling their children in Da Fo's market and of starved cadavers strung along the roads leading beyond Da Fo. Piled on top of these memories are those of famine disappearances: Bao Honglin's father fled to the coal mines of Tang Shan during the 1942 famine, never to be heard from again, and Bao Zhendao's father, Bao Chenyun's father and uncle, and Ruan Guocheng's uncle all migrated to Da Tong, where they found work for a while but were rumored to have perished before they could return to Da Fo.[68]

To these rural people, therefore, the Great Leap Forward was not simply a campaign to overcome the impasse in agricultural production and to move on to an improved livelihood. They saw in the Maoist call to arms a permanent solution to a historically embedded threat to their existence, and, to a significant extent, they interpreted the Great Leap as a millenarian war to abolish any possibility of famine in the future, to create a new China in which neither the plunder of foreign powers nor the indifference of Beijing officials could ever again jeopardize the shared food security of the forgotten and unwanted rural poor. Thus, it was easy for them to believe in the necessity of instilling popular confidence that the Mao-led 1949 revolution was going to afford fail-safe insurance against any future disaster and to join boss Bao Zhilong in adopting the cruel instrument of public criticism as a necessary means of manufacturing subjects who would join them in the battle to break the famine cycle of the past. Many of them had survived the last remembered famine in 1942 by joining Mao's revolution. Thus, it seemed rational to mobilize other villagers to this cause.

These explanations for Da Fo villagers' compliance with the state's desire for collectivization focus on reasons internal to the village, but they do not tell the entire story. The particular circumstances of provincial-level politics – a regional political battle that itself grew out of fractures at the center of the party – put extraordinary pressure on Da Fo's Communist leaders to herd the village into the commune, decisively turning them away from the free market and individual tillage and transforming them into zealots for collectivization.

To fully appreciate the importance of this development, we must grasp the political war that was raging between Henan first party secretary Pan Fusheng, the advocate of a pragmatic agrarian policy that cautioned against imposing collectivization on the countryside, and Henan second party secretary Wu Zhipu,

---

[68] Bao Zhidan, interview, June 26, 2001; Bao Honglin, interview, June 25, 2001; Ruan Yunchun, interview, July 15, 2000.

the messenger of Maoist-style mobilization. In the spring of 1957, Pan Fusheng returned to Henan province to seize on the Mao-led central government's hesitancy to go forward with collectivization. A key leader of the Pingyuan base area of which Dongle was a part during World War II, Pan was keenly aware of the consumer orientation of farm-based families and of the crucial role markets played in popular livelihood in this section of the North China Plain. He put forward policies to relax the collective measures that had stifled economic gains for small farmers, sanctioning withdrawal from the cooperatives, allowing private plots, and encouraging market expansion.[69] Determined to spare farmers a further dose of socialism, Pan even issued a provincial party committee directive to inhibit the launching of the anti-rightist campaign below the county level.[70]

As we have seen, farmers in Da Fo welcomed the institutional sanction of the retreat they had engineered from Maoist collectivization in the aftermath of the 1956 Wei River flood disaster and the collapse of the APC. By the summer harvest of 1957, they had dissolved the big collective, and by November 1957 they had placed the power to make decisions about the requirements of agriculture in the hands of small production teams.[71] Through most of this period, Pan Fusheng's star was on the rise in Da Fo.

In this same 1957 period, however, Mao launched the Socialist Education Movement and turned it into a campaign to abolish private landownership and move from cooperativization to collectivization in the countryside, all the while placing decisions about the organization of agricultural life in the hands of brigade party leaders. At this point, Wu Zhipu launched an attack on Pan Fusheng. Pan was accused of being a rightist who had supported popular resistance to state procurement and had foiled the state's plan to get more grain from the countryside.[72] By early 1958, Pan Fusheng was being criticized for halting the anti-rightist campaign in the countryside and thus violating the instructions of the Central Committee and Chairman Mao. Anti-Pan posters appeared on the sides of trains running from Beijing to Zhengzhou.[73] The *Henan Daily* created a special column to struggle against Pan. And anti-Pan big character posters (*da zi bao*) could be seen everywhere.[74] Clearly, Pan Fusheng had lost favor with the Maoist center. On May 18, the Central Committee replaced him with Wu Zhipu, and Pan quickly lost power in Henan province.[75]

In this period, the so-called right wing of the Henan party apparatus was subjected to criticism and purge. Wu Zhipu's faction implicated the prosperous independent smallholders in this wing. Hailing from this stratum of the peasantry,

---

[69] Domenach, *Origins of the Great Leap*, 30–34, 53, 110, 117–18, 124–27, 138, 158–59.
[70] Qiao Peihua, "Xinyang Shijian Fasheng de Yuanyin," 1–3.
[71] Zheng Yunxiang, interview, September 15, 1993.
[72] Qiao Peihua, "Xinyang Shijian Fasheng de Yuanyin," 1–3.
[73] Wemheuer, "Stone Noodles."
[74] Qiao Peihua, "Xinyang Shijian Fasheng de Yuanyin," 1–3.
[75] Ibid.

some of the party members in Da Fo and Dongle were accused by Wu and his followers of being "militants who entered the Communist Party at a time when the declared aim was not yet socialist revolution, but a 'new democracy.'"[76] "New democracy" was the code term for village people who would fight for proprietary rights and market freedoms outside the framework of CCP-dictated agricultural collectivization. In Dongle County, local community leaders who empathized with such people were branded "rightists" – opponents of Mao's socialist revolution – and were cashiered in the anti-rightist rectification movement launched by the Maoists in June 1957. By December this rectification had targeted 1,741 esteemed members of the rural elite, including township cadres, schoolteachers, and doctors and nurses.[77]

On December 15 the movement was extended down to the villages, where, according to Dongle County records, "right-wing farmers" responded by attacking the performance of the Communist Party after Liberation, publicly saying it was not a good party.[78] The so-called right-wing farmers blamed the leadership of the Communist Party for flawed collectivization and for the system of unified purchase and sale. They also expressed dissatisfaction with the government appropriation of the harvest. Understandably, many of Da Fo's party members were worried, because they had been part of a regional political circle in which Pan Fusheng and his associates were instrumental; key members of this circle had, prior to 1957, been able to provide Da Fo with both protection and patronage from various levels of the government.

These developments largely explain why, in the first quarter of 1958, only a few months after Wu Zhipu and Tan Zhenlin sponsored an early November 1957 conference in northern Henan to promote Mao's plan for agricultural cooperation on a grand scale[79] and only a few weeks after the December rectification movement reached the Dongle countryside, Bao Zhilong and his militia-based clients decided to heed the Maoist call to strengthen central state controls over the grain harvests. Boss Bao and his young allies were anxious not to be categorized as supporters of Pan Fusheng and included in the 16 percent minority of "die-hard right wingers." Muzzling longtime comrades whose predispositions resonated with the party line of loser Pan Fusheng, they went to great lengths to prove they were worthy cadres of Wu Zhipu's command to tighten upper-level supervision of lower social units, and they became militant supporters of large-scale projects pushed by the Maoist center.

The struggle between Wu Zhipu and Pan Fusheng divided party and village. "There were straw scarecrow figures along Da Fo's roads carrying slogans, saying

---

[76] Domenach, "Origins of the Great Leap," original unpublished manuscript in English translation, 240–49, 251.
[77] *Dongle Lishi Jilu*, 204–05, 207.
[78] Ibid., 204–06.
[79] Domenach, *Origins of the Great Leap*, 140–41, 148.

'Down with Pan Fusheng!' and 'Down with Wu Zhipu!'" recalls Bao Zhigen.[80]
Pan Fusheng had been popular in Da Fo because he had said people should be free
to leave the land-pooling association and the APC. Those who voiced Pan's view
ended up suffering. In mid-1957, for example, Bao Zhengda, the temporary Da
Fo Communist Party secretary, was branded a rightist because he questioned the
logic of the frenzied well-digging exercises and large-scale irrigation schemes. He
subsequently was dismissed by Bao Zhilong and the Liangmen district leaders,
who were already leaning toward Wu Zhipu.[81] Dissenters like Bao Zhengda were
among the first to be sent to Lin County to make steel (and less political trouble)
for the Maoist state in late 1958.

The political infighting between Wu Zhipu and Pan Fusheng – and its terrible
consequences for Pan's supporters throughout the region – goes a long way toward
explaining why Bao Zhilong and the other Bao lineage party members, who
had come out of the ranks of the land-poor salt producers and had joined the
Communist Party in quest of market justice prior to 1949, decided to go along
with the Great Leap collectivization plan despite its anti-market thrust. Their
decision was made easier by the fact that by the eve of the Great Leap, these Da
Fo party leaders identified less than they once had with the economic interest
of the poor farmers and petty traders who depended on the marketplace for a
living. Whereas nearly half of the ordinary villagers worked poor saline lands
and depended on marketing salt, nitrate, and other products for 10 to 50 percent
of their income, even in the mid-1950s, Bao Zhilong and party members in his
favor had received some of the richest agricultural lands in the village in the land
reform of 1945–47, and, with subsidies from the state, they were able to find
prosperity through cooperative-geared cereal production into the mid-1950s. At
the same time, Bao Zhilong and his cronies had become small-fry bureaucrats in
the Leninist articulated party-state apparatus, and their support for the market
shifted along with the sources of their power and personal financial interests. As
these core party leaders began to spend an inordinate amount of time on the
affairs of government at the village, district, and even county levels, they severely
cut back on their market activities. Their appreciation of the importance of the
market in the everyday livelihood of villagers faded to a point where they viewed
delivery of grain to the state under unified purchase and sale as the first and
correct order of politics. They apparently did not conceive the coming of the
people's commune as portending a complete break with popular market activity,
but they still were motivated by their own changed position, as well as Maoist
political language and propaganda, to enforce collectivization.

Between 1951 and 1958, Da Fo village followed its Communist Party leaders –
the agents of a new state – down a path that initially looked promising. At the

[80] Bao Zhigen, interview, July 21, 1994.
[81] Ruan Shaobing, interviews, September 1, September 11, 1993.

beginning of this journey, the farmers of Da Fo believed that their goals and the party's goals were the same: the new government of the PRC would protect their freedom to make and market earth salt and would defend their freedom to farm the land as individual tillers. As the decade wore on, however, it gradually became clear that the Communist Party under Mao's leadership was headed in a quite different direction that did not portend well for the tillers of the saline land of Da Fo. That they accepted the party's mandate to join the Liangmen People's Commune in 1958 even after the agricultural production cooperative had flopped can be attributed only partly to their faith in their leaders or to reciprocal patron-client relations with the regime. Whereas many scholars have analyzed the confrontation of top-down state forces and the bottom-up, survivalist-oriented peasantry, providing insightful detail about the patron-client ties that developed between high-level party-state actors and village-level party cadres, such an approach barely touches on the real nature of Leninist relations with the rural poor in China – and Da Fo.[82] In Da Fo, a mixture of "triumphalist pride" on the part of the party's local activist base, fear of ending up on the losing side of a national-cum-regional war over Great Leap policy, and a blind faith in Mao and the true believers who curried his favor allowed Mao and his regional inner-party agents to connect with previously marginalized and militarized young party activists like Bao Zhilong and his clients, but not with ordinary farmers at the village level.[83]

Thus, to understand why Da Fo's party leaders chose to take villagers down the path of disaster, we must look to the past – to their faith in a Leninist party that had done them many services and promised to deliver them from the political threat and privation of the past – to the politics of their present, which gave them good reason to fear political exile or worse if they brooked any protest of Mao's Great Leap plans; and to how Mao took advantage of their ambitions for the future. Secure in the knowledge of their party's mandate to rule the Chinese countryside, Da Fo's party leaders could not have comprehended that their actions over the next three years would damage that mandate irreparably at a substantial cost to the villagers.

---

[82] For this approach, see Scott, *Moral Economy of the Peasant*, 26–27. On the Soviet Union, see Fitzpatrick, *Stalin's Peasants*, 7–12, 268–79, 313–14, 319–20; Viola, *Peasant Rebels under Stalin*, 3–12, esp. 11–12; and Ledeneva, *Russia's Economy of Favours*, 1–4, 28–35, 104–05, 127–28. On China, see Friedman, Pickowicz, and Selden, *Chinese Village* and *Revolution, Resistance, and Reform*.

[83] In developing this point, I have benefited from personal correspondence with Charles Tilly, March 5, 2007, and with Edward Friedman, May 1, 2007, as well as from my many conversations with Da Fo residents.

4

The Mandate Abandoned

THE DISASTER OF THE GREAT LEAP FORWARD

Just before the June wheat harvest in 1958, party leaders in Da Fo responded positively to the central government demand to upgrade the movement for agricultural collectivization by galvanizing popular support to join with nineteen other villages in Liangmen district to form the Liangmen People's Commune. Four times the size of the failed five-village APC, this commune unit included Beitoucun, Wencaicun, Taigu, Da Weicun, Xiao Weicun, Minglizhuang, Shangdizhuang, Liangmen, Liangmenpo, Wanxiuzhuang, Xiangtianzhuang, Weiliancun, Shennongzhuang, Shichaomiao, and Jingweizhuang. The commune headquarters was in Liangmen, and Beitoucun was designated the commune's model production brigade. At the outset of the Great Leap, Zhou Enlai visited Beitoucun and declared the village a socialist pacesetter.

Many of Da Fo's party leaders played a critical role in the formation of Liangmen People's Commune. Bao Zhilong became the vice-director of the commune and a central player in commune affairs; Bao Peijian, one of the first party members in Da Fo, was placed in charge of the Commune Dispute Mediation Committee and also served as a member of the Commune Work Inspection Team; Bao Zhendao became the head of the People's Commune Bank; Bao Yibin, the son of PLA martyr Bao Yidai, was given the position of Commune Finance Director; and on and on it went. All of these Bao lineage Communist Party leaders worked and lived for extended periods in the people's commune headquarters in Liangmen, occasionally returning to Da Fo to tend to family matters and issues bearing on the village's relationship to the larger commune. Concerned that pacesetter Beitoucun was leaping ahead of their home village, they took it upon themselves to conduct Da Fo's affairs in a manner that would prove the worth of their village to the economic plan of the Maoist state.

But in striving to impress their party betters, to propel Da Fo toward a better future, and to avoid criticism or punishment, the Communist Party leaders of Da

Fo abandoned the mandate villagers had bestowed on them during the tumultuous years of occupation and civil war. They stripped the people of Da Fo of their private property, privacy, and many aspects of their traditional culture, herding them to live collectively in the fields, sleep in tents, and eat in public dining halls. They drove them to work nonstop, day and night, in the fields and on far-flung projects, depriving them of the time and energy they needed to participate in the market. And in return for the villagers' sacrifices, far from delivering the prosperity they had promised, the village's Communist cadres escalated the party's procurement claims until they precipitated a famine, taking all of the grain the farmers produced and giving them nothing in return except a small daily food ration inadequate for survival over the long term. Mobilizing the work style they had developed in the pre-1949 period in service of Mao's Great Leap Forward, Da Fo's party leaders coerced its residents to participate in Mao's deadly project using a combination of physical and verbal abuse, deprivation, and terror.

Farming and Living Collectively

If the management of agriculture was taken out of the hands of the heads of farm households in the stage of the agricultural production cooperatives, the Great Leap Forward compounded this practice. With the commencement of the Great Leap, the leaders of Liangmen People's Commune reaffirmed the socialist mantra of 1956, declaring that all private farmland belonged to the collective. In Da Fo, as in many other villages, family grain fields were placed in the preserve of the commune, and virtually all decisions involving agriculture were assumed by party brigade leaders beholden to commune superiors. These brigade leaders often structured decisions on when, how, and what villagers were to produce without prior consultation with the villagers. This usurped the decentralized day-to-day private land use decision-making authority of farm household heads and converted many leaders into "feudal lords."[1] Da Fo was especially hurt by this process, for its major feudal lord – party boss Bao Zhilong – was a key leader of Liangmen People's Commune.

In early August of 1958, the Da Fo party leaders called on villagers to turn in all of their cooking pots and all of their wheat harvest to the brigade. According to Bao Yuming, "The wheat harvest was not divided among the households. Instead, it was taken to the new public dining halls. Therefore, individual households did not have any grain left at this time."[2] The public dining hall system was an important factor structuring peasant life changes in the Great Leap Forward, one that was inseparable from the Maoist attempt to mobilize and regiment labor. Originally established to free up more people to join the workforce and to perform labor duties on huge water conservation and iron- and steel-making

[1] Zhou, *How the Farmers Changed China*, 14–16, 22–28, 48.
[2] Bao Yuming, interview, June 21, 2001.

projects, Da Fo's public dining halls were created in response to a mandate from Wu Zhipu, whose message was delivered by the Liangmen People's Commune party secretary, Qing Zhenxin. The dining halls, it was said, would bring "good things" to Da Fo and China. They would allow farmers to retain enough grain for themselves, and they would permit farmers to give more grain to the state so that Chairman Mao could pay off the national debt to the Soviet Union and China could be self-reliant. The Da Fo party leaders conveyed this message to villagers with a slight exaggeration: with the public dining halls established, no one need worry about hunger ever again.[3]

The public dining halls were set up with lightning speed, literally on the same day of the meeting in which Qing Zhenxin called for their establishment. Bao Dongzhi recalls that such immediate transformations were normal at the time, part of the Communist work style developed over the course of the occupation and civil war:

Right after I returned from the meeting with Qing Zhenxin we set up the public dining halls in Da Fo. There was no hesitation at all. All the county, commune, and village leaders were like that at the time. They would not argue with their superiors. They would not tolerate any delay. You had to do whatever they asked you to do without any hesitation.

This style of doing things had a long organizational foundation in China at the time. It was a very effective style developed during the war years. Most of the Liangmen People's Commune party leaders and some of the Da Fo leaders like Bao Zhilong, Bao Zhendao, and even myself had experienced the same style of work during the wartime period and the land reform. I never questioned it, nor did any of the other party leaders. We had unshakeable confidence in the Communist Party and the leadership of Chairman Mao.[4]

In rural China, the public dining hall assumed two distinct forms. The "regular form," with which most Western journalists and scholars are familiar, was usually housed in several buildings, where villagers came together to eat meals and to enjoy limited input on issues such as the timing of meals, amounts of grain to which they felt entitled, and the quality of food. In the second form, more common in the provinces where the radical Maoists prevailed, brigade-level party leaders collected, managed, and increasingly centralized all of the property and grain production of villagers within the dining hall system.[5] Within less than a year after their establishment, Da Fo's public dining halls became the locus of Maoist state power over village society, as party leaders confiscated and managed most of the property and grain of households and took power over fiscal decisions and food resources. The party leaders in charge of Da Fo's dining halls were hand-picked by Bao Zhilong, still the vice–party secretary of Liangmen People's Commune, and by Bao Yibin, the Da Fo party secretary. Throughout the Great Leap, they managed the mess halls to reinforce their dominance over

[3] Zheng Jintian, interview, June 22, 2001.
[4] Bao Dongzhi, interview, June 24, 2001.
[5] Thaxton and Wang, "Power, Disentitlement, and Life Chances."

village life and to make sure that villagers surrendered to the labor directives of the commune. This second type of public dining hall system engendered invasions of the villagers' households by party leaders, culminating in state confiscation of private family property for commune use. "Some of the village leaders actually came to the houses of villagers to take away their cooking utensils and grain personally," recalls Bao Yuming.[6] Within a year, the party leaders had torn down walls marking off private household boundaries, pulled down houses, and removed gates to courtyards and gardens.[7] Mao's ill-conceived Great Leap iron- and steel-making campaign, which encouraged Chinese farmers to turn over metal items that the state could use to produce iron and steel, accelerated this invasion of private household space. Once all of the metal items were confiscated, including the locks on household doors, "village leaders, or anybody for that matter, could walk right into anybody's house," says Bao Guangming. As the demand intensified for wood to fuel the smelting processes, even the doors were taken away from farmers' homes. After coming under this system, Bao Guangming explains, "the home was not a home – it was just a place for sleeping."[8]

In the first year of the Great Leap, party brigade leaders literally moved Da Fo's entire population into the collective fields. The village was divided into three harvest companies, each with its own dining hall.[9] By late 1958 the Da Fo brigade office and each of the company headquarters had been moved out of the village proper into the fields, where huge tents were set up for people to live in. Everyone ate, worked, and slept in the fields. No one could return to the once-vibrant village without permission, and Da Fo was abandoned for long stretches of time. The village as a site of visibly segmented private households no longer existed, as houses that formerly belonged to big landholders, affluent tillers, and even smallholders of modest means were dismantled, rebuilt, and merged for common use – particularly for administrative offices and for the public dining halls, but also for entertainment. At one point, the Liangmen Commune officials mandated that Da Fo's party leaders pull down private farmhouses and deliver their bricks and wooden beams for building a big commune theater – an order that incensed uncompensated farmers.[10]

A few of Da Fo's harvest company heads fought to prevent complete usurpation of private entitlements. At first, when the public dining halls were set up, Tang Guoyi allowed members of his company to keep small amounts of grain in their

---

[6] Bao Yuming, interview, June 21, 2001.
[7] Zheng Tianbao, interview, July 15, 2005.
[8] Bao Guangming, interview, July 12, 2000.
[9] The southwest part of Da Fo came under the First Harvest Company, led by Bao Dongzhi and Bao Zhigen; the Second Company drew its foot soldiers from the east of Da Fo and was headed by Ruan Renxing; and the Third Company, under Ruan Guoli and Tang Guoyi, commanded the north part of the village.
[10] Zheng Tianbao, interview, July 15, 2005.

houses.[11] When the Da Fo party leaders urged the harvest company heads to tear down some of their members' private homes and use the scavenged household materials and tools to build public dining halls, Ruan Renxing, also the head of a harvest company, attempted to foil the scheme. He told his members that they were free to use his personal official seal, without first seeking his permission, to confirm any party confiscation of household property on paper in order to create a record to be settled later. Ruan Renxing went further: he secretly led a group of his harvest company stalwarts to "steal back" building materials from the construction site of the Liangmen People's Commune Procurement Office. When his scheme was discovered, he was so afraid of being punished that he stayed inside his house for days on end, telling others that he was sick and unable to lead them in the autumn harvest campaign.[12]

Villagers also resisted the arbitrary adjustment of their village boundaries by Communist Party cadres who re-mapped natural village boundaries along lines that favored the labor conscription and control functions of the larger people's commune.[13] In the aftermath of the terrible Wei River flood of 1956, a debate had raged within Da Fo over whether to move the village to the high ground just east of Da Fo. It had been settled by compromise: the thirty most vulnerable families moved their homes to the outskirts of the old village. This put them a hair closer to Da Weicun than Da Fo, but they still were intimately connected with Da Fo by ties of kinship, marketing, and politics. When the Maoist call for establishing the public dining halls came, the Liangmen Commune leaders put these thirty families under the leadership of Da Weicun and its public dining hall system for the sake of administrative efficiency. This "state simplification," aimed at improving cadre legibility of the labor force by connecting villages or parts of villages into conveniently mapped public eating sites, ignored primordial affinities of the traditional village and villagers' emotional ties to place – ties that mattered greatly to local residents.[14] Bao Yuming provides a rare insight into how China's rural people saw the insensibility powering this Maoist managerial simplification and into how Da Fo's inhabitants responded to it:

Because the Liangmen People's Commune leaders thought we were about to enter communism, they did not care about which village we would belong to. But we villagers did not feel comfortable with changing our village affiliation. We resisted the idea of affiliating ourselves with Da Weicun, and we insisted that we have our own public dining hall. We fought with the commune leaders for about a month over this matter, and in the end we were allowed to have our own public dining hall.

We also opposed the idea of putting our land under the management of Da Weicun. The commune leaders wanted us to give up our land to Da Weicun, where we were scheduled to take our meals. But we did not agree. We wanted to keep it for ourselves.

[11] Bao Zian, interview, June 26, 2001.
[12] Zheng Jintian, interview, June 22, 2001.
[13] For this logic, see Schurmann, *Ideology and Organization*, 456–57, 471–73, 486.
[14] As Scott's work would anticipate. *Seeing Like a State*, 30–44, 232–33.

The commune leaders mostly came from other places, and many of them were not real farmers. They did not understand the mentality of farmers. In the autumn of 1958, we decided to cut the millet and other crops before the harvest was fully mature, so that the people from Da Weicun could not get our harvest first. With this harvest in hand, we set up our own public dining hall at this time. That is why our dining hall started one month later than the main dining halls in Da Fo.[15]

Bao Yuming's testimony reminds us that villagers' small acts of resistance did sometimes manage to affect changes in the Maoist plan in the early days of communal agriculture. Perhaps it was such small concessions, in combination with the uncommon abundance of food available in the public dining halls during their first months and the villagers' trust in their leaders' promise of an end to famine, that initially convinced Da Fo's villagers to go along with the larger, more radical transformations of the Great Leap Forward.

Runaway Procurement and the Causes of the Famine

As we have seen, Da Fo's villagers enjoyed the abundant food supplied by their public dining halls in the first months after they opened. In fact, there was a tendency in many villages across Henan and China for rural people to overindulge in the food supplied. Even in Da Fo, some of the poorest villagers listened to the party leaders who equated this pig-out with the promise of communism. If the old habits of austerity worked against wasting food, the free handouts sometimes did help prepare the way for future scarcity. In Wan Li village, Feidong County, Anhui province, for instance, the party cadres in charge of the public dining halls dispensed food to people without keeping tabs on supply, carelessly distributing the portion of the grain crop normally reserved for seed, thereby leaving the collective with little to plant for the next harvest.[16] In this instance, a burst of excessive consumption jeopardized the survival chances of villagers.

Taking such episodes to be indicative of a larger trend, Gene Hsing Chang and Guanzhong James Wen locate the primary cause of the famine of the Great Leap Forward not in the food availability declines and the entitlement failures to which classical theorists of famines point but rather in the failure of consumption efficiency, presumably associated with "irrational" food consumption habits fostered by the public dining hall system.[17] Perhaps there is some merit in this view; surely Da Fo's history is in keeping with one of its premises, summarized well by the late D. Gale Johnson: "The decline in food output . . . was not itself sufficient to precipitate famine."[18] In advancing this "irrational consumption" thesis, however, Chang and Wen make several other assumptions that must be tested against the everyday public dining hall encounters of rural people in a well-defined

[15] Bao Yuming, interview, June 21, 2001.
[16] Thaxton and Wang, "Power, Disentitlement, and Life Chances," 13.
[17] Chang and Wen, "Communal Dining" and "Food Availability," 157–66.
[18] Johnson, "China's Great Famine," 126.

rural place like Da Fo. For one thing, Chang and Wen assume that the traditional frugal subsistence-focused habits of Chinese farmers were supplanted by new habits of irrational and wasteful food use, so the irresponsible popular overconsumption of food available via the public mess halls became the primary trigger of the famine. Moreover, they assume that from the beginning to the end of the Great Leap Forward, villagers were able to consume as much of the freely supplied public dining hall food as they wished and that there was popular overconsumption of such grain well into the famine period – that is, right up until the dining halls were dismantled.[19]

Da Fo's Great Leap survivors hold a complex memory of the public dining hall system and its impact on survival that does not resonate well with the Chang-Wen thesis. For one thing, Da Fo, like many villages in Henan, Anhui, and Shandong, enjoyed a bumper wheat harvest in 1958, and villagers naturally celebrated by eating more in the aftermath of the harvest, which corresponded with the establishment of the public dining halls and the traditional autumn harvest dinner, often a community affair. But once this postharvest feast was over, people went back to frugal habits of food consumption, or so they say. In the autumn quarter following the 1958 bumper wheat harvest, people in Da Fo seldom ate more than was needed. Undoubtedly some food was wasted in this period of plenty, but this waste apparently was partly the product of popular discontent with the public dining hall takeover of the family management of food supply.[20] Bao Guangming explains:

At the beginning of the public dining hall, everybody was allowed to eat as much as he could.... Therefore, some people were less careful in preserving food, and some people threw food away carelessly. But some people were not happy with the public dining hall, and they threw away food intentionally to protest. Most people who were angry with the public dining hall could not speak out openly, because they would have been struggled in public [i.e., subjected to public criticism by the leaders]. They could only protest quietly and covertly.[21]

At this time, elderly villagers spread a quiet rumor, declaring that the Old God in Heaven would punish the leaders who carelessly promoted overindulgence. Reflecting on this wisdom of the elders many decades later, Lu Xiuli says, "they were proven right, for in the end we suffered great hunger."[22] At the same time, villagers suffered cultural violence, as these same Da Fo party leaders destroyed the Temple of the Lord of Heaven and dismantled its bell for the steel-making campaign.[23]

In Da Fo, grain rationing quickly put an end to the so-called overconsumption that occurred on the heels of the bumper wheat harvest of 1958. Zheng Jintian

[19] Chang and Wen, "Food Availability," 158, 163.
[20] Bao Zian, interview, June 26, 2001.
[21] Bao Guangming, interview, July 12, 2000.
[22] Lu Xiuli, interview, September 10, 2002.
[23] Yu Jianli, interview, September 20, 2002.

remembers, "In the beginning, people were happy about the public dining halls, as they were allowed to eat as much as they could. The food was not bad, and we ate more frequently than ever before. But it lasted only a few months before the public dining halls began to ration food."[24] Because dire hunger did not set in within Da Fo until a year later, we cannot correlate the overconsumption of public mess hall food with famine. By the time the desperation of early 1960 had arrived, overconsumption was a practice of at least three harvests past. Recalling the time when big baskets full of wheat bread were placed on the tables of Da Fo's dining halls and when villagers ate to their hearts' delight, Bao Dongzhi confirms the important aspect of this episode:

Within several months we consumed nearly all of our wheat bread supply. By the time we finished the autumn harvesting and planting [in 1958], we began to realize that we would not be able to eat like that for long. Therefore, we began to conserve our grain. Each person in Da Fo was given some grain coupons, and thereafter he got a share of food with the coupons. Equal to one *jin* of grain per day, the grain was enough for one steamed bun and one bowl of porridge, so it was enough to get by on.[25]

But was it really? The question begs a final qualification: the "freely supplied" food of the commons was actually the product of a tightly regulated system of state food distribution aimed at procuring the maximum amount of grain for the state by keeping rural people at bare subsistence – at best. Everyone in Da Fo knew that the delivery of family grain harvests to brigade party leaders was not a matter of choice: each household was ordered to turn over all of its grain. Few saw the food grain returned to them via the public dining hall as "free," for not only did the allocated grain ration not reflect the amount of grain taken away by the commune, its primary function was to restrict consumption.[26] Furthermore, the grain ration was not constant. The greater the harvest expectations of Wu Zhipu and the Henan provincial Maoists, the more grain Da Fo's party leaders gave up to the Liangmen People's Commune grain silos and the more the daily grain ration fell, from the promised minimum of one *jin* per day in the fall of 1958 to one-half *jin* following the summer of 1959 to one-fourth *jin* in the spring of 1960. Each cut correlated with an aggressive Maoist attempt to appropriate more of the harvest. The priority, now, was to produce a "grain surplus" for the requisitioning state at any cost.

Da Fo's history challenges not only Chang and Wen's overconsumption thesis but other scholarly attempts to explain the reasons for the Great Leap Forward Famine as well. On the eve of October 1, 1962, Zhou Enlai linked the Great Leap's failure with the impact of climate on agriculture. A number of pro-Mao commentators subsequently echoed the notion that bad weather conditions had

[24] Zheng Jintian, interview, June 22, 2001.
[25] Bao Dongzhi, interview, June 24, 2001.
[26] I agree with Li's wisdom that the grain ration actually placed a "limit on consumption," *Fighting Famine*, 357.

triggered a fall in crop yields in the North China region during the "three difficult years," claiming this was an important reason for the food crisis of 1960.[27] Even if this were true for North China in general, the impact of climatic change on the harvest output of specific counties, communes, and villages varied considerably. At no point between 1958 and 1961 did Da Fo village undergo a weather-related life-imperiling drop in crop yields. On the contrary, grain yields were good: 1958 saw bumper harvests for June wheat, summer corn, and October sorghum; 1959 saw good cereal yields across all three harvests; and 1960, even considering the minor drop in the amount of the autumn sorghum crop harvest, was on the whole good too.[28]

Let us ponder the year 1960 from the vantage point of two kinds of data: oral testimony derived from popular memory and published county records. According to villagers, the June wheat harvest of 1960 was good, and the September corn was also good, but due to heavy rains and minor flooding fall sorghum fell to only two-thirds of normal output. Overall, in their testimony, 1960 was a year in which crops were fair to middling. There was a spring drought in Dongle in 1960, but the drought did not affect Da Fo. In fact, the amount of rainfall for both Da Fo and Dongle in 1960 was 666 mm, or approximately 62 mm above the yearly average rainfall for Dongle County in the same period (604.1 mm for the period 1960–80). Compare this to the year 1966, when the turbulence of the Cultural Revolution combined with the rain god's stinginess (248 mm of rainfall) to threaten agricultural output in all of Dongle.[29] In this year of serious spring and autumn droughts, there was no significant decline in crop yield, and there was no food shortage, not to mention famine, in Da Fo. In short, something other than a climatic problem must have engendered the famine of the Great Leap Forward in Da Fo.

Whereas several insightful scholarly works have documented a fall in grain output per capita over the Great Leap period for China and a few of its provinces,[30] this claim has never been substantiated for a single Chinese village.[31] As we have seen, the notion that the Great Leap Forward Famine was due to falling grain yields does not hold up against the memory of Da Fo's inhabitants. Yields across the three years of the Great Leap averaged 200 *jin* per *mu* to 230 *jin* per *mu*, up 80 to 110 *jin* per *mu* over the pre-1949 period. Let us, therefore, focus specifically on

[27] On the Zhou Enlai speeches on inclimate weather, see Dutt, "Some Problems of China's Rural Communes," 125, 129; for the contention that bad weather contributed to the calamity, see Berger, "China Today: Walking on Two Legs," 352–55; Hinton, *Shenfan*, 229, 242–43, 303; and Liu, "China, Mao and Lincoln: Part 2, The Great Leap Forward Not All Bad."

[28] Pang Tinghua, interview, September 11, 1993; Jiang Weihai, interview, September 12, 1993; Bao Zhendao, interview, September 13, 1993.

[29] cf. Peng Youqiang, *Dongle Shilue*, 41–42, 44, 49.

[30] On Sichuan, see Bramall, *In Praise*, 318–19. On Henan, see Domenach, *Origins of the Great Leap*, 284.

[31] Friedman, Pickowicz, and Selden, *Chinese Village*, 242, is the partial but splendid exception.

1959, the year in which Da Fo's food supply crisis became critical, to determine as precisely as possible per capita food output versus per capita food availability and to flush out the relationship of Maoist rule to this crisis.

In the late autumn of 1958 Da Fo's cultivators planted 2,400 *mu* of wheat. The crop yield in the following summer was 230 *jin* per *mu*, or a total of 552,000 *jin*. In fact, however, the amount of harvested wheat was only 497,000 *jin*, because hungry villagers secretly ate 10 percent of the wheat crop prior to the harvest. According to Bao Yibin, the Da Fo party secretary at this time, the Liangmen People's Commune leaders, acting in the name of the Henan provincial government and the Maoist-led center, took 60 percent of the harvested wheat via procurement. The remaining 40 percent of the harvested grain (198,800 *jin*) was placed in a brigade granary – or so it was said. Actually, brigade leaders set aside 48,000 *jin* for seed and another 14,000 *jin* for animal feed. This left 136,000 *jin* of harvested wheat in the granary. But 4 percent of the 198,800 *jin* of stored grain was set aside as a famine relief fund, another 2 percent as a public welfare fund, and yet another 15 percent as an administrative fund. When this sum of 41,748 is subtracted from 136,000, Da Fo was left with 94,252 *jin* of grain for its subsistence needs, or about 64.1 *jin* per person.

Thus, if we compare the actual grain output with the amount of the harvested grain crop left in the village from the summer wheat harvest of 1959, we arrive at the conclusion that per capita wheat output was not falling. The crop yield was rising to 230 *jin* per *mu*, or 110 *jin* over the pre-1949 average high of 120 *jin* per *mu*, so the grain output per capita was at least 375.5 *jin*, or only 24.5 *jin* short of what villagers could get by on annually. However, grain availability *after Maoist state appropriation* stood at only 61.4 *jin* per capita from the summer harvest. In other words, the Communist Party–led state had appropriated nearly four-fifths of the harvested wheat of this Henan village in the second summer of the Great Leap Forward! It was for this reason, and not because the crop yield was poor, that people in Da Fo became fearful over the perceived lack of food supply in the summer of 1959.

A similar pattern of appropriation prevailed for the fall harvest of 1959, so per capita grain availability for the entire year was approximately 128.2 *jin*. That same fall, the daily grain ration in the public dining halls was reduced from 0.8 to 0.6 *jin* per person, leaving each villager with 60.8 *jin* per year. In practice, this meant that grain availability after harvest distribution – assuming that distribution was indeed equal – and after grain rationing was at best 190 *jin* per capita, so villagers were short approximately 210 to 220 *jin* of their minimum subsistence grain requirement. This formulation corroborates popular memory of the existential dilemma facing Da Fo residents on the eve of the Great Leap Forward Famine, for many villagers remember they were 217.5 to 220 *jin* short of basic subsistence grain in January 1960, right before the grain ration was reduced again in the spring of that year.

In studying rural Sichuan, Bramall discovered that food output did in fact decline in 1959.[32] However, the decline in and of itself apparently was not the key proximate cause of the Great Leap famine. The evidence on Da Fo suggests a different picture: food *output* by and large did not decline, but there was an astonishing loss of food *availability* associated with Maoist state appropriation. This opened the door to famine, and the problem was compounded by poor government planning in late 1958. According to Pang Yilu,

The government had plans to plant more wheat that year, and, in some cases, we did not have time to harvest the corn before we had to plant the wheat. That was due to the very bad leadership of the Da Fo party leaders. . . . As farmers we should have known better. Even if they told us to leave the corn in the fields to rot, we should not have listened to them. . . . We were not responsible. In the end, we were punished for our irresponsibility.[33]

Maoist pressure to produce more and more wheat for the state, neglecting Da Fo's long-standing pattern of diversified agriculture, further exacerbated the problem of food availability in the first year of the Great Leap Forward.

Given the fairly good harvest of 1959, Da Fo's inhabitants still hoped that their food supply would be sufficient, for the state supposedly was going to compensate them for grain delivered to its bins. This hope was dashed by the pressures within the hierarchy of the party-state to overreport the actual crop yield and the subsequent bloated harvest estimates of *fukua feng*, or "the wind of exaggeration." Although the harvest of 1959 was better than average, local harvest company leaders Bao Zhendao, Pang Haijin, and Ruan Renxing all overreported Da Fo's actual crop yields. Once commune officials received this blockbuster report they happily raised their procurement goals for Da Fo.[34] Zheng Tianbao recaptures the political fervor guiding the procurement excesses from the middle of 1959:

Actually, the party officials in Liangmen People's Commune decided how much grain was given over at the time. The village leaders overreported their production to the commune, as everyone was trying to overreport grain production. Why was this the case? At the time, if one production brigade head within Liangmen Commune reported that his village produced four hundred or five hundred *jin* per *mu*, and if yet another brigade leader reported only two hundred per *mu*, then the commune leaders would place the second leader on a platform and criticize him. They would compel him to confess why his village had produced less. In this political climate, everyone was afraid of becoming a target of criticism, so the brigade leaders overreported in both 1958 and 1959.

The Liangmen People's Commune leaders did it because they had pressure from the Dongle County government, and the Dongle County leaders did it because they were under pressure from the Henan provincial leadership. Our village and company leaders did it too, for they felt pressure to overreport to their superiors. In 1959 it was too late to reverse this trend. No one dared to resist it because at that moment there was an atmosphere of madness surrounding the government drive for grain collection.[35]

[32] Bramall, *In Praise*, 329, 333.
[33] Pang Yilu, interview, July 31, 2004.
[34] See also Chan, "Campaign for Agricultural Development," 65.
[35] Zheng Tianbao, interview, August 10, 1990.

It was this "atmosphere of madness," of pressure to please upper-level Henan politicians looking for promotions from Wu Zhipu's pro-Maoist hierarchy, that triggered the excessive grain procurement documented by Thomas P. Bernstein, Nicholas Lardy, and Alfred Chan.[36] Bao Yibin, Da Fo's key party liaison to Liangmen People's Commune during the Great Leap, has a keen understanding of the role of party-driven procurement in fostering the famine of 1960. "At the time," he says, "the commune authorities in Liangmen district were afraid that our village leaders would not report the true figures of their grain production. They compelled the leaders to report high production figures. To make sure of this, they came to Da Fo to see if the grain was hidden by our leaders."[37]

There was great urgency given to procurement in the "second radical phase" of the Great Leap Forward in 1959–60.[38] Thus, in the summer of 1959, after the better-than-normal wheat harvest, Liangmen People's Commune officials collected a record "surplus" of Da Fo's grain crop and shortly thereafter reduced the grain ration of villagers to half a *jin* per person per day. In the last half of this year people were allowed less than half the food needed for survival, and even those who previously were nonplussed by unified purchase and sale began to resent it bitterly.[39]

The experience of Ruan Baozhang's family suggests how the ill effects of the grain procurement system on Da Fo villagers snowballed during the Great Leap Forward.[40] Partly because his family had benefited from land reform and partly because he was the only young male laborer in an eight-person household, Ruan Baozhang had volunteered to participate in the early cooperative movement. His household needed four hundred *jin* per capita per year for subsistence. Prior to Liberation his father had made earth salt for the market to meet this figure; after land reform the family began to realize its requisite four hundred *jin* from grain production and melon sales and was secure at this level in 1951. In 1952, when the Ruan household joined the first elementary cooperative in Da Fo, its income dropped to three hundred *jin* per capita because one-half of the grain of the co-op was distributed according to the workforce of member households. In 1953 and 1954 the Ruan household got the same income, but only because of the charity of the co-op leaders.

In 1955–56, the first year of the APCs, the Ruans were still getting three hundred *jin*, but again with a handout from the cooperative, for now 100 percent of the cooperative harvest was distributed according to labor force input principles. Those with few working family members were given supplementary grain. Within the year, the APC movement in Da Fo proved incapable of meeting the

[36] Bernstein, "Stalinism, Famine, and Chinese Peasants"; Lardy, "Chinese Economy Under Stress"; Chan, *Mao's Crusade*.
[37] Bao Yibin, interview, August 15, 1990.
[38] Bernstein, "Stalinism, Famine, and Chinese Peasants," 368.
[39] Zheng Yunxiang, interview, September 15, 1993.
[40] Ruan Baozhang, interview, September 14, 1993.

grain requirements of the Ruan household – or any other. In July of 1956, one month after the Ruan family had reaped its wheat harvest, the Wei River flood engulfed Da Fo, spoiling the stored wheat. The CCP-led Dongle County government quickly came to the rescue, providing relief grain and a fresh supply of fish and fuel for the quarter following the flood. Thereafter, the Ruans, along with others, were given a coupon booklet that allowed them to acquire grain from the state at an affordable price. In 1957, with the APC disbanded, the Ruans got four hundred *jin* per member, putting them back at the pre-cooperative level. The reason grain income leaped back to subsistence level standards in 1957, according to Ruan Baozhang, is that the flood had enriched the land, making for a good wheat harvest that summer.

The bumper harvest of the first year of the Great Leap Forward was a different story. As Ruan explains, "In 1958 the wheat, peanuts, cotton, and corn all were bountiful, but we received little of the harvest because the public dining hall started in August. We were allowed to eat only one *jin* per day, which came from the collective dining hall."[41] Thus the yearly per capita grain intake of the Ruans fell approximately forty *jin* in 1958, the so-called "year of plenty." In 1959 virtually all of the harvest went to the collective, and the Ruans got all of their grain through the public dining hall. They were allowed to eat only 280 *jin* per person, which they supplemented by planting twenty *mu* of turnips and carrots and by secretly eating green corn prior to the fall harvest. Grain consumption was drastically reduced again the following year because the public dining hall ration was far less. Because the government took most of the harvest via procurement, recalls Ruan, there was no incentive to work in the fields and properly attend the wheat crop. Ruan Baozhang and his wife secretly ate more corn from the collective fields in 1960; they also borrowed money from a cousin, using it to purchase bread on the black market.

As Ruan's story makes clear, there is little reason to doubt that the stiffening terms of procurement seriously hurt villagers. If, however, we focus only on the exchange between state and village society that was implicit in unified purchase and sale – that is, the state price for grain that villagers turned over to the government – we cannot fully grasp the nature of the political appropriation that precipitated the radical decline in food availability in Da Fo during 1959–60. In this phase, something other than more efficient procurement, as it originally was intended, was at work in the Communist Party–state relationship with Da Fo. Unbridled revenue gathering by the Communist Party replaced any government giving, supplanting the two-way exchange system of procurement, which had been imbalanced but tolerable. Let us trace the progression of this development as it unfolded in Da Fo's relationship with the Liangmen People's Commune.

[41] Ibid.

In 1958, at the outset of the Great Leap, the price the commune level officials set for grain purchased from farmers in Liangmen district was 0.14 *yuan* per *jin* of wheat, which was sixteen cents less per *jin* than they would have earned from selling the wheat on the market.[42] Although Da Fo's farmers were not paid until six months after they had given up their crops, they were paid, and they were able to use the payments to buy grain back from the state if necessary.[43] This pattern of state purchase disappeared in the second year of the Great Leap Forward, when villagers waited in vain for the Liangmen People's Commune leaders to pay them for their summer wheat delivery to the commune. From roughly the second half of 1959 up to the end of 1960, Liangmen Commune officials did not pay villagers for their grain deliveries. The procurement system was taken over by the commune-level agents of the Henan Maoists, and Bao Zhilong, now a pivotal player in the commune, went along with this radical act of state greed.

Whereas the price of grain purchased by the state had never satisfied farmers, prior to 1959–60 at least there had been a price. Commencing late in the second year of the Great Leap, however, the amount of grain people were required to give up to the state had increased, while the price they received for their grain "sales" to the commune plummeted, reaching zero in the summer of 1960. Bao Zhigen, the leader of the First Harvest Company and an agent of the party-state appropriation frenzy in 1959–60, recalls: "The price of grain was decided by commune officials. Actually, we eventually received nothing for the grain, so it was no longer a matter of 'selling' the grain to the state. We just turned it over to them without getting anything in return."[44]

People in Da Fo have a good memory of the institutional origins of the deep subsistence crisis of 1960. They tell us that Da Fo's Communist Party leaders, heeding the cue of the party stalwarts who had moved into the leadership hierarchy of the Liangmen People's Commune, overreported the yields to make the commune and county leaders look good in the eyes of Wu Zhipu and the Mao-led national leadership.[45] They remember that Bao Zhilong, the Da Fo party patriarch who had assumed power in the commune, was a principal collaborator in this exaggeration. "Because Bao Zhilong was illiterate," says Pang Huiyin,

he did not fully understand the government's policy. Also, he was too eager to please Wu Zhipu and the upper government leaders. He boasted about our grain yields, and the commune government leaders thought we had more grain, and thus they came to take more and more grain from the village. Bao Zhilong could not contradict himself, and so he let the commune take more and more grain from us.[46]

[42] Bao Zhendao, interview, September 3, 1993.
[43] Bao Zhigen, interview, August 11, 1990.
[44] Ibid.
[45] Bao Yuming, interview, June 21, 2001.
[46] Pang Huiyin, interview, July 20, 2000.

Bao Yuming explains the consequences:

Thus, when the upper government officials came to procure grain based on these exaggerated production figures, they did not know what was really going on. Even though the upper officials felt they had left more than enough grain for the villagers, we actually did not have enough grain for survival. The party leaders under pressure said the yield was four hundred *jin* per *mu*. So when the upper officials said, "We took away two hundred *jin* per *mu* and left two hundred *jin* for you," they simply assumed that we had more than enough food. But actually the two hundred *jin* was all we had at the time. When the Liangmen People's Commune leaders first realized what was happening in the village, they promised us that we would have no less than one *jin* per day, and they said no one would starve. But they did not keep their promise. They reduced the ration to 0.4 *jin* per day, after which we had to search for tree leaves and wild vegetables.[47]

By early 1960 the Maoist leaders of the Liangmen People's Commune had shipped virtually all of Da Fo's grain crop to commune storage bins, simultaneously discontinuing any payment back to the villagers. They were left with no way to buy back grain from the state. There was hardly any harvest left in the village, and starvation loomed.

Da Fo brigade party leaders responded by organizing the women to forage and cook wild vegetables to supplement the reduced food ration of the public dining halls. By early 1960, according to Bao Yuming, the ration was cut to 0.4 *jin*, which was woefully short of the customary standard of subsistence. By mid-1960 most villagers were at least 220 *jin* short of their minimum yearly food grain requirement. The result for the preponderant majority was a state of semi-starvation. Tang Guoyi, survivor of the 1942 Henan Famine and the famine of 1960, recalls that "the suffering was comparable with that of 1942." In both famines, according to Tang, people had very little flesh left on their bodies. The difference was that in 1960 they still were required to work in the fields all day.[48]

Escalating Demands for Labor

Of all the Communist Party regulations aimed at regimenting the rural population, those ordering work life were the most harmful. The work regulations in Da Fo posed a constant danger to family survival, and people remember them with great pain. When they articulate their anger over the Great Leap Forward, they nearly always focus on the ways commune and brigade party leaders compelled them to work. "The problem with the Great Leap Forward," recalls Bao Honglin,

was not only food shortage, but also the demand for everybody to come to work in the fields or to work on a project. Some leaders became simply crazy. The Dongle County leaders declared that we had to mobilize everybody to work to build socialism. On the

---

[47] Bao Yuming, interview, June 21, 2001.
[48] Tang Guoyi, interview, September 15, 1993. Also see Ruan Jing, interview, May 7, 1994; Bao Zhanghui, interview, May 2, 1994; Bao Yuming, interview, June 21, 2001.

surface, there was nothing wrong with a slogan like this. However, the Liangmen People's Commune and Da Fo village leaders would then push this policy to the extreme, taking it to mean that literally everybody, including the blind, had to do something. As long as you could move your body, you had to work in the collective fields or appear to be working in the fields.[49]

In addition to ordering women who had suffered foot-binding to work in Da Fo's collective fields and to travel long distances to make steel in Lin County,[50] Bao Zhilong and the commune leaders even pushed blind people to perform labor. Determined to take possession of all the bodies in the village for Mao's Great Leap experiment,[51] Da Fo's party activists organized a Mao Zedong Blind People's Thought Propaganda Team made up of the blind people who previously had been storytellers and made a living by fortune telling. The cadres also sent the village's six blind residents to go stand in the sun-baked fields, responding when queried by one astonished field worker that the bodies of the blind needed to receive the energizing warmth of Chairman Mao's radiant thought, so that they too could give to the collective good.[52] Blind people also were made to sleep in the fields with the rest of the workers.[53] Obsessed with finding a clear productive role for the blind, the Da Fo party leadership called on Ruan Renxing, head of the Second Harvest Company, to come up with a plan to justify their food rations, and Ruan did not disappoint. Before the collective period, farmers in Da Fo had used donkeys to push the stone mill to grind the wheat, and blind people were enlisted to cover the beasts' eyes while they worked. Now, in the frenzy of the Great Leap, Ruan Renxing declared that the blind would pull the millstone themselves, in place of donkeys. By deploying their labor in this way, the collective would save the step of covering up the donkeys' eyes, which was said to cause delays in refining the wheat.[54] This mindless act pleased the commune labor inspectors, who insisted that no one could go idle and still eat the food of the collective.

Pushing villagers to work around the clock, the party leaders organized Da Fo's school-age children to march and demonstrate in the streets, shouting slogans: "We will work during the day, we will work during the night; we will work all day and all night!"[55] By late 1959 many villagers barely had the energy to walk or hold their heads up, and yet in the months to follow they were ordered to dig a half *mu* of land in the day and a half *mu* at night, as part of the deep plowing campaign, which was undertaken in the mistaken belief that the deeper the farmers plowed, the larger the root systems of their crops would be. The result was predictable:

[49] Bao Honglin, interview, June 25, 2001.
[50] Tang Weilan, interview, July 31, 2006.
[51] See Mueggler, "Spectral Subversions," for the general point.
[52] Bao Zhendao, interview, September 3, 1993.
[53] Lin Xiuqie, interview, September 1, 2002.
[54] Zheng Jintian, interview, June 22, 2001; Bao Honglin, interview, June 25, 2001.
[55] Bao Gaojun, interview, July 12, 2000.

only those who cheated survived. Pang Renjing was not one of them. Zheng Jintian recounts the story:

Pang Renjing died during the Great Leap Forward. He died of exhaustion, not starvation. He was sixteen years old at the time. The Liangmen People's Commune leaders selected young and capable people to do the deep digging of the soil. Everybody tried to cheat. Instead of deep digging, most villagers would simply dig up part of the soil and then cover up the rest with dirt to make it look like they had done the deep digging. Pang Renjing was not smart enough to do that. He was honest, and he dug earnestly. As a result, he fell behind others. He worked harder and harder. In the end, he suffered from overexhaustion and an intestinal disorder. People tried to send him to Dongle County hospital, but he died on the way there.[56]

According to Mike Davis, physicians have observed the "destruction of the lining membrane of the lower bowel" as a classic sign of starvation-related deaths.[57] The deadly "intestinal disorders" that Da Fo's inhabitants came to associate with overwork and death in the Great Leap episode thus can be taken as a folk memory that reflects well-established medical knowledge to which the rural poor were not privy.

Some of the most pointed verbal battles between ordinary villagers and party leaders in Da Fo occurred over the right to take adequate rest breaks and to take leave for illnesses related to overwork. This latter issue in particular permanently scarred party relations with villagers. Although many people were laboring day and night for the collective and working themselves into a state of poor health, Bao Zhilong and his party clients pressed them to work even when they fell ill from working the collective fields, injured themselves, or had to take care of pressing family chores, often ignoring their most basic requirements for recuperation and renewal. Shortly after the Great Leap started, for example, Tang Wenjie, the head of a production team, became sick from overwork, and he appealed to Bao Zhilong to allow him to go home for some rest. Bao turned him down.[58]

The administrative confusion of the Great Leap Forward contributed to the exhaustion of the rural labor force.[59] During the first two years of the Great Leap, each level of government, including the central, provincial, prefectual, county, and commune-level governments, started up its own independent irrigation project, and all of these projects made demands for labor on the villages. "Part of the problem with the Great Leap Forward," says Bao Xufeng, "was that there were too many irrigation projects going on at the same time."[60] This problem was reflected in the labor claims of Liangmen People's Commune leaders,

---

[56] Zheng Jintian, interview, June 22, 2001.
[57] Davis, *Late Victorian Holocausts*, 40.
[58] Ruan Yulan, interview, July 9, 2002.
[59] On this point, see Friedman, Pickowicz, and Selden, *Revolution, Resistance, and Reform*, 7. Here I am more interested in the impact at the sub-county level, particularly how this chaos put villagers at risk.
[60] Bao Xufeng, interview, July 15, 2002.

and it affected farmers in Da Fo. Villagers were given too many work assignments, some of which overlapped and required the same individual to report to one work site right before or after he or she had been sent to a different site. Hence villagers remember running to Ji County, Sun County, and Dongle County irrigation projects on short notice, with hardly any time to prepare. The upper-level Maoist officials in charge of this disorder often failed to provide grain for the workforce, so the workers were required to "supplement" official supply. Although the workers needed more food to keep pace with the physical demands of these projects, they often went hungry and had the appearance of walking skeletons.[61]

The imposition of collectivist principles on individual households dealt a near fatal blow to market-focused entrepreneurship. As many astute China scholars have pointed out, the people's commune obligated villagers to participate in agricultural production activities continuously, spending at least twelve hours a day working in the collective-secured fields.[62] The Liangmen People's Commune leaders did not attempt to stop Da Fo's inhabitants from pursuing the selling of earth salt in the first year of the Great Leap, but few people had the time to produce or peddle salt, and almost everyone gave up the market due to physical exhaustion in the year following the establishment of the commune.[63]

The public dining hall food ration was linked to a coupon system. Da Fo party leaders not only were in charge of printing the coupons, they also decided who received them and threatened to withhold them from apparent slackers. Under the pressures of the Maoist wind of exaggeration, this coupon system was used not only to control any sign of popular overconsumption but also to lock villagers into a submarginal food regime founded on repression. In the post-1958 Communist Party crackdown, the threat of withdrawing the food coupon was invoked to prevent villagers from resisting the Maoists' increasingly unbearable labor demands. Because the Maoists had already undercut two of the most important means whereby people had traditionally defended their families against famine, the threat was terrifying.

Agricultural work was reorganized to serve the Maoist propaganda machine that trumpeted the miraculous progress of the Great Leap Forward. In practice this meant that Communist Party brigade and commune leaders, under severe pressure to impress the officials sent to the countryside by first party secretary Wu Zhipu and his network with astounding production achievements, frequently ordered collective field workers to literally drop everything and rush to organize some Potemkin village assemblage of a spectacular harvest. This practice of assembling village farmers to create false impressions of agricultural development

[61] 2002 interviews with Bao Xufeng, July 15; Bao Jiping, July 15; Pang Zhanglin, July 16; and Bao Dongzhi, July 17.
[62] Domes, *Socialism in the Chinese Countryside*, 33–34; Friedman, Pickowicz, and Selden, *Chinese Village*, 227.
[63] Ruan Shaobing and Pang Qinli, interviews, September 1, 1993.

was accentuated by Russian-inspired conventions of national progress in building socialism.[64] At the time of the Great Leap, the Dongle County and Liangmen People's Commune leaders were in awe of the unprecedented Sputnik launch by the Russians. They felt that China's agricultural production had to reflect something equally impressive.[65] Wanting to wow their superiors in the Henan provincial government with news of their swift-paced accomplishments, the Dongle County and Liangmen People's Commune leaders launched their own *fan xingwei* (satellites) by making villagers live in the collective fields, demanding that they accomplish two days' work in one day, and assigning each individual worker a quota. Only those who finished on time were allowed to eat in the public dining hall.[66] Few brigade-level party secretaries dared to openly resist this rush into satellite production. In responding to Maoist urgings to shoot up satellites, Da Fo's party leaders often ignored common sense. In 1959, they were ordered to finish the turnip harvest within a single day. Knowing this was impossible, the village party leaders ordered villagers to whack off the top parts of the turnip plants, creating the illusion that the turnips had been harvested. Much of the turnip crop was lost in this madness.[67]

In addition to the irrigation projects, there were other large-scale work projects designed to build rural infrastructure for modern industrial development that placed unreasonable demands on villagers' labor. In August of 1959, Da Fo was ordered to simultaneously mobilize its stalwart workers for participation in the Lin County steel-production drive and the Ji County river dig project, known as the Tong Tin River Dig. The food grain ration promised to the local people who labored on these projects was forty-five *jin* per person per month, which at that point was nearly three times the daily grain ration allocated to each of Da Fo's residents. Not surprisingly, the project drew more than one hundred "volunteers" to Lin County and fifty to Ji County.

The Ji County project, which aimed to deepen and widen the riverbed so that it could accommodate the larger vessels that industrialization required, took six months, twice as long as planned, mainly because people in the camps did not have enough food. The forty-five-*jin* grain ration was insufficient to fuel the tremendous amounts of physical energy needed to do the work in the first place, and when the Anyang prefecture and Dongle County governments failed to provide this promised amount, the Liangmen People's Commune supervisors went ahead and reduced the ration while insisting that people work longer and harder. Moreover, according to Bao Hongwen, "the party leaders in charge of the public dining halls at the Ji County work site stole the grain, so ordinary

---

[64] Becker is excellent on this point. *Hungry Ghosts*, 84, 87.
[65] Bao Zhidan, interview, June 26, 2001.
[66] Bao Zhongxin, interview, June 23, 2001.
[67] Bao Zhendao, interview, September 3, 1993.

workers could eat only half of the promised daily grain ration."[68] Within a few weeks the workers at the river dig were asking relatives back in Da Fo to send food. Wives and children carried food packages to male family members at these labor camps, and forty days into the Tong Tin River Dig, Da Fo's party leaders organized thirteen horse-drawn carts to send its best food to the fifty river-site workers. Unfortunately, Bao Ziyan, the Da Fo party cadre in charge of the river-dig unit, was an alcoholic. The Communist Party leaders in charge of workers from other brigades discovered that if they could get Bao Ziyan drunk, they could steal some of the grain sent by Da Fo. "Consequently, although Da Fo sent a lot of grain to the river dig site," remembers Zheng Jintian, "our people were not able to benefit as much as planned."[69] By December 1959 food pilfering from the labor camp dining halls and taking unauthorized leaves of absence back to Da Fo had become commonplace. These two counteractions were associated with endless quarrels and confrontations with Bao Zhilong and the other Liangmen People's Commune officials overseeing the multi-brigade "volunteers," who by now understood they were entangled in a system of endless corvée labor.

Two other serious problems illuminate the threads of political madness that bound villagers to these labor camps. The projects were undertaken over long periods and continued regardless of changing weather conditions. In the Lin County steel-production drive of 1959, Da Fo's volunteers were forced to walk all the way to the project in a torrential rainstorm. Arriving wet, chilled, and exhausted, they immediately had to go to work. The situation in Ji County was even worse. The work on the Tong Tin River Dig lasted into the winter months of 1960, and former workers recall that they had to dig the icy river even when freezing and howling winds brought the first snowfall.[70]

And, on a psychological level, the atmosphere of the labor camps was dispiriting. The Maoist zealots in charge of the Ji County labor camp all but obliterated the cultural festivities and holiday celebration days that brought joy and reaffirmed community. Bao Yuming remembers:

We went to Ji County to dig the Tong Tin River on August 15 of the lunar calendar, the date of the traditional Chinese moon festival, a time of celebrating the harvest and family reunion. But the Great Leap Forward changed all of that, because immediately after the harvest we were sent to dig the river. Worse, the supervisors there came up with the idea of working four sessions per day. This would have been all right if it were only for one or two days, but when they forced us to do this kind of labor every day for long hours, few people were willing to work hard, especially during the holiday season. We farmers always took long holidays during the Chinese New Year. After a long year of hard work, we expected a long New Year's break to relax and enjoy good food with our families and

---

[68] Bao Hongwen, interview, July 11, 2000.
[69] Zheng Jintian, interview, June 22, 2001.
[70] Zhou Weihai, interview, September 1, 1993.

friends. But we were forced to stay in Ji County for the Chinese New Year. Perhaps this made sense for the party leaders, who wanted to finish the river dig project as soon as possible, but it did not make sense for villagers. As a result, we all slacked off. We were not able to eat dumplings, the traditional food for the New Year. Thus we were unhappy and troubled about working there.[71]

Hanging back from working hard was not an option, however. The Liangmen People's Commune labor supervisors in Ji County all but eliminated any opportunity for sleep. People were required to rise at four o'clock in the morning, walk one and a half hours from their village base camp to the Tong Tin River Dig site, work three full hours until they could take breakfast at 8:30 a.m., and then work a shift that went until midnight. A few of the key supervisors of this river dig project were from Da Fo, and they required Da Fo's contingent to work until 1:00 a.m. to show their "special enthusiasm" for the project. After this work shift there was always a one-hour meeting. By the time people went to bed it was already two in the morning, so they had only two hours of sleep. "It was all right for a few days," recalls Bao Peisun, "but it was simply impossible for an extended period. The whole project lasted nearly half a year. I only worked there for sixty days. It was too much for me."[72]

Virtually all of the Da Fo participants survived the Tong Tin River Dig project,[73] but some of their counterparts from other villages in Liangmen People's Commune did not. Several men from Taigu died of high fevers caught working in freezing water; one from Wanxiuzhuang died from eating bad white turnips served in the dining halls, which made everyone sick for several days. There were no reliable doctors assigned to the work site. The frightening possibility of dying, underscored by the spread of the condition of edema throughout the Ji County labor camp, sent a stream of Da Fo's weakened and underweight volunteers back home without permission in early 1960, despite the rumors that the food in Da Fo was inferior both in quantity and quality to that in Ji County.[74]

The extravillage work assignments took a significant toll on Da Fo's ability to sustain agricultural development and promote family health among its own villagers. Having sent nearly eighty strong male farm hands to the Lin County steel-production labor camp in the second half of 1958, for example, the workforce available to bring in the fall harvest was insufficient. The wheat to be harvested the following June, usually planted in early November, was neglected and not tended properly. "Villagers were asked to work day and night," recalls Zheng Xiaoquan, "but when people were too tired, they could not do a very good job."[75]

---

[71] Bao Yuming, interview, June 21, 2001.
[72] Bao Peisun, interview, September 15, 1995.
[73] One of the Da Fo workers died after contracting a disease in Ji County, but he died a few months after returning to the village. Bao Xiandai, interview, July 5, 2006.
[74] Ibid.
[75] Zheng Xiaoquan, interview, May 6, 1994.

Because they were sent away to the camps, some of the most competent younger adult members of Da Fo were unable to take care of their aged parents back in the village, who in some instances had to shoulder an inordinate burden of labor in harvest companies depleted of younger, stronger adults. When serious illness, commonly hunger-related, struck families, they were without healthy members to see to their needs. Reports of parents being injured after fights with company harvest leaders over food supplies often reached Lin County too late; as a result, by the time a son or daughter returned to look after his or her injured parent, it was too late.[76]

The Gender Bias of Maoist Forced Labor and the Attack on Motherhood

Gail Hershatter has pointed out that participation in the collectivization of the 1950s must be understood partly in terms of the tensions between the "campaign time" of party cadres and the "domestic time" of village women, many of whom were fearful of the danger posed by leaving the relatively secure space of the home.[77] In answer to Da Fo women's concerns about making the "leap" from domestic time to campaign time, party leaders drew women into the revolutionary space of the people's commune by promising them that it would lessen the burdens of domestic time. In return for leaving the home to participate in field work and far-flung river channel projects while entrusting their food requirements to the public dining halls and giving up their infants and small children to commune-sponsored day care facilities, Da Fo's women were reassured that they would be paid a fair wage for their labor, and, interestingly, that the ordinary burdens of household labor, such as leaving the village to gather firewood on back roads filled with untrustworthy strangers, would also be lifted from their shoulders. At the start of the Great Leap, these promises seem to have raised hopes that a new, more exciting and fulfilling life was in store for them.

In reality, however, women were treated worse and were even less protected than men. The Great Leap slogan in Dongle County was that men and women were equal, so women had to work like men and perform involuntary labor in the collective fields. Nonetheless, several women who worked in the fields day and night recall that "there was no salary and no payment," that by late 1958 the public mess hall was not providing enough grain to eat, and that day care services were inadequate.[78] Yet it seems that Da Fo's women actually played

---

[76] Ibid.
[77] Hershatter, "Gender of Memory," 2006, 3, 6.
[78] Interviews with Huang Fengyan, Zheng Fuqing, and Pang Aichen (all women who worked in Da Fo's collective fields and who were transferred to work in the fields of other brigades), September 12, 1993. These interviews suggest that once the Great Leap experiment got into trouble, women were not paid in work points but rather in public dining hall food, and that whether food would be paid to them and how much were decided at the whim of the dining hall food dispensers.

an even more important role in field work than men,[79] because so many of the males were sent to dig irrigation ditches and rivers and produce steel outside of the village. In the past, Da Fo's male farmers had used winter to recuperate and rest up for the agricultural cycle of the new year, but now they were sent to dig and repair irrigation facilities in the winter quarter. "Consequently," recalls Li Shulan, "most farm work was done by women, and women were not as good as men at farming. As a result, yields were very negatively affected by the lack of a sufficient labor force back in the village."[80]

Increasingly, women had to work in the collective fields for very long hours, and they too became victims of the Maoist regime of forced labor. Pressed by male harvest company heads to assume the burden of field work, the women were deprived of sleep. Ruan Yulan, a woman who at age twenty-two was pressured to serve as the head of a production team under Tang Guoyi, sheds light on just what this meant in practice:

During the Great Leap, I tried very hard not to be a production team leader because I did not want to lead the women in the team to work. At the time, people did not have enough food to eat, and they did not have enough time to sleep, so how could they be expected to work hard? I did not want to make hard feelings among the women in my team. But in the end, I had no choice.

Many women did not want to work, and they fell asleep in the fields frequently. I remember that one day most of the women in my team fell asleep in the sweet potato fields. Because we did not finish our work, Tang Guoyi and the other production team leaders began to complain about me – they said I was no good.

Still, we were so sleepy at the time that we often fell asleep while at work. Sometimes when we woke up we were so disoriented we did not know where we were. Many times we were forced to work so hard we had to take off our shirts. We had to compete with the other teams to see who could work the fastest. Visitors came here constantly. Whenever we saw these outsiders, we began to work harder, and we had to shout many slogans to show that we were enthusiastic about our work.[81]

For Da Fo's women, the Great Leap Forward delivered great damage to the most elementary of female rights. Bao Zhilong and the Da Fo party leaders repeatedly overlooked the need for women to suspend their field work duties when menstruating. Yin Fengxiu was thirty-eight at the start of the Great Leap. She remembers that "most of the women had to work in the fields like the men. They did not get any special treatment during their menstrual periods, because the leaders did not allow them to take a leave of absence."[82]

The duties of motherhood also came under attack. Though Dongle County leaders announced that new mothers would receive a fifteen-to-thirty-day maternity leave, this commitment was not always honored. Excepting a few Da Fo wives

---

[79] Gao, "China's Modernization," 80–83. Gao shows that women assumed more agricultural tasks in the Great Leap of the 1950s.
[80] Li Shulan, interview, July 18, 2002.
[81] Ruan Yulan, interview, July 9, 2002.
[82] Yin Fengxiu, interviews, July 10–11, 2002.

whose husbands worked for the Liangmen People's Commune, pregnant women had to work in the fields right up until a few days before giving birth, and, in comparison to the pre-collective period, when they performed light, household-based chores at a freely determined pace, this was extremely hard and physically debilitating labor, the terms of which were dictated by men who were not family members.[83] In much of rural China, women customarily sat out a month or so after giving birth, a practice known as *zuo yuezi*.[84] They were not allowed to do any work other than recover and nurture their newborns in this period. But Da Fo's Great Leap leaders pressed them to return to work in the collective fields only a week or so after delivery. Although the brigade-level units of Liangmen People's Commune supposedly provided day nursery services for infants, in reality some of the mothers of newborn babies had to breastfeed the infants in the fields, and elderly women assigned to the nurseries shuttled the babies back and forth for feedings, exposing both mothers and babies to the elements.[85] According-ing to the Dongle County government policy, the mothers of newborn children were entitled to better food, including a few pounds of sugar and wheat flour, but Ruan Yulan recalls that "sometimes people did not get it despite the government's policy that they should get it."[86] Some of these same mothers carried their babies on their backs while doing manual labor in the day and cuddled them at night under makeshift tents in the fields, all the while praying they would not be forced to supplant their breast milk with the dreaded public dining hall porridge – a common occurrence. "In fact," recalls Pang Guihua, "some women lost their babies to poor nutrition and hard work in the fields."[87]

Precisely because men were engaged in work outside of Da Fo for long stints and women assumed the burden of field work, taking sick leave was exceedingly difficult for women. Many remember bitterly that denial was the order of the day. In late 1958, Huang Fengyan, a member of the First Harvest Company under Bao Zhigen, fell ill from overwork. For five days, she could not even lift herself from bed to go to the collective fields. Through a friend, Huang was able to persuade the company cook to let her use her grain ration to nourish herself while resting in her home, thereby avoiding the stressful, energy-draining ordeal of taking her meals in the public dining hall, which was located a long distance from her quarters. But Bao Zhigen dispatched a female leader of the harvest company to Huang's bedside to ask how she could be sick for as long as five days. Huang was required to give back the grain and to take her meals with the masses. "I was so angry when this happened," recalls Huang, "that I was sick for seven more days."[88]

---

[83] I am indebted to Kimberley Ens Manning for educating me about how to interpret my oral history evidence in this section. Personal correspondence, August 3–4, 2006.
[84] See Evans, *Women and Sexuality*, 149.
[85] Yuan Suting, interview, September 22, 2002.
[86] Ruan Yulan, interview, July 9, 2002.
[87] Pang Guihua, interview, July 11, 2002.
[88] Huang Fengyan, interview, September 12, 1993.

Andrew B. Kipnis has stressed that *ganqing*, or feelings of human concern, contributed to wellness, perhaps lifting the spirits and thus speeding the recovery of the sick in rural China.[89] As Huang Fengyan's remarks imply, the Great Leap Forward all but obliterated the practice of *ganqing* and made it more difficult for villagers to recover from illnesses induced by forced labor.

The heartless denial of sick leave intensified the assault on motherhood, putting women in situations in which they could not properly take care of their infants. The result was sometimes tragic, as was the case for Du Rutai. Born in 1921, Du was thirty-seven years old in the first year of the Great Leap, one year after she had given birth to her sixth son. Already by the winter of 1958 Du had been subjected to public criticism for being late to work, the result of putting her obligation to take care of her many children before her duty to serve the commune. She therefore could not gain permission from Da Fo party bosses or production team leaders to take work leave when her youngest son fell ill. Consequently, Du informs us, "My sixth son died at the age of one. In 1958 he contracted measles, but the production team leader still insisted that I go work in the fields. I went to work in the fields with my son, and I should not have done that. He was sick all the time I was at work in the fields, and so subsequently he died."[90]

Mothers with three to five young children were especially at risk. Because their collective field work shifts lasted until midnight, they had to leave their children at home without any proper care for long stretches of time. To cope, they frequently would run into the village to see their children briefly during the lunch hour and then hurry back to do field work and dig irrigation channels for the collective. Because they were simultaneously trying to spare most of their own food for their children, this harried routine, in combination with overwork, wore them down. "In the end," recalls Lu Xiuli, "several of them died of small illnesses."[91]

Work regulations in Da Fo even undercut the rights of women to practice mourning properly by participating in the funerals of their family members. When Pang Aichen's husband died, Pang was not allowed to return home for the customary days of mourning. During this period, Da Fo's party leaders required her to continue working in the collective fields and to shuck the harvested corn. Former members of the First Company are still overtaken with disgust and indignation when remembering such attacks on family mourning rights.

Kimberley Ens Manning has shown that whether rural Chinese women reflect favorably on the Great Leap and its promised sexual equality and expansion of maternalist entitlements depends substantially on how they were positioned vis-à-vis village power holders with party and kin connections.[92] The majority

---

[89] Kipnis, *Producing Guanxi*, 23, 28–29.
[90] Du Rutai, interview, September 21, 2002.
[91] Lu Xiuli, interview, September 10, 2002; also Lin Guofang, interview, September 1, 2002, and Ji Danying, interview, September 2, 2002.
[92] Manning, "Marxist Maternalism," esp. 93, 105. Her argument resonates with Friedman, Pickowicz, and Selden, *Chinese Village*, and Ruf, *Cadres and Kin*.

of Da Fo's women field workers, situated on the margins of the dominant Communist Party network of party boss Bao Zhilong and his close kin and friends, suffered enormously. They were required to work harder for less food, were denied the rest and sleep needed to stave off exhaustion, and lost their ability to protect their young children and, in the end, sustain their reproductive health. In this village, ordinary women lost the entitlements of gender and motherhood, if not their lives, in the Great Leap.

Still, it must be pointed out that there was one way in which women achieved a significant measure of equality with men during the Great Leap: slow or careless workers, regardless of gender, were targets for cadre abuse. Bao Zhilong, along with the Da Fo party leaders, relied on people like Bao Zhigen to drive villagers to work. He beat and cursed those who did not work hard, and "many people feared him," recalls Bao Yuming.[93] The Henan provincial leaders and the Maoists at the center understood physical coercion as necessary for mobilizing labor.[94] By the end of 1959 Bao Zhilong, Bao Yibin, and the Maoists in Da Fo had begun to meet challenges to their mandate to mobilize "free labor" with a uniquely radical, senseless, and inhumane organizational strategy. At its core was the public criticism session.

Public Criticism

Many Western scholars assume that the Maoists sustained the mobilization of the Great Leap Forward mainly by ideological exhortations and exuberant promises.[95] Certainly they were part of the picture, but the means by which the party-state enforced its will were based not so much on the promise of a permanent solution to the age-old food security problem as they were on fear. Da Fo's Communist Party leaders promised villagers that by following their lead, the villagers would be protected from future hunger, but they also threatened that any villager who did not do as the party's agents directed would be physically punished as well as publicly criticized and shamed. In other words, the party used both the carrot and the stick to enforce its will in Da Fo.

As we have seen, the practice of public criticism began in Da Fo during the 1946–47 land reform and Civil War and was revived during the period of Maoist ideological obsession with the "rightist inertia" of rural smallholders, people whose conservative farming and marketing habits supposedly made it difficult to overcome the stagnation of grain production in the pre–Great Leap decade.[96] In the Hebei-Shandong-Henan border area where Da Fo was located, the Communist Party had relied on public criticism to hold the civilian population to its

[93] Bao Yuming, interview, June 21, 2001.
[94] Chan, *Mao's Crusade*, 229–30.
[95] Friedman, Pickowicz, and Selden, *Chinese Village*, 217–21; Chan, Madsen, and Unger, *Chen Village*, 25.
[96] Chan, *Mao's Crusade*, 24.

cause during the Civil War. Party leaders waged public "struggles" against those who either assisted the Kuomintang New Fifth Army or deserted the PLA.[97] The big Bao landholders who aided the Nationalist government troops when they invaded the Communist Party Hebei-Shandong-Henan revolutionary base in late 1946 and early 1947 were also subjected to public criticism. During the Mao-orchestrated anti-rightist campaign of 1957, which followed Mao's "Hundred Flowers" invitation for nonparty intellectuals to express their political dissent and which set the political tone for the Great Leap Forward,[98] Communist Party–directed public mass criticism became a key mechanism for mobilizing popular opinion against "rightist elements" that were labeled dangerous. Da Fo's Bao Zhongxin was accused of being a rightist for drawing cartoons lambasting the special food privileges and corruption of the Dongle County party secretary and several other officials. In one sketch, Bao had portrayed a county party leader as a tiger who snatched public property, and he had included a reference to Wu Song, a figure in the historical novel *Shui Hu* (The Water Margin) who had defeated a tiger with his bare hands, to urge people to bring down the official. For drawing this cartoon, Bao Zhongxin was subjected to public criticism in Dongle County town. Two years later, after Bao Zhongxin returned home as one of the "five bad elements," Bao Zhilong and the Da Fo party leaders made him regularly clean up the village streets without compensation, and he was able to survive the hunger of the Great Leap only by poaching the crops of the collective.[99] Thus, well before the Great Leap campaign started in 1958, the public criticism session was symbolically linked to Mao's relentless will to push the Communist Revolution forward even in the face of popular opposition and overwhelming odds.

To meet the expectation for superabundant harvests and to ensure that farmers would part with their crops, the Communist Party leaders in Liangmen People's Commune and Da Fo continued to rely on public criticism throughout the Great Leap Forward, and public denunciation became the principal means for compelling rural people to participate in the communal labor schemes of Wu Zhipu and the Henan Maoists. Commencing in late 1959, when the anti-rightist campaign reached high tide, this public whip of Maoist terror was used to combat all forms of popular resistance to greater work sacrifices for Mao's utopian communal order.

We can explain the heavy reliance on the public criticism session in Da Fo in part by reference to the work style of the village's second-pole leaders discussed in Chapter 2. Inspired by Wu Zhipu and other Maoist provincial officials, the public criticism sessions in Da Fo and other parts of rural Henan were carried out by young people who were haunted by memories of war, famine, and counter-revolutionary terror in the Republican era. Poorly educated, repeatedly drawn

---

[97] Zheng Jintian, interview, June 22, 2001.
[98] Meisner, *Mao's China*, 1999 ed., 166–67.
[99] Bao Zhongxin, interview, June 23, 2001.

into the habits of war, and left with hardly any family outside the CCP, these local Communist Party leaders were bereft of any popular Mencian or Confucian understanding of the human rights of fellow villagers. They connected the salvation of their disrupted Han Chinese families with the Communist Party's struggle to save the country from exploitation and ruin at the hand of outsiders and "others." As we have seen, the work style of militia commando Bao Zhilong and these young party leaders, formed in violent struggles with the Kuomintang state, the Japanese Puppet Army, and landlord *min tuan* (militia) forces, was characterized by bullying and coercion and grounded in emotional habits ranging from hot-headed condemnation of foes without any investigation, to unauthorized invasions of the households of suspected class enemies, to ostracism of villagers who failed to come to mass meetings, to sharp censure of people who spoke out in opposition to false accusations, and to severe punishments for even relatively small infractions against the Maoist transcript.

As Ruan Yunchen points out, this work style was embedded in the dominant party-nurtured patron-client network developed by Bao Zhilong after 1949 and was heightened during the Great Leap Forward:

All of Da Fo's village party leaders were chosen and cultivated by Bao Zhilong. Bao Zhilong was not educated. Most of the people who joined the party during land reform were not well educated either. At that time, the party needed people who were aggressive and who were ready to fight the landlords in the village. These qualities also were useful during wartime, but they proved to be bad during a time of peace. In the early years of Communist Party rule, these people were educated by the party gradually [in matters of policy], but their bad tempers and predisposition to struggle and fight with people remained. The Great Leap Forward provided a very good opportunity for these bad qualities to grow.[100]

Yet the question remains: Why did Da Fo's party leaders turn the public criticism session into a weapon for carrying out the Great Leap crackdown? To begin with, they were operating under the threat of physical duress. If Da Fo's party leaders did not yield to the pressure to report exaggerated yields to make the commune and county leaders look good in the eyes of Wu Zhipu and the Henan Maoists, they too stood to become candidates for public criticism. In the fall of 1959, as the Liangmen People's Commune began pushing for greater harvest returns, its cadres began staging mass criticisms against the brigade party leaders who called for more accurate reporting of the harvest and traditional cropping practices. Recalls Zheng Yunxiang:

We felt that the village leaders were obligated to take care of the villagers first, but they had to carry out the Liangmen People's Commune government orders for procurement. If they did not do what the commune leaders wanted, they would be punished. Some brigade leaders were punished for meeting the needs of villagers at the expense of government demands. Deng Zhengfa, the head of Wanxiuzhuang village, was a disabled PLA veteran, so he possessed great political capital. He was criticized for doing too much for his village

---

[100] Ruan Yunchen, interview, July 15, 2000.

at the expense of Liangmen People's Commune government. When the commune officials asked for one thousand *jin* of grain, Deng Zhengfa would say, "No, we will give no more than eight hundred *jin*." Later, Deng was subjected to public criticism for this practice. Nevertheless, he became popular in his village. Da Fo people thought him very capable and held him in high esteem.[101]

The leaders of Liangmen People's Commune came into Da Fo to check on work almost daily, and they convened mass meetings, mostly to criticize brigade party leaders, almost every night.[102] Many of Da Fo's party members attended the public criticism sessions for village leaders in surrounding villages, where they learned what was in store for them if they did not comply. Bao Dongzhi, a member of the Da Fo party committee in the Great Leap period, remembers:

It was not easy to be a leader then. The Liangmen People's Commune officials wanted us to accomplish so much every day. If village leaders were not able to accomplish what they were assigned, the commune leaders would come to Da Fo to hold a mass meeting to criticize us and denounce us. This kind of meeting was held frequently.... I once participated in one of these public criticism meetings in Dalu village, north of Da Fo, where the Liangmen People's Commune leaders were struggling one of the harvest company heads. He was forced to stand on a table, and people were criticizing him. Somebody kicked the table out from under him, and he fell down to the ground, breaking several of his ribs. It was a brutal and scary practice.[103]

Many of Da Fo's key party leaders, as well as its minor party figures, became aware of the political discipline they would face if they did not strive to promote Mao's Great Leap transcript, for the local grapevine was humming with news about the penalties administered even to party secretaries in public criticism sessions across Liangmen and other districts. Zheng Jintian was one of the villagers who brought such news back to Da Fo after 1958:

Once during a cadre meeting in Leigong People's Commune, at which I was present, a village party secretary was forced to go through public criticism. For failing to properly guard the grain harvest on the threshing ground, he was forced to bow his head and confess his crime. The village party leaders in Liangmen People's Commune also had to submit to public criticism. Huang Haiji, a leader in Jingweizhuang, in Liangmen district, was accused of plowing under the ears of corn instead of leaving them on the surface. At a public criticism meeting, he was forced to kneel down on the four legs of a stool that was turned upside down. When someone kicked the stool, Huang Haiji lost his balance and fell on the legs of the stool. His ribs were fractured.[104]

Fearful of being subjected to this kind of punishment, Da Fo's party secretary and his inner-party allies insisted that villagers meet the labor demands and procurement targets of the commune leadership. In this village, as in many others, the Communist Party secretary was a subwarden of a communal penal colony

---

[101] Zheng Yunxiang, interview, September 19, 1995.
[102] Bao Yuming, interview, June 21, 2001.
[103] Bao Dongzhi, interview, June 24, 2001.
[104] Zheng Jintian, interview, September 15, 1993.

system created by socialist collectivization. He lived in daily fear of being demoted into the world of ordinary villagers and conscripted peasant laborers. The key to keeping out of trouble was to maintain vigilance in the campaign to make villagers perform big sacrifices for Maoist state appropriation, cracking the whip on those who faltered in work assignments or who spoke out against the food regime of the public mess hall.

In an important sense, therefore, the public criticism session was the key instrument of Maoist terror, creating a climate of political hysteria, sycophancy, and aggression. As the pressures for more effective conscription of labor and for greater harvest yields mounted in late 1958 and early 1959, Da Fo's party leaders pushed villagers to perform at a superhuman pace and to exaggerate production, "because," says Bao Jiping, "if their performance was not as good as other villages in Liangmen People's Commune, they would be called to task at public criticism meetings."[105] As the modality of party rule became inseparable from public criticism, exaggerated harvests became commonplace. Bao Zhigen, the head of Da Fo's First Harvest Company, speaks of this new terrifying pressure to comply with unrealistic and misdirected procurement:

I had to lie. Otherwise, I would be criticized. Because I exaggerated production, I did not suffer. In the summer of 1959 my company produced only thirty thousand *jin* of grain, but I said that we produced fifty thousand *jin*. As a result, we had to sell more grain to the state. Thus we had to make very thin porridge and include a lot of wild vegetables in our diets. Our village leaders were in a dilemma. In order to avoid being criticized by the Liangmen People's Commune leaders, we had to exaggerate production, but when we exaggerated the villagers had to suffer hunger.[106]

Thanks to the protection of party boss Bao Zhilong, the deputy head of Liangmen People's Commune, Da Fo's party leaders were less frequently subjected to public struggle than their counterparts in other brigades. "Bao Zhilong did not allow the commune leaders to debate the party leaders from Da Fo," recalls Bao Dongzhi. "He was very protective of us."[107] If boss Bao spared the Da Fo party leaders in his snare, he nonetheless took the lead in bringing the whirlwind to party branches in other villages, like Jingweizhuang, where the party leaders were frequently criticized, forced to kneel down on stools, and beaten if they told the truth about crop yields.[108]

The punishments for disobeying work orders, for foot-dragging on work assignments, and for interfering with the state claim on the harvest in the Great Leap Forward took many forms, but clearly physical aggression, involving cadre beatings of villagers, was the principal one. "Those who did not finish their work on time, or who were caught doing a lousy job, would be beaten by the village

---

[105] Bao Jiping, interview, September 2, 1993.
[106] Bao Zhigen, interview, July 21, 1994.
[107] Bao Dongzhi, interview, June 24, 2001.
[108] Bao Zhigen, interview, May 11, 1990; Bao Yuming, interview, June 21, 2001.

leaders, and the village leaders often denounced such people for these reasons," recalls Bao Zhidan.

In the public criticism sessions, those people who had made negative comments or complained about their work assignments were forced to criticize themselves. The victim was forced to stand on a table, [kneel down], and confess to everyone in the crowd why he did not work hard enough, why other people could do the work and he could not do it. If he had complained, then he would be forced to explain why he had complained about certain things, and why other people had done their work without complaining. If the explanation was acceptable, then the person being criticized would be spared, but if the explanation was unacceptable, then the village leaders would beat the person. On some occasions, the village leaders would suddenly knock down the table on which the victim was standing, and the victim would fall to the ground and suffer injury. It was a very cruel practice.[109]

Bao Zhilong was a major proponent of turning the tables upside down on the targets of public criticism, something he did himself on frequent visits to the villages from his newfound perch in Liangmen People's Commune.[110]

The campaign to forge a unified popular commitment to Mao's revolutionary ascent, directed by Da Fo's trio of party leaders (each of whom served as party secretary at some point in the Great Leap), delivered relentless physical harm to those who underperformed, both within the public criticism sessions and outside them. These punishments were driven by utopian work performance expectations and useless work payment formulas, and villagers bitterly resented them. Da Fo brigade party secretary Bao Yibin was brutal in his treatment of villagers, particularly those charged with taking care of the collective animals. When one of the oxen hurt its leg in the autumn of 1959, Bao Yibin accused ox-watcher Bao Peicheng of sabotage and forced him to kneel down on bricks as punishment. In the following winter, Bao Xizhou was forced to take off his clothes and kneel down naked in the snow for neglecting the animals. For beating a disobedient ox in the spring of 1960, Bao Chuanshen was forced to kneel down on a table before a big public assembly, whereupon party secretary Bao Yibin kicked the table out from under him, knocking him to the ground.[111]

Villagers resented such treatment all the more because it highlighted the extent to which local cadres had usurped the villagers' rights to private property and then redefined their protest as criminal behavior. During the Great Leap Forward, an outbreak of animal theft and animal murder occurred in the villages of Xinyang, and animals in the vicinity of Da Fo – particularly oxen – also were targeted. This wave of violence correlated with the sharp hunger induced by the takeover of household grain staples and the collapse of the public dining hall food ration.[112] Although brigade-level party leaders meted out brutal punishments

[109] Bao Zhidan, interview, June 26, 2001.
[110] Bao Zhigen, interview, May 11, 1990.
[111] Bao Guishan, interview, July 19, 1998.
[112] On this point, I have benefited from reading Archer, *By a Flash and a Scare*, 198–215, 229, 231–32.

to the "poachers," it turns out that the so-called poachers sometimes were half-starved farm laborers who had been assigned to watch the oxen that the party leaders had confiscated from them, or other farmers, and transferred into collective livestock pens, where they awaited slaughter for beef dishes that the leaders devoured in hush kitchens. In many cases, the poachers killed the oxen mainly because they were desperate for food, and their acts gained popular legitimacy. Village Communist Party leaders who meted out brutal punishments to ox stealers were actually punishing them for reclaiming animals that had been private property before they were stolen by the local agents of the commune for their own benefit.

Punishments for protesting against the default on promised food rations in the Liangmen People's Commune regional labor camps were also brutal. In the winter of 1959–60, when Bao Zhilong and the other commune officials in charge of the Ji County river dig project reneged on the promise of forty-five *jin* per month, the hungry labor camp workers attempted to steal sweet potatoes and liquor from the commune kitchen. Bao Ziyan, the Da Fo party boss in charge of the work detail, responded cruelly: Bao Minglian was forced to kneel down and confess to his crime publicly; Tang Zelong was beaten with a big stick, injuring his back so badly that he missed two months of work; and Tang Youyi was bound to a window outside of the commune kitchen and left to freeze. On and on it went. Work project defections correlate strongly with the rise of these repressive measures, which occurred in the awful spring hunger of 1960.

These punishments were aimed at making workers sacrifice for the collective, but they also were about establishing the dominance of the Communist Party and, ironically, manufacturing the impression that the party took seriously its obligation to care for, not cheat, rural people. Zheng Jintian remembers an episode involving Bao Ziyan, the Da Fo deputy party secretary who was known for beating people while they were being struggled in public:

After we had completed the work on the Ji County river dig project, we walked all the way back to Da Fo. Bao Ziyan, the supervisor of the Da Fo work group in Ji County, wanted to look good back in the village. So he ordered Pang Yusong, the cook, to prepare two kinds of bread for our return trip, one with high quality wheat flour and the other with corn flour. Bao told Pang Yusong to give the corn flour bread to everybody first, and to dispense the wheat bread toward the end of the trip, so that when we entered Da Fo we could show our families that we had high quality food while laboring at the camp. But people were hungry. They implored Pang Yusong to give them the wheat bread first. He did. When Bao Ziyan saw that members all had wheat bread, he immediately lost his temper. He ordered Pang Yusong and Bao Xizhou to kneel down on the road. He slapped Pang twice and kicked Bao three times. We all tried to calm him down, but only when we promised we would not eat our wheat breads and definitely would show them to our families in Da Fo did he stop beating Pang Yusong and Bao Xizhou.[113]

---

[113] Zheng Jintian, interview, June 21, 2001.

Public criticism often took the form of humiliations dreamed up by the party leaders of any given village. Da Fo's inhabitants remember one that was invoked time and time again, relied on to make them observe the rules ordering the food allocation system of the people's commune. Pang Yilu remembers how it worked:

The public dining hall was the only place cooking was allowed. Villagers were forbidden to cook at home. My uncle, Pang Jingran, worked in the Liangmen People's Commune for a long period every day, and at day's end he was very tired and hungry. One day, while en route back to Da Fo, he stole a few sweet potatoes from the collective fields. He brought these home and began to cook them. Bao Yibin and the other party leaders saw smoke coming out of my uncle's chimney. They came to my uncle's house and took his cooking pot together with the sweet potatoes to the village headquarters, where they convened a public criticism session. They forced Pang Jingran to kneel on a stool, and they compelled him to swallow the stems of the sweet potatoes. His knees began to bleed from kneeling for so long, and when the stool was kicked out from under him, Pang's legs were badly injured. Still, the next day, they came to force him to work in the fields.[114]

This humiliating punishment, which also tore into the victims' gums and made their mouths bleed, was administered again and again as the Great Leap intensified.

In Da Fo one of the most feared aspects of the public criticism session was the accusation of being a "lazybones." Villagers who did not live up to labor standards were continuously threatened with the withdrawal of their grain ration coupon, which was printed by Da Fo brigade leaders themselves and issued every three days. Some of the villagers who starved to death were the victims of such threats and the terrifying forms of labor discipline with which they were associated. People who were publicly denounced as lazy were forced to wear a white ribbon, which carried a stigma that resulted in social isolation and sometimes proved too burdensome to bear, as Pang Qinli recalls in reference to the death of Bao Geng, a member of Bao Zhigen's First Harvest Company:

Bao Geng was about sixty years old in the Great Leap Forward. He was accused of being a lazybones and was forced to wear a white ribbon. At the time, when the head of a household had to wear the white ribbon, the family reputation was ruined. Consequently, it was very difficult for the sons to find a wife and get married. Before a woman would agree to marry, her family would come to the village to investigate the young man and his family. If her family discovered that the young man's father wore a white ribbon, she most likely would refuse the marriage proposal.[115]

Constantly harassed and shamed for inefficient work habits, Bao Geng fell sick, and in the end Bao died. Burdened with grief and shame, his wife, who was also ill, died shortly thereafter. The couple's elder son, Bao Zhangli, was so ashamed

---

[114] Pang Yilu, interview, July 14, 2000. This story was corroborated by Bao Yuming (interview, June 21, 2001) and by Bao Zhongxin (interview, June 23, 2001).

[115] Pang Qinli, interview, September 11, 1993. The "white ribbon" penalty might have been a local variant of penalties instituted by directives from up the party chain of command, for in other villages "white flags" were issued to perceived "slackers."

of the white ribbon label and so traumatized by his parents' deaths that he also died from what villagers recall as "a disease caused by too much anger."[116] Second son Bao Lianjie was able to survive only by leaving the village to live with his sister in Shadi village in Wei County, Hebei province.

Bao Lianjie took with him a dehumanizing piece of knowledge about the fate of his family: shortly after his father, mother, and brother were buried, Da Fo's brigade party leaders ordered their tombs leveled to clear the way for planting sweet potatoes on their old family burial ground. This shocking act of cultural violence served as notice to Da Fo's villagers that the party-state was capable of excluding from the community anyone who did not fully comply with its assertion of control over private landholdings and with its commands as well. Anyone who moved backward toward the old family-based mode of agriculture would be cut out of the CCP-led community. The white ribbon penalty was the means for transforming recalcitrants into unwanted elements.[117] Chinese villagers had always associated the color white with death and finality, and Da Fo party leaders who imposed this penalty knew that it implicitly threatened to terminate the family line. The sons of the "white ribbon households" were understood as alien, undependable, unmarriageable. The threat of this repressive penalty and its dreaded curse drove many a Da Fo father to work himself into a condition of utter exhaustion and ruined health.

The destruction of the Bao family tombs also showed that the party-state had the power to deny the psychological comfort associated with ancestor mourning. Villagers saw that the Maoist state had consigned Bao Geng to the fate of a wandering ghost, imprisoned in a violent cultural state that denied any hope for a future bliss to those who questioned the miracle of revolutionary socialism. Here Maoism derived its power in part from the knowledge that the brigade party leaders could obliterate the sacred space in which people could connect to the loss and recovery of ancestor origins and guidance.[118]

Political exile was another correlate of the public criticism session. Some of the extravillage work projects were, in subtle ways, transformed into surrogate *gulags*. In 1958, for example, Bao Zhengda, the Da Fo party secretary who had opposed the digging of more irrigation wells in 1957, was sent to Lin County to make steel. Liu Xuanyuan, the head of Liangmen People's Commune, had not forgotten that Bao Zhengda had quarreled with commune vice-director Bao Zhilong over the well-digging scheme, and he seized on the steel-making campaign as a means of getting rid of the troublemaker. Suffering from a stomach ailment, which worsened after his arrival in Lin County, Bao Zhengda pleaded with Liu Xuanyuan to allow him to return to Da Fo to work instead. But Liu replied, "If

---

[116] Bao Guishan, interview, July 19, 1998.
[117] Compare with Mueggler, "Spectral Subversions," 115.
[118] Here I have benefited from Santler, *Stranded Objects*, 130, and also from Mueggler, "Carceral Regime," 1–42, esp. 32.

you need to die, you must die here."[119] Similarly, Bao Ke, Pang Xiannai, and other so-called rightists were sent to labor reform camp sites to be taught subservience through hard labor. Conversely, the Da Fo party leaders did no manual labor on the sites. Bao Ziyan, who was in charge of Da Fo recruits, worked only in headquarters and "did not engage in any work, but was solely preoccupied with urging people to work harder."[120]

In the context of the labor camps, public criticism was an instrument for thwarting further dissent and preventing half-starved laborers from joining in a rebellion against the corrupted Maoists. At the height of the Great Leap Forward, for instance, most of the people who had been sent to Ji County knew that Shai Nian, the head of the public dining hall at the Tong Tin River Dig site, was stealing public grain and giving it to women in the surrounding villages in exchange for sexual favors. "But no one dared to speak about this," recalls Pang Yilu, "because Shai Nian could organize a public criticism session to punish whoever dared to challenge him. We kept quiet even though we hated him very much. If we had the chance, we would have killed him. But we dared not."[121]

By 1960 the Ji County irrigation project was equated with death, and most Da Fo inhabitants feared this assignment. New recruits had to pass through surrounding villages with graphic reminders of what could happen to those who were sent to this project. In the part of Ji County where Da Fo's contingent was based, for instance, usually only the male villagers participated in burial ceremonies, but because there were no males left in the villages, the women had to take up the responsibilities for burying the dead, and there was a constant procession of funerals of people who had died because of working on the project.[122] Better to avoid, or acquiesce in, public criticism than suffer this fate.

Reports on work life in the Lin County steel project are not much better. Many villagers who were hospitalized for serious injuries were required to go back to work immediately after treatment or to undergo public criticism. Some, like Pang Jinchun, died of a puzzling disease while working in Lin County in 1959.[123] In early 1960 a growing number of workers fled the project to find subsistence and security in the coal mines near Hebi city in Henan, returning to Da Fo only after the Great Leap Forward Famine had receded.

The sites of public struggle meetings were invariably inside or near the grounds of the public dining halls, which gave the party cadres in charge of the sessions a captive audience. Da Fo's conscripted field workers visited the public dining halls with great trepidation, for they knew that at any moment anxiety-stoking public criticisms could erupt. The dining hall was not a place where people ate in peace. Tang Guoyi often interrupted the dinner hour to harangue people about working

[119] Zheng Jintian, interview, June 22, 2001.
[120] Pang Yilu, interview, July 14, 2000.
[121] Ibid.
[122] Ibid.
[123] Pang Youqing, interview, August 30, 1995.

harder, and Bao Zhigen, one of the most hated of Da Fo's Great Leap–era leaders, is remembered for blowing a loud whistle to warn people who were eating in the dining hall that he might cut their ration.[124] During the spring hunger of 1960, people often collapsed in the dining halls from acute hunger, and everyone had to watch the pitiful attempts of relatives and friends to hang on for just one more day or week. Bao Yiwu yelled deliriously about his hunger on the street outside of the public dining hall before he died. Bao Sihai, the uncle of deputy party secretary Bao Yiming, died after a long period of malnutrition, during which he more than once publicly implored public dining hall leaders to help him get some bread.[125]

In the Great Leap Forward, some of the party activists in charge of the public dining halls held the public criticisms more frequently and conducted them with less mercy as the famine intensified.[126] Perhaps this was because the physical capabilities of conscripted laborers simply collapsed with the dramatic reduction of the grain ration in the fall of 1959; as a result everyday resistance to forced labor in the collective – unauthorized rest breaks and feigning field work – increased. Those who were accused of transgressing the work rules were guilty until proven innocent, and in fact there was no due process whatsoever. Bao Zhongxin remembers: "Although the public criticism session was called a public debate by the party leaders, it seldom if ever allowed the victim a chance to defend himself. It was mostly physical punishment by the village leaders and militiamen. People had to kneel down on the ground while others criticized them in harsh language."[127]

Few of the Da Fo party leaders who managed the dining halls made any allowance for dissent. Appealing to them for relief from hunger was out of the question, because anyone, including the party leaders themselves, who dared to say anything against the public dining hall system was at political risk. If someone complained, the party leaders said that he was digging a hole undermining China's Great Wall of Socialism and often responded by demeaning the complainant.[128] When Bao Zhidan complained to the head of Da Fo's public dining hall that he did not have enough food, he was told that his stomach was too big and that he therefore had nothing to complain about.[129] From the standpoint of the party faithful, such people were insulting Chairman Mao, who was unyielding in his insistence that his socialist polity was providing food for everyone and who equated any dissatisfaction with a "class struggle" waged by rightists who favored the private distribution of production.[130] No one was allowed to even

---

[124] Bao Zian, interview, June 26, 2001; Bao Honglin, interview, June 25, 2001.
[125] Bao Guangming, interview, July 12, 2000.
[126] Thaxton and Wang, "Power, Disentitlement, and Life Chances."
[127] Bao Zhongxin, interview, June 23, 2001.
[128] Thaxton and Wang, "Power, Disentitlement, and Life Chances."
[129] Bao Zhidan, interview, June 26, 2001.
[130] Gao Hua, "Da Ji Huang de 'Liangshi Shiyong,'" 73–74.

insinuate the truth, which was that the Mao-inspired people's commune system had engendered massive, life-threatening hunger.

Nevertheless, people did find ways to express this truth. Villagers' memories of the Great Leap Forward invariably travel back to jokes, poems, and doggerel deriding the bad food supplied by the public dining halls when they first suffered the hunger of the reduced grain ration. One doggerel in particular, made up by Tang Guoyi, seems to have taken up permanent residence in popular memory of the slide into the uncertainty of Mao's communist "utopia." In local native Chinese, it went like this: "*Sige yanjing, erge tou, youyou wawu youyou lou, yi chui yi ge lang tou, yi xi yi ge hui liu.*" It translates: "In the mirror provided by the thin porridge soup, one can see four eyes and two heads, / As well as the reflections of houses and buildings. / By blowing at the porridge, one can make a large wave in a small bowl, / And if you suck at it, you can hear a loud sucking sound." This doggerel, which Tang Guoyi titled "Zhao Ren Tang," or "The Satire on the People's Soup," enjoyed great popularity throughout the Great Leap for expressing what everyone knew: that the porridge supplied in the public dining halls was inadequate to sustain life – so thin and watery that you could see your own reflection in it. "Everybody talked about it at the time," Bao Zhongxin recalls, "and everybody still remembers it to this day."[131]

On Chinese New Year's Day, 1960, Bao Huajie wrote a two-sided couplet – a traditional New Year's activity – and pasted it on the door of his living quarters. Lambasting the substitute food of the public dining hall system, one side read: "*Qiqicai mimihao, hongshu yezi baocaibao, pinnong shenghuo gouxuan*" (Wild vegetables, wild buckwheat shoots, and sweet potato leaves go into the dumplings of the poor. How can we poor farmers get by on this excuse for food?). The other side went like this: "*Guoliao Zhongyue shi eryue, sanyue siyue shi yijie, guoguo*" (We can survive January and also February, but March and April pose a greater difficulty, and the spring hunger portends a great uncertainty). The implication of Bao's derisive wit was clear: it was a complaint against the adulterated food ration of socialist rule. On hearing of it, Da Fo's party leaders instantly called a meeting to criticize Bao in public, and people rushed to ask Bao what he meant by the couplets. "But nobody beat him," recalls Bao Honglin, "because almost everyone knew what he said was largely true."[132] Classified as a landlord, Bao Huajie was a tailor-made target for a blistering attack from Da Fo's Maoists, but his act of dissent went unpunished, a small but significant crack in the Great Wall of Da Fo's socialism.

The posting of doorway couplets (*duilian*) in Da Fo reflected a mode of resistance described by Patricia Thornton in her powerful essay on insinuation and political contention in pre-1949 China. According to Thornton, this mode of

---

[131] Bao Zhongxin, interview, June 23, 2001. Also confirmed by Bao Honglin, interview, June 5, 2001; Bao Zhidan, interview, June 21, 2001.

[132] Bao Honglin, interview, June 25, 2001.

protest derived its potency from its power to summon collective support for community standards of basic social morality and to rebuke the hypocrisies of unrighteous rulers.[133] By early 1960, most people in Da Fo by and large agreed that the food system of the public mess halls was morally bankrupt. The fact that they refused to embrace party leadership impulses to bring Bao Huajie to Maoist justice via public criticism underscores their disgust with and rejection of the so-called social guarantees of socialist rule. Sensing that Bao Huajie's doorway couplet had given expression to communitywide ridicule of the moral dilemma they had created, Da Fo's party leaders apparently worried that a strong retaliation might produce an even more contentious action. They backed off.

After Da Fo village joined the Liangmen People's Commune in 1958, life changed drastically for the worse for the farmers of Da Fo in just a few short years. As it was implemented by local Communist Party leaders, the Great Leap Forward deprived them of the rights to individual farming and market participation that they had associated with Communist Party victory and subjected them to excessive demands on their labor, offering them in return only a small ration of grain inadequate for survival. As we will see, their experiences with Mao's Great Leap turned the villagers of Da Fo against the Communist Party and particularly against its local agents, in whom they had earlier placed their trust. Yet as procurement escalated and famine loomed in 1959 and 1960, threats of public criticism, physical punishment, and social humiliation kept them from mounting any significant collective resistance.

Toward the end of the first year of the Great Leap Forward, when the grain ration was cut to one-half *jin* and the Da Fo party leaders began to block strategies of survival, villagers pondered other means of accessing food. They instinctively understood the importance of the "entitlement sets" that, as shown in the seminal work of Amartya Sen, had proved critical to acquiring food in times of crisis.[134] Many would have preferred to pursue two of the entitlement strategies they had relied on in past famines: selling off property and soliciting loans. The problem was that both of these strategies had come under attack in the previous decade, and the Great Leap Forward accelerated this attack. With family land turned over to the collective and with housing materials, tools and implements, and farm animals being converted to communal property, the first strategy was no longer viable. Only the landless poor had starved to death in the 1942 famine; now, in the Maoist Leap, everyone was landless. It was a frightening comparison. Nor was it possible to garner food through another familiar entitlement strategy: taking a loan from one of Da Fo's landlord patrons, now the dreaded (and vanquished) class enemy. The grain now stored in the twelve commune-level state grain silos in Dongle County, including that of Liangmen district, was not accessible on

---

[133] Thornton, "Insinuation, Insult, and Invective," 598, 600, 612–13.
[134] Sen, *Poverty and Famines*, 43–45.

any terms, because the commune leaders were holding it for Wu Zhipu and his Maoist allies in Zhengzhou and Beijing.

Deprived of all traditional household methods of coping with food shortages, villagers were still expected to comply with the work rules of the Liangmen People's Commune, knowing that even if they did, they would not necessarily survive. Prior to 1960 resistance was pursued mainly to minimize or avoid the harmful effects of the aggrandizement of the people's commune, not to challenge the legitimacy of the Maoist-led political center. This is not to say that villagers would always remain silent or refrain from challenging the regime of collectivization: such a challenge would emerge during the famine. In the years before the relentless labor regimentation and unrestrained harvest appropriation raised the specter of death, however, most people in Da Fo took virtually the same approach that Jean-Luc Domenach has documented as their response to the state attack on livelihood in Mao's "first leap" of 1955–56: Rather than rebel against the deprivation of collectivization, the great majority of villagers "simply endeavored to survive."[135]

[135] Domenach, *Origins of the Great Leap*, 64. Domenach makes it clear that the principal reason for the reluctance to rebel was fear – compare with pages 60–61.

5

Strategies of Survival and Their
Elimination in the Great Leap Forward

Written accounts of the Great Leap Forward often have a ring of fatalism. Here
was a Maoist state policy failure, followed by debilitating famine and unprecedented social devastation reflected in massive peasant death rates, which reached
appallingly high levels in rural communities under the thumb of radical Maoist
provincial governors.[1] Da Fo's history supplements, refines, and enriches this representation of the Great Leap, reminding us that the body count of the impending
famine was not solely determined either by Maoist conceived policy or by the
efforts of local Communist Party leaders to implement commune regulations.
Whether villagers succumbed to food shortages and whether mortality rates differed from one village to the next was also conditioned by local popular strategies
of survival.

In Da Fo, villagers pursued a number of survival strategies outside the formal
institutions of the party-state and occasionally even found succor with the aid of
government-run machinery. To be sure, the Great Leap quickly evolved into a
devastating social catastrophe, but the people of this village initially were able to
stave off its worst consequences. The survival strategies of most Da Fo farmers
initially were aimed at preventing zealous Maoist cadres from enforcing the state
monopoly of grain ever more tightly and from mobilizing the village labor force
for rural industrial projects associated with party-state goals. Few such strategies
are recorded in the standard Western scholarship on the famine, and of course
most are missing from the annals of official Communist Party history.

Though these strategies focused mainly on survival rather than defiance, it is
fair to classify them as forms of "everyday resistance," which James C. Scott has
defined as "the prosaic but constant struggle between the peasantry and those who
seek to extract labor, food, taxes, rents, and interest from them." This struggle

---

[1] Becker, *Hungry Ghosts*, 47–210.

takes place covertly, through "the ordinary weapons of relatively powerless groups: foot-dragging, dissimulation, false compliance, pilfering, feigned ignorance, slander, arson, sabotage, and so forth."[2] Much of the everyday resistance to state domination in Da Fo was initially little more than the dogged apolitical pursuit of time-honored strategies of coping with externally induced food shortages. Alarmed villagers saw these stratagems as *fan xingwei*, or survival-oriented countermeasures undertaken to temper and evade the radical claims of the state. The Chinese term "*fan xingwei*" implies a popular reaction to flaws and mistakes in the structure and administration of the people's communes, not outright resistance to the Maoist system of socialist rule per se.[3] This term, originated by Gao Wangling, is helpful in grasping the original nature of resistance in Da Fo, whose farmers at first opposed the shortages of the Great Leap Forward out of their family material interests but with no anti-state political agenda.[4]

How the leaders of the Communist Party in Da Fo and throughout the region perceived the villagers' *fan xingwei* actions is a different matter, however. Concluding that these survival strategies sabotaged the progress of Mao's Great Leap, they redefined them as forms of resistance and cracked down on one practice after another, often depriving villagers of many of the core social entitlements they relied upon in times of famine and crisis. This redefinition was surely cued by Mao's definition of actualized mass discontent with the people's commune's ration system as a rebellion for food.[5]

Foot-Dragging

Facing the escalating claims of the Maoists, Da Fo's farmers at first resorted to forms of self-exploitation as a means of security and survival.[6] By working above and beyond the call of duty in the collective fields, many of them hoped to solidify their right to the daily grain ration or to be given a larger-than-average grain ration for participating in far-flung, labor-intensive development projects organized by the Liangmen People's Commune. This, in part, explains why they sacrificed themselves in long day-and-night brigade field work vigils in the first year of the Great Leap Forward and why some of them gravitated toward the commune-directed labor camps in Lin and Ji counties in 1959–60.

The penury terms of working for the collective eventually overburdened villagers' capabilities and patience, however. When the leaders of Liangmen People's Commune lowered Da Fo's daily per capita grain ration from one to one-half *jin*

---

[2] The term is from Scott, "Everyday Forms of Resistance." Quotation from *Weapons of the Weak*, 29.

[3] Gao Wangling, "Guoji Bijiao de Yige An Li," 1–13. Also see Gao Wangling, *Renmin Gongshe Shiqi Zhongguo Nongmin "Fanzingwei" Diaocha*.

[4] On other such "everyday political behaviors" that do not necessarily involve intentionality and hierarchy, see Kerkvliet, *Everyday Politics in the Philippines*, 20–25.

[5] Gao Hua, "Da Ji Huang de 'Liangshi Shiyong,'" 73–74.

[6] Compare with Friedman, Pickowicz, and Selden, *Chinese Village*, 271.

in the summer of 1959, the social cost of collective work sacrifices for the escalating procurement claims of the Maoist party-state became unbearable. Protest against interminable labor in the collective fields and falling grain rations was voiced. Tang Guoyi, the head of Da Fo's Third Harvest Company, told brigade party leaders: "Nobody can work with half a *jin* grain consumption per day." There were heated arguments over this issue, often resulting in the dismissal of harvest company heads who spoke for the majority of their members. "I was dismissed as the head of the Third Harvest Company," recalls Tang Guoyi, "because [almost everyone knew that] what I said to the party leaders was true."[7]

Villagers remember they could only work so much harder while subsisting on less grain before they fell victim to a form of sleep disorder associated with work exhaustion. Many, including Zhou Weihai, suffered "involuntary sleep." Zhou Weihai was responsible for repairing village carts, so he often crossed paths with people from all quarters of the village. "In the first year of the Great Leap Forward," says Zhou, "villagers had to work very hard day and night in the fields. I remember that when people came to me, they would fall asleep right there on the spot."[8] Reports abound of villagers falling asleep at various odd times near the cart repair shop, by the village wells, and in the fields of the collective.

Bound to the collective fields each day from six a.m. until midnight, seven days in a row, by the fall quarter of 1959 people were able to survive only by taking unauthorized work breaks in the collective fields and by slowing down their collective work activities or avoiding them altogether. Increasingly, many villagers found ways to rest their shrinking, weary bodies while pretending to sacrifice for the collective. Foot-dragging became the order of the day. In this art of survival Da Fo's peasants were rather accomplished. Avoiding the eyes of Liangmen People's Commune labor inspectors was central to survival. According to Bao Peijian, a member of the Liangmen People's Commune government during the Great Leap Forward, the commune work inspectors were actually the foremen of a labor police force, party cadres who "pressed villagers to work without sleep" and undertook night patrols to make sure that people were working around the clock.[9] By mid-1959, people would sneak away to sleep at the edge of the collective fields. Bao Yuming remembers: "At the time, everybody was worn out, so we built many sheds from corn stalks for people to sleep in at night. Sometimes, when people got tired, they would slip away from their harvest companies to sleep in the sheds if the village leaders were not in the fields."[10] Apparently, Da Fo's leaders sometimes collaborated in these counteractions. "When we made the rounds at night," recalls Bao Peijian, "Da Fo's village chief often let the villagers avoid work. We were pressing them to work without sleep. But when the village chief saw

---

[7] Tang Guoyi, interview, September 15, 1993.
[8] Zhou Weihai, interview, September 1, 1993.
[9] Bao Peijian, interview, September 11, 1993.
[10] Bao Yuming, interview, June 21, 2001.

that the Liangmen People's Commune leaders were sleeping, he would signal to everyone that it was permissible for them to go to sleep too."[11] To hoodwink zealous labor inspectors, some villagers left lanterns in distant fields where they supposedly were toiling away for Chairman Mao and socialism.

There was yet another twist to this silent war for sleep. Before the June wheat harvest of 1959, the Liangmen People's Commune Labor Inspectorate created a bicycle police force whose members were charged with patrolling the twenty villages within the commune late at night, making certain that people were manning the mechanical irrigation pumps. Da Fo's collective field workers feigned compliance by placing the pumps in neutral gear and leaving them running. Hearing the pumps' click-click-click, the labor inspectors cycling by Da Fo assumed that its residents were working hard to set a good Maoist example and gave Da Fo good reviews in their reports. Villagers take great pride in the fact that the Liangmen party leaders did not learn about this ruse until 1985, three years after the disbanding of the people's commune.[12]

Remittances

With the grain ration cut drastically, by mid-fall of 1959 many of the ordinary collective farm workers in Liangmen People's Commune were feeling the first pinch of the food crisis. A small black market for grain developed, primarily among the politically dominant, comparatively well-off, and enterprising Bao lineage members – the sociopolitical base of local Communist Party leaders with connections to government, trades, and schools in Liangmen, Dongle, and neighboring counties, provinces, and the national capital. The money and means to acquire this black market grain was obtained largely through remittances, or the functional equivalent, from kinfolk.

During the first two years of the Great Leap Forward Da Fo's inhabitants relied on two different streams of remittance to ward off hunger. Yunxiang Yan has pointed out that those villagers with kinship-structured networks of *guanxi* (connections) in other communities had a better chance of obtaining food.[13] This finding rings true for Da Fo as well. A small number of villagers, spearheaded by some of the disgruntled carpenters who had been hurt by collectivization, had gone to Lanzhou, Gansu province, in August 1956, and found work building an electricity plant. At least half of the Lanzhou construction workers had returned to Da Fo by the first year of the Great Leap, but those who stayed in Lanzhou sent enough money by registered mail to support their parents, wives, and other relatives on a monthly basis up to early 1960.

[11] Bao Peijian, interview, September 11, 1993.
[12] Ibid.
[13] Yan, "Changes in Everyday Power Relations," 93–94. Also see his "Culture of *Guanxi*," 17–19, esp. 18.

160

The other major stream of remittance flowed into the village indirectly from the coffers of the party-state itself, via the small sums given to villagers by relatives who held positions in the new government. Whereas Yan found that poor villagers who had become Communist Party activists were bereft of *guanxi* networks, and hence more vulnerable to food scarcity in the Great Leap, political sociology worked differently in Da Fo.[14] Here former poor peasant households with political connections, and with records of political activism supportive of the CCP, were able to better mobilize resources to stave off hunger – at least before the terrible year of 1960. To some extent, Da Fo was saved from massive starvation during the early phase of the Great Leap by patronage derived from the official positions that many of its village party members had obtained through their pre-Liberation connections with the Communist Party.

This process was apparent at several levels above the village. Locally, more than a few of Da Fo's revolutionary Civil War heroes had gone on to government work in Liangmen district after Liberation. Their placements unexpectedly provided a form of temporary insurance during the Great Leap. PLA veteran Bao Lijun, for example, returned to Da Fo in 1950, joined the cooperative movement in 1953, and started work in the government cooperative shops in Da Fo, Shangcunji, and Liangmen. Receiving a steady salary of twenty-nine *yuan* per month, Bao Lijun was able to purchase some grain on the black market from a relative in Minglizhuang, Wei County, Hebei province, augmenting the dwindling food supply of his family in Da Fo. At the same time, Bao also drew on his government salary to secretly purchase some grain from a storekeeper in Jiucun. Bao used this grain to make bread loaves, selling them on the sly in the vicinity of Shangcunji.[15]

Da Fo was tied to the structure of Communist Party power and patronage regionally too, which proved useful to even nonparty villagers. In remembering the food shortages of the Great Leap famine, Tang Guoyi tells us,

No one in my family died of hunger. My two younger brothers were government employees. My second brother worked in Beijing, and my third brother was the Communist Party secretary of a commune in Shen County, Shandong province. During the worst moments of the famine, I went to live with my second brother for a while, and with my third brother on two occasions. They provided me with food and shelter and with some grain coupons to use after returning to Da Fo.[16]

Similarly, Bao Huayin, the Da Fo native who had served as the Communist Party secretary of the Dongle CCP during the Anti-Japanese War and climbed up the national Communist Party hierarchy to become the head of a PRC grain department in Beijing after Liberation, helped his father, Bao Shiying, survive by

[14] Ibid., 93–94.
[15] Bao Lijun, interview, September 12, 1993.
[16] Tang Guoyi, interview, September 15, 1993.

sending part of his salary to him in Da Fo all through 1959 and the first half of 1960. "In early 1958," relates Bao Huayin,

I had given my father a fine leather coat, but after the Great Leap Forward began he had to exchange it for a small amount of grain. During that period I gave my father about 20 to 30 percent of my income so he could purchase enough grain to pass through the famine. For the first years of the Great Leap Forward, he purchased grain secretly from peddlers involved with the black market of the Bao lineage in Da Fo.[17]

As many as one-seventh of Da Fo's households had a small income from remittances sent to them by family members or relatives who were employed outside the village, often by the party-state. Whereas remittances to villagers were never officially prohibited by the CCP during the Great Leap Forward, the pressure on the grain market, coupled with the dwindling ration of the public dining hall system, eventually reduced their efficacy. Work for the state did not provide secure protection against famine, moreover, as many of Da Fo's lower-level state employees learned. Bao Lijun, who still was on the payroll of the Liangmen Cooperative in mid-1959, recalls that once the public dining hall food ration was reduced in the fall of that year, his family began having difficulty finding enough food to eat. Bao earned twenty-nine *yuan* per month in his official position, but he needed one hundred *yuan* to purchase thirty *jin* of grain, so when he combined his household grain ration with his government salary he still was 2,136 *jin* of grain below his eight-person household's minimum annual food requirement. Because his government salary was not much help, in 1960 Bao gave up his salaried position. Using the proceeds from clandestine marketing to obtain grain on the black market, Bao was able to supplement his meager dining hall ration and his gains from gleaning to get through the following year.

Remittances from relatives on state payrolls or with salaried jobs in urban political hierarchies helped some villagers keep body and soul together throughout 1959, but by the winter of 1960 remittance prerogatives and connections to relatives in powerful state positions were insufficient to protect villagers against state-imposed scarcity. Even Bao Huayin, the highest-ranking Da Fo native in the central government in Beijing, could not save his father in the famine year of 1960. In that year, Bao remembers, "the Bao black market pipeline dried up and...the price of grain shot up to a point where my father no longer could get it. So he died of starvation."[18]

Migration

The pressure to move toward the mono-cropping of grain, coupled with the state closure of the market, prompted villagers to contemplate migration toward the

---

[17] Bao Huayin, interview, August 12, 1990. Notwithstanding his high state position in Beijing, Bao Huayin visited Da Fo himself every year until the Cultural Revolution, so his knowledge of the Great Leap was derived from talks with family and friends in his old home village.

[18] Ibid.

end of 1958. In the summer to follow, however, Da Fo's harvest company leaders passed the word that migration was prohibited. From this point forward, if people left the village without permission for more than a few days, they were reported to brigade and commune leaders. If they were apprehended, they were criticized in front of cohorts in their harvest companies.[19]

Some villagers did manage to move to other places. A few of Da Fo's inhabitants took advantage of party-directed mobilizations to enlist the "basic masses" in far-flung steel production, irrigation construction, and dam-building projects, including the Tong Tin River Dig in Ji County. The long-distance work projects temporarily freed them from the harsh Maoist labor regime of the transformed village and gave them a chance to address food insecurity within the brigade. Many people experienced their participation in these projects as a form of surrogate migration, and when project conditions, too, became unbearable, a number of workers abandoned them and migrated onward.

The picture of migration in the Great Leap is sketchy, and the pattern suggested by the interview data gathered in this study should be viewed as tentative for Da Fo. Although the Maoist state attempted to stem migration, hungry villagers still attempted to move their bodies to food security. In late 1959, when Da Fo's per capita grain ration was cut and when the pull of the labor camp assignments created greater work burdens for brigade-bound tillers, some of the younger villagers attempted to migrate. Bao Xiandai and several of his friends left and begged their way west into mountainous Shanxi, eventually arriving in Hongdong County, where population density was comparatively low and the projection of state power was relatively tenuous.[20] Apparently, too, China's rural northeastern frontier was associated with the possibility of freedom and survival. Tang Yinfa, for example, fled Ji County and the Tong Tin River Dig to Liaoning province, where he found a job in the Angang steel factory. Although the overwhelming majority of Da Fo's project workers did not migrate, this does not mean that there was not massive flight from the forced labor of the projects. Whether the Liangmen People's Commune authorities recorded such flight is not clear, but one point, on which still more evidence is desirable, is interesting: the old-timers in Da Fo tell us that, in the Ji County village where they lived during the river dig, the young people had run away *en masse* to escape the work demands of the commune authorities. "Only old men and old women were left in the village," recalls Bao Peisun, "and they could not do any work at all."[21] Several dozen village youths left Da Fo for Beijing, Tianjin, and other North China cities toward the end of year two of the Great Leap Forward to escape being drafted for these work projects, just before the household registration system was activated by the Maoist state to track down and seize illegal migrants.

[19] Bao Zhigen, interview, August 1, 1990.
[20] Bao Xiandai, interview, July 5, 2006.
[21] Bao Peisun, interview, September 15, 1995.

Many of the workers who fled the Ji County work project went into hiding in other regional villages, where they lived among relatives and kinfolk, if only long enough to recuperate and then contemplate an escape. But escape to where? Increasingly, the police were positioned at the chokepoints of regional transportation routes with orders to return all runaways. "Several people from Da Fo tried to run away from the Ji County Tong Tin River Dig project," recalls Bao Gaojun. "Bao Peizhi was one of them. He was very smart, and he ran away as soon as he realized the difficulty of surviving there. But he and others who tried to escape were caught by the police at the Anyang train station and sent back."[22] In late 1959, Zheng Yunxiang and Pang Zhenghao schemed to leave the Ji County labor camp to "visit relatives" in Shengyang. Anticipating that cadres and co-workers would be watching the performance of a Tianjin City Opera Group touring the commune work sites "for the peasantry," they stole away from the work camp, intending a rendezvous in a village three miles away. But Zheng lost his way. Intercepted by police in Handan seven days later, Pang Zhenghao was able to convince them he was on his way to the Fengfeng Electricity Station to visit his younger brother, who eventually took him in for a week, gave him some grain coupons, and convinced him to abandon the plan to flee to Shengyang. When Pang's brother escorted him back to Anyang, Liangmen People's Commune cadres were waiting at the train station to return the runaway to the Ji County work camp. Zheng Yunxiang, who already had returned to the camp, had covered for them, saying they had planned a visit to friends.

More and more, as hunger gripped the work project sites, workers fled for Da Fo itself. Da Fo's project workers were somewhat favored in this strategy, for they were assisted by strategically placed local party leaders. Even so, most of them arrived back in Da Fo exhausted, hungry, and armed with harrowing tales of the horrendous terms of work life and the heightened conflicts between press-ganged workers and Communist Party labor supervisors over food supply. One of them, Pang Yilu, who worked on the Tong Tin River Dig from October 1959 to February 1960, recalls being constantly hungry:

We were given one *jin* of dry wheat flour, but it still was not enough for one meal. . . . We did not get paid for doing the work, and there was no compensation to the families of those who died while digging the river. One person from Xiangtianzhuang died at the Ji County river dig site as a result of the hard work and poor nourishment. My family occasionally sent me a coupon worth three *jin* of grain, and I bought corn flour with it. I made corn flour bread. I could finish all three *jin* of the corn bread in one meal. But I exercised self-control in order to let the corn bread last a little longer.

Pang and the other workers were forced to work long hours in the freezing river: "Winter was much colder then. Still, we had to work with our bodies partly submerged in icy water. We worked all day. We got off work at midnight or at

[22] Bao Gaojun, interview, July 12, 2000.

one o'clock in the morning, but we were so hungry that we could not go to sleep right away." Subjected to such torture, Pang "became a skeleton" and grew "too tired and too weak to continue working in Ji County." He remembers: "When I returned home I was unrecognizable – my family could not recognize me, and I could not recognize them." Dismissed by the project leaders, he and three other exhausted workers had to make their way back to Da Fo:

The four of us were given six bread loaves each as travel expenses. We sold four of the loaves and got twenty-four *yuan*. We used this money to take the train to Anyang. From Anyang, we took a bus to Chu Wang town. We got off the bus at eight o'clock in the morning. We then walked all the way to Da Fo, arriving long after midnight. This fifteen kilometer journey took us nearly twenty hours to finish.[23]

Increasingly, such workers were in double jeopardy. They were left without any food guarantees if they did not abide by the work regulations of the commune labor camp supervisors; people who stole turnips or sweet potatoes from the dining halls in Ji County were publicly scolded and deprived of food. Unless they were severely injured, they were not allowed to leave the labor camps, either. Bao Guangming was sent to Lin County in August 1958. His job assignment was to carry bricks, coal, and stones to the Lin County steel-making site. By the middle of November, when Bao hurt himself while on assignment, the terms of work life had become a threat to survival. "There were quotas," recalls Bao, "and we had to work day and night. If we did not fulfill our quotas, we were not given any food to eat."[24]

From the end of 1959, several political developments raised the stakes of migration for even the daring minority of villagers. At the national and regional levels, state household registration controls, or *hu kou*, made it more difficult to secure the registration card that was necessary for obtaining work in a city or for taking up residence in a new place. The *hu kou* system was implemented in Da Fo in 1955, and this system of residential permits, aimed at keeping rural dwellers from leaving the collectivized land for the better living conditions in state-controlled urban locales, was enforced by public security between 1955 and 1958.[25] Villagers say that in the first year of the Great Leap Forward it was still possible to migrate to regional cities, since *hu kou* controls on migration were still loose. During the following year, however, migration became increasingly difficult. Zhou Weihai recalls, "There were some young people who tried to flee the village to seek a better life in the cities. But at that time, it was not an easy thing to do. When caught in the cities, they would be detained as '*liucuanfan*' [wandering criminals] and would be sent back to the village."[26]

[23] Pang Yilu, interview, September 5, 1993.
[24] Bao Guangming, interview, September 4, 1993.
[25] Solinger, *Contesting Citizenship*, 35–36, 42–44.
[26] Zhou Weihai, interview, September 9, 1993.

In 1960 Bao Yibin, the Da Fo party secretary, made it clear that anyone who left the village for an extended period without an official *hu kou* certificate would not be able to get food outside the village and would risk losing his or her share of the village grain ration. Nonetheless, Bao Zhentian wandered to Shaanxi, and Pang Zhen fled to Shanxi. Both men were sent back by the police when they were arrested for stealing food and property in the cities.[27] Caught in the jaws of hunger, Ruan Yijun, Ruan Ying, and Ruan Qinwang also took to the migration trails to distant provincial cities, but police and party leaders relied on the *hu kou* system to return them to the village.

At the provincial level, the Communist Party authorities in Anyang, the prefecture to which Liangmen district was assigned, issued an order to Liangmen People's Commune officials that further slowed migration out of villages: Food would not be given to any household with a member missing from harvest company work for more than a few days. The Da Fo brigade and harvest company leaders were urged to discourage migration and if necessary to apply coercion to stop it. The harvest company heads helped apprehend those who left Da Fo for more than a few days and severely criticized them in front of their cohorts. Bao Zhigen, the leader of the First Harvest Company, admits his role in carrying out this crackdown: "In 1960 people tried to migrate. I was strict about this matter. If people tried to migrate, then I would beat them."[28]

Few people dared to risk migration without political authorization in the November 1959 to April 1960 period – the first desperate months of the Great Leap. Most stayed put, scrounging food from tree leaves, wild vegetables, and pilfered crops. Whereas some villagers had died of starvation in the famine of 1942 because they could not migrate to food security, in the Great Leap, the party-state made it even more difficult for villagers to pursue migration without incurring beatings, criticisms, or banishment. In the past, few villagers who migrated had sold their homes, because they counted on coming home when a famine was over. Temporary migration had been the dominant pattern for Da Fo's people in the previous two great famines of the twentieth century. The commune-based Maoist party-state took away this choice, equating migration with a betrayal of the shared work norms of the socialist collective and threatening those who left with permanent exile.

In late 1959 and early 1960 Liangmen Commune officials started to clamp down on the tendencies toward secret in-region migration associated with the growing tide of labor camp defections. From late September 1959 until late December 1959, Da Fo party secretary Bao Yibin was preoccupied with sending workers who had deserted the Tong Tin River Dig project back to the work camp, as an alternative to either hiding them in the village or helping them find

---

[27] Bao Jenming, interview, July 4, 1994.
[28] Bao Zhigen, interview, August 11, 1990.

succor elsewhere. Bao Yiming, who fled the camp, reflects on his reception by party secretary Bao:

I fled back to Da Fo in late September 1959. I arrived back here exhausted, hungry, and angry. We felt cheated. Never mind the lack of pay. We had nothing to eat, and yet we had to work all day. We could not voice our anger. If we did, Bao Ziyan, the Da Fo party leader in charge of the group that was sent to dig the Tong Tin River, would organize criticism sessions and punish us. At this point, after two and a half months, I fled, and I began wandering about the countryside. I went to Zhaogong village in Wei County, where my grandparents lived; then I went to my aunt's house in Shunfeng village, also in Wei County. Finally, I returned to Da Fo and went directly to party secretary Bao Yibin. Bao said I was supposed to be criticized, but he skipped the criticism on my assurance that I would go back to Ji County for ten more weeks.[29]

Increasingly, Liangmen People's Commune, and its attendant labor camp locations, were places where politics worked against the freedom to move outside the orbit of Maoist dictatorship, for here a dense political network of party-directed associations linked villagers with county, prefectural, provincial, and national Communist Party surveillance activities. The party-state used this network to inhibit escape from the bondage of the work camp. By early 1960 the cadres in charge of the Tong Tin River Dig were not only working with regional police forces to apprehend migrants, they were intercepting telegrams urging camp captives to return to Da Fo to help family members stave off starvation. "If they saw the telegrams," says Zheng Yunxiang, "they knew we would run away."[30]

Da Fo work camp stewards also relied on the Maoist whip of public terror to make their starving captives stay put. Yet, as Pang Yilu recalls, people still were determined to escape:

They had political meetings to educate people not to run away, but many people did run away. At the Ji County work site the leaders liked to debate people. Tang Mofu from Da Fo ran away, and they denounced him publicly. They asked him why he ran away, and he said that he did not have enough food to eat. The leaders began to beat him. He was forced to kneel down on a stool, and somebody kicked the stool and he fell down very badly. They did not allow him to eat. In the end, he ran away again.[31]

Not only was mobility systematically restricted during the Great Leap, but many Da Fo natives who had found party-structured employment outside the village were sent back there to live. The Maoist-inspired rustification of millions of people only recently located to urban work places, which was termed "*xiafang*," exacerbated the conditions for famine.[32] The party-state vigorously promoted downward migration from the commune headquarters itself, from low-profile

---

[29] Bao Yiming, interview, September 12, 1993.

[30] Zheng Yunxiang, interview, July 14, 1998.

[31] Pang Yilu, interview, July 12, 2002.

[32] For an excellent overview, see MacFarquhar, *Origins of the Cultural Revolution*, 3:23–36.

regional county towns, and from prefectural cities to the countryside. The intent was to alleviate the financial burden of provisioning the cities and to add managerial expertise to the socialist experiment at the village level. In Da Fo, this emergency measure had two tragic results. It sent down people who had been a source of remittances for their families in Da Fo at the very time when such remittances were most needed, and it added more hungry bodies to a village already caught up in a situation of semi-starvation.[33]

Zheng Tianbao, along with a host of Liangmen People's Commune staff appointees, came back to Da Fo to stay in 1960, because the salary from his commune position was too small to support him and his family. Ruan Tianhan, who had been sent to work in the Anyang Cotton Station in the first year of the Great Leap, returned to Da Fo's collective fields in the fall of 1961. The flood gates opened in 1962: Pang Guihua, a worker in the Shangcun Cotton Station, had to return to Da Fo that year after the staff of the station was downsized from 180 people to 30. Pang Canshen, a state cadre who sold pesticides, fertilizers, and farm implements for the Dongle County Commercial Bureau, "volunteered" to give up his employment in 1962 because, he says, "my salary could not support my five young children." Bao Jingan, who had found work in the Anyang Steel Company, was sent back to Da Fo to become a farmer in 1962. In 1963 Ruan Yindao, the deputy-director of the Liangmen Commune Irrigation Department, gave up his government position, with its 27.5 *yuan* per month, to come back to the village and serve as the accountant of the fifth production team.[34] And on it went.

The statements of villagers' willingness to sacrifice for Mao's "good intentions" in the Great Leap Forward and for China's national security needs notwithstanding, compliance with *xiafang* engendered bitterness among recently ascended rural people. These upwardly mobile people felt betrayed not only because they had been sent back to the village but also because the Mao-led party-state had reneged on its promise to compensate them for service and for loyalty.

Jun Chengshang's story illustrates the consequences of the Great Leap–era *xiafang* initiative. He settled in Da Fo around the period of land reform. After his father joined the PLA and participated in the Korean War, Jun dropped out of primary school and worked as a cook at the Number One Middle School in Handan. The position of state cadre in a regional town like Handan carried enormous

---

[33] Mark Selden, Roderick MacFarquhar, and several other astute observers of contemporary China have taken 1961–62 as the takeoff period for this state-engineered migration from cities to the countryside. The *xiafang* for Da Fo residents who had taken state jobs also accelerated in 1962. However, the history of Da Fo suggests that there was a progression of *xiafang* that first began with the great subsistence crisis induced by the Maoists in the Great Leap Forward. Commencing with the unbearable hunger of early 1960, it picked up in 1961 and became the 1961–62 tidal wave identified by Selden and MacFarquhar. Cheng and Selden, "Origins and Consequences"; MacFarquhar, *Origins of the Cultural Revolution*, 3:30–32.

[34] 1993 interviews with Zheng Tianbao, September 7; Ruan Tianhan, September 15; Pang Guihua, September 20; Pang Canshen, September 7; Bao Jingan, September 16; and Ruan Yindao, September 24.

prestige and was considered a great leap up a ladder of success in the new China of the 1950s. Shortly after supporting his younger brother's education in Handan, Jun finished primary school, then high school, and went on to technical school in Shijiazhuang. In 1954 Jun was promoted to office clerk in a state-run Handan technical school unit, and he worked there for forty *yuan* per month until 1962 – the year his life fell apart. According to Jun, "Facing economic difficulties, the state adopted some stringent policies in 1962 and tried to reduce the number of employees in the urban areas. My wife and my three children all lived with me in Handan. My family and I were forced to go back to Da Fo." Continues Jun:

At the time, the leaders told me that we should go back to Da Fo village for two to three years in order to help the state cope with temporary difficulties. When the state overcame its difficulties they would bring us back. I took them at their word and I left Handan. We returned to live in Da Fo with my parents. I had worked for the state for twelve years, from 1950 to 1962, and in the end I was driven home without compensation. Some people in my situation did receive some kind of economic compensation from the state. I tried to get some compensation too. But each time I went to Handan to talk with people in charge of this matter, I was sent back with empty words. In our country, honest people often have been shortchanged.[35]

When Jun returned to Da Fo, the public dining hall had already been disbanded. His family was given two *mu* of private land on which to till food crops, but in the first months of his homecoming they did not have enough to eat. They became one of the poorest families in the village. Jun's sister, who still worked in Handan, sent money with which Jun was able to purchase some grain.[36] Still, grain was hard to come by; people like Jun had to get by on difficult-to-digest soybean and corn seeds for half the year.

The *xiafang* initiative, beyond being an economizing gesture, was also a vehicle of disguised repression. Many of its "sent-down" individuals were ascended rural people who had expressed their views that the growing scarcity of the Great Leap Forward was linked to Maoist state policy and had spoken out against its social consequences.[37] Much like Pan Fusheng, the Henan provincial governor who had criticized Wu Zhipu's officials for exaggerating the harvest, the Maoists sent these people back down to the countryside in order to silence them. Bao Zeng, a Da Fo native who had risen to become the head of the Department of Civil Affairs of the Anyang Municipal Government after Liberation, was one of them. Pang Yilu recalls Bao Zeng's fate:

To villagers, Bao Zeng was a high official and very powerful at the time of the Great Leap Forward. However, just like Pan Fusheng, in 1959 Bao Zeng was labeled a rightist simply because he said that village people did not have enough to eat. Bao Zeng was from Da Fo,

---

[35] Jun Chengshang, interview, September 16, 1993.
[36] Ibid.
[37] I am indebted to Mark Selden, who helped me develop my understanding of *xiafang*. Personal conversation, October 29, 2001.

and he came back to visit once in a while, so he knew what was going on in the countryside. After being labeled a rightist, Bao Zeng lost his position and power, and in late 1959 he was sent back to Da Fo to work as an ordinary farmer for three years. He almost starved to death.[38]

Apparently, the Maoist state also attempted to structure migration out of the region to serve its Great Leap agenda, and its controls on frontier land, in combination with food shortages in the agricultural interior, both pulled and pushed villagers to participate in its agenda. In late 1959 several Da Fo villagers answered the Anyang prefectural government's call for one thousand volunteers to open up state-captured farmland on the grasslands of Qinghai province. The stated grain ration was twice that in Da Fo, and so the lure was strong. But the Qinghai climate proved to be bitter cold, the grain harvests were poor, and the collective farm, though subsidized by the state, did not prosper. Furthermore, the nomadic people of the province resented outsiders and complained to the state farm cadres that the state-sponsored migrants were damaging the grassland ecosystem. Da Fo's migrants felt unwanted, but they stayed "because," according Bao Wenchou, "it was better than Da Fo as far as food was concerned."[39] They returned home to Henan only when the state farm collapsed and closed in the wake of the Great Leap famine, by which time half of the volunteers had run away. In short, even state-structured migration did not work so well for desperate villagers.

The Black Market

Many villagers had given up full-time earth salt trade in the early 1950s, partly because the benefits of land reform had permitted them to become tillers and grain traders and partly because the onerous, time-consuming participation in the cooperative movement of the 1951–57 period had often proven incompatible with the demanding routines of production, transportation, and sale of earth salt. Nonetheless, at least 50 percent of Da Fo's households had continued to produce salt for the market intermittently up to 1955–56, well into the middle phase of Maoist collectivization. Many villagers naturally went back to this strategy of acquiring food during the first months of the Great Leap dearth, secretly accentuating it in the second half of 1959 after the socialist state took away most of the wheat harvest. Aimed at circumventing the suffocating market controls of the party-state, this counteraction bore a striking resemblance to the evasive day-to-day mode of survival villagers had pursued in their pre-1949 struggles to avoid the social consequences of Kuomintang state interference with their market way of life.

[38] Pang Yilu, interview, July 14, 2000.
[39] Bao Wenchou, interview, September 1, 1995.

Zheng Xu was one of many villagers who produced and sold earth salt during the Great Leap years. He describes his reasons for doing so:

I made earth salt during the Great Leap Forward. At the time, I had to work in the collective fields during the day; but during the evening I made earth salt. The reason was that I had many people in my household. I was able to obtain a little grain from the government, but I wanted to make certain that I could support my family. Therefore, I had to go out and steal dirt from other places to make the salt, and I had to make the earth salt in the wee hours of the morning.

My wife sold the earth salt in Da Fo. Occasionally, the farmers from Peihe village in Wei County came to Da Fo to buy our stored earth salt. They wanted it to produce *jiang* [a product used in making bean curd]. We used the money from selling the salt to secretly purchase grain in Hebei province, where peasant livelihood was better.[40]

At the outset of the Great Leap Forward it was still legal to produce earth salt for the market – but only as a member of the collective. Because quite a few Da Fo party leaders were unclear about state policy regarding the making and selling of salt on an individual basis, it was often tolerated. After late 1958, when production for the market was pronounced illegal by Liangmen People's Commune authorities, the local commune authorities suspended salt making, because, according to commune vice–party secretary Bao Zhilong, "they wanted us to focus labor entirely on field work."[41] Henceforth, Bao and his Da Fo party clients warned that the practice was taboo. Nonetheless, old habits persisted. In the spring of 1959, when Da Fo's harvest companies stopped organizing salt making, there was a rush into the private black market, and a year later, during the spring hunger of 1960, hundreds of desperate villagers turned to secretive earth salt production to ward off starvation, selling it on the sly in Xiaolu, Shengdianji, and Shangcunji.

Even some villagers with family connections to the CCP and positions in the Liangmen People's Commune itself were implicated in this illicit trade. Zheng Tianbao, who held a position in Liangmen district government, tells us: "I made earth salt myself during the Great Leap Forward. At the time party leaders issued a policy to stop us from making salt for private sale. However, I secretly made it after midnight in my courtyard in order to sell it here and in surrounding villages. I could sell it without difficulty as long as this did not affect my work for the commune."[42] Zheng continues:

I worked in Liangmen People's Commune for two years before I went back to Da Fo. The salary of my job at the commune was small, and I could not support myself and my family with that money in 1960.

I had nine people in my household, including my mother, wife, and six children. After I came back to the village in the spring of 1960 I worked hard in the collective field during

[40] Zheng Xu, interview, September 13, 1993.
[41] Bao Zhilong, interview, May 6, 1990.
[42] Zheng Tianbao, interview, August 10, 1990.

the day. At night I slept to one o'clock in the morning and then got up to collect the salty earth until dawn. After breakfast I went to work in the fields. During lunch time I would make the earth salt, then rush back to participate in the field work in the afternoon. At the end of the day, after I finished working in the fields, I would go peddling in the surrounding villages, selling the salt even when it was dark. I remember I lit a match to see the scale. There were other villagers who did the same thing I did in this period.[43]

The number of people in pursuit of the salt market shot up with the first signs of dearth in late 1959. Forty percent of Da Fo's households produced salt for the market in the first half of the famine year to follow, most of them secretly. Many had Communist Party connections or party backers, and until the market crackdown of early 1960 they were able to come and go from the village without exciting notice. At that point, when the Maoist-inspired grain seizures threatened minor local party leaders as well as ordinary villagers, they had shifted 80 percent of their illicit trade out of Da Fo's former periodic market to points well beyond the village.

There was a similar surge in nitrate production for the market, most of it sold to the state cooperative in Shangcunji. Da Fo's chemists received one *yuan* and eight cents per *jin*, enough to feed one family member for several months. The nitrate production was limited to a handful of villagers, however, and they were unable to fully reactivate their old market connections to the Zhanbeitun fireworks makers.

In addition to producing salt and nitrate, villagers secretly conducted other small businesses during the Great Leap, though they were technically forbidden to do so. The sellers of small foodstuffs, such as fried cakes and steamed breads, began offering their products on the sides of roads leading away from Da Fo's outskirts.[44] Just getting to these alternative impromptu market spots required cunning and courage. Disguising their food baskets and pretending they were on the way to till collective fields or going to gather firewood or embarking on a trip to visit a relative, they departed Da Fo secretly.[45] Displaying only a few bread loaves or fried cakes alongside the secondary dirt roads, they often hid the greatest part of their stock in nearby fields in order to minimize their losses if caught.[46]

With the post-1958 ban on salt making for the market, on nitrate trade, and on other forms of petty commerce, people in Da Fo issued a spate of appeals to harvest company heads and the brigade party secretary, aimed at gaining approval for the pursuit of carpentry, stonecutting, and braid rope making without party-state interference. The sideline activity that ensued sputtered along over the next half-year but was duly suppressed by Liangmen Commune agents.

The Maoist attack on Da Fo's market during the period of collectivization took many forms. After the establishment of the agricultural production cooperatives

---

[43] Zheng Tianbao, interview, September 13, 1993.
[44] Bao Jiping, interview, September 2, 1993.
[45] Pang Tinghua, interview, September 1, 1993.
[46] Compare with Solinger, "Marxism and the Market," 201.

in 1956, farmers had to seek approval from the cooperative leaders before they could make salt for the market. Those who were granted permission had to purchase work points from the cooperative in order to compensate those who stayed on in the village to shoulder the burdens of collective field work. The villagers who took this market path still made small profits, but there was a challenge: in order to purchase the work points and gain permission to leave the village for the market, they had to cultivate special *guanxi* with the production team leaders and harvest company heads who had the power to deny them access to the market. Even before the Great Leap, the decision to pursue a market-focused strategy of survival had been taken away from villagers.

During the crackdown of 1959 and 1960, permission to conduct business in the market was seldom given, and the party-state ban on the private market was extended to the earth salt trade. Daily markets, periodic markets, and market fairs were declared anti-socialist and unwholesome. According to Bao Yibin, the secretary of the Da Fo CCP, those who made earth salt at night without official permission were singled out and criticized by brigade party leaders for their poor work performance during the day.[47] Just before the June wheat harvest of 1959, the party-state clampdown on the marketing of earth salt was coupled with a wide-scale attack on trading in grain, oil, and cotton, and from this point on small business was routinely discouraged. "At this time," recalls Bao Yinbao, "if you missed half a day's work in Da Fo's fields to carry on small business, then you had to miss one meal as well."[48] The restriction on petty trade was aimed at restraining people from leaving the collective fields for markets when the harvest was good, and a special high business tax was announced any time brigade party leaders anticipated a good harvest. In fact, the tax was a "management fee" charged by the Communist Party cadres of the Bureau of Industry and Commerce, and Da Fo's brigade party leaders brought these cadres to the households of those who engaged in small business.[49] Consequently, fewer and fewer people openly chose to engage in business.[50]

Beginning in late 1959, the party-state policing of the market was extended to even the most minor forms of petty trade pursued by desperate villagers. Da Fo's peddlers and petty traders were constantly harassed by the anti-commercial agents of the commune, and they seem to have waged a small guerrilla war to avoid these agents into the famine year to follow. In the first half of 1960, officials from Liangmen People's Commune's Bureau of Industry and Commerce were seen chasing the peddlers of bread loaves and fried cakes through Da Fo's streets and into the fields. Elderly villagers still remember the capture of saleable food products by commerce bureau inspectors.[51] Ironically, the targeted victims of

[47] Bao Yibin, interview, September 15, 1993.
[48] Bao Yinbao, interview, September 16, 1993.
[49] Bao Zhigen, interview, September 10, 1993.
[50] Pang Chuanjian, interview, September 16, 1993.
[51] Bao Jiping, interview, September 12, 1993.

this harassment called the roadside spots where they sold their small offerings of breads and cakes the "frontline areas" and dubbed the off-the-road places where they hid their baskets full of marketable foods "*genjudi*," or "base areas" – a term that the Communists, in the era when they needed the support of rural people to survive, had used to describe places that were safe from the reach of the Kuomintang's anti-market police forces and armies.[52]

At the start of the Great Leap, the Liangmen People's Commune leaders had also moved to strengthen their hold over the prized occupational sidelines through which many Da Fo households generated off-farm income. Reacting to the clamor of Da Fo's carpenters to be allowed to continue private contracting, party secretary Bao Yibin demanded that the private carpentry association become public and work for the brigade as a collective. In 1959, Bao Zhendao, now the head of the Liangmen Commune Cooperative Bank, had convened a meeting of Da Fo's carpenters and declared himself the head of the carpenters' association. All private carpentry was prohibited. Thirty percent of the carpenters' income was to go to the brigade and 70 percent to the carpenters to buy work points from the brigade. In theory, buying work points was a party-sanctioned way of obtaining release to participate in the private market. Even this was a sham, however, for although the actual value of one work day was only ten cents, the brigade party leaders required the carpenters to pay one work point valued at one silver dollar per work day. To a man, carpenters say they were cheated out of ninety cents on the dollar. Before disbanding back into a private carpenters' association in 1961, there was resistance of a sort, but Bao Yiming is quick to point out its limits: "What kind of resistance could we offer? We complained as a group of ten and said it is not a good idea. But Bao Zhendao ignored our complaint and dismissed me as the head of the association, telling the other carpenters to come to him. He was so ignorant he had to come and ask me for the estimates."[53] Throughout late 1959 and early 1960 the carpenters were required to construct palatial buildings, repair bridges, and mend farm tools for the Liangmen People's Commune Headquarters at a loss to their already inadequate household incomes.

Prior to the Great Leap, Da Fo's market had been one of sixteen markets in western Dongle, and in 1958 it still was the biggest market for people residing on the floodplain of the Wei River. It served the people of two provinces, as villagers from Henan and Hebei came to Da Fo to buy grain, salt, nitrate, organic fertilizers, fried cakes, and peanuts.[54] Since 1947, when the PLA had driven out the Kuomintang Army, the market fairs of Da Fo had bustled. Over the course of a ten-day market cycle, as many as forty to fifty thousand people came to Da Fo to exchange goods. During late 1959 and early 1960, the leaders of the Liangmen People's Commune set out to capture Da Fo's market under the pretext

---

[52] Bao Zhigen, interview, September 10, 1993.
[53] Bao Yiming, interview, September 11, 1993.
[54] Ibid.

of ridding Liangmen district of illicit trade. Enviously, they complained that many township government seats were located at the same place as key markets, and that Liangmen had been the exception to this pattern.[55] They set up an alternative market in Liangmen on the same days as Da Fo's periodic market. To facilitate this artificial transfer, they first raised taxes on small business stalls in Da Fo, then sent in market management agents to harass and drive away the peddlers in Da Fo's market.[56] Da Fo's market persisted even during the famine, but it shrank for several years, as people crossed the border to conduct trade on the sly in Hebei.

Then came the scheme to facilitate the redirection of rural trade. Historically, the prosperity of Da Fo was due to its location, as well as its much-desired products. Because, prior to 1949, there had been no bridge connecting Shangcunji to the east with the villages of Liangmen district on the west bank of the Wei River, local people preferred to buy, sell, and barter in Da Fo. Prior to the Great Leap Forward, few people chose the inconvenient ferry ride across the sometimes-turbulent Wei River to Shangcunji. Even during the mid-1950s, farm animals were drowned and farmers seriously injured in ferry accidents at this river crossing. Toward the end of the Great Leap, around late 1961, the central government Ministry of Finance built a modern bridge across the Wei River. Ostensibly, this project was designed to modernize the archaic infrastructure of rural Dongle's highways. However, the Liangmen People's Commune officials saw it as a chance to shift the flow of rural trade to Shangcunji, which only recently had become the site of the state-run collective shops on the eastern bank of the river. These shops favored townspeople and sold government maritime salt, the price of which was only slightly higher than privately produced earth salt. As a result of this change, the people of Da Fo lost half of their periodic salt market clientele to Shangcunji. The private markets for vegetables and melons also went south. "Our market was surpassed by Shangcunji after the bridge was built," Ruan Renxing says.[57]

Although Da Fo's market was never completely obliterated during the early collective period, it was badly damaged. There was a prolonged decline in the wealth previously generated from the village's periodic market for local grain, salt, nitrate, and pork. In the two decades following the Great Leap, people substituted clandestine market runs outside of Da Fo for the small trade they had conducted in village streets abutting their own households. Perhaps the village also lost its reputation as a place of thriving rural enterprise and trade. When I first discovered Da Fo and asked Dongle County government leaders about its history, few of them remembered it as a market village. The implementation of the Great Leap Forward in Da Fo had disrupted the traditional periodic market routines and the impromptu commercial transactions that villagers had long engaged in beyond Da Fo's boundaries. Popular trade was driven underground to persist only in

[55] Tang Degao, interview, September 2, 1995.
[56] Bao Jieshi, interview, September 1, 1995.
[57] Ruan Renxing, interview, September 14, 1993.

tiny and impoverished forms. There is little doubt that loss of entitlement to this non-farm income, however small, to Communist Party repression was a critical factor inducing the subsistence crisis of 1960.

Begging

The fate of begging was linked to that of the market. Historically, approximately 30 percent of Da Fo's inhabitants, the poorest one-third of the village, regularly turned to begging as a way of coping with natural disaster and famine, a pattern witnessed in both the 1920–21 North China Famine and the Henan Famine of 1942. Following the drastic cut in the public dining hall food rations in 1959, Zheng Tianbao returned to Da Fo to find villagers begging. The number of people engaged in begging never reached 30 percent, however, largely because the structure of the communal food supply system inhibited them. Bao Lijun elaborates:

If everyone in every village was dependent on the public dining halls, where could you go to beg? You could not even find a place to beg. Nor could you depend on soliciting food from your friends. Bao Minglian, for example, had gone begging with his mother to Wei County, Hebei, in 1942. They ended up eating their way through the famine with the help of his aunt in Maiqiu village. But there was little hope of begging at the time of the Great Leap Forward. It was all but impossible to beg outside of the village because the whole border area was in the public dining hall system. Even the government employees had to abide by this system. There were no private restaurants. So there was no place to beg.[58]

What begging did occur was at the margins of a food distribution system that increasingly was controlled by a predatory socialist regime, making it a far riskier enterprise than in the Republican past.

Bao Zhidan says, "During the famine of 1942 we were so famished and thin that a strong wind could knock us down. I do not know how we survived these difficult years. The market in Da Fo helped us a lot. There were some commercial activities in the Da Fo markets, and it was relatively easy to go to the market *then* and beg for some food there."[59] But at the height of the Great Leap, the formal village market was no longer a place to beg. Beginning in late 1959 the CCP leaders of Liangmen People's Commune imposed a small but severe penalty on villagers who begged. Bao Zhilong and other commune party leaders considered begging shameful, an act that disgraced a People's China in which Chairman Mao and the Communist Party assured a subsistence grain ration to everyone. People who begged were ungrateful to Mao, anti-egalitarian. In Da Fo, males seldom went begging, for Da Fo's brigade leaders played on the culturally ingrained idea that it was a greater shame for adult males to beg than for females and children. Although there was an upsurge of begging among women and children in the

[58] Bao Lijun, interview, September 5, 1993.
[59] Bao Zhidan, interview, June 26, 2001.

176

middle of 1960, when raging hunger overrode fears of the political consequences of defiance, this strategy of survival was still considered risky, for the Da Fo party activists began holding public criticism sessions to struggle the women who begged – Chen Chunfang remembers that the militia seized and humiliated her in 1960, when the famine drove her to beg.[60]

The evolving political terms of begging during the subsequent famine year are reflected in the experience of Zheng Tianbao's household, which had a chronic history of begging prior to Liberation. In the worst moments of 1960 Zheng Tianbao's wife secretly went to Shengdianji, another market village, where she begged for a few daylight hours, returning to Da Fo just before nightfall. Begging, coupled with the hidden benefits of crop watching and illegal salt trade, enabled the Zhengs to prevent their children from starving. But they paid a severe penalty, for each day the wife was absent, her daily one-half *jin* food ration was taken away. "Because of this later constraint, less than 20 percent of the village went begging in 1960," Zheng Tianbao remembers.[61]

That Zheng Tianbao's family was penalized for begging was significant, for it was perceived as a betrayal of the long-standing friendship of Zheng Tianbao's father, Zheng Daqing, with CCP boss Bao Zhilong and of the friendship that had infused party relations with poor people in the pre-1949 period. Zheng Daqing was a revolutionary martyr who hailed from the ranks of Da Fo's "poor peasants," and prior to 1945 he had been a good comrade of Bao Zhilong. Zheng Tianbao himself had made heroic sacrifices for the CCP in its Anti-Japanese War of Resistance and in the Civil War, and he was a Liangmen People's Commune leader, both of which factors should have enabled his family to beg for food outside the village without reprimand – at least, this was how most villagers saw it.[62] That the Zheng household was penalized for begging was received by Da Fo's denizens as a stern warning that begging would no longer be tolerated. The great majority heeded this warning. Pang Chuanjian remembers: "Virtually no one begged . . . during the three years of economic difficulties. What we did was to eat the green crops in the fields. . . . We also stole a lot of grain."[63] Crop theft was escalating with the party blockage of less risky strategies of survival, and it too was dealt with harshly.

Crop Theft

With its off-farm income, its tradition of specialized side-occupations, and its own periodic market, Da Fo seldom had been plagued by internal crop theft. Although it was a prized target of crop pilfering and petty banditry by outsiders in the Republican period, villagers took great pride in the fact that they did not indulge

---

[60] Chen Chunfang, interview, September 11, 2002.

[61] Zheng Tianbao, interview, August 10, 1990.

[62] Ibid.

[63] Pang Chuanjian, interview, September 16, 1993.

in stealing the crops of insiders or of other villages. However, the economic depression of the Great Leap Forward transformed its proud, independent tillers and traders into reluctant crop thieves. Crop theft within the village reached its highest level during the Great Leap, testimony to the increasing effectiveness of official restrictions on the market and migration.

Still, internal crop theft did not increase substantially until the fall of 1959, several months after the daily per capita grain ration was pared to one-half *jin*, when the Liangmen People's Commune leaders in charge of the public dining hall system replaced the lost grain ration with a porridge made of barely edible wild vegetables and soaked wheat stalks. Before the autumn harvest of 1959 and 1960, commune leaders reported an upsurge in crop pilfering. Increasingly, Da Fo's field workers got into the habit of stealing a few ears of Indian corn, hiding the corn in the waistbands of their trousers, and then spiriting it back to their households.[64] This practice, along with raids on the collective pumpkin patches, became widespread. By the close of 1959, Da Fo's harvest company leaders were assigning crop watchers to the collective fields and posting guards at each of the village's three gates.

By the autumn of 1960, when Da Fo's inhabitants were so hungry that they felt as though each day was their last on earth, crop theft had assumed a collective dimension and triggered conflict with other brigades. At this time, the Second Harvest Company was implicated in a hair-raising crop raid organized by Bao Yinyuan, a returned PLA soldier who persuaded scores of fellow villagers to join him in taking sorghum crops from Minglizhuang brigade fields, over the border in Wei County, Hebei province.[65] Bao and several conspirators secretly approached Zheng Yunxiang, a member of the Da Fo militia and the guardian of the grain supply of the Second Harvest Company, pleading with him to join with them in a scheme to steal crops. Nine out of ten people were engaging in crop theft, they said, and those who did not steal would starve. Zheng Yunxiang gave in, joining them (with his rifle) in a nocturnal raid on Minglizhuang, just a few *li* from the Dongle County line. The raid, according to Zheng, "was well planned. Fifty-three people went, including some party members like Bao Jiping."

"However," he continues,

we got into a fight with the crop watchers of Minglizhuang at the sorghum fields. Ten of us rounded up six crop watchers at the southern end of the field. The rest started cutting the heads of sorghum. While we were detaining the crop watchers someone from Da Fo hit one of them over the head with his cudgel. When the wounded crop watcher cried out, we panicked, and in this moment of panic one of the crop watchers escaped. We knew that he quickly would bring reinforcements from Minglizhuang. So all of us, including those who were cutting the sorghum, fled.[66]

---

[64] Tang Jinlin, interview, August 10, 1990.
[65] Pang Guihua, interview, September 20, 1993.
[66] Zheng Yunxiang, interview, September 15, 1993.

Police units from both Wei County and Dongle descended on Da Fo to investigate the incident. Liangmen People's Commune officials assisted them in confiscating weapons from the suspects, then issued a warning against stealing the crops of the "people's government." Bao Yinyuan and three of the crop thieves were arrested and detained for arraignment and trial.

In 1960 the Liangmen Commune officials began a crackdown on crop theft in Da Fo with a new show of force. The old arrangements had sprung a number of serious leaks. Those who worked the collective fields had found ways to enter the village with stolen crops without passing through the main gates. Worse, from the standpoint of the surveillance of the commune, Da Fo's crop watchers by and large proved soft-hearted (and politically savvy). They reported only the habitual offenders, for those who repeatedly took the crops of the collective threatened the chances of others to steal just a little now and then without being caught.[67]

Hence the Liangmen People's Commune leaders ordered the activation of brigade-level militia patrols. At first the Da Fo militia did not respond enthusiastically to this order, for many of its own members were stealing crops to feed their families. However, the pressure of Bao Zhilong and other commune officials was relentless. By the summer harvest of 1960 the Da Fo militia was stopping field workers to search their baskets, increasing the risk of returning with even a few wheat spears or ears of corn. There were militia-ordered public criticisms of people who took even a pinch of flour while grinding it. Pang Siyin remembers twenty such criticisms in one day alone. The suspects were forced to kneel down on a long narrow stool together; if one of them fell down, everyone else fell with him, bodies colliding and bones cracking. Recalls Pang, the Da Fo militia "even went to individual homes to search for stolen crops."[68] Pang Siyin should know, for when Shu Jianchou picked up a melon from the collective field and spirited it home for consumption, vice–party secretary Pang led the militia charge to take it away from him. Shu Jianchou subsequently died of starvation.

The Da Fo militia was ordered to use force. Bao Zhigen, the head of Da Fo's First Harvest Company, relates his role in carrying out this crackdown:

In 1960 some people were hungry and stole crops. Crop stealing was widespread at the time. So I organized a small militia unit to catch the crop thieves. We used iron-fisted methods to prevent crop theft. We carried pistols to stop it. Qing Zhenxin, the CCP secretary of Liangmen People's Commune, gave his pistol to me and told me to use it to stop the crop thieves, so I used it to do this. If they stole the crops I beat them. Thereafter, no one dared to fight back.[69]

---

[67] Interviews with Zheng Yunxiang, September 15, 1993; Pang Siyin, September 9, 18, 1993; Zheng Tianbao and Bao Yibin, July 5, 2002; Bao Zhigen, August 11, 1990.

[68] Pang Siyin, interview, September 9, 1993.

[69] Bao Zhigen, interview, August 11, 1990.

The leaders of the Second and Third harvest companies were not so vigilant, however. Their families, too, were hungry, and crop pilfering within, and occasionally beyond, the boundary of Da Fo continued all through 1960. In the middle of 1960 the special People's Commune Public Order Force (Renmin Gongshe Zhiandui) was set up to suppress crop theft in Liangmen district. Ruan Shaobing, a resident of Da Fo and the head of the Liangmen People's Militia, was asked to form this force. "At the time," recalls Ruan, "the commune leaders called on the people in Liangmen district to stop stealing the crops. So virtually every village [eighteen of twenty] sent a crop thief to our Public Order Force. We paraded these crop thieves through the villages and into the fields, and we told the crowds of people what they had done."[70] At first Da Fo did not send a crop thief to Liangmen. But when the Public Order Force marched into the village, Bao Zhigen, commander of the First Harvest Company, sacrificed Bao Xichuan to be paraded around Liangmen district with the other thieves.

As external crop theft became rampant, new draconian measures to deter raiding of collective fields in other brigades, districts, and counties of Henan province hurt Da Fo. After the raid on Minglizhuang's sorghum fields, the police units from Dongle and Wei counties were joined by police from the Liangmen People's Commune. The police confiscated twenty-three rifles from Da Fo and went on to seize scores of rifles in surrounding villages. Then they arrested the four ringleaders. PLA veteran Bao Yinyuan, who had conceived and led the raid, was sentenced to two and a half years in prison. Zheng Yunxiang, the co-leader of the raid, was subjected to public criticism by commune vice-director Bao Zhilong and then paraded through each of the brigades with a heavy bag of grain on his head. All of the minor crop thieves implicated in the raid on Minglizhuang were required to walk to Wei County to apologize personally to Minglizhuang's residents and were ordered to give some gifts to settle the dispute. How these half-starved and dispossessed people acquired such gifts is not clear.[71]

Theft of stored food grain, along with crop theft, reached such alarming heights in early 1960 that the commune leaders called in the police to investigate. Although the Da Fo militia was not quick to enlist police support, Da Fo was repeatedly the target of such investigations. The party-state forced the issue, and a rising tide of repression against theft of stored grain followed. After the June wheat harvest of 1960, for example, the police entered Da Fo to investigate the theft of a few bags of grain from the storage bin of the sixth production team. Bao Heshan, who lived near the bin, was a prime suspect. Although Bao Heshan knew the identity of the thief, he did not want to expose him. Repeatedly pressured to reveal the name of the thief, Bao Heshan hanged himself. By late 1960 and early 1961, the police were visiting Da Fo more and more frequently, and even

---

[70] Ruan Shaobing, interview, September 14, 1993.
[71] Interviews with Zheng Yunxiang, September 15, 1993; Bao Chentang, July 17, 2002; and Bao Zhigen, September 10, 1993.

former PLA members and party leaders were being apprehended and criticized for theft of stored grain.[72]

An increase in animal theft began in 1960 as well in Da Fo. Each morning's discovery of a missing sheep, goat, or ox spread suspicion through the village, as people from different production teams reported suspects to public security chief Bao Jingan. Thieves from within the village occasionally were caught, but those who came from the east bank of the Wei River got away with heist after heist. Villagers remember that one of them was especially cunning. "He put some cotton-soled human shoes on the sheep's feet, and on the ox's feet, so that there were no animal footprints to be found," recalls Pang Qinli.[73] Many villagers still owned goats that grazed in the collective fields. With this spate of theft, people became even more concerned about keeping tabs on prized animals. But these animals were increasingly threatened by the party as well, as Da Fo's party leaders redefined animals grazing in the collective fields as crop thieves. Within a few months, Bao Yiming, the Da Fo deputy party secretary, caught several villagers with their goats on the collective fields. In a fit of rage, Bao Yiming took all of the goats to the village square and systematically killed each one with a big chopper in front of a huge crowd. Such violent acts were not forgotten.

Gleaning

As the central government increased pressure to meet procurement quotas and Henan Maoist Wu Zhipu pushed harder for spectacular harvest reports from county governments, the Liangmen People's Commune tightened its grip. Da Fo's farmers resorted to yet another food-garnering strategy: the secret expansion of gleaning, which, superficially, seemed to suggest cooperation and compliance with collectivization. Whereas gleaning might seem an impotent response to external state extraction, villagers consider their attempt to convert gleaning into a low-profile non-contentious means of coping with the growing threat of runaway procurement one of their cleverest defenses against the harvest appropriations of the Great Leap Forward.

Zheng Tianbao remembers that this strategy of survival allowed villagers a reprieve from the impending crisis of food supply losses in the first years of the Great Leap campaign: "We used to glean the wheat fields along the Wei River," recalls Zheng,

into Huangdeng village, in Wei County. We gleaned like this in the 1950s and continued to the early 1980s, when our wheat crops improved. But in 1958 we had to resort to secret gleaning here, and then over in Wei County, because of the Great Leap Forward. Because the Liangmen People's Commune leaders wanted everything for the collective, they did not want the individual farmers to glean and bring the wheat back to their old homes,

[72] Bao Gaojun, interviews, September 1, 4, 14, 1993.
[73] Pang Qinli, interview, September 1, 1993.

and the Da Fo brigade party leaders thought that if we were allowed to glean, then there would be no one left to work in the collective fields. Therefore, in late 1958, Bao Zhilong began to carry out the orders from the Liangmen People's Commune to halt the gleaning in Da Fo village.[74]

As Wu Zhipu and his loyal followers accelerated the Great Leap in the summer of 1959, this strategy of coping with state harvest seizures grew even more popular. In June, Liangmen People's Commune officials ordered the Da Fo brigade to cut the wheat harvest as rapidly as possible. Shortly thereafter, people proceeded to harvest by what Kenneth Lieberthal has called a "shock-force work style," cutting the crop in a hurried, less than meticulous fashion.[75] Da Fo's farmers intentionally left much of the crop in the fields in order to enhance their prospects for gleaning after the collective harvest, when the harvest company leaders would be preoccupied with threshing, crop reports, and grain deliveries to commune headquarters.

Following the logic of Jean C. Oi, who has insightfully analyzed the popular evasion of state grain controls in contemporary China, the excessive waste of the harvested grain (and, increasingly, tuber crops such as sweet potatoes) during 1959, 1960, and 1961 was indeed the product of a rational peasant scheme to leave a great deal of the crop in local fields for later gleaning. Referring to one such evasive tactic in the 1970s, Oi surmises: "The grain that remained in the fields either through carelessness or on purpose was not wasted. Once the official harvest had been completed and the 'state grain' had been accounted for, peasants were very careful and thrifty about recovering this grain."[76] In Da Fo this evasive practice was first pioneered in an attempt to survive the onset of dearth in the Great Leap Forward. People say they were fairly successful in relying on gleaning to restore a portion of their lost food supply. Bao Chuanshen recalls:

During the Great Leap Forward we were ordered to finish certain harvest work within an impossible time frame, so we harvested the peanuts and sweet potatoes in a very hurried manner. It was the same with the wheat and maize crops. The leftovers were gleaned by the people who did the harvesting. I was the one who picked up the wasted crops.

At the time, there was only one harvest company leader. He usually was away from the fields doing something else, like holding village meetings, running back and forth to Liangmen People's Commune, or ordering people to work. So he could not see those who gleaned the crops. The peanuts and sweet potatoes grew underground, so when they were harvested carelessly a lot was left over. Later, when we plowed the fields, we turned up a lot of these crops. Thereafter, the villagers could glean them.

It is true that we benefited from the wasted harvest. The person who plowed up the fields, like me, got as much as one thousand *jin*. Of course those who harvested the crops . . . did this in order to keep themselves alive. They slipped back to the fields themselves to pick up the leftover crops.[77]

[74] Zheng Tianbao, interview, May 8, 1990.
[75] Lieberthal, "Great Leap Forward," 306.
[76] Oi, *State and Peasant*, 119.
[77] Bao Chuanshen, interview, September 12, 1993.

Strategies of Survival and Their Elimination

Similarly, Bao Minglian elaborates on the moment when gleaning was transformed into an important means of inflecting the influence of Great Leap procurement:

A lot of the wheat and corn that was left over from the hurried harvests rotted in the fields. Since people were not desperate in 1958, they did not pay much attention to gleaning the wasted crops. But starting in 1959, when the grain that was rationed at one *jin* per day fell to half a *jin* per day, people were desperate. During the harvests they intentionally dropped the wheat and corn in the fields, or left the crops on the stalks. As much as 30 to 50 percent of the grain was wasted, and field workers got half of this by gleaning. Starting with the summer wheat harvest of 1959, everyone began to resort to this kind of gleaning.[78]

There were several differences in gleaning during the Great Leap Forward in comparison to the pre-collective era. For one thing, in the past much of the gleaning had been undertaken by women and children, but during the stark years of the Great Leap adult males joined the ranks of the gleaners: Bao Chuanshen, Pang Qingcai, Bao Jinfeng, and Zheng Tianbao all took up gleaning in 1959–60. For another, although nearly two-thirds of Da Fo's residents had gleaned local fields prior to the early 1950s, gleaning had been essential to the survival of only the most poorly endowed families. Bao Lijun, with only 2.5 *mu* of land prior to 1945, says his family got one-fourth of its summer and fall food supply from gleaning the fields during the pre-Communist era. In the throes of the Great Leap, however, nearly everyone in the village, including the former smallholders who once owned twenty and thirty *mu*, became dependent on gleaning. Whereas my interview data do not reveal sharp conflicts over who would glean how much of the wasted harvest, competition for the leftover crops was doubtless greater than in the past. Finally, the traditional practice of inter-village gleaning was threatened by the pressure of the impending famine. Previously, several hundred people from surrounding villages had joined Da Fo's residents in gleaning wheat, corn, and sorghum fields, but, when hunger threatened in late 1959, Da Fo's insiders made certain they got first dibs on gleaning their own fields. The harvest company leaders actively enforced commune restrictions against gleaning by outsiders, and production team leaders were less and less inclined to extend their arts of evasion to people from other villages.

By the last quarter of 1959 the Liangmen People's Commune leaders had been alerted to the practice of secretive gleaning. The villagers' feigned harvest inefficiencies of that year were associated with poor work performance and poor harvest results. Pressing ahead with state procurement claims, Liangmen People's Commune officials declared a ban on gleaning.[79] A familiar political figure enforced this ban, or so recalls Pang Siyin: "Bao Zhilong was the one who carried out the orders from Liangmen People's Commune to halt the gleaning at the

[78] Bao Minglian, interview, September 12, 1993.
[79] Zheng Tianbao, interview, May 8, 1990.

183

time. The commune leaders wanted everything for the collective, so they wanted to stop individual farmers from going out and gleaning and bringing the wheat back to their houses."[80] Henceforth, gleaning in Da Fo and other commune brigades was a less efficacious strategy of survival. Between the fall of 1959 and the fall of 1960 commune leaders did not allow families to cook anything gleaned from village fields inside their households. New regulations against sojourning and scavenging food beyond the village were routinely enforced.

By early 1960 gleaning within Da Fo had become risky. Villagers were warned that gleaning the fields after the collective harvest would bring a penalty. The heads of the harvest companies were ordered to prevent villagers from picking up the peanuts, sweet potatoes, and turnips that were left in the fields after the initial harvest, and party leaders moved to make sure this regulation was understood. Following the peanut harvest of 1960, several people who gleaned peanuts from Da Fo's fields were seized and forced to publicly swallow the stems of peanuts, a punishment that carried the risk of choking. Whereas many people were so hungry they went right back to gleaning despite the risks, some took the shame to heart. In 1960 Wei Laoshu was caught "stealing" the collective peanuts after the harvest for the state was completed. The Da Fo party leaders held a public meeting to criticize Wei Laoshu for crop theft before his friends and harvest company companions. After this public criticism Wei Laoshu was too ashamed to continue residing in Da Fo, and Wei and his family walked the migration trails to Shanxi, never to return.

The Liangmen People's Commune prohibited gleaning in all twenty villages within its territorial boundaries. The commune militia, which was now more integrated with the brigade-level "shock force" harvest companies, was posted to prevent villagers from going outside Da Fo to exercise customary gleaning rights. Whereas perhaps ten of the one hundred households under the Second Harvest Company still secretly gleaned fields along the Wei River in 1960, the majority of Da Fo's inhabitants were forced to find other ways of surviving the famine.[81] Da Fo's denizens recall this interlude in which they were forbidden to glean their own crops with great disbelief, for something baffling and outrageous happened at this point: gleaning was given up to outsiders. According to Pang Qinli, "The crops mostly were picked up by the people from Hebei province."[82] Because Hebei's party leaders did not push the Great Leap as hard as the Henan Maoists, villagers reasoned that Da Fo, which had been under the jurisdiction of Hebei in Republican times, was now a victim of the politics of place and plunder. Such a development – closing part of the village's food resources off to insiders rather than outsiders – angered villagers.

[80] Pang Siyin, interview, May 8, 1990; story corroborated by Zheng Tianbao, interview, May 8, 1990.
[81] Zheng Tianbao, interview, August 10, 1990.
[82] Pang Qinli, interview, September 18, 1993.

Grain Concealment

One strategy that helped to tide over villagers who were forbidden to glean was grain concealment. Concealment occurred at three levels: the individual farm household, the harvest company, and the village, or production brigade, itself. As Tang Jinlin recalls, there was a tit-for-tat struggle between families and party leaders over the concealment of grain throughout much of the Great Leap Forward, lasting up to the party clampdown of 1960:

During the Great Leap Forward the harvest belonged to the collective. In the case of most households, all of the grain was taken away. Some smart people did hide some of their grain. But individual cooking was not allowed. The people's militia monitored each household, and if someone's chimney was smoking, the militia would come to check. Those who were caught cooking at home had to engage in public self-criticism. If the criticism was unacceptable, the person would not be allowed to eat for a full day.[83]

Toward the end of 1959, when Da Fo's private grain market was pronounced dead by villagers and when Liangmen People's Commune grain inspectors stepped up their harassment of grain-concealing households, another form of concealment began to be practiced by harvest company leaders. The leaders of Da Fo's three harvest company hierarchies secretly gathered one thousand to three thousand *jin* of wheat from different parts of the village after the first threshing and spirited this grain away to hidden storage places without reporting it to the production brigade storekeeper for weighing. They used this concealed grain to add to the one-half *jin* grain ration of late 1959 in order to increase the size of the bread loaves prepared for their members by the public dining hall kitchens. Additionally, beginning in late 1959, each harvest company leader concealed the deaths of company members, continuing to collect their grain rations for the living. The Second Harvest Company, for example, concealed the deaths of seven of its members, giving the extra ration to those who had to gather firewood and fuel and to transport items for the company outside of Da Fo.[84]

Da Fo's brigade leaders conspired with fellow villagers to cheat the people's commune. Officially, the village had 3,800 *mu* of land, a figure Da Fo leaders always had reported to upper-level government grain tax officials – to the officials of the Qing dynasty, the Kuomintang, and the Japanese Puppet Army. In fact, they underreported by four hundred *mu* of hidden land. Whereas the early Communist Party leaders of Da Fo surely knew of this discrepancy, they maintained the practice of hiding the additional four hundred *mu* from the state, and they attempted to rely on grain sown on this land to cope with the pressures of requisitioning. Whatever grain was reaped from this hidden land, however, was insufficient to prevent widespread hunger in the second year of the Great Leap.

[83] Tang Jinlin, interview, August 10, 1990.
[84] Ruan Renxing, interview, September 14, 1993.

The concealment of grain harvested from Da Fo's publicized land base reached its zenith in the late fall of 1959. Bao Yibin, Da Fo's acting Communist Party secretary, initiated an underground countermovement to conceal the amount of grain produced by the village. Bao's actions give us a glimpse of the tricky political world of brigade party leaders caught between the demands of the communal arm of the Maoist state and the concerns of sub-county leaders genuinely worried about the possibility of popular discontent turning into riot and rebellion.

In late 1959 Bao Yibin attended the Five Village Crop Inspection Conference in Wencaicun, sponsored by the Liangmen district government. After going on a tour to inspect the millet crops of Wencaicun, Bao Yibin returned to the Wencaicun village office, where he saw an internal report to the Liangmen People's Commune that put the acreage of Wencaicun's fall millet crop at 167 *mu*. Knowing he had just seen 300 *mu* of millet under cultivation, good Communist Bao pointed out the possibility of production brigade concealment to Liangmen district leader Sun Yunqi, who, in turn, conveyed the concern to Qing Zhenxin, the Communist Party secretary of Liangmen People's Commune. To Bao Yibin's surprise, in the meeting that followed secretary Qing Zhenxin exclaimed that the precise area of a village's planted land could not possibly be known to anyone. Further, although Qing waxed eloquent about the obligation to fulfill the quota of state procurement to the *jin*, he also paid homage to the importance of taking care of the livelihood of local people. The half a *jin* of grain had to be guaranteed, and there was to be no shortage of seed or animal feed, he explained. If this were not done, Qing Zhenxin warned the brigade party secretaries present, all of them would be cashiered for creating too much popular discontent.

Apparently, this sobering message inspired Bao Yibin to initiate his own village-based concealment scheme. "As soon as I returned to Da Fo, I called an emergency meeting of the village accountant, the party vice-secretary, and the three harvest company heads. At the meeting I asked each harvest company head to hide five thousand *jin* of the fall grain crop. I also said there should be enough grain for people to celebrate the Spring Festival."[85] A wave of concealment swept Da Fo village. By the first quarter of 1960 the Second Company had stashed away 26,000 *jin*, and the village's three companies together concealed 70,000 *jin* of grain. "The villagers planned to eat this concealed grain in the months of the spring hunger," says Ruan Renxing, "and to use it to add two ounces to the inadequate official grain ration for our bread loaves."[86]

Party-state pressures against concealment by individual households first surfaced in the inaugural year of the public dining hall system, which was set up after the wheat harvest in 1958, a time of plenty. Although villagers ate to their satisfaction in the dining halls that year, and although the Da Fo leaders kept a reserve grain supply after the October harvest, at the end of autumn skeptical

[85] Bao Yibin, interview, September 15, 1993.
[86] Ruan Renxing, interview, September 14, 1993.

villagers still attempted to store away enough grain for a family emergency.[87] Once food rationing began, pressure mounted to give up all household grain to the commune and rely on the public dining hall system. By the fall of 1959, the militia was searching each household, often seizing hidden family grain; by early 1960 people found to be hiding grain were threatened with fines.

In early fall of 1959, as Mao's anti-rightist campaign unfolded in rural Henan, the pressure on personal grain concealment was extended to production team concealment. Liangmen district work teams came to Da Fo to search for hidden grain. Subjected to state pressure, the leaders of several production teams revealed the location of the hidden grain, which was carted away to the commune granary.[88] In this period, right before party secretary Bao Yibin began to organize concealment at the village level, local party leaders collaborated with Liangmen Commune officials in monitoring concealment and reported the offenses of production teams and harvest companies to their political superiors.

By mid-autumn of 1959 officials had extended harvest policing to virtually every conceivable act of grain concealment, as the leaders of Da Fo's Second Harvest Company learned. In the previous year, the company leaders had raised three pigs to be slaughtered at the New Year's Festival so members could find a little meat in their dishes on this festive occasion. Grain converted into pot-bellied oinkers, they hoped, would not be taken as concealment. However, Da Fo's ever-vigilant party leaders reported this scheme, and the commune officials came to Da Fo to confiscate all three pigs. The heads of the Second Harvest Company were denounced for stealing public grain to feed to pigs. The meatless festival of 1960 served as a bitter reminder of the growing power of Mao's collective polity to curtail even food supply techniques that had the force of custom behind them.[89]

The most spectacular advance of state appropriation came toward the end of 1959, when Mao's vicious anti-rightist campaign intimidated rural officials to such a degree that their extraction of grain from the villagers more or less precipitated the famine of 1960.[90] In November Wu Zhipu initiated a provincewide anti-grain hoarding movement. The campaign reached Liangmen district in early 1960, and Da Fo became one of its prime targets. Several days before the New Year's Festival, a team of Liangmen People's Commune grain inspectors arrived in Da Fo, accompanied by an armed militia. Using public criticism to exert pressure on party and nonparty villagers, and promising immunity for confessions and revelations of concealment, they made Bao Jiping crack, and he revealed the whereabouts of seventy thousand *jin* of hidden grain. By April of 1960 Da Fo had lost most of its *harvested* grain to Maoist state appropriation. Edema set in.

---

[87] Zhou Weihai, interview, September 1, 1993.
[88] Pang Siyin, interview, September 1, 1993.
[89] Zheng Yunxiang, interview, September 15, 1993.
[90] This history resonates with Bernstein, "Mao Zedong and the Famine."

Famine settled over the village, and the old strategies for coping meant political trouble. Villagers had the look of bare sticks, and they were frightened.

The Nature of Resistance in the Early Years of the Great Leap

The oral history interviews from Da Fo village gathered for this study underscore an important point: rarely seen as acts of intentional resistance by their instigators, these popular counteractions were not connected with a conscious strategy of individual or collective contentious opposition to the new Mao-led polity. Between the June harvest of 1958 and the imposition of extra-village labor camp assignments in August 1959, Da Fo denizens seldom questioned the right of the Maoist party-state to exist or to extract resources from them. For the most part, they saw their survival efforts as temporary deviations from collective projects organized by a national central government whose ideas and goals they still accepted – even if with growing skepticism.

If, therefore, intentionality is one criterion for "everyday resistance," not all of these deviations constituted resistance per se.[91] Many were mundane attempts to adapt to and modify the rules of the party-state without mounting resistance. To be sure, the organized raid on the sorghum fields of Minglizhuang brigade seems to meet the criterion of intentionality, but it is important to stress that such organized crop theft occurred more frequently *after* the summer of 1959, when the authorities escalated their crackdown on more mundane forms of adaptation to acute hunger. Thus it seems that most instances of "everyday resistance" in Da Fo occurred only *after* Mao's cadres launched a comprehensive attack on virtually all of the pedestrian adaptive strategies of Da Fo's farmers in the anti-rightist campaign of late 1959.

Still, it is important to ask: Why was there little, if any, outright contentious resistance at the outset of the Great Leap Forward in this village? Two factors weighed heavily; both involved memory and politics. Remembering that the Communist Party had provided them with aid in the aftermath of the 1956 Wei River flood, many villagers still had faith that the Mao-led socialist state would rescue them from any disaster and that in the event of a crisis they would be allowed to exit the people's commune, which, even with its flaws, represented a Mao-championed government attempt to serve the public good. Zheng Jintian sums up the perceptions of the great majority of Da Fo denizens:

When the Liangmen People's Commune was set up in 1958, the village party leaders announced that we did not need to worry about hunger any more. Ever since the Communist Party had come to power, there were new experiments happening almost every year. Some worked well, and some worked relatively well. But when the huge flood engulfed Da Fo in 1956, the government stepped in with generous help, and we did not suffer at

---

[91] For the criterion of intentionality, see Scott, *Weapons of the Weak*, 29, 32–33, and Scott, "Everyday Forms of Resistance," 7–8, 21–30.

all. The mindset of ordinary villagers was heavily influenced by the way the government handled this event, and they began to think that the government was good and could do no wrong. That was [one reason] why there was no resistance in Da Fo.[92]

This recollection discounts the role individual household market pursuits played in the recovery from the Wei River flood, but this is not surprising given that Da Fo party leaders manufactured confusion about how villagers actually got beyond the disaster, miscrediting rescue from this crisis solely to a Communist Party bailout. In the first year of the Great Leap, few villagers challenged this interpretation.[93]

More powerfully, the founding of the national government of the Communist Party under Mao's guidance was still intimately tied up with the pre-1949 fate of many Da Fo families, and popular biases rooted in family sacrifices in the struggle to defeat the Kuomintang, which had attacked the social rights of Da Fo's inhabitants, were deeply rooted. It was not just that villagers feared a return of the Taiwan-based Kuomintang and the threat it posed to their day-to-day existence: the development of the new Maoist polity was essential if Da Fo's Communist Party members were to secure the political careers and material advancements to which their family sacrifices entitled them. In time, the famine would underscore the cost of their identification with Mao's war-borne state, but the fate of Bao Zhongxin underscores how powerful this identification with the new revolutionary order was at the start of the Great Leap.

In 1946, when the Nationalist troops were attacking pro-CCP villagers in Dongle County, fourteen-year-old Bao Zhongxin entered a school for the children of the cadres of the party. Then, when the Civil War broke out, Bao joined the PLA and participated in the Battle of Huaihai, by which time he had been promoted to deputy head of the Mapping Department of General Liu Bocheng's 129th Division. Right after this battle, Bao Zhongxin was chosen to be a founding member of a new PLA-organized air force. It seemed like a splendid opportunity. Bao was afraid of airplanes, however, and when the PLA train carrying air force recruits for flight school training in Northeast China stopped in Jinan, he deserted.

The young Bao dared not go home. His father, Bao Yizhao, had joined the CCP in 1938, and he worshipped Mao Zedong. Bao and his brother had roamed with his father's army troop during the Anti-Japanese War of Resistance "because," he recalls, "we did not have enough food to eat at home." His second uncle was the head of the Da Fo Peasant Association, and his fourth uncle was the CCP secretary of Dongle County. Fearing that desertion from the PLA would destroy the honor of his family, Bao Zhongxin chose to hide at his elder sister's house in Shangdizhuang, not far from Da Fo. But the sister reported him to their father, and Bao Yizhao declared his intention to kill his son. Bao Zhongxin had not only

[92] Zheng Jintian, interview, June 22, 2001.
[93] On misattribution, see Schacter, *Seven Sins of Memory*, 94–95.

189

disgraced the family, he had also thrown away his opportunity to advance with his father and uncles, all of whom had risked death in the Civil War. Spared only by the last-minute intervention of a third uncle working in the CCP-led Hebei-Shandong-Henan base area government, Bao Zhongxin was stripped of his party membership and blacklisted from any future government service. His father refused entreaties from his subordinates to help rehabilitate his son well into the years of collectivization.[94]

Believing that Mao's new polity was the first government in history to care for poor rural families like his and that the revolution would enhance the relationship that bound villagers together as kin, Bao Yizhao exhibited a party-structured loyalty that influenced his understanding of the Great Leap Forward. Although shaken by the scarcity and disorder of late 1958 and early 1959, Bao Yizhao, like many of the veterans, reasoned that Mao and his allies in Beijing did not know rural people were exhausted and facing hunger. He presumed the flaws of the Great Leap were associated with the mistakes and distortions of powerful sub-national officials who colluded to subvert Mao's goal of feeding the people, and this memory bias, rooted in his pre-1949 political experience, quelled impulses to translate doubts about the Great Leap experiment into defiance and resistance – until, as we see in Chapter 6, it was too late.[95]

To be sure, resistance did develop and eventually became interwoven with some of the strategies of survival fashioned by small groups of kin and small clusters of friends in the first year of the Great Leap Forward. The important question is: How did the popular *counteractions* on which survival depended evolve into *resistance*? Such counteractions were "redefined" as counterrevolutionary resistance by Wu Zhipu and the Henan provincial Maoists, whose ranks were filled with ideological and ignorant local party cadres. Under pressure from the Mao-led center, these party activists twisted popular rational efforts to survive the appropriation and aggrandizement of the people's commune into "political opposition" and began to clamp down on all of the activities that allowed Da Fo's farmers to avoid starvation. It was this repression that ushered in the Great Leap famine and placed an outlandish strain on the cooperative survival strategies of close-knit families and friends who lacked connections to power.

Although the CCP attempted to systematically shut down the ability of villagers to pursue strategies of survival, it did not entirely succeed in Da Fo. People in this village continued to try to engage with those strategies, both individually and collectively, whenever they could. Of course, throughout history small groups of kin and friends have attempted to cooperate in sustaining these strategies against the intrusions of the powerful – and Primo Levi has documented such

---

[94] Bao Zhongxin, interview, June 23, 2001.
[95] On memory bias, see Schacter, *Seven Sins of Memory*, 138.

cooperation even in concentration camps.[96] In this sense, Da Fo was no exception, but, on the other hand, here the Mao-led party-state placed an extraordinary burden on kinship and friendship, and in some cases the pressure from above severely tested the bonds of cooperation that tied people together in resistance. Although families and friends did not entirely give up trying to survive via mutual help, they had to respect the limits placed on this mutuality by the party-state agents locally, and to reshape their strategies in response. If, as Chapter 6 shows, the villagers of Da Fo were fairly successful in making such an adaptation, these small group-based survival strategies were all but eliminated by state agents in other places – particularly in Xinyang, whose fate became known to informed people in Da Fo.

Political Repression and the Lesson from Xinyang

The Maoist party-state crackdown on household strategies of survival was paralleled by a campaign to suppress dissent, which gained momentum in the anti-rightist movement of 1959. People who criticized the politics of the Great Leap Forward were silenced, harassed, and punished. Sometimes they were stigmatized in ways that ruined their lives forever, as the stories of Tang Guoyi and Bao Zhang illustrate.

In late 1959, Tang Guoyi, a minor village leader, was chosen to attend as a deputy a meeting to elect the head of Dongle County government. The opening speech at this meeting was given by Zhang Yusan, the Dongle County magistrate. In this speech, Zhang urged the deputies to make sure villagers had enough to eat in order to ensure they would work hard for socialism. Tang Guoyi openly challenged Zhang by declaring that a half a *jin* of grain per day (the ration at this point) was not sufficient for current workloads. Zhang Yusan scornfully told the assembly that Tang had "spoken like a child" and publicly suggested that he should be dismissed from his position as the head of one of Da Fo's harvest companies. Subsequently, the Dongle County government stripped Tang Guoyi of his right to serve as a people's deputy, and when he returned to Da Fo, party boss Bao Zhilong subjected him to three days of verbal harassment and public criticism. Boss Bao then made Tang accompany him to Liangmen People's Commune to apologize to the leaders there.[97] After this incident, few people openly voiced criticism of the worsening subsistence crisis.

During the full-blown famine of 1960, food became a daily topic in Da Fo. Because talk about food was defined as political talk, it was neither tolerated nor forgiven by party leaders. Sometimes it resulted in permanent tragedy, affecting

---

[96] Thanks to Charles Tilly for making me think harder about this issue. See Levi, *Survival in Auschwitz*, 54–57, 71–72, 145–46, 155, 166–68, 172, 179–80.

[97] Tang Guoyi, interview, September 20, 1995.

the social choices of villagers into the contemporary period. The fate of Bao Zhang and his family is a case in point. In the spring hunger, several of Da Fo's desperate inhabitants declared that in a war they would support whichever army could give them food. Bao Zhang added a thunderous footnote. He said that if Chiang Kai-shek would give him a bag of grain, then he would say that Chiang was a good person. In 1960, in 1968–69, and again in 1982 (while on his death bed), Bao Zhang was severely criticized by village party leaders. Bao was stigmatized as disobedient, contentious, and disruptive. Even after the Great Leap Forward few people dared to say anything good about his family. No one would introduce their young daughters to Bao Wudao, Bao Zhang's son, who was condemned to seemingly permanent bachelorhood, a fate he attempted to avoid in 1993 by purchasing for marriage a woman from outside of Da Fo. The woman, it turns out, was a swindler, and left Bao high and dry after fifteen days. In 1995, forty-year-old Bao Wudao was still looking to buy a wife, for the legacy of the Great Leap had made it impossible for him to get one any other way.[98]

The most politically significant episode of repression in Da Fo focused on the courageous dissent of Bao Yizhao, who attempted to reverse the damage inflicted by Mao's violently utopian allies in Henan province.[99] One of the most dedicated Communist Party leaders in Da Fo, Bao Yizhao had joined the party with his four brothers in 1938, fought underground against the Japanese and their Puppet Army in northern Henan during the early 1940s, and helped the PLA achieve victory against the Kuomintang in the Civil War. Right after the founding of the PRC in January 1950, Bao Yizhao became the head of the Liangmen district government. His stature was even higher than that of Bao Zhilong – soon to be the district vice-director. Quickly elevated to the Disciplinary Committee of the Anyang prefectural CCP, Bao was an ardent disciple of Mao Zedong. By 1957 he had been promoted to the deputy chairmanship of the Disciplinary Committee of the Henan provincial CCP. When the struggle between Pan Fusheng and Wu Zhipu commenced, Bao Yizhao sided with the moderate Pan, aligning himself with the party leadership faction that opposed Wu Zhipu's radicalization of agricultural policy.

As Wu Zhipu and his followers increasingly exaggerated production figures in 1958 and then attempted to impress Mao by accelerating the Great Leap, exhausting the rural workforce, encouraging harvest seizures, and promoting widespread hunger, rumors of terrible human suffering circulated in parts of rural Henan – especially in Xinyang prefecture. In early 1960, Bao Yizhao led one of several inspection teams of the Henan CCP Disciplinary Committee from Zhengzhou to Xinyang prefecture in southeast Henan to investigate these rumors. During the following months Bao focused on the political transactions between Communist

---

[98] Zheng Yunxiang, interview, September 21, 1995.

[99] On this point and the Maoist push for communization in Henan province, see Chan, *Mao's Crusade*, 48, 68–71.

Party cadres and farmers in Xinyang. Bao's mission was to report the committee's findings on the course of the Great Leap in Xinyang back to Wu Zhipu himself.

What Bao Yizhao learned about the disaster that would later be called the "Xinyang incident" horrified him.[100] Beginning in 1957–58, Wu Zhipu had begun to persecute as a "rightist" any party cadre who disagreed with him. Responding to pressure from Wu, just after the summer 1959 Lushan Conference, wherein Mao cashiered Great Leap opponent Marshal Peng Dehuai, Lu Xianwen, the CCP secretary of the southern Henan region, had promoted the Henan provincial committee's anti-rightist movement to find unreported grain and property in the counties and villages of Xinyang prefecture. The party cadres who could not fulfill the goals of procurement had been labeled "little Peng Dehuais" and subjected to harsh public criticisms such as those endured by "landlords" under land reform.[101] Tragically, the campaign had gotten out of hand, as the county-level party committee meetings were transformed into public criticism assemblies. Ma Longshan, the first party secretary of Guangshan County committee, led a struggle against Zhang Hongfu, a "rightist" party leader who had failed to meet the procurement target. Ma personally beat Zhang Hongfu in front of a large gathering of cadres, who joined in the fray, tearing Zhang's scalp from his head and kicking him to death. The carnage spread to the village level. In Huaidian People's Commune, Liu Wencai, the county party secretary, relentlessly criticized and assaulted villagers, and more than forty farmers were beaten to death. Bao Yizhao discovered that party discipline in Xinyang had completely broken down, as 90 percent of the first-grade cadres of the Chinese Communist Party had joined the Guangshan beatings.[102]

In 1958 Wu Zhipu had pushed a "great leap" in the construction of large-scale irrigation works and in iron and steel production in the Henan countryside. In calling for 15 million people to participate in irrigation construction projects, Wu had thrown the agricultural workforce into a civil engineering scheme that was equivalent to building forty-eight Panama Canals. This quickly wore out much of the rural workforce in Xinyang. But there was more. Wu made Henan the cradle of a revolution in iron and steel making, mobilizing one-eighth of the farming population in the fall of 1958 and again in the autumn of 1959. Fall harvesting was neglected, crops rotted in the fields, and trees were cut *en masse* to burn in the charcoal-making process, leaving no leaves or bark for people to scavenge when the famine hit in 1960.[103]

---

[100] Whereas the Xinyang incident was not made public until 1982, evidently it is not true, as Jasper Becker contends, that the Henan provincial party inspection teams were prevented from collecting facts about the famine. These teams were armed, and their advanced delegations, including the one led by Da Fo's Bao Yizhao, gathered copious information. See Becker, *Hungry Ghosts*, 120.

[101] Becker, *Hungry Ghosts*, 113; Kang Jian, "Chu Chu Dou You Yanwang Dian."

[102] Kang Jian, "Chu Chu Dou You Yanwang Dian."

[103] Xu Ming, "Wu Zhipu," 37–38, 41–42.

Seeking to impress Mao and the central leaders with Henan's progress in grain production, Wu Zhipu encouraged wild exaggeration. In 1958 the grain production for all of Henan was only 281 million *jin*, but authorities estimated 702 million *jin*, which led to large purchases by the central government from the province and created pressure for local party cadres to punish farmers who did not meet their quotas. Although tillers were working day and night to produce at least 201 million *jin* – or, by some miracle, an even greater yield – Wu Zhipu and his clients announced that a super-abundant harvest of 450 million *jin* was at hand. They then brought pressure on local party organizations to find the missing 249 million *jin*, which were supposedly being concealed by crafty villagers.[104] Lu Xianwen, the first party secretary in Xinyang, followed suit, doubling the real amount of the harvest and trying to make up the difference by pushing the anti-hoarding campaign initiated by Wu Zhipu.[105]

Liu Junchao, an official in the Henan provincial Department of Foreign Trade, was sent down to work in Xinyang prefecture during the Great Leap Forward, supposedly to help the people leap into a better future. Liu's recollections help us grasp the link between official exaggeration and the famine of the Great Leap: "The local county officials lost their heads," he says. "They thought they were doing good things for the cause of the revolution, but it all seems so stupid today." Guangshan County party leaders claimed to have tripled grain production and tried to turn over twice as much as the 8 million *jin* requested by the Henan provincial government. After learning that some farmers were concealing grain for consumption, the county party leaders launched an anti-concealment campaign and eventually turned over 24 million *jin* to the Henan authorities – three times as much as the state had asked for. Liu remembers:

They had taken all the grain they could lay their hands on, and the people in Guangshan were starving. Even some of the Henan provincial officials felt too much grain had been taken from the county, and they offered to give grain back. When the county leaders refused, they were told they should not feel badly about taking the grain back. But they refused again. These county leaders were completely indifferent to the suffering of local people.[106]

Tales like this one spread via the grapevine in the Henan countryside throughout 1959 and 1960, reaching Zhengzhou, Anyang, Dongle County, Liangmen district, and Da Fo village through a network of people who had left their homes to serve the Maoist state. Bao Yizhao was the leader of this network, and he would transmit all of the mounting details of Xinyang's fate to kin, friends, and party members back in Da Fo.

Bao Yizhao's inspection team uncovered several important shreds of evidence regarding why the Great Leap had produced a social crisis in Xinyang. In their desire to become the number-one pacesetter in the Maoist commune movement,

[104] Xin Xi, "Lishi de Laji," GLFA, December 19, 2000.
[105] Becker, *Hungry Ghosts*, 113.
[106] Liu Junchao, interview, July 22, 2000.

the Wu Zhipu loyalists in the Xinyang party committee had utterly ignored the exigencies of agriculture. In the late summer quarter of 1959 a severe drought settled over most of the counties in Xinyang. The land received no rain from July 15 to December 1. Anticipating that this intense drought would threaten the crops, Zhang Shupan, the Henan commissioner of agriculture, convened an August meeting to urge local party leaders to take preventive measures, but the Xinyang party committee subjected his instructions to ideological debate. The committee not only did not implement any of Zhang's instructions, it refused to relax its procurement claims in the face of a withering fall harvest – all of this in order to impress Wu Zhipu, whose political ambitions demanded that any obstacles to greater production were not obstacles at all but actually were attributable to the mistakes of "right-wing opportunists." Responsible leaders who spoke of the need to take careful measures to cope with the crisis were ignored or silenced.[107]

Indeed, following the Lushan meeting with Mao, Wu Zhipu returned to Henan to strike up an anti-concealment campaign. In Xinyang this campaign was conducted with ferocious cruelty and made no allowance for the drought. Commune-level party cadres, many in a state of panic, were pressured by provincial and county leaders to lead anti-hoarding task forces into villages to ferret out hidden food. In Suiping County these task forces stormed into homes and courtyards, compelling farmers to help them uncover dried sweet potatoes stashed in holes inside of homes, soybeans concealed inside house walls, wheat shells stored in jars and buried in courtyards, sesame seeds hidden in plastic bags and submerged in the vats of toilets, and grain hidden inside birds' nests. When Lu Xianwen, the party boss in the Xinyang region, called Suiping in mid-November to push the campaign to a climax in the months ahead, many village party secretaries were stricken with unbearable anxiety. They knew there was hardly any food left. But the Maoists were relentless. To achieve compliance, party members, accountants, and production team members were split into different discussion groups in separate rooms and then urged to self-report about the food they had concealed. Incentives were offered to induce village party leaders and villagers to expose one another. By the first snowfall of December, scores of Suiping villages did not have even a trace of food. Faced with starvation, villagers seized and ate the seedlings and animal fodder. In the spring hunger of 1960, the public dining halls in Suiping and Xinyang stopped providing any food grain ration, so whole villages were left without any grain in the ten weeks prior to the June wheat harvest.

When these radical measures ignited outrage by brigade party leaders and farmers in Xinyang, Wu Zhipu used the instrument of public criticism to violently suppress any form of resistance. Worse still, as Bao Yizhao discovered, public criticism had been transformed into an instrument of deadly torture. In Suiping

---

[107] Qiao Peihua, "Xinyang Shijian Fasheng de Yuanyin," 7–9.

County, it had been wedded to "corrective labor camps" in which so-called rightist farmers, teachers, and landlords were subjected to life-threatening ordeals every night for the slightest deviation. In Shengqiao village, for example, ox-watcher Li Shaoqing was severely criticized because he had eaten the ox's food, leaving it to starve instead of him, and then criticized even more severely for climbing the camp wall and sneaking back home at night. In Tushan village, Yang Baoquan was subjected to criticism and beaten badly for saying that the food in the public dining hall was not fit for a dog. And, in Changhan village, the party cadre orchestrating public criticism beat Hu Tianyu until he could not get up, simply for saying that he had no strength left to work.[108] In the razor-sharp hunger of 1960, when all of the edible grain had been transferred to the Suiping County and Xinyang prefectural communal granaries and nothing was left in the villages, villagers and party leaders began to consume any of the substitute foods they could find in order to survive. Those who were caught were subjected to merciless public criticism and ruthlessly tortured until they confessed – or died.

Jia Yanmin's study of mortality in the Chayashan People's Commune underscores the above-mentioned point: In this commune, located in Suiping County in the Xinyang area, many rural people died from the terror whip of the Great Leap's agents, not simply from hunger. According to Jia, approximately 12 percent of the total population of 40,929 died in the Great Leap famine, and in some villages all of the inhabitants died. Although the main cause of death apparently was starvation, among the 4,605 people who perished between June 1959 and June 1960, the year Mao renewed the anti-rightist movement, 398 were beaten to death, 148 were driven to suicide, and 105 were frozen to death after being stripped of their clothing and exposed to the bite of winter. Many of these cruel acts were carried out by CCP militia captains – the counterparts of Bao Zhilong, the former Da Fo CCP militia chief and the vice-director of Liangmen People's Commune in Dongle County. Afflicted with Mao's anti-rightist fever, they turned public criticism into an instrument of justifiable torture, and their victims account for 14 percent of the total number of people who perished in this year of the Great Leap Forward.[109] All of this in a commune that Mao Zedong had touted as the national pacesetter for China's progress toward communism.

Wu Zhiupu used the revenues and riches generated by the Great Leap Forward in Xinyang to build up the power of his own party network and curry favor with Mao. Even when massive numbers of rural people were dying of starvation, Wu Zhipu had been striving to achieve his one great ambition: to host the National CCP Representative Conference in Zhengzhou. He directed the construction of a luxurious garden villa estate near the Yellow River within easy reach of

[108] Kang Jian, "Chu Chu Dou You Yanwang Dian."
[109] Jia Yanmin, *Dayuejin Shiqi Xiangcun Zhengzhide Dianxing*, 221–27, 230–31. Li Huaiyin more or less confirms that at least 10 percent of the population in the Chayashan People's Commune died in the Great Leap disaster. See his "Village China Under Socialism and Reform," chapter 4, p. 16 (unpublished manuscript in progress).

Zhengzhou, using money gained from procurement and the appropriation of agrarian harvests. Inside the villa was a building complex with suites for every one of the top-rank Communist Party Central Committee members in Beijing and a separate villa for each of the seven key leaders in the party. The size of each villa increased in accordance with the rank of its anticipated guest. While this estate was being constructed, fields were neglected, villages evacuated, families ruined. In Xi County alone 100,000 people died, and 639 villages disappeared. Family lineages were completely wiped out as entire households succumbed to starvation. Many other families had only orphans left. According to statistics from Xi, Huangchuan, and Guangshan counties – all three in the Xinyang theater of Mao's Great Leap into war communism – the total number of orphans was more than twelve thousand.[110]

The Xinyang incident had occurred in a well endowed agricultural prefecture. In this prefecture, where 20 percent of Henan's population resided,[111] more than one million people perished. Astonishingly, this was at least half of all the Great Leap–era excess deaths in the province,[112] and apparently this one prefecture accounted for a disproportionate percentage of the excess mortality rate nationally.[113] In short, the Maoists had turned most of rural Xinyang into a disquieting graveyard, in which the small last-ditch acts of beggars, orphans, and bare sticks constituted the only signs of human communion.[114]

Meanwhile, Bao Yizhao and the Disciplinary Committee delegation further discovered that Xinyang's high party leaders had attempted to cover up their complicity in the disaster and that Lu Xianwen, a key Wu Zhipu loyalist, was implicated in the cover-up. Lu had insisted that people were starving not from lack of food but due to the incorrect political thinking of opponents of the party's anti-concealment activity in the villages, and he had attempted to prevent the spread of information about the carnage by preventing besieged farmers from exiting Xinyang's communes and by clearing its roads of desperate beggars.

Stunned by his horrific findings, Bao Yizhao summoned the courage to do his duty and, so he presumed, to save the Mao-led party from the mistake of its provincial arm. He reported aspects of the rapidly developing social disaster in Xinyang to Wu Zhipu, emphasizing that the exaggeration of harvest production had opened the door to hunger, famine, and hell. He said that the oxen were so thin and weak they were about to drop, that the farmers did not have enough

[110] Xin Xi, "Lishi de Laji," GLFA, December 19, 2000.
[111] Becker, *Hungry Ghosts*, 128; Wemheuer, "Stone Noodles."
[112] Compare with Yang, *Calamity and Reform in China*, 75–76.
[113] From Yang, *Calamity and Reform in China*, 37–39; Becker, *Hungry Ghosts*, 267, 272, 274; Peng, "Demographic Consequences," 646–49; and Michelson, "Deprivation, Discontent, and Disobedience." Wemheuer has turned up a report that claims 2.4 million people starved to death in Xinyang alone. I will leave the full story to his indefatigable scholarship. Personal correspondence with Wemheuer, April 5–6, 2005.
[114] Xin Xi, "Lishi de Laji," GLFA, December 19, 2000.

food to eat, that people were starving to death. "Wu Zhipu did not want to hear that," recalls Bao Yizhao's son.

He tried to force my father to repent and write a self-criticism. But my father refused. He said that he had seen precisely what was unfolding with his own eyes. Then Wu Zhipu organized a team to examine my father and wrote up some false reports [about Xinyang] for him to sign. But my father refused. My father's truthful and responsible report was in disagreement with Wu Zhipu's representation of the Great Leap Forward in the rural areas. So Wu Zhipu punished my father for telling the truth.[115]

Bao Yizhao was labeled a rightist, kicked out of the Communist Party, and assigned to a low position in Loyang city government, but he rejected the assignment. He refused to work for the revolutionary socialist state any longer and returned home to Da Fo early in the worst year of the Great Leap Forward Famine. Mao Zedong reportedly did not learn of the severity of the Xinyang disaster until late October 1960, and the Xinyang incident was not made public until 1982.[116] But the villagers of Da Fo knew about it, and the news surrounding Bao's return struck fear into their hearts, delivering a stark political message to all: what had happened in Xinyang could happen in Dongle County, even in Da Fo.

In short, Mao's political network had abandoned the Mandate of Heaven and delivered a chilling social disaster to scores of counties and villages within the Xinyang area. Somehow, Da Fo party leaders and villagers had to find a way to keep Wu Zhipu and the provincial radicals from ruining their chances to survive. What they needed was a strategy of food acquisition that would save them from socialist-induced starvation. This strategy, which involved ingesting the harvest before the agents of the Henan provincial government and the Liangmen People's Commune were able to appropriate it, underscored the deepening crisis in Maoist party-state relations with China's rural people.

---

[115] Bao Zhongxin, interview, June 21, 2000.

[116] On when Mao first learned of the Xinyang disaster, see Huang Jun, "1960–61 Mao Zedong dui Lianghuang Wenti de Renzhi Jiqi Zhengce Diaozheng," 10. Also see Becker, *Hungry Ghosts*, 112.

6

The Escape from Famine and Death

Between the autumn harvest of 1959 and the spring hunger of 1960, the existential situation of Da Fo's inhabitants deteriorated sharply. Reduced to one-fourth *jin* (4.2 ounces) of food per day – the equivalent of about two cups of rice or a few slices of bread – in the spring hunger of 1960, the public dining hall grain ration in Da Fo was a quarter of the daily ration during the killer Madras Famine in India of 1877.[1] Yet most people in Da Fo survived the ensuing terrible year of the Great Leap Forward Famine. If grain concealment, the black market, and gleaning rights were all but eliminated and if the Liangmen People's Commune and Da Fo party leaders had usurped the household entitlements of the past, such as selling off family land and property to purchase food or seeking hunger loans from landlord patrons, how did villagers escape death?

China's rural people, including the tillers of Da Fo, avoided losing all of their crops to state procurement during the Great Leap famine by eating the crops of the collective *before* the harvest.[2] People from all three of Da Fo's harvest companies say that 90 percent of their members survived primarily by relying on *chi qing*, as villagers call the practice of eating immature or unripe crops. This means that if we focus mainly on the amount of the harvest taken by commune officials *after* the harvest was reaped rather than the struggle over the harvest within the fields of the collective, we cannot grasp the most effective survival strategy when starvation threatened in 1960 and 1961.

Because *chi qing* deprived Maoist state procurement agents of a substantial portion of the grain crop before they could move it to the threshing ground and

---

[1] Davis, *Late Victorian Holocausts*, 38–39.
[2] Though he does not mention this practice specifically, Kerkvliet talks about the attempts of Vietnamese peasants, burdened by socialist collectivization, to get the harvest from the fields before the state appropriated it for public ends. See *The Power of Everyday Politics*, 237–38.

take it to the public dining hall and the commune granary, this survival strategy was also an elementary form of popular resistance, implicitly challenging the Maoist ideological transcript of the Great Leap, which held that development was dependent on putting the production of state revenue by the big collective before the basic food security of rural people dependent on the smaller units of family and village.[3] By focusing on *chi qing*, we can begin to grasp why the *fan xingwei*, or apolitical counteractions described in Chapter 5, turned into everyday resistance and, in the end, contention: the sheer desperation and injustice delivered by Mao's Great Leap altered the political content of villagers' survival strategies.[4]

Chi Qing: *The Most Effective Hidden Strategy of Resistance*

Well before the Great Leap Forward, villagers were accustomed to nibbling a few green wheat spears or a few ears of unripened corn. "Before Liberation in 1945," says Zheng Xu, "this was a common practice, but it became more pronounced in 1959 and 1960, the worst years of the famine."[5] By late 1959, with the tacit approval of the Da Fo harvest company heads, scores of villagers in each harvest company had taken up this strategy of survival. Zheng Jintian remembers:

At least four hundred to five hundred people in each company ate the wheat crop raw in the fields. As soon as Ruan Renxing was not watching, we would begin to eat the crop. Actually, Ruan Renxing knew what we were doing, because everybody was eating the crops the same way. We would pick the wheat, grind it with our hands, blow the husks away, and then put the sweet and soft green kernel into our mouths. This practice increased in the Great Leap Forward. During the famine years it became our main food source. Prior to 1959 we had eaten only a little of the standing crop, so as to not ruin the harvest, but during 1959 and 1960 we ate the crops without concern for ruining the collective harvest. I remember that in 1959 over a period of just ten days we ate 5 to 10 percent of the entire wheat harvest.[6]

Without *chi qing* the people of Da Fo would not have lived through the famine. Two political developments drove villagers to this strategy. In early 1960 the Liangmen People's Commune Communist Party leaders took away all private plots reserved for family vegetable gardens, sweet potato crops, and melon patches, further reducing the supplemental food supply of every household.[7] A great fear seized tillers: With the land there was assurance that even in the darkest of winters there always would be life, but now they had little hope. At the outset

---

[3] Friedman, Pickowicz, and Selden, *Chinese Village*, chs. 7–9.

[4] I am indebted to Benedict Kerkvliet for helping me see this change. Personal correspondence, April 9, 2006.

[5] Zheng Xu, interview, September 13, 1993.

[6] Zheng Jintian, interview, September 13, 1993.

[7] Bao Peisun, interview, September 15, 1995. In some villages, farmers still owned their vegetable gardens inside their courtyards or close to their home villages before and after the Great Leap started, and these plots had not been given over to the collective previously.

of 1960 each person received a public dining hall grain ration of only ninety *jin* per year, enough to sustain him or her for only three months. At this point, recalls Zheng Tianbao, the crop watcher of the Second Harvest Company for much of 1960, people went to the grain fields day and night and ate as much as possible. Villagers remember deriving at least 60 percent of their total subsistence grain supply from the unripened wheat and corn crops of the collective. In combination with scavenging leaves and wild vegetables and eating the thin porridge offered at public dining halls, this practice saved them.

When first told of *chi qing*, I doubted that villagers could have garnered much of their food supply from the standing crops, for I assumed that *chi qing* occurred over too short a time span to enable villagers to meet their subsistence needs. However, Da Fo's old-timers say *chi qing* actually began prior to the June wheat harvest, continued through the months linking the early autumn corn harvest, and went on into the sorghum (or millet) harvest of late October. Furthermore, they remember carrying a lot of the crops they took in the pre-harvest periods home to dry and secretly storing them for future use.

Chi qing was facilitated by planting the most durable – as opposed to the highest quality – grain crop at the outset of year two of the Great Leap. In early 1959, Da Fo's harvest company and production team leaders decided secretly to increase the acreage sown to corn. The principal reason for this decision was to maximize the output of the grain crop that would be edible in the fields. There was also local concern for concealing from Liangmen Commune officials the loss of grain targeted for state procurement to such crop-eating sprees. Consequently, by the summer of 1959, some of the land previously slated for wheat, beans, cotton, and peanuts was being sown in corn, and more spring corn was planted to supplement the fall crop. Zheng Xu reflects on the logic behind this decision:

At the time, 10 percent of the corn was lost to eating in the fields, so it seemed wise to plant more corn because this was not incompatible with the national orders to increase wheat and corn production. We planted more land to corn because the output per *mu* was greater than the output of wheat. The corn was able to withstand the storms. It was our sturdiest crop, so it was likely to be there for eating in the fields. Also, corn was more versatile than wheat. We used it for eating in the fields, for corn porridge, and for feeding our animals.[8]

Moreover, the tall, thick rows of corn provided good cover.

The decision to eat the standing crops was a spontaneous decision by peasant household members. People just did it when the opportunity presented itself. This strategy was taken up at dusk, at midnight, and at the early dawn, and it occurred in many different villages simultaneously. Though the Liangmen People's Commune officials managed to impede virtually all other survival strategies, they were

---

[8] Zheng Xu, interview, September 13, 1993.

at a loss to deflect this one in any systematic way. The speed and secretiveness of *chi qing* made it safer than other strategies. Bao Zhongxin says:

There were so many hungry people doing it that there just was no way the leaders could stop it. They had to settle for trying to stop people from taking the green crops home to eat. If people did not eat the crops from the collective fields they would have starved to death. So the [unstated] rule was that if you just ate the crops in the fields it would be fine.[9]

Chi qing expressed a moral decision to give one's family a subsistence portion of the harvest before provisioning the Maoist state, but it was more than that: Da Fo's denizens also saw it as an entitlement.[10] Bao Zhongxin expresses it this way:

The reason very few people died of starvation in Da Fo during the three years of economic difficulties was that people were able to get the crops from the collective fields. The collective fields were, after all, different from private fields. *Everybody felt that they were entitled to eat the green crops from the public fields.* Even though eating the green crops was sort of like stealing from the collective, we did not really feel that we were stealing. We were taking our share of the green crops, *a share that belonged to every one of us.* Why should we have gone hungry when the crops were standing there in the fields?[11]

The pressure of the famine itself created the political conditions for collusion between ordinary villagers and the Da Fo brigade, harvest company, and production team leaders who were responsible for complying with state harvest claims. The acutely serious food problem of 1960 sent virtually every person in Da Fo to the fields to eat the green crops until the start of the summer harvest. Whereas neither party boss Bao Zhilong nor secretary Bao Yibin took up the practice, their spouses and children survived the spring hunger of 1960 by practicing *chi qing*. To be sure, Bao Yibin spoke for the claims of the commune, but he had to live among kin, neighbors, and fellow villagers whose guarantees of minimal food security had collapsed. Bao was dependent on ordinary villagers for his salary and operating expenses, and Bao Yibin's family food supply came from Da Fo's grain fields, not from the people's commune, so his family too was reduced to near-starvation by the severe reduction in the grain ration.[12]

This point is worth dwelling on: like every government of China that came before it, the party-led government of the PRC could not afford to pay its government employees at the local level. At least 70 percent of Communist Party cadres – including the leaders of the communes and their lower-level operatives – were paid by the commune. If the commune and, more to the point, the villages that these operatives supervised did not produce a surplus, the operatives could

---

[9] Bao Zhongxin, interview, June 23, 2001.
[10] Compare with Scott, *Moral Economy of the Peasant*, 15.
[11] Bao Zhongxin, interview, June 23, 2001.
[12] Jean C. Oi informs us that brigade cadres were dependent on sub-commune tillers for their food supply. See *State and Peasant*, 106–07.

not be paid. This created a problem of double loyalties in low-level cadres, who were charged with squeezing resources out of the villages for the party-state and were inclined to line their own pockets, but who also were conditioned and constrained by their ties to local villagers and had the power to offer them some protection from the center.[13] In the crisis months of 1960, therefore, Bao Yibin faced a dilemma: If he strictly enforced requisitioning by cracking down on *chi qing*, he would be doing his duty to the state and perhaps securing his position, but he risked the very survival of his own household. Bao opted not to do this, and, according to him, "No village leader was serious about stopping villagers from eating the green crops."[14] Even those party leaders who cruelly suppressed villagers' other survival strategies could not repress *chi qing* too harshly, because many of them and their family members relied on it to survive in the harsh months of 1960–61.

What proved decisive was Da Fo's blood tie to the leadership of the commune, for Bao Yibin was able to rely on his relationship with Bao Zhilong, still the vice-director of the Liangmen People's Commune, to prevent any severe crackdown on *chi qing*. Da Fo was politically fortunate. In some parts of China – like Laoqu village, Dingyuan County, Anhui province – villagers who had neither blood ties nor party-based connections to the leadership of the people's communes found that Maoist officials overthrew kinship-based village leadership arrangements and used repression to back up orders to prevent people from eating the green crops, and the death rate soared to 20 to 50 percent in these places.[15]

In Da Fo, *chi qing* had strong approval from most village-level Communist Party and nonparty leaders and followers. As Bao Jiping explains, "There was solidarity among the villagers and production team leaders. They all ate the green crops, and there was no need for them to hide this from one another. They only tried to hide the consumption of the green crops from a few major village leaders."[16] Seldom did Da Fo's leaders betray this solidarity, for the pressure for it came from below, and reputations could be damaged by attempting to stop it. Bao Dongzhi, a client of Bao Zhilong and the formal head of the First Harvest Company during the Great Leap Forward, explains:

At the time eating the green crops was widespread, especially among women. They would take toilet breaks once in a while, but in fact they just disappeared into the fields and ate the crops during the breaks. I had to warn them not to eat too much. But I had no way to stop them. Everybody was hungry. If I reported them to the village leaders, they would be criticized in public, and I would have offended them. I could not afford to offend everyone in the production teams. Therefore, I had to turn a blind eye.[17]

[13] Compare with Shue, *Peasant China in Transition*, 113.
[14] Bao Yibin, interview, September 15, 1993.
[15] Chen, "Memory and Survivorship," 3, 8–9, 16–17.
[16] Bao Jiping, interview, September 2, 1993.
[17] Bao Dongzhi, interview, September 7, 1993.

Bao Zhigen, the *de facto* head of the First Harvest Company, did great damage to his reputation by beating Bao Wending's mother for taking green crops from the collective fields. In the aftermath of the famine, Bao Wending occasionally fought with Bao Zhigen and cursed him in public, and four decades later villagers still have not forgiven Bao for this beating, which they took as an attack on a shared entitlement.[18]

Virtually all of Da Fo's village leaders, including those with Communist Party membership, sanctioned *chi qing* by pursuing it themselves. Apparently they too felt that eating the crops in the fields was a traditional inalienable right and were unwilling to give it up to the central state drive for more grain-based revenue. Zheng Tianbao, a crop watcher for Da Fo's maize fields, says he ate as much corn as possible from the fields he guarded at night and that this practice enabled him to get through the famine year of 1960. Zheng and his crop-watching counterparts never reported any of the nocturnal "eat-ins" of the other village corn-eaters during the terrible year of 1960. Recalling the role of Da Fo CCP brigade leaders in regulating *chi qing* once the famine worsened in early 1960, Tang Degao adds an important note:

The village leaders knew everybody was hungry. They knew it was very bad to eat the green crops, because the more they ate the unripened crops, the poorer would be the harvest. But they had to let the villagers eat in order to keep themselves alive. They did assign militia to walk around the fields and inspect the people's baskets at the entrance of the village, but it was impossible to stop hungry people from eating, and I do not think that village leaders really tried very hard.[19]

Because Da Fo villagers could sustain *chi qing* at a comparatively minimal risk, by midsummer of 1960 the practice had expanded to a far greater scale.[20] Only half of the June wheat crop found its way to Da Fo's threshing grounds in 1960.[21] Worse, from the standpoint of the commune authorities, villagers extended *chi qing* to other crops. Pang Chuanyan says: "We ate everything, including corn, sorghum, peanuts, and sweet potatoes. Some of these crops were eaten up completely before the harvest."[22]

In the famine months, roughly the late fall of 1959 to the early spring of 1961, villagers gained knowledge of the spreading practice of *chi qing* and of the Maoist state difficulty in containing it through news coming from telephone calls made from the Liangmen People's Commune to countless villages within Liangmen district itself. The telephone lines in Dongle County were shared party lines, so if someone picked up a receiver in Da Fo, he could listen in on the conversations between party leaders in Liangmen People's Commune

---

[18] Bao Zhongxin, interview, June 23, 2001.
[19] Tang Degao, interview, September 2, 1995.
[20] See the logic of Scott, *Domination and the Arts of Resistance*, 189–94.
[21] Pang Qinli, interview, September 1, 1993.
[22] Pang Chuanyan, interview, September 6, 1993.

headquarters and party leaders in all of the twenty brigades. Many of Da Fo's curious residents did precisely this, getting news of the reports of crop theft, *chi qing*, and other forms of forbidden behavior spreading throughout the countryside and then passing on details to fellow villagers. When villagers listened in on these official telephone conversations, they heard commune leaders voicing alarm to brigade party secretaries about their losses to *chi qing*. These reports enhanced the villagers' confidence that they could continue eating the green crops without punishment.

That the Liangmen People's Commune officials only loosely controlled the village-based militias, whose members also were exposed to sharp hunger, gave even more impetus to *chi qing*. "During the Great Leap Forward," remembers Bao Honglin, "the Da Fo militia had thirty guns and assigned four people to watch the crops day and night. I went to the fields to watch the crops at the time. Being in the militia was beneficial. Those of us in the militia could eat as much of the green crops as we pleased without worrying about being caught. Our family members could also eat much more than others, because they knew that we would not try to catch them."[23] As the militia relaxed its crop-watching controls in mid-1960, at the height of the famine, villagers followed suit, and some were so bold as to bring home the green crops to store for consumption at a later date.[24]

Throughout 1960, Bao Zhilong and the Liangmen People's Commune crop inspectors pressed party secretary Bao Yibin to address *chi qing*. Although a few villagers gratefully recall that former party secretary Bao Yibin did "a very poor job of stopping the practice of eating the green crops," this practice was the target of a short-lived repression.[25] In Da Fo, the most feared agent of this repression was Bao Zhigen, the toady of commune vice-director Bao Zhilong. In this time of famine, Bao Zhigen beat several elderly hungry women, including the mother of party secretary Bao Yibin, because they pilfered green crops from the collective fields.[26]

Everyone also seems to know the story of Ruan Linqing, the "green crop thief" who was publicly disciplined in order to placate the Liangmen People's Commune authorities and to keep the commune crop inspectors from subjecting Da Fo's grain fields to closer scrutiny. Ruan Shaobing tells it:

In 1960, villagers ate nearly all of the wheat crops before the time for the harvest. The fall crop would have met with the same fate if the brigade leaders had not taken measures to inhibit the villagers from eating the green crops. As an emergency measure, the brigade leaders began to discipline those who were apprehended in the act of consuming the green crops, punishing them by taking away their household belongings. Ruan Linqing started to eat the fall millet crop very early in the season. He was the first person to be caught,

---

[23] Bao Honglin, interview, June 25, 2001.

[24] Ruan Yindao, interview, September 14, 1993.

[25] Bao Guangming, interview, September 4, 1993.

[26] Bao Zhongxin, interview, June 23, 2001.

and his household belongings were taken away. Ruan Linqing's wife persuaded him to let her go back to her parents' home. They separated without the knowledge of the brigade leaders, and the woman never came back to her husband.[27]

The tragedy that Ruan Linqing suffered for *chi qing* reminded everyone that, even when rendered ineffective, the people's commune still posed a serious threat to the form of social organization they most cherished: the family.

As the famine intensified in 1960, some of the Da Fo party leaders increasingly targeted the women who had to rely on *chi qing* for survival, and they were inclined to mistreat those whose husbands were away, a process that also destroyed marriage and family. Ruan Yulan explains:

> One of my cousins was married to Ruan Yin. One day, this cousin was eating an ear of green corn, and she was caught by Bao Yiming. He took the corn from her and threw it right onto her face. She was so humiliated and so angry that she left Da Fo with her young son and ran all the way back to her mother's home village.
>
> Ruan Yin, her husband, . . . had just returned from Ji County, where he had been digging the river for a long time. He was so starved that he could barely walk. So he did not fully grasp how much humiliation his wife had suffered. My cousin did not see any hope in Da Fo, and she told Ruan Yin that they should temporarily divorce so she could take her son to a better place. Ruan Yin did not know that she would leave him forever, and so he agreed. After the divorce, my cousin married somebody else in a different village. Ruan Yin was never able to marry again, and his family remained a broken family. He died a couple of years ago, in 2000, childless, without anyone in Da Fo noticing his death until several days after he died.[28]

The breakup of these two families underscored the life-and-death struggle in which China's rural people were involved and cautioned prudence. From the fall harvest of 1960, therefore, Da Fo's production team and harvest company leaders warned villagers against eating green crops too prematurely, in broad daylight, or within the purview of top party loyalists with strong ties to the Liangmen People's Commune. Simultaneously, Bao Yibin discreetly let it be known that he did not want to be troubled by the branch party leaders bringing such behavior to the attention of commune authorities.

In Liangmen district, *chi qing* was so widespread that it crippled the capacity of the commune officials to enforce procurement in accordance with Maoist state claims. There is little doubt that this practice, taken cumulatively, went a long way toward inhibiting the grain revenue campaign of the Henan provincial arm of Mao Zedong's central government. Pang Tinghua says: "The practice of eating the green crops was so prevalent that some of the crops were completely ruined. The corn, for example, was stripped bare and had no seeds. This practice ruined the harvest, and thereafter the government was not able to collect any grain tax."[29] Ironically, the village people who brought on this ruin were labeled

---

[27] Ruan Shaobing, interview, September 11, 1993.
[28] Ruan Yulan, interview, July 9, 2002; story corroborated by Pang Yilu, interview, July 12, 2002.
[29] Pang Tinghua, interview, September 1, 1993.

rightists by the Da Fo party leaders who had become operatives of the commune. Bao Dongzhi, the only person who actually gained weight from eating the green crops, was said to be the leading "tough-stomached rightist" in Da Fo.[30] What this meant, of course, was that tough-stomached Bao was leading the popular retreat from the famine made by the Mao-led leftists.

The Death Rate in Da Fo

Chi qing enabled many of Da Fo's villagers to survive the Great Leap Forward Famine, but it could not save everyone. The dilemma of Da Fo worsened all through 1960, and by mid-year the signs of great human suffering were every-where. By late 1960 the stench of death permeated Da Fo's streets, edema ran rampant, and despair gripped its households. Precisely how many people died of starvation is not easy to determine. Villagers are reluctant to venture an educated guess, and the acts of local party leaders in the thrall of the Maoist collective experiment themselves work against our attempts to get at the truth. In Da Fo it was a custom when someone died for the family to place a strip of yellow paper before the earth god temple (*tudi miao*). This public expression of grief informed everyone in the village of the family's loss. Because this custom was discontinued by party leaders who pushed the Great Leap, and because such leaders kept villagers in the collective fields from dawn to midnight for months on end, people say it is difficult to know who, outside of their immediate fami-lies, fell victim to the famine. Collectivization, ironically, promoted solitude and estrangement.

When asked about the famine's mortality rate, villagers disagree. Some parrot the vague standard Communist Party version of village history: a dozen or so elderly people died of hunger in 1960. But this is not true; in fact, it does not even accord with statements of loyal party leaders. Bao Zhendao, the Da Fo vice–party secretary during the three years of the Great Leap Forward and someone who is in the habit of lying about any conceivable aspect of the Great Leap, claims that no one died of famine.[31] Bao Yibin, the party secretary in this same period, estimates that thirty people died in 1960. "Most of them," says Bao, "were old folks, people who were vulnerable to poor nutrition. Many of them could not eat and digest the tree leaves and other substitute food."[32] By contrast, Bao Huayin, the ex–Dongle County wartime party secretary whose father died of starvation in 1960, informs us that at least sixty villagers became the victims of the famine that followed the Great Leap Forward. Nearly all of them died in the acute hunger of 1960.[33]

---

[30] Bao Yibin, interview, September 15, 1993.
[31] Bao Zhendao, interview, May 10, 1990.
[32] Bao Yibin, interview, August 10, 1990.
[33] Bao Huayin, interview, August 12, 1990.

If Bao Huayin's estimate is the accurate minimum number of villagers who died from a lack of food, as I believe is the case, it contrasts starkly with the early historiographical assumptions that the Great Leap resulted in only "generalized malnutrition" stemming from critical food shortages.[34] Much to their credit, Meisner, Lardy, Lieberthal, and Friedman, Pickowicz, and Selden have corrected this representation, and Lardy more or less sums up their view in stating that "extremist CCP policies of the Great Leap engendered a famine of proportions unprecedented."[35] These studies, however, provide little by way of microlevel evidence on mortality rates in rural villages caught in the death grip of the famine. The human suffering in Da Fo apparently was indeed unprecedented in the twentieth century. The Great Leap Forward Famine in this rural market village was at least as devastating as had been the Henan Famine of 1942, which did serious damage to the legitimacy of Chiang Kai-shek's Nationalist government in Henan province during World War II.[36]

Still, the estimate of sixty deaths does not include deaths from miscarriages, abortions, or infanticides associated with the desperation of female famine victims. Nor does it include newborn children who died from malnutrition. Recalls Zhou Weihai: "The newborn children were particularly vulnerable, because their mothers were too poorly nourished to breast-feed them, and there was hardly any other suitable food available for the babies. When they died, they just died. People here did not say they died of hunger because it did not sound right."[37]

Whereas the oral history data on famine mortality is largely anecdotal, it tends to correspond with the findings of Lillian Li on the factors shaping the age distribution of deaths. Li's data suggest that children under ten were among the major victims of famine; in Da Fo most of the children who died in the 1960 famine were between the ages of one and five, a finding that corresponds more to the pattern of mortality among village children in the Sudan Famine of 1984–85.[38] When Da Fo's inhabitants say, as they often do, that they were able to save their children from the famine of the Great Leap by taking them along to eat the green crops and setting aside most of their family's public grain ration for them, they are talking about children between the ages of six and twelve, for only children in this age group were allowed to accompany adults to the collective fields, were able to digest the green crops, were able to bear the risks of these poor food supplements as well as survive the prevalent bacterial diarrhea, and thus ultimately were able to scavenge for tuber crops and wild vegetables.[39]

[34] Buck, *Food and Agriculture*, 9; Fairbank, Reischauer, and Craig, *East Asia*, 912; and Meisner, *Mao's China*, 248–50.
[35] Meisner, *Mao's China*, 250–51; Lardy, "Chinese Economy Under Stress," esp. 370–71; Lieberthal, "Great Leap Forward"; Friedman, Pickowicz, and Selden, *Chinese Village*.
[36] White and Jacoby, *Thunder Out of China*.
[37] Zhou Weihai, interview, September 1, 1993.
[38] Li, "Life and Death," 500–01; de Waal, *Famine that Kills*, 178.
[39] Bao Jieshi, interview, September 1, 1995.

The soaring death rate was, according famine survivors, accompanied by a marked decline in the birthrate and by delayed births linked to a decline in fertility.[40] Amenorrhea, the failure of menstruation and the onset of infertility in women plagued by extremely poor nutrition, was prevalent in Da Fo from late 1959 through early 1961. In referring to the strong relationship between amenorrhea engendered by radical dearth and a falling rate of conception, Le Roy Ladurie stresses that rising death rates, declining marriages, and falling birth rates "all interact with machine-like regularity" in times of famine.[41] Tang Jinlin observes: "At that time, family planning was not yet in vogue. But during the famine, because of poor nutrition, many women stopped their menstrual period. Hence they did not need birth control."[42] Zheng Fuqing, Huang Fengyan, and Pang Aichen, women who were 42, 38, and 43 years old respectively in 1958, all say their menstrual periods stopped in the famine year.[43] A few Da Fo villagers see the cause of the drop in the number of village births as much in politics as in physiology. "The birthrate," says Zhou Weihai, "dropped a great deal. Only people who had income from outside and people who were [party] leaders were able to have children and keep them alive too. Ordinary folk did not give birth to children, and if they did the chance of the baby dying of hunger was nine in ten."[44]

The estimate of sixty famine deaths also does not include the village people who succumbed to a growing number of famine-related diseases and conditions, which critically affected the life chances of previously healthy adults, especially elderly farmers. The most prevalent of these conditions was edema. People from every quarter of the village, every age group, every occupational category, and every political background and rank suffered from what villagers refer to as "swollen leg disease," which became pandemic after the half-*jin* daily grain ration was reduced by the Liangmen People's Commune leaders. By early 1960 Da Fo had established a small hospital for edema sufferers. Patients could eat a little better than people outside the hospital. Clearance for hospital stays was a matter of contention, for by the spring hunger of 1960 it had become perfectly obvious that the hospital was, from the standpoint of basic food security, a far safer place to be than in the "healthy society" nurtured by the collective dining hall system. The line between the deserving and undeserving hospital candidates became more and more difficult to establish. Many of those waiting for admission died.

So did many of those who actually were admitted, and it is clear from the testimony of Tang Degao, whose father died of dropsy while in the brigade's

---

[40] Li, "Life and Death," 502.
[41] Ladurie, "Amenorrhea in Time of Famine," 265–69, esp. 267. See also Friedman, Pickowicz, and Selden, *Chinese Village*, 201.
[42] Tang Jinlin, interview, August 10, 1990.
[43] Zheng Fuqing, Huang Fengyan, and Pang Aichen, interviews, September 12, 1993.
[44] Zhou Weihai, interview, September 1, 1993.

makeshift hospital, that these deaths were not unrelated to *chi qing*. Recalls Tang,

I remember the date of my father's death because that day was also the moon festival. My father was sixty-seven years old that year [1960]. Quite a few people died in the village that year. The old people were more vulnerable to the hunger than the younger ones, as their stomachs could not digest the green crops they were eating. Also, they did not work in the fields, and they did not have the same easy access to the fields as others.[45]

In this first year of hunger a dozen elderly Da Fo villagers died of starvation, and twenty others perished in early 1961.[46] Tang Weilan, who was twenty-five in 1960, confirms the estimate of approximately thirty deaths among the aged. "During the two years of public dining halls, there were about twenty to thirty villagers who died of malnutrition. Most of them were old folks."[47] Tang Weilan's grandfather was also admitted to the hospital – called the Happiness Garden Infirmary – when he became sick from malnutrition. Tang Weilan recalls:

My grandfather suffered from swollen legs at the time. He was accused of 'doing nothing' by Bao Yiliao, the head of the infirmary, and not allowed to eat his full share of food, and he also was beaten by someone. Three days before he died, they asked us to take him home. He died at home. My family was very angry with his death. But we did not dare complain at the time.[48]

Not surprisingly, therefore, we learn from Bao Jiping, the vice–party secretary of Da Fo in 1956–57, that "during the three years of the Great Leap famine, close to one hundred people died of hunger, or a combination of hunger and diseases."[49] There were at least 1,470 people in Da Fo in 1958, so it seems likely that 6.8 percent of them perished in the famine of the Great Leap.

But even this estimate is probably too low, as a host of lesser known factors raised the death rate. The estimate of 6.8 percent, which adds forty edema-related deaths to the sixty starvation deaths, does not address the presumption, which permeates Western scholarship, that very few middle-aged villagers died of hunger during the Great Leap Forward Famine. Prior to 1949, quite a few men in the thirty-to-fifty age group in Da Fo had survived a strain of tuberculosis still present in the village, and they apparently pursued normal work lives into the early period of collectivization. But once the protein deficiencies, energy drains, anxieties, and pneumonias of the late 1950s took their toll, many of them were beset by symptoms associated with the tubercle bacillus that had affected them in the past and that was still incurable in rural China. I have uncovered six victims of this pattern of heightened vulnerability in Da Fo, but more doubtless existed. Surely this factor added to the death toll of the Great Leap famine.

[45] Tang Degao, interview, September 21, 1995.
[46] Bao Tanger, interview, September 1, 1995.
[47] Tang Weilan, interview, September 20, 1995.
[48] Ibid., July 14, 2002.
[49] Bao Jiping, interview, September 2, 1993.

There is also the question of how many people died from collectivist labor-related accidents. Field production and labor camp campaigns disrupted the normalcy of rural work life, sometimes radically altering well-known work routines and village landscapes in ways that jeopardized physical safety. The frantic mobilization of local people to instantly and continuously meet impossible production goals sometimes resulted in fatalities that are not usually inferred to be the product of the party-state drive for collectivization in the Great Leap, but, as Zhang Yimo's motion picture adaptation of Yu Hua's novel, *To Live*, reminds us, they often were linked to the acute sleep deprivation induced by the unceasing rush to increase production. There were two such tragedies in Da Fo. After the fall harvest of 1958, Zhou Weihai's wife, exhausted from her labors, fell asleep while breast-feeding her child and inadvertently smothered the infant to death. In early 1960, Bao Meizhe, worn down from overwork and loss of sleep, accidentally fell into one of many recently constructed, unmarked earthen wells in Da Fo's snow-covered collective fields while stealing crops at night and drowned.[50]

The frantic rush to instantly apply unfamiliar and unused modern technology to increase agricultural production, seemingly without consideration for increased catastrophic accident risks, was an important part of the mortality toll. In the first year of the Great Leap Forward, farm people, farm animals, and farm machinery all had to rely on ferry boats to cross the Wei River. On the occasion of the arrival of the first Russian-made tractors in Dongle County, the Liangmen Commune leaders jammed the heavy-wheeled vehicles onto a ferry carrying a crowd of farmers and animals. Loaded over the safe weight limit, the ferry capsized during the crossing, taking both the tractors and human traffic into the river. This incident prompted an investigation by the Dongle County Communist Party secretary, but the responsible parties were not reprimanded, and the death toll went unreported.

The public criticism sessions also increased the death rate in several ways. In the first case, blows to the body caused internal injuries that, in combination with physical emaciation and acute hunger, could induce death. After stealing two cabbages from Da Fo's fields in the summer of 1959, for example, Pang Ranxi was apprehended by party secretary Bao Yibin and taken to brigade headquarters, where Bao called a mass meeting to publicly criticize the culprit for half a day. "Pang Ranxi was so exasperated and exhausted there was nothing he could do to defend himself," remembers Pang Yilu. "After that Pang Ranxi collapsed and fell ill, and he never recovered."[51] A similar fate awaited people sent to the labor camps. "Most of the strong-bodied Da Fo youths sent to the Ji County river dig camp were able to survive the harsh conditions there," recalls Bao Yuming, "but there was a person from Wanxiuzhuang who died. He was in poor

[50] Zhou Weihai, interview, September 2, 1993.
[51] Pang Yilu, interview, July 14, 2000.

health and could not work very hard. The leaders struggled him once before he died."[52]

In the second case, the traumatic experience with vulgar and demeaning verbal assaults, in combination with the punishment, threatened or actual, of taking away the dining hall food ration, induced a kind of life-threatening anxiety attack and triggered a paralyzing fear that any future encounter with the public dining hall would bring death. For some, this experience was too much to bear, and it induced death by heart attack or, more likely, a stroke – farmers describe that the victims of these encounters had high blood pressure and brain bleeding.[53] Without food, the recipient of this kind of public criticism knew he or she was going to die, and that fear, in combination with social isolation and inability to express and quickly release anger over public chastisement and humiliation, could accelerate death.[54]

Yet a third result of the public criticisms was suicide. In some Chinese villages the frequency of suicide increased as the famine loomed, and apparently it was inseparable from the sting of these criticism sessions. The public beatings and humiliations left villagers with a sense of shame, and many of them felt they had no way to stand up against the disgrace other than to deprive the Maoist labor bosses of their bodies. Lu Xiuli, who witnessed many public criticism sessions in Da Fo during the Great Leap, remembers the trauma of one in particular:

I was never struggled against during the Great Leap Forward. However, there was a woman in the village who was caught taking the green crops [from the collective fields] by village leaders. She was struggled. The leaders forced her to eat sweet potato vines because she had stolen the sweet potatoes. The practice was to force people to eat the stems or vines of the crop they stole. She was so humiliated that she tried to kill herself by jumping into a well. But she did not die. People saw her and rescued her just in time.[55]

To some extent, the spate of attempted suicides in Da Fo village seems to have accompanied the anti-rightist/anti–grain concealment campaign of late 1959, and there is little doubt that Bao Zhilong and his men, including merciless hustler Bao Zhigen, were implicated in bringing the pressure that pushed villagers to the brink.

Let us briefly revisit the story of Tang Weilan, whose grandfather died of mistreatment during his stay in the Happiness Garden Infirmary. In late 1959, Tang Weilan was beaten by Da Fo party leaders for running away from the Ji County river dig, and then compelled to work on the satellite of Beitoucun, the commune's model brigade. While in Beitoucun, Tang received word that his edema-stricken father, Tang Jintao, had been accused of hiding grain in his Da Fo

[52] Bao Yuming, interview, June 21, 2001.
[53] I am indebted to Susanne Weigelin-Schwiedrzik for making me pay closer attention to the terms Da Fo's farmers used to describe this phenomenon. Personal correspondence, July 7, 2006.
[54] See Thaxton and Wang, "Power, Disentitlement, and Life Chances." The research of Robert A. Anderson, M. D., suggests a strong relationship between inability to express anger and let it disappear quickly and elevated risk of myocardial infarction. See "Psychoneuroimmunoendocrinology Review," 50–51.
[55] Lu Xiuli, interview, September 10, 2002.

household by Bao Zhigen. Reportedly, Bao Zhigen and members of the militia had struggled Tang Jintao in public, and then overthrown all due process. Bao had searched and destroyed much of Tang Jintao's house, all the while beating the elder Tang. Refusing to listen to Tang Jintao's denial, Bao Zhigen ordered the public dining hall to cut off Tang's food ration until he revealed the whereabouts of the hidden grain, which in fact did not exist. Bao Zhigen then incarcerated Tang in a small, dark room, where Tang hanged himself in protest, only to be rescued by neighbor Bao Xugan. On hearing this shocking news, Tang Weilan hurried back to Da Fo from Beitoucun to challenge party boss Bao Zhilong to either find the grain in his parents' house or arrest the entire family. Upon investigating the matter, boss Bao denounced Bao Zhigen for setting up an "illegal court" and contemplated informing the police, which would have resulted in a five-year prison sentence for Bao Zhigen. At this juncture, however, the modality of Communist Party rule took over the case. Bao Zhigen secretly bribed boss Bao's wife, and she persuaded boss Bao to go easy on Bao Zhigen and to release Tang Weilan's parents in order to calm Tang's anger, though this response did not placate Tang Weilan, whose repeated challenges caused Bao Zhigen to scheme to assign Tang to work outside of Da Fo.[56]

Apparently, the threat of suicide was a weapon of the weak, and in some cases it did give party leaders pause. Speaking of the terrible winter of 1960, Tang Fuyin tells us, "We went to dig carrots in the fields. The ground was frozen already. We hid the big carrots under our clothes. When nobody was around, we would eat them raw in the cold. One woman had two big carrots in her waistband, and she was discovered by others. They said they would hold a public meeting to criticize her. She was very angry, and she threatened to kill herself. The meeting was cancelled for that reason."[57]

In the course of the Great Leap Forward, Da Fo apparently had only a few suicides, but many villagers contemplated it or wished that some act of fate might relieve them from their suffering. This tendency was evident in the young, lonely, and angry men who had been subjected to forced labor and public criticism beyond the village. Bao Zhongxin is haunted by his memory of the ordeal of work life in the Ji County labor camp during 1960. "I was hungry all the time," says Bao,

and the main reason was that the work there was too hard. Because the work was so hard, during that period I often wished that one day I would die in an accident at the work site. If I were killed, then I would not have had to bear the suffering I endured. I had this thought many times, but I could not tell my parents back in Da Fo because they would have worried too much about me if they had known how really difficult my situation was.[58]

The Communist Party leaders in charge of the Da Fo public criticism sessions seldom if ever recorded struggle-related deaths for what they were. But clearly, Mao's politics combined with other factors, including the reduction of the public

[56] Tang Weilan, interviews, July 14, 2002, July 25, 2004, and July 31, 2006.
[57] Tang Fuyin, interview, July 20, 2003.
[58] Bao Zhongxin, interview, June 23, 2001.

food ration and exhaustion from overwork, to make spurious the claim that rural people died from a hunger that was not related to the lethal public whip of state terror in the Great Leap Forward. We have compelling evidence of this point from Wu Yongkuan, a native of Gao Dadian village, Guangshan County, Henan province, who courageously published a memoir of his ordeal with the Great Leap famine in the October 2004 issue of *Beijing Spring*:

I turned 15 in 1959. In my memory, those were days of sorrow and horror.

At the time, in order to build socialism, the central government espoused the Three Red Flags – the Final Path [or Final Solution], the People's Communes, and the Great Leap Forward. It was unimaginable that this socialist experiment, with its wind of exaggeration (*fukua feng*), not only would fail but also would promote social chaos. From top to bottom, this was a time when those who boasted of great results were the "red" achievers.

The anti-rightist movement was in full swing, and public condemnations of non-disclosure of private production and private property were spreading. If you spoke the truth, you were compelled to put on a hat [wear a label] and accused of being a right-wing opportunist, interrogated, beaten and tortured, and even hung up by a rope.

You had to confess your guilt. Otherwise, you were beaten to death. For example, Wu Derong, one of my production team members, once said: "There is plenty of grain here, so why not distribute it among our members?" Just because of this single sentence, he was beaten for several days and nights until he died. To give another example, when Wu Detong chastised the brigade leader Wu Yongshou a little, Wu Yongshou, the brigade leader, called on several men to beat him to death. When the vice-director of the brigade, Wu Rongguan, said that the Great Leap Forward was endangering many lives, he was beaten to death at the brigade headquarters after an official brigade meeting.

My father, Wu Dejin, was an honest and kind person. He was the accountant of the production team. He said it was a shame that in spite of a bountiful harvest, the team members were not allowed to have a share of it. After being subjected to public struggle by the brigade party chief, Wu Yongshou, he died at 5 p.m., November 3rd due to his anger and starvation. I lost my beloved father at the age when I needed parental care. With my dear father gone, I had to drop out of school, I had no way to get treatment from a doctor when I was sick, and this loss hurt me all through my life.

In 1959, our production brigade [village] enjoyed a bountiful harvest. In the summer, the wheat harvest reached 12,000 *jin*, while soy was at 3,500 *jin*. These crops, as well as cotton, were all transferred to the national silos. Every person was allowed to keep 30 *jin* of the summer wheat harvest as well as 30 *jin* of the autumn rice crop for consumption. However, although we were told we could keep this much of the harvest, shortly thereafter the anti-concealment campaign [of late 1959] commenced. Although we gave up our remaining food, the authorities went a step further and demanded that we surrender food provisions that we allegedly had kept for ourselves. In fact, we did not have a single kernel of grain left. Yet from that point on, the production brigade office was turned into an office for beating people. There were daily struggle meetings, and those who did not turn in enough crops were verbally abused and beaten.

At this point, everyone began to panic, for with no food left we had to eat wild grass and tree bark to sustain ourselves. Soon the wild grass and tree bark were gone, and people had to eat *kangzhai* [rice husk sediment], and subsequently they lost their ability to defecate. People died of starvation, and every day the death count rose. In some cases, the dead children were eaten by adults, and the adults then died of *huangzhongbing* [an exceptionally severe case of edema]. In less than half a month, more than 70 persons died in our village of 120 people.

214

In retrospect, this tragedy was caused by the anti-rightist movement of the central government, which spiraled out of control. From top to bottom, the country was run ... through anti-rightist propaganda, deceitful reports, and political labels, ... and this allowed bad-natured people with the worst intentions to climb into leadership positions. The result was a train of abuse and a massive loss of life.[59]

Da Fo shared a similar, though less horrible, fate under Mao's fanatical party whips. After the Great Leap, Mao attempted to deny that the fanaticism he had whipped up in his cadres was responsible for the party's alienation from rural people, and he usually omitted the human costs of this fanaticism as it unfolded in public criticism.[60]

Explaining Da Fo's Escape from the Great Leap Forward Famine

That the Great Leap Forward Famine killed about 128 people, or 8.70 percent of the population of Da Fo village, indicates that approximately 90 percent of villagers managed to escape the famine's death grip. The scholarship on the Great Leap Forward is by and large silent on the subject of how the people of any specific village escaped, and Da Fo's history provides an important clue to this puzzle – a clue worth comparing with the two major explanations for how the famine ended, both of which assign a significant role to reformers in the central government.

Jasper Becker asserts that reformist policy measures conceived by leading Communist Party opponents of Mao saved China's villagers by ending the Great Leap Forward Famine.[61] Because of the failure of the Great Leap, Mao was forced to give up his chairmanship of the PRC. Though Mao remained the chairman of the CCP until he died, in 1976, after the Great Leap, Liu Shaoqi served as head of state, and Mao's power was challenged by Liu Shaoqi, Deng Xiaoping, and other reform-minded politicians in the central party leadership. Implementing the *sanzi yibao* (three freedoms, one contract) policies that approved the resumption of small plots for private household use, sanctioned market-focused petty trade in non-grain products, and allowed cooking in private homes, Liu and Deng purportedly brought the famine to a close.[62] These reforms did not entail the abandonment of communal farming or the resumption of private landownership, but they did allow villagers to return to farming small parcels of land individually, raising their own livestock, and engaging in small trade. With the introduction of *baochan daohu*, or the household contract responsibility system, tillers had to agree to sell a certain amount of the grain they raised to the state, but they were

---

[59] Wu Yongkuan, "Lishi Jianzheng," 36–37.
[60] Selden, *People's Republic of China*, 480–81; compare with Chang and Halliday, who claim that Mao pushed for less mercy, more brutality (*Mao*, 394).
[61] Becker, *Hungry Ghosts*, 238–53.
[62] Apparently Friedman, Pickowicz, and Selden share Becker's assumption. See *Revolution, Resistance, and Reform*, 13–14.

allowed to keep or sell the remainder.[63] Supposedly, these reforms enabled them to grow enough surplus grain to meet their subsistence needs, thus rescuing them from starvation.

The Becker argument doubtless holds up for many rural locales in China, because *sanzi yibao* restored popular incentives and provided the institutional framework that encouraged famished tillers to go back to private food production. However, the Becker thesis cannot explain the timing or the method of Da Fo's escape from the famine. There was a considerable gap in time between when this Liuist reform policy decision was taken and the time villagers needed to grow food for their families.[64] Da Fo party leaders did not implement the Liuist *sanzi yibao* policy in 1961. This policy was not put into practice in Da Fo until after the third year of the Great Leap, in 1962.[65] By the time the reform policy measures began to take hold during the first part of 1962, desperate villagers already had invented ways of coping with hunger. For the most part, therefore, the delayed social benefits of *sanzi yibao* only supplemented a host of locally conceived devices that Da Fo's tillers had come to rely on: eating the green crops, gathering tree leaves and wild vegetables, and pilfering collective melon and pumpkin fields.

Tragically, too, the Liu-Deng efforts to supplement *sanzi yibao* by providing relief grain to the countryside were apparently confused and compromised by Mao. It was not until the second half of 1960 that Mao and his rivals in the upper party leadership fully realized the severity of the food crisis in the countryside, and by then the central government did not have enough food to relieve the disaster – and Da Fo's farmers apparently could not count on government relief grain to escape the famine.[66] In mid-1960, the central government launched a campaign to increase the amount of "substitute foods" available in the countryside. The campaign lasted for the next year, but for Mao the ultimate goal of this campaign was to make China's village people reserve as much good food grain for the state as possible so that the state could use it to provision the cities and sustain exports, and this made it more difficult for Liu and Deng to get relief efforts going in the villages.[67] It is no wonder that most of Da Fo's farmers have trouble linking their escape from starvation to state-delivered substitute food. In order to recover from edema, for

---

[63] Becker, *Hungry Ghosts*, 239.

[64] I am indebted to Kimberley Ens Manning for helping me better understand my interview evidence and develop this argument. Personal correspondence, October 3, 2007.

[65] Bao Guangming, interview, July 12, 2001.

[66] Former first-pole party leader Bao Huayin reportedly visited Da Fo in late 1960. On finding villagers starving, Bao supposedly wrote a letter requesting that the central government order the Henan provincial government to provide relief grain for the village. However, there is no evidence that the provincial government followed up, or that it did so rapidly and efficiently. Even if the provincial leaders attempted to provide relief, the recipients and managers of this grain would have been the same brigade party leaders who were implicated in the Great Leap famine and who were inclined to direct food to their families and party-based friends. This interpretation is based on my reading of all of the four hundred Da Fo interviews, and also on my doubts about the sketchy, contrarian recollections of Bao Xiandai, interview, July 5, 2006.

[67] All of this relies on Gao Hua, "Da Ji Huang de 'Liangshi Shiyong,'" 71–81.

example, villagers remember eating a soup recipe based on the skin of winter melons, which they secretly took from the collective fields when "nearly everybody was starving" in 1960, so the official substitute relief foods delivered from the forests of Guangxi and Yunnan provinces more than a year later played a minor, belated role in nourishing them.[68] Villagers confirm that they benefited from the Liuist reform (which they dubbed "the big collective with small freedoms"), but they mostly remember that the reforms helped them put greater distance between themselves and a disaster from which they already had begun to escape.[69]

Dali Yang provides a somewhat different explanation of how reform helped China's rural people to resolve the Great Leap food crisis. Downplaying the importance of any top-level central government policy design, Yang argues that many tillers, in veiled collusion with local county- and brigade-level Communist Party leaders, established household contracting on their own prior to receiving government authorization, quietly pledging to deliver a specified percentage of the harvest to the government in return for the right to set aside private land parcels for individual household management and to practice animal husbandry for family gain. Rural famine survivors, according to Yang, credited the household responsibility system "for saving their lives."[70] This system was later redefined and sanctioned by the Liu-Deng reformers in order to rejuvenate agricultural production.[71] No doubt Yang's argument identifies an important aspect of the politics allowing many rural Chinese communities to escape from Mao's great famine.

In Da Fo, however, there was no household contracting. Wu Zhipu punished local party leaders who advanced the household responsibility system in rural Henan.[72] Therefore, Liangmen People's Commune and Da Fo brigade leaders did not actively embrace the responsibility system.[73] Nor did villagers clamor for the adoption of the household responsibility system, which was founded on the premise that rural farmers would be able to produce enough grain both to fulfill the quota and to reap a gain on the above-contract amount – an unlikely outcome in Da Fo, with its unproductive saline lands. To Da Fo's inhabitants, whose off-farm incomes remained suppressed, the household responsibility system seemed like a mechanical scheme to facilitate state control over how much of the crop they consumed and, worse, for high state rulers to reassert their claim to the grain crops lost to preemptive consumption – that is, to *chi qing*. Perhaps *baochan daohu* was a less authoritarian mechanism for appropriating the harvest than unified purchase and sale through the collective, and this arrangement did promise an

---

[68] Bao Honglin, interview, June 25, 2001; Pang Youqing, interview, July 18, 2000.

[69] Bao Honglin, interview, June 25, 2001.

[70] Yang, *Calamity and Reform in China*, 149–52, 155–60, quotation on 150.

[71] Yang, "Surviving the Great Leap Famine," 284. The word "later" is important because, according to Yang, both Liu and Deng were initially cautious about endorsing independent farming and the household responsibility system. See ibid., 284–88.

[72] MacFarquhar, *Origins of the Cultural Revolution*, 2:302–03; Yang, "Surviving the Great Leap Famine," 271–72, 293.

[73] Compare with Zhou, *How the Farmers Changed China*, 49.

end to starvation. Nevertheless, this particular retreat from the extremism of the Great Leap was a retreat *within* the collective system – it was not designed to restore private landownership or to liberate the energies of farm households. While making a concession to household-based agriculture, its aim was to ensure continued state claims on the production of tillers, and ultimately to restrict mobility and market entry.[74] Not surprisingly, therefore, the people of this village saw it as a state ploy to get them to give up their right to eat the standing crop without addressing critically related issues: harvest irregularities, the whims of corrupt local cadres, or the potential for the Henan provincial Maoists to take over *baochan daohu* and wed it to an only slightly diminished form of collective appropriation.

And, in truth, they recognized something that many China scholars have not: *baochan daohu* was not merely a mutually collaborative economic arrangement designed to bolster the income returns of famine-stricken farm households, it was a device of power designed to contain conflict among a desperate, angry, and rebellious peasantry precisely when Mao's famine had destroyed all trust in the Communist Party.[75] The purpose of the household responsibility system was to redefine the conflict over the failure of the Communist Party to provide food security through collective agriculture in a manner that would encourage rural people to accept the idea that those who remained loyal to the party and its socialist path of development would be saved by cooperating with cadres to remake the collective to serve both society and state, not merely the latter. Party leaders strove to convince farmers that there was a way to handle food security issues within the Leninist system of which they were a part. But Da Fo's residents and many other rural dwellers refused to give up *chi qing* and reengage the harvest extraction processes of the party-state because they had been conditioned by their experiences of the past decade to believe that more work could not bring more grain and more production could not result in more food to consume. They had concluded that if the greedy and corrupt party leaders were taking almost all of the grain they harvested for the state, then their only chance of surviving was to eat the raw crops in the fields. Hence, they would not trade *chi qing* for party-state harvest extraction without a plan that gave them greater control over the harvest and put food in their stomachs *before* putting it into the granaries of the commune. In short, villagers were looking to renegotiate the taking relationship that had endangered their survival during the Great Leap. They rejected *baochan daohu* and reemphasized the practice of *chi qing*. In Da Fo, then, the reforms

[74] Teiwes and Sun make it clear that Mao was opposed to this concession and that he feared it would encourage a drift back to individual farming and undermine his commune-based vision of socialist rule. They, and also Dali Yang, make it clear that the party leaders did not conceive the household responsibility system in order to empower village dwellers. See Teiwes with Sun, *China's Road to Disaster*, 218–29, and Yang, *Calamity and Reform in China*, 84–97, esp. 93–94.

[75] Patricia Thornton's exceptional work offers examples of farmers' reluctance to accept the household responsibility system and of the conflicts between farmers and cadres over this system. *Disciplining the State*, 146–47.

that emerged from the conflict between Mao on one side and Liu Shaoqi and Deng Xiaoping on the other did not result in the villagers' rescue from the worst ravages of the famine. Da Fo's villagers rescued themselves.

Chi qing was, in popular memory, "the most important method used to survive the famine."[76] To be sure, *chi qing* flourished only in agricultural counties where tillers could get seeds to sow and where the climate was favorable to grain crops. Da Fo, and most of the villages in Liangmen People's Commune, were fortunate, for they preserved their seeds up until 1960. By way of comparison, few villages in nearby Anyang People's Commune had seeds left in 1960, because people ate the entire standing crop, forcing villagers to turn to begging or banditry in other rural places and cities. Most people in Da Fo knew that everyone stood to suffer if *all* of the standing crops were eaten too early in the season. In the second half of 1960, when the famine was intensifying, villagers became alarmed that a small minority were gorging themselves without regard for future community food availability; this is why the same villagers who were grateful that Da Fo party leaders did not come down hard on *chi qing* prior to this critical point were upset when they let a handful of people eat too many of the green crops too early. In response, hungry villagers developed their own informal rules to regulate *chi qing* so that it did not quickly evolve into a blindly desperate lose-lose expedient inadequate to prevent starvation. Ironically, *chi qing* reflected the ability of famished villagers to cooperate even in the worst of times, and this jeopardized the Maoist attempt to exploit the countryside for primitive capital accumulation.[77]

This practice is all the more significant if juxtaposed with central government policy adjustments to the Great Leap crisis – or the lack thereof. In July 1960 Da Fo disbanded its public dining hall system, a move that occurred almost simultaneously with the July 1960 Beidaihe Work Conference in which Mao Zedong had mounted a *defense* of the value of the public dining hall system.[78] Mao himself did not sanction the disbanding of the public dining halls until the spring of the following year. The unsanctioned closing of the public dining hall system in Da Fo was, indirectly, the result of growing peasant resistance to draconian grain rationing and the inequalities of the public dining halls. In early 1960, before the pandemonium of *chi qing* compelled the Maoist state to relax its controls and before villagers found hope in the economic liberalization of Mao's opponents, an episode of collective action occurred in Da Fo that had all the marks of contentious protest.[79] The incident grew out of popular disenchantment with the corruption of the public dining hall food entitlement by the Da Fo party leaders, including commune vice–party secretary Bao Zhilong, party secretary Bao Yibin, and corrupt accountant Pang Lang. By early winter of 1960 these

---

[76] Zheng Yunxiang and Ruan Shaobing, interviews, September 19, 1995.

[77] My grasp of this point owes a great debt to Alfred Chan, personal correspondence, June/July 2006.

[78] Yang, *Calamity and Reform in China*, 73–74.

[79] For terminology and the conception, see McAdam, Tarrow, and Tilly, *Dynamics of Contention*, 7–8.

leaders not only were eating more and better food than ordinary villagers, they also were allowing the cooks to withhold grain rations from villagers. It was a time of sharp hunger and great fear, and many villagers voiced their anger. Lu Xiuli recalls, "On New Year's Eve of 1960, villagers went to Pang Lang's house to harass Pang and the leaders. They went there without a leader, and *it was like a rebellion*. Pang Lang was very frightened. He apologized to the villagers, and afterward he was much less aggressive toward them. We did not take anything from him, but we humiliated him."[80]

The protesters had called for a restructuring of the food allocation process and demanded accountability from the party leaders in charge of the public mess hall system, at the same time asserting their desire for independence from the commune food chain and threatening to turn things upside down if no one listened to them. Following this so-called disturbance (*naoshi*), Da Fo's party leaders were a bit more reserved about plundering the public food supply, and they temporarily relaxed their restrictions on eating green crops. This challenge from below left villagers feeling that they could influence the course of the Great Leap campaign. It sent a signal to party leaders in Da Fo and Liangmen that desperate rural people could and would act together to defend their rights to survival. Throughout the remainder of 1960, villagers continued to engage in crop theft, concealment, and, most importantly, *chi qing*, all of which alerted Henan government officials to a massive popular disengagement from the food distribution system of the commune. By late 1960, in Da Fo and throughout Liangmen district, this disengagement posed a serious challenge to any state collection of the harvest, raising the possibility of popular struggle from below putting the state in a serious fiscal crisis.

By the last quarter of 1960, members of the upper party leadership of Da Fo, Liangmen district, and Dongle County had fallen prey to the food-deprivation physical condition of edema. Even the Henan party work team leaders from Anyang prefecture who stayed in Da Fo had "swollen leg disease."[81] These local politicians began to understand that the public dining hall system was a failure. Many of them belonged to the network of Liu Jianxun, a reform-minded Henan provincial Communist Party secretary who replaced radical Maoist Wu Zhipu – part of the shakeup in party leadership that began to take place following the public exposure of the extent of the famine. The disbanding of Da Fo's public dining hall was undertaken with the tacit consent of these edema-stricken local party leaders, including a contingent in Liangmen district government, all of whom now called the public dining halls the *jibopi*, or "skin strippers."[82]

The case for doing away with the public dining halls came neither from Liangmen People's Commune leaders nor from the Da Fo party bosses, however. It came from local villagers' communications with Dongle County government. In

[80] Lu Xiuli, interview, September 10, 2002.
[81] Zheng Jintian, interview, September 13, 1993.
[82] Ruan Shaobing, interview, September 19, 1995.

The Escape from Famine and Death

November 1960, the Dongle County magistracy invited each village in Liangmen district to send one party member to the county seat to give a truthful assessment of the public dining halls. Da Fo sent Bao Jiping, a twenty-nine-year-old villager whose poor five-person family had received thirty-two *mu* of land through land reform. Originally a confidant of Da Fo party chief Bao Zhilong, Bao Jiping seemed a politically safe party choice, and indeed he initially behaved cautiously before county leaders. On hearing delegates from surrounding villages criticize the public dining hall system, Bao was emboldened to tell county leaders that Da Fo villagers had so little food that they were reduced to eating cotton seeds and a host of other food substitutes, from which they had fallen sick. And there was corruption. The grain ration, Bao revealed, "was being reduced as the grain passed through the hands of the Da Fo brigade party leaders, accountants, the head cook, and the secondary cooks."[83] Corroborating statements from scores of village leaders participating in this "public opinion meeting" prompted the Dongle County officials to order the public dining halls to relax their controls over the grain ration. Specifically, they were to allow villagers to take the grain home to cook for their families, so that the ration would be used more efficiently.[84] Significantly, these orders were put forth *before* Liu Shaoqi's reformist policy edicts were issued.

There is a consensus among Da Fo's inhabitants that life began to improve not long after the disbanding of the public dining halls, and Bao Tanger agrees.[85] At the same time, Bao Tanger attests,

The dining halls were not good, but they did give us something to hold on to. After they were dissolved, things became even harder for some time. There were twenty people who died in this period. Most were old. Poor nutrition was a factor behind their deaths. Small children also were vulnerable. The old and young did not have the same opportunity to eat the green crops in the fields as the stronger adults.[86]

These seemingly conflicting memories reflect the multifaceted reality of how the people of Da Fo survived the excruciating hunger between July 1960 and the autumn harvest of 1961. During this desperate fifteen-month stretch, according to Da Fo's Bao Zhidan (who helped manage the Liangmen People's Commune granary), the commune granary contained a lot of grain, but the commune leaders did not let people eat it because the state had earmarked most of it for transfer to other regions.[87] A few weeks after the close of the public dining halls, there was a strong upsurge in the practice of *chi qing*. Pang Furong recalls: "I came

---

[83] Bao Jiping, interview, September 2, 1993.

[84] Bao Jiping, interview, September 2, 1993; Zheng Jintian, interview, September 13, 1993.

[85] Bao Jiping, interview, September 2, 1993; Zheng Jintian, interview, September 13, 1993; and Bao Tanger, interview, September 1, 1995. Perhaps this was because the dining halls specialized in inferior food and corrupt management and also were situated in dirt fields far from the homes of tillers.

[86] Bao Tanger, interview, September 1, 1995.

[87] Bao Zhidan, interview, July 26, 2001.

back to work in the village in early 1961, not long after the public dining halls were disbanded. At the time, people did not have enough food to eat. I remember that everybody was eating the crops in the collective fields. As long as there were crops in the fields, we could eat them and not go hungry."[88] In short, what started out as a popular strategy of supplementing the grain ration of the public dining hall had replaced that system *in toto*. With the collapse of the dining hall system, eating the green crops was the key to survival. Many of those who suffered most were the ones who tried to live only on the food from the public dining halls and did not go to eat in the fields.[89]

In this same critical period villagers benefited from another important political change: a deflation in the power of the Maoist engineers of the Great Leap Forward. With the overthrow of Wu Zhipu, a campaign known as the *fan wufeng*, or Anti–Five Winds, reached Dongle County in early 1961. Focused on rooting out corruption and correcting the bad political behavior of the brigade party leaders, this campaign was extended to the villages in the month prior to the Spring Festival. Da Fo was a prime target. Twenty-four of Da Fo's sixty party members – its key leaders – were taken to a detention center in Dongle County town, where they were interrogated along with party leaders from Jingweizhuang and Beitoucun. Some went through political studies, acknowledged their misdeeds, and were released. Others, who refused to immediately confess wrongdoing, were subjected to special training. The rest, made up of incorrigibles oblivious to the seriousness of their offensive practices, were sent to the Public Security Bureau and then sentenced to seven months in a thought reform camp, which, in effect, was a prison. Few members of the "Da Fo 24," as this group was dubbed locally, confessed to any wrongdoing.[90]

The seven-month imprisonment temporarily removed party boss Bao Zhilong and Da Fo's strong-armed brigade party leaders who had restrained *chi qing*. Ruan Shaobing, who led the people's militia in this period, remembers that the escalation in *chi qing* in early 1961 was dependent on a diminishment in the presence of the party-state in Da Fo and other villages. "The villagers suffered the most right after the public dining halls were dissolved," says Ruan.

They did not have anything to eat, and they were looking for leaves and wild vegetables to pass over the spring hunger. When the wheat crop became edible toward the end of the spring 1961, they finished all the wheat crops before they reached the threshing ground. Another reason that the wheat crops were finished that year was that the old party leaders who were tough in enforcing rules in the village were all rounded up and taken to the Dongle study camp. Consequently, there was nobody in the village to take care of the interest of the collective.[91]

[88] Pang Furong, interview, September 3, 1995.
[89] Bao Dongzhi, interview, June 24, 2001.
[90] Ruan Shaobing, interview, September 19, 1999; Zheng Yunxiang, interview, September 21, 1995.
[91] Ruan Shaobing, interview, September 19, 1995.

Zheng Yunxiang confirms that people seized on this power deflation to practice *chi qing*:

Before the New Year of 1961 most of the village leaders were taken away from Da Fo to participate in the reform camp in Dongle County. These old village leaders were brutal in enforcing government policies, and enforced the rules [of procurement] more strictly. After they were taken away, a Dongle County work team began to denounce the mismanagement of the public dining halls, and the dining halls were done away with. Without public dining halls providing the little food they had provided in the past, and without the old leaders to watch the collective crops, villagers had the freedom to eat whatever they wanted to eat. In a way, the famine of that year was greatly diminished by the eating of the green crops.[92]

In March 1961 Da Fo's inhabitants also engineered a pullback from collective agriculture. Small parcels of collectivized land were reallocated to individual households for use in family-based crop production. Whereas official CCP history attributes this pullback to the Liu Shaoqi–guided policy reform, there was another history at work. The decision to divide the land into family land was initiated by the production team leaders, not the Da Fo party leaders, who did nothing to stop it.[93] Still, Da Fo's farmers did not call it "household contracting," or *baochan daohu*. Each individual took 0.2 *mu* of private land to sow to grain, giving a household of five one *mu* of land for grain production. Whereas this division roughly anticipated the trajectory of the Liuist *sanzi yibao* policy, it contributed little to the survival of Da Fo's farmers at first. Villagers were not able to harvest a secondary grain crop until the fall of 1961, and the first wheat harvest on this land, taken in June 1962, was "not so good."[94]

What made a much greater difference than the establishment of these small plots of allegedly "contracted land" was *hongshu jiedi*, or borrowed sweet potato land. Each person was allocated half a *mu* to plant this supplementary tuber crop, and virtually everyone made the most of it. Bao Yufa remembers how villagers came into possession of the *hongshu jiedi*: "At the end of the Great Leap Forward, the village gave each person half a *mu* of land to grow sweet potatoes. It was a trick by the village production team leaders. They did not want other people to see it as an effort to divide the land to the individual households. Therefore, they said that they had lent the land to the villagers to grow sweet potatoes."[95] Bao Yufa's recollection of this "trick" indicates that Da Fo's farmers understood the importance of making it seem as though their resistance was occurring *within* the framework of the party-controlled people's commune, while in fact the "borrowing" of the small plots was a transgressive move back to private, individual household production for the family first: though this sweet potato land was technically not privately owned by the villagers, they could eat all of the food

---

[92] Zheng Yunxiang, interview, September 21, 1995.
[93] Zheng Jintian, interview, September 12, 1993. To his credit, Marc Blecher anticipates this counter-history in "China," 193–94.
[94] Bao Guangming, interview, July 12, 2000.
[95] Bao Yufa, interview, July 25, 2006.

they produced on it themselves without having to allocate some portion of it to the state. "In name the land was for sweet potatoes," recalls Pang Haijin, "but in fact villagers could grow anything they wanted . . . for themselves."[96] By early 1962, one-third of the village land had been given over to *hongshu jiedi*.

In planting sweet potatoes, the tillers of Da Fo protected themselves from any potential state attempts to capture their crops: because sweet potatoes grow below ground, they were more difficult for agents of the state to capture than above-ground crops like corn or wheat.[97] Moreover, the state considered sweet potatoes to be "non-essential foodstuffs," and, according to Shu-min Huang, paid less attention to these crops than to rice and wheat.[98] Sweet potatoes also relied less on fertilizer and irrigation than other food crops, were better able to resist drought and minor flooding, and were easier to preserve.[99] It was at this point in the Great Leap famine that sweet potatoes replaced corn as the major food crop of the poor. Pang Tinghua's family of five was able to use its 2.5 *mu* to grow sweet potatoes for two seasons and turnips and pumpkins for one season each. "After this," says Pang, "the famine was basically over. We had enough to eat."[100] The private sweet potato plots villagers had gained remained in their hands for the next five years, and they were able to use these parcels of land to serve their family interests.

There is little doubt that the half-*mu* of private land (*siliudi*) entrusted to each person was a key factor permitting local people to reduce their reliance on *chi qing* in 1962 and regain some food security.[101] Zheng Yunxiang remembers: "As soon as the new crops came in, people stopped eating the green crops."[102] In the fall of 1961 Da Fo's tillers still ate most of the crop while it was in the field, and this, in combination with the dry-well storage of the good sweet potato harvest of that autumn, tided them over to the summer wheat harvest of 1962. The move to sweet potato land was significant not only because it helped end the famine but also because it dealt a small structural blow to collectivization. Speaking of this land, Zheng Jintian recalls: "We got more crops than we appeared to get from the production team, and it represented a kind of concealed 'private sprout' within the production team."[103]

---

96 Pang Haijin, interview, September 18, 1993.
97 I am indebted to James C. Scott for urging me to pay attention to the importance of sweet potato land in peasant strategies of coping with famine. Personal conversation, April 1, 2005.
98 Huang, *Spiral Road*, 61.
99 Bao Xueyang, interview, July 28, 2006.
100 Pang Tinghua, interview, September 1, 1993.
101 The important point here is that *chi qing*, in combination with the recovery of private household plots, was the key to escaping the famine. Furthermore, the recovery of private lands not only did not occur *first*, the June 1961 Central Committee decision to return private lands was structured in part by the pressure of *chi qing* on state revenue.
102 Zheng Yunxiang, interview, September 21, 1995.
103 Zheng Jintian, interview, September 12, 1993.

Actually, this "private sprout" of sweet potato production saved more than a few members of the Dongle County government from extinction during the Great Leap famine. By year three of the Great Leap, the collective, as well as every household, had a deep underground cellar for sweet potato storage, and the county police, who were suffering hunger, repeatedly encouraged young villagers to bring them sweet potatoes from Da Fo's sweet potato cellars. By meeting this request – often through pilfering the sweet potatoes of the collective – villagers ensured themselves protection against county-level police support for commune-level militia crackdowns on the preemptive consumption of the green crops, including sweet potatoes, which were sprouting up everywhere. Villagers remember that the police were smart to not ask any questions about where they got the tubers. Both sides understood that the disaster of Maoist state formation had driven a wedge between county- and brigade-level agents of the commune.[104]

To a lesser extent, popular survival was dependent on the reinstatement of still another entitlement of household-based agriculture: the freedom to glean family fields. In March of 1961, just after the breakup of the public dining halls, villagers reached a silent agreement to go back to the old pattern of gleaning. Zheng Yunxiang and Zheng Xu, leaders of the sixth production team of the Second Harvest Company decided, without consulting Da Fo's brigade party leaders, to allocate the land to be gleaned on a household basis. The reform was taken up by other production team leaders. Brigade leaders sanctioned it, and many households benefited. Zheng Tianbao's household was one of them. "The crops that were gleaned after the harvest were not counted as part of our food ration," says Zheng, "so we got more food, and the food we got was free. This was good for individual families, but it hurt the state. Sometimes my household got as much as 1,500 *jin* of sweet potatoes from gleaning."[105] Indeed, there was a rush to expand collective sweet potato production in this period, and it seems that villagers were able to glean far more of this crop than wheat or corn in the last year of the famine.[106] By mid-1961, *chi qing*, in combination with gleaning and the renewed cultivation of small private plots, pointed toward the recovery of basic food security.

Market reentry also facilitated villagers' recovery. The first half of 1961 saw a renewed burst of petty trade. According to Zheng Jintian, "In 1961, after the public dining hall system had disbanded, earth salt production for the market took off again. Nearly 80 percent of the people in Da Fo made it again."[107] Proceeds from this salt trade were used to earn income to purchase grain for family sustenance. With this off-farm income, along with a less pronounced

---

[104] Compare with Bao Zhanglin, interview, July 6, 2006, and Bao Jinsong, interview, July 12, 2006.
[105] Zheng Tianbao, interview, September 7, 1993.
[106] Bao Chuanshen, Zheng Jintian, and Zheng Tianbao, interviews, September 12, 1993.
[107] Zheng Jintian, interview, September 13, 1993.

chi qing, and with crops from private strips of land and gleaning, villagers began to uplift their households into subsistence. By late fall, Da Fo's salt market was invigorated again, and private business focused on non-farm income began to pick up.

Significantly, the renewal of popular trade corresponded with the departure of two major institutions of the collective. Bao Jenming recalls:

After the disbanding of the public dining halls and the dissolution of the harvest companies, private business was very much alive again, because the collective did not demand as much of our time as before. I started a small fruit business. I went to Pulizhuang in the early morning and came back in the evening with peaches and other fruits. The next day I would sell them in Da Fo and other nearby places. I could make a profit of twenty to thirty *yuan* each trip. I did not pay any tax on my business, and nobody tried to stop me.[108]

As we will see in subsequent chapters, many of the low-profile forms of averting state-induced food deprivation during the Great Leap Forward Famine influenced popular strategies to resist the renewal of predatory rule in the post–Great Leap Forward decade. *Chi qing* remained the centerpiece of popular strategies of survival well into late 1962, and in the long aftermath of the famine people in Da Fo stood ready to return to eating the unripe field crops when hunger threatened. The small plots of privately held sweet potato land were not returned to Da Fo's production teams until 1966, and even then the harvests from these lands continued to go to individual farm households until pro-Mao outsiders attempted to confiscate them for the collective in 1970.[109] Similarly, the gleaning of small parcels by families persisted until 1982, when the Liangmen People's Commune was disbanded and individual households openly farmed their own shares of land with the formal sanction of village leaders. The march back into the salt market continued with only one brief interruption into the early 1990s, by which time countless private, family-based commercial undertakings were reflected in the flurry of small entrepreneurial transactions in Da Fo's revived periodic market. All of these popular strategies of surviving the famine originally were undertaken without the permission of high state rulers and, as David Zweig's astute work suggests, constituted subsurface forms of resistance to Maoist state appropriation and domination.[110]

Chi Qing *as a Form of Anti-State Resistance*

Villagers were cognizant that *chi qing* was a means of compelling the Liangmen People's Commune government to bring its claims on village food resources in

---

[108] Bao Jenming, interview, September 11, 1993.

[109] Madsen, *Morality and Power*, 202–03; Ruan Tianhan, interview, September 11, 1993; Bao Yinbao, interview, September 12, 1993.

[110] Zweig, *Agrarian Radicalism*, 86–96, 122, 132, 137–38, 143–44, 191–200.

line with the "subsistence first" principle of local society.[111] Zheng Yunxiang explains,

After the year in which *chi qing* ruined the crops, the local officials no longer exaggerated the output. The procurement policy of the central government remained the same, but the amount taken by the commune government was adjusted in accordance with changes in the harvest. The procurement was more dependent on the harvest. When the harvest was poor, the Liangmen Commune officials took less; when it was better, they took more.[112]

Few Da Fo villagers use the word "resistance" in talking about their strategies of famine survival. But Bao Guangming speaks for the majority of Da Fo inhabitants when he says of *chi qing*, "Of course we undertook it exclusively for survival, but we also were aware that it would hurt the government."[113] According to China scholar Wang Shaoguang, there was a significant drop in central government revenue in 1961.[114] Surely *chi qing* was a factor in this decline. Surely too the evolution of this strategy of survival into a modality of resistance spurred provincial Communist Party leaders to reconsider strict enforcement of policies that had induced food shortages, suffering, and death. Zheng Yunxiang is referring directly to *chi qing* when he recalls,

In the spring of 1961, when we ate all of the wheat crop and most of the corn, there was nothing left of the harvest. Needless to say, there was nothing to give the government, and the Henan provincial government did not receive any harvest from the villagers. In the end, the Liangmen district government had to provide Da Fo with some additional seeds obtained from other places, and the central government had to bring in relief grain from the Northeast. So eating the green crops was the best form of resistance.[115]

In the case of *chi qing*, we are dealing with a strategy of survival grounded in the arts of "preemptive consumption." Its practitioners may not have intended it as resistance in any overtly political sense. In order to identify whether *chi qing* was a survival strategy, a form of resistance, or both, we need to better conceptualize the difference between strategies of survival and forms of resistance. Consider first the difference between eating wild vegetables and *chi qing*. Villagers were permitted by the state to gather and eat wild vegetables, but they were not permitted to eat the unripe crops of the collective. Engaging in forbidden actions is a form of resistance, regardless of whether it is resistance for the sake of survival or resistance for the sake of harming the state. With this in mind, let us now differentiate *chi qing* from *tou qing*, or stealing the crops of the collective. Party leaders used these two terms as if they described different phenomena. *Tou qing* was clearly perceived as a form of resistance by both villagers and party leaders. But whereas stealing crops was clearly an illegal act, villagers who engaged

---

[111] Scott, *Moral Economy of the Peasant*, 15–20.
[112] Zheng Yunxiang, interview, September 19, 1995.
[113] Bao Guangming, interview, September 19, 1995.
[114] Personal correspondence, 1994.
[115] Zheng Yunxiang, interviews, September 15, 1993; September 19, 1995.

in *chi qing* could pretend they were doing nothing wrong. *Chi qing* was a much more subtle act than *tou qing* – a carefully devised form of preemptive consumption of crops to which the collective had laid first claim, but one that villagers could pretend was not pilfering or stealing. Much more so than *tou qing*, Da Fo's inhabitants could rely on *chi qing* to survive while protecting themselves from state penalty and public criticism by the village party bosses. Whereas popular remembrances of this practice occasionally do include the notion of resistance, it was largely *chi qing*'s unintended or secondary consequence – the undermining of the party-state's ability to expropriate the grain crop at the expense of food security – that made it transgressive, giving the agents of Mao's grasping polity a pretext to impose a new definition of "resistance" onto this humble and desperate attempt to preempt its seizure of the harvest. Nonetheless, viewing *chi qing* as a form of silent popular resistance to state appropriation illuminates the political reality that the Henan provincial Maoists sought to cover up: *Chi qing* posed a serious threat to the Maoists' ability to generate the revenue needed to maintain Communist Party government, fund the PLA, bolster national security, industrialize China, and service debt to the Soviet Union. The same villagers who were eating their way out of the Great Leap famine via *chi qing* were also eating away at the fiscal base of the central government. By 1960 the party agents of procurement were involved in an undeclared war with China's rural people, whether intentional or not.

Knowledge of this war and its political significance is so far missing in Western scholarship, but the Maoists were keenly aware of it. On September 7, 1960, the Central Party Committee issued an urgent order to reduce the food rations of people in the cities and the countryside, insisting that farmers had to be convinced to give up more food for the nation. This report sounded alarm over the severity of the phenomena of stealing crops (*tou qing*) and eating unripened crops (*chi qing*) in Henan, Shandong, Anhui, Jiangsu, and Shanxi, which were said to result from overestimates of production and overconsumption of food at the beginning of the June wheat harvest.[116] Clearly, Mao and his allies were agitated by state losses to *chi qing*.

Hence, they repeatedly criticized and refused to respond constructively to local Communist Party loyalists who carried out investigations of the famine's destruction and passed up reports on how it was damaging party relations with village people. Top-secret reports of provincial, county, and district party officials in Henan, Anhui, and Shandong speak of an alarming number of popular strategies of resistance, including *chi qing*. The deputy party head of Liu Jiazhuang Commune in rural Shandong might well have been speaking of Da Fo and much of the Henan countryside when he reflected in an urgent report on the

[116] Liu Haifan, *Zhonggong Zhongyang Guanyu Yadi Nongcun he Chengshi Kouliang Biaozhun de Zhishi*, 2676–78.

"disastrous life situation" of rural people and the rise of popular resistance to Maoist progress:

> Our strategy of seizing the grain from the farmers was doomed from the beginning. The farmers are the masters of their land. From planting to harvesting, from threshing to storage, they have complete control over the grain crop. . . . If we attempt to take the grain before it is threshed, they will seize it before the crop is ready to harvest. If we attempt to seize the grain crop from the fields, they will take the crop before it matures – when the seedlings first sprout. And if we coerce them further, they will take the seeds and may not plant anything.[117]

Rural tillers' silent resistance from below, in combination with the paralysis of the increasingly divided national Communist Party leadership, enabled them to survive state plunder and Maoist famine. The unofficial political history of the Great Leap famine in Henan province is that rural people gave up *chi qing* only in return for official reassurances that the draconian requirements of agricultural collectivization would be suspended and farmers would be left to pursue their own devices in putting the famine behind them. By early 1961 the people of Da Fo began returning to household-based farming, and they also began re-entering once-familiar local markets. These undertakings, in combination with *chi qing*, enabled them to make it through the spring hunger of 1961.

Apparently, there was more to this resistance than meets the eye. Along with Beijing's inability to grasp the magnitude of death from starvation and the center's failure to provide increased amounts of edible food to villagers, it reflected a deep political crisis for Mao and top party leaders in Zhongnanhai. In his seminal work *Famine Crimes*, Alex de Waal has written of "the paramount duty of the state" to assist its population in a time of famine, stressing the importance of an anti-famine contract between state officials committed to relieving starvation and rural people who speak up for their basic social rights and demand that such officials lay claim to legitimacy by addressing *the political causality of famine*.[118] By the Qing period, the Chinese state had a rich history of forging such contracts with local people, frequently relegitimating its presence in the process of addressing famine conditions.[119] The Mao-led party-state failed to institute such an anti-famine contract, however, and thus ruined its chance to salvage its mandate to govern. The ensuing crisis of legitimacy, which correlated with the worst period of the Great Leap famine, was so dangerously acute that top Communist Party officials, including General Song Renqiong, who had joined Mao's Red Army in 1927 and assumed the directorship of the PLA's General Cadre Department,

---

[117] Du Shixun, "Gei Dang Zhongyang Mao Zhuxi de Baogao," 26–27.
[118] De Waal, *Famine Crimes*, 11–12, quotation on 11.
[119] Will and Wong, *Nourish the People*; Wong, *China Transformed*, 97–98, 118–19.

were fearful that a new rebel emperor would arise from a mass revolt in rural China and replace Mao and his government.[120]

In short, prior to the end of 1961, the Maoist state failed to relieve the starvation of the Great Leap, and Mao's Great Leap Forward and his anti-rightist campaign of 1959 did so much damage to the system of disaster reporting and relief, as well as to agricultural production, that the Liu-Deng group actually did not have the means to effectively arrest the famine. Apparently, it was not until National Celebration Day (October 1) of 1962 that food supply in the cities improved, and the cities remained the priority – which explains why October 1, 1962, was hardly celebrated in village China.

Well into 1962, people in the remote interior of rural China had to save themselves – unless, of course, they were living in state-favored model villages. In Da Fo, they did so by recapturing small family-centered entitlements unreachable by high socialist rulers. In so doing, they pursued a parallel mode of livelihood that had little, if anything, to do with official reform from above (*sanzi yibao*) or below (*baochan daohu*). As a form of "peasant resistance," *chi qing* not only preceded the Communist Party endorsement of *baochan daohu* in particular, it also compelled the Maoists to retreat from their radical grab of local food resources and silently moved China ever closer to the brink of rebellion.

In an important sense, however, the success of this strategy of resistance in part explains why Chinese villagers did not openly rebel during the famine of the Great Leap. Da Fo's farmers, like their counterparts in many other villages, chose to pursue low-profile resistance that allowed them to get their hands on the crops they produced before the Maoists could usurp them for state use. As Gao Wangling reminds us, the fear that the Mao-led party-state would increase its claim on the harvest motivated starving villagers to claim it first.[121] In Da Fo, this quiet version of contentious resistance, carried out under the radar of national state power, both frustrated the Maoist party-state's efforts to impose its policies of massive extraction and opened a channel that offered a way out of Great Leap–style madness – until Mao attempted to vindicate his Great Leap strategy in another great upsurge of militant politics known as the Cultural Revolution.

---

[120] Gao Hua, "Da Ji Huang de 'Liangshi Shiyong,'" 78–81.
[121] Gao Wangling, "Guoji Bijiaode de Yige An Li," 10–13.

7

Indignation and Frustrated Retaliation

THE POLITICS OF DISENGAGEMENT

Whereas it is well established that the absence of any institutionalized checks on the Maoist abuse of centralized state power subjected villagers to socialist famine,[1] one school of thought, expressed eloquently by Dali Yang, argues that the Great Leap famine delegitimated *only* the people's commune while leaving the legitimacy of the party-led state itself more or less intact in the minds of rural people.[2] The memories of Da Fo's famine survivors illuminate, however, that Dali Yang's thesis does not hold for this Chinese village, where villagers came to see local party leaders as illegitimate due specifically to their poor leadership and political misbehavior during the Great Leap Forward, not simply because of their association with the commune. People understood their behavior was inseparable from the party-state to which they were loyal.

The behavior of the party's representatives in the aftermath of the famine only compounded the problem. If a famine-subjected state must forge an anti-famine contract with its people in order to retain its legitimacy, as Alex de Waal has argued, then it was incumbent upon the government of the PRC in the wake of the Great Leap Forward Famine to make its disgraced leaders at all levels accept accountability for their errors, to introduce greater institutional openness and transparency, and to transfer regulatory power over food into the hands of famine-vulnerable farmers, returning to them the prerogative of provisioning themselves before the state.[3] None of this happened. Though a post–Great Leap reform movement within the Communist Party resulted in attempts to punish and rehabilitate the worst offenders in the village, CCP rulers in Beijing failed to correct the deceitful and violent political habits of the sub-national party leaders

---

[1] Friedman, Pickowicz, and Selden, *Chinese Village*, 282.
[2] Yang, *Calamity and Reform in China*, 240–42, 246.
[3] De Waal, *Famine Crimes*; Thaxton, "How Famines End."

who had perpetrated the Great Leap's horrors. Instead, the same group of Communist Party leaders was lightly disciplined and returned to power. Thus, even as rural people recovered from Mao's famine, they had no one whom they could trust to negotiate a political contract against future famine.

In consequence, villagers' memories of the Great Leap famine and of the savage leadership that pushed it convinced them to pursue disengagement aimed at impeding and deflecting the demands of the agents of Maoism. In Da Fo, this disengagement took the form of resistance to the local perpetrators of Mao's famine and exploded during the Cultural Revolution, which began in 1966 as an attempt by Mao to recapture control of the CCP from Liu, Deng, and his other rivals and which brought China to the brink of civil war in the decade prior to Mao's death in 1976. Villagers endeavored to use the Cultural Revolution to bring the perpetrators of the Great Leap famine to justice, but their effort was compromised by the disgraced party leaders Bao Zhilong and Bao Yibin, who manipulated the incendiary rhetoric of the era to discredit their rival networks and return themselves and their clients to power. Though boss Bao Zhilong regained power in the end, his triumph had devastating consequences for the long-term legitimacy of his party in Da Fo village.

Alienation and Disengagement during the Great Leap Forward

Although collectivization was the brainchild of urban-based Maoist party cadres and not of the country people, Da Fo's farmers were more alarmed by the way in which local party leaders carried out collectivization in the Great Leap than they were by the concept per se. Chinese villagers, like people anywhere, will put up with a great deal of corruption as long as their corrupt leaders are competent and deliver needed services. The basic concern of Da Fo's villagers was food security. How could they ensure that those who played by the rules of the collective would receive enough food for survival? How could they ensure that Da Fo's party leaders would uphold minimum standards of fairness in food distribution? How could they ensure that those who labored the longest and hardest would be fed first and given a fair portion of superior protein-rich food, whereas those who shunned field work would eat last and least? The sparks of popular disengagement from the reach of the Liangmen People's Commune originated in its politically ordered food insecurity and in how farmers saw the causes of this insecurity. From the viewpoint of villagers, Da Fo's party rulers helped the party-state collective take away virtually all of the harvest while also taking over the distribution of the skimpy food supplies that were allocated to the village by Liangmen People's Commune. Despite their lip service to the principle of equal distribution, Bao Zhilong and the Da Fo Communist Party leaders invariably placed their families' food requirements ahead of the security of the rank-and-file peasantry, who had given up the crops of their households and their production teams to the commune. It was their leaders' failure to deliver basic food security in exchange for the many sacrifices the Maoist project demanded of them that angered villagers the most and magnified every other violation of their trust by the party's local agents.

We have seen that the Great Leap Forward Famine was induced by Maoist state repression as well as party-mandated harvest exaggerations and excessive state extraction. We have also seen that the notion that Mao's famine directly reflected the unreasonable popular consumption of "free food" in the common mess halls is questionable – at least for Da Fo. Villagers associate the starvation of the Great Leap with the skewed redistributive politics that passed only a few crumbs down to the remote, poor villages of backward, interior agricultural provinces like Henan. Several aspects of this flawed system of food distribution, of which villagers were clearly aware, structure popular memory of the Great Leap.[4]

There were different kinds of public dining halls, each with a different standard of food supply. At the commune level, party cadres not only received more food than the people in the brigade or village, they also were allowed to eat portions exceeding their own scheduled ration. They could obtain food from Liangmen People's Commune itself and from the public dining halls in Da Fo and other brigades under their supervision. The leaders of the village-level public dining halls were often so eager to please the commune leaders that they did not even ask for their coupons. Meanwhile, the farmers of Da Fo brigade could get food only from their public dining halls. This in part explains why the death rate in the Liangmen People's Commune public mess halls was much lower than in brigades dependent on a single pipeline of public food.

The Communist Party leaders in charge of the rural communes, brigades, and production teams frequently used the excuse of working overtime to obtain more food. In Da Fo and the Liangmen Commune, many of the party leaders took overtime for political study, for chatting and conducting meetings, and for playing card games past midnight. Da Fo's farmers had no overtime option. No matter how long they labored for the collective, their food ration was unchanged.

A privileged order of food allocation prevailed, moreover, involving spatial connections and special titles. Homes of key brigade Communist Party leaders often were storehouses for food designated for the public dining hall, so leaders who lived near the main artery of food supply had enough to eat. Well into the most terrible months of the famine, Da Fo party leaders Bao Zhilong, Bao Yibin, and Pang Siyin and their clients all enjoyed substantially greater food security than ordinary villagers.[5] The inner circle ate far more than its share of grain, and they extended this privilege of "food grabbing" to their subordinates and families. According to Bao Jiping, "The heads of the harvest companies could eat more. They just came to the kitchen and grabbed a few bread loaves after returning

---

[4] I am indebted to Wang Shuobai, "Guanyu Zhongguo," 1–4, for the conceptual underpinnings and historical analysis of this phenomenon.
[5] Pang Siyin, interview, September 12, 1993.

from brigade or commune meetings, and nobody could stop them. The head cook and the other cooks all ate more than their share too."[6] Pang Chenglan, head of Da Fo's Second Harvest Company during the famine, recalls, "Even during the grain shortage of 1960, my family did not suffer from hunger at all."[7] Party leaders had privileged access to food at a time when the danger of starving to death was so pronounced that, according to Bao Zhendao, "Some people were grabbing food from other people's hands and then deliriously running away with it."[8] Every handful of food taken via privilege pushed those on the lower rungs of the rationing system closer to a level of malnutrition from which they could not recover.

The politics of the Communist Party takeover of the food supply produced a new category of people whose special titles enabled them to acquire more food, to claim first dibs on food grain, and to get superior food. The relationships of the chefs with the food privileges to Da Fo party leaders was of no small significance. Because Da Fo's party leaders were dominant in the Liangmen People's Commune government, the Dongle County and the Liangmen Commune leaders treated them favorably. Thus, whenever the commune government was looking for a worker or a cook, party boss Bao Zhilong would send a runner to enlist a Da Fo resident. Eight of the chefs in the commune-level government were recruited from Da Fo, and they were favored in the struggle for survival. Recalling that "villagers did starve" during the Great Leap Forward, Bao Zhidan notes, "Of course I did not starve myself. As a cook in the Liangmen People's Commune grain department, I could eat as much as I wanted."[9] A similar pattern prevailed at the brigade level, where the chefs were positioned to serve their families and their party-based patrons. Pang Qinli recalls: "Bao Changsan, the head cook [of the brigade], knew how to please the leaders. The best company food was reserved for the leaders and for the leaders' families by him."[10] The chef assignment was the most envied in Da Fo, for the cooks were able to give their children a little more food all through the three difficult years.

The public dining halls maintained two sets of kitchens in many villages, including Da Fo. According to Ruan Shaobing,

The big ones prepared food for villagers in general. There was also a small kitchen which was supposed to prepare food exclusively for the Liangmen People's Commune leaders who came to the village to inspect work. The small kitchen had better food, like pork and steamed wheat bread. When the visiting commune leaders came, company harvest leaders would eat with them. When the outside leaders did not come, the company leaders still would eat a special meal there once in a while.[11]

[6] Bao Jiping, interview, September 2, 1993.
[7] Pang Chenglan, interview, July 21, 1994.
[8] Bao Zhendao, interview, September 3, 1993.
[9] Bao Zhidan, interview, June 26, 2001.
[10] Pang Qinli, interview, September 1, 1993.
[11] Ruan Shaobing, interview, September 19, 1995.

Indignation and Frustrated Retaliation

The existence of this second "hush kitchen," whose chefs prepared pork and vegetable dishes for Bao Zhilong and his Da Fo allies, stirred much resentment when the dining hall rations of the main kitchen were reduced, though villagers dared not speak out against it for fear of punishment. Later on, when the famine was in force, the second kitchen closed, but the chef continued to extend favorable treatment to Bao Zhigen and other harvest company heads. "I did not need to stand in the food line. The cook would bring my food to the table. Other people could eat only so much," he said. "But I could eat as much as I wanted."[12]

Until early 1960, Da Fo's party stalwarts, Bao Zhilong and Bao Yibin, handled the money that was periodically allocated by the bigger commune unit to buy grain for villagers and also handled the grain that Liangmen district officials allocated back to the village for its daily grain ration. Villagers claim that all of these safety dispensations from above were distorted locally and that the distribution was unequal.[13] The truly important source of redistributive injustice, however, was systemic. It lay in the grain allocation policy of urban-based provincial and central government politicians. People in marginal hinterland villages like Da Fo were receiving the grain left over after the party-state had taken care of provisioning cities – places where its upper-level cadres dwelled. Recall that between 1959 and 1961 the daily per person grain ration for Da Fo decreased from one *jin* to one-half *jin* and finally to one-quarter *jin* per day, or from about thirty *jin* per month to about eight. In this same period, an ordinary factory worker in urban Henan had his grain ration reduced from twenty-eight to twenty-one *jin* per month, and a party official working in an office in Zhengzhou saw his ration fall from about thirty-two to twenty-four *jin* per month. This gave the city-based party cadre, who did little if any manual labor, three times more food than his counterpart in Da Fo brigade.[14] This state-level grain distribution system created the massive imbalance in food supply that contributed to the starvation deaths of millions of country dwellers in Henan, including most of the villagers who died in Da Fo. The villagers remember, correctly, that the public dining halls were only part of the problem and that the local party leaders who were implicated in this failed system had not created the problem: they only worsened it by infusing it with local patronage, favoritism, and corruption.

In the end, the pronounced unfairness of the Maoist public dining hall system produced envy and, more important, a loss of popular faith in the public dining hall as an institution of socialist entitlement. Zheng Xiaoquan makes this point succinctly: "Villagers had to eat a little less than they were entitled to eat."[15] In corrupting this entitlement, Bao Zhilong and the leaders of the Da Fo Communist Party destroyed its appeal for ordinary villagers, who in the end clamored for the

---

[12] Bao Zhigen, interview, July 21, 1994.
[13] Bao Guangming, interview, September 4, 1993.
[14] Han Dongping, personal correspondence, November 8, 2001.
[15] Zheng Xiaoquan, interview, May 6, 1994.

replacement of the public mess halls with a return to family-supplied food and home cooking.

Not only did Da Fo's Communist Party leaders eat more than their nonparty counterparts, they also worked less. The ethic of total sacrifice for the Maoist collective was imposed on villagers by party leaders who often exempted themselves from incessant and excessive labor assignments. Zheng Jintian touches on this important point: "Some leaders did not work themselves. But they urged the villagers to work even harder when the villagers did not have enough to eat and when the village leaders, and sometimes their families, had more to eat. When the villagers had to eat the green crops, they had to hide from the village leaders. If only the leaders would have eaten and worked on the same terms as we common folk, I would hold nothing against them for my suffering."[16]

We have seen that villagers were pushed into famine not only because of lack of food but also because they were forced to start work at the crack of dawn and were given little if any time to sleep. Da Fo's harvest company leaders blew their whistles every day before dawn to wake people up to go work in the fields and then went back to sleep.[17] Such behavior underscored the unfairness of the labor regime and stimulated bouts of verbal contention. Pang Guihua, a member of the First Harvest Company, remembers:

Our company head was Bao Zhigen, and the deputy head was Tang Sujing – a woman. Bao Zhigen and Tang Sujing would wake up before dawn and blow their whistles. As soon as one heard the whistle, one had to get up and come out to work. Their whistles were very loud. Anybody who did not rise quickly enough stood to be subjected to public criticism and condemnation. However, Bao Zhigen and Tang Sujing themselves only came to the fields occasionally to see what was going on. . . . Therefore, many people hated Bao Zhigen and Tang Sujing.[18]

On top of this, many of the wives of top Da Fo party members went to the fields only when it suited them or not at all. Liang Xiaolu, the spouse of party boss Bao Zhilong, refused to work in the fields and was allowed to cook at her own home because of her husband's position. When she became pregnant during the Great Leap, she demanded extra grain for herself from production team leaders. To make matters worse, Liang relied on sycophant Bao Zhigen to harass marginal nonparty women who spent most of their time in the collective fields, and she accused people she did not like of hailing from "bad family backgrounds."[19]

Party leaders' failure to labor alongside villagers in the collective fields might have been overlooked had they acknowledged the villagers' work sacrifices for the people's commune, but they did not. One of the most troublesome and destructive aspects of the Great Leap Forward in Da Fo was the extent to which its

---

[16] Zheng Jintian, interview, September 15, 1993.

[17] Pang Guihua, interview, July 11, 2002; Yin Fengxiu, interview, July 10, 2002.

[18] Pang Guihua, interview, June 27, 2001.

[19] 2002 interviews with Ruan Yulan, July 9; Yin Fengxiu, July 10; and Bao Rulong, July 5.

Communist Party stewards constantly accused people of neglecting their work duties. Party boss Bao Zhilong seems to have specialized in making villagers feel unappreciated. Zheng Jintian relates one incident:

During the Great Leap Forward, Bao Zhilong was not a village leader anymore. He was a Liangmen People's Commune leader. But he often came back to Da Fo, and he liked to behave as if he was still a village leader. Once, he saw villagers resting in the fields. He immediately went into a rage and cursed them. He said: "We provided you with food and drink, but you do not work. The food and drink might as well be fed to the dogs."[20]

News of this insult spread through the collective fields like wildfire, stirring moral indignation in many of Da Fo's workers.

The same top-level party leaders who urged people to work themselves to death for the common good were simultaneously throwing overboard popular conventions of normal decency. During the Great Leap, there was an outbreak of lasciviousness among Communist Party activists and accomplices in Liangmen district. Many of the disputes that the Liangmen People's Commune Dispute Mediation Committee had to settle during the Great Leap years were brought by men required to labor in the fields who learned that local political leaders had taken advantage of the laborers' absence to coerce their wives to have sex with them.[21] Such disputes were a particular problem in Da Fo. The main agent of this lechery was the lustful party-appointed head of the First Harvest Company, Bao Zhigen. Most villagers abhor Bao, who repeatedly left his work detail to seduce the wives of his co-workers, including the wife of Bao Zhengda, his distant cousin. Whereas it was not uncommon for men in Da Fo to pursue sexual affairs with the wives of known wife beaters like Bao Zhengda, Bao Zhigen used his political status (his two brothers were martyrs of the pre-1949 Communist Revolution) and his political power (he could issue or refuse grain ration coupons and he could issue white ribbons) to force three harmoniously married women to have sex with him, and he drew a total of at least five village women into sexual intercourse with him during the Great Leap Forward.[22]

Bao Zhigen's heated quarrels with the men whose wives had been forced into unfaithfulness never reached the Commune Dispute Mediation Committee, for Bao Peijian, the head of the committee, was a member of Bao Zhigen's First

---

[20] Zheng Jintian, interview, September 15, 1993.

[21] Bao Peijian, interview, September 11, 1993.

[22] Tang Weilan has revealed the names of each of these women, though I have chosen not to give them here. Interviews of July 14, 2004, and July 31, 2006. To be fair to Bao Zhigen, there is a somewhat different interpretation of his sexual relations with women in the Great Leap. This view is found among some male farmers whose families had served in the PLA. According to Ruan Zhaoyin, for instance, Bao Zhigen did not actually rape anyone. Instead, because Bao was young and handsome, without a wife after his divorce, and a company head with access to food grain, a number of women went to his house and bed willingly, and some wanted to live with him. Even if this were the case, Ruan still concedes that "with his power and authority, Bao Zhigen was able to give his favored women some small benefits, such as a little food and light job assignments." Ruan Zhaoyin, interview, June 17, 2006.

Harvest Company. Wanting no trouble, Bao Peijian was reluctant to process complaints about his superior's behavior. Understandably, some of these quarrels generated impulses for legal suit. But here too there was an obstacle to justice. As Ji Danying, who married into Da Fo in 1955, recalls:

At the time of the Great Leap Forward, my husband worked in Shangcun Cooperative, and I worked in the public dining hall of a cooperative farm in Wencaicun. Bao Jiping took advantage of me. After this, I dared not come home at night. Bao Jiping was a village leader. My husband and I planned to sue him. But Bao Jiping was the cousin of Bao Zhilong, and so I did not win in the end. Instead, they forced me to kneel down on bricks for suing Bao Jiping.[23]

The opulent lifestyle of the leaders of Liangmen People's Commune during the Great Leap Forward and its famine also set a bad tone for party-villager relations. In late 1958, Qing Zhenxin, the Liangmen People's Commune party secretary, issued an order to construct a palatial set of buildings for the commune. Qing ordered Da Fo's seventeen production teams and each of the teams of sister villages to send one cart to Shangcunji to transport limestone back across the Wei River to Liangmen, all in a winter day's time. This ill-conceived order caused a serious cart jam at the river ferry, and some farmers lost their animals to hypothermia in the delay. Villagers were so incensed they pressed Da Fo party secretary Bao Yibin to report the incident to the Henan provincial government. Officials came to Da Fo to consider the matter, but they never disciplined the commune secretary, and villagers were not compensated for their losses.

In the next year, Deng Renping, a vice-director of Liangmen district, assigned each brigade within the Liangmen Commune to provide a quota of bricks and wooden beams to be used in building a commune theater hall. Bao Yibin protested that Da Fo would not be able to fulfill the quota and asked Deng to explain how villagers would live if their houses were dismantled for supplies. A quarrel erupted. Bao Zhilong intervened and stopped the dispute, but Deng Renping ultimately got his way: Da Fo's bricks and beams began showing up at the Liangmen theater construction site. In this small but flagrant example of the indecency of socialist appropriation, the building of a state-directed collective function-hall mandated tearing down the homes of local people. Such instances of abuse on the part of Da Fo's Communist Party leaders are not special cases but rather examples of the normative predatory corruption that was a hallmark of "everyday Maoism" in the Great Leap era and afterward, which characterized the modality of socialist rule at the village level.

As F. G. Bailey has argued, political organizations must go the extra mile "to earn dignity and become institutions instead of mere organizations, thus being recognized as ends in themselves and commanding selfless service."[24] During the

---

[23] Ji Danying, interview, September 2, 2002.
[24] Bailey, *Kingdom of Individuals*, 184.

Great Leap period – the capstone years of the critical first decade of Communist Party–led state building – this did not happen. Instead, local party leaders, acting like arrogant patriarchs who stood for the egocentric interests of "their" party, suppressed villagers to a point at which the much-celebrated dignity of Mao's CCP was seriously damaged in villagers' eyes. So why did Da Fo's party leaders, only a short decade after the revolution, become surprisingly unrevolutionary, treating villagers with contempt and abusing their power to satisfy themselves at the expense of ordinary people? Certainly, multiple factors produced this outcome. The wars of the 1930s and 1940s had displaced and shredded kin groups, thereby weakening the ability of many villagers to rely on social weapons to counter the acts of local party leaders backed by a Leninist center,[25] and the U.S. exclusion of the PRC from the international community made certain that Mao and his followers were not significantly influenced by global human rights norms for keeping state abuse of the rural poor at a minimal level.

Yet there were two more powerful factors at work, and each can be fully appreciated only by reference to Mao as the principal agent of a rushed collectivization. For one thing, as pointed out in Chapter 3, Da Fo's leaders clearly engaged in a path-dependent process of learning wartime habits and applying these to the postwar period; as a result, after the war they drew on habits of coercion to maintain their power and privileges. Mao's unwillingness to promote democratic checks on high and low party leaders only served to justify a culture of state privilege and to reinforce the perception that special privilege, as well as full citizenship, was derived from service in war – and so the war theater of the Great Leap became a training ground for acquiring such privileges.[26] For another thing, Mao, as the principal agent of China's developmental course, was obliged to ensure that his local party agents were taught self-restraint, but in reality he loosened disciplinary controls on the use of force in dealing with rural-dwelling people to such a point that local party leaders were left to enforce his Great Leap policies without any sense of "combat morality" – a process that allowed, if not encouraged, them to ratchet up coercion and terror in ways that all but destroyed accountability and jeopardized party legitimacy.[27]

Thus it is hardly surprising that Da Fo's party leaders specialized in crafting the most institutionally damaging form of misrule imaginable: using punishments to humiliate villagers. The assumption that such punishments would strengthen party authority proved false. Many of the public disciplinary actions aimed at preventing villagers from interfering with state material accumulation provided villagers with vivid examples of how blind devotion to the party could produce forms of abuse that destroyed the dignity of the collective's victims.

---

[25] As Porter notes was the case of Germany after World War I. Porter, *War and the Rise of the State*, 215–20. I have benefited greatly from Porter in developing this section.

[26] Ibid.

[27] For this point, I have drawn on the wisdom of Mitchell, *Agents of Atrocity*, 176–81, 185–87.

Zheng Yunxiang's punishment by Bao Zhilong after he attempted to steal wheat to add to the bread loaves his team members received is especially poignant. Zheng recalls: "I was ordered to attend a public criticism theater meeting at Wanxiuzhuang. Three persons from Da Fo were criticized at this meeting.... We had to carry a bag of bread loaves on our backs for what we did." As they prepared to leave the village with the bread loaves, Bao Zhilong decided that their load was not heavy enough and ordered that it be increased. At the public criticism meeting, Bao Zhilong publicly relieved Zheng Yunxiang of his post of harvest company head. According to Zheng, "Bao Zhilong lied at the meeting. He said that our plan was to sell the stolen wheat in Hebei province at a price of thirty-five cents per *jin* and to use the money to buy a bicycle."[28] Zheng would have been punished even more severely if Bao's false claims had been verified. Fortunately, the head of Liangmen People's Commune, Zhu Cunjie, softened the case against Zheng by permitting the participants in the Wanxiuzhuang assembly to decide the punishment. In the end, they decided the case was a "contradiction among the people" and ordered no further punishment. Bao Zhilong had gone too far. Still, the damage to Zheng's personal dignity could not be erased. Many people in contemporary Da Fo date their first impulses to disengage from brigade and commune party leaders with the suffering they endured from precisely this kind of contemptuous and contrived punishment, which was meted out repeatedly during the Great Leap Forward and the ensuing famine and which caused them to feel lasting humiliation.

The physical bashings delivered by party bosses during public criticism sessions created a sense of betrayal among villagers and set party leaders apart from ordinary folk. Although villagers submitted to such aggression, the oral history evidence from Da Fo makes it clear that in the long run coercion produced hatred for their tormentors. The physical injuries suffered from beatings or from falling off stools during public shaming for "stealing" the collective peanut or sweet potato crops stirred deep, lasting anger. Apparently, the memories village people have of injuries suffered from these insulting punishments are seldom separable from their memories of the process of state expropriation.[29]

Not only did Bao Zhilong and other CCP leaders physically punish and humiliate Da Fo's villagers, they also lied to them repeatedly and betrayed their trust, destroying their credibility and eroding the popular belief that the party was the trustworthy friend of the common people. The first shocking lie, as we have seen, was the broken promise of "procurement with subsistence." Villagers gradually grasped that the same party leaders who, in the pre-1949 period, had found ways to protect their households had become instruments of state appropriation. In their new roles as commune agents, Bao Zhilong and his political clients showed a dangerous propensity to assist Maoist state superiors in extracting as much grain

[28] Zheng Yunxiang, interview, September 15, 1993.
[29] Compare with Scott, *Domination and the Arts of Resistance*, 188.

as possible without initially paying attention to the social consequences.[30] Worse still, they extracted this grain while pretending they did not eat more than their fair share of the public grain ration. This pretending, as Sissela Bok's study *Lying* would argue, was designed to mask the critical advantage village party leaders created for themselves in the competition for food and survival.[31] But some villages saw through the mask. "The leaders ate more food secretly, but people could very easily tell if they had eaten more or not from their physical appearance," says Bao Jiping.[32] Not surprisingly, villagers began to ask how they could trust party leaders whose primary focus was on fulfilling quotas of state appropriation and who reacted to the suffering their actions engendered only after villagers began to resist state grain requisitioning.

Party-state relations with villagers were also increasingly fraught with a kind of organizational lying. Much of this was aimed at preventing villagers from revealing the public theft of party leaders and was carried out under the pretext of the normal functioning of communal government. Militia member Zheng Xu, for example, discovered while on routine patrol in 1959 that Pang Chunzhi, a CCP member and production team leader, was stealing flour from the public dining hall. When Zheng Xu was about to report this matter, however, he suddenly was given an unexpected assignment outside of Da Fo. Zheng Xu and his nonparty friends knew that the real motive was to remove someone who could expose the "dirty hands" behind the dwindling food supply.[33] Villagers understood that the same deceitful brigade party leaders who had transferred Zheng Xu were the people who were penalizing those who did not give up their family grain to the dining halls and were strictly enforcing disciplinary measures against those who "stole" public crops. Why should they trust such leaders?

The lying of major Da Fo party figures taught minor party members that deceit was permissible in relations with ordinary villagers, giving license to those who were at risk in the famine to prey on their nonparty peers. This phenomenon, and the subtle disengagement from party authority it stimulated in villagers, is best illustrated by the ways in which villagers strove to resolve disputes over party violations of proprietary rights. Villagers assumed correctly that the brigade leaders would tolerate such transgressions, allowing the perpetrators to plunder without serious punishment. When there was a rash of petty theft of small property by some Bao party members in the famine months of 1960, for example, few people trusted Da Fo's party bosses to conduct honest inquiries into the cases or make the offenders compensate them in any way. They often attempted to solve the cases of theft by themselves, occasionally outsmarting the obstinate party leaders who let these petty crimes slide. In 1960, for example, Zheng Yunxiang's goat was

---

[30] Compare with Bailey, *Kingdom of Individuals*, 112–13.
[31] See Bok, *Lying*, 118.
[32] Bao Jiping, interview, September 2, 1993.
[33] Zheng Xu, interview, September 13, 1993.

stolen, and he discovered some of its bloody remains under a bed at the home of half-starved PLA veteran Bao Lieri. After Bao told him that his father-in-law had bought the goat for him, Zheng quickly raced to Pingchuan village, where the father-in-law lived, and asked him whether he had purchased a goat for his son-in-law's family, arriving less than an hour before Bao Lieri's wife, who also was bicycling to Pingchuan village to warn her father-in-law that he should go along with his son's false story. When the father-in-law, unaware of the lie, denied that he had purchased a goat, Zheng got the Pingchuan village security chief to write up the story, reported it to the commune, and won compensation for his stolen property.[34] That the local Da Fo party leaders had not themselves punished Bao for stealing the goat was not a case of the Bao lineage protecting a client within its kinship-centered network, for Bao Lieri was on bad terms with Bao Zhilong and the dominant party leadership in Da Fo. This was a matter of villager relations with the party whips of the Maoist communal state: villagers had no illusions that political justice could be obtained within the power domain of party leaders. Because Bao Lieri was both a party member and a PLA veteran, Zheng Yunxiang placed no faith in obtaining justice from Da Fo party leaders. Their lying had made them untrustworthy.

Despite their untrustworthiness, Communist leaders in Da Fo demanded respect regardless of their performance. They forbade disagreement, all the while expecting villagers to pay homage to their way of ordering local society and economy. In her scholarship on "everyday Stalinism" in the Soviet Union, Sheila Fitzpatrick has written that the regime's inexperienced and incompetent political militants shared a presumption that they "were always right" in their efforts to manage even the minor details of everyday work life.[35] The same premise was evident in relations between party leaders and villagers in rural China during the Great Leap Forward. In Da Fo, it diminished the respect villagers had for the party itself.

Several examples from Da Fo's history illustrate how party leaders defeated their own purpose during the late 1950s by exalting themselves. The first has to do with one of the major themes of the Great Leap Forward: the acceleration of "socialist accumulation" by mobilizing rural dwellers to develop local technologies for agricultural production and economic prosperity. Maurice Meisner notes: "The Maoist solution was deceptively simple and perhaps simplistically utopian: the masses of peasants . . . themselves were to master modern technology."[36] The "master technician" in Da Fo was none other than Bao Zhilong, and the technology in question was well-drilling. In the winter of 1955 local party leaders of the agricultural production cooperatives organized a large-scale well-digging project in Liangmen district. Under the leadership of party boss Bao Zhilong,

---

[34] Zheng Yunxiang, interview, September 15, 1993.
[35] Fitzpatrick, *Everyday Stalinism*, 6, 14–17, 28–29, 33.
[36] Meisner, *Mao's China*, 225.

Da Fo villagers alone constructed ninety-seven earthen wells.[37] Digging these wells in winter was hard, bone-chilling work: some old-timers say their joints still ache from this work. The work also required courage. The crude shaft used in constructing the wells was constantly shaking, so someone had to go down inside each well to steady it, risking death in the event of a cave-in. Bao Zhilong repeatedly led Tang Yuxin, Ruan Yindao, Ruan Weiming, and Bao Zhengshou down into the well shafts, thereby demonstrating his conviction that prosperity was dependent on working hard for the collective under harsh conditions.[38] By early 1956 the well-digging experiment provided irrigation for nearly 90 percent of Da Fo's fields, and many villagers were praising Bao Zhilong and the well-digging team as "socialist labor heroes." In the summer flood of 1956, however, water quickly filled in the shallow earthen wells, ruining virtually all of them.[39] Although a few wells were salvaged and used to irrigate vegetable gardens, villagers had to rely on the rain-fed Wei River to irrigate the croplands, just as in ancient times. Those who had voiced skepticism about the well-digging experiment now seemed wiser than Bao Zhilong.

Reluctant to admit the mistake of constructing shallow earthen wells, boss Bao and Da Fo party leaders again set out to promote well-digging during the Great Leap Forward. In late 1957 to early 1958, they led a campaign to construct dozens of new deep wells using wooden drill pump technology. Party leaders asserted that this well-drilling technology could irrigate 95 percent of Da Fo's cropland, but they overlooked an important detail: When these wells were constructed, just after the 1956 Wei River flood, the water table was at a high point. Using this as the baseline, the team struck the wells to a depth of approximately twenty to thirty meters and positioned the drill pumps to reach down several additional meters. In 1958 the water table began to go down, in 1959 it fell again, and in 1960 it fell yet again, to a depth of eighty to ninety meters. As villagers discovered that the wells could not cough up the underground water, and as the physical labor took its toll on those assigned to power the water pumps, dissent over the well-drilling mania was expressed openly. Bao Zhengda, the Da Fo party secretary in 1957, did not agree with the well-digging. When he quarreled with Bao Zhilong and the commune party leaders about this matter in the months leading up to the Great Leap, he was dismissed and replaced by Pang Xinzhen. The importance of digging was reiterated without further discussion.[40] No one in the upper reaches of the Da Fo party hierarchy dared to correct this foolhardy experiment. When the new wells failed to make a difference in yields during the subsistence crisis of 1960, the well-digging fiasco became a target of popular condemnation. Disgusted with Bao Zhilong's dictatorial methods, villagers quipped that boss Bao was an expert only in making errors and denying their occurrence.

[37] Pang Yilu, interview, September 5, 1993; Bao Peijian, interview, September 11, 1993.
[38] On this point, see Friedman, Pickowicz, and Selden, *Chinese Village*, 167.
[39] Pang Yilu, interview, September 5, 1993.
[40] Ruan Shaobing, interview, September 1, 1993.

The utter disregard for basic common sense in the Great Leap strategy of agricultural production fostered more disrespect for leaders. The Great Leap approach to boosting agricultural surpluses for party-state appropriation was predicated significantly on the military-style mobilizations of the Anti-Japanese War of Resistance – the so-called Yenan way of rousing rural people to sacrifice for the national interest.[41] In August 1958, during an expanded session of the Politboro, Mao emphasized the importance of combining Marxism with the iron-fisted discipline of Qin Shi Huangdi, the first emperor of China, and said that collective life in the people's communes would be achieved via military-style mobilization.[42] The Liangmen People's Commune officials who impressed this Maoist approach on Da Fo saw themselves as competent agronomists. In contrast, villagers saw the militarization of agricultural operations as nonsensical.

One example was the "great turnip field war" of late 1959 discussed in Chapter 4, during which commune leaders ordered production to be carried out in accordance with the principles of a military campaign. Farmers were ordered to complete certain field tasks in a fixed time frame. One such order called for the harvesting of the turnip crop within twenty-four hours. "It was like the army ordering a company to take a military position," recalls Pang Yilu. "If you did not do it, you had to suffer the consequences. If the village did not complete the task in time, the harvest company leaders would be criticized. In order to avoid being punished, the leaders often adopted silly measures."[43] To finish the harvesting on time, Da Fo's villagers frantically broke off the turnip leaves and stems, leaving the edible plant in the ground. This deceived the commune turnip harvest inspectors, but it wasted a great deal of this supplemental crop at a time when the bulk of village grain supply was being lost to hyper-procurement. The waste from the hurried turnip harvesting left individual gleaners to compete with the collective for the leftover crops. Because turnip porridge replaced steamed bread loaves as Da Fo's major public mess hall staple, fatal hunger for those who lost out cannot be separated from the turnip field war. Survivors still remember people dying in snowbound fields where they were searching for lost turnips in the dead of night. "Bao Sihai, who died of hunger in the famine," recalls Bao Jiping, "yelled for a turnip at his last minute."[44] Villagers condemn the idiocy that drove this politically induced starvation as a profound moral failure.

As we have seen, villagers also place part of the blame for runaway procurement on local party leaders. They do recognize that high Maoist regime pressure on local party leaders to exaggerate harvest output was real and that it intensified with the anticipated harvest benefits from various state irrigation projects. But whereas such exaggerations misled Liangmen People's Commune officials about harvest

[41] Lieberthal, "Great Leap Forward," 294, 299.
[42] Gao Hua, "Da Yuejin Yundong Yu Guojia Quanli de Kuanzhang," 50; Wemheuer, personal correspondence, 2003 and 2004.
[43] Pang Yilu, interview, September 5, 1993.
[44] Bao Jiping, interview, September 2, 1993.

surpluses, prompting them to mismanage procurement, it made little difference whether the gales of *fukua feng* strengthened or subsided, because no matter how accurate or inaccurate the reports, the commune officials still collected as much of Da Fo's grain crop as they could, without honoring any of the terms of payment implicit in the order of procurement. One point is critical: Although Liangmen Commune leaders knew of the exaggerations of Da Fo's output, after the summer harvest of 1959 they did not strictly adhere to these figures when it came time to take delivery of the grain crop. If, for example, harvest company heads reported the wheat harvest at five hundred *jin* per *mu* when in fact there was a yield of only two hundred *jin* per *mu*, the Liangmen Commune grain collectors did not necessarily request a delivery based on the inflated estimate. *Instead, they simply took all of the grain that they presumed was surplus* and relied on the brigade storekeeper, who was the only person who actually weighed the grain carefully, for the total actual harvest figure. Thus, the sharp upswing in excessive grain extraction in 1959 and 1960 was not solely due to the *fukua feng*.

In other words, it was not simply the policy of procurement alone, or the wild exaggerations of harvest output, that locked villagers into the death grip of 1960. The upswing in grain requisition, which exceeded even the most utopian procurement-related formulas in the second and third years of the Great Leap, was also the product of Mao's leftward turn after his Great Leap adventure was attacked by Peng Dehuai at Lushan in July 1959, and hence was substantially due to Mao's revival of anti-rightist pressures to push the Great Leap even harder.[45] In this political atmosphere, the local party leaders of Liangmen People's Commune continued to treat Da Fo's grain crop as if the commune owned all of it. They sold the grain to the Henan provincial arm of the Maoist state without using the proceeds to pay villagers back. The commune leaders did not even inform Da Fo as to whether they received a payment from the provincial authorities, and neither the provincial nor the prefectural authorities knew whether the commune leaders withheld payment.

Neither reliable agents of procurement policy nor trustworthy brokers for the food interests of villagers, the leaders of the Liangmen People's Commune (including Bao Zhilong) apparently used the political structure of the commune, and the resumption of Mao's radical Great Leap policies, to build up their internal political capital and political power, leaving village people with virtually no grain for consumption.[46] That this pattern became serious enough for upper-level Maoist state leaders to attend to is underscored, among other things, by the fact that in late 1960, when the "Da Fo 24" were arrested as part of the Anti–Five

---

[45] I am indebted to Thomas P. Bernstein for helping me grasp this development. Personal correspondence, April 16, 2007.

[46] The scholarship of Siu and Zweig anticipates this pattern. Siu, *Agents and Victims*, 193; Zweig, *Agrarian Radicalism*, 193. On the political autonomy of the commune, also see Hinton, *Shenfan*, 215. See Friedman, Pickowicz, and Selden, *Chinese Village*, 224–25, 279, for a powerful statement on the dangers of the autonomous development of big collective units.

Winds Campaign, Liangmen People's Commune leaders Qing Zhenxin, Chen Yichen, and Deng Renping all were also seized and subjected to a lengthy rectification campaign. These arrests must have given the tillers of Da Fo reason to hope that the party-state was about to rectify its Great Leap mistakes – a hope that would prove to be false.

Resentment Unalleviated: The Anti–Five Winds Campaign and the Four Cleanups Campaign

During the Great Leap, the people of Da Fo did not engage in open revolt against their local party tormentors with links to Liangmen People's Commune. The political and physical danger of opposing the regime was extremely high. Vice-director of Liangmen district Bao Zhilong was also the titular head of the commune militia. Da Fo party secretary Bao Yibin was connected with the Dongle County police force. First Harvest Company head Bao Zhigen publicly displayed the pistol given him by the party secretary of the commune. These police agents of the commune spent much of their time in Da Fo. Because the militia confiscated all of the weapons they could find after 1951, the physically exhausted and virtually weaponless villagers of Da Fo were not prepared to pursue aggressive retaliation. The balance of local and national power left them little choice but to rein in their collective anger. Preoccupied with all the prudent maneuvers of survival during the famine itself, many villagers bided their time until a power shift significantly decreased the risks of retaliation.[47]

James C. Scott suggests that subordinate, powerless rural people who are cowed into deference and compliance may, after a distant political reform, "be tempted to risk acting on their own anger." As they begin to sense that they can get away with acts of counter-aggression in a new power situation, their resistance may turn into a swelling tide of "infrapolitics" in which politically marginalized groups move in a low-profile manner against political tyranny, not only creating a small sanctuary against state domination but also perhaps replacing locally dominant rulers without declaring open rebellion.[48] This pattern of infrapolitics characterized villager interactions with Da Fo party leaders in the immediate aftermath of the Great Leap Forward Famine. It was a central factor shaping popular tendencies to cooperate with or challenge the party leadership of the village in the decade following the famine (and even during the post-Mao era). Although villagers were reluctant to mount a political movement visibly expressive of anti-socialist sentiments, neither did they blindly follow local party leaders. Instead, their indignation and resentment took the form of a silent, undeclared war of disengagement from the Da Fo party leaders who imposed the Great Leap Forward

---

[47] This section owes an immense debt to Scott, *Domination and the Arts of Resistance*, 192–93, esp. n. 21, p. 193.
[48] Ibid., 192–201, esp. 198–99.

and who continued to press for collectivization. This war for disengagement also had a second front, as villagers looked to gain revenge for the indignities and injustices suffered under the great catastrophe of Maoist rule.

In the first post–Great Leap Forward decade, the villagers' acts in waging this war were largely invisible forms of resistance designed to cover the footprints of people who still had few, if any, institutionally guaranteed political rights.[49] Some of their acts will never be known to outsiders, partly because some of the resisters have perished and partly because, in Da Fo, memory of this resistance sometimes informs and directs present-day resistance. Some villagers continue to be naturally hesitant to discuss such resistance, not to mention its agents, with outsiders. Nonetheless, oral history establishes empirically that there was resistance in the immediate aftermath of the Great Leap famine. This resistance occasionally took on a life of its own and tested party schemes to contain it. It had serious implications for the continuity of Communist Party rule.

After the initial shock of discovering the Great Leap's destruction – especially the death toll in Xinyang, Henan province, where Wu Zhipu's zeal to impress his CCP superiors by relentlessly pushing the agenda of the Great Leap Forward led to massive death – complacent Central Committee leaders in Beijing started a damage-control campaign. They sent an investigation team to rural Henan province, and its members reported that Wu Zhipu had transformed the Henan party apparatus into an independent kingdom (*duli wangguo*) in which rural people had been slaughtered and starved.[50] In late 1960, an inner party struggle erupted in Beijing over how to address the anger toward the party's rural political base. One faction, located in the Ministry of Internal Security, proposed to execute three to five party leaders in each village, and later the Central South Regional Committee also insisted that some of the cadres who were responsible for the Great Leap disaster should be put to death. However, there was a problem: Mao Zedong not only refused to set a precedent for executing local party leaders, he also pardoned the very cadres who had driven rural villagers to death.[51] To be sure, after the exposure of the carnage in Xinyang, some intermediate-level cadres were given prison sentences.[52] But Wu Zhipu, the leader of Mao's Leninist system in Henan province, got off lightly; he was demoted to second party secretary in 1961 and then transferred to play a role in the secretariat of the Central South Bureau of the CCP. Although this demotion served as a warning to Bao Zhilong and the major Da Fo party branch leaders, Wu's personal fate also reassured them that Mao would not allow his people to be thrown to the wolves.[53]

---

[49] Ibid., 198–99.
[50] *Xinyang Shibian*, ch. 22.
[51] Ibid., ch. 28.
[52] Jia Yanmin, *Dayuejin Shiqi Xiangcun Zhengzhide Dianxing*, 238–40.
[53] I am indebted to Alfred Chan for this information about Wu Zhipu and for helping me to grasp the dual significance of his punishment. Personal correspondence, June/July 2006.

At the village level, the wounded survivors of the Great Leap's mayhem wanted revenge, and the party needed to find a way to address the popular alienation from its rural leadership base and persuade villagers that it was going to get rid of or rehabilitate the "bad elements" who had usurped the party's leadership and turned the Great Leap into a tragedy of good intentions. The result, as we have seen, was the national damage-control movement known as the *fan wufeng*, or the Anti–Five Winds Campaign. This movement was launched toward the end of 1960 by Liu Shaoqi and Deng Xiaoping, both of whom had succumbed to Mao's Great Leap vision in early 1958.[54] The *fan wufeng* campaign was aimed specifically at party leaders who exaggerated harvest yields, used their privileged status to acquire too much public grain, resorted to blind commandism in directing agricultural production, practiced arrogance and physical abuse, and engaged in illicit sexual affairs with village women – a good summary of the political behavior of boss Bao Zhilong and his network in Da Fo during the Great Leap and its famine.[55] The political goal of the *fan wufeng* campaign was to rebuild trust with villagers and to reestablish party hegemony among the very rural people whom Mao's radical followers had ruined.

Thus, in early 1961, after the abandonment of the public dining halls, the Dongle County government sent a work team to Da Fo. Headed by Qi Shijun and joined by Communist Party cadres from Anyang prefecture, the work team was charged with investigating the misdeeds of village party leaders during the Great Leap Forward. Its primary mission was to assign responsibility for the famine in order to reestablish the credibility of the Communist Party locally. This task required that work team leaders find ways to persuade villagers that party activists undergoing "rectification" in the Dongle study camp were capable of being redeemed. In Da Fo, this was utopian. Here the *fan wufeng* campaign escaped the controls of the Dongle County and Anyang prefectural work team leaders. Unanticipated popular resistance to Da Fo's Maoist party rulers sometimes spilled beyond the zone of public criticism and dissent in which the work team cadres were authorized to operate and took the form of vehement condemnation and violent retaliation against the perpetrators of the famine.

Although the work team leaders were confident that all of the Da Fo party leaders responsible for Great Leap abuses had been taken to the Dongle reform camp, villagers were not. Some said Bao Yilin was also implicated in the catastrophe of collectivization and that he was still roaming Da Fo freely and passing

[54] I am indebted to Thomas P. Bernstein for reminding me that Liu and Deng surrendered to Mao's utopian vision in the first half of 1958. Personal correspondence, April 16, 2007. On the timing of this campaign, see Friedman, Pickowicz, and Selden, *Revolution, Resistance, and Reform*, 12. The origins of this campaign seem complex. According to Teiwes and Sun, in November 1960 Mao wrote to provincial party secretaries asking them to correct the "five winds" among cadres. But whether Mao subsequently pushed this campaign remains to be seen. Personal correspondence, February 2, 2008.

[55] On the Anti–Five Winds Campaign and the work styles it sought to rectify, see MacFarquhar, *Origins of the Cultural Revolution*, 2:324, and Joseph, *Critique of Ultra-Leftism*, 95–102.

word about the independent political activities of villagers to party leaders serving camp sentences. Under popular pressure, work team leaders agreed to place Bao Yilin in the study camp.[56] Villagers also insisted on bringing the perpetrators of the famine back to the village in order to "struggle" them.[57] One of these returned leaders was Bao Zhilong. People lambasted boss Bao for his sordid, disgraceful behavior during the famine, when he had not suffered hunger, and gave him the opportunity to apologize to fellow villagers – though he did not take it. No one physically abused Bao Zhilong at this point. After a few days of public scolding, boss Bao was taken back to the Dongle study camp.

Other party leaders were not so fortunate. Some were subjected to severe punishments. Bao Yiliao, the head of the Happiness Garden Infirmary during the 1958–61 famine, was beaten severely during a mass public criticism meeting. Recalls Tang Weilan: "Some people died in the Happiness Garden Infirmary while Bao Yiliao was in charge. The children of these people said that Bao mistreated their fathers or grandfathers.... Some of them got excited and beat Bao with their fists."[58] Throughout 1961, incarcerated village party leaders were repeatedly taken back and forth from Dongle to Da Fo and subjected to similar violent outbursts, a phenomenon driven as much by the embittered memory of the famine's survivors as by work team agents of the enlightened, reform-minded central government led by Liu Shaoqi.

Most Da Fo leaders, like Bao Yibin, were to serve only seven months in the Dongle reform camp, but villagers insisted that some stay longer. The lecherous and brutal Bao Zhigen was imprisoned for a full year. After release from the Dongle County reform camp for incorrigible elements, Bao Zhigen came back to Da Fo and went to every family in the village, imploring each to forgive him for his behavior during the Great Leap Forward. No one did.[59] Instead, people cursed him behind his back, calling him a "son of a bitch." Many villagers hoped that Bao would die an unnatural death, and the sooner the better.[60]

The upper-level work team leaders, responding in part to demands for justice from below, allowed the people in Da Fo to broaden the scale of *fan wufeng*, including Liangmen People's Commune party leaders who had incurred popular wrath. In attempting to settle scores with the corrupted labor masters of the Ji County irrigation project, for example, they seized Shai Nian, the dining hall chef who had used their food to win sexual favors from desperate women, and repeatedly abused him in criticism sessions.[61] Commune party secretary Qing Zhenxin, also arrested and taken to the Dongle County reform camp, was returned to Da Fo for public struggle, during which villagers accused him of scoffing at their

---

[56] Tang Weilan, interview, September 20, 1995.
[57] Ibid.
[58] Ibid.
[59] Bao Zhongxin, interview, June 23, 2000.
[60] Bao Honglin, interview, June 25, 2001.
[61] Pang Yilu, interview, July 14, 2000.

inferior noodles during the famine – food that was not good enough for secretary Qing. Unable to shoulder this pressure, Qing Zhenxin later committed suicide.

Nonetheless, the 1960–61 *fan wufeng* campaign was more or less taken over by popular skepticism. Although Dongle County leaders emphasized that the Da Fo party leaders were imprisoned in the county labor camp for reeducation and reform in order to alleviate popular anger over their wrongdoings, some villagers suspected that the county leaders had a somewhat conflicting agenda: they wanted to reprimand Da Fo's party leaders for undermining the Great Leap by all sorts of subterfuge, including grain concealment.[62] Hence, many villagers were unsatisfied by the Dongle reform camp punishments rendered to the "Da Fo 24" during the *fan wufeng* campaign. Some felt that life in the camp was not severe enough, because each of the incarcerated "Da Fo 24" leaders was allowed a grain ration that was nearly twice as much as the public grain ration allocated to villagers during most of 1961. That Bao Yibin and the party leaders who had committed the crimes of the Great Leap were better fed than their victims back in Da Fo was the subject of endless bitter village gossip.

Furthermore, the *fan wufeng* campaign seemed inadequate for addressing the anguish felt by the survivors of the Great Leap famine. Many villagers were predisposed to avenge their suffering and could only begin to release their desires for revenge through this initiative. Tang Weilan, one of the victims of Bao Ziyan's merciless beatings at the Ji County Tong Tin River Dig labor camp, experienced this sense of frustration with *fan wufeng*, as Pang Yilu explains: "After the Great Leap Forward, Bao Ziyan paid a price for his cruel treatment of villagers while he was in charge of the Ji County river dig project. He was sent to a labor reform camp in Dongle County for his misdeeds. That made Tang Weilan feel a little better, but it did not reduce his hatred against Bao Ziyan."[63]

When the *fan wufeng* campaign came to an end in 1963, Bao Zhilong was returned to his village leadership position, and his clients returned to power the following year. Da Fo's villagers' distrust of their local leaders and the Communist Party had not been replaced with trust, and their anger had not disappeared. The remembered ineffectualness of *fan wufeng* would come back to haunt everyone – particularly the party leaders who perpetrated hunger and loss in the Great Leap – during the Cultural Revolution, just a few years away.

In 1964–65, Da Fo's party leaders caught wind of a campaign known as the Four Cleanups (*Siqing*). Modeled after the Taoyuan village experiment promoted by Liu Shaoqi and his wife, Wang Guangmei, it required village-level party leaders to compensate villagers for goods taken in the years of food shortages and placed new controls on the spending of public funds by brigade and production team leaders. This campaign swept into Da Fo in late 1964, but was put on hold by Bao Zhilong and the party members in his network.[64] Shortly after the Spring Festival of 1965,

[62] Bao Guangming, interview, July 12, 2000.
[63] Pang Yilu, interview, July 14, 2000.
[64] Bao Peisun, interview, September 1995.

the Dongle County government sent a work group to lead its development in Da Fo. Led, like the last work team, by Qi Shijun, its members stayed in the village continuously for two months, organizing mass meetings and encouraging village participants to openly expose the illegal practices of party leaders.

No one did. Instead, cautious villagers anonymously reported the wrongful conduct of boss Bao Zhilong, Bao Yibin, and a few of their clients during the Great Leap famine. Subsequently, the county work team took action to compensate villagers for party misconduct during the famine. Bao Zhilong's side-house was dismantled, and the building materials were given to several people; Bao Jiping's elm trees were transplanted to the courtyards of famine victims; and on it went.[65] The recipients never acknowledged that they had accepted these items as compensation for famine-related deprivation. It was said that the redistribution was something the outside political authorities had conceived and that villagers were playing along only to obey Dongle government orders.

This was not how the Four Cleanups movement had been conceived by Liu Shaoqi. Its purpose was to eliminate the aggression and corruption of local party leaders implicated in the Great Leap famine.[66] County- and commune-level work teams made up of party outsiders were charged with stage-managing the participation of villagers in exposing and confronting the bad political behavior of village party leaders.[67] In Da Fo, the reformist transcript of Liu Shaoqi was undercut by entrenched party leaders, partly because party secretary Bao Zhilong still had close ties with Liangmen Commune leaders and partly because Mao Zedong had launched an attack on Liu's agenda, attempting to shift the focus of the Four Cleanups from fighting corruption to fighting "capitalism" and finding "class enemies," giving entrenched "local emperors" like Bao Zhilong a chance to avoid, or even take over, the movement.[68] Bao Zhilong not only avoided the sting of the Four Cleanups, he actually worked behind the scenes with the Da Fo leaders designated by the outside work teams to run this campaign. By this point, Bao Zhilong and party members in his network were in control, and Bao shrewdly used the campaign to further bolster his power in the village. The principal target of the Four Cleanups became Bao Yibin, the party secretary *in situ* during the Great Leap Forward in Da Fo. Bao Zhilong seized the opportunity to cashier Bao Yibin and shift the blame for the famine to his former client and his Da Fo–based accomplices.

Bao Yibin had become vulnerable to Bao Zhilong's attack due to a major mistake he made in 1963. Right after yet another Wei River flood had spilled over

---

[65] Bao Jiping, interview, September 2, 1993.

[66] Friedman, Pickowicz, and Selden, *Revolution, Resistance, and Reform*, 59–60.

[67] For a superb, ground-level study of the Four Cleanups, see Chan, Madsen, and Unger, *Chen Village*, 41–65. In Chen village, in contrast to Da Fo, the party secretary and deputy party secretary were cashiered for some of the same abuses of office that Bao Zhilong was able to engage in without serious penalty in the Four Cleanups. See ibid., 61–62.

[68] On Mao's counterattack on Liu's Four Cleanups, see Gao Hua, "Da Ji Huang Yu Siqing Yundong de Qiyuan," in *Zai Lishi De Fengling Dukou*, 174–80.

into village croplands, at a time when villagers were still short on food and reeling from the material losses and physical diminishment of the famine, Bao Yibin built a brand-new, three-room brick house. People were incensed, because villagers knew that the grand house was beyond the reach of Bao Yibin's official salary. An indignant villager sent an anonymous letter to Dongle County government about the house, which not only seemed an insult to struggling villagers but the building of which also violated a party prohibition against house building. When Liangmen People's Commune was ordered to investigate this "problem," the commune leaders asked Bao Zhilong to preside over the investigation.[69]

Bao Yibin felt that he was framed by Bao Zhilong, who was itching to get back in power. When Liangmen People's Commune had prohibited any house construction, commune leader Bao Zhilong had neglected to inform Bao Yibin of this regulation. As a matter of fact, Bao Zhilong had called a party branch meeting to give Bao Yibin a piece of collective land on which to construct his new house. When the Dongle County party leaders investigated the matter, Bao Zhilong denied that he had approved the construction, leaving Bao Yibin to face the music alone. Bao Yibin was removed from his position as party secretary, and his party membership was suspended for two years, for which, says Bao Yibin, "I hated Bao Zhilong."[70]

To add to his troubles, Bao Yibin was discovered to be having an affair with a Da Fo woman. Bao Zhilong's wife, Liang Xiaolu, leaked the news to Bao Yibin's wife, who got into a fight with her rival, cursing her in front of villagers. Skirmishes like this were not uncommon, and usually they were not taken too seriously by villagers. However, after the fight, Liang Xiaolu secretly went to Bao Yibin's lover and encouraged her to sue Bao Yibin's wife for beating her. The subsequent lawsuit, brought in the Liangmen People's Commune government, exposed Bao's affair, and he was further disciplined by the party, increasing his resentment toward Bao Zhilong and his wife.[71]

With the exception of Bao Yibin, not one key party leader was dismissed from his post during the Four Cleanups campaign. Instead, the Four Cleanups group worked closely with Bao Zhilong to shift the focus of the campaign to the reinstated production team leaders. The production team leaders were investigated, audited, interrogated, and in some cases dismissed on charges of embezzlement. In auditing the accounts of the team headed by Bao Yiming, for example, Tang Weilan and the Four Cleanups group discovered that Bao Deyan, the accountant, did not keep any accounts at all and that he owed the production team three hundred *yuan*, a substantial sum. He was proven guilty of embezzling the collective's money and was dismissed from his post.[72] Bao Zhilong gathered the evidence from the Four Cleanups group and announced to each production team that its

[69] Bao Rulong, interview, July 5, 2002.
[70] Bao Yibin, interview, May 4, 1994.
[71] Ruan Shaobing, interview, September 12, 1995.
[72] Tang Weilan, interview, September 20, 1995.

leaders were going to be replaced and that the former team leaders had to compensate the team for what they had embezzled. This wholesale replacement of the production team leaders made it more difficult to persuade qualified persons to serve as production team heads, and it also drove a wedge between these heads and the Da Fo party leadership.

In the end, the "peasant mobilization" of the Four Cleanups, far from introducing a measure of justice in village relations with party leaders and addressing villagers' anger, was appropriated by Bao Zhilong and his clients. The pattern of petty tyranny and corruption that had characterized their leadership during the Great Leap continued.[73] This is not to say that the Four Cleanups did not have a few unanticipated twists and turns, however.[74] Late one night, while the Four Cleanups group was auditing the accounts in the production team office, Bao Zhigen's house was set on fire. A rumor spread that the arsonist was the husband of Bao Zhigen's recently divorced wife, who lived three *li* away in Huicun. After the divorce from his wife in the Great Leap, Bao Zhigen had ordered her to bring food and other items to his house in Da Fo without her new husband's knowledge, and she did so, partly out of concern for her son's well-being. The husband had retaliated, or so it was rumored.[75] But other villagers assumed that the arsonist was using the moment of power deflation engendered by the state-delivered famine and the Four Cleanups campaign to retaliate for Bao Zhigen's lechery and cruelty in the Great Leap. To some, the incident was an indication of a political fire smoldering below, an act that portended a retaliation that would take on a life of its own when the political situation was right.

The Cultural Revolution and Its Complexities

The third round of retaliation against the Da Fo perpetrators of the Great Leap famine came during the Cultural Revolution, in the years 1967–70. The early 1960s were frustrating for Mao Zedong. In these years, Mao gave his party opponents, as well as growing numbers of rural people, reason to doubt his judgment. Apparently, he and some of his central party allies still believed that "great harvests" were occurring in every part of the country, and they maintained that edema, which by 1960 had become the number-one disease in the People's Republic of China, was due to problems of digestion and consumption of dirty food rather than requisition-induced malnutrition. In these years of great demoralization in village China, Mao instructed party cadres to correct the thoughts of farmers who desired to take back more land in order to acquire more food.[76]

---

[73] Patricia Thornton has pointed out that Wang Guangmei's July 5, 1964, report to the Central Committee argued that the Four Cleanups had failed and that powerful local party bosses had subverted its intent, a claim that is substantiated by Da Fo's history. See "Memory Palace," 11. Also see Thornton, *Disciplining the State*, 171, 176–77, 185–87.

[74] On this process, see Chen, "Differing Motivations."

[75] Tang Weilan, interview, September 20, 1995.

[76] Gao Hua, "Da Ji Huang de 'Liangshi Shiyong,'" 73–74.

The Maoists had lost credibility with rural people as well as party-based reformers, but Mao was not about to give up. Looking to regain power to initiate and implement central state policy, after 1964–65 Mao Zedong began to rely on "revolutionary mobilization" to transform the polity and revive his Great Leap strategy. This mobilization, known as the Cultural Revolution, began with the May Politburo Conference and the May 16 Circular of 1966, and it reached Dongle County and Liangmen Commune in early 1967.

The Cultural Revolution had two agendas. Mao's first goal was to destroy his Liuist opponents. Secret reports on the Great Leap Forward from his secretary, Tian Jiaying, confirmed the massive starvation caused by the Great Leap and documented official and unofficial opposition from local people.[77] Mao believed that the desires of rural dwellers to reestablish the securities of time-honored family-based agriculture and to return to cultural practices that brought joy and affirmation (such as posting couplets on household doors, participating in temple pilgrimages and market fairs, and joining in competitive martial arts contests) represented a petit-bourgeois slide backward toward a way of life that undercut the progress of revolutionary socialism. For Mao, the Cultural Revolution was a way of removing these oppositionist elements, including local commune- and brigade-level party leaders who stood in the way of the resumption of big Great Leap–type experiments with the rural economy.[78] The Cultural Revolution, then, was also a way of resuming the Great Leap and of promoting a struggle to eradicate the anti-communitarian influences of bourgeois individualism in the countryside – influences that inhibited uncritical faith in Mao's transcript for agricultural progress.

In Mao's view, he had offered Chinese villagers a "field of dreams" (to borrow Roderick MacFarquhar's apt term)[79] inside the people's communes, giving them a chance to free themselves from the drudgery of farm life and dependency on the earth through collective struggle.[80] Never mind that they had risked death in the fields of flawed collectivization. It was the class enemies, Mao believed, who had foiled the Great Leap. Landlords, rich peasants, teachers, rightists, and counterrevolutionary local officials had allowed the family-based foot soldiers of the Great Leap Forward to cling to tiny farm parcels, take up clandestine marketing, conceal grain from the collective, and even consume the standing crops before the party-based agents of the Maoist state could take them away for the "public good." The Cultural Revolution was aimed at rooting out these elements too, for their strategies of survival had subverted Mao's version of socialism and national strength.

---

[77] I am indebted to Yixin Chen and Edward Friedman for this line of logic. Personal conversations, November 1, 2001.

[78] As Becker has pointed out, the Cultural Revolution was a purge of those leaders who had brought an end to Mao's Great Leap famine. *Hungry Ghosts*, 253.

[79] MacFarquhar, *Origins of the Cultural Revolution*, 3:470.

[80] Friedman, "Mao Tse-tong," 314–15, 319.

When the Cultural Revolution arrived in Da Fo, few, if any, villagers were fully aware of the complex political issues it targeted. That Mao needed to shift attention away from the fact that he and his provincial clients had pressured local officials and local party leaders to exaggerate harvest yields[81] or that he had knowingly tolerated the corrupt and coercive work styles of provincial-, county-, commune-, and brigade-level party leaders, thereby steering the Great Leap toward disaster,[82] was not yet established in popular consciousness. Likewise, few villagers understood that Mao still ardently insisted that the Great Leap Forward had been a great, noble experiment that had been sidetracked only by those who had lost faith in his wisdom.

Officially, therefore, Mao and the party cadres who sought to regain the authority and privilege they had lost to the excesses of the Great Leap transcribed the Cultural Revolution as progress. There was, however, an unknown Cultural Revolution transcript that, as Hong Ying's memoir would suggest, "belonged to the country folk" who seized on the fissures created by the power struggle between Mao Zedong and the Liu Shaoqi–led reformers to avenge the injustices of the Great Leap Forward.[83]

Indeed, in much of Liangmen district, the Cultural Revolution developed into something other than what Mao had intended. In the hands of village people it became an antidote to the problems of the Great Leap famine, particularly to the problem of brigade-level party leadership. When we trace the evolution of the Cultural Revolution at the village level, we discover that local people seized the early moments of Maoist-sanctioned upheaval to openly voice grievances that originated with the Great Leap Forward and to publicly shame and secretly strike back at the key party bosses who had manufactured food shortages and made families suffer. In short, the Cultural Revolution in this rural Henan village, where there had been virtually no change of leadership during the post–Great Leap readjustment period, was transformed into a force to correct the work style of the Communist Party leaders who imposed the famine and to settle scores with the agents of its pain. In order to engineer this correction, villagers appropriated a familiar instrument of Maoist politics: the public criticism session.

Although it is often presumed that the Maoists had some kind of natural hold on public criticism and that it was an organic, direct instrument of Maoist authority, in reality the Cultural Revolution saw multi-polar contention over who would control this mechanism of politics. The Maoists of course wanted to take charge of public criticism and use it to push for another great leap, this time in the realm of culture, so that they could mobilize a new rebel discourse against the highest-level party "renegades," Liu Shaoqi and Deng Xiaoping. At the same time, the Liu-Deng reformers wanted to take command of public criticism to further reform

---

[81] Yixin Chen, personal correspondence, November 1, 2001.
[82] Chan, *Mao's Crusade*, 3, 92–93.
[83] Hong, *Daughter of the River*, 174–75.

the work style of the Communist Party cadres who had perpetuated the Great Leap disaster. They needed this instrument to quickly discipline non-repentant local pro-Mao leaders who were foot-dragging on reform and to regain some measure of their own credibility with the embittered survivors of the famine. The common people had their own plans for public criticism. They wanted to appropriate it to settle scores with the Maoist perpetrators of the famine, to promote authentic community-based discourse on village self-governance, and to bolster the everyday forms of resistance to the continuing CCP attempt to make them surrender their family-based farm economies to state monopoly.[84]

Longtime village leader Bao Zhilong was the main target of the villagers' wrath. According to Bao Shanguang, "At the time of the Cultural Revolution, many villagers hated Bao Zhilong. He had been village party secretary for too long, and he had offended too many people. Those who hated Bao used the opportunity provided by the Cultural Revolution to get back at him. He was beaten frequently at mass struggle meetings."[85] In early 1967, villagers took Bao to task for destroying individual farming and taking away their personal family property – often to benefit himself or his clients. They made this former militia chief and party secretary stand on a stage, crouch submissively, and listen to people accuse him of exceptional cruelty, tyranny, and greed. Angered by the deaths of relatives, famine survivors threw porcelain food bowls and other objects at Bao. They also reached out to the wounded residents of other villages within Liangmen district to settle scores with this commune and brigade party champion of the Maoist catastrophe. Zheng Yinchang recalls the humiliation to which Bao was subjected:

Bao Zhilong suffered the most during the Cultural Revolution. He was paraded in the village with a tall hat. At a mass meeting one night he was beaten. Not only people from this village tried to beat him. There were people from other villages who wanted to struggle him too.

During the Cultural Revolution, the people whom Bao Zhilong had hurt in the past came here to get him in order to struggle him. Usually, when people from other villages came to Da Fo, they had to ask permission before they could take anyone from the village. Because we hated Bao Zhilong, and because we were the dominant group in the village, we almost always let other people take him away to struggle against him. Bao Zhilong's family was frightened to death during the peak months of the Cultural Revolution, for they thought that anyone who came to their home was there to get Bao again.[86]

Throughout 1967, the sins of the Great Leap Forward Famine came back to haunt boss Bao. Cartoons ridiculing him and his lackey Bao Zhigen appeared on Da Fo's walls. Bao's enemies threw manure on the doors of his house – an act that was considered an insult and a curse. (This stinky curse found its way onto

[84] Thaxton and Lu, "Public Whip of Maoist Terror," 27.
[85] Bao Shanguang, interview, July 13, 2000.
[86] Zheng Yinchang, interview, May 3, 1994.

the doors of Bao Zhilong's counterparts in other North China villages during the Cultural Revolution. The people of Guojiaxiang in eastern Shandong still remember that on the lunar New Year of 1967 the relatives of the village party secretary arrived to find manure smeared on the doors of their powerful kinsman, who had taken advantage of a small "hush kitchen" to eat more than others during the Great Leap hunger.)[87] They later dismantled the front entrance to Bao Zhilong's house, sold the doors, and divided the bricks among themselves. On one occasion, villagers paraded Bao Zhilong around Da Fo's streets in a white paper funeral hat, a symbol that he had killed his own reputation as an honorable person.[88]

Denounced for taking too much grain from the collective for himself, taking bribes from production team leaders during the Great Leap, and diverting money from a commune-level grant fund to rebuild a local dam following the 1963 Wei River flood, Bao Zhilong also was paraded in the streets with the characters for "political pickpocket" (*zhengzhi paishou*) scrawled on his back, signifying he had used his power to steal from villagers. They were especially livid over boss Bao's willingness to allow his wife, Liang Xiaolu, who adopted the political language and symbols of male party leaders, to secure privileges at their expense. Anger over one particular privilege exploded in the Cultural Revolution when Ruan Zhaoyin, a production team accountant in the Great Leap, revealed during a public struggle session that Liang Xiaolu had demanded that Ruan give her extra grain when she was pregnant in 1959. When Ruan refused, Liang Xiaolu called her husband back from a big irrigation work site. The next day, boss Bao Zhilong fired Ruan. When the Cultural Revolution irrupted, Ruan seized the chance to publicly denounce boss Bao for this nepotism – an act that had great appeal to those whose prospects for procreation had been destroyed by the perpetrators of the Great Leap.[89] On several occasions, after the nighttime public criticisms against Bao Zhilong, someone blew out the lamp near Bao's home and attacked him in the dark. Finally, in late 1967, toward the end of the first phase of the Cultural Revolution, Bao Zhilong was relieved of his position of village party secretary. Too many anonymous accusation letters had found their way to Dongle County authorities.[90]

Popular retaliation against Great Leap leaders again broke out in the second phase of the Cultural Revolution, but this time it was entwined with a power

---

[87] Personal correspondence with Han Dongping, November 15, 2006.

[88] Interviews with Bao Rulong, July 5, 2002; Bao Jenming, September 14, 1993; Ruan Yindao, May 11, 1994; and Ruan Yulan, July 9, 2002. This humiliation all but destroyed the young first son of Bao Zhilong, who ran away from home.

[89] Ruan Zhaoyin, interview, July 17, 2006. On popular resentment that tends to well up over women who usurp the power of male husbands and adopt the attributes of "male" power holders, see Blok, "Female Rulers," 225–27.

[90] Interviews with Bao Wending, May 2, 1994; Pang Guihua, July 11, 2002; Bao Hongwen, July 24, 2004; Bao Jiping, September 2, 1993; Ruan Shaobing, September 12, 1995; Bao Guangming, September 19, 1995; and Ruan Shaobing, September 19, 1995.

struggle between Da Fo's Communist Party leaders that challenged the notion of the party as an institution wherein fraternal solidarity and mutual protection of members prevailed. The climactic incident involved Bao Yibin and Bao Zhilong, his former mentor. On regaining his party membership during the Cultural Revolution, Bao Yibin moved to settle the score with Bao Zhilong. In 1968 he joined in the ongoing village campaign to criticize Bao Zhilong. For the next two years, the dispute between these two Communist Party leaders and kinsmen more or less eclipsed the popular struggle to rectify the deadly errors of Great Leap leadership. Bao Zhilong was paraded around Da Fo's streets by different units of Red Guards, a mass movement of young people mobilized by Mao Zedong to carry out the Cultural Revolution – a movement that fractured into many competing armed factions. One of these Red Guard units, the *Hongyi* (Red Artists), was organized by Ruan Shaobing, Bao Zhenghai, Ruan Baofa, Bao Yiming, and Zheng Yinchang; Bao Yibin was the ringleader. Tang Huangdao, a member of a Red Guard unit that refrained from attacking Bao Zhilong, recalls: "Soon after the Cultural Revolution started, Bao Yibin became the most powerful person in the village. Bao Yibin operated behind the scenes, however. When Da Fo's Village Revolutionary Committee was set up, people from Bao Yibin's Red Artist faction in Dongle County town dominated it. Ruan Shaobing and Ruan Baofa, the head and deputy-head of the committee, were friends of Bao Yibin."[91]

In late 1969 Bao Yibin led the Red Artists to Dongle County town to join a like-minded faction in a fight against another Red Guard unit. When the Red Artist faction returned to Da Fo, its members were carrying iron bars and wearing military helmets. Although there was no Red Guard fighting in Da Fo, Bao Zhilong was beaten more than once by the Red Artists.[92] By late 1969, three years into the Cultural Revolution, villagers were frightened, and with good reason. Although no one was seriously injured from Red Guard infighting in Da Fo prior to 1970, a worker in the Dongle County machine tool factory had been killed in Red Guard wars. Closer to home, a person was killed when one faction of the Red Guards stormed the stronghold of another faction in Shangcunji.[93]

Worse yet, villagers' entitlement to practice *chi qing* had been attacked by the Red Guards, bringing back unwelcome memories of the Great Leap. In the spring of 1967, Ruan Shaobing, a key player in Bao Yibin's militant Red Artists network, began to suspect that villagers were hiding green crops in their baskets. Without the approval of either the commune or the brigade leaders, he and the Da Fo security chief implemented the search and seizure of those returning to the village from the fields. "Because of their strict policy, very few people stole the green

---

[91] Tang Huangdao, interview, September 11, 1995.
[92] Bao Peisun, interview, September 15, 1995.
[93] Ruan Yindao, interview, May 11, 1994.

crops during this year of the Cultural Revolution," remembers Bao Guishan.[94] Da Fo's wheat harvests were not good in the years 1962–68, and this attack portended a return to a bitter past and to hunger. Villagers were appalled and angered. They wanted nothing to do with the Red Artists' attempt to rush back to Mao's collective revival, and they found the definition of *chi qing* as a political crime that cheated the socialist state to be incomprehensible.[95] A renewed war over first rights to the standing crops evolved.

A few years later, in early 1970, Bao Yibin's Red Artists unit entered into a half-year alliance with Guo Weili, a Dongle County Highway Department party cadre. In the decade building up to the Great Leap disaster, Guo Weili had been the young leader of the Duidao village militia, and his reputation for violence against villagers preceded him: it was said that he liked to beat people.[96] On arriving in Da Fo to organize the campaign to suppress corrupt elements and counterrevolutionaries, forty-year-old Guo set up a torture chamber in the village. He enlisted Bao Yiming and Ruan Shaobing – both clients of Bao Yibin – to coerce the enemies of the Red Artists to confess their political wrongdoings.[97] Their major target was Bao Zhilong. Under Guo Weili's protection, Bao Yibin twice secretly encouraged Ruan Shaobing, Bao Zhenghai, and others to aid in the torturing of Bao Zhilong. Bao's house was sealed, all of his belongings were taken away, he was beaten during mass criticisms, and he was repeatedly taken out of his house and paraded around Da Fo while he shouted that he would not confess to any wrongdoing, even if it meant death.[98]

Death was a real possibility. Bao Yibin instructed the Red Guards in his Red Artists network to expose Bao Zhilong as the number-one agent of the anti-Mao party faction. Such absurd accusations had become commonplace by this point in the Cultural Revolution, as power struggles between various groups and individuals were fought in the revolutionary language of Maoism. Bao Zhilong, Bao Yibin, and many of the Da Fo party leaders were all connected to the Mao-led regime by an administrative system of patronage that had been damaged by the Great Leap Forward Famine. The hunger they had imposed in the Great Leap had marked them as grain-seizing terrorists. Now, badly split, they competed to use the chaos produced by the Cultural Revolution to regain supremacy and to help Mao stave off an imagined anti-Communist rebellion in Da Fo and the Henan countryside. The question, from their standpoint, was how to prove themselves super-loyal to Mao, the supreme leader of the most revolutionary people on earth.

[94] Bao Guishan, interview, July 19, 2000.
[95] In Da Fo this second development replicated some of the features of the Class Ranks Campaign that Richard Madsen has written about in Chen village, in faraway Guangdong. Madsen, *Morality and Power*, 178–81. Compare Hinton, who presents a similar example of this but an incomplete understanding of its political significance and dynamics. *Shenfan*, 454–58.
[96] Qian Chunlei, interview, September 15, 1995.
[97] Bao Mingsan, interview, September 18, 1995.
[98] Ruan Guobang, May 5, 1994; Tang Huangdao, September 11, 1995.

The political rhetoric of the Maoists ripped Da Fo apart for months in 1967 and then again briefly in 1970, as the ultra-leftist faction under Bao Yibin took Mao's call to expose capitalists and counterrevolutionaries as an excuse to persecute villagers whose actions were not in accord with socialist political conduct. Moral anarchy and political lawlessness swept the village. Bao Yibin's Red Guards organized public struggle meetings in which Bao Zhilong was questioned about why he supported senior CCP leader Liu Shaoqi's policy of individual farming – a blatant misrepresentation of Bao's post–Great Leap record. They hung an effigy of Liu Shaoqi around his neck, and they made him wear a heavy board across his torso with his name and that of Liu Shaoqi inscribed on it, with the characters for Bao Zhilong covered over by a red cross – the mark reserved for criminals scheduled for state execution.[99]

This phase of the Cultural Revolution was led by a campaign to cleanse the class ranks, with its emphasis on striking down hidden counterrevolutionaries, that is, people who were covering up bad class backgrounds (i.e., "landlords" or others who could be painted as bourgeois or associated with the Kuomintang) and plotting to complicate Mao's march toward socialism.[100] Because there were no obvious targets for the campaign in Da Fo, the Red Artists leaders pulled stereotyped candidates out of thin air, and for a few months in 1970 they subjected five or six villagers to harassment, isolation, and public criticism. There was not a shred of evidence that any one of the accused was plotting to undermine the party's leadership of the revolution.[101] It was impossible for the innocent victims of this imagined pogrom to defend themselves, and tragedy ensued.

Under the influence of Guo Weili, Bao Yiming, Ruan Shaobing, and the Da Fo Red Artists began a search for former Kuomintang members. Liu Jing, the wife of imprisoned Bao Sunyuan, the former party secretary of the Dongle County Kuomintang Committee prior to 1949, was targeted. Ruan Shaobing and the Red Artists pressured Liu Jing to generate a list of villagers who had secretly joined the Kuomintang when Bao Sunyuan was a Kuomintang leader.[102] As other people learned about this, a few secretly told Ruan that certain villagers, like Bao Hedian and Bao Zhiwang, were Kuomintang members. Ruan Shaobing believed their accusations. If the accused would not confess to his alleged crime and to plotting, he was subjected to public criticism and forced to kneel down on the ground in front of Guo Weili and Ruan Shaobing, who would burn his fingers with a lighter if he did not say what they wanted. Bao Hedian was one of several victims of this terror.[103]

[99] Bao Rulong, interview, July 7, 2002. On this political practice and its deadly consequences, see Friedman and Selden, "War Communism," 25.
[100] Madsen, *Morality and Power*, 178–81.
[101] Madsen differs and gives the radicals the benefit of the doubt. Ibid., 181.
[102] Pang Zhonghua, interview, July 21, 2000.
[103] Bao Guishan, interview, July 19, 2000.

Indignation and Frustrated Retaliation

Once the targets were tortured in public criticism meetings, Ruan Shaobing compelled Liu Jing to frame her testimony to match accusations the Red Artists had made. Some of the Red Artists secretly went to Bao Sunyuan in Jiaozuo prison and pressed him to write a statement in support of the list of accused Kuomintang members, which Ruan Shaobing used to further justify any methods to make the accused confess. The campaign grew so ferocious that Ruan Shaobing and the Red Artists resorted to beating people in order to obtain confessions. Through most of 1970 all civility disappeared: the war communism of the Great Leap had returned in spades.[104]

Many of Bao Zhilong's party clients came under attack during this phase of the Cultural Revolution. Bao Mingsan, a close family connection, remembers that the Red Artists spread unfounded rumors that his grandfather was a member of the Kuomintang and that his father was a member of Chiang Kai-shek's Sanqingtuan. Fearing persecution, the grandfather fled Da Fo. He was wise, for those who stayed were tortured. Bao Hedian, one of more than a dozen people labeled Kuomintang, had his fingers burned with a lighter by the Red Artists, after which he was hanged from a beam of Guo Weili's torture chamber.[105] The Red Artists sometimes hurt villagers who were neither beholden to party boss Bao Zhilong nor former members of the Kuomintang. They wrote to Quzhou County in Hebei province, where Bao Mingsan's second uncle was a party commune secretary, saying that the uncle was an unreliable element. A demotion followed. Under Guo Weili's influence, the house of Bao Wending was sealed, the trees in his courtyard were cut down and taken away, and his family was forced to live in a temporary shelter for forty days.[106] And on and on it went. To avoid penalty, torture, and exile, many people admitted to false political labels and bore cartoon tattoos that read "class enemy" as they swept Da Fo's streets.[107]

Bao Yibin's spurious linking of Bao Zhilong to Liu Shaoqi confused and ultimately derailed the struggle of the famine-scarred victims of Mao's Great Leap to bring party boss Bao to justice. During the Cultural Revolution, everyone in the power structure of the Da Fo Communist Party wanted to be seen as the purest of pro-Mao radicals, so the history of the Great Leap Forward Famine was twisted and moved off of center stage – which is precisely what Mao Zedong wanted. This inner-party political struggle frustrated the famine's living victims' efforts to seek justice and settle debts with all of the party leaders of the Great Leap Forward Famine: after all, the Red Artists also were implicated in the famine's carnage.

---

[104] Just as the seminal work of Friedman and Selden has shown. "War Communism," 2; Friedman, Pickowicz, and Selden, *Revolution, Resistance, and Reform*, 132, 139–41, and 145–50.

[105] Ruan Guobao, interview, May 5, 1994.

[106] Bao Wending, interview, May 2, 1994.

[107] Bao Mingsan, interview, September 18, 1995.

Da Fo's farmers drew two conclusions from this Cultural Revolution episode. First, Bao Zhilong, who refused to publicly acknowledge that his Great Leap mistakes had driven villagers to starvation and persisted in the belief that villagers depended on him and his understanding of the Communist Party, was beyond redemption. Villagers concluded they would have to wait and settle scores with Bao Zhilong and the other perpetrators of the famine later. Da Fo's villagers also concluded that the Communist Party was a politically dangerous organization. The ferocious infighting between Bao Yibin and Bao Zhilong taught villagers that the party managed politics by "internecine factional violence," just as Lowell Dittmer's conception suggests,[108] and that in this vicious system loyalty to government did not count. Virtually everyone in the village knew that Bao Zhilong had treated Bao Yibin better than his own son from 1945 to 1955 and that the two were very close until 1963–64, when Bao Yibin was disciplined by the party. Bao Yibin's father, Bao Yidai, had been the popular head of Da Fo's Peasant Association and had died a PLA hero, and it was common knowledge that Bao Yidai had entrusted the upbringing of his son to his comrade Bao Zhilong before he left for the South China battlefront.[109] Some said Bao Zhilong had set up his own son; others said Bao Yibin lacked gratitude. Their infighting and vendettas did nothing to heal the hurt of the Great Leap famine or to improve living standards, and they destroyed what respect remained for party authority in Da Fo and in Liangmen People's Commune. The villagers who had participated in the political struggle against the leaders of the Great Leap and its famine began thinking about ways to get beyond this damaging, pathological mode of local party rule.

The Price of Restoring Order: Bao Zhilong Is Returned to Power

In the winter quarter of 1969, when the Soviet Union was massing hundreds of thousands of troops on China's border and the resumption of good relations with the United States became imperative, the central government, acting in accordance with Premier Zhou Enlai's wisdom, moved to bring the Cultural Revolution to a close.[110] The PLA, which had itself come under attack from the Cultural Revolution left, was ordered to help rein in the radical Red Guards and assist provincial and sub-provincial committees in reestablishing order in the countryside. In Da Fo the move away from moral chaos and the restoration of a party apparatus that could elicit some measure of popular acceptance did not occur without a fight. It was led by Da Fo native Pang Zhonghua, a PLA veteran who had served as an officer in the Korean War.[111] Assigned to Jiuquan,

---

[108] Dittmer, "Chinese Cultural Revolution," 261.
[109] Ruan Xuetian, interview, May 8, 1994; Bao Jingxian, interview, May 1, 1994.
[110] Meisner, *Mao's China*, 376–77, 382–83, 388–89.
[111] Pang Zhonghua, interview, July 21, 2000.

Gansu province, at the outset of the Great Leap, until 1970 Pang Zhonghua had worked in the top-secret field laboratory where PRC scientists experimented with nuclear weapons. He returned to Da Fo during the campaign to oppose the illegal activities of the Cultural Revolution.

Pang Zhonghua immediately clashed with Guo Weili. After criticizing Guo for attacking, falsely accusing, and punishing too many villagers, Pang found that Guo had organized twenty party members to criticize *him*. Pang was accused of supporting Bao Zhilong, of being absent from Da Fo for too long, of not knowing what Bao Zhilong had done during the Great Leap Forward, and of not taking enough time to acquaint himself with the progress of the Cultural Revolution activities, which pointed toward a radiant future. But after this attack, which took place during a closed all–Da Fo party branch meeting of fifty party members, Pang struck back:

I told them that I was pleased that there were party members willing to criticize me, but then I turned to Guo Weili and cursed him very loudly. I pounded on the table and I yelled at him. I exclaimed that during the Cultural Revolution the PLA had a very high reputation, and that Chairman Mao once said that the whole nation should learn from the army. Since I had just retired from the army, the people in the village had to respect my right to voice my opinions. When I began to yell at Guo everybody fell quiet, including Guo himself. Guo Weili did not know how to deal with me. He did not know my background, and so he was really scared. . . . The next day, after I spoke against Guo Weili, I went to Liangmen People's Commune to report what I had understood was unfolding in the village, and my army reputation gained me the respect of the commune leaders.[112]

Pang Zhonghua did not have much evidence against Guo Weili and the Red Artists, but his articulation of their recklessness and ruthlessness in Da Fo prompted the commune leaders to reconsider their plan to make Guo the deputy head of the Revolutionary Committee of Liangmen People's Commune. Guo Weili fled Da Fo, and Pang Zhonghua accepted the position of Da Fo party secretary, serving in this capacity from 1970 until the end of 1972.

Pang Zhonghua moved to right the wrongdoings of the Cultural Revolution. He relaxed the militia controls on eating the green crops, and he worked day and night to clear villagers who had been falsely accused of being Kuomintang members and conspirators against Mao's revolution. But this latter task proved difficult. Guo Weili, Ruan Shaobing, and the Red Artists had used the testimony of Liu Jing to accuse a number of villagers of counterrevolution. Pang set out to make sure that Liu Jing's testimony was accurate and that she had not given it under duress. "I went to her house to talk with her," he recalls,

but her dinner was still placed on the table and she was not at home. I left, and I went back again. But she still was not at home. I was a bit concerned, and I looked for her in the village. Later, after organizing a search team, I found her body at the bottom of a well in the northwest corner of Da Fo. I was certain that Liu Jing had been murdered and

[12] Ibid.

thrown into the well by somebody who feared she would tell me the truth about what had been going on in the village. . . . I reported the incident to the commune and to the county government. But no one cared to investigate the matter at all. Liu Jing had no one in Da Fo to defend her.[113]

No one except Pang Zhonghua, that is. Pang persisted. He sent investigators into the prison where Liu Jing's husband, Bao Sunyuan, was held, to talk with Bao about Kuomintang membership in Da Fo. Bao Sunyuan, who had been coached by Guo Weili's factional clients to reaffirm the accusations of Guo Weili, Ruan Shaobing, and the Red Artists, now sent out countersignals, and on the basis of new information Pang Zhonghua was eventually able to clear everyone who had been accused of being a Kuomintang plotter.

While investigating Bao Sunyuan's countersignals, one shred of information about Liu Jing's case prompted Pang Zhonghua to lay down the law to the Red Artists. Pang was curious as to whether Bao Sunyuan had actually implicated those who had been accused, tortured, and murdered. He demanded that the Liangmen People's Commune send one of its leaders to the Jiaozuo prison to get additional testimony from Bao. Originally, Red Artists members Pang Haijin and Bao Dongzhi had interrogated Bao Sunyuan in the prison after the first accusation against the "Kuomintang plotters" was aired. Bao Sunyuan had written the names of the suspects, giving details of when they had joined and sworn oaths to the Nationalist Party. Later, however, Da Fo sent a second team of investigators, including some of the Red Artists in the first team, to the prison. This time, Bao had written down the same testimony, adding the two Chinese characters *mei you* in brackets. On reviewing this evidence, Pang Zhonghua went to visit a detective in the Dongle County police bureau, and the detective suggested that the bracketed characters possibly signified that Bao had left the door open for a retreat. Hence, Pang asked for a third prison interview with Bao. But Pang did not even talk to the accused. Instead, he remembers,

I talked with the prison guards and asked them if the people who came there the first time had used violence when they interrogated Bao Sunyuan about the Kuomintang membership list. They told me that Pang Haijin had kicked and cursed Bao for not telling the truth, and that the Red Artists had shouted that the villagers already had confessed and demanded to know why Bao Sunyuan was still lying about the matter.[114]

Pang needed no more evidence. He overthrew the accusations, exonerated Liu Jing, and thus prevented other innocent villagers from being hurt by Red Artists violence.

Pang Zhonghua was angry with Ruan Shaobing, Bao Yiming, and the Red Artists, for they had allowed Guo Weili, an *outsider*, to beat fellow villagers. This had created an impression that the Communist Party was a party of outsiders, of

[113] Ibid.
[114] Ibid.

alien politicians, an impression Pang now had to overcome if he was to gather popular support and move beyond the destruction of the Cultural Revolution. This was not easy. The "unreformed rich peasants" whom the Red Artists had repeatedly beaten and some of the accused Kuomintang plotters would begin to shake when Pang approached them or asked them to come to the Da Fo party office. Patiently and compassionately, he assured them that the political situation had changed and beatings were a thing of the past.

Pang Zhonghua also moved to prevent local party leaders from implementing central government policy with their own biases. Ever since the Great Leap, Da Fo party leaders had persistently implemented policy without following the written documents of superiors. Ruan Shaobing in particular had ignored the central government instructions that suspected "bad elements" could only be accused of any wrongdoings after witnesses, material evidence, and *voluntary* personal confessions were in place. Pang gives us an insight into the political mentality of the violent Cultural Revolution left:

His [Ruan Shaobing's] kind of revolutionary enthusiasm was common among people of my generation, for they grew up during land reform and went through many political campaigns. Ruan Shaobing actually said that if somebody verbally accused someone of being a Kuomintang party member, this fulfilled the criterion for a human witness. Furthermore, since Bao Sunyuan had given his testimony to back up the accusations, this was taken as sufficient evidence. With this evidence in hand, Ruan thought he was justified in confronting people to demand that they confess. If they refused, then using force to obtain the confession was permissible. When I saw Guo Weili, Ruan Shaobing, and the Red Artists beating the villagers I tried to persuade them to let the villagers go. I told Ruan that he could not rush to judgment in legal matters of such importance, I urged him to take ample time in dealing with these people, and I emphasized that we could not assume they were Kuomintang members before we finished the investigations.[115]

Many of the victims of the Red Artists wanted to retaliate against Ruan Shaobing and Bao Yiming by beating them, but Pang Zhonghua refused to allow any Da Fo party member to beat anyone during his tenure. Even though he despised Ruan Shaobing and the Red Artists, Pang protected them from this swell of vigilante emotions.

During his short tenure as party secretary, Pang Zhonghua restored a sense of community and security in village life. But it was short-lived, and it ended with a perplexing development. A month before the Spring Festival of 1973, Pang Zhonghua decided to leave Da Fo and become a state employee. The Liangmen People's Commune party committee solicited his recommendation for a good candidate for Da Fo party secretary. Looking to restore order and stability, Pang wanted a party leader who could handle the factions and bring the villagers back together. He declares: "I said that Bao Zhilong was the only person who could handle it."[116]

---

[15] Ibid.
[16] Ibid.

At first, this may seem an odd choice: most Da Fo villagers opposed party boss Bao; most party members found him barely acceptable. But the tradition of Mao-crafted Leninist dictatorship and fidelity to the Communist Party was the crucial factor deciding who ruled the village, and the process of leadership selection was determined solely by the party. Pang Zhonghua had invited the commune leaders to Da Fo to discuss who would be the best candidates for party secretary. After choosing these candidates, an election was held to determine which party members had the most popular support, but, in the final analysis, it was the recommendation of the previous brigade party secretary that carried the day. "In Bao Zhilong's case," recalls Pang, "my recommendation was crucial. There was no way he would have become party secretary again without it. He had been disgraced in the village."[117]

Despite his disgrace, two factors pointed toward Bao Zhilong. As the research of Andrew Walder and Bobai Li would anticipate, Bao's early Communist Party membership had placed him on a career track, and the party favored "poor peasants" whose sacrifices had lifted it to revolutionary power.[118] In this respect, Bao Zhilong's selection was structured in part by an early ascription that had elevated him to a district administrative position – no small accomplishment for a semi-landless and uneducated member of a marginalized interior village. In addition, Pang Zhonghua and most of the Da Fo party members were keenly aware that Bao Zhilong was one of the few party leaders who had mastered the arts of party patronage. Prior to and after the Great Leap fiasco Bao had gathered expertise in securing much-needed resources from the authorities in Liangmen district and Dongle County.[119]

Because there was no doubt about Bao Zhilong's political loyalty, the upper-level party officials deemed him a trustworthy collaborator in restoring order and someone who could move beyond his Great Leap mistakes. Many villagers found this logic absurd, but, to the Da Fo party leaders concerned about Da Fo's relationship with administrative power, it was the only sensible way to quickly move from the disorder of the Cultural Revolution back to discipline and patronage. The Cultural Revolution was fading, the PLA had restored a sense of order and security, and the Mao-led terror was being replaced by renewed discourse, by euphemisms about Mao's great mistake, and by renewed efforts to exit the collective via the market. Villagers and village leaders wanted to move beyond the lingering impoverishment and depressed living standards of the Great Leap Forward Famine.

In an important sense, Pang Zhonghua had saved the Da Fo Communist Party, but at a hidden price. The trauma of the Great Leap Forward Famine was unresolved,

[117] Ibid.
[118] Walder and Li, "Career Advancement," 1371–76, 1378–79.
[119] On the importance of this factor, see ibid., 1371–72, 1380.

the Cultural Revolution had piled on a new trauma, and the man chosen to help Da Fo get beyond the latest Maoist disaster was none other than one of the two principal local party agents of the Great Leap disaster. It was not a matter of Maoists versus Liuists. The choice was between the least tainted of the Maoist party leaders, who had perpetrated acts of extraordinary political evil and human suffering. Repackaged as a strong man who could sustain Pang Zhonghua's efforts to save the party and rule Da Fo as if it were a big collective family in which fair play would replace factionalized hell, Bao Zhilong was more than eager to prove he did not deserve the verdict of the Cultural Revolution. But the decision to bring Bao Zhilong back would complicate the party's ability to regain popular legitimacy through reform. In the long run, it left Da Fo's Communist Party vulnerable to the dangerous popular memory of suffering and loss in the Great Leap Forward Famine.

Photo 1. Dai Ruifu (the author) before the "people's heaven" – the earth's harvest – circa 1989.

Photo 2. The entrance road to Da Fo village.

Photo 3. The rhythm of rural life: a farmer on the way to market, during the first decade of post-Mao reform.

Photo 4. Cutting the June wheat crop.

Photo 5. A village threshing and milling ground.

Photo 6. A wagon driver and August corn, Da Fo village, 1990.

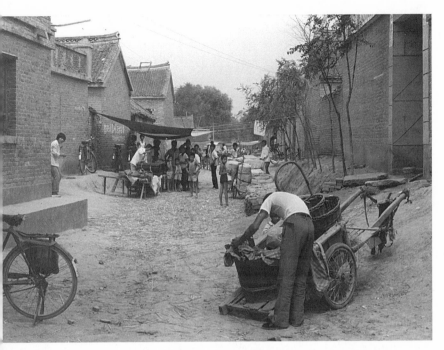

Photo 7. A small, early-morning market, Da Fo village, 1990.

Photo 8. A rural villager and Dai Ruifu (the author), Hebei-Shandong-Henan border area, first decade of post-Mao reform.

8

The Market Comes First

THE ECONOMICS OF
DISENGAGEMENT AND THE ORIGINS
OF REFORM

Following the Great Leap famine, Deng Xiaoping and Liu Shaoqi had promoted a package of reforms designed to relieve suffering in the countryside by pulling back from Mao's radical socialism, among them the retreat from fully collective agriculture entailed in *baochan daohu*, or the household responsibility system of farming. When Deng and Liu were removed from power during the Cultural Revolution, their reforms were systematically attacked by Maoists, who attempted to eliminate all individual farming and reemphasize the collectives. Following Mao's death in 1976, Deng effectively took control of the party-state. Many scholars have linked the emergence of market forces in post-Mao China to the agrarian reform announced two years later at the Third Plenum of the Eleventh Party Congress in December 1978, when the Deng Xiaoping leadership dealt a decisive blow to Maoist remnants. Minxin Pei's celebrated version of this interpretation claims that the momentum for reform came from mass pressures to escape the economic deprivation of the commune system and from government encouragement of a reform program that China's rural dwellers transformed into their own household responsibility system, a system that opened the door to decollectivization, private business, and market entry.[1]

---

[1] Pei, *From Reform to Revolution*, 94–97. Pei's study finds support in the works of other scholars. Dali Yang argues in *Calamity and Reform in China* that the process of reform was the product of high state policy shaped in response to the disastrous legacy of the Great Leap Forward, that is, by the acknowledgment of the Maoist leadership that the social consequences of collectivism had unleashed popular demands to loosen the state's grip on family-based farming. Yang writes "The official concessions fell short of the peasants' demand for household based farming, to be sure, but they represented a dramatic retreat from the utopian people's communes" (2; cf. 164–67). According to this interpretation, what *presumably* saved China's farmers from the disaster of Maoist collectivization was the household responsibility system, which villagers and provincial rulers experimented with in the aftermath of the Great Leap but which the Central Committee of the CCP reluctantly endorsed only after 1980. Kate Xiao Zhou has echoed this interpretation, arguing

The Market Comes First

To a certain extent, this interpretation is correct, because village-based farmers did shun the artificial collective and return to private farming after the Great Leap famine, and this spontaneous and instinctive process led naturally to village markets and rural-based market fairs.[2] But the experience of Da Fo – which of course is only one tiny star in the galaxy of China's million villages – is not exactly in accord with the above explanation of the origins of reform. Still reeling from the setback of the Great Leap famine, Da Fo's farmers launched themselves into private trade and began to reclaim market space *before* the Cultural Revolution had ended, *before* the CCP's Eleventh Congress, and *before* the *baochan daohu* system gained acceptance by the party's Central Committee. They also rejected all central and county government attempts to enlist their participation in the household responsibility system between 1979 and 1982, engineering their own silent land-to-the-tiller movement in this period. Only in light of villagers' resistance to state attempts to re-bind them to the collective and of the relationship of the black market to this resistance can the origins of reform in Da Fo be understood. Local initiatives began not with the move to *baochan daohu* in the 1979–82 period but rather with a spate of small, sometimes hidden changes that they initiated in the early 1960s and sustained throughout the Cultural Revolution and its aftermath. Invisible to Western observers and unknown to high state rulers, these small changes often were the product of a daily struggle for survival that impeded the attempt of party bosses to implement collectivization. Da Fo villagers' perspective on the development of this struggle defies the usual serialization of the process of Chinese reform.[3]

Aware that the post–Great Leap Forward strategy of Liu Shaoqi and Deng Xiaoping pointed toward a state-framed process of decentralized agricultural decision making for management of the people's communes, Da Fo's inhabitants also remember that party bosses often acted to inhibit them from returning to household-governed strategies of livelihood and acted to keep them from withdrawing from the collective. Nonetheless villagers – sometimes acting with the tacit support of village and sub-village leaders – carried out reforms outside of the realm of high state politics. These reforms did not always sit well within the framework of socialist collectivization. Driven from below, they reflected the market initiatives of an emergent social movement forming outside Mao's socialist political order. Indeed, they reflected Da Fo villagers' attempts to disengage economically from the party-state at the same time that they disengaged politically

that in the post-1978 period farming households were able to regain autonomy in agriculture largely by "using the knife of *baochan daohu* to free themselves from the controls of party cadres" and by extending their subsistence-oriented farm activities to the market. Zhou, *How the Farmers Changed China*, 4, 76.

[2] I am indebted to Alfred Chan for helping me develop this point. Personal correspondence, June/July 2006.

[3] This is as one might expect from reading the insightful work of Lynn T. White. See *Unstately Power*, 11–16.

in the years following the Great Leap Forward. Disenchanted with their local Communist leaders and their millennial promises, the people of Da Fo found their own ways to return to the forms of market participation and individual tillage that had served them so well in the past.

Hidden Smallholding within Collectivization

Although all the land in Da Fo is now farmed by individual households, the household responsibility system was never put into practice there. As we saw in Chapter 6, toward the end of the Great Leap Forward Famine, as an emergency measure, the production teams in Da Fo began "lending" half a *mu* of sweet potato land to villagers to farm themselves. At this time, 1961–62, villagers called this land taken out of collective production *hongshu jiedi*, or "borrowed sweet potato land." No one used the term *baochan daohu* to describe the farming of this land, and, indeed, the two systems were quite different, as farmers who engaged in household responsibility farming had an obligation to deliver a set amount of grain to the state, and the delivery of this amount took precedence over their own subsistence needs. *Baochan daohu* was collective agriculture in a different guise: the land that each household farmed was part of the collective, and the crops they grew on it were not fundamentally their own, though they might get to keep some portion of them. The *hongshu jiedi*, on the other hand, consisted of private plots (*siliudi*) that villagers had reclaimed from the collective, often in collaboration with their production team leaders. Such private plots sprouted up like weeds in rural China in the period after the Great Leap Forward Famine. Those who cultivated them had no responsibility to give up their produce to the team, brigade, or commune or to any tax arm of the Maoist party-state.[4] Families cultivated the land strictly for their own benefit.

The Lilliputian "sweet potato" plots reclaimed for survival at the peak of the Great Leap famine were used to grow food for recovery. Well into the mid-1960s Da Fo's farmers used them to grow wheat, sweet potatoes, turnips, and pumpkins for family consumption, and they refused to give them up either at the behest of the Liu-Deng government during the Four Cleanups campaign or during the Cultural Revolution, when Mao declared such farming practices "politically unacceptable."[5] Following Mao's call to re-collectivize these lands, the Dongle County government sent a work team to Da Fo to recall the private household "sweet potato" plots. Terrorist Guo Weili, its leader, decided Da Fo's farmers should cut the wheat on these plots collectively and ordered them to deposit the

---

[4] Apparently, there was so much demoralization after the Great Leap famine that many farmers simply left the commune and practiced individual farming or *dangan* (go it alone) by dividing land among themselves. I suspect the borrowed sweet potato land movement was related to *dangan*. Thanks to Alfred Chan for pointing out the *dangan* phenomenon. Personal correspondence, June/July 2006.
[5] Compare with Yang, *Calamity and Reform in China*, 94.

June harvest on the collective threshing ground. Villagers resisted. On hearing of Guo's decision, many people harvested the wheat planted on these plots before the local officials could take possession of the crop in the name of the collective. Pang Zhonghua, the Da Fo party secretary, had been away from the village at the time of Guo Weili's decision; when he came back many people complained to him about it. Pang declared that anyone who had lost their private field harvest to the collective threshing ground could take it back. Local party leaders saw no way of overcoming popular hostility to re-collectivization, and the Guo Weili proposal was not adopted.[6]

Still, the Maoist pressure on the private plots did not let up, and by the end of 1970 they had been returned to the production teams to be farmed on a collective basis. Yet even during this period, villagers say, they retained rights to their plots' produce.[7] Zheng Xiaoquan explains, "During the Cultural Revolution, the collective took over the actual farming of the private plots, but villagers still could get grain from the collective as if they were farming the private plots themselves."[8] The persistence of these small private landholdings during the Cultural Revolution was the product of a popular struggle that had widespread community support. According to Bao Renqing, "Most people felt very good about this system, because under it they did not need to worry about losing their private plot."[9]

Production team leaders played a large role in protecting the sweet potato plots and the other interests of their team members after the functions of the brigade were reduced: the team leaders became de facto representatives of their fellow villagers and seldom enforced the orders from brigade- or commune-level party-state leaders strictly. Lineage ties or kinship bonds alone cannot fully explain this phenomenon, because such ties were partially emasculated during the high tide of the socialist agricultural surgery of the 1950s and 1960s. It appears that the eroding legitimacy of the Maoist state at all levels, including its structural and ideological power over popular norms that argued for survival-oriented petty trade, was a key factor – sweet potatoes were easily peddled in black markets and were in great demand. In any case, Da Fo's production teams prevented Cultural Revolution radicals from dismantling the veiled system of harvest rights on formerly private plots. Many of the team leaders also moved to prevent the power struggles and political rallies of the Cultural Revolution from disrupting the agricultural production of both households and teams, so that food security was not seriously jeopardized by the same overzealous labor mobilization offensives of the Great Leap period.

---

[6] Interviews with Pang Benwin, September 1, 1993; Bao Jiping, September 2, 1993; and Pang Furong, September 3, 1995.
[7] Bao Wending, interview, May 2, 1994; Zheng Xiaoquan, interview, May 6, 1994.
[8] Zheng Xiaoquan, interview, May 6, 1994.
[9] Bao Renqing, interview, May 30, 1995.

Two small retreats from the frenzy of the Great Leap stand out. Production in home village fields was given priority over participation in the extra-village public works projects that had in the past drawn labor out of the village during critical points in the agricultural cycle. People were to stay put and cultivate their tiny household plots and the crops of their teams. Physical energy was to be reserved for farm work. There was to be no repeat of the radical Maoist political mobilization that produced the exhaustion, sleep disorders, and poorly focused agricultural work performances of the Great Leap disaster. Pang Tinghua recalls:

During the Cultural Revolution years, I was the head of the third production team. At that time, I made a rule. Everybody was allowed to participate in the Cultural Revolution on one condition, which was that they had to do it at night. If they wanted to make revolution during the working hours, they would not get work points, and if they did not get their work points, they would not be able to get as much grain as those who worked in the fields. My rule did not intend to interfere with people's desire to make revolution, but I had to make sure that production was not adversely affected so that at harvest time every member of the team would get enough grain to survive.[10]

Pang Tinghua's team had been one of the best in Da Fo. Its members were accustomed to getting more grain than those on other teams, and Pang himself had pressure, as well as support, from below to sustain this performance – which is precisely what he did.

Similarly, caring for the crops during the important junctures of the agricultural seasons came before political campaigns. Production team leaders insisted that political meetings be held in winter, so that Cultural Revolution activities were finished by the time the busy June wheat harvest season was upon them. Even in winter, when revolutionary meetings were frequent, the team leaders suspended meetings to feed the wheat. Pang Canshen says: "Villagers knew very well that they had to make sure their crops were doing fine. Otherwise, they were the people who were going to suffer."[11] That the Cultural Revolution did not harm production in this Henan village was partly the result of the embodied memory of suffering from compliance with recent collective political mobilization: the great fear of a return to the disruptions introduced during the Great Leap Forward strengthened the resolve of villagers to resist any attempt to shift power over production from the team to the brigade. If sub-brigade production team leaders appreciated the Cultural Revolution purges of Bao Zhilong and the Great Leap radicals, they also asserted the rights of their members to manage the day-to-day process of production without party-state interference.

Throughout the late 1960s and early 1970s, it was also common for Da Fo's production teams to conceal production figures from brigade leaders. "It was in their interest to tell the village leaders that their production figures were lower

---

[10] Pang Tinghua, interview, September 1, 1993.
[11] Pang Canshen, interview, May 9, 1994.

than they thought," says Bao Guishan. Moreover, some teams divided the wheat secretly without the knowledge of brigade leaders.

The policy was that the production team members could not divide the wheat among themselves before they first paid the tax to the government. But the production team leaders always tried to get around the policy. They would tell the Da Fo brigade leaders they did not divide the wheat harvest and say they only let the members borrow some wheat from the team to eat during the harvest season. They would argue that the team members did not have any grain left to eat, and they would contend that without the grain the team members could not work in the fields. The brigade leaders usually would allow the team leaders to get away with this.[12]

Party brigade leaders, accompanied by production team leaders, did inspect the crops, but villagers say that there always was room for little ways to conceal some of the yield. By 1969–70 another form of concealment had evolved. During the Cultural Revolution each of Da Fo's production teams had about four hundred *mu* of land, but the leaders only reported three hundred *mu*, leaving each team about one hundred *mu* of extra land that was not taxed. Ninety percent of its June wheat, August corn, and October sorghum harvests were distributed equally across the households of team members, while the production team leaders used the remainder to maintain a small welfare fund and an agricultural reinvestment fund for each team.[13]

These various strategies of preserving villagers' entitlements helped to alleviate the privations of collective agriculture, which failed to deliver sufficient returns to villagers throughout the decade of the Cultural Revolution. Partly because Mao's retreat from the radicalism of the Great Leap Forward proved only half-hearted, grain production and grain prices stagnated in many parts of rural China during the years 1966–76.[14] Between 1966 and 1978, most production team members in Da Fo received about 300 to 320 *jin* per person annually from the collective.[15] Crop yields had improved little by little over this decade, with wheat increasing from 200–250 to 240–350 *jin* per *mu* and corn improving from 300 to 400 *jin* per *mu*, translating into some relief from hunger. However, for the members of ten of Da Fo's thirteen production teams, the average per capita annual grain consumption in 1978 was 300 to 320 *jin*, which was 100 *jin* short of the 400 *jin* villagers had historically managed to garner in disaster-free years. Actually, the situation was even worse, for the makeup of the 300 to 320 *jin* signified a bitter memory of the Great Leap: for the poorest teams, which composed 70 percent of Da Fo's population, 220 *jin* of the 300–320 *jin* came from corn, while the prime wheat went mostly to the favored production teams, the brigade leadership, and

---

[12] Bao Guishan, interview, September 9, 1995.

[13] Zheng Yunxiang, interview, July 14, 1998; Ruan Shifan, interview, July 17, 1998.

[14] Friedman, "Maoism and the Liberation," 409; Unger, "Decollectivization," 588. Also see Lardy, *Agriculture*, and Lin, "Collectivization." For a different take on this issue, see Yang, *Calamity and Reform in China*, 109–11.

[15] Zheng Xiaoquan, interview, May 6, 1994.

commune officials.[16] In this period, "corn was the staple food for the common people," recalls Zheng Xu.[17] The reason corn dominated the diet of the poor was directly linked to the continuing fear of another Great Leap. Corn had been one of the crops villagers had emphasized to avoid the Maoist craze for wheat and to survive the famine. Even in 1978, according to Bao Wending, people did not want to work hard in the wheat fields of the collective, because the state had first claim to wheat before villagers and took wheat before corn.[18]

The distribution of disappointing harvest returns by the collective left villagers at the margins of subsistence throughout most of the Cultural Revolution. Crop theft was rampant, and some people, including members of the militia, stole cabbages, spinach, and sweet potatoes from the collective fields at night in order to make ends meet.[19] But even more important was the one hundred *jin* of grain per person that villagers managed to grow on their veiled private plots, which did not appear on the books of the production teams.[20] The persistence of this private land arrangement was critical in sustaining popular acceptance of collective production in the late 1960s and early 1970s. The production team leaders allowed the harvests from these plots to go to villagers in order to give them an incentive to stay within the larger framework of collective agriculture, and villagers took care of these plots first, putting family labor and fertilizer into them before they invested in the fields of the collective. This invisible partial withdrawal encouraged popular tolerance of the collective.

The Land Division of 1982

The present system of family-based landownership in Da Fo is an outgrowth of resistance to those modes of surplus extraction that engendered famine and to the subsequent party-state attempt to encumber grain production and food availability via household responsibility systems. Villagers agree that Deng Xiaoping should be credited with the impetus for decollectivization. Pang Huiyin recalls, "It was the central government leaders who asked the village to divide the land. We were not given an opportunity to express our opinion about the decision to divide the land. It was imposed from above."[21] Pang Guihua echoes this understanding: "When Deng Xiaoping became the national leader, we thought that he might do something different. But people were a little surprised when we found out that we actually were to farm the land on the basis of individual households."[22]

The first full-fledged land division in Da Fo occurred in the fall of 1982. Deng Xiaoping's officials had actually issued the directive to divide the land of

[16] Bao Wending, interview, May 2, 1994.
[17] Zheng Xu, interview, May 12, 1994.
[18] Bao Wending, interview, May 2, 1994.
[19] Bao Guangming, interview, July 18, 1998.
[20] Pang Canshen, interviews, May 8–9, 1994.
[21] Pang Huiyin, interview, May 16, 1994.
[22] Pang Guihua, interview, May 14, 1994.

the collective in 1980. In the fall of 1981, Da Fo party leaders announced that each person would be given half a *mu* of land to grow food for his or her own consumption. The rest of the land was to be divided according to the number of working bodies on a production team and rented to individual farmers to cultivate grain for the state. The farmers were to be given work points in accordance with how much land they farmed and with the yields from this "responsibility land."[23] This version of the household responsibility system was not put into practice in Da Fo, however, because villagers refused to agree to adopt it.[24] To be sure, they eagerly accepted the half-*mu* of "food land," which was clearly an extension of a private, politically uninhibited land system that had long been in place. What they did not accept was the division of the remaining collective land into parcels of "responsibility land" on which teams of workers would produce grain for the state on a contractual basis. The villagers said that it was not easy to measure precisely how much effort each farmer put into the land simply according to the yield. Because the quality of land varied considerably, several households might put the same effort into the land with disparate harvest results. Public opinion soon turned against the idea of dividing the land according to the number of people in a production team, a practice that discriminated against smaller families and labor-short households. If there was to be an annual quota of grain production per *mu* for delivery to the state, these villagers refused to take back the land.

All through late 1980, 1981, and early 1982, a debate raged in Da Fo over the criteria for dividing the land and the terms on which the land to be received would be farmed. In the fall of 1982, Da Fo party leaders, in open consultation with all of the production team leaders, agreed that the land was to be divided by the number of people in the village, and each individual, regardless of age, was given an equal share. In the end, the process of land division was taken over by villagers. "It was the production team leaders who decided how to divide the land," says Tang Guoyi, "But they had to ask the approval of the villagers."[25] Da Fo's cultivators also elicited a promise from party leaders to redivide the land every three to five years to reflect the changing demographic circumstances of each household and got party leaders to agree that the divided land would carry no quota, convincing labor-short households to consent to work the land.[26]

To distrusting villagers, only a complete break with the collective and its state-captured harvests could serve the interest of individual families. Furthermore, the political significance of freely growing one's own food in family-managed fields was burned deeply in the memory of all villagers. Maoist zealots had used food as a weapon to hurt them during the Great Leap Forward, and the move to a mode

[23] 1994 interviews with Zheng Yinchang, May 13; Tang Canjun, May 15; and Pang Chenglan, May 16.
[24] 1994 interviews with Bao Wending, May 2; Zheng Xiaoquan, May 6; and Pang Chenglan, May 16.
[25] Tang Guoyi, interview, September 20, 1995.
[26] Zheng Yinchang, interview, May 13, 1994.

of land division that favored individual household food management made it much harder for party leaders to repeat this history.[27] Apparently, Da Fo's party leaders went along with this system of independent smallholding for reasons of their own, one being the costly time demands required for managing the household responsibility system.[28] There was another factor motivating village leaders to accept, and even advocate, land division on a per capita basis, however: the lingering fear of a return of social insecurity. According to Zheng Yunxiang, "The people who openly defended Deng Xiaoping's directive to divide the land were [still] scared of the food shortages of 1960; they thought that it would be a good thing to farm the land on an individual basis."[29]

In short, whereas the 1982 land division was given impetus by central government policy, once subjected to village discourse the division policy took a form that encouraged the resurgence of intensive farm production by smallholder families. The villagers had perceived the proposed introduction of a household responsibility system as an unenlightened remnant of state-directed collective agriculture,[30] and they were right, in a sense, because state procurement continued under the household contracting arrangements of the post–Great Leap era.[31] (Even the less collective *da baogan* system of household contracting, while allowing farmers to keep the harvest after paying taxes and meeting a procurement quota, did not guarantee subsistence protection in the event of a serious harvest problem – its major purpose was to temper and thereby sustain procurement, in part by providing an incentive to maximize output.) To be sure, other locales abandoned the experiment with the household responsibility system after 1982,[32] but Da Fo farmers refused to participate in such an experiment in the first place. Instead, they went back to family-based farming without the leftover paraphernalia of party-state collective management (contracts, quotas, and work points) as early as 1983. By the following year, they had gained a clear advantage vis-à-vis the party-state in determining how much of their harvested crops would remain with their households for consumption, savings, or exchange. Speaking of this "premature" supplanting of collective agriculture by a smallholder-based system of family farming, Tang Canjun recalls, "After we divided the land in this way, the Dongle County government leaders thought we had gone too far. They

[27] Zheng Yunxiang, interview, July 14, 1998.
[28] Bao Tanghui, interview, May 2, 1994.
[29] Zheng Yunxiang, interview, September 21, 1995.
[30] On the Western conception of the household responsibility system as "replacement," see Putterman, "Incentive Problem," 104; Netting, *Smallholders, Householders*, 250–51.
[31] I am indebted to Thomas P. Bernstein for bringing this important point to my attention. Personal correspondence, April 16, 2007. According to Tang Wenjie, procurement in the post-Mao 1980s was resented up into the 1990s. Apparently, the Liangmen township government did not pay Da Fo's farmers for the grain they sold to the state, but rather issued worthless paper IOUs, which some farmers said "was like robbery." Tang Wenjie, interview, July 1, 2006.
[32] Hartford, "Socialist Agriculture," 38.

came to the village twice to correct our mistakes, but there was nothing they could do to make us utilize the household responsibility system they had suggested. In the end, they accepted what we had done."[33]

The landholding system that has prevailed since 1982 in Da Fo, in which land is allocated in accordance with the number of people in each household, is an extension of a family-centered household land management system that found expression in the actualized escape from the Maoist disaster of 1958–61. Bao Pei-jian says: "What we are doing right now is exactly the same thing that Liu Shaoqi and Deng Xiaoping wanted to do in 1961 and 1962. At that time, it was stopped by the Socialist Education Campaign and the Cultural Revolution. Nowadays we have gone much farther than Liu and Deng might have anticipated."[34]

Hidden Market Reentry within Collectivization

Just as Da Fo's farmers, motivated by fear of another Great Leap–style disaster, reconnected with traditional household farming prior to state-inspired decollectivization, they also reentered the market well in advance of the Third Plenum of the Eleventh Party Congress in order to keep privation at bay. In 1963, Da Fo's farmers learned that Liu Shaoqi was encouraging people to participate in the free market. More of them started to sell peanuts, sweet potatoes, fried cakes, melons, and other foodstuffs. With the improvement of yields on the private lands and profits from family businesses, life was a little better, people recall. In the fall of 1963, however, the Wei River flooded again, and the crop was lost. After the flood, the government provided each person a half-*jin* of grain a day until the next crop was harvested.[35] As in the aftermath of the 1956 Wei River flood, the government again encouraged villagers to engage in different commercial activities, and many families were able to recover, meet the government requirement of paying back the relief loans, and get on with their lives, mainly by pursuing small businesses. Bao Wenchou recalls, "My father continued with his peanut business on the market. I worked in the collective fields and took care of the crops on the private plot. So, all in all, the flood did not cause great suffering."[36]

The evidence of these market-opening realities exposes the fraudulent nature of the Maoist ideological stress on "peasant self-reliance" under socialism. In Da Fo, the Maoist party-state repeatedly attempted to prevent villagers from pursuing small trade in order to maximize appropriation of agricultural surpluses, but every time there was an economic crisis, whether because of the flawed operation of the collective itself or because of natural disasters, local party leaders went

[33] Tang Canjun, interview, May 15, 1994.
[34] Bao Peijian, interview, May 3, 1994; see also Bao Gui, interview, May 1, 1994.
[35] Tang Guoyi, interview, September 20, 1995.
[36] Bao Wenchou, interview, September 1, 1995.

ahead and relaxed market controls, allowing villagers to reenter the market in order to save themselves and then hailing such initiatives as the "self-reliance" of socialism. The only problem was that Maoist rulers could not always put the genie of such popular market initiatives back into the bottle. By the late 1960s the pursuit of the market had gained a momentum of its own, swelling into a silent community-based challenge to collectivization.

In Da Fo, as in many other villages, the pursuit of the market in the aftermath of the Great Leap famine was seen by Mao and his party allies as an "irrational remnant" of petty-bourgeois fanaticism. Yet this "fanaticism" managed to sustain itself, for several reasons. The surveillance apparatus of the Liangmen People's Commune, and for that matter the Da Fo brigade, suffered a severe power defla-tion after 1961, so the party-state was less able to keep track of villagers' economic pursuits. Also, a good many villagers, having outwitted and outlasted the party-state repression that had brought them face-to-face with death in the Great Leap famine, were less fearful of the local party leaders who threatened penalties for petty trade. They were now more willing to "go it alone" and to contest the anti-market commands of high state policy agents.

Although the production teams, often led by kinsmen, gained some autonomy and provided some measure of security in the aftermath of the Great Leap debacle, villagers remained unhappy with the way their leaders made decisions on the issue of a living wage. The leaders decided who got how many work points, and the same number of work points was not always given for the same task. There were constant arguments with production team leaders over procedures for dividing the harvest. Bao Guangming recalls: "If there was a big pile of sweet potatoes, including big ones and small ones, everybody wanted to get the big ones. In order to be fair, we usually drew a lottery to decide who was first to get his share, and from which side of the sweet potato pile. Still, it was not always fair."[37] Some of the leaders of Da Fo's poorest production teams were lazy and corrupt: "They were found to be taking a little more than their fair share," complains Bao Guishan, "and they treated people unequally, assigning the best jobs to their friends."[38]

To counter this unfairness and the food insecurity it fostered, 60 percent of the members of Da Fo's production teams engaged in some kind of surrepti-tious market activity. Many of the poorest members expressed their discontent by doing a poor job in the fields, which prompted official investigations. This, coupled with state pressures to increase production, resulted in team leaders leav-ing their positions, after which production dropped and the value of work points decreased. If the Liangmen People's Commune officials blocked market entry at this point, they had to deal with poor and hungry team members who had only one meaningful chance for survival, which was to pilfer the crops of the collective, and by now the militia was lax when it came to controlling crop theft.

[37] Bao Guangming, interview, July 18, 1998.
[38] Bao Guishan, interview, July 19, 1998.

278

Disenchanted with Maoist dearth and mindful of the punishment of Bao Zhilong and the Great Leap radicals, Da Fo's party leaders gave in.

Bao Xuexing was a member of the first production team, one of Da Fo's poor teams in the late 1960s. The grain his family received from the team averaged only about three hundred *jin* per person per year. "It was not enough for us," recalls Bao, so he began to make and sell jellied foods, dried noodles, breads, and fried cakes in the Da Fo market and in surrounding villages. Bao explains why he was allowed to engage in these types of activities:

The village and government leaders did not encourage people to do small businesses like this, for a very good reason. If they encouraged people to do it, there would be very few people who wanted to work in the collective fields. They wanted to prevent people from leaving the collective fields. But it was not a secret among my neighbors or fellow villagers that my family was engaging in small business. The production team leaders and the brigade leaders all knew what was going on. They did not do anything to stop us from doing small business. . . . Everybody in Da Fo knew that I had a big family to support and needed the small business endeavors to make extra money.[39]

The local brigade and production team leaders were all Da Fo natives. They did not want to offend fellow villagers by stopping them from engaging in small business, and in fact they had no personal interest in doing so. Thus, they turned a blind eye.[40]

Poor families could obtain permission to operate a small business legally if they applied to the Dongle County Business Management Office, but few did. Even those who did never notified the office when they actually were in pursuit of the market, so that they seldom if ever paid a tax. They were rarely apprehended, because there were only a small number of tax officials per county, and these officials wore clearly identifiable uniforms that made it easy for market-goers to elude them. Even when villagers were caught, they often found ways of avoiding fines. Caught by tax officials while selling fried cakes in Zhanbeitun, Bao Xuexing simply gave up his basket full of cakes and fled the market; because the tax officials did not know who Bao was or where he was from, they had no way of following him or fining him.[41]

In the first three years after the Great Leap famine, Liangmen Commune officials apparently did not stop villagers from selling their own surplus grain on the village market and did not prohibit them from buying grain within Da Fo for their own use, but this liberalization had its limits. In 1964 the CCP-led Liangmen district government stepped up efforts to discourage small business and petty trade, particularly in grain, for which there were legal restrictions on intra-village exchange. Each year, the commune government banned all grain sales in the months before and after the June wheat harvest. Thereafter, it allowed

---

[39] Bao Xuexing, interview, September 15, 1995.
[40] Ibid.
[41] Ibid.

families to sell their surplus grain and buy grain for their households. Agents of the Liangmen People's Commune tried to stop virtually all profit taking in grain trade and were especially vigilant in their attempt to ban trade beyond the village. "The government wanted to stop those people who traveled a long distance to buy grain and sell it for a profit. This kind of trade was considered illegal speculation and it was banned," recalls Bao Tanger.[42]

Nevertheless, petty trade in long-distance grain markets was not completely obliterated. According to Bao Tanger, "There still were many loopholes in the blockade and people could easily get around it. The state only set up checkpoints on one or two major roads to stop people carrying large amounts of grain. People could get around the checkpoints. I do not know many Da Fo people who were caught by the checkpoint police."[43] Throughout most of the Cultural Revolution period, growing numbers of bicyclists carrying small bags of grain could be seen leaving Da Fo for long-distance market trade.

One of these traders was Bao Gui. In 1967 there were four people in Bao Gui's family. Altogether, they got about 300 *jin* of grain per family member. Because Bao Gui was the only member of his household working in the collective field, the family grain allocation was below average. Seldom did they have enough to eat, and they often ate pumpkin dishes given to them by relatives to survive. "After eating the pumpkin," recalls Bao Gui, "I felt very ashamed that I could not obtain enough food for my family." Bao's escape from this predicament was predicated on market entry: he borrowed money, used it to rent a bicycle, and pedaled to Shandong, where he purchased grain to sell back in Da Fo. The small profit from this venture enabled his family to survive the period of dearth before the next harvest. Though the police lectured Bao in an attempt to dissuade him from making such trips to trade in grain, he continued to do so.[44] By 1978 Bao Gui's household was getting about 360 *jin* of grain per person from the collective, but its guarantee of food security was located in the market: in this same year, Bao's wife began making two rolls of straw braid daily, which brought thirty cents a day, enough to cover all daily living expenses. This, coupled with Bao Gui's intermittent peddling, freed up family income to invest in a pig. Later, Bao began a sesame oil business in addition to his grain trading. By 1984, his household was earning four thousand *yuan* a year from trade.[45] This income gave them security they had not experienced since before the Great Leap Forward.

It also enabled the Baos to invest in their land, enhancing crop production with fertilizers and irrigation equipment. "The productivity of the land improved significantly," Bao says. In 1985 he bought a tractor jointly with a neighbor; in 1986 he bought his first television set. In 1987 the Baos rebuilt their house, and

---

[42] Bao Tanger, interview, September 1, 1995.
[43] Ibid.
[44] Bao Gui, interview, May 1, 1994.
[45] Ibid.

with two small bank loans they built new houses for their sons and financed the wedding of one family member. By 1993 there were nine people in the household, and the Baos still farmed only seven *mu* of land, but they earned 2,800 *yuan* from agricultural income. Bao Gui's eldest son worked in the local brick factory and brought home 2,000 *yuan*; his youngest son collected and sold recyclable items, also bringing in 2,000 *yuan*. Bao had given up his grain trade but had joined with his nephew to make and sell *baozi* (steamed dumplings) in Anyang, deriving a profit of 1,000 *yuan*. The yearly non-agricultural income of the Bao household now stood at more than 5,000 *yuan*, and this sum did not include the small streams of income from straw braid making, pig raising, and a new chicken-egg business. Whereas Bao Gui attributes this improvement partly to new agricultural inputs and new farm infrastructure, he says that the major variable facilitating this progress was the decreased power of party leaders to decide what kind of work villagers would be required to do. The most significant change of all, in this regard, was doubtless the loss of the leaders' authority to prevent local people from withdrawing from collective-mandated labor duties in order to pursue the temptations of the market.

Other Da Fo villagers tell similar stories. The evidence shows that the resurgence of popular market activity even in the grain trade, which was one of the most tightly state-regulated trade arenas, preceded the removal of government market controls after the Third Plenum of the Eleventh Party Congress.[46] Clearly, this unauthorized market activity was a factor moving families beyond food insecurity and providing a small, economically secure platform from which farm households could diversify into private sidelines in the years immediately spanning the 1982 land division. Importantly, too, this popular market surge was a threat to the deep political structure of collectivization. Da Fo denizens' attempts to re-enter the market between 1965 and 1975 entailed both hidden and open forms of resistance to the Maoist state. Tang Huangdao, who began illegally selling fried peanuts and cakes when he was twenty-seven, explains that he hid his activities from government authorities by frying the peanuts and cakes at night and selling them from the side of the road to travelers. He hid most of his wares in the fields by the road, keeping only a small quantity with him to sell. He explains what happened if he was caught: "In the years of collectivization, I was caught only once selling peanuts and twice selling fried cakes. The peanuts and cakes were confiscated and then sold cheap by the Business Administration officials from neighboring Hebei province. There was no other punishment."[47] According to villagers, the Henan provincial government did not have enough personnel to enforce policy across the broad expanse of the triprovincial border area. Therefore, says Tang Huangdao, "The officials were largely dependent on the willingness of people to listen to them. Many people ignored the anti-trade rules

---

[46] See Chan and Unger, "Grey and Black," 456.
[47] Tang Huangdao, interview, September 11, 1995.

and pursued various kinds of business."[48] Because profits were relatively high, villagers seldom protested when caught and simply would lay low for a few days before resuming their petty trade.

As the testimony of Pang Chenglan, the head of the third production team from 1961 to 1965, suggests, the determination to re-enter the market also sometimes gave rise to defiant acts. Pang sold *baozi* and cooked sweet potatoes in surrounding villages. Such trade was risky, in part because vendors had no redress if their goods were confiscated or stolen. One day, when Pang was selling *baozi* in Shuidi, Hebei, the village head, confiscated all of his wares. Pang relates what happened next:

I counted how many *baozi* I had in my basket and left for home. But the next morning after breakfast, I took my wife and all my children to Shuidi. I found out where the head of the Shuidi production brigade lived, and I entered his house and settled my family down inside. I told the head of Shuidi production brigade that we were going to live there from that time on. I said he could keep my *baozi*, and it would be alright. But I politely warned him that we were going to eat whatever he and his wife were eating for lunch that day and sleep wherever he and his family would be sleeping that night. I said that since he did not want me to sell the *baozi*, surely he must have come up with another way for me to support my family and that I was very grateful for the gift of his support.

In the beginning, his wife did not know what I was talking about. When she discovered what her husband had done to me, she grew angry with him and cursed him for taking away my *baozi*. She said he should mind his own business. What did it matter to him, she asked, if I was doing small business in Shuidi? Of course his wife was more worried that my family would really live with her family. I had counted on this.... After being cursed by his wife, and after seeing that I really intended to live with them, the leader of Shuidi brigade returned everything to me.

This method proved very successful. So I was prepared to use it on anybody who tried to stop me from doing small business. I was willing to use it against government officials who wanted to stop me from selling. They were afraid of my methods. Consequently, I did not meet any village leaders who were willing to stick by the collective principles in such situations. It did not hurt them to let me go my own way.[49]

This kind of bold assertiveness was not primarily a response to a relaxed Maoist state policy, nor was it the by-product of the Deng Xiaoping–approved household responsibility system and market reform system. Families who had survived the Great Leap Forward Famine intact often found a way to force the issue of market participation while Mao was still waging a war against the market.[50]

How was such resistance possible under Maoist dictatorship, especially when, as oral history evidence shows, many villagers were caught by the agents of the Maoist state's anti-commerce agency? Apparently, rural people initiated a strategy of "middle zone" resistance to foil the Maoist attempt to establish a tight state monopoly on rural grain transactions, for those who were apprehended by government agents usually could manage to get their grain back with a letter

[48] Ibid.
[49] Pang Chenglan, interview, May 16, 1994.
[50] See Friedman, "Maoism and the Liberation," 420.

from village leaders saying that the grain was for family use. The history of this everyday village-cum-kinship-based resistance is all but lost, but Zheng Yunxiang remembers how it worked in Da Fo during the last years of collectivization:

I used to go to Daming to buy grain, and I transported it back here to sell. However, the government did not allow people to deal in grain then. The officials set up checking stations on the roads and stopped people carrying large amounts of grain for questioning. I was caught several times, and each time they confiscated my grain. But this was not exactly confiscation. They would purchase my grain at the state price. I had two options. I could either let the government keep my grain, and I would take a loss, or I could return to Da Fo to ask village and commune leaders to write a letter to plead my case. In the letter they would say that I bought the grain for my family's own use, not to sell it for profit. Then, after I showed the letter to the government, the grain would be returned to me.[51]

Zheng went right ahead selling his retrieved grain for profit, and so did other villagers. With the profits from this quasi-legal grain business and from a spate of unauthorized petty trade activities, villagers were able to live a little better.

These "letters of licit trade" did not always do the trick, however. Anti-grain trade agents occasionally confiscated villagers' bicycles, making them walk the thirty-five *li* from Daming back to Da Fo. When villagers went back to Daming several days later, the market officials had already sold the grain, sweet potatoes, and other confiscated items at the state-determined price. Not surprisingly, therefore, another strategy, pursued outside of state-regulated approvals, became prevalent. This involved traveling on rural back roads where the Dongle County and Daming County highway police were absent. "That kind of trade," says Bao Tanger, "was considered speculation and was banned by the state. But still there were many loopholes, and people could easily avoid the surveillance. . . . In fact, I do not know many people in Da Fo who were ever caught."[52]

When it came to enforcing controls on grain transactions, state agents focused primarily on stopping caravans of eight and ten people who were traveling a long distance with big loads of grain. Individuals with inconspicuous amounts of grain, sweet potatoes, and apricots seldom were stopped. Hence a third strategy: short multiple trips in which a solo bicyclist carried one or two small bags right past the checkpoint personnel. There were at best loose political controls on this kind of cross-county trade, particularly because the county governments hired local people from nearby villages to serve as monitors. Such people, sympathetic to the petty trade of the poor, were paid the same amount of work points for their service no matter whether they stopped one, ten, or one hundred "speculators" a day, and they gained nothing by monitoring traffic aggressively. Many Da Fo villagers thus were able to make twenty to thirty of these short market sorties, which brought in quick, handsome profits.[53]

---

[51] Zheng Yunxiang, interview, July 23, 1994.
[52] Bao Tanger, interview, September 1, 1995.
[53] Zheng Yunxiang, interview, September 21, 1995.

The expansion of trade in the post–Great Leap famine period was underwritten by the continuous accentuation of salt making for the market, which Da Fo's inhabitants revived to escape the starvation of 1960–61 and accelerated to cope with the Wei River flood in 1963. Ultimately, therefore, the engine driving petty capitalism in and around Da Fo was the ageless semi-legal market activity that villagers had traditionally pursued in order to generate off-farm income outside of state regulations – the same activity they had emphasized to survive Kuomintang state making. Bao Tanger explains salt making for the market and the link between this hidden enterprise and the revival of far-flung rural petty trade:

During the collective years, we had just enough food most of the time, but we did not have enough cash income from the collective to pay for household expenditures. Sometimes when the harvest was not good we needed money to buy grain from the market. Salt making was the only way I knew to get this money. . . .

During the three winter months we could make very good money from this traditional enterprise. We usually left the village to collect the salty earth and came back the same day. We went as far as Yueguang People's Commune in Dongle County, which was seventy *li* from Da Fo. I usually left the village at dusk and came back in the early morning. During the day, my family would make the salt from the saline earth I collected at night. From one cart of this salty earth we could produce about twenty *yuan* worth of products, including salt, nitrate, and *lu shui*.

. . . We carried on this kind of enterprise for twenty to thirty days during the winter, and we made about four hundred *yuan* for the whole season. That was a lot of money, more in fact than an ordinary worker's annual salary. And it made a great difference in our life. We used the money from these selling trips to buy grain to supplement the grain we got from the collective and pay other household expenses. . . . The income from salt trade kept my family well fed.[54]

Anita Chan and Jonathan Unger have documented a "gray zone" in which people in rural Guangdong carried on semi-legal trade after sundown, when those from poor villages smuggled commodities across county lines under cover of darkness while state market control agents were asleep.[55] Da Fo's earth salt found its niche in this gray zone, the profits from which could be used to underwrite black marketing of grain – a commodity in which trade was strictly forbidden.

The production teams exempted the most important money-earning market activity of their members from collective engagement, protecting the individual pursuit of the salt and nitrate market for profit as long as participants fulfilled their obligations to the team. Thus Pang Furong remembers,

During the Cultural Revolution, there were many people in the village who also engaged in making salt and nitrate. They usually got up earlier and went a long way to the surrounding villages to collect dirt with a high content of salt and nitrate and came back to Da Fo in time to work in the fields. Since they did not stop working in the production team, the

---

[54] Bao Tanger, interview, September 1, 1995.
[55] Chan and Unger, "Grey and Black," 452, 458.

team did not interfere with their market activities. And they did not need a license to do that either. Therefore, they did not pay any tax on income derived from marketing these items.[56]

The importance of maintaining this market habit cannot be overemphasized. It always had been associated with disengagement from state taxation, had provided roughly half of smallholder household income prior to collectivization, and had enabled more than a few households to escape the famine of the Great Leap Forward. Just as they had done in the Republican period, when the Kuomintang state attempted to obliterate this black market activity, Da Fo's inhabitants moved to exploit the administrative inefficiency of the party-state apparatus charged with keeping them from profitable petty trade.

If Maoist holism, in which brigade party leaders pressured villagers to see the interest of the collective, or the "public good," as greater than the sum of their individual family interests, was still powerful and inclined some to see those active in country markets as enemies of the public good,[57] such ideology did not command a mass following in Da Fo. Admittedly there was tension between the individual villagers who pursued distant markets and the collective agendas of Da Fo leaders, but below the brigade level there was unarticulated popular support for individual interests, far more than there was for the regimented, artificially constructed moral community that the Maoists wanted. Bao Jieshi alludes to this support and reminds us that individual petty traders still felt obligations to society:

During the collective years, everybody on the production team knew everybody else, and everybody also knew how important and urgent the work in the collective fields was during the busy season. Most people depended on the collective for their grain; so during the busy season one did not take days off without asking for permission. Still, one had to be reasonable; one did not work for the production team leader or for the state only. One worked for oneself. If you took off days and made money for yourself, that was alright. If you did too much of this kind of shrewd business activity and took advantage of your friends and neighbors, however, you could not expect respect from others.[58]

Just as they helped to protect team members' small private plots of sweet potato land, then, production team leaders conspired with members to circumvent the government ban on market activity. The pretext, and the template, for this hidden market activity was kinship. Production team leaders who shared the same lineage as their members gave in to kinship-based excuses for exiting the collective. Recalls Zheng Yunxiang,

According to the rule, one needed to tell the production team leaders that one could not come to work for the day, because the leaders needed to make out work assignments for different tasks each day. If you asked to go to market too many times, you aroused

---

[56] Pang Furong, interview, September 3, 1995.
[57] Chan, Madsen, and Unger, *Chen Village*, 247–48.
[58] Bao Jieshi, interview, September 1, 1995.

suspicion of the production team leaders, so they might not grant permission. Therefore, many people simply went to the market for the whole day, and when they came back to Da Fo they told the production team leaders that they had visited a relative or friend for some reason. It was easy to find an excuse, and the production team leaders did not want to pursue the matter any further.[59]

Except during the busy planting and harvesting seasons, production teams in Da Fo did not forbid villagers from undertaking trade. If a team member had enough family members working in the collective fields, he usually was granted permission to disengage from collective farming in order to pursue small business. Those who did not have enough family members laboring on the collective lands had to buy work points with part of the profits derived from doing business. The price of these "going-to-market" work points was much higher than their face value. But, according to Pang Furong, local people perceived this practice to be fair, because given the lower price of collective grain, there was hidden value in the work points. "For a person who was skillful in doing small business, it was still a good deal," says Pang. "He did not need to buy more than 1.5 *yuan* worth of work points per day. If he could make more than this in the market, then he would still be better off than working in the fields."[60] The majority of production team members in Da Fo regularly requested approval from their teams to take these "buy-out-leaves" to engage in market activities, and they usually were approved quickly.

By 1970 there were hundreds of illegal business operators in Da Fo, and underground market activity was on the rise. Dongle County authorities ordered brigade leaders to round up and fine these secret operators. The fine was to be paid to the brigade. Yet many production team members say that they do not know if there was a system of fines aimed at punishing people who took days off from working in the collective fields. Apparently, the Da Fo brigade leaders charged with enforcement did little more than shout warnings through loudspeakers.

Indeed, many of Da Fo's earliest market hounds in the collective era were production team leaders for whom the task of shouldering the burdens of leadership proved too great a sacrifice. Pang Chenglan, the head of the third production team prior to 1965, was one such leader. "The head of the production team," he says "was the most difficult job in the village. It was the most demanding, and yet it bestowed the least authority. It was like being a company army commander with all kinds of assignments but with no authority to get them done. Not many people in the village wanted this position." Pang left his position to start up a small business in selling Popsicles, fried peanuts, watermelon seeds, and straw braids. Pang explains why he was better off than many of his production team counterparts. "If I was head of the production team, I would not have been able to conduct small business at all. How could I do any small business if I was leading

---

[59] Zheng Yunxiang, interview, July 14, 1998.
[60] Pang Furong, interview, September 3, 1995.

others to work in the fields every day?"[61] Pang Chenglan was not unique. Many other Da Fo production team leaders, disgruntled because land-bound duties to the collective inhibited market involvement, repeatedly complained to brigade party leaders and plotted ways to conduct forbidden business. The defections of such leaders signaled to ordinary team members that they too could pursue the market without penalty.

When they felt that their leaders were insufficiently sympathetic to their market needs, villagers would use foot-dragging as a way of sabotaging production and forcing the issue. Bao Rechen remembers that there were villagers who "lacked community spirit, and they did not associate their well-being with their performance in the collective fields."[62] They neither showed up for work on time nor stayed in the fields until the end of the work day, and they found excuses to escape work assignments. According to Tang Degao, the head of Da Fo's ninth production team, many of the members simply would not work at all without Tang, or production team committee leaders, literally taking them to the fields each day.[63] Surely this lack of commitment to the collective was a factor behind the unimpressive grain crop yields of the late Maoist era.

And just as surely there was a link between popular evasion of party-state controls relegated to the production team and the popular fear of a recurrence of the excessive state extraction that brought on the famine of the Great Leap Forward. Tang Degao complains that "many people did not work hard enough" because "they thought that if we produced more grains the government would have them taken away." Tang believed that excessive state procurement was a phenomenon limited to the Great Leap Forward years and that subsequent state procurement "did not hurt the village too much," and he lamented, "It was too bad that some of the villagers did not understand this."[64] Actually, the "some villagers" constituted the great majority, and the people making up this majority by and large understood the nature of Maoist state-taking. They refused to work harder for a state that had only modified the basic structure of its revenue gathering process – a process that had inflicted unforgivable loss. Villagers say that the team members who expressed their discontent by doing a poor job in the fields knew they were engaging in an act of political consequence. When the yields went down, brigade leaders would investigate. At this point, team members would voice complaints to the Da Fo brigade leadership and demand an election of new leaders.[65] In other words, if production team leaders did not allow their members in the market, the latter could induce a cycle of agricultural poverty that would replace those leaders with ones who might be more permissive about mixing agricultural production with petty trade.

---

[61] Pang Chenglan, interview, May 16, 1994.
[62] Bao Rechen, interview, September 20, 1995.
[63] Tang Degao, interview, September 2, 1995.
[64] Ibid.
[65] Bao Wenchou, interview, September 1, 1995.

Da Fo's denizens utilized their market access to underwrite yet another important strategy of coping with the poverty of agricultural collectivization: the overloading of the better-off production teams. Ruan Shaobing, the head of the tenth production team, whose members always had more than enough to eat when other teams barely had enough food, remembers this phenomenon. Because of their hunger, he says,

> many people in other teams would come to my team. These people came to work with us in the fields whether we gave them permission or not, and regardless of whether we gave them work points or not. Some of them worked in our fields for as long as fifty days per year without getting work points. During the day they worked alongside us like everyone else, and at night they came to my house and pleaded with me to let them stay in my team. I was in a very difficult situation. It was hard to turn these people down. But there were too many of them.[66]

The people who attempted to piggyback on the better-off teams usually brought with them their share of land but did not bring collective property to their "new team." Although more information on this interesting phenomenon would be desirable, two points are clear. First, these people were invariably from the poorest teams and engaged in the market when they attempted to jump to a better-off team. Second, they persisted in such jumping attempts, for although team leaders like Ruan Shaobing turned many "jumpers" away, they also speak of such people swelling their teams to unmanageable sizes of three and four hundred people in the late 1960s and early 1970s.

More significant, these so-called poor villagers were mobile petty traders whom the state required to belong to a production team.[67] In Da Fo, they were able to use profits from market activities to persist in attempts to join richer teams and still cover any home team costs incurred by their extended absences. The reason they persisted in underwriting leaps to the better-off teams is that in joining these teams, with their superior harvests, they not only could avoid the poverty of the home team, they also could purchase food rations from the rich team while plying markets on a full-time basis. This kind of transference was common in Da Fo from 1966 to 1970, and it persisted, if only in small unofficial mutual agreements between teams, after the central government attempted to restrict the splitting of teams in the early 1970s.

The struggle to reenter the market during the last decade of Maoist rule was fueled in part by memory of the loss of market access in the Great Leap period. Significantly, after Bao Zhilong was reinstated as Da Fo party secretary in 1973, this struggle escalated, resulting in a quid pro quo relationship with party leaders that further weakened the hold of the Communist Party over villagers, especially the production team leaders. Bao Zhilong returned to his post at a time when Mao Zedong was scheming to once again push a rural development plan that was

---

[66] Ruan Shaobing, interview, September 19, 1995.
[67] Chan and Unger, "Grey and Black," 467.

The Market Comes First

based on the same logic as the Great Leap; as a result many villagers feared that the cancer of the Great Leap had only gone into remission and might return at any time. They were right. Once he resumed local power in 1973, Bao Zhilong consistently attempted to prevent the most talented and accomplished villagers from leaving the village. He wanted them to take on the jobs of the collective: teachers, accountants, barefoot doctors, and production team leaders. Accepting such a position made it even more difficult to pursue the market or find work outside of the village, which for the poorest villagers was still the key to survival. Consequently, villagers frequently struggled with Bao Zhilong and the Da Fo party leaders to quit these state-captured positions after only a year or two of service and move into the market. Bao Zhilong was compelled to give in or risk a collective mobilization of the same democratic village forces that had challenged his monopolist, corrupt work style in the aftermath of the Great Leap famine.

In 1973, for instance, Bao Wending, whose family had made and marketed *baozi* to escape the famine, was told he could not do this anymore, so he stopped and began working Da Fo's collective fields. After a year of profitable moonlighting, Bao Wending was elected head of the second production team, a decision influenced by Bao Zhilong's power network. Bao Wending recalls:

After one year, I refused to serve as the production team head any more. Yet the members of the second team elected me all the same. But I refused to accept it. Bao Zhilong came to persuade me to accept the result of the election. I did not take his advice. I told him it was time for someone else to serve as production team head. Bao Zhilong was very tough. He insisted that I had to accept the result of the election. Bao Zhilong did not understand why I did not want to be the head of the team. I wanted to do a small business on my own. In the end, Bao Zhilong had to give in. The team had to elect somebody else. As soon as I quit the position, I started a small business.[68]

Such courage to take the risks necessary to engage in petty trade sustained the popular escape from the poverty of the collective. In Da Fo – and one suspects countless other rural Chinese villages – "party emperors" like Bao Zhilong had to accommodate this courage if they were to secure temporary commitments from skilled villagers to serve the public good, which of course the cadres of Mao's authoritarian state-building movement took to mean the interests of their own political network. Participation in the market promised liberation from this inherited pattern. Ironically, the party accommodation of the market would in the long run only reinforce popular disdain for the "public good."

The chaos of the 1982 land division, which in Da Fo signaled the climax of decollectivization, informed villagers that their instincts about how Maoist rulers understood "the public good" were correct. Bao Zhilong and the Da Fo party activists, along with a handful of well-connected production team leaders, declared that the property of the collective was to be given to those who could lay their hands on it first, and they began grabbing farm tools and planters, farm

[68] Bao Wending, interview, July 22, 1998.

289

animals, and stored grain. "All of this collective property, which Chairman Mao had worked so hard to accumulate for the village, was taken away in a robbery in a matter of a few hours," recalls Pang Canshen.[69] Indeed it was an act of robbery, which to villagers recalled the entire episode of Maoist collectivization and particularly its corrupted, crowning achievement: the Great Leap Forward and its theft of life, fairness, and liberty.

Vivienne Shue argues correctly that Maoist party-state controls over village society were not as tight in the post–Great Leap years as many Western observers have concluded.[70] What loosened the grip of the Mao-led party-state in this period was not simply that, among other things, local party leaders secretly collaborated with inward-looking tiller schemes to avoid government harvest claims – a phenomenon that, in the case of Da Fo, did occur at the sub-village level. What ensured the survival of people in this state-impoverished village was the upsurge of illicit trade in market networks positioned in the shadowy interstices of commune and brigade administration. It was this hidden popular trade, which sub-brigade, and even brigade, party leaders occasionally abetted, that provided the people of Da Fo with a weapon to oppose, and continuously escape, the tentacles of the Maoist party-state.[71]

To be sure, as Lev Timofeev's account of Soviet peasants would argue, the Maoist version of the Kokholz system undermined the productivity of the farm household and violated any notion of a "living wage," and popular efforts to survive in this system often involved self-exploitation.[72] Nonetheless, in Da Fo this process unfolded in ways that helped tillers combat state capture. In response to the Great Leap famine, they put their best energies into working their little sweet potato plots, into coming up with excuses to engage in "purchased absenteeism" from the collective fields, and into selling the products from their small plots in the marketplace.[73] Of course, life within this system still exacted a heavy social toll, including chronic fatigue from working one job in the collective sector and another in the market sector and constant stress from dealing with village party stewards and their thugs, but locally this system also fostered a strange interdependence.[74] The commune-based collective economy was able to sustain itself only by tolerating the efforts of small farmers to reclaim their right to subsistence in a semi-legal underground economy. Oddly, the collective political economy rested on a system of underground petty trade that supposedly did not exist in

---

[69] Pang Canshen, interview, May 9, 1994.

[70] Shue, *Reach of the State*.

[71] See Shue, who sees the market but does not fully appreciate it as a weapon of the weak (ibid., 77), and Unger, who sees the market and appreciates it but underplays its evolving pre-1978 importance in popular strategies of combating Maoist despotism (Unger, "State and Peasant," 132–34).

[72] Timofeev, *Soviet Peasants*.

[73] Jim Scott, in Gross, "Symposium on *Soviet Peasants*," 118–19.

[74] Tim Luke, Alexis Berelowitch, Jim Scott, and G. L. Ulmen, all in Gross, "Symposium on *Soviet Peasants*," 110–11, 119–20, 121, 123–24.

late-Mao China. Apparently, this latter economy was expanding through everyday resistance, and this resistance was slowly but surely eroding the base of the socialist economy it helped sustain.

With footprints extending back to the escape from the Great Leap famine, popular market-driven resistance was refined in the decades prior to the ascent of Deng Xiaoping. It prepared the ground for the seemingly rapid switchover to family-based farming and market-focused enterprise. Moreover, it came first – that is, it *provided* the economic platform for the takeoff in household-based farming. The center did not lead; it scurried to catch up with this process and to create mechanisms to inhibit a full-scale abandonment of the collective system. In Da Fo, where villagers had turned away from the economics of Mao (and Deng) in the collective years, the center failed. It did so during a long period when the local party leaders who had imposed Mao's Great Leap famine were being reprimanded by agents of the party-state itself and were being repudiated by village-bound petty traders. As a result, popular submission to the party-state was no longer automatic or total. Villagers would take advantage of the post-Mao reform agenda of Deng Xiaoping to amplify their resistance, challenging the attempts of imprudent township and county government officials to impose their version of the central state policies guiding reform from above.

9

Persistent Memories and Long-Delayed Retaliation in the Reform Era

The return of Bao Zhilong to the post of party secretary in 1973 marked the end of the Cultural Revolution in Da Fo village. Villagers waited to see if Bao would attempt to atone for his Great Leap Forward sins or retaliate against his tormentors. Like Deng Xiaoping, who became the leader of the party-state following Mao's death in 1976, Bao Zhilong had been hurt by the Cultural Revolution. Both men faced a serious political dilemma: the Great Leap Forward and its attendant famine had all but destroyed their party's claim to legitimacy, the claim that had equated socialist rule with the recovery of the decent standard of living that had been threatened under the Kuomintang and with the end to the violent disorder that had prevailed during the Japanese invasion. Somehow, the Communist Party had to quickly restore its reputation for revolutionary virtue. The key to this process, from the perspective of the party propagandists in Beijing, was to take charge of the discourse on the Great Leap fiasco in order to remake the popular memory of this catastrophe. The party leadership sought to reassert its authority and rescue its legitimacy by a practice known as *yiku sitian* (remembering the bitter past and savoring the sweet present), that is, a moralistic discourse that framed history to serve its own political ends.[1]

Familiar with the ritualized pressures of *yiku sitian*, villagers had typically surrendered to this movement. Now, however, the Da Fo party agents of this initiative were also the agents of the Great Leap disaster it was aimed at obliterating, and their actions spoke louder than the political education of *yiku sitian*. While proclaiming his support for Deng's enlightened reform policies, Da Fo party boss Bao Zhilong nonetheless resumed the same day-by-day work style that had put the radicalizing dynamic of Mao's Great Leap theory into practice locally.

---

[1] On *yiku sitian*, I rely on Beja's informative essay, "Forbidden Memory, Unwritten History," 1–5; I also am indebted to Wu, "Remembering the Revolutionary Past."

Time and time again, villagers experienced everyday betrayals of pacts entered into with Bao, reminding them of the trail of broken promises that had destroyed their trust in the party during the Great Leap years and further alienating them from Bao and his network. Villagers might have tolerated most of these transgressions, but Bao Zhilong also made no attempt to reconcile the crimes of the Great Leap with any member of the village; indeed, he seemed to behave as if the famine had never happened, and he complied with all of the state campaigns to erase or alter the memory of the famine.

Far from rehabilitating the image of the Communist Party in the 1970s, 1980s, and 1990s, then, Bao's leadership merely damaged it further. Over the course of this period of reform, as civil society began to take root again in rural China and Bao and the leaders of the Great Leap era no longer had total control over the village, the long-held grievances with local Communist leaders began to surface. The slow burn of discontent and anger over the Great Leap Forward years was transformed into outbursts of violence, arson, and public protest. Having failed to reclaim their political reputations or renew an anti-famine contract with villagers after the Great Leap famine, Da Fo's local Communist leaders were finally forced to pay for their past mistakes.

The process whereby rural dwellers succeeded in dislodging the local party agents of the Great Leap is still not adequately understood. Kevin J. O'Brien and Lianjiang Li have traced the origins and nature of reform-era resistance in Chinese villages to "policy-based resistance," that is, to popular efforts to make local party leaders follow official reformist policy directives, which were backed by laws of governance and intended to incorporate claim-making within a zone of loyal opposition.[2] Popular resistance in post-Mao Da Fo, however, was sparked far more often by the desires hidden within a persistent and powerful memory of the destructive violence of village party leaders in the Great Leap famine. The power of this memory to keep alive a righteous struggle for remedial justice and to throw up contentious challenges to party legitimacy long after the Great Leap is unquestionable, and thus until we understand how Da Fo's villagers retaliated against their Great Leap–era leaders twenty and even thirty years after the famine came to an end, we cannot fully understand the villagers' relationship with the party-state, past or present.

The State Campaign to Manage the Memory of the Great Leap Forward Famine

The first post–Great Leap act of institutional memory crafting occurred only three years after the famine had subsided. In 1964 a work team entered Da Fo to push the Socialist Education Movement, aimed at creating a *yiku sitian* dialogue

[2] O'Brien and Li, "Politics of Lodging Complaints," 159, 167, 170, 174, 177; O'Brien, "Rightful Resistance," 28–61; and O'Brien and Li, *Rightful Resistance in Rural China*, 1–14.

designed to supplant the memory of a massive disaster with the idea that the suffering of rural people was miniscule when compared to suffering in the pre-Communist era and that in the end the party-state had relieved hunger. *Yiku sitian* was a form of official political socialization wherein Communist Party cadres and local party leaders were to collaborate in mobilizing villagers to recall the bitterness of the pre-1949 period and to savor the sweet good life of the present. It was an explicit attempt of the party-state to manipulate popular memory in ways that would help the party cast the Great Leap Forward as an episode in the continuing party-championed struggle to improve popular livelihood and save the nation.[3]

Several times in the past, beginning with the land reform of 1947, *yiku sitian* had served the Communist Party well. Dongle County and district leaders had invited people to talk about their past suffering in order to unite villagers to struggle against landlords and to persuade them to go along with unified purchase and sale from 1953 to 1955, and in some parts of rural China party leaders had used *yiku sitian* to pressure villagers to participate in the Great Leap Forward. In the campaign for unified purchase and sale, for example, Qing Zhenxin, the party leader of Liangmen district, had convened an *yiku sitian* meeting to convince villagers they should sell more grain to the state to support its construction projects as well as its war in Korea.[4] "At the time," recalls Yin Fengxiu,

> many people did not want to sell grain to the state. The price was low, and people felt uncomfortable with not storing enough grain at home.... But the leaders said that poor farmers should not forget that they were able to live better today because the Communist Party had led them to get the land from the landlords. If they did not support the state, they might be forced to suffer again, as they had in the old days.[5]

The *yiku sitian* movement attempted to distort the remembrance of how people suffered and survived under Mao's famine, as Bao Wending's recollection makes clear. Bao, who was a hungry schoolboy in Liangmen primary school during the famine, remembered villager Bao Wudao declaring that

> he did not care if Chairman Mao was good, and he did not care whether the Communist Party was good or not. He said that whoever would give him two bags of grain would be good. With two bags of grain, Bao Wudao said he would not be hungry and his family would not go hungry. When villagers passed Bao Wudao, they would ask if he really mean what he said. He would respond that he really did mean it. They would then ask him: Wha if Chiang Kai-shek offered him two bags of grain now? He would respond that he woul then say that Chiang Kai-shek was a good person.

---

[3] I am indebted to Vivienne Shue's essay, "Legitimacy Crisis in China?" 27–31, 35, for the conceptua framework here. Also see Wong, *China Transformed*, 93–98, cited in Shue, "Legitimacy Crisis i China?" and Selbin, "Agency and Culture," 8.

[4] Tang Weilan, interview, July 25, 2004.

[5] Yin Fengxiu, interview, July 27, 2004.

Persistent Memories and Long-Delayed Retaliation

Bao Wending recalls thinking "that Bao Wudao was brainless to say that Chiang Kai-shek was a good person just for two bags of grain," because to him, "Chiang Kai-shek always had been a bad person." When the Socialist Education Movement began in 1964, Bao Wudao came to regret his Great Leap Forward heresies. Bao Wending describes what happened:

The village leaders cooked a big pot of wild vegetables to serve a meal for the whole village, and everybody in the village came to eat out of this big pot. While we were eating, the old folks would tell us how hard life was before Liberation. Some people told us their experience of begging from door to door and how they could not get enough food to eat. Bao Wudao began to cry very hard. He said to the whole village that he felt very bad thinking about what he had said in the 1960s during the Great Leap Forward. Before Liberation, he declared, he had begged and never had enough food to eat. In the 1960s, the Mao-led state had some economic difficulties, and the whole nation was hungry. He blamed himself for saying that he would proclaim Chiang Kai-shek a good person just for two bags of grain. Bao Wudao said that he had forgotten that even with the extreme difficulty of 1960, the Communist Party had not turned its back on farmers completely. Under Mao, the state still provided some food for the villagers to tide them over the time of economic difficulty. Even though it was not enough, Bao Wudao asked us to "Just compare this with the situation before Liberation, when I was begging from village to village, and from door to door. Just who gave me anything to eat?" His words won a great deal of applause from the villagers.[6]

Though they applauded, many of Da Fo's villagers had not forgotten that begging was prohibited during the Great Leap Forward and that Chiang Kai-shek's government had not inhibited them from scavenging and begging in the countryside – just as they had not forgotten *chi qing*. Virtually everyone was painfully aware that it was eating the green crops of the collective, not relief grain from the national government in Beijing, that had permitted them to escape the death grip of the famine.

The efforts to implant a false memory of Mao's famine gained momentum in the Cultural Revolution, when a Da Fo Red Army veteran and Communist Party leader, taking cues from the work teams, began planting politically correct memories in classrooms. Bao Chaoqun, a Da Fo first grade teacher in 1966, describes the arrival in her classroom of Bao Wuqing, a Communist Party member and a member of the Peasant Association's School Management Committee. According to Bao Chaoqun, Bao Wuqing told her students about "how hard life was before Liberation." Bao Chaoqun recalls:

Bao Wuqing talked about the famine of 1942 in Da Fo village. She said that in that year there was no harvest because of the drought and the locusts in the fields, and the poor villagers had to migrate to other places to survive, and many people begged and died on the way. She also said that under the leadership of the Communist Party and Chairman Mao villagers had a much better life after Liberation. Even during the difficult year of 1960, when everybody was hungry and starved, nobody starved to death in Da Fo. The

Bao Wending, interview, July 22, 1998.

government made sure that everybody got the food required for everyday survival. Even today, I still can remember what these people told the students.[7]

At the heart of the Mao experiment in managing popular memory was an attempt to produce a false memory of the Great Leap Forward and, to borrow a phrase from Elizabeth F. Loftus, to create a memory of "a past that never was."[8] The emphasis was on erasing the most obstinate memory of the Great Leap as a death trap – the memory of family members and fellow villagers dying in the streets and the fields from overwork and starvation. Loftus has demonstrated that it is possible to instill false memories in the minds of subjects in controlled research environments and that the subjects often are confident that the implanted memories are real.[9] But after the Great Leap the Communist Party had less control of its rural subjects, and villagers viewed the party's intentions as, to say the least, highly suspect. Thus the creation of false memory was easier if the party could find people whose Great Leap experience had walled them off from the reality of the famine's devastation. Bao Chaoqun was a perfect candidate. A graduate of Shangcun middle school, she had been away in middle school in the bad years of 1958–61, and she was connected to a party-favored family. Though she had to eat sweet potato leaves in 1960, she received a significant remittance from her brother – the secretary of the Communist Youth League in Shangcun, and her family had not suffered as much hunger as other Da Fo families. Her opinion that "nobody really starved to death in the bad years," based on hearsay and on the message of *yiku sitian*, was easily tethered to the party's effort to plant a false understanding of the famine's social toll.[10]

Others were not such ideal candidates. Bao Hongwen, who participated in the *yiku sitian* meetings a couple of times, tells us:

The activity usually was held by the Da Fo Peasant Association. The idea was to educate people to remember the past hard life and value the current good life. I did not suffer at all before Liberation. But I did remember the hardship of the Great Leap Forward. I was in my teens at the time. I was so starved that I did not have the energy to move at all. I was listless all day. I knew of more than ten people who died during the Great Leap Forward. . . . The truth is that whichever village followed the government policy more strictly, the more it suffered as a consequence. Our village leaders did not want to deceive the upper government leaders. As a result, we suffered more severe hunger than other villages.[11]

For people who were directly in the path of the Great Leap calamity, *yiku sitian* could not supplant popular awareness of its political dynamic. Their memory-based understanding of the Maoist past posed an enduring problem for the party-state.

[7] Bao Chaoqun, interview, July 6, 2002.
[8] Loftus, "Memories of a Past That Never Was," 60–65, 74. Also see Loftus, "Make-Believe Memories," and Loftus, Bernstein, and Vernika, "Altering Traumatic Memory."
[9] Ibid.
[10] Bao Chaoqun, interview, July 6, 2002.
[11] Bao Hongwen, interview, July 5, 2004.

Persistent Memories and Long-Delayed Retaliation

One central strategy for dealing with the memories of the Great Leap's horrors was to shift the blame for the dearth and hunger to Russian pressure to pay off the debt of the Korean War, climatic downswings and bad weather, and the overzealous acts of local political actors who had incorrectly implemented Mao's developmental policies – to portray the Great Leap Forward as a tragedy of the Mao-led Communist Party's good intentions.[12] In the short term, reconstructing the political causality of the Great Leap disaster was an antidote to the persistent memory of Mao's role in designing it. In Da Fo, this new construction worked in two ways. First, villagers were constantly told by outside work teams that the Communist Party, in contrast to previous regimes, had their interest at heart. Second, they were repeatedly informed that local party miscreants had upended Mao's plan to improve peasant livelihood: the disaster was not denied, but the agency of disaster was shifted from top to bottom.

Tang Degao, a survivor of the Great Leap and the carrier of a memory of some of its everyday traumas, reflects the short-term Maoist success in reproducing a party-state hegemony based on an official Maoist rendition of how the Great Leap turned into a tragedy. Tang is convinced that "the Communist Party is much better than the Kuomintang," for a number of reasons. He explains: "The Communist Party divided the landlords' land to the poor peasants in the villages and helped them to organize to achieve prosperity. It was true that during the difficult years of 1958, 1959, and 1960 we suffered hunger. . . . But the government's intention was good. It did not want the people to suffer at all. It wanted people to live a better life." Tang continues: "The Communist policy toward the villages was very good on the whole. The party always took things very seriously and designed its policies very carefully. But the people at the lower level completely messed things up. If leaders at this level messed things up, then can we blame it on the Communist Party as a whole? Can we blame it on Chairman Mao? No, I think that every word Chairman Mao had uttered was reasonable and good for us villagers."[13]

Implicit in the state-packaged memory of Mao's role in the Great Leap gone awry was the message that local party zealots were too eager to please Mao and the upper leaders, who were kept in the dark about the reports of exaggerated yields by the brigade leaders, about how much grain was being extracted from villages by commune leaders, and about how many people were starving to death. Bao Zhongxin communicates this politically implanted memory when he says:

Many people blamed Mao for the failure of the Great Leap Forward. Yes, Mao was [partly] responsible for the failure of the Great Leap. But China is a big country. So how could Mao be held responsible for all of the actions of local officials? Ultimately, the local officials had to be more responsible for what happened in their localities. . . . Wu Zhipu was ultimately

[12] Compare this argument with Bo Yibo, who insinuates that China's rural people forgave Mao and the CCP for the Great Leap because they knew it was driven by "good intentions." "Ruogan Zhongda Juece Yu Shijian de Huigu," 26–36. Also see Joseph's brilliant analysis of this line of party-conceived propaganda, "Tragedy of Good Intentions," 8, 33–34.

[13] Tang Degao, interview, September 2, 1995.

responsible for what happened in Henan province. He was overzealous and was too eager to see results of his policy in the beginning. But in the end his actions bordered on criminal behavior – he tried to hide the fact that people in some parts of Henan were starving just to save himself from embarrassment. In contrast, Chairman Mao served the people with his heart and soul all of his life. Even his mistakes were committed with good intention. This is why we never blamed Chairman Mao for our problems.[14]

The emphasis on how impossible it had been for Mao to control the party's crazed local agents was accompanied by a campaign to purge evidence of Mao's active complicity in the catastrophic outcome of the Great Leap Forward – that Wu Zhipu had been a graduate of Mao's Peasant Institute; that Mao had favored Wu Zhipu in removing the moderate pro-smallholder, anti–big collective unit Henan party leader Pan Fusheng; that Wu Zhipu had taken his cues for creating a Communist utopia from Mao;[15] and that Mao had allowed Wu to push ahead with the Great Leap even after receiving evidence that it was causing great human misery in the Henan countryside. All this was purged from the Maoist remaking of this "memory of hindsight" of the Great Leap Forward.[16]

The new Maoist version of the Great Leap tragedy nearly always implied that genius Mao would have solved the problem if only he had received the right information in time. Bao Honglin, who had been in the network of party boss Bao Zhilong and party lackey Bao Zhigen, articulates this rescripted memory and the power it achieved over villagers:

Of course farmers suffered most from hunger in Da Fo during the Great Leap Forward. But nobody in the countryside believed it was Chairman Mao's policy to starve us. Chairman Mao cared about the well-being of farmers. I do not think that Chairman Mao even knew that we were suffering from hunger. I blame all the trouble on the leaders of the people's commune. They should be held responsible. They were the lowest-level government officials. They were supposed to know what was going on in the villages and report this to the upper government. But they exaggerated their achievements by reporting higher yields to the Dongle County government, and then they forced the village party leaders to report yields that were not in accord with the actual output. . . . The top leaders in Beijing did not know what was going on in the countryside, and the information they got was the exaggerated information from the lower-level officials.[17]

In the short term, this new representation of the Great Leap as a tragedy proved relatively effective in producing misremembering. The oral history evidence suggests, however, that it was more effective for a select group of villagers: those with no education, those who had joined the Da Fo militia (or in a few cases the PLA) in the pre-1949 period, those with special connections to party chief Bao Zhilong, those who had spent their lives entirely inside the village, and those with a need to forget a particularly damaging loss in the famine.[18] For this last group

---

[14] Bao Zhongxin, interview, June 23, 2001.
[15] Chan, *Mao's Crusade*, 68–69.
[16] On the dictatorship of biased memory, see Schacter, *Seven Sins of Memory*, 138–49.
[17] Bao Honglin, interview, June 25, 2001.
[18] Compare with Schacter, *Seven Sins of Memory*, 175–77.

especially, the Maoist recasting of the famine as a tragedy of good intentions helped blur reminders of its horror. Tang Degao, for instance, had lost his father to starvation at the height of the famine in 1960, a heartbreaking experience he could make better sense of within the framework of the new official memory of the Maoist state. The notion that people died needlessly for the required sacrifices of a badly flawed Maoist conception of nation building was too much to bear.

But some villagers refused to give Mao the benefit of the doubt. Bao Huayin, the former first-pole Da Fo party leader who rose to a high position in the PRC and whose father starved to death in 1960, told me that he hated Mao Zedong for continuing the Great Leap even after he became aware of its human costs.[19] It may be that highly educated cadres like Bao Huayin, who had sacrificed to make China a secure county with a bright future, who felt betrayed by the Great Leap, and who traveled in highly informed political circles, were more inclined than others to directly link Mao to the famine. Indeed, a rural Anhui villager who had joined the PLA and fought in Korea, had studied to become a primary school teacher, and then had moved up the county-level educational hierarchy only to watch Maoist zealots destroy the learning environment after 1958, remembers that the cruelty of Mao's dictatorship in the Great Leap was "not inferior to Qin Shi Huangdi" and that the hunger of the Great Leap was directly the product of Mao's will.[20]

The issue of whether ordinary farmers, without ties to the CCP, blamed Mao, or village party leaders, or both for a situation that was framed, and substantially controlled, by Mao and high-ranking Communist power holders is complicated and difficult[21] – I will revisit this issue in greater psychoanalytic depth in the sequel to this volume. For now, it seems that some of Da Fo's ordinary farmers, especially those with little, if any, education, still revered Mao and were more inclined to blame their suffering in the Great Leap on bad local party leaders with ties to the people's commune, a finding that would lend some support for Dali Yang's claim that the Great Leap famine created a disaggregated legitimacy crisis, damaging only the authority of the commune while leaving the legitimacy of the upper end of the Mao-led party-state intact.[22] Whether this finding holds up for the majority of nonparty tillers in Da Fo, or elsewhere, is unclear, both because of the sensitivity of the issue of "blame" and the limitations on the data at hand.

My own reading of this issue is that many of Da Fo's farmers saw the actions of local party leaders as inseparable from the Mao-led party-state, and that they did not exempt Mao at the top end from association with the local party-state and its ground-level whips. In the case of this village, and I suspect countless other villages in China, there were reasons why this blame was not apparent in

---

[19] Bao Huayin, interview, September 15, 1993.
[20] Anhui, interview, 2006.
[21] This section has been stimulated, and in part constructed, by helpful exchanges with Gail Hershatter (September 19, 2007) and Edward Friedman (September 25, 2007).
[22] Compare with Yang, *Calamity and Reform in China*, 240–42, 246.

the aftermath of the Great Leap disaster – why many farmers chose to remain silent about the matter.

For one thing, despite the reform-era nostalgia for Mao, including all of the Mao shrines and Mao remembrance halls, China's rural people, like human beings anywhere, were in the grip of a deep-seated biological need to forget: the all-too-human need to get on with reclaiming the right to live a normal life invited forgetting and silence. It was difficult to blame Mao for a famine that disgraced China without opening up closets of painful memories about how his policies drove people to desperate and sometimes agonizing and guilt-producing acts that subsequently were difficult to reconcile with kin, friends, and neighbors. People protected themselves against this pain and guilt by keeping silent about Mao.

Many villagers also protected themselves by blaming the agents of the emperor, rather than the emperor himself – as Mao wanted them to do. The political cost of openly blaming Mao in the post–Great Leap era, when Mao was determined to distance himself from the famine, was high. China was still under a single-party socialist dictatorship, and popular fears of the workings of this authoritarian system, with its local informants, spies, and thugs, compelled many villagers to silently accept the official version of Mao's Great Leap in order to survive; the Great Leap went awry because of bad village party leadership – a phenomenon that Da Fo's farmers experienced firsthand. Few dared to say that Mao had violated, and overthrown, the principles of good paternal governance. People chose to forget – especially in public – and this of course created the impression of a "disaggregated legitimacy," in which village party leaders were labeled illegitimate and Mao was retained as a legitimate imperial father figure.

The silence did not tell the real story, however.

In the wake of the Great Leap, many rural dwellers blamed Mao *and* the Communist Party when they discussed the famine in private, and they implicated Mao directly in their suffering. Few of these private conversations found their way into the public sphere, but apparently some did. According to Gao Hua, in the early 1960s, when Beijing required every rural party branch to lift high the Red Flag of Mao's thoughts, to stress the achievements of the first decade of Mao's rule, and to squelch rumors from "class enemies" that rural people had starved to death under socialism, farmers dared to voice dangerous thoughts about Mao's Great Leap experiment with their lives. Those in Xuancheng, Anhui, a county that had been hit very hard by the Great Leap famine, muttered that Chairman Mao stank more than the cover of a chamber pot and that he was to blame for their hunger.[23] Some of their counterparts in Jing County, also in Anhui, grumbled that Mao did not know how to manage a country because he was a dictator and that he was to blame for the famine – and after Mao died they openly said that

---

[23] Gao Hua, "Da Ji Huang de 'Liangshi Shiyong,'" 80.

Mao only cared about grabbing power and that he had ruthlessly disregarded the most basic interests of tillers.[24] Condemning, altering, and wiping out such blasphemy was precisely what *yiku sitian* was designed to achieve. Da Fo's Maoists, understanding the challenge of this goal, borrowed the language and premises of this political campaign to justify the party's presence and purpose to ordinary villagers all through the post-famine decade.

Obstacles to Creating a New Memory of the Great Leap Forward Famine

Because the Great Leap disaster had all but destroyed the legitimacy of the Communist Party in the countryside, Mao attempted to prevent any discourse about the famine. As Susanne Weigelin-Schwiedrzik has pointed out, the famine was a topic of official taboo in the PRC.[25] Although a subject of inner-party strife, to some extent Mao was able to suppress inner-party debate and dissent over the failure of the Great Leap, thus complicating attempts of the Liu-Deng group to create in the wake of the famine an official national communicative memory of the so-called three difficult years, and evidently the term "Great Famine" (*da jihuang*) was not even used in official party historiography until after Deng Xiaoping's 1978 ascent.[26] Nonetheless, the effort to silence and transform the memory of the famine years in China's villages was challenged in both the private and public spaces of the famine's survivors.[27] The popular memory of death during the famine cast a long shadow over the Maoist attempt to create a new memory of the Great Leap Forward. In Da Fo the memories of social loss and physical diminishment from the famine were vivid, coloring efforts to return to normalcy, especially in the fifteen years following the Great Leap. The memories persisted in both silent and whispered forms, keeping alive the bitter experience derived from the Great Leap engagement with Maoist state power and diluting the party's attempt to convert the haunting dream of the famine into a non-lethal, morally ambiguous tragedy.

Silent and Embodied Memories

The most powerful silent memory of the famine – the death of beloved family and friends – permeated everyday life. Each time a meal was eaten, the absence of a family member who had died from hunger reminded families of loss and of the homeless, tormented soul of the deceased, who often had been buried

---

[24] Anhui, interview, 2007.

[25] Weigelin-Schwiedrzik, "Trauma and Memory," 41–61.

[26] Ibid., 41–42.

[27] I am indebted to Rubie S. Watson for making me think harder about this point. See *Memory, History, and Opposition*, 10.

improperly.[28] The Great Leap also had disordered the normal architectural pattern of the household, and daily interactions with this disorder kept alive the memory of the famine's death toll. For instance, the loss of house doors lingered on as a reminder of the carnage. In many cases, the doors' iron hinges had been confiscated for use in the Great Leap steel-making campaigns. In other cases, the doors were used to make surrogate coffins for those who succumbed to hunger and overwork. The missing doors haunted family survivors: every time they entered or left their houses, they were reminded of family desperation and of those who had perished during the famine. Even after the 1961–64 recovery, most of Da Fo's families still lived a hand-to-mouth existence. Into the late 1970s, families worried that food supply might dry up, that edema might return, that another outbreak of radical procurement and forced labor might drive someone they cherished to death.

Another side of silent memory had to do with long-term damage to the bodies of famine survivors. When I first began field work in Da Fo and a dozen other villages in northern Henan in 1985–90, I was struck by the shrunken torsos and frail bodies of fifty- to seventy-year-olds who had barely escaped starvation. Many were much thinner and at least three to six inches shorter than some of the privileged Da Fo Communist Party leaders who had gorged on steamed bread, tea, pork, eggs, and vegetables in the secret kitchens of the brigade and commune public dining halls while imposing the excesses of the Great Leap. Most of Da Fo's famine survivors looked like toothpicks in comparison to boss Bao Zhilong, a brawny man six feet in height. There is little doubt that Da Fo's shrunken famine survivors also linked their physical deformities to the Great Leap famine. Comparing the frail, thin body of a family member or friend with the strong, healthy body of Bao and other party leaders who had imposed the famine triggered flashbacks of food deprivation and physical depletion and kept alive a bitter memory of the unjust food distribution imposed by the Maoists.

Even more troublesome for Da Fo's Maoist famine perpetrators was the appearance of villagers who had suffered physical violence. Survivors of the bone-shattering public criticism sessions, left with wrongly mended rib and ankle breaks, stooped or limped. Others bore scars from the hangings, beatings, and burns incurred under the forced labor regime of the river-digging and steel-making campaigns. Victims of the relentless labor assignments in the Lin County steel-making campaign saw the socialist state through the damage its cadres had done to their bodies. Bao Gaojun, a farmer who had participated in this campaign, was so exhausted while working in Lin County that he dozed off and fell into the burning embers of a campfire. Fortunately, Bao was saved by a fellow worker, but still carries an unhappy memory of the incident on his body. "I still have a

---

[28] Compare with Mueggler, *Age of Wild Ghosts*. This book is an exemplary study of suffering and death in and after the Great Leap.

scar on my left arm from that accident," says Bao, "and whenever I see this scar it reminds me of my days in Lin County."[29] Being in constant touch with such bodily damage surely sharpened the powers of people like Bao to distinguish between the *yiku sitian* representations of the party as compassionate and caring and the specific, localized Great Leap interactions that had put them in harm's way and left them to deal with the consequences. Some of the victims of hunger, edema, and torture in the Tong Tin River Dig camp were able to walk only with the aid of stick canes after the Great Leap.[30] Their deformities, scars, and disabilities – and those of many other Da Fo villagers – nurtured a long, embodied memory of the destructive terror of the Maoist state, undermining party attempts to instill through semantic propaganda a hegemonic memory of the Great Leap Forward as the tragic act of a well-meaning parential order.

The *yiku sitian* propaganda of the Maoists was aimed at altering famine memories presumably stored in areas of the brain that could be affected by semantic Pavlovian conditioning, a process designed to damage the discriminating power of episodic memory – that is, the memory of specific events of life. This was an important key to producing what psychobiologists call "retrograde amnesia," a severe memory deficit of the Great Leap famine's damage to everyday life. Yet the memory of bodily pain developed in the course of surviving the Great Leap episode often worked against the repetitive *yiku sitian* campaign to remind villagers of the sweetness of Maoist rule. The latter was largely a semantic-cum-visual process without direct connection to the villagers' bodies that were the products of the Great Leap's deprivations, whereas the former was a biological process involving more or less permanently embodied memories that trumped the presumed amnesic effects of *yiku sitian*.[31]

Naturally, for most villagers, the most powerful embodied memory of the Great Leap era was that of stomach-ravaging hunger; as a result the memory of surviving the famine by acquiring food on their own was carried deep in the physical gastrointestinal tract for many years after the famine was declared officially over. Ironically, even one of the sweetest victories that sustained everyday life in this time of food scarcity – the recovery of sweet potato lands – created physical problems that kept alive mnemonic understandings of the lasting harm of Mao's fundamentalist attack on agriculture and life. As we have seen, at the semantic level, villagers voice happy memories of this aspect of their resistance to Maoist rule in the Great Leap. But relying on sweet potatoes to relieve the pressure of hunger apparently had unhappy consequences for the gastric system, and these frequently endured for decades after the Great Leap famine officially ended, creating a widely shared embodied memory of the famine that the Maoists

[29] Bao Gaojun, interview, July 12, 2000.
[30] Tang Weilan, interview, July 14, 2002.
[31] For this section, I have relied on the conceptual knowledge of John P. J. Pinel. See *Biopsychology*, 210–11, 371–74, 394–95, 397, 479–80.

could not master: the memory of gastric ulcers and painful starburst lesions in the lining of the stomach.

Most of Da Fo's farmers tell us that during the Great Leap famine and for many decades afterward, sweet potatoes made up 70 percent of their food supply and that their improvised daily menu was composed primarily of all kinds of sweet potato foods: the sweet potato itself, sweet potato vines, sweet potato noodles, sweet potato dumplings, sweet potato soup, and *mostly* sweet potato bread. The problem was that over-reliance on sweet potato flour breads damages the stomach lining, causing ulceration and bleeding of the stomach; as a result many farmers also say they continued to experience day-to-day stomach pain long after the famine ended.[32] As Tang Weilan informs us, this pain served as a constant reminder of the Great Leap and its damage: "I do not want to plant sweet potatoes again unless I have to. The sight of sweet potatoes makes me sick. My stomach starts to churn up sour liquids when I think about sweet potatoes. I have some ulcers in my stomach that were left over from eating sweet potatoes too much and too often in the Great Leap Forward years."[33] Sweet potatoes, an important symbolic reminder of how villagers had in fact survived Mao's famine, were also associated with an episodic-specific memory of how the famine's fallback foods tore away at the body, making a mockery of the efforts of local party leaders (who had eaten well during the Great Leap and thus who most likely were not even aware of their victims' gastrointestinal pain) to cultivate a pre-1949 memory of a food regime that was worse than that of Maoist rule. This embodied memory was transmitted within families, and sometimes among farmers from different households, all through the 1960s and 1970s, and it persisted into the reform era, seemingly unchanged by the sweet political talk of Da Fo's Maoists.

There were other signs of the Great Leap's long-term damage to the body, notably in the realm of post-famine funerals for villagers who succumbed to tuberculosis. A train of death from this disease silently plowed through the village in the ten years following the famine.[34] Tuberculosis apparently was the number-one killer in Da Fo into the Deng Xiaoping era, for as late as 1979 Da Fo's barefoot health workers did not have the knowledge to administer tuberculin tests or the means to gain access to the penicillin that was necessary for treating it. In the early years of my field work in Da Fo, roughly 1989–92, this disease was once again rampant.

Memories of what happened to dead bodies – that is, of what happened to bodies after death – also resonated in Da Fo. One of the most powerful challenges to the CCP's attempt to relegitimate its institutional presence through *yiku sitian* propaganda lay in the persistent memory-spun tales of how the Great Leap had disrupted the funerary rites and death rituals of families, and some of these stories

---

[32] Bao Fabao, interview, July 29, 2006; Tang Weilan, interview, July 31, 2006.
[33] Tang Weilan, interview, July 31, 2006.
[34] Bao Yuming, interview, June 21, 2001.

had political salience that was at odds with the official narrative. We have seen that, in confiscating private lands, the leaders of Liangmen People's Commune deprived some farm households of private burial sites. In the Great Leap, the local Da Fo party leaders also refused to release collective field workers from their work assignments to attend funerals for more than short stints; villagers report that during the famine they had to wear their white funeral garments to work in the collective fields, and they often voice their disgust over having to attend funerals of deceased kin in soiled clothing. People were dismayed by this undignified practice. But what seems to have aroused even greater popular discomfort and disdain for the political agency that delivered the Great Leap famine was its direct, or indirect, interference with the funeral rituals that protected the household from the demonic forces of the universe.

A common theme in Chinese funeral rituals involves sending the deceased off with offerings to present to various powers in control of access to the *yingjian* (heaven). The specific offering varied from place to place – a coin or pearl in the mouth in one village, a fried cake or steamed ball inserted in the hand of the deceased in another.[35] In Da Fo, the custom was for surviving family members to place a fried cake in the hand of the deceased parent or grandparent. Da Fo's farmers believed that someone who died would be met by Tiangou, a vicious barking dog who stood at the gates of the *yingjian*.[36] To pass into this desirable place, the soul of the deceased person had to placate Tiangou with the cake, thereby silencing the guardian of the *yingjian*. If the soul did not gain entry to the *yingjian*, the ghost of the deceased would drift about, inviting misfortune into the lives of its living family members for years or decades until the dilemma could be resolved.[37] This kind of death ritual, in which the living would enable the soul of the physical body in the grave to pass through a "demonic spiritual cosmos," whose guardians had counterparts in China's official imperial order, was a major reason why Da Fo's families spent so much on funerals: the dilemma of being stranded in the zone of demonic forces was to be avoided at all cost.[38] Hence, even in a time of famine, it was imperative to serve Tiangou with a fried cake.

In the Great Leap Forward, however, procuring offerings to enable entry into the *yingjian* often became highly problematic for Da Fo households, and for decades after the famine many villagers relied on troubling memories to spread rumors about the fate of famine-ravaged families. Some of these rumors survived the multiple waves of Maoist *yiku sitian* propaganda and persisted well beyond the

---

[35] On this point, I have relied on Mueggler, personal correspondence, March 1, 2007; Fei Deng, personal correspondence, March 10, 2007; and Yu Honglian, personal correspondence, March 15, 2007. I have also relied on Watson and Rawski, *Death Ritual*, 194.

[36] Ruan Zhaoyin, interview, June 17, 2006.

[37] Mueggler, personal correspondence, March 1, 2007.

[38] Compare Day, *Chinese Peasant Cults*, 117–19; Groot, *Religious System of China*, 6, 931, noted in Kuhn, *Soulstealers*, 104–05; Feuchtwang, *Popular Religion in China*, 43–51; and Smith, "Talking Toads," 411–19.

first two decades of reform. One memory in particular unleashed a rumor of wandering "famine-corpse ghosts," which seemed to keep alive a shared community belief that questioned the ability of socialist governance to deliver food security and spiritual bliss – the core elements of *yiku sitian* propaganda. The case that inspired it seems to have reflected popular anxieties over the continued effects of the souls barred from the *yingjian* during the famine, and the rumor points to the deep stain on this particular famine-traumatized family. At the height of the Great Leap famine, so the rumor goes, Bao Song, one of Da Fo's overworked farmers, had starved to death.[39] When Bao Song died, his family members, who themselves were starving, could not afford a proper funeral. Nonetheless, they managed to place a small fried cake in his hand to placate Tiangou. The hunger of Bao Song's daughter was so assailing, however, that she snatched the cake and ate it during the makeshift funeral ceremony – a shocking transgression that angered Tiangou and left the ghost of Bao Song stranded in the dark underworld of imperial judges, spies, and police who stood in the way of the eternal bliss of the *yingjian*.

Rumors like this one held a critique of the power that was behind *yiku sitian* and made it impossible for the CCP to retire the memories that challenged its representation of socialism as the progressive realization of materialist utopia. Worse, this particular rumor circulated in the context of, and reinforced, stories and rumors that pointed to Mao and his party as the source of the disaster that had destroyed the rituals that connected the living with the dead,[40] implying that the party-state itself was a dark force that threatened food security, operated through the sinister deception of "socialist betterment" talk, and actually produced what it preached against: chaos and instability for the living and the ancestors. The party agents of *yiku sitian* were unable to prevent the periodic mobilization of such memories and rumors, which provided farmers in Da Fo with alternative ways of comprehending the Great Leap famine as an attack on a culturally rooted search for personal dignity and family peace and stability.

Semantic Memories

In addition to the physical reminders of the famine, there were memories expressed in everyday stories, rumors, common knowledge, and persistent questions. Virtually everyone in Da Fo village knew that Mao had astutely and cleverly conducted rural investigations into the conditions of village life in the late 1920s and early 1930s, well before the party came to power, giving the Communists the edge in their efforts to address farmer grievances and win popular support in the countryside. Why had Mao not applied this method to the Great Leap Forward, when he was in power? As people learned more about Wu Zhipu's role in pressing local party leaders to exaggerate production figures and about Wu's

[39] Ruan Zhaoyin, interview, June 17, 2006.
[40] Smith, "Talking Toads," 422, 426.

connections to Mao, they wondered how much Mao really knew. They asked themselves why Mao had let Bao Zhilong and the commune-level cadres and village party leaders get away with corruption and blatant coercion during the Great Leap. If Chairman Mao was indeed a genius, how could he not have known what was going on in the rural areas? How could he not have known that the commune and village leaders were lying about harvest output and concealing their brutal political behavior?

Yin Fengxiu, who was thirty-eight at the start of the Great Leap, recalls the process by which villagers became disillusioned with the party:

The Communist Party started the Great Leap with a lot of enthusiasm from the local people. People thought that Chairman Mao and the party leaders were always right, that they wanted the common people to benefit from the policy. Most people in Da Fo listened to the party. Our village leaders were mostly party members, and so they too listened to the party. Those who did not would get into trouble with the village leaders. But looking back, we were very naïve at the time. We learned that Chairman Mao and the Communist Party could make mistakes too. They made mistakes because they no longer knew what was going on in the rural areas, where most people lived. Of course the village leaders did not tell the truth to the government, but they were forced by their superiors to exaggerate the harvest production figures.[41]

Everyone in Da Fo knew that the supreme leader of the CCP was Chairman Mao Zedong himself, and people like Yin Fengxiu still remembered that Mao had directed them into disaster, after which their enthusiasm for Maoist rule was lost.

In the two decades following the Great Leap Forward, people in Da Fo voiced both personal memories and family-cum-community memories by storytelling. Such narratives kept alive a social memory of the Great Leap Forward as the product of a morally debased socialist order. Personal stories were passed on to trusted family and friends and repeated time and time again in the post–Great Leap Forward decade, promoting solidarity among famine survivors and casting doubt on the Maoist-crafted official memory of the famine.

Families who had survived the famine passed on personal memories of the Great Leap hunger to their children. At the center of these stories was a lesson: Be very grateful for the food before you, for there was a time when we did not have enough to eat – a time when we went hungry, when we almost starved. Bao Xueyang, for example, was born in 1965, three years after the famine abated, but in recalling that he and his family still lived on sweet potatoes until 1978, he reveals,

I first heard of the Great Leap Forward when I was about ten years old. At that time, my father told me about it. He said that during the Great Leap Forward some leaders exaggerated the crop yields, and the government took away a lot of grain.... In the end, people in our village faced starvation and ate mostly sweet potatoes and sweet potato vines.

---

[41] Yin Fengxiu, interviews, July 10–11, 2002.

Also, in these years my grandparents did not want us to complain about the bad food. So whenever we said that we did not like the food, they would tell us stories of the food scarcity of the Great Leap Forward.[42]

Bao Fabao also remembers his parents telling him not to waste food: "They would say that if I did not value food, a food shortage like that of the Great Leap Forward might occur again."[43] Such stories damaged the legitimacy of the collective experiment itself, for they were frequently told with an important footnote about Tang Guoyi's satire on the "mirror porridge" served in the public dining hall, which was so thin you could see your reflection it. Everyone knew the story, and it resonated with the history of missing kinfolk and playmates who had succumbed to the mess hall system's woefully inadequate rations. Another form of storytelling focused on how Da Fo's young Maoists had threatened the storyteller with violent public assault and how he or she had avoided or survived the danger of public criticism. Across the decades linking the famine with reform, many women filled their daily household conversations with references to such memories.

Husbands who had been away from the home intermittently during the Great Leap learned of the fears still haunting their spouses into the post-Mao era. Bao Zhidan was one of them. "A couple of years ago, in 1998," says Bao,

my wife and I were talking about her experience of being caught by the Da Fo militia when she took the green corn to eat. Who would eat an ear of raw green corn today?! During the Great Leap Forward, people seized and ate the corn because they were hungry. But the Da Fo militia caught her. They took her to the village leaders, and the leaders talked about debating her in a public meeting. My wife was very scared. She promised the village leaders that she would not do it again. In the end, they decided not to debate her.[44]

The memory of these brushes with the Maoist whip of the Great Leap outlasted Deng as well as Mao. Their understated but widely understood message was that the village party leaders had violated the moral economy of *chi qing*, while they themselves had their subsistence guaranteed through the institutionally privileged food chain of the public dining halls.

For a long time after the famine ended – well into the mid-1980s – many villagers did not compare notes about the Great Leap past or the suffering they had experienced. Locally and nationally, talk was still dangerous. Herman and Schacter both point out that disaster victims often seek to avoid talking about their traumatic encounters.[45] Many of Da Fo's victims too largely kept quiet, a strategy that accorded with what the Maoists preferred. The Cultural Revolution was, after all, a Maoist ploy to stop any such talk or thinking. Nevertheless, long before Deng Xiaoping attempted to defuse the dangerous memory of the Great Leap by

[42] Bao Xueyang, interview, July 28, 2006.
[43] Bao Fabao, interview, July 29, 2006.
[44] Bao Zhidan, interview, June 26, 2000.
[45] Herman, *Trauma and Recovery*; Schacter, *Seven Sins of Memory*, 175.

pursuing decollectivization and allowing greater dissent, young students who were sent down to the countryside sometimes heard villagers angrily and tearfully pour out their grief.[46] They heard these emotional conversations in Dongle villages too, and the conversations picked up once Mao was gone. In Da Fo, collective memory of the famine surged to the front of popular discourse in the Deng Xiaoping era, when villagers found the energy, time, and space to engage one another about their common suffering and loss.

From 1985 on, sharing stories of the past became more widespread. Stories about Great Leap–era brigade leader Bao Yibin circulated widely. Villagers remembered that party secretary Bao Yibin had joined with Bao Ziyan in subjecting people to public criticism and forcing them to kneel down on the ground, on bricks, and on tables.[47] Many villagers knew that in 1960, while the Great Leap famine was raging, Bao Yibin had denied his mother his pet rabbit's leftover noodles. But the full story began to circulate only after decollectivization, around 1985. It went like this: in the 1961 *fan wufeng* campaign, Bao Yibin was approached by friends of his mother's family. They told Bao that he should practice filial piety and help his mother and younger brother, as both were emaciated and short on food. Bao Yibin gave his mother a bottle of cooking oil. His mother was so very happy with her son's turn of heart that she began telling the good news to everyone she knew. However, when Bao Yibin's wife caught wind of this news, she began to quarrel with Bao Yibin's younger brother, Bao Hongwen, about the gift. Bao Hongwen recounts the story:

I was sleeping on the bed, and she rushed in and grabbed my penis so hard that she almost killed me. Later my penis turned black and blue. When my mother came back home, she discovered what my sister-in-law had done to me. She became very angry. . . . She got into a big fight with my sister-in-law. My sister-in-law was young and strong, and she beat up my mother on the street. My brother, Bao Yibin, was too afraid of his wife to stop her. Consequently, my brother gained a very bad reputation in Da Fo. Many villagers hate him and his family. Of course all of the village leaders offended some people in one way or another. But my brother had more enemies than most of the others.[48]

By permitting the starving and beating of his own helpless mother, Bao Yibin placed himself in an unforgivable moral predicament – the predicament of the Da Fo Communist Party.

In Da Fo, this predicament also enveloped the CCP's relationship with the key institution of state power, the PLA, as the case of Zheng Daqing attests. The son of a poor farmer and salt producer, Zheng had fought against the Kuomintang salt police, joined the CCP-led resistance army, and fought with his three sons against the Kuomintang Army in the Civil War. His eldest son, a commander in the New Fourth Army, had died in the Battle of Huaihai. Officially designated a

[46] Weigelin-Schwiedrzik, "Trauma and Memory," 4.
[47] Zheng Xianyi, interview, July 14, 2000.
[48] Bao Hongwen, interview, July 11, 2000.

"martyr family" after Liberation, Zheng's household was entitled to special treatment by the party-state. When Zheng Daqing was ravaged by hunger in the Great Leap famine, he appealed to Da Fo party secretary Bao Yibin for relief, but he was denied – even his old comrade Bao Zhilong, who had access to the commune's food supply, refused to help – and he starved to death. News of this abandonment shocked other PLA veterans and spread rapidly through the village.

This shocking news stayed with PLA veterans long after the famine's end, and it created a memory that competed with and in the end defeated the attempt of *yiku sitian* to promote amnesia. To better grasp this point, we return to Bao Hongwen, the son of Bao Yidai – one of Da Fo's most celebrated PLA martyrs. Bao Hongwen had joined the PLA during the Cultural Revolution to escape the lingering impoverishment of the Great Leap famine, and, on demobilizing, he was compelled to participate in the *yiku sitian* meetings of the post-famine decades. He found that this method of making people forget the past did not work so well for him. Bao held a counter-memory he could not give up:

After my father died in the Civil War, my mother, who was pregnant at the time, had to take care of my elder brother and elder sister by herself. Of course, my family received some special treatment, because my father had died for the revolution. We received a three-*yuan* monthly support allowance for my mother, and my mother was provided with one kilo of candy and permitted to buy a pig to celebrate the New Year. But in fact we did not receive much help. In 1960, the worst year of the famine, my mother was starving. I had to quit school, and I lived with my mother. Like most villagers, I was starved very badly. I did not have the energy to walk or speak, and I always looked down because I did not have the energy to look up.[49]

I later participated in the *yiku sitian* meetings a few times. These usually were held by the village Peasant Association. The idea was to educate people to remember the past hard life and to value the current good life. We were asked to eat bread made of tree leaves and wild vegetables. I did not suffer before Liberation, but I did remember the hardship of the Great Leap Forward, [so] I was not strongly impressed by the *yiku sitian* meetings.[50]

Under the pressure of another political disappointment, by the late 1980s Bao Hongwen had given up the idea that socialism had delivered a sweet life. In 1987, his mother was diagnosed with cancer and hospitalized in Anyang. "I went to the Dongle County government Civil Affairs Department and asked them to help with my mother's medical bills," says Bao. "They refused. When my mother died that same year, I went there again to ask for help with the funeral cost. Again they refused. It seemed that my father had died in vain."[51]

Such daily storytelling of the post-Mao era helped villagers connect with the uncensored version of the famine, overriding all official memory of the disaster. This memory from below had tremendous moral appeal. Such stories reminded them that they were part of a community engaged in a long-term, hidden practical

[49] Ibid.
[50] Ibid., July 5, 2004.
[51] Ibid., July 11, 2000.

struggle against continuing political domination by the same party agents who had broken all of the basic rules of civility in the Great Leap Forward. Each retelling reconfirmed that the purpose of this struggle was not just to get even but also to get rid of the local party agents who wanted the victims to forget the recent past.

Habitual Memories

The persistence of memories associated with the everyday performances on which Da Fo's farmers had relied to get through the Great Leap famine and that had allowed them to recover in its long aftermath also provided a powerful daily anti-dote to the rituals of *yiku sitian*. Two such memories stand out, reminding us that unauthorized popular efforts to endure the famine created lasting forms of resis-tance that were, cognitively speaking, in direct competition with Maoist efforts to line up everyday experiences of villagers with messages about the benevolence of the Da Fo party leaders or the central government.

Despite the post–Great Leap *yiku sitian* claims that the collective had saved villagers from the famine by "giving them" land on which to grow tuber food, Da Fo's wretched famine survivors understood that the production team leaders had only claimed to be "lending" them the land to grow sweet potatoes in order to cover up their division of collective land for private use – a division that Mao and his commune-level agents opposed – and all of Da Fo's farmers knew that life had improved dramatically due to their own efforts to plant tubers in the midst of the famine. Long after the Great Leap famine officially ended, moreover, they continued to rely on sweet potato production to cope with food shortages, and this habit surely made less appealing Maoist invitations to eat the "inferior" root and tuber crops of the pre-Liberation era as a way of grasping that Mao's revolution had alleviated poverty. The daily production and consumption of sweet potato–based foodstuffs in the post-famine period only served to remind villagers that life in the present was dependent on continuing the resistance of the recent past.[52]

How villagers remembered the way in which they engaged in clandestine market habits also hindered the case of Mao's *yiku sitian* activists in Da Fo. Some of the farmers who secretly engaged in forbidden petty trade to escape and recover from the Great Leap famine in 1960 and 1961 accentuated this practice after the famine was over, and a few held on to their memories of the famine years by keeping the material instruments that had allowed them to pursue the market in the worst years of Maoist scarcity. Zheng Yunxiang was one of them. Speaking of the two-wheeler he had habitually relied on to purchase sweet potatos in Shandong and wheat stalk in Hebei for resale around Da Fo during the famine and its aftermath, Zheng says: "I had my own bicycle then. It was a steady one. That

---

[52] I am indebted to Bao Yufa, whose testimony about sweet potatoes, though not directly in reference to *yiku sitian*, helped me with this point. Interview, July 25, 2006.

bicycle helped me earn a lot of money in the past."[53] This old bicycle represented the memory of how Zheng Yunxiang had survived the Maoist attempt to take away the market – an empowering memory that ran counter to the Maoist *yiku sitian* support for communal farming over petty capitalism – and Zheng would not let go of it. When I interviewed him in the early and mid-1990s, the old, dirty bicycle from his black market days occupied a special place in his household. It sat alongside two new bicycles, but Zheng made it clear that he could not rely upon them. He was saving the instrument that had helped him to survive more than three decades earlier, just in case he needed it to get through another state attack on his family's food security.

Settling the Score

Although there was no open rebellion against the Da Fo Communist Party branch after the Great Leap disaster, the days of political acquiescence were numbered. The long memory of abuse, suffering, and loss in the Great Leap provided the wellspring for popular indignation and resentment, which took the form of a silent, undeclared war against the party bosses who continued to press for collectivization. This war's primary goal was to exact revenge for the indignities and injustices villagers had endured under the old-guard Maoists during the Great Leap and its famine.

In the first post–Great Leap Forward decade the acts villagers undertook in waging this war were largely disguised forms of resistance that covered the footprints of people who had few political rights.[54] We have seen that the resistance of the post–Great Leap decade occasionally took on a life of its own and tested schemes of Maoist state capture and containment. If the process of party-state cooptation had been fairly complete, then the memory of the Great Leap would not have posed a threat to the local Maoist party leaders in the last years of Mao's regime, and the transition to reform socialism would have been assured. This was far from the case.

The most prevalent and threatening form of semi-hidden protest against Da Fo's Great Leap leadership reared its head in the late 1980s and early 1990s, nearly three decades after the Maoist disaster. This was the rash of arson directed against the persons and property of village party bosses directly responsible for the appropriation, greed, and brutal repression that brought on the Great Leap famine. Arson became – and remains – the major weapon of choice among powerless villagers intent on settling scores with Bao Zhilong and the local party rulers and on stoking forms of political discourse through which they might realize certain basic rights. As an episode of resistance, arson in this village had little to do with

[53] Zheng Yunxiang, interviews, September 1 and September 21, 1995.
[54] Compare Scott, *Domination and the Arts of Resistance*, 198–99.

the policy reform of the Deng Xiaoping–led center.[55] Nor does it seem to have primarily been the product of violence by jealous poor farmers who suffered from envy against well-to-do farmers who displayed wealth derived from specialized economic activities.[56] Bao Zhilong, one of the major targets of arson, was hardly a well-to-do farmer. Though, as will become evident, Bao did profit in ways that stoked resentment, he did not intentionally flaunt whatever gains he made under reform. Instead, this episode of reform-era resistance had everything to do with the efforts of famine survivors to reconcile the wounding and losses of the past.

According to Lucien Bianco, if there was one primary "weapon of the poor" in rural China, it was the use of fires, or arson, against the houses and headquarters of officials and their agents, a regular practice in the last years of the Qing dynasty. The burning of residential houses in particular occurred sporadically until the Communists took power, and in the Great Leap episode rural people sometimes challenged communist rule by torching the homes of party cadres.[57] The arson started up again under reform, when villagers used this weapon to express anger with detested officials. Such fires, according to Bianco, foretell the next rubric: vengeance.[58] Looking back, perhaps there was a hint that villagers would, in the absence of a multiparty system and autonomous elections, use arson as a way of punishing and dislodging the party leaders who had delivered Mao's disaster. In 1977, for instance, Zheng Peifu, Bao Zhilong's choice to head the second production team, was compelled to resign under pressure of arson, which destroyed all of his team's hay.[59] In one sense, the outbreak of arson was the product of a "chosen trauma," that is, the conscious impulse of the living victims of the Great Leap famine to find a relatively safe way to set things right;[60] it was the product of a memory-centered identity formed around a preoccupation with righteousness. This obsessive concern with righteousness called for undoing the harm of the past and, simultaneously, legitimated what Anthony Robben calls the "self-righteous exercise of violence" against the known agents of the Great Leap trauma.[61] A "hidden transcript" of righteous contention, formed in popular memory during and long after the Great Leap Forward Famine, summoned villagers to strike back at party leaders.

Not surprisingly, the primary objects of popular arson in Da Fo were the three most resented oppressive agents of its Communist Party branch: party secretary Bao Zhilong, vice-secretary Bao Yibin, and toady Bao Zhigen. Between

[55] Thus, it cannot be explained by the policy-based resistance paradigm of O'Brien and Li. See *Rightful Resistance in Rural China*.
[56] For this view, see the interesting work of Burns and Rosen, *Policy Conflicts*, 273.
[57] For this section, I have relied mostly on Bianco and Hua, *Jacqueries et révolutions*, 59, 84, 114–15, 138–44, 302–03, 372, 381–82, 480, 615, esp. 138–44, 480; on the post-1949 period, see Domes, *Socialism in the Chinese Countryside*, 69.
[58] Bianco and Hua, *Jacqueries et révolutions*, 59, 84, 114–15, 138–44, 302–03, 372, 381–82, 480, 615, esp. 138–44, 480.
[59] Zheng Peifu, interview, September 10, 1995.
[60] On chosen trauma, see Robben, "How Traumatized Societies Remember."
[61] Mueller, "Memory and Power"; Robben, "How Traumatized Societies Remember," 9.

313

the winter of 1989 and the summer of 1993, there were at least forty-seven cases of undisclosed nocturnal arson in Da Fo. Occasionally, there were several in the same night, and on more than one occasion all were directed at these political actors.

In January of 1989, in the spring of 1991, and in March of 1993, Bao Zhilong's house was torched. Pang Qinli's testimony gives us reason to surmise that the emotion-laden memory of the Great Leap hurt surfaced in the reform era to play a role in shaping the political actions of villagers in the contemporary period:

There are many people in the village who hate Bao Zhilong because they felt he took more than his fair share during the hunger of the Great Leap Forward. A few years ago his new house was burnt down the very night it was finished. Someone climbed into his courtyard and set his house on fire again this year. The person locked the house doors from the outside in order to prevent him from escaping. However, Bao Zhilong and his wife were rescued by other people.[62]

Arson was extended to some of the key minor Communist Party leaders who had collaborated with Bao Zhilong. In March of 1989, for instance, the house of Bao Yiming, the widely resented vice–party secretary (and bad-tempered goat killer) of the Great Leap period, was torched. Bao Chuanshen's home was burned down in 1991. On returning to Da Fo for field work in 1993, I saw the charred walls of the red brick houses of at least forty former Communist Party leaders.

If the failed rule of the village party leaders in the Bao lineage came under attack as a result of their past misdeeds, then Bao Yibin, who in 1993 was returned to the post of vice–party secretary in Da Fo, would logically have been the second of the primary targets of retaliatory protest and revenge. And indeed this was the case. But in addition to arson, Bao Yibin was the target of another form of anonymous resistance: crop-cutting. In May of 1993, someone entered Bao Yibin's wheat fields under the cover of darkness and cut the crops before they could ripen, leaving Bao to try to survive by eating what was left of the green crops – that is, to suffer the fate of the hungry, half-starved poor in the Great Leap famine. Bao Yibin could not find anyone in Da Fo who would identify the culprit; people still hated him for denying his mother leftover noodles. Moreover, villagers understood the deeper, non-verbal political message of the crop cutting: the next act might be far more aggressive, such as torching his home or even a threat on his person.

Arson and cutting the premature green crops were increasingly accompanied by another retaliatory strategy: property theft. In the spring of 1993, Bao Zhigen's cart was stolen, and the thief also stole eight hundred catties of wheat (close to a thousand pounds) from Bao Donger's fields, using the cart to haul away the crop.[63] Clearly, the intent was not only to retaliate against Bao Zhigen but also to create divisions within the ruling party clique by implying that one leader had taken the crop from another. Such a diversion was also a political precaution, for Bao Zhigen, the pistol-wielding lecher of the Great Leap past, remained the

[62] Pang Qinli, interview, September 1, 1993.
[63] Ibid.

only Da Fo leader authorized by Dongle County authorities to carry a gun, and villagers had to be extra cautious in attacking him.

If we are to interpret such actions as "infrapolitics,"[64] as a kind of delayed retaliation for the Great Leap famine, then we must explain why such resistance did not irrupt earlier in the reform era – in 1978, 1980, or 1986. The answer lies partly in the redevelopment of a rudimentary civil society in Da Fo during the first decade of reform. Small groups of kinsmen, friends, and neighbors operating independent of the power network of Bao Zhilong and the control of the Da Fo party branch were gradually able to compete with the weakened revolutionary state-controlled public associations of the collective era – the militia, the Peasant Association, the harvest company, and the public criticism session. Slowly but surely they were able to create and defend spaces of home, neighborhood, and temple that had been penetrated by the Maoists in the Great Leap.

Villagers' newfound material gains also helped them to assuage the pain of the Maoist past. After all, what villagers wanted was to live a happy life – to chitchat over *mahjong*, seek blessings for new infants in temple fairs, enjoy long and joyous rest breaks over the New Year Festival, get their children into middle schools and high schools, save for spectacular weddings and funerals, and secure decent living quarters for their married offspring. Some of the villagers who experienced economic advancement in the first decade of reform (1978–88) used the material gains from their off-farm market dealings to recreate the ramparts of personal, family, and community defense against the hated leftover Communist Party leaders.

In 1986 several villagers began to rebuild temples to Guangong, the war god, on the streets near their households. When I first entered Da Fo in August 1989, virtually every family had a small shrine in its courtyard or a picture of the war god on its door. The revival of the war god tradition, with its symbolic approval for resisting bad rulers, did not bode well for Bao Zhilong and his ilk, especially because this process was entwined with, and indeed stimulated, the popular attempt to acquire an old weapon of empowerment that had been lost to the Great Leap Forward – a weapon Da Fo's Maoist bullies had feared.[65]

In the Republican era, Dongle County had sponsored an annual martial arts contest, and Da Fo's martial artists had several times won the countywide championship. Once collectivization accelerated, exhaustion from overwork, combined with the loss of income necessary for undertaking martial arts training, forced the abandonment of the sport. From the standpoint of Communist Party leaders, this development proved politically convenient, for without martial arts training it became far more difficult for male villagers to defend themselves and family members against Great Leap berating and beatings. With subsistence and strength regained in the 1980s and with money saved from petty trade, however,

---

[64] See Scott, *Domination and the Arts of Resistance*, 183–92, 199–201.
[65] Zheng Puyi, interview, August 22, 1989.

village people took up training under martial arts masters, and once again Da Fo became a major site of *gong fu* contests. But few villagers took up martial arts merely for leisure. The training had a specific political purpose: villagers took it up to empower themselves in confrontations with Da Fo party leaders so that the latter could no longer place them in threatening situations without paying a price. Between 1985 and 1990, scores of Da Fo families sent two and three sons to train under local martial arts teachers, and they did so for the unstated but understood purpose of hitting back at Bao Zhilong and his power network. By 1986 several Da Fo martial artists whose families bore grudges from the Great Leap period were making it difficult for Bao Zhilong to rule the village. They challenged Bao more frequently and occasionally threatened to beat the daylights out of his family members if he attempted to interfere with their affairs.

Bao Zhilong responded by sending his sixteen-year-old son, Bao Rulong, to the famous Shaolin Temple Academy, in Henan's Loyang, to study martial arts for a year. Bao Rulong explains: "My father supported me, partly because both my father and I knew that I had to be prepared to fight for my family and myself. If people knew that I was strong and had martial arts skills, they would be less likely to mess with me and would show me respect."[66] But Bao Rulong became the laughingstock of people whose respect he craved when villagers discovered that his Shaolin martial arts teachers were imposters. Nearly one thousand *yuan* had been wasted on his so-called training, and he could not defend his father. Faced with ailing health and worn down by a spate of martial arts challenges from the sons of families he had offended in the Great Leap, Bao Zhilong offered to retire from his post as party secretary in 1986, only to be told by Liangmen People's Commune leaders that he had to stay on a few years and mentor his successor, Bao Wanqing.[67]

By 1992 the martial artists had captured space throughout the village, both for their periodic training sessions under Da Fo's master teachers and for their daily impromptu run-ins and skirmishes with party leaders. From this point on, the martial artists defended their households by issuing threats against party leaders, began to supplant party leaders previously charged with mediating villager disputes, and refused to cooperate with party leaders in carrying out the orders of the Liangmen township leaders. Without the whip of the public criticism session or the automatic support of the Dongle County police, Bao Zhilong and his sons were the constant target of threatened beatings from the young men who had taken up martial arts, often the sons of victims of party-inflicted abuse.[68] Faced with a riot of arson and fearing the rising threat of the marital artists, Bao Zhilong insisted that Liangmen township find someone to replace him. Some

---

[66] Bao Rulong, interview, July 5, 2000.
[67] Ibid.
[68] In developing this section, I have profited from McAdam, Tarrow, and Tilly, *Dynamics of Contention*, 22–32.

villagers speculate that such threats caused his debilitating stroke in 1992, the year of the next attack on the party leaders of the Great Leap. In any event, the incidents of arson escalated in the early 1990s, making it difficult for Bao Wanqing, the hand-picked vice–party secretary of Bao Zhilong, to establish credibility, win trust, and implement policy in a manner acceptable to villagers, thus throwing the Da Fo party branch into a succession crisis.[69]

The small gains that Da Fo's villagers made toward the creation of a healthy civil society and traditional culture during the reform era gave them strength to retaliate. People who had risked emotional damage and physical harm by standing up to challenge Da Fo's party leaders and who had had no choice but to keep quiet and submit to retaliation no longer had to fear being struggled in public criticism meetings or isolated from villagers who might support them. From the mid-1980s, they could begin to count on selective companions and confidants to support them in conflicts with Da Fo party leaders.

Many of these people shared mutual hatred of the perpetrators of the Great Leap famine, and they occasionally banded together to defend their families and friends against the petty tyrants of the Maoist past. In the mid-1980s, for example, Great Leap rapist Bao Zhigen resumed his old sexual habits, pinching the bottoms of young women and luring wives, daughters, and sisters into illicit sexual intercourse. "But this time," says Bao Hongwen,

Bao Zhigen was frequently beaten by villagers, and his face was covered with blood. One time, when Bao Zhigen slept with Zheng Shan's elder sister, Zheng Shan and his two younger brothers beat him up with iron bars. Bao Zhigen almost died. On several other occasions, when Bao Zhigen was beaten, he lay on the village streets for a long time. He still was one of the most hated persons in Da Fo.[70]

Such dramas did not simply punctuate the normalcy that was being recovered in the first post-Mao decade, they paved the way for it. In some of these skirmishes, the villagers who stood up to Bao Zhigen angrily shouted at him while he was lying on the ground bleeding, on one occasion asking him, "Now, do you still think it is the Great Leap Forward?!"

The devolution of central government power that occurred with centrally sanctioned reforms in the post-Mao era also weakened the structure of surveillance and force previously available to the Da Fo party leaders, working to the advantage of villagers and their hidden mode of resistance. By the end of the 1980s, the Da Fo militia had been disbanded, public criticism – the whip of Maoist terror – was put aside, and village party leaders could no longer automatically mobilize the militia-based policing functions of the commune to impose their will. In fact, the Dongle County police seemed more and more reluctant to assist the attempts of the Bao party bosses to thwart or beat back many forms of resistance. On countless occasions the Dongle County police were called to

---

[69] Bao Renqing, interview, September 15, 1993.
[70] Bao Hongwen, interview, July 11, 2000.

Da Fo to investigate acts of arson, but the police refused to come to Da Fo at all unless the plaintiffs – in this case Bao Zhilong and the old-guard Maoist party leaders – paid them gas money, and they refused to carry through on arson investigations without receiving under-the-table money from the besieged party leaders. People charged with crimes, including arson, could reduce any fine as long as they could make a substantial payoff. Corruption became a "weapon of the weak," an instrument in the hands of villagers bent on getting even for the misrule of collectivization.[71] Apparently, widespread local knowledge of the weakened enforcement apparatus of the party-state below the level of Dongle County government only encouraged Da Fo's resentful denizens to retaliate against the perpetrators of the Great Leap.

Behind the escalation of retaliatory protest was the obstinate memory of the outrageous conduct of Da Fo's Communist Party activists during the Great Leap Forward and afterward. By the late 1980s, it had become clear to villagers that Bao Zhilong and the leaders of the Great Leap past were beyond redemption. After he returned to power toward the Cultural Revolution's end, Bao Zhilong soon took up his old tricks. He chose Pang Lang, the corrupt accountant and target of popular anger in the desperate hunger of 1960, to serve as Da Fo's vice–party secretary, a post Pang held until 1986. He put villagers in situations in which they had to curry favor and give him gifts in order to obtain permission to engage in important routines of livelihood. As Howard Giskin has pointed out, Chinese villagers subscribe to the notion that "good persons . . . do not look for gifts but simply go about their daily chores without thought of gain."[72] Bao's tendency to expect gifts in return for favors stoked the memory of similar misdeeds in the Great Leap period. Moreover, from 1973 until 1985, Bao Zhilong made it difficult for talented young people to leave Da Fo in order to pursue a better life, but in this same period he secured jobs outside of the village for his own sons. And Bao discriminated against villagers who had spoken out against his Great Leap wrongdoings during the Cultural Revolution.

The relationship between villagers and party leaders was infused with hostile criticism and contempt, and Bao's misbehavior only made matters worse. The slow-but-sure disengagement of previous decades seemed to be spawning a divorce. In September 1993, during a Beijing interview, Bao Huayin, the wartime Communist Party secretary of Dongle County, revealed how memory of the past had come to structure the contentious present. Bao explains the dilemma created by Bao Zhilong's bad track record during the Great Leap:

In 1961, at the end of the Great Leap Forward and the famine, Bao Zhilong knew the villagers in Da Fo were dissatisfied [*bumanyi*] with him. He wanted to be forgiven. *However,*

---

[71] The term is from Scott, *Weapons of the Weak.* Also on this point see Scott, "Socialism and Small Property." Bao Zhendao, interview, September 3, 1993. Zhou, *How the Farmers Changed China,* predicts this development.

[72] Giskin, "Using Chinese Folktales," 30.

they were not willing to forgive him. His house was torched in early 1989, and again in March of 1991. Even so, people are still resentful and hateful of him. When Bao Zhilong held power right after 1961 no one dared to commit arson against him. But now that his power has slipped they are not afraid to torch him.[73]

Villagers would not forgive Bao Zhilong and the leaders of the Great Leap, and, by the same token, the former party bosses of the village were reluctant to publicly apologize and seek forgiveness for the plunder and carnage of the Great Leap. Mutual empowerment was not possible. Consequently, from 1989 to 1995, Da Fo's former party leaders often went on the defensive and invited a kind of infra-resistance that reeked of disrespect, insubordination, and the desire for revenge, all of which culminated in contentious actions that drove those same disgraced party leaders into further denial and isolation.[74]

It would be wrong to suggest that the arson, beatings, and other expressions of hostility visited upon Bao Zhilong and his Great Leap accomplices derived entirely from their conduct in the crisis famine years rather than from the accumulated grievances of villagers at the misbehavior of these party leaders over a much longer span of time. Both factors were at work, and in the reform era the corrupt behavior of Bao Zhilong and his clients surely added fuel to the fire. Let us look at two examples of accumulative grievances over corruption, one involving land, the other grain.

Some villagers suspected that Bao Zhilong's house was torched because of the way he had corrupted the village government process of reassigning building lots to farmers in the reform era. Bao Zhilong, and his client Bao Zuoming, took charge of this process in 1988–89. The two men schemed to assign the most treasured lots in Da Fo to their households, and Bao Zhilong built his new house on one of these lots. But Bao went further, committing an act of greed that many perceived to be a blatant abuse of power: while others were waiting for the remaining open ground in the village to be assigned for them to build homes, Bao Zhilong deliberately left the open ground in front of his house – a space half the size of a football field – out of the process and did not assign it to anyone. According to Bao Zuoming, "Some thought that Bao Zhilong was going to annex that open ground to his yard someday. Whether that was true or not, no one knows. The fact is that the open ground should have been assigned to somebody, but it was not. People were angry."[75] Some villagers figured that the arsonists had torched Bao's new house to express this anger.[76]

Actually, Bao Zhilong had used his power to assign building lots arbitrarily to villagers all through the collective period, and people who refused to give him gifts to secure a lot usually did not get one or received the worst lots in Da Fo.

---

[73] Bao Huayin, interview, September 16, 1993.
[74] I am indebted to John Gottman, "Why Marriages Succeed or Fail," for the conceptual underpinnings of this point.
[75] Bao Zuoming, interview, July 26, 2006.
[76] Ibid.

Consequently, there were heated disputes in Da Fo over building lots all through the Mao years, and many poor farmers, like Bao Jinguang, hated Bao Zhilong for his corrupt work style.[77] Thus, the graft that began in the collective era continued into the reform era, mutating into nakedly money-based corruption, for in the latter period Bao Zhilong and his clients began selling the lots to different buyers on different terms. There was no fair play in the process. Some people received lots right away, whereas others had to wait and wait; some were sold big pieces of land, whereas others got smaller ones for the same price; and some – the friends and favorites of Bao and his men – paid less than one hundred *yuan* per lot, whereas others had to pay three hundred *yuan*. This reassignment process only reminded many villagers that Da Fo's power holders were determined to serve their favored clients first and had little, if any, sense of duty to serve those who were marginal to party-based community – as had been the case in the Great Leap Forward.[78]

In the reform era, villagers attempted to engage Bao Zhilong and the Da Fo party leaders in a conversation focused on access to Da Fo's grain storehouse. In 1967, during the second year of the Cultural Revolution, villagers had attempted to publicly debate the issue of who was to have a key to the grain storehouse. The consequences of the lack of public oversight of the granary during the Great Leap were fresh in popular memory – Bao Zhilong and his followers held the keys, which enabled them to acquire grain for personal consumption while others starved. In the post–Great Leap decade, therefore, the Da Fo party secretary was required to make two keys to the storehouse lock, one of which was to be placed in the hands of a representative chosen by ten production team leaders in a public meeting. Subsequently, throughout the 1970s, this representative slept in the grain storehouse every night, so that the party secretary and his cronies could not gain entry to the storage grain without public knowledge. This "sleep-in" practice was aimed at creating oversight and accountability and was intended to inhibit party leaders from skimming public grain – a practice that had contributed to the food inequities in the Great Leap. This oversight practice was discontinued in the 1980s, when the collective was disbanded and everyone began storing grain in private households. But between 1985 and 1990, Bao Zhilong and the subsequent Da Fo party secretaries stored collected tax grain in their homes, as if this public grain were their private property. Many villagers, including Pang Youqing, the Da Fo deputy party secretary, were upset that the township leaders allowed Bao Zhilong and his men to dismantle the post–Great Leap check on party corruption in this way. But, as in the Mao era, Bao and his clients refused to answer questions

[77] Bao Jinguang, interview, September 10, 1995.

[78] In constructing this argument, I have benefited from Xiaobo Lu, whose *Cadres and Corruption* brilliantly demonstrates that corruption in contemporary China is entwined with the historically embedded work style of local party leadership; from Heidenheimer, Johnston, and Levine, *Political Corruption*, 155–60; from Pei, "China's Governance Crisis," 107, and Pei, "Long March Against Graft"; and from Sun, *Corruption and Market*, 22–25, 160–71.

or respond to complaints about the use and disappearance of public stored grain. To villagers, Bao's lack of accessibility reflected a township-sanctioned adaptation of corrupt Mao-era methods to the Deng-led decentralization. Their anger over this practice was piled on to past hatreds of Bao's leadership style.

In short, the Great Leap was not the only factor that stoked anger and invited aggressive behavior toward Da Fo's party leaders. Reform and the way such leaders manipulated it also provoked anger and resistance. But the abuses of the Great Leap years invariably came to the forefront of villagers' memories when they responded to questions about why Bao Zhilong was targeted in the early 1990s, and virtually no villager linked the acts of arson solely or mainly to the reform-era behavior of secretary Bao and his party-based clients. Furthermore, as the above two examples suggest, many villagers linked the attacks on the households of the powerful to reform-era misdeeds that in fact were connected to some of the egregious injustices of Maoist dictatorship.

The goal of the resistance of the late 1980s and early 1990s was not simply revenge; it also worked to deny the party leaders of the past any role in contemporary political life. With the escalation of protest in the early 1990s, alienated and angry villagers focused on the office of the party secretary and his lackeys, aiming to drive unwanted leaders from the administrative space of the village and to exclude the morally repulsive agents of the state from the political terrain of Da Fo. We have already seen how the combined pressure of arson and physical attack by martial artists drove Bao Zhilong from power and made it difficult for his successor, Bao Wanqing, to operate as party secretary. The second attack came on Bao Yibin and was aimed at denying him any role in local political decision making. It started with Bao's attempted comeback as a reformist party leader in 1992 and escalated until he was publicly disgraced in 1994. In the early 1990s, when Bao Wanqing proved inept at managing public affairs, the newly appointed Da Fo party secretary, Bao Xueliang, reinstated Bao Yibin as vice–party secretary, so that Bao would help complete the division of village lands to households and assist party leaders with taxation; Bao Yibin subsequently became an important village party leader again, because Bao Xueliang, like Bao Wanqing, did not know how to carry out the land reform directive issued by Liangmen township. At the time, there was a consensus among party branch members (and many villagers, including some of Bao Yibin's detractors) that the land division had stalled and that Bao Yibin had the ability to accelerate it. Most villagers hated Bao Yibin. Still, nearly all were objective when it came to judging his ability: as far as knowledge of household land boundaries, negotiation of conflicts between production teams, and ensuring that the division was not totally dictated by Liangmen township leaders was concerned, Bao Yibin was the logical choice to break the impasse of reform.

Although Bao took up the post of vice-secretary, the obstinate memory of his track record in enforcing the transcript of Maoist plunder and pain in the Great Leap and beyond remained. Few villagers would speak to him about anything, including the land division that was in their short-term material interest. In 1993 they launched a verbal counterattack against Bao, which combined elements of confrontation and confinement. Villagers often came to his house and challenged him to come out to face them, while hurling stones and cursing him. According to Zheng Tianbao,

Bao Yibin had to swallow his pride and stay in his house. Still, they threw stones into his courtyard and tried to break into his house, and they openly challenged him to come outside to fight like a brave man. Other villagers tried to stop the challengers. Yet Bao Yibin's enemies persisted for three days. Bao had to take the insults and keep quiet until his opponents calmed down. If Bao had come out, he would have been beaten, and it's very unlikely that he would have gotten justice from the village or township government.[79]

Bao Yibin began locking himself inside his house for extended periods. This impeded his ability to roam the village and build the support needed to implement reform, and it further damaged his reputation, branding him a political coward. He relinquished his position of vice-secretary in 1994.[80] Several years later, on the eve of the Chinese New Year, Bao Yibin was reminded of the danger of an attempted political comeback: someone poured gasoline on his household door and set fire to it. The entrance to Bao's household was burned down. Subsequently, he dared not venture out of his house, no matter who came to call on him.[81]

The increasingly open struggle against the old-guard Maoists took place on a linguistic front, too. In the Great Leap, the rules governing how emotions were released in public were dictated by party leaders and their lackeys, particularly Bao Zhigen, who was infamous for his tantrums and whistle blowing, angrily cursing those who did not comply with his commands to work harder in the collective fields. With the demise of the collective in the early 1980s, villagers cursed Bao in small circles of trusted friends. Bao Wending, whose mother had been beaten by Bao Zhigen for "stealing" green crops, openly cursed him in Da Fo's streets. On one occasion, when Bao Zhigen got into an argument with Bao Zuoming over use of the village storeroom, he lost his temper and tried to win the argument by verbal abuse. The argument spilled into public space, where Bao Zuoming told Bao Zhigen that this was no longer the time of the Great Leap Forward, that he was no longer afraid of him, and that he could no longer expect to frighten people into compliance by losing his temper. Caught off guard and embarrassed by this bold challenge, Bao Zhigen relented, publicly demonstrating that he no longer had the power to enforce the informal ad hoc orders of the party. By 2001, villagers had begun to stand up and openly challenge party leaders still influenced by the habits of Mao-era rule.[82]

---

[79] Zheng Tianbao, interview, May 10, 1994.

[80] Bao Jinguang, interview, September 10, 1995.

[81] Bao Hongwen, interview, July 11, 2000.

[82] Zheng Jintian, interview, June 22, 2001; Pang Guihua, interview, June 27, 2001. For the new literature on the emotion-driven struggles over public space among nondemocratic groups, see Aminzade and McAdam, "Emotions and Contentious Politics," 47–50.

In Da Fo, the struggle to dislodge the local party agents of the Great Leap was powered by a desire for righteous revenge, a tradition that the Chinese call *bao chou* and one that has deep roots in village China. Da Fo's political history suggests that this tradition was very strong. And indeed, this makes sense. Rural China, where there was no state-guided reconciliation after Mao's famine crime, is a place where this problem of revenge was prominent in popular memory into the reform era. As a result, one round of violence begat another round, even if the temporal distance between the two was three decades. The round of incendiary hostility against secretary Bao Zhilong and his clients in the early 1990s expressed justice-seeking revenge rooted ultimately in deeply held memories of the earlier round of brutality and violence against villagers by party-based zealots in the Great Leap era.[83]

For villagers, resistance was aimed at delivering this message: "We have not forgotten your complicity in the Great Leap atrocity. We have not fallen for your revised narrative of how to remember the famine. We have been waiting for a chance to voice our anger, and now you will hear us. We are going to remedy the indignity and ruin of the past, and there will be no legitimacy in the future without this remedy. We are going to include ourselves in making the political community of reform, and we will summon force to continuously separate you, the perpetrators of the terrible past, from our future."[84] The collective acts of Da Fo's protesters were not prescribed by post-Mao political authorities. They were unmistakably transgressive, for they were linked to the hidden episode of barely contained and forbidden resistance aimed at settling scores with, and escaping from, the party-based agents of Mao's Great Leap Forward Famine.

Challenging the right to rule the village of Bao Zhilong and the Communist Party leaders who still professed to be the agents of the upper government, the manifestation of this unofficial, righteous memory in transgressive protest activities in the early 1990s opened the door to an era of dangerous contention.[85] As I will show in a future volume, in Da Fo the contentious acts of arson, the confrontations of the martial artists, and the challenges of stone-throwing crowds during the early 1990s established the political latitude within which party leaders

---

[83] I am indebted to both Steven I. Levine and Susanne Weigelin-Schwiedrzik for helping me to develop this important point. Levine, personal correspondence, February 11, 2006; Weigelin-Schwiedrzik, personal correspondence, July 8, 2006. China's great literary figure Mo Yan is not the only astute writer to explain one round of violence as the result of an earlier episode. Also see Richard Madsen's essay on how poor villagers sought vengeance in the Cultural Revolution for past damage to their interests and how Mao's policies "incited" such revenge while attacking the norms that were necessary for constraining it. Madsen, "Politics of Revenge," esp. 189–90.

[84] Here I am building on the instincts and concepts of Mueller, "Memory and Power" and drawing from the wisdom of Robben, "How Traumatized Societies Remember," 8–11, and Feldman, "Punition, Retaliation," 7.

[85] I am indebted to McAdam, Tarrow, and Tilly for helping me achieve some conceptual clarity on this point. See *Dynamics of Contention*, 7–8.

could operate in the future and invited new acts of popular resistance that threatened to spread the rebellion from the village to the township, which replaced
the commune under Deng Xiaoping's leadership. The still-hated site of socialist
extremism, the Liangmen township government was seen as the arm of radical
innovation stemming back to the early 1960s and a threat to gains won through
resistance in the aftermath of the Great Leap disaster and the Cultural Revolution. Villagers were prepared to defy the attempts of its officials to impose their
version of the policy reforms of rulers in Beijing.

In short, in Da Fo, as in many other rural Chinese villages, the reform era saw
new hatreds piled on the old memories of the Great Leap catastrophe. To be
sure, the new issues and grievances were not always the same as the old ones, and
indeed the new ones often had as much salience as those with roots in the radical
Maoist past. But in Da Fo, the new ones occasionally dialed up the past; as a result
even as villagers bid farewell to Mao's hunger, the deeply etched memories of his
radical Great Leap experiment with their lives continued to influence the ways
in which they received and responded to reform. Even as reformers in Beijing
attempted to put the Maoist past behind the Chinese people, the greatest crime
of that past was still present in the lives of those who had survived the famine
and memories of it, particularly of its break with long-accepted rules of humane
and just governance, sometimes informed resistance and contention.

Conclusion

So what does this case study of Da Fo village allow us to conclude about rural China, and on what matters is it merely suggestive? To be sure, we cannot generalize from such a microlevel case study to all of macrolevel China. Nonetheless, it is possible to offer some tentative reflections about the extent to which Da Fo's history does or does not resonate with the lessons we have learned from leading China scholars about how other parts of rural China were ruled in the Great Leap period, what caused the Great Leap famine, how memories of the Great Leap–era wreckage affected state legitimacy in the immediate and long-term aftermath of the famine, and whether the memories of this episode of Mao-era rule influenced the upsurge of resistance against the perpetrators of the famine in the post-Mao period.

As many top-rank China scholars have concluded, the Great Leap Forward was the product of Mao's determination to rapidly transform China's economy and society and build up a strong socialist state by relying on a disciplined Leninist party. The result was a leftist political frenzy that enveloped villagers in a great famine. Da Fo's political history clearly reveals that entrenched local party cadres willingly aided Mao in his war against the civil and social rights of rural dwellers. Still, it also reaffirms that Mao was the major causal agent of the Great Leap calamity – not the local party cadres who were blamed and scapegoated by Mao and allies at the center of the party. If the Great Leap Forward was a mistake of leftism, it was China's ultra-leftist emperor, Mao Zedong, who was mainly responsible for relentlessly pushing leftism to a point at which it engendered a systematic assault on the time-honored survival strategies of village people.

The oral history of Da Fo also teaches us that the rural people of this village, at least, see the socialist polity through their lasting memories of the ruin delivered by Mao Zedong and his willing accomplices during the Great Leap Forward and the famine that accompanied it. The Communist Party exercised power during

the Great Leap in a manner that encouraged local party leaders to violate tradi
tional morality, engendering a disaster that persisted in what Robert Goodfellov
calls the "durational memory" of famine survivors.[1] This absolutely ruinous pas
framed the way in which villagers received and related to socialist power holder
who sought to manage and manipulate the post-famine chaos and the order o
post-Mao reform, complicating and hindering the efforts of China's socialist stat
to reestablish its legitimacy with rural people in the short-term aftermath of th
famine. Naturally, in the 1960s the broken trust of the Great Leap was fresh i
the minds of Da Fo's farmers, and their post-famine resistance was structure
by memories of a communist polity in which both the policy mistakes of centra
government leaders and the conduct of local party cadres fostered hunger, aban
donment, and death. The evidence from this village indicates that rural people di
not trust that the state had any strategy to relieve the famine, which is why the
took matters into their own hands and proved reluctant to accept at face value th
household responsibility system of the Liu-Deng reformers. Though certainl
an improvement over Mao's all-out plunder, such a system was not the key t
escaping famine. It only aided an ongoing escape based on desperate strategie
of secretly eating the crops of the collective before the party-state could spiri
them off to the commune and of covertly taking back private sweet potato lands
and, in the end, it did little more than promote a silent truce between state an
society – a truce that did not fully settle the question of who had first claim t
the harvest to the satisfaction of farmers.

In Da Fo, the memories of Great Leap–era mistreatment by local party leader
and their vigilante networks directed and cued resistance against the agents of th
famine well into the post-Mao period; as a result the demise of the Communis
Party's power and authority locally was not just the product of the central gov
ernment's policies of decollectivization and the rapid shift of economic resource
from the state to rural society via the market.[2] Rather, politics and history i
contemporary China are more complex: the voices of Da Fo villagers tell us tha
during the Great Leap, the Maoists institutionalized forms of structural coercio
and corruption that ruined villagers and left a legacy of bitter memories as we
as an arsenal of weapons of coping and resistance that survived through variou
previously hidden processes of transmission.[3] The rise of collective resistanc
and protest over local government misconduct in the reform era cannot be sep
arated from this larger, long-term political legacy of institutional caprice an
decay. Thus, in an important sense, central government attempts to revive th
unreformed, pathological institutions of socialist rule are likely to arouse popu
lar fears about the restoration of autocratic party rule and thus stoke even mor

---

[1] Goodfellow, "Forgetting What It Was," 42.
[2] For this view, see Pei, *From Reform to Revolution*, 207.
[3] I am indebted to Steven I. Levine for helping me to better grasp this point. Personal correspondenc
   January 31, 2003.

profound and widespread resistance.[4] This study reveals that such fears are sustained in part by memories of the systematic degradation rural people suffered at the hands of ruthless local cadres and their autocratic party superiors during the Great Leap and its famine, a traumatic political experience that taught villagers to equate the agents of the state with deceit, viciousness, and grave danger.[5] As we will learn in the sequel to this volume, resistance to the way in which local party leaders have managed reform in Da Fo since the 1990s has been significantly driven by such fears, which, in combination with the persistent lack of institutional arrangements for the adequate expression and redress of social grievances,[6] sustain the enduring governance crisis of the regime even half a century after the catastrophe of Maoist rule.

In concluding this project, on which I have spent two decades, I now want to turn to some of its specific findings and draw out the broader issues at stake in this investigation of the political history of Da Fo village. I believe that these issues go to the heart of whether a China that has opened itself to the world is a stable or unstable country and whether the Leninist ruling group will be able to hold on to state power and survive the impact on its rural subjects of its great leap into the capitalist world order – a question that the next volume will address in some detail. Let us begin with the origins of war communism.

War Communism and Lumpen Leadership

Tragically, the war communism that defined Mao's Great Leap Forward was driven not only by Mao's penchant for radical transformation but also by the violently anti-democratic habits of his party's local political base. In Da Fo, pre-1949 predatory banditry, brutal Japanese occupation, and zero-sum civil war gave birth to a bellicose and brutal home guard militia. The self-styled heroes of the Communist-sponsored resistance increasingly equated revolutionary citizenship with membership in their murderous network. Mao's reliance on such vigilante militias further bolstered their power and enhanced their political status locally, more or less exempting them from adhering to the non-exploitative, non-coercive rules governing regular army relations with rural dwellers.[7] The political work

Compare with Minxin Pei's brilliant analysis in "China's Governance Crisis," 96–109. Pei does not focus on the Great Leap era and its heritage, but his essay lends support for such a hypothesis.
This point also finds support in the seminal ethnography of Mueggler. See *Age of Wild Ghosts*, 2–8, ch. 6. On the promise of Ethan Michelson's brilliant use of survey research methodology and historical evidence, see his "Deprivation, Discontent, and Disobedience." On the fear of openly expressing this understanding of the state, see Pocha, "Huge Dam Costly to Farmers," *Boston Globe*, A1, December 25, 2006.
On this point, which also underscores popular fears of state interference and the possibility of such fears being directed against the CCP, see Whyte, "Chinese Social Trends," 148–49.
I am much indebted to Elizabeth J. Perry's insightful comparative scholarship on militias for making me think harder about this point. See *Patrolling the Revolution*, 321–25. Whereas Perry says that the wartime militias were combined with the CCP-led regular army in the 1940s and 1950s, she also

style that evolved among the men who became Da Fo's Communist Party leaders was, in essence, the product of an addictive counter-violence that was necessary for surviving the years of war, occupation, and bloodshed. In this part of rural China, the key unspoken lessons internalized by the Communist-sponsored militia in the course of embracing Maoist insurgency were profoundly simple: force trumped reason, and war and politics were synonymous. When combined, they justified the repression and killing of opponents.

Whereas official CCP historiography more or less separates the violence of the wartime period from the factors mediating and facilitating the establishment and development of rural governance in the PRC, villagers articulate a different memory. To them, the violent state transgression of elementary civil dignities and democratic rights (including a minimal voice in decisions impacting guarantees of protection against search and seizure, assurances of due process, and security from arbitrary violence to personhood and property) in the years building to and culminating in the Great Leap catastrophe had roots in the toxic work style of the pre-1949 revolutionary process, conditioning the way in which Da Fo's Maoists treated ordinary tillers for decades thereafter.

To be sure, during most of the Republican era, and especially in the early phase of Communist Party development, the Da Fo militia tended to support the independent household production initiatives of farmers imperiled by the reach of the Kuomintang revenue state, as well as the local village system of democratic self-governance that had been corrupted in the Nationalist period. In popular memory, the Mao-commanded insurgency was supposed to rescue rural dwellers from threats to this ideal political life.[8] But Mao's failure to rein in the power and prerogatives of home-grown militia actors proved disastrous. We have seen that villagers remember a pre-1949 land redistribution process that became a pretext for militia aggrandizement, and we have also seen that the militia-based leadership received the lion's share of state-derived subsidies for cooperative development in the first years of socialist collectivization. Above all, villagers remember that the monopoly power of the CCP allowed the young vigilantes who had taken over the party branch to silence and punish challenges to their corruption, which were interpreted as a denial of the sacrifices that entitled them to the spoils of revolutionary war. The newly empowered militia leaders conceived of such repression as a rational defense of a revolutionary epoch that justified – indeed mandated – the violent suppression of the enemies of a Mao-led national revival that would include the poorest of the rural poor. In this

notes that the PLA "was never able to exercise unquestioned command over the militias" (321). Perry's work focuses mainly on urban-based worker militias, but her point seems to hold for Da Fo as well, and it might be fruitful for someone to conduct a systematic investigation of whether rural-based "peasant militias" operated with the same kind of semi-autonomous impulses that Perry has documented for the urban militias in China's post-1949 era.

[8] See Thaxton, *Salt of the Earth*, chs. 7–9 and conclusion.

Conclusion

political context, the cadre-spawned corruption of the Great Leap was both path-dependent and deadly.[9]

Ironically, Da Fo's history teaches us that many of the poor wartime militia leaders became the new political overlords of the peasantry. In a seminal study, Franz Schurmann conceived the Chinese Communist Party as the functional equivalent of the landed gentry elite.[10] The status of this elite, he maintained, was based on its adherence to Confucian principles that enabled it to mediate conflicts between state and rural society. The Schurmann argument is predicated on the assumption that Liu Shaoqi and enlightened Communist Party moderates effectively curtailed the terror of the 1947 land reform, thereby placing party-based controls on the process of arousing the poor to facilitate the replacement of the old elite;[11] however, Da Fo's farmers hold a different memory. The actors who engineered the violent replacement of Da Fo's Republican-era landholding elite were poor semi-peasants, and they were by no means the functional equivalent of the former gentry. Villagers remember them as poorly endowed, uneducated, quick-tempered, perfidious hustlers and ruffians who more often than not operated in an arbitrary and brutal political manner in the name of the Communist Party. These marginalized people had not been schooled in the arts of enlightened, benevolent governance by Da Fo's Republican-era landholding elite – and they certainly were not the equivalent of a new elite.

The voices of Da Fo's Great Leap famine survivors leave no doubt that it was such undesirables who willingly facilitated the Maoist effort to dismantle China's system of private household proprietorship and to destroy the practices and institutions that historically made for mutual discourse between educated village elites and state officials – a discourse that enhanced the possibility of some measure of village self-rule and political stability. The structural replication of militant local party-cum-militia leaders as the "landlords" they had destroyed was the result of Mao's decision to pursue a course of war-directed state development that destroyed local self-governance and that depended on "people's militias." The militia was a repressive institution, and Mao needed it to repress the countless rural dwellers who were resisting disentitlement by the agents of the people's commune.[12] Da Fo's farmers remind us that the marginal and militant village-level agents of Communist revolution enthusiastically helped Mao steer the revolution down the path of the "yellow bomb road," enforcing the Communist Party's simplification of agricultural production, its regimentation of village work life, its monopolization of food supply, and ultimately its repression of

---

[9] On the institutional basis of path dependency, see North, *Institutions*, vii, 59, 78–84, and Dugger, "Douglass C. North's New Institutionalism," 453–58.

[10] Schurmann, *Ideology and Organization*, 8–11.

[11] Ibid., 434–37.

[12] Schurmann calls Mao a "prime mover" in mobilizing militia elements to enforce his Great Leap transcript. See ibid., 571.

popular resistance to runaway appropriation. In Da Fo, this decision soured the party's relationship with farm households in the years building to the Great Leap and ultimately ushered in the calamity of the Great Leap itself.

How this could have happened in Da Fo, with its rich and proud heritage of relatively united and successful resistance to unjust state intrusions, remains a mystery. Perhaps a partial answer lies in the scholarship of Qin Hui, who has found that China's affluent farmers invariably were the ones who started rebellions against high-and-mighty state intruders.[13] This was Da Fo's modern history too. The young returned students who started the Communist Party branch in this village during the Anti-Japanese War were the educated and enlightened offspring of affluent farmers. But under the pressures of invasion and war, many of them made an early exit from the political stage, and Communist Party success in the revolutionary Civil War pulled their counterparts out of the village to serve in new, urban-based state hierarchies. Thus, in the end, Da Fo's elite relinquished leadership of its party branch to the poor, capricious, militia-based fringe elements.[14]

There was more than the heritage of war at work, however. The post-1949 Maoist inclusion of these quasi-*lumpen* fighters into village-level governance and the Mao-led Communist Party's pressure to replace the affluent, educated, and conservative village leaders (including the small gentry, lineage heads, and smallholders) who traditionally had brokered the claims of the state on behalf of honest and hardworking farmers with these base and fierce elements[15] opened the door to the possibility that they would turn Mao's plan for rushed economic development and state aggrandizement into a disaster. It is important to once again emphasize, as Da Fo's history illustrates, that the previously marginalized men who took over important village-level party and militia posts were not centered in the universe of popular Confucian reason, so, as Lu Huilin points out, their elevation to positions of leadership effected a profoundly radical transformation in the structure of basic rural governance.[16] These men were practically the perfect candidates to tear apart civil society and destroy human purpose: this study indicates they had a lot in common with the Khmer Rouge in Cambodia, with Ceausescu's militias in Transylvania, and with the Janjaweed in the Darfur region of Sudan. In rural China of the late 1950s, as in these other killing field environments, such men were backed by state power. Thus this book's findings resonate with Franz Schurmann's discovery that, in Henan during the Great Leap, the

---

[13] Qin Hui, *Pastorals and Rhapsodies*, 5.

[14] On militias as "wayward" institutions with their own impulses, see Perry, *Patrolling the Revolution*, 184.

[15] On this point, see Lu Huilin's "Weixing Shi Ruhe de Shang Tiande," 3–5. Lu advances this point by consulting the reliable studies of Fei Xiaotong, Sidney D. Gamble, and Prasenjit Duara, all of whom are astute observers of rural China.

[16] Ibid., 3–7. Lu's work recognizes that it was Mao's push against the conservative rural people who were reluctant to endorse collectivization that brought the "poor peasants" into the policy implementation process at the millet-roots level in the years building to and spanning the Great Leap Forward.

militias, whose leaders were composed of low-life characters who had no respect for the rule of law, "were bitterly hated by large elements of the population."[17]

Surely the everyday repression of the Great Leap era – and hence the reluctance of conservative and increasingly disempowered farmers to rebel openly – could not have occurred had not Mao and his provincial clients allowed, if not encouraged, such violent and base semi-*lumpen* elements to act with impunity against the village-level enemies of a collectivization experiment designed to serve the Leninist state hierarchy and its urban-dwelling constituency, and surely the famine's death rate would not have been so high without such repression. Actually, it was Mao who, at the outset of the Great Leap Forward, advanced the notion that the militia was *the armed force of all the people* (*quanmin wuzhuang*) and the basic organizational template of the big commune.[18] The militia therefore was to play a critical role in helping the Great Leap to achieve liftoff, and Mao celebrated it as the industrial army of the socialist state and the nation. Thus he more or less authorized its young and war-hardened members to move smallholders into large-scale agricultural production, which was fundamentally incompatible with the routines of rooted tillers and the highly personal and humane tradition of village-centered political discourse and governance. It was this Maoist ideological exultation, along with his party's break with popular elite-based village governance, that gave such youthful zealots license to rule villagers with arbitrary brutality and that cast the die for the killer famine of the Great Leap Forward – and, one might add, transformed the militia into a competitor for power with the PLA and set the stage for the militia violence in the post–Great Leap–cum–Cultural Revolution period.[19]

The Repression and Theft of Entitlement

The way in which Da Fo's famine survivors remember the causality of the Great Leap Forward and the famine that followed it is at odds with PRC state efforts to create an "official memory" of these events. Whereas the party's 1981 "Resolution on Some Questions Concerning the History of the Party since the Establishment of the PRC," published in *People's Daily*, attributed the famine to climatic downswings, the loss of Soviet aid, and the usurpation of central party policies by leftist cadres in the countryside,[20] these conditions are downplayed or missing in the

[17] Schurmann, *Ideology and Organization*, 567. For confirmation of Schurmann's argument, see Jia Yanmin, *Dayuejin Shiqi Xiangcun Zhengzhide Dianxing*, 224–28.

[18] Wang Yanni, "Cong Macheng Kan Gongshihua de ABC," 24–27.

[19] On the militia as a competitor with the PLA, see Schurmann, *Ideology and Organization*, 568, and for further evidence of internal PLA opposition to Mao's Great Leap policies, see Mao, *Jianguo Yilai Mao Zedong Wengao*, 8:342–43. On militia violence in the 1960s and the Cultural Revolution, see Friedman, Pickowicz, and Selden, *Revolution, Resistance, and Reform*, 137–50.

[20] "Guanyu Jianguo Yilian Dang de Ruogan Lishi Wenti de Jueyi" (Resolution on Some Questions Concerning the History of the Party since the Establishment of the People's Republic of China), *Renmin Ribao* (People's Daily), July 1, 1981.

memories of Da Fo farmers who survived the Great Leap famine. They focus on two other powerful causal factors: the systematic repression of long-accepted, legal, family-centered food acquisition endeavors and the systematic corruption of the socialist political institutions designed to shift food acquisition from private household production and private market exchange to acquisition through collective entitlement.

As Edward Friedman, Paul G. Pickowicz, and Mark Selden have demonstrated in *Chinese Village, Socialist State*, the Great Leap Forward was precipitated by Mao's warlike attack on the peasant household economy, for Mao believed that the success of socialist collectivization depended on the destruction of the ability of tillers to secure food through habits that legitimated a long-standing pattern of minimalist state intervention in rural life.[21] The war communism of the Great Leap was a war against the private landownership and land use rights villagers had attempted to reaffirm in the land redistribution of the late 1940s. In speaking of the assaults of this war, Da Fo's famine survivors – particularly those without party affiliation – remember the starvation of the Great Leap as a product of the party's comprehensive attempt to dispossess them of their customary right to exercise power over the acquisition of food. This is why they are still burdened by recollections of the party's invasions of their private household food supplies in the anti–grain concealment campaign of late 1959 and early 1960 and recollections of the party's assaults on their dignity and bodies in the intensifying public criticism sessions of the same terrifying period.

Their spoken memories tell us that acute starvation was not the result of a poor harvest, missing Soviet aid, or a cadre's leftist bent pure and simple, but rather the result of the Communist Party's relentless use of coercion to stop them from pursuing their own household strategies of acquiring food. If this popular memory is valid, then, drawing on the wisdom of Amartya Sen, the Great Leap famine might be more accurately conceived of as a famine caused by malevolent political disentitlement[22] imposed by Mao and his local party loyalists. Of course, the suffering and ruin of farmers and their families that resulted was by and large left out of official political discourse,[23] so that those who were humiliated, beaten, and tortured for insisting on their basic right to survival were discouraged from seeing their political disentitlement as Mao's famine crime. This study of Da Fo, however, shows that the famine of the Great Leap Forward belonged to the state-driven campaign of the Great Leap and that the two events were not separate.

As the voices of villagers also indicate, the corruption of the Communist Party itself, particularly its institutionally conceived mechanisms of food supply, further

---

[21] Friedman, Pickowicz, and Selden, *Chinese Village*, 227.
[22] See Sen, *Poverty and Famines*, chs. 4–5, esp. 39–41, 45–47.
[23] Wemheuer, "Regime Change of Memories," 13.

contributed to the hunger, starvation, and death of the Great Leap period.[24] In mapping what Sen might refer to as the shift from private to public food supply,[25] Mao and his party-based clients failed to create transparent, democratic checks on the proclivities of local party leaders to use their political connections to generate food privileges for their family networks; as a result, the public dining hall system in particular became an instrument of cadre privilege and a weapon of cadre power. The farmers who were not part of the ruling party network were not so fortunate. The amount of food that the commune provided most of them actually declined over the course of the Great Leap, hitting a mark below the original promise of subsistence, which was itself below the level of customary food entitlement. This decline was associated significantly with the relentless pressure of Maoist procurement, but it was also caused by local party leaders who distorted the transfer and distribution of food to villagers by stealing. In combination with the repressive crackdown on private landownership and private market exchange, party leaders' corruption subjected villagers to a sudden, two-dimensional entitlement failure that made the famine of the Great Leap a "double-barreled" famine, that is, a famine that struck *both* the private and public food entitlements of rural people simultaneously. Da Fo's history gives us reason to conclude that this duality most likely explains why the Great Leap famine was so uniquely frightening and lethal.

The voices of its survivors also nudge us to reconsider whether the Great Leap famine was in fact a "tragedy of good intentions." If this was a double-barreled famine, both barrels were loaded by the same regime. Not only this: the famine associated with the failed promise of collective entitlement – that is, the public commune–sector famine on which most Western scholarship associated with the "good intentions" thesis has focused – was actually the second consequence of an institutionally designed mobilization process that aimed to build state power at the expense of rural dwellers. It is a mistake to misidentify this second-barrel effect as a Mao-conceived good policy gone wrong. Such a conception ignores, and indeed obliterates, the previously existing party-state-driven assault on private household entitlement that began in the early 1950s and culminated in the Great Leap infliction of the first-barrel famine of the household farm – a malevolent state-ordered dispossession that left farm households with little choice but to turn to the people's commune for subsistence entitlement. The important point is that without the previous sequence of Maoist state–engendered dispossession, villagers would not have been so nakedly vulnerable to the collapse of public entitlement under the people's commune. To argue otherwise is to obscure the

---

[24] The CCP subsequently failed to resolve this institutional problem with its rural political base, so that it persisted into the post-Mao period with still harmful but less deadly consequences. Compare with Lu, *Cadres and Corruption*, and Sun, *Corruption and Market*, 9–11, 21–22, 168–71, 184–85.

[25] Sen, *Poverty and Famines*, 49–50.

principal cause of the Great Leap famine and to confuse the political sequence that entrapped farm households in the vice of Great Leap collectivity in the first place. There was only one principal cause: Mao's anti-democratic politics. But there were two effects, and the second, which was the collapse of the public food base of the commons, represented the final stage in a process that involved the party-state putting farm families at high risk and then pushing them along a path toward socialist colonization, subhuman forms of labor, and starvation.

Resistance, Memory, and Communist Party Legitimacy

For a long time, the received wisdom among most China scholars was that there was no resistance during the Great Leap Forward – supposedly, popular challenges to Mao's communal polity "disappeared" after 1957.[26] The phenomenon of Great Leap resistance was of course politically sensitive and difficult to discern. The Communist Party represented its organization as the champion of mass resistance in the pre-1949 period, and the CCP derived its authority and legitimacy in part from its claim to have transformed resistance into revolutionary victory. So who could speak of resistance to Mao's post-1949 plan for China's leap into the modern world? Yet this study illustrates that the resistance to unified purchase and sale and to advanced collectivization, which Mao and his men anticipated[27] and which formed in response to Mao's determined pursuit of the yellow bomb road in the mid-1950s, welled up again in the Great Leap Forward. Apparently, in Da Fo this resistance was a response to the double-barreled disentitlement famine to which the Maoists introduced the farmers whom they had already impoverished.

To be sure, a lot of the everyday resistance to state disentitlement that formed early in the Great Leap Forward, be it foot-dragging, concealment of harvested grain, pursuit of the black market, or clandestine migration, was what Michael Adas calls "avoidance protest."[28] In Da Fo, this resistance was taken up to avoid the socially devastating consequences of disentitlement. Those who engaged in it seldom viewed their actions as radically contentious; they were merely trying to survive and to keep the Maoist state threat to survival at bay. Nonetheless, two points jump out of the memories Da Fo villagers hold of their Great Leap–era resistance. First, resistance was not prompted by Maoist-style mass campaigns that called for rural people to participate in "class struggle." It was neither encouraged nor justified by Maoist state policy and official party-guided political discourse.[29] Second, looking at Da Fo through the historical memory of

---

[26] Li, "From Righteous to Rightful: Peasant Resistance to Agricultural Collectivization in China in the 1950s," 36. On this point, also see Lu Huilin, "Weixing Shi Ruhe de Shang Tiande," 6.

[27] Bo Yibo, *Ruogan Zhongda Juece Yu Shijian de Huigu*, 271–72.

[28] Adas, "From Avoidance to Confrontation."

[29] In other words, this resistance cannot be explained by the policy-based resistance paradigm to be found in O'Brien and Li's powerful book, *Rightful Resistance in Rural China*, xi–14.

Conclusion

ts famine survivors, we can see that their resistance reflected an enduring tradition of righteous opposition to state tyranny.[30] That is, the resistance was aimed at preserving the core "righteous governance" precepts of popular Mencian and Confucian thought.[31] These precepts legitimated a "just rebellion" against rulers who exercised state power to brazenly violate the wisdom of the adage *guo yi min wei ben, min yi shi wei tian*, which in popular thought translates, "The people are the foundation of the country, and food is the people's Heaven."[32] Most likely, such low-profile resistance frequently preceded and became entwined with the outbreak of rebellion in rural China; I suspect it was the long-hidden fuse to the explosion of more visible challenges to tyrannical imperial power. The Great Leap Forward seems to have posed a serious threat to rural China's long-standing tradition of righteous governance. The Maoist penetration of village society, along with the destruction of its autonomous, elite-backed system of articulating popular grievances to government officials through deferential politics and petitions, made it increasingly difficult, if not impossible, for Da Fo's farmers to defend their social entitlements by resistance within the bounds of Maoist-style mass campaigns and mass criticism, which were designed to monitor, report, and crush the independent pursuit of household entitlement outside of the collective and to deny the right of tillers to withdraw from the people's commune.

Clearly, the Maoist threat to long-standing household entitlements alienated villagers and prompted them to disengage from the party's experiment with collectivization. Even so, the political history of Da Fo cautions that villagers initially were reluctant to turn to outright resistance – not to mention contention. It was the Mao-led CCP's repressive response to quotidian efforts to evade its damaging reach that turned villagers toward resistance, and it was the revved-up repression of this "everyday resistance" that turned it into an episode of contention at the height of Mao's Great Leap. At the center of this contention was a struggle to resist starvation – a struggle that was articulated as righteous resistance. Whereas some have argued that the center's slow response to the social crisis of 1960 had something to do with bottled-up channels of communication between city and countryside, this study reveals that Mao's mass line dictatorship actually was intended to stifle and conceal righteous resistance to his party-based accomplices, and that the party activists in command of public criticism used food as a weapon to discourage, disaggregate, and wipe out such resistance. Surely, therefore, it was this draconian modality of rule that activated a popular oral tradition in which party-inflicted disaster would be transmitted as the act of bad rulers who had lost the Mandate of Heaven. Such an interpretation resonates with the expression of

[30] Perry, "Challenging the Mandate," 164–65.
[31] On how Mencian political thought justified rebellion against unrighteous officials and the relationship of this concept to the Mandate of Heaven, see de Bary, introduction to de Bary and Tu, *Confucianism and Human Rights*, 8, 13, and 22.
[32] I am indebted to Andrea Janku's excellent paper for helping me develop this point. "Publicized Disasters," 6.

primal memory in Da Fo and in other rural villages where Mao's agents were dominant.[33]

Whatever success the Communist Party has enjoyed in exercising control over memory in the post–Great Leap famine era, the case of Da Fo shows that many rural people retain their own personal memories of how the disaster ended. For one thing, they tell us that there was a full-blown episode of collective resistance to the famine. At the center of this resistance was the unauthorized individual and community practice of *chi qing* (eating the premature crops of the collective), a last-ditch response that turned into a weapon of preemptive consumption used to combat the injustice of Mao's scheme to impose his version of administrative colonization on the countryside.[34] *Chi qing* proved to be the only weapon dispossessed farmers had left in a great famine that was, to appropriate a phrase from Mike Davis, a "war over the right to existence."[35]

It seems clear that denial of the freedom to move out of the orbit of Maoist dictatorship drove the desperate inhabitants of this rural Henan village to accentuate their only remaining weapon of preemption. Yet in their largely invisible undertaking, they had two advantages. One was geographical. A long way from the reach of the power of the provincial arm of the urban-based Maoist state, people in Da Fo, as in other remote villages, could use *chi qing* to exercise control over the harvest of the collective while also attacking Maoist procurement. The other advantage had to do with local political sociology. The fact that nearly all of Da Fo's party leaders were native village insiders and that some had risen within the administrative structure of the commune evidently allowed ordinary villagers to mobilize widespread emotional support for preemptive consumption from the ground-level agents of the party-state, thereby limiting regime violence against autonomous contention from below in the crisis moments of the famine.[36]

Of course, we need to revisit the question of precisely which particular activists proved less loyal to the Mao-led center. In the case of this village, we are not talking about the quasi-*lumpen* militia elements who became party leaders, but rather the local village leaders who were most susceptible to siding with tillers – the lower-tier production team leaders, not the party secretary and his closest allies. Surely they were less loyal to Mao and his communal polity because they and their families were starving, as they were at too low a level to be able to take advantage of the communal food distribution chain for their own households. Compared to them, the village party secretary and his allies were sitting well up the pyramid of sacrifice and were favored in the scramble for food supply, and these local power holders by and large stood with Mao and did the dirty work of his Great Leap. Nonetheless, when the Great Leap famine hit home and there

[33] Compare with Wemheuer, "Regime Change of Memories," 20–21.
[34] Compare with Scott, *Seeing Like a State*, 194–95.
[35] Davis, *Late Victorian Holocausts*, 13.
[36] In forming this interpretation, I have benefited from Sewell, "Space in Contentious Politics," 79–83, and also from McAdam, "Harmonizing the Voices," 224–25.

was less and less food to grab for their families, they too proved to be less than completely loyal to the Maoist center. Preemptive consumption could limit the famine's death toll in remote places where such local party big men were similarly able to provide protection to villagers.[37]

Although the work of Jasper Becker; of Edward Friedman, Paul G. Pickowicz, and Mark Selden; and of Dali Yang would suggest that the Great Leap famine was curtailed and ended by administrative intervention – and to some extent by resistance from below[38] – in fact it was the practice of preemptive consumption and the political circumstances that allowed it to mushroom, not official relief or reform, that saved the rural people of Da Fo from the starvation of the Great Leap famine. In popular memory, policy-driven relief and reform were insufficient to enable villagers to escape the famine. Given this situation, the Communist Party could not create an official narrative of how the Great Leap famine ended that resonated with the socialist state's promise to abolish poverty and prevent starvation, for the public sphere of China's recovering village society was flooded with popular counter-memories of self-generated salvation and extrication. Many Western-trained China scholars, as well as many of the shaken Chinese intellectual allies of the Communist Party center, have presumed that Beijing's rulers renegotiated an ambiguous legitimacy in the wake of the Great Leap. But deep in the countryside in remote, politically battered villages like Da Fo, it seems that the local party leaders were unable to manufacture an authenticating legitimacy for their superiors – which is why most studies of model villages, where the negative impact of Mao's war communism was comparatively muted, are not useful guides to understanding the unbridgeable chasm that had developed between the socialist state and rural society.[39] The unofficial memory of *chi qing* fostered popular skepticism about state legitimacy all through the post–Great Leap period, interdicting the socialist state's efforts to recover a political mandate based on any public record of collective food security. By failing to address the causality of the Great Leap famine and the badly politicized and flawed state effort to end it by administrative intervention, the Communist Party was unable to establish an anti-famine political contract with scarred famine survivors, perpetuating mistrust and further complicating the recovery of legitimacy.[40]

[37] See Scott, *Seeing Like a State*, 207.

[38] For my review of their positions, see Thaxton, "How Famines End," 11–12.

[39] And yet the brilliant scholarship of Friedman and his associates and of Bruce Gilley, both on model villages, indicates a pattern of party-based thug rule locally. Moreover, Friedman and his associates point out that the violence and harm delivered by this kind of regime most likely were greater in villages enjoying less state protection and patronage. Friedman, Pickowicz, and Selden, *Chinese Village*, 270, and *Revolution, Resistance, and Reform*, 148; Gilley, *Model Rebels*, 73–79, 145–49, 178.

[40] Building on the work of Charles Tilly, *Trust and Rule*, and John A. Hall's review of Tilly's book, the second volume of this study will show why and how villagers have attempted to rebuild their own trust networks locally through forms of contention, and it will shed light on how the Communist Party has further damaged the social trust of its own political network, partly by perpetuating its corrupt mode of rule and partly by attempting to corrupt and dismantle village-level contention, including the democratic electoral process through which villagers seek to place limits on party

The oral history evidence suggests that this was so, at least in Da Fo, because the lines of political accountability for famine relief aid were mainly between the center and local party operatives, not between the government and ordinary villagers. The state failed to place the acquisition, delivery, and distribution of food relief supplies under popular democratic supervision. Village party secretaries and their clients took over this process, and they made sure their families benefited first and foremost from it. In Da Fo, many of these actors were the same party-based activists whose lies about food crop yields, food availability, and food distribution to their privileged networks had exacerbated the state-engendered subsistence crisis of the Great Leap. Small wonder that rural people did not consider such local party leaders capable of providing the honest leadership that was a prerequisite to preventing, or fighting, food shortage and another famine. Neither Mao nor Liu nor any of the warring factions of the center ever corrected the corrupt and deceitful political habits of sub-county party leaders who had perpetuated the Great Leap's horrors.[41] In this context, Da Fo's farmers, and I suspect many of their counterparts in other Chinese villages, had little reason to trust that the reformist policies and reintegrative contractual production arrangements introduced by the socialist state to help ease the pressure of the Great Leap's hunger would not fail them again, subjecting them to severe economic hardship and leaving them to find their own way out of famine.

Popular attitudes toward the household responsibility system, then, reflect skepticism born of Great Leap deprivation and institutional failure. In the view of villagers, the household responsibility system was conceived by socialist rulers under great pressure to correct their miserable record of managing rural landownership and land use issues, and as a device of power this system was designed to contain the famine-ignited conflict over private land and harvest rights. Many of Da Fo's farmers saw the household responsibility system as the act of retrograde socialist rulers looking to reattach those who were disengaging from collectivization to a drawn-down contractual obligation to guarantee the state a portion of their harvest. Although some top-rank China scholars have seen the system as part of a process whereby the central government reduced its control over the countryside,[42] this reading is foreign to the memory of village people who had come to associate socialism with starvation and the agents of the party-state with the specter of death. What, they reasoned, was so beneficial about a contracting

corruption and coercion. It also will explain how this process, and the struggle it has spawned, is connected to popular memory of the party-state betrayal of society in the Great Leap and to a lingering, strong popular distrust of state power, as well as to the fear that in carrying out a state-guided, capitalist-oriented economic reform the party will abandon its commitment to the public, just as it did in carrying out its experiment with a communist economy in the Great Leap era.

[41] Again, the two outstanding sources on this failure to reform the corrupt work style of cadres are Lu, *Cadres and Corruption*, and Sun, *Corruption and Market*.

[42] See Zweig, *Freeing China's Farmers*; Unger, *Transformation of Rural China*; and Weigelin-Schwiedrzik, "Distance between State and Rural Society."

system that reintegrated them with a system of commune-based state power that had utterly failed them? They were intuitively skeptical of any program that required them to first meet quotas set by the party-state and then – and only then – allowed them to use the remaining portion of the harvested crop for family consumption. It seemed that socialist rulers were still bent on stabilizing the income of the state at tillers' expense, which is why Da Fo's farmers rejected this unrighteous official rigmarole and continued to rely on *chi qing* and private field sweet potato production to escape the Great Leap famine.

And, in fact, as Da Fo's farmers recollect, the Great Leap famine did not really end in 1961 or on October 1, 1962, the date when Beijing's rulers celebrated the end of the food supply crisis. In remote and agriculturally poor Da Fo, Mao's famine was just downgraded to a low-intensity, category-one famine that lasted across the decades building toward the Deng Xiaoping–led reform. In this period, Da Fo's farmers faced acutely embedded and exacerbated poverty, which they coped with by relying largely on the same inferior tuber crops that had saved them from starvation, a practice they did not give up until the late 1970s.[43] The prolonged reliance on starchy and problematic fallback foods provided evidence not only of the remains of Mao's Great Leap famine in their daily lives but also of the failure of the Liu-Deng reformers to effectively relieve the annual food shortages they faced in the agonizing years that followed – and, most significantly, of the continuing lack of an anti-famine contract with socialist power holders. I suspect that the state's failure to provide such a contract is one reason why Peter Ho has discovered that the pursuit of customary landownership continues to be an explosively charged issue in rural China[44] and why Vivienne Shue has found that China is characterized by great popular ambivalence about state legitimacy.[45]

In short, the way in which the Great Leap famine ended in Da Fo village did little to alleviate the deep legitimacy crisis produced by Communist Party–directed state taking. Anguished tillers rejected the household responsibility system because they thought it inadequate to resolving this crisis. What they wanted was a state guarantee against future starvation, but power holders in Da Fo and the party-state hierarchy were unwilling to provide it.

The Cultural Revolution and Its Link to the Great Leap Famine

Official representations of the Cultural Revolution often suggest a great radical break with history, with Mao as the innovative, life-giving protagonist of a China besieged by the darkness and oppression of an antiquated past. Yet the voices of Da Fo's past leave no doubt that there were important historical continuities

---

[43] The oral history data on Da Fo accord with Gao Hua's claim that the food problems of China's farmers were not resolved until 1980 and the early years of the Deng-led reform. See Gao Hua, "Da Ji Huang Zhong de 'Liangshi Shiyong,'" 80–81.

[44] Ho, "Contesting Rural Spaces," 93.

[45] Shue, "Legitimacy Crisis in China?" 43.

between the Cultural Revolution and the Great Leap Forward, and indeed the history of these two Mao-initiated movements seems to be intimately connected in the minds of many villagers. In both movements, the Maoists attempted to push collectivization by destroying private household entitlements to land and harvest; by shutting down private market trade; by containing dissent in the public sphere through Leninist-orchestrated, pseudo-democratic mass criticism meetings; and by subjecting innocents to torture and death. This book shows that beneath the Maoist propaganda of a great populist upsurge in support of the two movements, conservative farm people actually were struggling to recover social entitlements that had been taken away by party-based vigilantes. In the case of Da Fo, the argument for continuity is strong, for the people of this village took the Cultural Revolution as an opportunity to settle debts with the local party leaders who were responsible for the personal and family crises that had arisen out of the Great Leap famine, and, furthermore, to erect internal defenses against a repeat of the nightmare.

This is not to say there were no differences. For one thing, it appears from Da Fo's history that the Great Leap and its famine proved far more traumatic to village people than did the Cultural Revolution.[46] I am not prepared to make this argument for all of rural China, because the Cultural Revolution also unleashed terrifying violence against untold numbers of village as well as city dwellers and sometimes resulted in politically motivated mass killing in the countryside.[47] Nonetheless, in contrasting the two movements in Da Fo itself, we can see that the Great Leap initially was more or less forged in an atmosphere of Leninist-style political consensus, whereas the Cultural Revolution was motivated by Mao's power struggle against his colleagues in the center – politicians who had gone along with Mao's great policy mistake only to discover that it had produced a catastrophe of major scale for both their party and its rural constituency. The Great Leap–era damage inflicted on the Communist Party's political base in this particular village proved more serious than that of the Cultural Revolution, in part because the social disentitlement caused by the Great Leap famine was far more ruinous than that of the Cultural Revolution and in part because the Liu-Deng leadership could do nothing to aid the recovery dynamics of the wounded victims of the famine except to feebly endorse a strategy of "materializing the old wounds" with limited economic concessions.

The Great Leap famine's damage to Communist Party legitimacy was more serious for another reason: For China's socialist rulers to admit the "great policy

[46] In constructing this section, I have followed the wisdom of Wu Jieh-min, given to me in his critical reading of a draft of one of my research proposals on the Great Leap Forward and popular memory. Personal correspondence, August 1999.
[47] For some of the grisly details, see Pomfret, *Chinese Lessons*, 18–25. For a recent insightful work on the unknown history of the Cultural Revolution, see Esherick, Pickowicz, and Walder, *Chinese Cultural Revolution*, especially Yang Su, "Mass Killing in the Cultural Revolution," which deals with mass murder in the rural communes and brigades of three different provinces.

mistake" of the Great Leap famine would have eliminated the *raison d'être* of the Communist Party and encouraged a democratic explosion of politically incorrect memories that were fundamentally at odds with future party efforts to expand nationally authenticated socialist controls over rural society. The Cultural Revolution was a comparatively easier policy mistake for the Liu-Deng opponents of Mao's regime to admit, and so they had less trouble containing popular memories of the Cultural Revolution's harm and in reconciling with rural people for the Cultural Revolution than for the Great Leap and its famine.

The differences between the two state-orchestrated movements should not obfuscate the important political connections between them. The Cultural Revolution reflected Mao's attempt to create a hegemonic structure of deafness to memories of past violence at the hands of his socialist polity, particularly the callous violence of the cadres who had imposed his Great Leap transcript on village China. As Da Fo's history underscores, the memories of this violence and loss were still tightly wrapped around the hearts of villagers during the Cultural Revolution, which explains the period's fantastic potential for popular unrest, protest, and upheaval. Retaliatory collective actions could irrupt during this period, for the divided center was no longer able to exercise control over distant villages and its repressive apparatus was too engaged with its own internal divisions to crack down on resistance or to prevent indignant and aroused villagers from appropriating the mechanisms of public criticism and control. In this respect, the suppression of popular dissent was a far more difficult task for Mao's loyal cadres in the Cultural Revolution than it had been during the Great Leap episode. Why this was the case here and elsewhere in rural China requires further study. But surely, as this study of Da Fo shows, by the late 1960s, the villagers who had survived the holocaust of the Great Leap were less preoccupied with sheer physical survival and were less vulnerable to the political language and public rituals of the high Maoist regime, whose Great Leap track record of arbitrary rule and abandonment had destroyed its claim to revolutionary paternalism and legitimacy and underscored the awful price of passive acquiescence.

If the history of this small place is any guide to the history of village China under the Cultural Revolution – and, again, it may not be – then we are talking about a country that was a powder keg of frustrated popular desires for justice in the last years of Maoist rule. That is, judging from the history of this village, Mao's Cultural Revolution was also an effort to rationalize and anesthetize the effects of the Great Leap famine, to disempower popular cultural efforts to translate suffering and loss in the famine into popular Confucian terms that equated its terror with political monstrosity and that justified subjecting its perpetrators to retributive justice. Mao succeeded to the extent that this retributive process, which in Da Fo took the form of retaliatory protest, was cut short by factionalized party infighting and Red Guard ravages, but the memories of the Great Leap's wounding and the Cultural Revolution's incomplete efforts to settle scores with its Maoist agents lingered on, giving rise to resistance and contention under reform – a topic to be explored in detail in a future volume. For now, the important point is that the fuse of some of the resistance that would explode in the post-1978 reform period was ignited many decades earlier in the inhuman episode of the Great Leap war on society, that the true nature of this state-society conflict never found its way into official history, and that the failure of state-orchestrated memory campaigns to convince the famine's survivors that it actually was not the result of systemic political malice provided the emotional material for a renewed outburst of resistance when the repressive institutions of the Maoists disintegrated after 1978.

The Great Leap's Legacy and Reform

The legacy of the Great Leap Forward Famine is also intertwined with another major landmark of contemporary Chinese political history: economic reform. By the early twentieth century, small landholders active in market trade constituted the most significant social group of the petite bourgeoisie in the section of the North China Plain that was home to Da Fo. The Communists could not have won state power without the support of these people.[48] As we have seen, their aspirations for the unimpeded pursuit of market profit, no less than for family-governed, fertile private farmland, accounted for their unswerving commitment to the pre-1949 Maoist insurgency. How then do we explain why the party-state betrayed them? Of course the state's hostility to petit bourgeois smallholders and their market proclivities grew out of an ideological commitment to important aspects of the anti-capitalist principles of Marxist regimes elsewhere in the world. Mao, like Lenin, feared the persistent obstacle conservative independent tillers posed for a rapid transition to industrial capitalism and progress, and he shared Stalin's contempt for small, affluent farmers whose self-conceived capitalist exploits were at odds with socialist-planned agricultural collectivization, so apparently Mao was determined to go after the very small property holders he had previously counted on for support.[49]

Yet the oral history of Da Fo village sheds light on several other factors that made for this Maoist betrayal. The monopoly on power that the Communist Party achieved following the Civil War put the fiscal agencies of Mao's socialist order on a collision course with smallholders, who simply were not prepared to give up the very things that made them members of the petite bourgeoisie: private household landownership, highly specialized crop production, flexible self-determined work schedules, penny profits generated from innovative petty trade activities, and the use of savings for family survival, joy, and advancement.[50] If the people of Da Fo originally had reason to equate the Communist Party's purpose with their perpetual struggle to protect their household-generated farm

[48] Thaxton, *Salt of the Earth*, chs. 7–9 and conclusion.
[49] See Evans, "Accursed Problem," 73–76. Evans does not speak of Mao, but he spells out the rather consistent anti-peasant, anti-capitalist bent of socialist regimes.
[50] Scott, "Socialism and Small Property," 185–91.

Conclusion

products and market profits from the tributary impulses of the powerful,[51] this popular expectation was interpreted as an "accursed problem" by Mao and China's new socialist leaders in the early 1950s, when they sought to impose revenue claims on smallholding villages via collectivization. Frustrated by the successful efforts of small farmers to hold on to harvests for family needs first and to sell whatever portion they could of their food crops in free markets rather than to state bureaus and cooperatives, Mao redefined them as exploiters of an imaginary poor tilling population and declared their mobility incompatible with a socialist polity supportive of local social prosperity and national state wealth, and he then relied on the leaders of people's militias, whose party-based privileges attenuated their commitment to protect the market prerogatives of small farmers, to make them serve the collective first.

In addition, it seems that the pre-1949 Communist insurgency in Da Fo invigorated a simmering, long-term struggle between small-scale commodity producers and the state for market control, thereby validating the popular notion that market recovery was essential to sustaining a community-sanctioned mode of survival. In the early 1950s, the party faced a serious problem in pushing collectivization over market-based commodity exchange. Not only was the market inseparably linked with the day-to-day survival of these smallholders, many of them treasured it as an arena of autonomous political contention. It was here that independent entrepreneurship found collective political voice.[52] Clearly, in the case of Da Fo, the new Maoist state confronted a social community that was potentially in political competition with its efforts to seize the harvest and exert control over small farmers. I submit that this most likely was a key reason why Mao was so bent on rapidly moving villagers into the cellular structure of people's communes: this advanced form of state collectivization was intended to supplant and destroy the market as a mechanism of community empowerment and anti-state resistance. My guess is that this resistance was even more tenacious and widespread than is conveyed by this case study and that its tenacity in part explains why the Maoists chose to rely on vigilante militia elements to suppress it.

Bringing in the voices of the petty traders who weathered the massive socialist transgression of market entitlement, this study of Da Fo suggests that rural people found their way out of the Great Leap catastrophe in part by opening up market space in the interstices of the cellular economy of the people's communes, founding a "second economy." To be sure, the post-Mao reforms officially approved the revival of free markets in rural China. But official party historiography never acknowledged that this underground second economy was a social movement to which the rural poor were drawn in order to recuperate the power they had lost

---

[51] Compare with ibid., 193, and Thaxton, *Salt of the Earth*, chs. 7–9 and conclusion.
[52] Just as Skinner's work on rural periodic markets and the market as a source of community would anticipate. See "Marketing and Social Structure," 1:3–44, 2:195–228, and 3:366–99, and especially "Chinese Peasants," 270–81. See also Thaxton, *Salt of the Earth*, especially the conclusion.

during the Great Leap and its famine. The reason Deng spoke of the urgency of
reform was that the center understood that the petit bourgeois survivors of the
Maoist catastrophe were winning the inch-by-inch, day-in-and-day-out struggle
against the failed economy of the collective era, and the spillover effects of this
process signaled a rise in the autonomous power of courageous villagers to contest
the party's authoritarian hold locally, in Da Fo and elsewhere in rural China.[53] In
this situation, Deng had to take hold of this movement and use policy to celebrate
its material advantages while symbolically drowning out the memories that its
rank-and-file activists held of his party's attempt to cut them off from the market.

Reform and Revenge

By the early 1990s, the grain harvests of farmers in Da Fo were more than double
the best yields of the collective era. Furthermore, many had stored enough grain
in private household bins to get through a two-year-long food shortage: fears of
another killer famine died hard. So why did revenge-seeking political behavior
irrupt in the reform period, taking the form of violence against the victimizers
of tillers who had begun to benefit from the recovery dynamics of the Deng-led
reform? The new governance paradigm of the post-Mao state does not even recognize this as a relevant, let alone legitimate, question. Yet it goes to the heart
of the hidden legitimacy crisis in Da Fo and, one suspects, countless other poor
Chinese villages struck hard by the Great Leap famine. The spate of arson that
broke out in Da Fo in the early 1990s was a form of resistance to the traumatiz-
ing state-led mobilization characteristic of the high Maoist regime, which had a
lingering effect on the recovery process of the post-1978 economic reform.

Villagers took the linkage between the distant suffering of the Great Leap
famine and their desire for revenge in the reform era for granted: locally and
nationally, reform-era Communist Party leaders had done nothing to right the
wrongs of the Great Leap carnage, so revenge was, in an important sense, a
response to "justice gone awry."[54] They took revenge, in other words, as a natural
human response to the perceived institutional failure of the state to evolve a legal
system that could effectively address past abuses of power and assume the burden
of retribution for Mao's famine crime,[55] thereby fostering a reciprocal healing
process between state leaders and village people. Without this legal process in
place, the memory of the Great Leap's hurt focused popular urges to settle scores
with its perpetrators on pent-up fantasies of revenge, and local party leaders in
Da Fo were hard pressed to keep the infrapolitics of the post-Mao period from
irrupting in verbal profanity, physical altercations, arson, and other forms of

[53] Compare with Pei, *From Reform to Revolution*, 21. I have benefited from Pei here, though this is
not exactly his point.
[54] Bloom, "Commentary," 2.
[55] Ibid., 13, 17.

aggression.[56] The psychiatrist Sandra L. Bloom emphasizes that "When justice is not forthcoming from a higher authority, people will and do take justice into their own hands. Acts of vengeance are the result."[57] The memories of many of Da Fo's famine-battered farmers resonate with this logic.[58]

Of course with the passage of time, the villagers who best remembered the Great Leap's terrible injustices were getting older, and Da Fo had new leaders and younger denizens who were not as motivated by the trauma of the famine years to seek revenge against the old-guard Maoists. At the same time, however, as the center's reform engine stalled in the mid-1990s and as corrupt village party cadres with ties to the former Maoist vigilantes seized state reform programs to benefit their households, new claims against the party-state's abuses began to pile up. Some of these claims had their roots in the same poor, unreliable governance style that had contributed to the Great Leap's ruin, and this resented modality of cadre rule mobilized collective defiance and popular critiques of reform that were entwined with and energized by dangerous memories of past socialist state performance.

As far as the early 1990s were concerned, two factors fueled the tendency of villagers to exact "Heaven's revenge" by their own devices, each structured by the official culture of the Communist Party and its cadre base. The absence of a party-sanctioned apology to the victims of the Great Leap's violent excesses meant that no institutionalized process diminished the negative perception villagers held of the Great Leap's perpetrators. Thus, well into the period of arson, many of Da Fo's farmers were stuck in the damning memory they held of the party secretary refusing to redeem himself by apologizing for his unrighteous Great Leap behavior when his feet were held to the fire during the Anti–Five Winds Campaign and in the Cultural Revolution. An official campaign of apology led by Beijing was out of the question, largely because this would have constituted an admission of an inconceivably monstrous abuse of state power, but, by the same token, by not addressing the issue, the post-Mao leadership unwittingly invited the retaliatory protest that had exploded in the Cultural Revolution to gravitate to extra-institutional revenge against its unapologetic party base. It was no accident that the party actors and clients who were least prone to admit wrongdoing and ask forgiveness for their Great Leap malevolence in Da Fo became the major targets of arson.[59]

The failure of the CCP under Deng to engineer a democratic political reform also left intact the authoritarian political work style that had crystallized in the Great Leap era; as a result, all through the reform era villagers not only had to live side by side with the perpetrators of the Great Leap's abuses but also had

[56] For the conception, I am following Scott, *Domination and the Arts of Resistance*, 191.
[57] Bloom, "Commentary," 13.
[58] As does Scott's work, *Domination and the Arts of Resistance*, 191–93.
[59] Bloom, "Commentary," 1, 7–8.

to suffer the same kind of political misconduct that had led them into famine: the arbitrary, brutal, corrupt, and deceitful habits that had subjected villagers to labor servitude, physical attacks, food shortages and food inequities, and excessive procurement all remained part of the culture of the established party branch and its leadership.[60] The continuity of institutionally appointed local party leaders whose authoritarian style of governance was still aimed at capturing as much of society's resources as possible for themselves and their superiors smacked of a pattern of state behavior that, to use the words of Lu Xiaobo, "put the interests of the regime above those of more intimate secondary and primary groups."[61] Thus even in the reform period, many everyday encounters between villagers and Da Fo's powerful Communist Party leaders evoked bad memories of the cost of the political work style of Great Leap–era party leaders, and these memories were energized by the tendency of village party leaders to fall back on habits of humiliating, shaming, and bullying ordinary villagers in their efforts to realize the reform policies of the post-Mao center. In the sequel to this study, we will see how villagers launched individual and collective challenges to these habits and how such challenges were influenced by memories of misrule in the Great Leap era.

With no redemptive potential in the official CCP narrative or approach to the Great Leap's harm, rural people had to find a way to deal with the unspeakable past on their own empowering terms. The arson in Da Fo was thus more than revenge acts against the immediate and specific local party agents of the Great Leap. The volcanic blazes in the night sky, the anguished disbelief and hysterical cries of the haughty and dominant arson targets, and the charred outer walls of the homes of party leaders all offered material evidence of a story that villagers wanted to tell. It was a story that contested the national official memory of the Great Leap Forward, in which they could not locate the losses they had suffered during their most horrific experience with socialist rule.[62]

It would be a mistake to not include this story, and the memories that house it, in our efforts to understand the dynamics of political contention in contemporary rural China. In Da Fo and in much of deep China, we can only begin to fully appreciate contention by turning to William Faulkner, who has taught us that "The past is not dead. In fact, it's not even past."[63] The villagers of Da Fo are to a certain extent stuck in the past, forced to live with memories of the Great Leap that continue to influence contention in the period of post-Mao reform, just as they did in the last decades of Maoist rule.[64] Without introducing democratic reform and

---

[60] Compare with ibid., 9–10, 14–15.

[61] The quotation is from Lu, *Cadres and Corruption*, 23.

[62] I am indebted to Peter Fritzsche for the conceptual leads for much of this section. See his "Case of Modern Memory," esp. 24–31.

[63] From Gavin Stevens. Faulkner, *Requiem for a Nun*, Act 1, Scene 2.

[64] Eric Mueggler's brilliant work, *The Age of Wild Ghosts*, anticipates much of my main argument here. See 3, 7–8, 263. Although Mueggler does not systematically probe the issue of pre–Great

fostering reconciliation, it is unlikely that Beijing will be able to avert the political consequences of this living past. So much is this the case that by the late 1990s, Da Fo village, which had seen the Communist Party–led township government subvert its experiment with electoral democracy, also witnessed the resurgence of household-centered war god shrines justifying opposition to oppressive rulers, the revival of the epic tale of *Shui Hu* (The Water Margin) rebels who challenged the corrupt officials of the Song dynasty, and the reproduction of late Qing underground geomancy booklets predicting a sixty-year reign of apocalypse and rebellion. Following the practice of Qing officials, the Dongle County Public Security Bureau banned the geomancy booklets. Rulers sought to impede the search for historical justice. But, as was the case in the late Qing period, they could not banish the memories through which rural people understood the present.[65]

Leap militia development and focuses mainly on the Cultural Revolution, he does say at one point that when villagers attempted to settle scores with the Great Leap Forward's official agents, they blamed and targeted the brigade's "militia secretary" and vice–party secretary for the Great Leap famine's injustice (263). Mueggler also emphasizes that the vengeance of the Cultural Revolution was driven by the painful memory of the Great Leap famine (268).

[65] On this point, also see Gilley, *China's Democratic Future*, 103, 220–21.

Bibliography

Chinese Written/Print Sources

Bao Huayin. "Huiyi Dongle Xian Kangri Zhanzheng" (My Memory of Dongle County During the Anti-Japanese War of Resistance), July 15, 1985.

Bo Yibo. *Ruogan Zhongda Juece Yu Shijian de Huigu* (Reflections on Several Important Policies and Events). Beijing: Zhonggong Zhongyang Dangxiao Chubanshe (Central Party School Press), 1991, 1993, 1997.

Cao Shuji. "1959–1961 Nian Zhongguo de Renkou Siwang Jiqi Cheng Yin" (The Death Rate of China's Population and Its Contributing Factors during 1959–1961). *Zhongguo Renkou Ke Xue* (China's Demographic Science), No. 1, 2005.

Chen Dabin. *Ji E Yinfa De Biange* (Reforms Originating from Hunger). Beijing: Zhonggong Dangshi Chubanshe (Central Chinese Communist Party History Press), 1998.

Chen Lian, ed. *Kangri Genjudi Fajian Shilue* (A Sketch History of the Anti-Japanese Base Areas). Beijing: Jiefangjun Chubanshe (People's Liberation Army Press), 1987.

"Chuan Guo Nongmin Yundong" (The National Peasant Movement). *Zhongguo Nongmin* (The Chinese Tiller), No. 1, December 1926.

Da Jihuang Dang An (The Great [Leap] Famine Archive), Xin Guancha (New Observations), 2000. http://www.xgc2000.com.

"Dongle Canan Shanhou." *Da Gong Bao*, April 17, 1935.

Dongle Lishi Jilu (Dongle County Historical Records). Confidential published source, 1962.

Du Shixun. "Gei Dang Zhongyang Mao Zhuxi de Baogao" (A Report to the Central Party Committee and Chairman Mao). *Ji Mo Xianzhi* (Ji Mo County Gazetteer), March 1961.

"Gansu Shengwei Jiancha Jiejue Tongwei Deng Sange Xian de Naoliang Wenti" (The Communist Party Committee of Gansu Province Checked and Resolved the Conflict over Food Problems in Tongwei and Two Other Counties). *Xinhuashe Neibu Cankao* (New China News Agency, Internal Reference). March 5, 1960.

Gao Hua. "Dayuejin Yundong Yu Guojia Quanli de Kuanzhang: Yi Jiangsu Sheng Weili" (The Great Leap Forward Campaign and the Expansion of State Power: A Case Study of Jiangsu). *Ershiyi Shijie Pinglun* (Hong Kong: The Magazine of the Twenty First Century), Issue 48, No. 4, 1998.

———. "Da Ji Huang de 'Liangshi Shiyong Zengliang Fa' Yu Dai Shipin" (Methods to Increase Edible Grain and Substitute Food during the Great Famine). *Ershiyi Shijie Pinglun*. (Hong Kong: The Magazine of the Twenty First Century). Issue 72, No. 4, 2002.

———. "Da Ji Huang Yu Siqing Yundong de Qiyuan" (The Great Famine and the Origins of the Si-qing Campaign). *Ershiyijie Pinglun* (Hong Kong: The Magazine of the Twenty First Century), Issue 62, No. 4, 2002.

———. *Zai Lishi De Fengling Dukou* (At the Fengling Ferry of History). Shidai Guoji Chuban Youxian Gongsi. Hongkong: Times International Publisher, 2006.

Gao Wangling. "Jitihua Shidai Zhongguo Nongmin Fan Xingwei de Diaocha Yu Sukao" (An Investigation and Reflection on the Era of Collectivization and the Counteractions of Chinese Farmers). *Min Bao Yuekan*, No. 8, Hong Kong, 2002.

———. "Guoji Bijiao de Yige An Li: Zhongguo Nongmin 'Fan Xing Wei'" (The "Counteractive Behavior" of Chinese Peasants: A Case for International Comparison). Unpublished paper, 2001 (2003/04).

———. *Renmin Gongshe Shiqi Zhongguo Nongmin "Fanzingwei" Diaocha* (An Investigation of the "Rebellious Counter Actions" of Chinese Farmers During the Era of the People's Commune). Beijing: Zhonggong Dangshi Chubanshe (Chinese Communist Party History Press), 2006.

"Guanyu Jianguo Yilian Dang de Ruogan Lishi Wenti de Jueyi" (Resolution on Some Questions Concerning the History of the Party since the Establishment of the People's Republic of China). *Renmin Ribao* (People's Daily), July 1, 1981.

Huang Jun. "1960–61 Mao Zedong dui Lianghuang Wenti de Renzhi Jiqi Zhengce Diaozheng" (Mao Zedong's Perception of the Food Shortage Problem and His Policy Changes in 1960–61), Part II. Paper presented at the Great Leap Forward Conference, University of Vienna, November 3–5, 2006.

"Ji-Lu-Yu Bianqu Dangshi Dashiji" (A Record of the Great Historical Events of the Communist Party in the Hebei-Shandong-Henan Border Area). No Date.

"Ji-Lu-Yu Bianqu Gongzuode Chubu Zongjie" (A Preliminary Summary of the Work of the Hebei-Shandong-Henan Anti-Japanese Border Area). In *Zhonggong Ji-Lu-Yu Bianqu Dangshi Ziliao Xuanbian* (A Selection of CCP Hebei-Shandong-Henan Anti-Japanese Border Area Party History Materials). Vol. 2 (1941–1943). Henan Renmin Chubanshe (Henan People's Press), 1988.

Jia Yanmin, *Dayuejin Shiqi Xiangcun Zhengzhide Dianxing: Henan Chayashan Weixing Renmin Gongshe Yanjiu* (A Typical Example of Rural Politics during the Great Leap Forward: A Study of Henan's Chayashan Satellite Commune). Beijing: Zhishi Chanquan Chubanshe (Intellectual Property Rights Press), 2006.

Jia Zongyi. "Dui Dongle Xian Diwei Gongzuode Huiyi" (Memories of Enemy Puppet Work in Dongle County). *Zhonggong Dongle Dangshi Ziliao* (CCP Dongle Party History Materials), Vol. 2, 1985.

Jiang, Peizhou, Shen Dexi, and Jiu Quan. *Lao Xinwen 1959–1961*. Tianjin: 1998.

Jiefang Ribao (Liberation Daily), May 5, 1945.

Jin Hui. CASS. 1993.

Kang Jian. "Chu Chu Dou You Yanwang Dian: Chayashan de Wa Liang Yundong" (There Are Hells Everywhere: The Food Digging Movement at Chaya Mountain). In Kang Jian, *Huihuangde Huanmie – Renmin Gongshe Jinshi Lu* (The Glorious Dissolution: The Revelation of the People's Commune). Da Jihuang Dang An, Xin Guangcha (Great Famine Archive, New Observations), January 23, 2000.

———. "Hei Ye de Tang, Ying Yueliang: Chaya Shan Ji Huang Can Jing" (Moon Reflected in the Soup in the Night: The Sorrowful Famine Ordeal at Chaya Mountain). Da Jihuang Dang An, Xin Guangcha (Great Famine Archive, New Observations), January 23, 2000, and February 16, 2000.

"Lai Han Zhao Deng" (Letter to the Publisher). *Da Gong Bao*, April 17, 1935.

Li Ruojian, "Dayuejin Yu Kunnan Shiqi de Shehui Dongdang Yu Kongzhi" (Social Turbulence and Social Control During the Great Leap Forward and the Period of Difficulty). *Ershiyi Shijie Pinglun* (Hong Kong: The Magazine of the Twenty First Century), Issue 62, No. 4, 2002.

Ling Zhijun. *Lishi bu Zai Paihuai, Renmin Gongshe Zai Zhongguo de Xingqi he Shibai* (History Is No Longer without Direction: The Rise and Fall of the People's Communes in China). Beijing: Renmin Chubanshe (People's Press), 1997.

Liu Haifan, ed. *Zhonggong Zhongyang Guanyu Yadi Nongcun he Chengshi Kuoliang Biaozhun de Zhishi* (Instructions Regarding Reducing Food Ration in the Cities and Rural Areas from the Central Party Committee). Issued September 7, 1960. Zhongyang Wenxian Chubanshe (Central Document Publishers), 2005.

Lu Huilin. "Weixing Shi Ruhe de Shang Tiande? Xiancun Jiceng Ganbu he Dayuejin" (How Were the Satellites Launched? The Village-Level Cadres and the Great Leap Forward). Unpublished paper, Beijing University Sociology Department, 2005.

Mao Zedong. *Jianguo Yilai Mao Zedong Wengao* (Manuscripts of Mao Zedong since the Founding of the State). Vol. 5 (1955) and Vol. 8 (1959). Beijing: Zhongyang Wenxian Chubanshe (Central Party Literature Press), 1991 and 1993.

Peng Youqiang, ed. *Dongle Shilue* (A Brief History of Dongle County). Ed. Lingpeng Cao and Peng Youqiang. Henan Sheng Dongle Xian Difang Shi Bianwei Hui Zhongbian (Chief Editorial Office of the Local History Editorial Committee, Dongle County, Henan Province), 1986.

Peng Youqiang. *Dongle Xianzhi Xiaozhu* (Annotation to Dongle County's Annals). Jinan: Shandong University Press, 1989.

Peng Zhen. "Lun Ji-Lu-Yu Hongqianghui Gongzuo" (On the Work in the Hebei-Shandong-Henan Area Red Spear Associations). *Qunzhong* (The Masses), May 1938. In Chen Zhuanhai, et al., eds., *Henan Hongqianghui Ziliao Xuanbian* (An Edited Selection of Materials on the Henan Red Spear Society). Zhengzhou: Henan Renmin Chubanshe (Henan People's Press), Henan Sheng Difang Shizhi Bianzhuan Weiyuanhui (Henan Province Local History Records Compilation Committee), 1985.

Qiao Peihua. "Xinyang Shijian Fasheng de Yuanyin" (The Causes of the Xinyang Incident). Paper presented at the Great Leap Forward Conference, University of Vienna, November 3–6, 2006.

Song Zhixin, ed. *1942 Henan Dajihuang* (1942: The Great Famine in Henan). Wuhan: Hubei Renmin Chubanshe (Hubei People's Press), 2005.

Wang Shanzheng. "Dongle Hongqianghui de Xingqi yu Xiaowang" (The Rise and Fall of the Dongle County Red Spear Society). In Wei Puzhen and Zhang Junhua, eds., *Dongle Wenshi Ziliao* (Dongle County Cultural History Materials). Vol. 2. Zhongguo Renmin Zhengzhi Xieshang Huiyi Dongle Xian Weiyuanhui Wenshi Ziliao Weiyuanhui (The Committee of Historical Records of the Chinese People's Consultative Committee of Dongle County), 1987.

Wang Shuobai. "Guanyu Zhongguo 1959–1961 Nian Da Jihuang Fasheng Genben Yuanyin de Yanjiu Baogao" (A Research Report Regarding the Root Causes of the 1959–1961 Famine in China). An unpublished report from research undertaken by Wang Shuobai and Dai Ruifu, presented to the Brandeis East Asian Studies Colloquium, April 4, 2001, and to a panel of the National Association of Asian Studies, 2001.

Wang Yanni. "Cong Macheng Kan Gongshihua de ABC" (Looking at the Fundamentals of Communism from the Standpoint of Macheng). Paper given at the Great Leap Forward Conference, University of Vienna, November 3–5, 2006.

Wu Yongkuan. "Lishi Jianzheng" (Witnessing History) – "Huiyi Yijiuwunian Liangshi Guan" (Remembering the Famine Ordeal of 1959). *Beijing Zhi Chun* (Beijing Spring), No. 137, October 2004.

Xinyang Shibian (The Xinyang Incident). No Date.

Xin Xi. "Lishi de Laji – 'Xinyang Sijian'" (The Rubbish of History – The 'Xinyang Incident'). Da Jihuang Dang An, Xin Guancha (Great Famine Archive, New Observations), December 19, 2000.

Xu Ming. "Wu Zhipu Yu Henan Dayuejin Youndong" (Wu Zhipu and the Great Leap Forward Movement in Henan Province). *Ershiyi Shijie Pinglun* (The Magazine of the Twenty First Century), Issue 48, No. 4, 1998.

Yu Xiguang. *Dayuejin Kurizi Shangshuji* (A Collection of the Petitions Made during the Hard Times of the Great Leap Forward). Hong Kong: Shidai Chaoliu Chubanshe (The Tide of the Times Press), 2006.

Zhang Huaiwen. "Ji-Lu-Yu Kangri Genjudi Gonggu Yu Fazhande Yuanyin Chutan" (An Exploration of the Reasons for the Consolidation and Development of the Hebei-Shandong-Henan Anti-Japanese Base). *Henan Dangshi Yanjiu* (Henan Party History Research), Nos. 2–3, 1987.

Zhang Letian. "Guojia Huayu de Jieshou Yu Xiaojie – Gongshe Zhong de 'Jieji' He 'Jieji Douzheng'" (Acceptance and Disappearance of State Language: "Social Class" and "Social Class Struggle" in the Context of the People's Commune). 2001.

Zhang Linzhi. "Yinian Laide Dang Yu Qunzhong Gongzuo" (Party and Mass Work in the Past Year). In *Zhonggong Ji-Lu-Yu Bianqu Dangshi Ziliao Xuanbian* (A Selection of CCP Hebei-Shandong-Henan Anti-Japanese Border Area Party History Materials). No. 2 (1943–1945). Henan Renmin Chubanshe (Henan People's Press), 1998.

Zhonggong Henan Shengwei Dangshi Yanjiushi (Henan Province Party History Research), ed. *Henan Kangzhan Jianshi* (A Short History of the War of Resistance in Henan). Zhengzhou: Henan Renmin Chubanshe (Henan People's Press), 2005.

Zhonggong Henan Shengwei Dangshi Ziliao Zhengji Bianzuan Weiyuanhui Bian (CCP Henan Provincial Party Committee Party History Compilation Committee), ed. "Ji-Lu-Yu Bianqu Kangri Genjudi Henan Bufen Gaishu" (A Brief Survey of the Henan Part of the Hebei-Shandong-Henan Anti-Japanese Base Area). In *Ji-Lu-Yu Kangri Genjudi* (The Hebei-Shandong-Henan Anti-Japanese Base Area). No. 1. Henan Renmin Chubanshe (Henan People's Press), 1985.

Western-Language Sources

Adas, Michael. "From Avoidance to Confrontation: Peasant Protest in Precolonial Southeast Asia." *Comparative Studies in Society and History*, Vol. 23, 1981.

Aminzade, Ronald R. et al. *Silence and Voice in the Study of Contentious Politics*. Cambridge: Cambridge University Press, 2001.

Aminzade, Ronald R., and Doug McAdam. "Emotions and Contentious Politics." In Ronald R. Aminzade, et al., eds., *Silence and Voice in the Study of Contentious Politics*. Cambridge: Cambridge University Press, 2001.

Anderson, Robert A. "Psychoneuroimmunoendocrinology Review and Commentary." *Townsend Newsletter for Doctors and Patients: The Examiner of Medical Alternatives*, August/September 2004.

Bibliography

Archer, John E. *By a Flash and a Scare: Incendiarism, Animal Maiming, and Poaching in East Anglia, 1815–1870.* Oxford: Clarendon Press, 1990.

Ash, Robert. "Squeezing the Peasants: Grain, Extraction, Food Consumption and Rural Living Standards in Mao's China." *China Quarterly,* Vol. 188, December 2006.

Babbie, Earl R. *Practice of Social Research.* Belmont, CA: Wadsworth, 1979.

Bailey, F. G. *The Kingdom of Individuals.* Ithaca, NY: Cornell University Press, 1993.

Bannister, Judith. "An Analysis of Recent Data on the Population of China." *Population and Development Review,* Vol. 10, No. 2, June 1984.

———. *China's Changing Population.* Stanford, CA: Stanford University Press, 1987.

Barme, Geremie. *In the Red: On Contemporary Chinese Culture.* New York: Columbia University Press, 1999.

Bearman, Peter S., and Katherine Stovel. "Becoming a Nazi: A Model for Narrative Networks." *Poetics,* Vol. 27, 2000: 69–90.

Becker, Jasper. *Hungry Ghosts: Mao's Secret Famine.* New York: The Free Press, 1996.

Beja, Jean-Philippe. "Forbidden Memory, Unwritten History." New Century Net, August 4, 2003.

Berger, Roland. "China Today: Walking on Two Legs." *Nation,* Vol. 199, November 16, 1964.

Bernstein, Thomas P. "Stalinism, Famine, and Chinese Peasants: Grain Procurements During the Great Leap Forward." *Theory and Society,* Vol. 13, 1984.

———. "Mao Zedong and the Famine of 1959–1960: A Study in Willfulness." *China Quarterly,* Vol. 186, June 2006.

Bernstein, Thomas P., and Lu Xiaobo. *Taxation Without Representation.* New York: Cambridge University Press, 2003.

Bianco, Lucien. "Peasant Movements." In John King Fairbank and Albert Feuerwerker, eds., *The Cambridge History of China: Republican China, 1912–1949.* Vol. 13, no. 2. Cambridge: Cambridge University Press, 1986.

———. "Peasant Responses to Communist Party Mobilization Policies in the Anti-Japanese Bases: Some Western Views." Unpublished paper delivered to the Second International Symposium on the History of Chinese Base Areas During World War II, Nankai University, Tianjin, China, 1991.

———. *Peasants without the Party: Grass-Roots Movements in Twentieth-Century-China.* Armonk, NY: M.E. Sharpe, 2001.

Bianco, Lucien, and Chang-Ming Hua. *Jacqueries et révolutions dans la Chine du le XXe siècle.* Paris: Martinière, 2005.

Blecher, Marc. "China: State Socialist Iconoclast." In W. Phillips Shively and Steve J. Mazurana, eds., *Comparative Governance.* New York: McGraw Hill, 1995.

Blok, Anton. "Female Rulers and Their Consorts." In *Honour and Violence.* Cambridge: Blackwell, 2001.

Bloom, Sandra L. "Trauma Theory Abbreviated." *The Final Action Plan: A Coordinated Community-Based Response to Family Violence,* October 1999.

———. "Commentary: Reflections on the Desire for Revenge." *Journal of Emotional Abuse,* Vol. 2, No. 4, 2001.

Bok, Sissela. *Lying: Moral Choice in Public and Private Life.* New York: Pantheon Books, 1978.

Bramall, Chris. *In Praise of Maoist Economic Planning.* Oxford: Oxford University Press, 1993.

———. "The Role of Decollectivization in China's Agricultural Miracle, 1978–1990." *Journal of Peasant Studies,* Vol. 20 (2), January 1993.

Buck, John Lossing. *Food and Agriculture in Communist China.* Stanford: Hoover Institution Publications, 1965/66.

Burns, John P., and Stanley Rosen, eds. *Policy Conflicts in Post-Mao China*. Armonk, NY: M.E. Sharpe, 1986.

Chamberlayne, Prue, Joanna Bornat, and Tom Wengraf, eds. *The Turn to Biographical Methods in Social Science: Comparative Issues and Examples*. London: Routledge, 2000.

Chan, Alfred L. "The Campaign for Agricultural Development in the Great Leap Forward: A Study of Policy Making and Implementation in Liaoning." *The China Quarterly*, March 1992.

_____. *Mao's Crusade: Politics and Policy Implementation in China's Great Leap Forward*. Oxford: Oxford University Press, 2001.

Chan, Anita, Richard Madsen, and Jonathan Unger. *Chen Village*. Berkeley: University of California Press, 1984.

Chan, Anita, and Jonathan Unger. "Grey and Black: The Hidden Economy of Rural China." *Pacific Affairs*, Vol. 55, No. 3, 1982: 452–71.

Chang, Gene Hsin, and Guangzhong James Wen. "Communal Dining and the Chinese Famine of 1958–1961." *Economic Development and Cultural Change*, Vol. 46, No. 1, October 1997: 1–34.

_____. "Food Availability Versus Consumption Efficiency: Causes of the Chinese Famine." In Bruce Reynolds, ed., "China's Great Famine." Special issue, *China Economic Review*, Vol. 9, No. 2, 1998.

Chang, Jung, and Jon Halliday. *Mao: The Untold Story*. New York: Knopf, 2005.

Chen, Yixin. "Memory and Survivorship in the Great Leap Forward Famine, with Special Reference to Cadres and Kinship in Three Rural Anhui Villages." AAS paper, revised 2001.

_____. "Differing Motivations for Peasant Rebellion in the Cultural Revolution: Cases in Three Anhui Villages." Paper presented to the Association for Asian Studies, Annual Meeting, San Diego, CA, March 4–7, 2004.

Cheng, Tiejun, and Mark Selden. "The Origins and Consequences of China's Hukou System." *China Quarterly*, Vol. 139, September 1994.

Cohen, Myron L. "Lineage Organization in North China." *Journal of Asian Studies*, Vol. 49, No. 3, 1990.

Connerton, Paul. *How Societies Remember*. Cambridge: Cambridge University Press, 1989.

Craig, Anne L. *The First Agraristas: An Oral History of a Mexican Reform Movement*. Berkeley: University of California Press, 1983.

Crook, David, and Isabel Crook. *Revolution in a Chinese Village: Ten Mile Inn*. London: Routledge and Kegen Paul, 1959.

Cushman, Thomas. "Anthropology and Genocide: Some Notes on Conceptual Practices of Power." *Anthropological Theory*, Vol. 4, No. 1, March 2004.

Davis, Mike. *Late Victorian Holocausts: El Nino Famines in the Making of the Third World*. London and New York: Verso, 2001.

Day, Clarence Burton. *Chinese Peasant Cults*. Taipei: Ch'eng Wen, 1969.

De Bary, William T., and Tu Weiming, eds. *Confucianism and Human Rights*. New York: Columbia University Press, 1998.

De Waal, Alexander. *Famine that Kills: Darfur, Sudan 1984–1985*. New York: Oxford University Press, 1989.

_____. *Famine Crimes: Politics and the Disaster Relief Industry in Africa*. Bloomington: Indiana University Press, 1997.

Diamant, Neil J. "Between Martyrdom and Mischief: The Political and Social Predicament of CCP War Widows and Veterans, 1949–66." In Diana Lary and Stephen MacKinnon, eds., *Scars of War: The Impact of Warfare on Modern China*. Vancouver: University of British Columbia Press, 2001.

Dickson, Bruce J. "Dilemmas of Party Adaptation: The CCP's Strategies for Survival." In Peter Hays Gries and Stanley Rosen, eds., *State and Society in 21st-Century China: Crisis, Contention, and Legitimation*. New York: Routledge Curzon, 2004.

Dittmer, Lowell. "The Chinese Cultural Revolution Revisited: The Role of the Nemesis." *Journal of Contemporary China*, Vol. 5, No. 13, 1996.

Domenach, Jean-Luc. *The Origins of the Great Leap Forward: The Case of One Chinese Province*. Trans. A. M. Barrett. Boulder, CO: Westview Press, 1995.

_____. "The Origins of the Great Leap Forward: The Case of One Chinese Province." Unpublished manuscript, no date.

Domes, Jurgen. *Socialism in the Chinese Countryside: Rural Societal Policies in the People's Republic of China, 1949–1979*. Trans. M. Wendling. Montreal: McGill-Queens University Press, 1980.

Dongping, Han. *The Unknown Cultural Revolution*. (Series ed. Edward Beauchamp.) New York: Garland Publishing, 2000.

Duara, Prasenjit. *Culture, Power and the State: Rural North China, 1900–1942*. Stanford, CA: Stanford University Press, 1988.

Dugger, William M. "Douglass C. North's New Institutionalism." *Journal of Economic Issues* 24, No. 2, June 1995: 453–58.

Dutt, Gargi. "Some Problems of China's Rural Communes." In Roderick MacFarquhar, ed., *China Under Mao: Politics Takes Command*. Cambridge, MA: MIT Press, 1966.

Ekman, Paul. *Emotions Revealed*. New York: Henry Holt/Owl Books, 2003.

Esherick, Joseph, Paul G. Pickowicz, and Andrew G. Walder, eds. *The Chinese Cultural Revolution as History*. Stanford, CA: Stanford University Press, 2006.

Evans, Grant. "The Accursed Problem: Communists and Peasants." *Peasant Studies*, Vol. 15, No. 2, Winter 1988.

Evans, Harriet. *Women and Sexuality in China: Female Sexuality and Gender Since 1949*. New York: Continuum, 1997.

Fairbank, John K., Edwin O. Reischauer, and Albert M. Craig. *East Asia: Tradition and Transformation*. Boston: Houghton Mifflin, 1973.

Faulkner, William. *Requiem for a Nun*. New York: Random House, 1951.

Feldman, Allen. "Punition, Retaliation and the Shifting Crises of Social Memory and Legitimacy in Northern Ireland." Paper prepared for the Harry Frank Guggenheim Foundation workshop on revenge, Madrid, Spain, December 15–17, 1995.

Feuchtwang, Stephan. *Popular Religion in China: The Imperial Metaphor*. Richmond-Surrey: Curzon, 2001.

Fitzpatrick, Sheila. *Stalin's Peasants: Resistance and Survival in the Russian Village after Collectivization*. New York: Oxford University Press, 1994.

_____. *Everyday Stalinism: Ordinary Life in Extraordinary Times: Soviet Russia in the 1930s*. New York: Oxford University Press, 1999.

Friedman, Edward. "Mao Zedong, Backwardness and Revolution." Unpublished manuscript, Department of Political Science, University of Wisconsin, June 1976.

_____. "Mao Tse-tong, Twentieth Century Innovator." In Dick Wilson, ed., *Mao Tse-tung in the Scales of History*. Cambridge: Cambridge University Press, 1977.

_____. "Maoism and the Liberation of the Poor." *World Politics*, Vol. 39, 1987.

_____. "Learning About a Chinese Village in a Leninist-Party Authoritarian State." *Journal of Contemporary China*, Vol. 15, No. 47, 2005.

Friedman, Edward, and Mark Selden. "War Communism." Yale University Program in Agrarian Studies Colloquium paper, October 22, 2004.

Friedman, Edward, Paul G. Pickowicz, and Mark Selden. *Chinese Village, Socialist State*. New Haven, CT: Yale University Press, 1991.

———. *Revolution, Resistance, and Reform in Village China*. New Haven, CT: Yale University Press, 2005.

Fritzsche, Peter. "Review Article: The Case of Modern Memory." *Journal of Modern History*, Vol. 73, March 2001.

Gao, Xiaoxian. "China's Modernization and Changes in the Status of Rural Women." Trans. Katherine Campbell. In Christina K. Gilmartin, et al., eds., *Engendering China Women, Culture, and the State*. Cambridge, MA: Harvard University Press, 1994.

Geertz, Clifford. *Local Knowledge: Further Essays in Interpretative Anthropology*. New York: Basic Books, 1983.

Gilley, Bruce. *Model Rebels; The Rise and Fall of China's Richest Village*. Berkeley: University of California Press, 2001.

———. *China's Democratic Future: How It Will Happen and Where It Will Lead*. New York: Columbia University Press, 2004.

Giskin, Howard. "Using Chinese Folktales in the Classroom." *Education About Asia*, Vol. 17, No. 3, Fall 2002.

Goodfellow, Robert. "Forgetting What It Was to Remember the Indonesian Killings of 1965–66." In Kenneth Christie and Robert Cribb, eds., *Historical Injustice and Democratic Transition in Eastern Asia and Northern Europe/Ghosts at the Table of Democracy*. London: Routledge Curzon, 2002.

Gottman, John. "Why Marriages Succeed or Fail." (1994) Preview. *The Boston Globe*, A3, November 11, November 22, 1993.

Groot, J. J. M. de. *The Religious System of China*. 6 vols. Leiden: Brill Publishers, 1910.

Gross, David. "Symposium on *Soviet Peasants*." *Telos*, Vol. 68, Summer 1986.

Guha, Ranajit. *Elementary Aspects of Peasant Insurgency in Colonial India*. Durham, NC: Duke University Press, 1999.

Halbwachs, Maurice. *On Collective Memory*. Ed. and trans. Lewis A. Coser. Chicago: University of Chicago Press, 1992.

Hall, John A. "Review of *Trust and Rule*, by Charles Tilly." *Canadian Journal of Sociology*, January–February 2006.

Hanks, Lucien. *Rice and Man: Agricultural Ecology in Southeast Asia*. Chicago: Aldine Atherton, 1972.

Harding, Harry. *China's Second Revolution: Reform After Mao*. Washington, D.C.: Brookings, 1987.

Harris, Marvin. *Cows, Pigs, Wars and Witches: The Riddles of Culture*. New York: Vintage, 1974.

Hartford, Kathleen. "Socialist Agriculture Is Dead: Long Live Socialist Agriculture! Organizational Transformation in Rural China." In Elizabeth J. Perry and Christine Wong, eds., *The Political Economic of Reform in Post-Mao China*. Cambridge, MA: Harvard University Press, 1985.

Hedges, Chris. *War Is a Force That Gives Us Meaning*. New York: Public Affairs Press, 2002.

Heidenheimer, Arnold J., Michael Johnston, and Victor T. Levine, eds. *Political Corruption: A Handbook*. New Brunswick: Transaction Books, 1990.

Heilig, Gerhard. "Presentation on 'Poverty Alleviation in China.'" Unpublished paper, Brandeis University, October 17, 2005.

Herman, Judith Lewis. *Trauma and Recovery*. New York: Basic Books, 1992.

Hershatter, Gail. "The Gender of Memory: Rural Chinese Women and the 1950s." *Signs: Journal of Women in Culture and Society*, Vol. 28, No. 1, 2002.

Bibliography

———. "The Gender of Memory: Rural Women and Collectivization in 1950s China." Yale University Program in Agrarian Studies Colloquium paper, November 17, 2006.

Hinton, William. *Shenfan: The Continuing Revolution in a Chinese Village*. New York: Random House, 1983.

Ho, Peter. "Contesting Rural Spaces: Land Disputes, Customary Tenure and the State." In Elizabeth J. Perry and Mark Selden, eds., *Chinese Society: Change, Conflict and Resistance*. London: Routledge Curzon, 2000.

Hofheinz, Roy, Jr. "Rural Administration in Communist China." In Roderick MacFarquhar, ed., *China Under Mao: Politics Takes Command*. Cambridge, MA: MIT Press, 1966.

Holloway, Wendy, and Tony Jefferson. "Biography, Anxiety, and the Experience of Locality." In Prue Chamberlayne, Joanna Bornat, and Tom Wengraf, eds., *The Turn to Biographical Methods in Social Science*. New York: Routledge, 2000.

Hong Ying. *Daughter of the River*. Trans. Howard Goldblatt. New York: Grove Press, 1997.

Huang, Philip. *The Peasant Economy and Social Change in North China*. Stanford, CA: Stanford University Press, 1985.

Huang, Shu-min. *The Spiral Road: Change in a Chinese Village Through the Eyes of a Communist Party Leader*. Boulder, CO: Westview, 1989.

Janku, Andrea. "Publicized Disasters in Nineteenth Century China: The Experience of Famine, the Organization of Relief, and the Image of the Nation." Paper presented to the ICAS conference in Berlin, August 9–12, 2001.

Jing, Jun. *The Temple of Memories: History, Power and Morality in a Chinese Village*. Stanford, CA: Stanford University Press, 1996.

Johnson, Chalmers. *Peasant Nationalism and Communist Power. The Emergence of Revolutionary China*. Stanford, CA: Stanford University Press, 1962.

Johnson, D. Gale. "China's Great Famine: Introductory Remarks." In Bruce Reynolds, ed., "China's Great Famine." Special issue, *China Economic Review*, Vol. 9, Fall 1998.

Joseph, William A. *The Critique of Ultra-Leftism in China, 1958–1981*. Stanford, CA: Stanford University Press, 1984.

———. "A Tragedy of Good Intentions: Post-Mao Views of the Great Leap Forward." *Modern China: An International Quarterly*, Vol. 12, No. 4, October 1986.

Kelliher, Daniel. *Peasant Power: The Era of Rural Reform, 1979–1989*. New Haven, CT: Yale University Press, 1993.

Kerkvliet, Benedict J. Tria. *Everyday Politics in the Philippines*. Berkeley: University of California Press, 1990.

———. "Village-State Relations in Vietnam: The Effect of Everyday Politics on Decollectivization." *Journal of Asian Studies*, Vol. 54, No. 2, May 1995.

———. *The Power of Everyday Politics: How Vietnamese Peasants Transformed National Policy*. Ithaca, NY: Cornell University Press, 2005.

Kipnis, Andrew B. *Producing Guanxi: Sentiment, Self, and Subculture in a North China Village*. Durham, NC: Duke University Press, 1997.

Kleinman, Arthur. "How Bodies Remember: Social Memory and Bodily Experiences of Criticism, Resistance, and Delegitimization Following China's Cultural Revolution." *New Literary History*, Vol. 25, Summer 1994.

Kuhn, Philip. *Rebellion and Its Enemies in Late Imperial China: Militarization and Social Structure, 1796–1864*. Cambridge, MA: Harvard University Press, 1970.

———. *Soulstealers: The Chinese Sorcery Scare of 1768*. Cambridge, MA: Harvard University Press, 1990.

Ladurie, Emmanuel Le Roy. "Amenorrhea in Time of Famine." *The Territory of the Historian*. Trans. Benard Sián Reynolds. Ch. 15. Chicago: University of Chicago Press, 1979.

Lane, Robert E. *Political Life: How and Why People Get Involved in Politics*. New York: Free Press, 1959.

Lardy, Nicholas. *Agriculture in China's Modern Economic Development*. New York: Cambridge University Press, 1983.

_____. "The Chinese Economy Under Stress, 1958–1965." In Roderick MacFarquhar and John King Fairbank, eds., *The Cambridge History of China*. Vol. l4, part 1. Cambridge: Cambridge University Press, 1987.

Lary, Diana. *Chinese Common Soldiers, 1911–1937*. Cambridge: Cambridge University Press, 1985.

Ledeneva, Alena V. *Russia's Economy of Favours: Blat, Networking, and Informal Exchange*. Cambridge: Cambridge University Press, 1998.

Levi, Primo. *Survival in Auschwitz*. New York: Touchstone/Simon and Schuster, 1996.

Levine, Steven I. *Anvil of Victory: The Communist Revolution in Manchuria*. New York: Columbia University Press, 1987.

Li, Choh-ming. "Economic Development." In Roderick MacFarquhar, ed., *China Under Mao: Politics Takes Command*. Cambridge, MA: MIT Press, 1966.

Li, Huaiyin. "The First Encounter: Peasant Resistance to State Control of Grain in East China in the mid-1950s: Research Report." *China Quarterly*, Vol. 185, March 2007.

_____. "From Righteous to Rightful: Peasant Resistance to Agricultural Collectivization in China in the 1950s." Yale University Program in Agrarian Studies Colloquium paper, November 16, 2006.

_____. *Village China Under Socialism and Reform*. Unpublished manuscript in progress, 2008.

Li, Lillian. "Life and Death in a Chinese Famine: Infanticide as a Demographic Consequence of the 1935 Yellow River Flood." *Comparative Studies in Society and History*, Vol. 33, 199l.

_____. *Fighting Famine in North China: State, Market, and Environmental Decline, 1660s–1990s*. Stanford, CA: Stanford University Press, 2007.

Lieberthal, Kenneth. "The Great Leap Forward and the Split in the Yenan Leadership." In Roderick MacFarquhar and John King Fairbank, eds., *The Cambridge History of China*. Vol. 14, part 1. Cambridge: Cambridge University Press, 1987.

Lin, Justin Yifu. "Collectivization and China's Agricultural Crisis in 1959–1961." *The Journal of Political Economy*, Vol. 98, No. 6, 1990.

Lin, Justin Yifu, and Dennis Tao Yang. "Food Availability, Entitlements, and the Chinese Famine of 1959–1961." *The Economic Journal*, Vol. 110, January 2000.

Link, Perry. "China's Core Problem." In Tu Wei-ming, ed., *China in Transformation*. Cambridge, MA: Harvard University Press, 1994 (Originally in *Daedalus*, Vol. 122, No. 2, 1990).

_____. "China: The Anaconda in the Chandelier." *New York Review of Books*, April 11, 2002.

Liu, Henry C. K. "China: Mao and Lincoln: Part 2, The Great Leap Forward Not All Bad." *Asia Times Online*, April 1, 2004.

Liu, Xin. *In One's Own Shadow: An Ethnographic Account of the Condition of Post-Reform Rural China*. Berkeley: University of California Press, 2000.

Loftus, Elizabeth. "Memories of a Past That Never Was." In "Memory as the Theater of the Past: The Psychology of False Memories." Special issue, *Current Directions in Psychological Science*, Vol. 6, No. 3, June 1997.

_____. "Make-Believe Memories." *The American Psychologist*, Vol. 58, No. 11, November 2003.

Loftus, Elizabeth, Daniel Bernstein, and Nourkova Vernika. "Altering Traumatic Memory." *Cognition and Emotion*, Vol. 18, No. 4, June 2004.

Lu, Xiaobo. *Cadres and Corruption: The Organizational Involution of the Chinese Communist Party*. Stanford, CA: Stanford University Press, 2000.

MacFarquhar, Roderick. *The Origins of the Cultural Revolution*. 3 vols. New York: Columbia University Press, 1974–97.

Madsen, Richard. *Morality and Power in a Chinese Village*. Berkeley: University of California Press, 1984.

_____. "The Politics of Revenge in Rural China During the Cultural Revolution." In Jonathan N. Lipman and Stevan Harrell, eds., *Violence in China: Essays in Culture and Counterculture*. Albany: State University of New York Press, 1990.

Manning, Kimberley P. E. "Marxist Maternalism, Memory, and the Mobilization of Women in the Great Leap Forward." *The China Review: An Interdisciplinary Journal*, Vol. 5, No. 1, Spring 2005.

McAdam, Doug. "Harmonizing the Voices." In Ronald R. Aminzade, et al., eds., *Silence and Voice in the Study of Contentious Politics*. Cambridge: Cambridge University Press, 2001.

McAdam, Doug, Sidney Tarrow, and Charles Tilly. *Dynamics of Contention*. Cambridge: Cambridge University Press, 2001.

McCord, Edward Allen. "Burn, Kill, Rape and Rob: Military Atrocities, Warlordism, and Anti-Warlordism in Republican China." In Diana Lary and Stephen MacKinnon, eds., *Scars of War: The Impact of Warfare on Modern China*. Vancouver: University of British Columbia Press, 2001.

Meisner, Maurice. *Mao's China and After: A History of the People's Republic*. 3rd ed. New York: The Free Press, 1999.

Merridale, Catherine. "The Collective Mind: Trauma and Shell-Shock in Twentieth-Century Russia." *Journal of Contemporary History*, Vol. 35, 2000.

Michelson, Ethan. "Deprivation, Discontent, and Disobedience in Rural China: The Case of Southeastern Henan." Unpublished paper presented to the Conference on Reclaiming Chinese Society, University of California–Berkeley, October 27–28, 2006.

Mitchell, Neil J. *Agents of Atrocity: Leaders, Followers, and the Violation of Human Rights in Civil Wars*. New York: Palgrave-MacMillan, 2004.

Mo Yan. *The Republic of Wine: A Novel*. Trans. Howard Goldblatt. New York: Arcade, 2000.

Mueggler, Erik. "A Carceral Regime: Violence and Social Memory in Southwest China." *Journal of Asian Studies*, Vol. 57, No. 4, 1998.

_____. "Spectral Subversions: Rival Tactics of Time and Agency in Southwest China." *Comparative Studies in Society and History*, Vol. 41, 1999.

_____. *The Age of Wild Ghosts: Memory, Violence, and Place in Southwest China*. Berkeley: University of California Press, 2001.

Mueller, Jan. "Memory and Power." Paper presented at the Frontiers of Memory Conference, Institute of Education, London, September 17–19, 1999.

Nee, Victor. "Peasant Household Individualism." In W. L. Parish, ed., *Chinese Rural Development*. Armonk, NY: M.E. Sharpe, 1985.

Netting, Robert C. *Smallholders, Householders: Farm Families and the Ecology of Intensive, Sustainable Agriculture*. Stanford, CA: Stanford University Press, 1993.

North, Douglass C. *Institutions, Institutional Change and Economic Performance*. Cambridge: Cambridge University Press, 1990.

O'Brien, Kevin J. "Rightful Resistance." *World Politics*, Vol. 49, No. 1, October 1996.

O'Brien, Kevin J., and Lianjiang Li. "The Politics of Lodging Complaints in Rural China." *China Quarterly*, Vol. 143, September 1995.

———. "Villagers and Popular Resistance in Contemporary China." *Modern China*, Vol. 22, No. 1, January 1996: 28–61.

———. *Rightful Resistance in Rural China*. Cambridge: Cambridge University Press, 2006.

Oi, Jean C. *State and Peasant in Contemporary China: The Political Economy of Village Government*. Berkeley: University of California Press, 1989.

———. *Rural China Takes Off*. Berkeley: University of California Press, 1999.

Parish, William L., ed. *Chinese Rural Development: The Great Transformation*. Armonk, NY: M.E. Sharpe, 1985.

Pei, Minxin. *From Reform to Revolution: The Demise of Communism in China and the Soviet Union*. Cambridge, MA: Harvard University Press, 1994.

———. "China's Governance Crisis: More Than Musical Chairs." *Foreign Affairs*, Vol. 81, No. 5, September/October 2002.

———. "The Long March Against Graft." *Financial Times*, December 10, 2002.

Peng, Xizhe. "Demographic Consequences of the Great Leap Forward in China's Provinces." *Population and Development Review*, Vol. 13, No. 4, December 1987: 639–70.

Pepper, Suzanne. *Civil War in China: The Political Struggle, 1945–1949*. Berkeley: University of California Press, 1978.

Perry, Elizabeth J. "Rural Collective Violence: The Fruits of Recent Reforms." In Elizabeth J. Perry and Christine Wong, eds., *The Political Economy of Reform in Post-Mao China*. Cambridge, MA: Harvard University Press, 1985.

———. "Challenging the Mandate of Heaven." *Critical Asian Studies*, Vol. 33, No. 2, 2001.

———. *Challenging the Mandate of Heaven: Social Protest and State Power in China*. Armonk, NY: M.E. Sharpe, 2002.

———. "'To Rebel Is Justified': Cultural Revolution Influences on Contemporary Chinese Protest." In Kam-yee Law, ed., *Beyond Purge and Holocaust: The Chinese Cultural Revolution Reconsidered*. New York: Palgrave Press, 2003.

———. *Patrolling the Revolution: Worker Militias, Citizenship, and the Modern Chinese State*. Lanham, MD: Rowman and Littlefield, 2006.

Pinel, John P. J. *Biopsychology*. 4th ed. Needham, MA: Allyn and Bacon, 2000.

Pocha, Jehangir S. "Huge Dam Costly to Farmers." *Boston Globe*, A1, December 25, 2006.

Pomeranz, Kenneth. *The Making of a Hinterland: State, Society and Economy in Inland North China, 1853–1937*. Berkeley: University of California Press, 1993.

Pomfret, John. *Chinese Lessons: Five Classmates and the Story of New China*. New York: Holt, 2006.

Porter, Bruce D. *War and the Rise of the State*. New York: Free Press, 1994.

Putterman, Louis. "The Incentive Problem and the Demise of Team Farming in China." *Journal of Development Economics*, Vol. 26, 1987.

Qin Hui. *Pastorals and Rhapsodies*. Beijing: 1999. David Kelly translation of the Preface to the Korean edition, 2002. This English translation can be found in Qin Hui, "The Common Baseline of Modern Thought." In David Kelly, ed. and trans., "The Mystery of the Chinese Economy: Selected Writings of Qin Hui." Special issue, *The Chinese Economy*, Vol. 38, No. 4, September 2005.

Robben, Anthony. "How Traumatized Societies Remember." Paper presented to the Harry Frank Guggenheim Workshop, Portugal, December 1997.

Ruf, Gregory A. *Cadres and Kin: Making a Socialist Village in West China, 1921–1991*. Stanford, CA: Stanford University Press, 1998.

Bibliography

Santler, Eric. *Stranded Objects: Mourning, Memory, and Film in Post-War Germany*. Ithaca, NY: Cornell University Press. 1990.

Schacter, Daniel L. *The Seven Sins of Memory: How the Mind Forgets and Remembers*. Boston: Houghton Mifflin, 2001.

Schoenhals, Michael. *Saltationist Socialism: Mao Zedong and the Great Leap Forward, 1958*. Stockholm: University of Stockholm, Institutionen for Orientaliska, 1987.

———. *Doing Things with Words in Chinese Politics: Five Studies*. Berkeley, CA: Institute of East Asian Studies, 1992.

Schurmann, Franz. *Ideology and Organization in Communist China*. Berkeley: University of California Press, 1968.

Schwarcz, Vera. *Bridge Across Broken Time: Chinese and Jewish Cultural Memory*. New Haven, CT: Yale University Press, 1998.

Schwartz, Benjamin I. "Modernization and the Maoist Vision – Some Reflections on Chinese Communist Goals." In Roderick MacFarquhar, ed., *China Under Mao: Politics Takes Command*. Cambridge, MA: MIT Press, 1966.

Schweiger, Irmy. "The Inscription of Trauma." Paper presented to the 2nd International Conference of Asian Studies, Berlin, Germany, August 9–12, 2001.

Scott, James C. *The Moral Economy of the Peasant: Rebellion and Subsistence in Southeast Asia*. New Haven, CT: Yale University Press, 1976.

———. "Socialism and Small Property – or – Two Cheers for the Petty Bourgeoisie." *Peasant Studies*, Vol. 12, No. 3, Spring 1985.

———. *Weapons of the Weak*. New Haven, CT: Yale University Press, 1985.

———. "Everyday Forms of Resistance." In Forrest D. Colburn, ed., *Everyday Forms of Peasant Resistance*. Armonk, NY: M.E. Sharpe, 1989.

———. *Domination and the Arts of Resistance: Hidden Transcripts*. New Haven, CT: Yale University Press, 1990.

———. *Seeing Like a State*. New Haven, CT: Yale University Press, 1998.

Selbin, Eric. "Agency and Culture in Revolutions." In Jack A. Goldstone, ed., *Revolutions: Theoretical, Comparative, and Historical Studies*. Toronto: Wadsworth, 2003.

Selden, Mark. *The Yenan Way in Revolutionary China*. Cambridge, MA: Harvard University Press, 1971.

———, ed. (with Patti Eggleston). *The People's Republic of China: A Documentary History of Revolutionary Change*. New York: Monthly Review Press, 1979.

Sen, Amartya. *Poverty and Famines: An Essay on Entitlement and Deprivation*. Oxford: Clarendon Press, 1981.

Sewell, William, Jr. "Space in Contentious Politics." In Ronald R. Aminzade, et al., *Silence and Voice in the Study of Contentious Politics*. Cambridge: Cambridge University Press, 2001.

Seybolt, Peter J. *Throwing the Emperor from His Horse: Portrait of a Village Leader in China, 1923–1995*. Boulder, CO: Westview Press, 1996.

———. "The War Within a War: A Case Study of a County on the North China Plain." In David P. Barrett and Larry N. Shyu, eds., *Chinese Collaboration with Japan, 1932–1945: The Limits of Accommodation*. Stanford, CA: Stanford University Press, 2001.

Shue, Vivienne. *Peasant China in Transition: The Dynamics of Development Towards Socialism, 1949–1956*. Berkeley: University of California Press, 1980.

———. *The Reach of the State: Sketches of the Chinese Body Politic*. Stanford, CA: Stanford University Press, 1988.

———. "Legitimacy Crisis in China?" In Peter Hays Gries and Stanley Rosen, eds., *State and Society in 21st-Century China: Crisis, Contention, and Legitimation*. New York: Routledge Curzon, 2004.

Bibliography

Simon, Roger I. *The Touch of the Past: Remembrance, Learning and Ethics.* New York Palgrave-MacMillan, 2005.

Siu, Helen F. *Agents and Victims in South China: Accomplices in Rural Revolution.* New Haven CT: Yale University Press, 1989.

Skinner, G. William. "Marketing and Social Structure in Rural China." *Journal of Asian Studies*, Vol. 24, Parts I, II, and II, 1964–65.

———. "Chinese Peasants and the Closed Community: An Open and Shut Case." *Comparative Studies in Society and History*, Vol. 13, No. 3, 1971.

Smil, V. "China's Great Famine: 40 Years Later." *British Medical Journal*, Vol. 7225, 1999

Smith, S. A. "Talking Toads and Chinless Ghosts: The Politics of 'Superstitious' Rumor in the People's Republic of China, 1961–1965." *American Historical Review*, Vol. 111 No. 2, April 2006.

Solinger, Dorthy J. "Marxism and the Market in Socialist China: The Reforms of 1979-1980 in Context." In Victor Nee and David Mozingo, eds., *State and Society in Contemporary China*. Ithaca, NY: Cornell University Press, 1983.

———. *Contesting Citizenship in Urban China: Peasants, Migrants, the State and the Logic of the Market.* Berkeley: University of California Press, 1999.

Spence, Jonathan. *Mao Zedong.* New York: Viking-Penguin, 1999.

Stoller, Paul. "Embodying Colonial Memories." *American Anthropologist*, Vol. 96, No. 3 1994.

Strauss, Julia. "Morality, Coercion and State Building by Campaign in the Early PRC Regime Consolidation and After, 1949–1956." *China Quarterly*, Vol. 188, December 2006.

Su, Yang. "Mass Killing in the Cultural Revolution: A Study of Three Provinces." In Joseph Esherick, Paul G. Pickowicz, and Andrew G. Walder, eds., *The Chinese Cultural Revolution as History*. Stanford, CA: Stanford University Press, 2006.

Sun, Yan. *Corruption and Market in Contemporary China.* Ithaca, NY: Cornell University Press, 2004.

Teiwes, Frederick, and Warren Sun. *China's Road to Disaster: Mao, Central Politicians, and Provincial Leaders in the Unfolding of the Great Leap Forward, 1955–1959.* Armonk, NY M.E. Sharpe, 1999.

Thaxton, Ralph A., Jr. *Salt of the Earth: The Political Origins of Peasant Protest and Communist Revolution in China.* Berkeley: University of California Press, 1997.

———. "How Famines End: Some Reflections on Processes, Implications for State Legitimacy, and a Few Cases, with Special Reference to the Famine of Mao's Great Leap Forward." Paper presented to the annual National Association for Asian Studies meeting. San Francisco, CA, April 6–9, 2006.

Thaxton, Ralph A., Jr., and Lu Huilin. "The Public Whip of Maoist Terror: Criticism, Accusation, and Condemnation in Rural China under Maoist Rule, with Special Reference to the Great Leap Forward." Paper prepared for the University of Vienna conference on "As China Meets the World: China's Changing Position in the International Community, 1840–2000," Vienna, Austria, May 17–19, 2004.

Thaxton, Ralph A., Jr., and Wang Shuobai. "Power, Disentitlement, and Life Chances in China's Great Leap Famine: Some Reflections on Memory Based Knowledge from Rural Anhui, with Special Reference to the Wisdom of Amartya Sen." Paper presented to the fifty-third annual meeting of the National Association for Asian Studies, March 22–25, 2001.

Theidon, Kimberly. "How We Learned to Kill Our Brother: Memory, Morality and Reconciliation in Peru." Draft of paper presented at the University of Virginia conference, Charlottesville. Published in *Bulletin de l'Institut Français d'Etudes Andines*, Vol. 29, No. 3, 2000.

Bibliography

Thompson, Paul. *The Voice of the Past: Oral History*. New York: Oxford University Press, 2000.

Thornton, Patricia M. "Insinuation, Insult, and Invective: The Threshold of Power and Protest in Modern China." *Comparative Studies in Society and History*, Vol. 44, No. 3, July 2002.

_____. "Comrades and Collectives in Arms: Tax Resistance, Evasion, and Avoidance Strategies in Post-Mao China." In Peter Hays Gries and Stanley Rosen, eds., *State and Society in 21st-Century China: Crisis, Contention, and Legitimation*. New York: Routledge Curzon, 2004.

_____. "The Memory Palace of Wang Guangmei: Memory, Will and Policy in the Aftermath of the Great Leap Forward." Paper presented to the Brandeis University East Asian studies colloquium on "History, Memory, and Power in Maoist and Post-Maoist China," April 6–7, 2005.

_____. *Disciplining the State: Virtue, Violence, and State-Making in Modern China*. Cambridge, MA: Harvard University Asia Center Monograph, 2007.

Tilly, Charles. *The Contentious French*. Cambridge, MA: Harvard University Press, 1986.

_____. *Trust and Rule*. New York: Cambridge University Press, 2005.

Timofeev, Lev. *Soviet Peasants: Or, the Peasants' Art of Starving*. Ed. with an introduction by Armando Pitassio and Victor Zaslavsky. Trans. Jean Alexander and Alexander Zaslavsky. New York: Telos, 1985.

Tong, Yanqi. *Transitions from State Socialism: Economic and Political Change in Hungary and China*. Lanham, MD: Rowman and Littlefield, 1997.

Tsou Tang. "Revolution, Reintegration, and Crisis in Communist China: A Framework for Analysis." In Ping-ti Ho and Tsou Tang, eds., *China in Crisis*. Vol. 1, book 1. Chicago: University of Chicago Press, 1968.

Unger, Jonathan. "Decollectivization in a Guangdong Village: An Interview." In John P. Burns and Stanley Rosen, eds., *Policy Conflicts in Post-Mao China: A Documentary Survey, with Analysis*. Armonk, NY: M.E. Sharpe, 1986.

_____. "Review Article: State and Peasant in Post-Revolution China." *The Journal of Peasant Studies*, Vol. 17, No. 1, October 1989: 114–36.

_____. *The Transformation of Rural China*. Armonk, NY: M.E. Sharpe, 2002.

_____. "The Cultural Revolution at the Grass Roots." *The China Journal*, Issue 57, January 2007.

Viola, Lynne. *Peasant Rebels under Stalin: Collectivization and the Culture of Peasant Resistance*. New York: Oxford University Press, 1996.

Wakeman, Frederic, Jr. *Strangers at the Gate: Social Disorder in South China, 1839–1861*. Berkeley: University of California Press, 1966.

Walder, Andrew G., and Bobai Li. "Career Advancement as Party Patronage: Sponsored Mobility into the Chinese Administrative Elite, 1949–1996." *American Journal of Sociology*, Vol. 106, No. 5, March 2001.

Watson, James, and Evelyn Rawski, eds. *Death Ritual in Late Imperial and Early Modern China*. Berkeley: University of California Press, 1988.

Watson, Rubie. *Memory, History, and Opposition Under State Socialism*. Santa Fe, NM: School of American Research Press, 1994.

Weigelin-Schwiedrzik, Susanne. "Taking the Heat Out of a Problem: Party Historiography and Traumatic Experiences in Modern Chinese History." Paper presented to the Association for Asian Studies, Boston, MA, March 1999.

_____. "Trauma and Memory: The Case of the Great Famine in the People's Republic of China (1959–1961)." *Historiography: East and West*, Vol. 1, No. 1, 2003.

_____. "The Distance between State and Rural Society in the PRC: Reading Document No. 1." Unpublished paper, February 2004.

Wemheuer, Felix. "A Policy of Destruction – Memories of Chinese Intellectuals on the Rural Great Leap Forward (1958–1961)." Unpublished paper, 2004.

_____. "Stone Noodles: Rural Memories of the 'Great Leap Famine' in Henan Province (1958–1961)." Paper presented to the East Asian Colloquium, Brandeis University April 6, 2005.

_____. "The Grain Problem Is an Ideological Problem: Discourses of Hunger in the Socialist Education Campaign in 1957." Unpublished paper delivered to the annual meeting of the Association of Asian Studies, March 24, 2006.

_____. "Regime Change of Memories: Creating Official History of Ukrainian and Chinese Famine Under State Socialism and the Cold War." Unpublished paper, University of Vienna, 2006.

White, Lynn T. III. *Unstately Power: Local Causes of China's Economic Reforms*. Vol. I Armonk, NY: M.E. Sharpe, 1998.

White, Theodore, and Anna Lee Jacoby. *Thunder Out of China*. New York: William Sloane Associates, 1946.

White, Tyrene. "Domination, Resistance and Accommodation in China's One-Child Campaign." In Elizabeth J. Perry and Mark Selden, eds., *Chinese Society: Change, Conflict and Resistance*. London: Routledge, 2000.

Whyte, Martin King. "Chinese Social Trends: Stability or Chaos?" In David Shambaugh ed., *Is China Unstable?* Armonk, NY: M.E. Sharpe, 2000.

Will, Pierre-Etienne, and R. Bin Wong, eds. *Nourish the People: The State Civilian Granary System in China, 1650–1850*. Ann Arbor: University of Michigan Center for Chinese Studies, 1991.

Wong, R. Bin. *China Transformed: Historical China and the Limits of the European Experience* Ithaca, NY: Cornell University Press, 1997.

Wu, Kaming. "Remembering the Revolutionary Past." Unpublished paper presented to the Association for Asian Studies, 2005.

Yan, Yunxiang. "Changes in Everyday Power Relations – A View from a North China Village." Unpublished paper given to the conference "Political Consequences of Departures from Central Planning," Arden, Homestead, NY, August 26–30, 1992.

_____. "The Culture of *Guanxi* in a North China Village." *The China Journal*, No. 35 January 1996.

Yang, Dali. "The Impact of the Great Leap Famine on Rural Policy in China: 1959–1976." AAS paper, March 25–28, 1993.

_____. *Calamity and Reform in China: Rural Society and Institutional Change Since the Great Leap Famine*. Stanford, CA: Stanford University Press, 1996.

_____. "Surviving the Great Leap Famine: The Struggle Over Rural Policy, 1958–1962." In Timothy Cheek and Tony Saich, eds., *New Perspectives on State Socialism in China* London: M.E. Sharpe, 1997.

Yang, Dali, and Fubing Su. "Food Availability Versus Consumption Efficiency: Causes of the Chinese Famine." In Bruce Reynolds, ed., "China's Great Leap Famine." Special issue, *China Economic Review*, Vol. 9, No. 2, Fall 1998.

Zhou, Kate. *How the Farmers Changed China: Power of the People*. Boulder, CO: Westview 1996.

Zweig, David. *Agrarian Radicalism in China, 1968–1981*. Cambridge, MA: Harvard University Press, 1989.

_____. *Freeing China's Farmers: Rural Restructuring in the Reform Era*. New York: M.E. Sharpe, 1997.

Index

Adas, Michael, 334
agricultural production cooperatives, 4,
90, 101–06, 119, 242–43. *See also*
land-pooling associations; Liangmen
People's Commune; mutual aid
groups
agriculture, 25–26, 27, 244. *See also* grain
crop; management of agriculture
alkaline land, 25
animal theft, 181. *See also* crop theft as
survival strategy
Anti–Five Winds campaign, 222, 245–50
anti–grain concealment campaign, 332
Anti-Japanese War of Resistance, 39,
52–53, 58, 63–64, 66–67. *See also*
Eighth Route Army
anti-rightist movement, 4, 115, 144, 193
armaments factory in Da Fo village, 55, 64
armies. *See* Eighth Route Army; Japanese
invasion and occupation; Kuomintang
Army; People's Liberation Army
arms smuggling, 64, 65
arson as retaliation, 312–14, 344, 346
avoidance protest. *See* resistance politics

Babbie, Earl R., 16
Bai Huqian, 77
Bailey, F. G., 238
banditry, 28–29, 35, 38, 43
Bao Bingqing, 36–37
Bao Chaoqun, 295–96

Bao Chenyun, 113
bao chou (righteous revenge). *See* retaliation
Bao Chuanshen, 148, 182, 183, 314
Bao Deyan, 252
Bao Donger, 314
Bao Dongzhi
and Bao Sunyuan, 264
brother's death during famine, 113
and *chi qing*, 203, 207
and harvest companies, 121
and mutual aid groups, 91
on public criticism, 146
on public dining halls, 108, 120
Bao Fabao, 308
Bao Gan, 42
Bao Gaojun, 164, 302–03
Bao Geng, 150
Bao Guangming, xviii, 121, 124, 165, 227,
278
Bao Gui, 41, 58, 280–81
Bao Guishan, 272–73, 278
Bao Hedian, 260, 261
Bao Heshan, 180
Bao Honglin, 113, 132, 205, 298
Bao Hongwen, xviii, 136–37, 296, 309,
310, 317
Bao Huajie, 154
Bao Huayin
and anti-Japanese resistance, 40
on Bao Zhilong, 318–19
biographical information, xviii

Index

Bao Xueliang, 321
Bao Xuexing, 279
Bao Xueyang, 307–08
Bao Xuqing, 60, 62, 94
Bao Yibin
  and Bao Zhilong, 258–59, 260, 262
  and beating of his mother, 309
  biographical information, xvii
  and *chi qing*, 202–03
  on death rate during Great Leap
    Forward, 207
  and food privileges for party leaders,
    233–34
  and the Four Cleanups campaign,
    251–52
  on government procurement, 127
  and grain concealment, 186
  as head of Red Artists, 258–60
  and Ji County river dig project, 166–67
  and land division (1992), 321
  and Liangmen People's Commune, 118
  on migration attempts, 166
  on overreporting of crop yields, 129
  retaliation against, 314, 321–22
  on salt trade, 173
  and use of violence, 143, 148, 246
  as village party secretary, 111
Bao Yidai, 73, 81
Bao Yiliao, 249
Bao Yilin, 63, 72, 73, 248–49
Bao Yiming, 153, 167, 174, 258, 259, 260,
  314
Bao Yinbao, 173
Bao Yinyuan, 36, 38, 48–49, 178–79, 180
Bao Yiwu, 153
Bao Yizhao, xviii, 77, 189–90, 192–98
Bao Yufa, 223
Bao Yuhua
  and anti-Japanese resistance, 40
  as benefactor of Da Fo village, 33–35, 61
  biographical information, xviii
  and education, 35, 37
  feigned collaboration and cooperation
    with Yang Faxian, 61
  and Henan Famine, 61
  marginalization of, 53, 111
  and protection from bandits, 35
  spared public criticism, 74
  survival of, 49
  and village defense corps, 42

Bao Yuming
  on changing village boundaries, 122–23
  on confiscation of private property, 121
  on elimination of festivals and holidays,
    137–38
  on foot-dragging, 159
  on overreporting of crop yields, 131–32
  on public dining halls, 119
  on rationing, 132
  on violence, 143
Bao Zhang, 192
Bao Zhangli, 150
Bao Zhendao
  on Bao Yuhua, 34
  on Bao Zhihai, 35
  and carpenters, 174
  on death rate, 207
  father's death during famine, 113
  on food shortages, 234
  and land-pooling associations, 93
  and land reform, 72
  and Liangmen People's Commune, 118
  on murder of Bao Shiyan, 59
  on overreporting of crop yields, 128
  on Yang Faxian's puppet regime, 55
Bao Zhenfa, 55
Bao Zheng, 27, 31
Bao Zhengda, 116, 151–52, 243
Bao Zhenghai, 258
Bao Zhengshou, 243
Bao Zhentian, 166
Bao Zhenxiu, 93
Bao Zhidan, 57, 113, 147–48, 153, 176,
  234, 308
Bao Zhigen
  and beatings, 204, 205
  biographical information, xvii
  on crop theft, 179
  on grain prices, 131
  and harvest companies, 121
  house fire, 253
  on land-pooling associations, 93
  lessening power of, during Reform Era,
    322
  on loan from Bao Yuhua, 61
  on migration attempt, 166
  as part of Bao Zhilong's ruling group,
    111
  on public criticism, 99
  and public dining halls, 153

Bao Zhigen *(cont.)*
punishment of, 249
retaliation against, 314–15
and sexual abuse of women, 237, 238,
   317
on struggle between Wu Zhipu and Pan
   Fusheng, 115–16
and Tang Jintao, 213
and use of violence, 143, 246
and work privileges for party leaders,
   236
Bao Zhihai
abuses of, 35–37
and education, 37
house commandeered, 53
and militias, 42
and murder of Bao Tiancai, 74
opposition to anti-Japanese resistance,
   48–49
targeted for criticism, though dead,
   73–74
and village defense corps, 42
Bao Zhilong
and agricultural production
   cooperatives, 103
and Anti–Five Winds campaign, 222
and arms smuggling, 65
on Bai Huqian, 77
and benefits to Da Fo village, 147, 203,
   234
biographical information, xvii, 40–41
on black market salt trade, 171
career of, 109–12
and the Communist Party, 39, 94–95,
   116, 293
consolidation of power, 82
corruption of, 318, 319–21
feigned collaboration and cooperation,
   60
and food privileges for party leaders,
   233–34
and the Four Cleanups campaign,
   251–53
and land-pooling associations, 93–94
and land reform, 71–72
and large landholders, 73
and Liangmen People's Commune, 118
as local Communist Party secretary, 81
and local market economy, 288–89

loss of power, 316–17
methods unchanged in Reform Era,
   292–93
and militias, 43, 44, 48, 62–63, 68–70,
   76
and mutual aid groups, 91
and the Nationalist government, 75
and overreporting of crop yields, 131
and patronage system, 266
and the Peasant Association of Da Fo,
   81
and the People's Liberation Army, 76
and politics of war, 69, 86–88
power struggle with Bao Yibin, 258–60,
   262
public criticism of, 249, 256–57
and resistance to taxes, 31, 62
retaliation against, 262, 313, 314
return to power, 265–67
on sale of temple land, 45
and salt police raids, 31
on Shi Dehai, 77
support for anti-rightist movement, 115
trust in and betrayal of trust, 109,
   240–41
underground resistance activities,
   63–64, 66
and use of violence and abuse, 69–70,
   84–85, 145, 246
and well-drilling, 242–43
and women laborers, 140, 143
and work style of war, 84
and Yang Faxian's puppet regime,
   59–60, 67–68
and Zheng Yunxiang, 239–40
Bao Zhitan, 42, 43
Bao Zhiwang, 260
Bao Zhongxi, 91
Bao Zhongxin, 144, 153, 189–90, 202,
   213, 297–98
Bao Zhouchuan, 79
Bao Ziyan, 137, 149, 250
Bao Zuoming, 319
baochan daohu. See household contract
   responsibility system
beatings
to achieve Great Leap Forward goals,
   143
anger and resentment due to, 240

Index

of Bao Yibin's mother, 309
for *chi qing*, 204, 205
and violence during Great Leap
Forward, 147–51
Becker, Jasper, 215, 337
begging as survival strategy, 27, 176–77,
295
Beidaihe Work Conference, 219
Beitoucun village, 101, 118
Berger, Roland, 125
Bernstein, Thomas, 129
bian (commemorative board), 36
Bianco, Lucien, 313
birthrate, declining, 208–09
black market as survival strategy, 160–62,
170–76. *See also* local market economy
blind people and forced labor, 133
Bloom, Sandra L., 345
Bo Yibo, 297
Bok, Sissela, 241
bond tax, 29
borrowed sweet potato land, 223–25,
270–74, 311. *See also* family-based
crop production; landownership,
private
Bramall, Chris, 128
burial customs, 151, 304–06

cadres, abuses of, 1–2, 239
Calamity and Reform in China (Dali Yang), 8
carpenters, 174
censorship, 12, 13–15
Chan, Alfred, 129
Chan, Anita, 284
Chang, Gene Hsing, 123
Chen Daobing, 28, 65
Chen Xinmeng, 28
Chen Yichen, 246
Chen Yun, 98
Cheng Guan village, 13–14
chi qing
and beatings, 204, 205
after closing of public dining halls,
221–22
forbidden by Red Guards, 258–59
as form of resistance, 199–207, 226–30,
336
during Great Leap Forward, 295
internal regulation of, 219

not seen as crop theft, 227–28
as survival strategy, 199–207, 224
and women, 205, 206
childbirth, 140–41
children, selling of, 57, 113
children during Great Leap Forward, 133,
142, 208
Chinese Communist Party. *See also* Eighth
Route Army; local Chinese
Communist Party; People's
Liberation Army; People's Republic
of China; retaliation
abuses by cadres, 1–2, 239
alienation from, 155, 247–50, 262, 307,
321
and anti-Japanese resistance, 39–41
anti-Nationalist propaganda, 74–75
and Bao Zhilong, 39, 94–95, 116, 293
betrayal of early supporters, 342–43
and corruption, 337–38
and the educated elite, 329, 330
and elections, 337–38
explanation of Great Leap famine,
331–32
failure to protect people from famine,
229–30, 332–33
fears of revolt, 229–30
founding of, in Da Fo village, 45
and "good intentions," 296–99, 333–34
and Japanese invasion and occupation,
52–53
and land redistribution, 74–75
language used by, 15–16, 87, 98
legitimacy of, 231, 334–39, 340–41
and memories of famine, 5–6, 325–26
no acknowledgment or apologies for
failures, 345
and official memory, 11, 292, 337
policies toward captured Nationalist
officers, 77
policy of village work for county
leaders, 112
pressure to overreport crop yields,
128–29, 131–32, 147, 194
and private landownership, 329–30
reasons for joining, 63
and resistance in Da Fo village, 58–70
and rural population, 149, 290–91
and rustification campaign, 167–68, 170

Index

floods on Wei River, 104–05, 130, 188–89, 277

food security as entitlement, 232–33, 331–34

food shortages. *See also* family-based crop production; Great Leap famine; procurement; rationing; survival strategies
  alleviated by local market economy, 281
  after closing of public dining halls, 221–23
  and corruption, 332–33
  during Cultural Revolution, 274
  embodied memory of, 303–04
  food used as weapon against resistance, 335
  and the Great Leap Forward, 112–13, 129–30
  and inequitable distribution of food, 89–90, 233–36
  and irrational consumption theory, 123–24
  lasting long past Great Leap famine, 339
  and mistrust of government, 101
  and public works projects, 136–39, 164–65
  and resistance politics, 335
  and return to family-based crop production, 223–24, 225
  subsistence levels inadequate, 99–100
  and weather conditions, 125–26

foot-dragging as survival strategy, 158–60, 287

forced labor. *See* labor

Forty-Seven Village Working Pacification Committee, 60

Four Cleanups campaign, 250–51, 253

Fourth Detachment, 44

Friedman, Edward, 8, 208, 332, 337

fukua feng (the wind of exaggeration), 128

furniture redistribution, 73

Gao Hua, 300

Gao Wangling, 158, 230

geomancy, 347

Gilley, Bruce, 13

Giskin, Howard, 318

gleaning as survival strategy, 181–84, 225

gongzhai (bond tax), 29

"good intentions" and the Chinese Communist Party, 296–99, 333–34

Goodfellow, Robert, 325–26

grain concealment as survival strategy, 185–88, 332

grain crop. *See also chi qing*
  average yield, 25
  bumper harvest (1958), 124
  corn *versus* wheat, 201
  and the Cultural Revolution, 272–73
  and gleaning, 181–84, 225
  grain distribution system, 235
  grain trading, 279–80, 282–83
  during Great Leap Forward, 126–28
  and Henan Famine, 56
  initial overconsumption of, 123–24
  and land-pooling associations, 94
  and manpower shortages, 138–39
  and mutual aid groups, 92
  under Nationalist government, 25–26
  nationalization of grain market, 4
  and North China Famine of 1921, 26
  pressure to overreport harvests, 128–29, 131–32, 147, 194
  and procurement, 244–45, 276
  and public dining halls, 120, 124
  and Republican period, 25
  storage of, 320–21
  underreporting of, 272–73
  and unified purchase and sale, 97, 101, 131

grain loans, 28, 34–35, 61, 155

Great Leap famine. *See also* survival strategies; three freedoms, one contract policies
  background information, 1–5
  Communist Party explanation of, 331–32
  and damage to legitimacy of Communist Party, 340–41
  desire for retaliation against perpetrators of, 21–22, 246–50, 253–62, 315, 344–47
  end of, in Da Fo village, 215–26
  and failure of communes, 231
  and "good intentions," 296–99, 333–34
  illnesses and deaths, 134
  and long-lasting food shortages, 339
  memories of pain and loss, 10–11, 19, 301–12
  physical effects on survivors, 302–03